The Editor

EVAN GOTTLIEB is Associate Professor of English at Oregon State University. He is the author of *Feeling British: Sympathy and National Identity in Scottish and English Writing, 1707–1832, Walter Scott and Contemporary Theory,* and *Romantic Globalism: British Literature and Modern World Order, 1750–1830.* He is coeditor of *Approaches to Teaching Scott's Waverley Novels* and *Representing Place in British Literature and Culture, 1660–1830: From Local to Global.* He is also a regular contributor to the Huffington Post Books blog.

NORTON CRITICAL EDITIONS
Age of Enlightenment

For a complete list of Norton Critical Editions, visit
wwnorton.com/nortoncriticals

A NORTON CRITICAL EDITION

Tobias Smollett

THE EXPEDITION OF HUMPRHY CLINKER

AN AUTHORITATIVE TEXT
BACKGROUNDS AND CONTEXTS
CRITICISM

SECOND EDITION

WITHDRAWN

Edited by

EVAN GOTTLIEB
OREGON STATE UNIVERSITY

W · W · NORTON & COMPANY · *New York* · *London*

Copyright © 2015, 1983 by W. W. Norton & Company
All rights reserved
Printed in the United States of America

Production Manager: Vanessa Nuttry

Library of Congress Cataloging-in-Publication Data

Smollett, T. (Tobias), 1721–1771.
    The Expedition of Humphry Clinker : an authoritative text, backgrounds and contexts, criticism / Tobias Smollet; edited by Evan Gottlieb, Oregon State University. — Second edition.
        pages cm. — (A Norton Critical edition)
    Includes bibliographical references.
    ISBN 978-0-393-93671-1 (pbk. : alk. paper)
    1. Travelers—Fiction.   2. Great Britain—Fiction.   3. Picaresque literature.   4. Epistolary fiction.   I. Gottlieb, Evan, 1975— editor.
II. Title.
    PR3694.H8 2015
    823'.6—dc23

                                        2014037478

W. W. Norton & Company, Inc., 500 Fifth Avenue, New York, NY 10110-0017
wwnorton.com

W. W. Norton & Company Ltd., Castle House, 75/76 Wells Street, London
W1T 3QT

1   2   3   4   5   6   7   8   9   0

Contents

Illustrations

Preface

Tobias George Smollett was both famous and quite ill when he wrote what would be his final novel, *The Expedition of Humphry Clinker*. He and his wife, Anne, had already left Britain for Italy's warmer climate in a vain attempt to forestall the tuberculosis that would eventually kill him. In fact, Smollett had not lived in Scotland, his birthplace, since leaving Glasgow almost thirty years earlier to seek his fortune in England and beyond; nevertheless, shortly before his final voyage abroad—and perhaps with the seeds of *Humphry Clinker* already germinating in his mind—he made a point of revisiting many of the "North British" places and people dear to him as well as his former homes, Bath and London. As a result, the descriptions of these locations in *Humphry Clinker* are not merely the nostalgic productions of a dying man's imagination, as some reviewers originally suggested; they also have fair claims to topicality and sociopolitical relevance. Combined with Smollett's formidable authorial skills, honed over a lifetime of creative and journalistic writing, the fictionalized tour of mid-eighteenth-century Great Britain that became his final novel is unmatched for its virtuosic blend of historical interest and narrative attractions.

Before *Humphry Clinker*, Smollett had tried his hand at every major genre of eighteenth-century writing, frequently with great success. Trained as a doctor but determined from an early age to be a professional author—especially after witnessing firsthand the ravages of warfare as a ship's surgeon in the British navy—Smollett's first found literary success with *The Tears of Caledonia* (1746), a sentimental poem publicly mourning the Jacobite defeat at the Battle of Culloden, which ended hopes for the Stuart monarchy's return to power (as well as for an independent Scotland). Smollett's first novel, *The Adventures of Roderick Random* (1748), was subsequently published the same year as Samuel Richardson's epistolary (novel in letters) masterpiece, *Clarissa, or, The History of a Young Lady*, and just two years before Henry Fielding's equally influential *The History of Tom Jones, A Foundling*. Smollett was thus a key participant in the so-called rise of the novel, and although he remains on the periphery of some critical accounts of the novel's generic ascension—due in part, at least, to his decision to write primarily in the picaresque mode, an older, Romance-based form that relies on the singularity of a main character rather than a carefully shaped plot for its degree of narrative coherence[1]—he seems to have been keenly aware of writing at an important moment, aesthetically as well as politically.[2] In this spirit, Smollett's preface to *Roderick Random* not only carefully explains his decision to make its first-person narrator a Scotsman, thus implicitly encouraging sympathy for his countrymen in the wake of the failed rebellion and its harsh reprisals, but also opens with a classic assessment of prose fiction's generic capabilities to be both "entertaining" and "universally improving."

Smollett would subsequently spend much of his career writing nonfiction, including the popular multivolume *Complete History of England*, and editing journals like the prominent *Critical Review*. Nevertheless, he repeatedly returned to the novel as his medium of choice for reaching a broad audience. His prefatory dedication to *The Adventures of Ferdinand Count Fathom* (1753) contains his best-known description of the genre:

> A novel is a large diffused picture, comprehending the characters of life, disposed in different groups, and exhibited in various attitudes, for the purposes of an uniform plan, and general occurrence, to which every individual figure is subservient. But this plan cannot be executed with propriety, probability, or success, without a principal personage to attract the attention, unite the incidents, unwind the clue of the labyrinth, and at last close the scene, by virtue of his own importance.

Here, Smollett's loyalty to the picaresque—he published several influential translations of European versions of the form, including Cervantes' *Don Quixote* and Le Sage's *Gil Blas*—is joined by a growing appreciation of the author's ability, indeed responsibility, to use prose's formal resources to shape as well as reflect her or his social reality.

More successfully than any of Smollett's previous novels, *Humphry Clinker* brings together his repertoire of novelistic tones and

---

1. The phrase *the rise of the novel* was popularized by Ian Watt in his study of the same name, *The Rise of the Novel: Studies in Defoe, Fielding, and Richardson* (Los Angeles and Berkeley: University of California Press, 1957). As its subtitle suggests, Smollett plays little role in Watt's influential story of the genre's eighteenth-century consolidation; however, more recent histories of the British novel by scholars such as Deidre Lynch and John Richetti have gone some way toward correcting this omission.
2. Franco Moretti points out that, considered purely as a publishing phenomenon, the novel actually rises in Britain most noticeably starting in the 1770s; see "Graphs," in *Graphs, Maps, Trees: Abstract Models for Literary History* (London and New York: Verso, 2005), 6–7 figs. 1–2; and "Style, Inc.: Reflections on 7,000 Titles (British Novels, 1740–1850)," in *Distant Reading* (London and New York: Verso, 2013), 188 fig. 7. Correlations between these numbers and matters of artistic innovation, however, remain murky at best.

narrative techniques (picaresque, epistolary, satirical, and sentimental) and consolidates them into a satisfying whole. Instead of restricting himself to just one or two letter writers as narrators, however, Smollett creates five distinct primary correspondents. We are encouraged from the start to direct our attention to Matthew Bramble, the ailing patriarch whose commentary on everything and everyone around him, as he and his extended family entourage travel through England and Scotland before returning to their Welsh home, forms the brightest thread for readers to follow. But by supplementing Matt's often jaundiced perspective with those of his niece, nephew, sister, and sister's maid, Smollett fills his novel with a kaleidoscopic multiplicity of voices that opens up new vistas for literary representation. Two additional characters who join the Bramble party along the way—the opinionated Scottish former lieutenant, Obadiah Lismahago, and the humble servant-turned-Methodist preacher Humphry Clinker—also lend their voices to the novel, although they write no letters themselves. In this way, *Humphry Clinker* anticipates one of the phenomena identified by Mikhail Bakhtin as central to both the aesthetic and ethical dimensions of the modern novel in general: *heteroglossia*, the inherently democratic representation of competing voices, none of which is finally dominant.[3] In a more historical vein, we can also see Smollett aligning sociable letter writing with the circulation of characters—understood as both the pages of text mailed by his characters and those letter writers themselves—along the routes of Britain's developing infrastructure, such that the Bramble's party's vectors of travel and communication become coextensive with the shape of the nation itself.[4] A fictionalized travel narrative, the unusual noun *expedition* in *Humphry Clinker's* full title suggests a quest or pilgrimage—older iterations of today's popular road-trip genre, which likewise combines geographical adventure with self and communal discovery—that is happily concluded by its final pages.

Smollett's characters do not just communicate and travel, however; they also change and grow psychologically in recognizable modern ways. Over the novel's course, Bramble becomes healthier in both body and mind, Jery Melford outgrows much of his immature caddishness, and Lismahago's rough edges are worn smoother by repeated exposure to the Brambles' company. Less appealing, especially to contemporary readers, is Smollett's treatment of his female

3. See M. M. Bakhtin, *The Dialogic Imagination: Four Essays*, ed. Michael Holquist, trans. Caryl Emerson and Michael Holquist (Austin: U of Texas P, 1981), esp. 261–74.
4. See Deidre Lynch's observations on the ramifications of the eighteenth-century epistolary novel's form in *The Economy of Character: Novels, Market Culture, and the Business of Inner Meaning* (Chicago and London: U of Chicago P, 1998), esp. 42–43. Lynch's insights into the historical conditions informing readers' understandings of (and expectations for) the nature of literary characters also inform the start of the next paragraph.

characters, who remain far more static and are given far fewer opportunities to voice their perspectives than are their male counterparts. Yet even as Tabitha Bramble's shrewish shallowness and Lydia Melford's enthusiastic naïveté may be objectionable, they tell us a great deal about mid-eighteenth-century gender stereotypes; moreover, the malapropisms that fill the creatively spelled letters of Tabitha and Win Jenkins provide unparalleled moments of wit and humor, albeit frequently at their putative author's expenses. (In regard to the annotations of their letters in particular, this edition tries to provide just enough editorial commentary to elucidate their idiosyncratic spellings, without ruining Smollett's sometimes risqué jokes via over-explanation.)

In addition to offering a formally experimental series of character studies, *Humphry Clinker* continues to hold interest for modern readers thanks to its abundance of colorful depictions of eighteenth-century Britain. As the Bramble entourage makes its circuit around England and southern Scotland, its members reference a cornucopia of persons, places, and events that Smollett's original readers would likely have known and that contemporary readers will find elucidated in this edition's notes. Nevertheless, *Humphry Clinker*'s evocations of the sights, sounds, and especially smells of Bath, London, Edinburgh, St. Andrews, and many places in between are as vivid now as ever. (Readers with weak stomachs may still find some descriptive passages rough going, a fact that no doubt would have pleased Smollett.) By having his letter writers describe these places in overlapping sequences, moreover, Smollett conveys their many dimensions without having to settle on a single "correct" perspective. Bath is thus "the very center of racket and dissipation" for Bramble, for example, whereas Lydia finds it full of "gayety, good humour, and dissipation"; likewise, in Bramble's letters London is "an immense wilderness . . . of luxury and corruption," while for Lydia the crowds, carriages, bridges, and buildings of London and Westminster mean that "the imagination is quite confounded with splendour and variety." Critics have long noted, however, that once the travelers move north into Scotland, their responses to their surroundings finally begin agreeing with one another. Thus upon recovering his health, thanks to the sociability of the Scots as well as to the apparent healthfulness of their climate and food, Bramble hails Edinburgh as "a hot-bed of genius," and Jery likewise declares himself so charmed that "If I stay much longer in Edinburgh, I shall be changed into a downright Caledonian." This hard-earned perspectival consensus is matched by an increase in familial harmony as well. By the time the party is ready to return to Wales and Brambleton Hall, the domestic discord that dominates the novel's early pages has largely been overcome: Clinker has assumed his rightful place in the Bramble family, and has in turn impressed on them his distinctive brand of moral and spiritual integrity; Tabitha and Lismahago have found happiness together, however comical; and Bramble is now mentally and physically able to help his old friend Dennison, rather than require constant assistance of his own.

If the multitude of voices introduced in *Humphry Clinker* lends Smollett's novel much of its verve, so too does the variety of professional, spiritual, and trade discourses to which readers are exposed. We meet not just members of the landed gentry and their servants but also lawyers, doctors, shopkeepers, farriers, writers, politicians, dancing masters, professors, sailors, preachers, prisoners, and messengers, many of them drawn from or based on Smollett's own acquaintances. The jargons and vocabularies of their various professions and trades saturate the novel until we feel personally acquainted with the variety of ranks, classes, professions, and trades at work and play in eighteenth-century Britain. (Several of the selections in this volume's Criticism section explore in more depth the novel's engagement with particular professional and sociopolitical discourses.) Taken together, they underscore the extent to which we are invited to corroborate one of Jery's final statements, made as he takes stock of what he has learned during his travels: "Without all doubt, the greatest advantage acquired in travelling and perusing mankind in the original, is that of dispelling those shameful clouds that darken the faculties of the mind, preventing it from judging with candour and precision."

Yet alongside this message of tolerance—and notwithstanding the novel's experimental formal features—*Humphry Clinker* encodes several strongly conservative dynamics. In addition to its old-fashioned episodic structure, it follows closely the time-honored plotting of prose romances, which customarily conclude with heirs discovered, estates restored, marriages brokered, and traditional hierarchies reestablished. Because these conventions correlate strongly with the maintenance of patriarchal social structures, it is no coincidence that Tabitha and Win Jenkins in particular are routinely revealed as ignorant, materialistic, and sexually repressed—qualities associated with women by the eighteenth-century masculine imagination—or that Bramble literally and figuratively "cleans house" for Dennison after the death of the latter's manipulative, frivolous wife. Equally reactionary in spirit are many of the novel's bawdy episodes, which frequently entail not just bodily humor but also humiliations involving physical disabilities (real or fake), scatological materials, and sexual innuendo delivered with varying degrees of misogyny. From Win Jenkins mistaken for a prostitute, to Lismahago tricked into exiting an upper-story window so that everyone on the ground can see up his nightshirt, these episodes generally take place under the sign of what Simon Dickie calls "the unsentimental eighteenth century."[5] Rather than condemn or ignore them, however, we may see them as symptomatic of an older cultural sensibility still prevalent in the mid-eighteenth century, even as it was being displaced by bourgeois norms of appropriateness. At the same time, given the prevalence in contemporary popular culture of gross-out comedies and self-consciously stupid Internet videos, today's readers may once again be primed to find in these scenes the humor and cathartic release that escaped more easily offended nineteenth- and early-twentieth-century readers.

Finally, alongside both the comedy and the commentary there is a discernable vein of pathos in *Humphry Clinker* that returns us to the biographical matters with which this introduction began. At irregular intervals, both the gritty realism and the stylized romance of the novel retreat, and we are left with the novelist's profound affection for his native Scotland as well as his apparent desire to take peaceable leave of his readers at the conclusion of a long and sometimes contentious public writing career. For Smollett's final novel contains an unusual number of personal touches: it includes his own poem "Ode to Leven-Water," with its unselfconscious celebration of that "Pure Stream! In whose transparent wave / My youthful limbs I wont to lave"; conciliatory portraits of several former enemies and rivals, including the irrepressible Irish stage actor James Quin; and an otherwise superfluous subplot that reunites and redeems characters from *Ferdinand Count Fathom*. It also contains an extraordinary cameo by Smollett himself, who appears in Jery's letter of June 10 as "Mr. S——," the veteran author and benefactor of a host of lesser-known writers. In this episode, Bramble and Jery are invited to Smollett's home in Chelsea, on the outskirts of London, where they witness firsthand his hospitality and patronage. After reporting that Smollett's home is "a plain, yet decent habitation, which opened backwards into a very pleasant garden," Jery expresses his surprise at his host's lack of pretension: "I saw none of the outward signs of authorship, either in the house or in the landlord, who is one of those few authors of the age that stand upon their own foundation, without patronage, and above dependence." In this final literary self-portrait, Smollett asks to be remembered primarily on the basis of his independent mind and generous spirit. Tellingly, he has Jery subsequently observe that "If there was nothing characteristic in the entertainer, the company made ample amends for his want of singularity." Over two hundred years later, the many characters, locales, and adventures of *The*

5. See Simon Dickie, *Cruelty and Laughter: Forgotten Comic Literature and the Unsentimental Eighteenth Century* (Chicago and London: U of Chicago P, 2011).

Expedition of Humphry Clinker continue to provide us with unparalleled company.

The text of this edition is based on the text of the first Norton Critical Edition of *Humphry Clinker*, prepared by James L. Thorson from the Zimmerman Library copy of the three-volume first edition of 1771 (Volume I, misdated 1671) at the University of New Mexico. While preserving Thorson's typographical modernizations, this edition corrects several errors that crept into the previous text via crosschecking with the University of Georgia Press edition prepared by Thomas R. Preston. The illustrations included here are those designed by Thomas Rowlandson for the 1793 two-volume edition of the novel. Smollett provided two notes for the original edition of *Humphry Clinker*, which have been retained and identified; all other notes in the novel, "Backgrounds and Contexts," and "Early Reviews and Criticisms" sections are the editor's. (Notes in the "Contemporary Criticism" section are those of the individual authors of the essays or excerpts.) Only clearly fictional or unidentified characters have not been noted. Most of the locations mentioned in the novel are real and noted as such, except where the geographical references are clear in the text or by reference to the map.

The Text of
THE
EXPEDITION
OF
HUMPHRY CLINKER

THE

EXPEDITION

OF

HUMPHRY CLINKER.

By the AUTHOR of

RODERICK RANDOM.

IN THREE VOLUMES.

VOL. I.

——Quorſum hæc tam putida tendunt,
Furcifer ? ad te, inquam———— HOR.

LONDON,
Printed for W. JOHNSTON, in Ludgate-Street;
and B. COLLINS, in Saliſbury.
MDCLXXI.

1. **Quorsum . . . inquam:** From Horace's *Satires* (2.7.21–22), in which a master who is being lectured by his servant asks "To what end does all this nonsense drive, rogue?" The answer is given: "To you, I said."
2. MDCLXXI: The first volume of the first edition of Smollett's novel is misdated 1671.

The Expedition of Humphry Clinker
April–November, ca. 1770

Key
— Actual Route
···· Conjectured Route

Mull
Iona
Jura
Islay

Loch Lomond
Stirling
St. Andrews
Kinghorn
Glasgow
Edinburgh
River Leven
Berwick-upon-Tweed

Dumfries
Carlisle
Durham
Morpeth
Newcastle upon Tyne

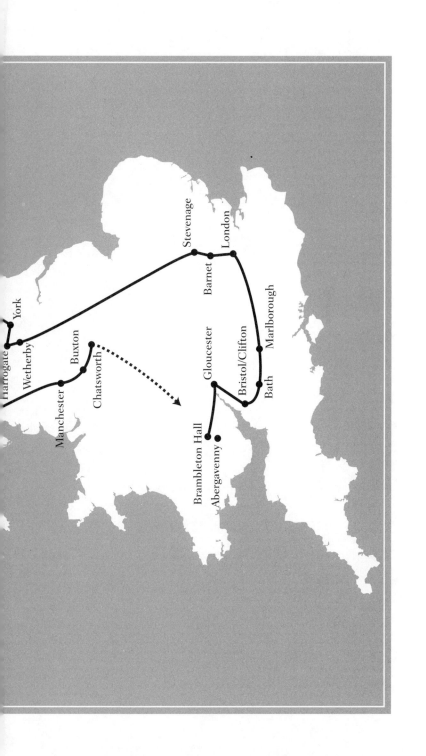

Volume I

To Mr. Henry Davis, Book-seller, in London.

Abergavenny,[3] Aug. 4.

Respected Sir,

I have received your esteemed favour of the 13th ultimo, whereby it appeareth, that you have perused those same Letters, the which were delivered unto you by my friend the reverend Mr. Hugo Behn; and I am pleased to find you think they may be printed with a good prospect of success; in as much as the objections you mention, I humbly conceive, are such as may be redargued,[4] if not entirely removed—And, first, in the first place, as touching what prosecutions may arise from printing the private correspondence of persons still living, give me leave, with all due submission, to observe, that the Letters in question were not written and sent under the seal of secrecy; that they have no tendency to the *mala fama*, or prejudice of any person whatsoever; but rather to the information and edification of mankind: so that it becometh a sort of duty to promulgate them in *usum publicum*.[5] Besides, I have consulted Mr. Davy Higgins, an eminent attorney of this place, who, after due inspection and consideration, declareth, That he doth not think the said Letters contain any matter which will be held actionable in the eye of the law. Finally, if you and I should come to a right understanding, I do declare in *verbo sacerdotis*, that, in case of any such prosecution, I will take the whole upon my own shoulders, even *quoad* fine and imprisonment, though, I must confess, I should not care to undergo flagellation: *Tam ad turpitudinem, quam ad amaritudinem pœna spectans*[6]—Secondly, concerning the personal resentment of

---

3. A town in northwest Wales, about six miles (ten kilometers) from the English border, near where the fictional home of Matthew Bramble is located.
4. Refuted.
5. For the public good (Latin). "*Mala fama*": bad reputation (Latin).
6. A punishment aimed to produce shame as much as bitterness (Latin). The wording is somewhat flawed, and although the italics suggest it is a quotation, it remains unidentified. "*In verbo sacerdotis*": in the words of a priest (Latin); i.e., on my honor. "*Quoad*": with respect to (Latin).

Mr. Justice Lismahago, I may say, *non flocci facio*—I would not willingly vilipend[7] any Christian, if, peradventure, he deserveth that epithet: albeit, I am much surprised that more care is not taken to exclude from the commission all such vagrant foreigners as may be justly suspected of disaffection to our happy constitution, in church and state—God forbid that I should be so uncharitable, as to affirm positively, that the said Lismahago is no better than a Jesuit in disguise; but this I will assert and maintain, *totis viribus*, that, from the day he qualified, he has never been once seen *intra templi parietes*,[8] that is to say, within the parish church.

Thirdly, with respect to what passed at Mr. Kendal's table, when the said Lismahago was so brutal in his reprehensions, I must inform you, my good sir, that I was obliged to retire, not by fear arising from his minatory reproaches, which, as I said above, I value not of a rush; but from the sudden effect produced by a barbel's row, which I had eaten at dinner, not knowing, that the said row is at certain seasons violently cathartic, as Galen observeth in his chapter περί ιχθυζ[9]

Fourthly, and lastly, with reference to the manner in which I got possession of these Letters, it is a circumstance that concerns my own conscience only; sufficeth it to say, I have fully satisfied the parties in whose custody they were; and, by this time, I hope I have also satisfied you in such ways, that the last hand may be put to our agreement, and the work proceed with all convenient expedition; in which hope I rest,

respected sir,

your very humble servant,

JONATHAN DUSTWICH.

P.S. I propose, Deo volente, to have the pleasure of seeing you in the great city, towards All-hallow-tide,[1] when I shall be glad to treat with you concerning a parcel of MS. sermons, of a certain clergyman deceased; a cake of the right leaven, for the present taste of the public. *Verbum sapienti*,[2] &c.

J.D.

---

7. Belittle. "*Non flocci facio*": I don't care about it (Latin; proverbial).
8. Within the walls of the temple (Latin). "Jesuit": a member of the Roman Catholic order, known formally as the Society of Jesus. According to their opponents, they were typically crafty and intriguing. "*Totis viribus*": with all [my] might (Latin).
9. Of fish (Greek). "Minatory": threatening. Galen (129–ca. 200), Roman physician and philosopher, whose writings make no specific mention of the roe ("row," eggs) of the barbel, a type of freshwater fish.
1. The season of All Saints' Day, commemorating those who have attained direct communion with God; celebrated in Western Christianity on November 1. "*Deo volente*": God willing (Latin).
2. A word to the wise (Latin).

To the Revd. Mr. JONATHAN DUSTWICH, at ————.

SIR,

I received yours in course of post, and shall be glad to treat with you for the MS. which I have delivered to your friend Mr. Behn; but can by no means comply with the terms proposed. Those things are so uncertain—Writing is all a lottery—I have been a loser by the works of the greatest men of the age—I could mention particulars, and name names; but don't chuse it—The taste of the town is so changeable. Then there have been so many letters upon travels lately published—What between Smollett's, Sharp's, Derrick's, Thickness's, Baltimore's, and Baretti's, together with Shandy's Sentimental Travels,[3] the public seems to be cloyed with that kind of entertainment—Nevertheless, I will, if you please, run the risque of printing and publishing, and you shall have half the profits of the impression—You need not take the trouble to bring up your sermons on my account—No body reads sermons but Methodists and Dissenters[4]—Besides, for my own part, I am quite a stranger to that sort of reading; and the two persons, whose judgment I depended upon in these matters, are out of the way; one is gone abroad, carpenter of a man of war; and the other has been silly enough to abscond, in order to avoid a prosecution for blasphemy—I'm a great loser by his going off—He has left a manual of devotion half finished on my hands, after having received money for the whole copy—He was the soundest divine, and had the most orthodox pen of all my people; and I never knew his judgment fail, but in flying from his bread and butter on this occasion.

By owning you was not put in bodily fear by Lismahago, you preclude yourself from the benefit of a good plea, over and above the advantage of binding[5] him over. In the late war,[6] I inserted in my evening paper, a paragraph that came by the post, reflecting upon the

---

3. An authentic list of recent travel books: Smollett's *Travels through France and Italy* (1766), Samuel Sharp's *Letters from Italy* (1766), Samuel Derrick's *A Collection of Travels through Various Parts of the World* (1762), Philip Thicknesse's *Useful Hints to Those Who Make the Tour of France* (1768), Frederick Calvert, Baron Baltimore's *A Tour in the East in the Years 1763 and 1764* (1767), Guiseppe Baretti's *An Account of the Manner and Customs of Italy* (1768), and Laurence Sterne's *A Sentimental Journey through France and Italy* (1768). Sterne was publicly associated with the title character of his novel, *The Life and Opinions of Tristram Shandy, Gentleman* (1759–67). In *A Sentimental Journey* he satirizes Smollett as "the learned Dr. Smelfungus."
4. English Christians who separated from the Anglican Church (Church of England) in the 16th through 18th centuries. "Methodists": vigorously evangelical Christians who follow the teachings and example of John Wesley (1703–1791).
5. In England and Wales, someone "bound" by a magistrate (a judge or other state officer) can be required to return to court at a later date or to refrain from certain activities for a designated period, or face arrest or penalty.
6. The Seven Years' War (1756–63), which was driven primarily by long-standing rivalries between Great Britain, France, and Spain.

behaviour of a certain regiment in battle. An officer of said regiment came to my shop, and, in the presence of my wife and journeyman, threatened to cut off my ears——As I exhibited marks of bodily fear, more ways than one, to the conviction of the byestanders, I bound him over; my action lay, and I recovered. As for flagellation, you have nothing to fear, and nothing to hope, on that head—There has been but one printer flogged at the cart's tail these thirty years; that was Charles Watson; and he assured me it was no more than a flea-bite. C—— S—— has been threatened several times by the House of L——;[7] but it came to nothing. If an information[8] should be moved for, and granted against you, as the editor of those Letters, I hope you will have honesty and wit enough to appear and take your trial——If you should be sentenced to the pillory, your fortune is made—As times go, that's a sure step to honour and preferment. I shall think myself happy if I can lend you a lift;[9] and am, very sincerely,

yours,

London, Aug. 10th.   HENRY DAVIS.

Please my kind service to your neighbour, my cousin Madoc— I have sent an Almanack and Court-kalendar, directed for him at Mr. Sutton's, bookseller, in Gloucester,[1] carriage paid, which he will please to accept as a small token of my regard. My wife, who is very fond of toasted cheese,[2] presents her compliments to him, and begs to know if there's any of that kind, which he was so good as to send us last Christmas, to be sold in London.

H.D.

---

7. The House of Lords, the upper house of the British Parliament, still meets in the palace of Westminster in present-day London. "C—— S——": Charles Green Say, a London printer who worked in Ludgate Street.
8. In legal parlance, an official complaint or charge against an individual lodged with a court or magistrate to initiate criminal charges without a formal indictment.
9. Help you achieve a better position.
1. An ancient cathedral city in southwest England, near the border with Wales. "Court-Kalendar": annual handbook of royal families and their courts.
2. A traditional Welsh dish.

The
Expedition
of
Humphry Clinker

To Dr. Lewis.

Doctor,

The pills are good for nothing—I might as well swallow snow-balls to cool my reins[3]—I have told you over and over, how hard I am to move; and at this time of day, I ought to know something of my own constitution. Why will you be so positive? Prithee send me another prescription—I am as lame and as much tortured in all my limbs as if I was broke upon the wheel: indeed, I am equally distressed in mind and body—As if I had not plagues enough of my own, those children of my sister are left me for a perpetual source of vexation—what business have people to get children to plague their neighbours? A ridiculous incident that happened yesterday to my niece Liddy, has disordered me in such a manner, that I expect to be laid up with another fit of the gout—perhaps, I may explain myself in my next. I shall set out to-morrow morning for the Hot Well at Bristol,[4] where I am afraid I shall stay longer than I could wish. On the receipt of this, send Williams thither with my saddle-horse and the *demi pique*.[5] Tell Barns to thresh out the two old ricks, and send the corn to market, and sell it off to the poor at a shilling a bushel under market price.—I have received a sniveling letter from Griffin, offering to make a public submission and pay costs. I want none of

---

3. Kidneys. An adaptation of Sir John Falstaff's complaint, "for my belly's as cold as if I had swallowed snowballs for pills to cool the reins," in Shakespeare's *Merry Wives of Windsor* (3.5.22–23).
4. The Bristol Hot Well and Pump Room, demolished in 1822, stood at the start of Saint Vincent's Parade, a row of houses still standing above the River Avon. Although natural hot springs had been used since classical times, the addition of increasingly elaborate pump rooms to dispense the waters for drinking was an early-18th-century development.
5. A saddle about half the height of a traditional war saddle.

his submissions; neither will I pocket any of his money—The fellow is a bad neighbour, and I desire to have nothing to do with him: but as he is purse-proud, he shall pay for his insolence: let him give five pounds to the poor of the parish, and I'll withdraw my action; and in the mean time you may tell Prig to stop proceedings.—Let Morgan's widow have the Alderney cow, and forty shillings to clothe her children: but don't say a syllable of the matter to any living soul—I'll make her pay when she is able. I desire you will lock up all my drawers, and keep the keys till meeting; and be sure you take the iron chest with my papers into your own custody—Forgive all this trouble from,

Dear Lewis,

Your affectionate
M. BRAMBLE.

Gloucester, April 2.

To MRS. GWYLLIM, house-keeper at Brambleton-hall.

MRS. GWILLIM,

When this cums to hand, be sure to pack up in the trunk male that stands in my closet, to be sent me in the Bristol waggon without loss of time, the following articles, viz. my rose collard neglejay, with green robins, my yellow damask, and my black velvet suit, with the short hoop; my bloo quilted petticot, my green manteel, my laced apron, my French commode, Macklin head and lappets,[6] and the litel box with my jowls. Williams may bring over my bum-daffee, and the viol with the easings of Dr. Hill's dock-water,[7] and Chowder's lacksitif. The poor creature has been terribly constuprated ever since we left huom. Pray take particular care of the house while the family is absent. Let there be a fire constantly kept in my brother's chamber and mine. The maids, having nothing to do, may be sat a spinning. I desire you'll clap a pad-luck on the wind-seller, and let none of the men have excess to the strong bear—don't forget to have the gate shit every evening before dark.——The gardnir and the hind may lie below in the landry, to partake the house, with the

---

6. A lace cap with streamers, of the variety made in Mechlin, Belgium. Tabitha may also be thinking of the actor Charles Macklin (ca. 1699–1797). "Trunk male": a trunk heavy enough to require that taxes be paid on it, usually spelled "mail." (For more on the unconventional spellings in Tabitha Bramble's and Win Jenkins's letters, see the Preface, p. xii, and the "Contemporary Criticism" section. Footnotes to these letters will be restricted largely to cases where the intended words need further explanation.) "Commode": a tall, elaborate, old-fashioned headdress.
7. Essence of waterdock, a common herb, sold by the apothecary and writer John Hill (1716–1775), who ran the *British Magazine* from 1746 to 1750 and was an editorial rival of Smollett's. "Bum-daffee": derived from Daffey's Elixir, named after another infamous quack doctor.

blunderbuss and the great dog; and I hope you'll have a watchfull eye over the maids. I know that hussy, Mary Jones, loves to be rumping with the men. Let me know if Alderney's calf be sould yet, and what he fought—if the ould goose be sitting; and if the cobler has cut Dicky, and how the pore anemil bore the operation.—No more at present, but rests,

Yours,

Glostar, April 2.   TABITHA BRAMBLE.

To Mrs. MARY JONES, at Brambleton-hall.

DEAR MOLLY,

Heaving this importunity, I send my love to you and Saul, being in good health, and hoping to hear the same from you; and that you and Saul will take my poor kitten to bed with you this cold weather.—We have been all in a sad taking here at Glostar—Miss Liddy had like to have run away with a player-man, and young master and he would adone themselves a mischief; but the squire applied to the mare, and they were bound over.—Mistress bid me not speak a word of the matter to any Christian soul—no more I shall: for, we servints should see all and say nothing—But what was worse than all this, Chowder has had the misfortune to be worried by a butcher's dog, and came home in a terrible pickle—Mistriss was taken with the asterisks, but they soon went off. The doctor was sent for to Chowder, and he subscribed a repository, which did him great service—thank God he's now in a fair way to do well—pray take care of my box and the pillyber,[8] and put them under your own bed; for, I do suppose, madam Gwyllim will be a prying into my secrets, now my back is turned. John Thomas is in good health, but sulky. The squire gave away an ould coat to a poor man; and John says as how tis robbing him of his parquisites.[9]—I told him, by his agreement he was to receive no vails;[1] but he says as how there's a difference betwixt vails and parquisites; and so there is for sartain. We are all going to the Hot Well, where I shall drink your health in a glass of water, being,

Dear Molly,

Your humble servant to command,

Glostar, April 2d.   WIN. JENKINS.

---

8. Pillowcase.
9. The fringe benefits conventionally associated with a given position or job, now commonly called perks.
1. Tips, bonuses.

To Sir Watkin Phillips, Bar^t.
of Jesus college, Oxon.[2]

Dear Phillips,

As I have nothing more at heart than to convince you I am incapable of forgetting, or neglecting the friendship I made at college, I now begin that correspondence by letters, which you and I agreed, at parting, to cultivate. I begin it sooner than I intended, that you may have it in your power to refute any idle reports which may be circulated to my prejudice at Oxford, touching a foolish quarrel, in which I have been involved on account of my sister, who had been some time settled here in a boarding-school.—When I came hither with my uncle and aunt (who are our guardians) to fetch her away, I found her a fine, tall girl, of seventeen, with an agreeable person; but remarkably simple, and quite ignorant of the world. This disposition, and want of experience, had exposed her to the addresses of a person—I know not what to call him, who had seen her at a play; and, with a confidence and dexterity peculiar to himself, found means to be recommended to her acquaintance. It was by the greatest accident I intercepted one of his letters; as it was my duty to stifle this correspondence in its birth, I made it my business to find him out, and tell him very freely my sentiments of the matter. The spark[3] did not like the stile I used, and behaved with abundance of mettle. Though his rank in life (which, by the bye, I am ashamed to declare) did not entitle him to much deference; yet as his behaviour was remarkably spirited, I admitted him to the privilege of a gentleman, and something might have happened, had not we been prevented.—In short, the business took air, I know not how, and made abundance of noise—recourse was had to justice—I was obliged to give my word and honour, &c. and to-morrow morning we set out for Bristol Wells, where I expect to hear from you by the return of the post.——I have got into a family of originals, whom I may one day attempt to describe for your amusement. My aunt, Mrs.[4] Tabitha Bramble, is a maiden of forty-five, exceedingly starched, vain, and ridiculous.—My uncle is an odd kind of humorist,[5] always on the fret, and so unpleasant in his manner, that rather than be obliged to keep him company, I'd

---

2. Jesus College at Oxford University was founded by Queen Elizabeth I in 1571 at the request of Hugh Price, a Welsh lawyer and clergyman. "Bar^t.": baronet, the lowest step in the hereditary British peerage.
3. A lighthearted or foolish young man.
4. Commonly used as a title of respect for unmarried as well as married women in the 18th century.
5. Since classical times, medical practice relied on a theory of four principal humors or types of fluids—blood, yellow bile, black bile, and phlegm—believed to make up the body. In a healthy person, these substances were thought to be balanced; imbalances were believed to cause physical discomfort, disease, and psychological abnormalities.

resign all claim to the inheritance of his estate.—Indeed his being tortured by the gout may have soured his temper, and, perhaps, I may like him better on further acquaintance: certain it is, all his servants and neighbours in the country, are fond of him, even to a degree of enthusiasm, the reason of which I cannot as yet comprehend. Remember me to Griffy Price, Cwyn, Mansel, Basset, and all the rest of my old Cambrian[6] companions.——Salute the bed-maker in my name—give my service to the cook, and pray take care of poor Ponto, for the sake of his old master, who is, and ever will be,   Dear Phillips,

Your affectionate friend,

and humble servant,

Gloucester, April 2.   JER. MELFORD.

To Mrs. JERMYN, at her house in Gloucester.

DEAR MADAM,

Having no mother of my own, I hope you will give me leave to disburthen my poor heart to you, who have always acted the part of a kind parent to me, ever since I was put under your care.—Indeed, and indeed, my worthy governess may believe me, when I assure her, that I never harboured a thought that was otherwise than virtuous; and, if God will give me grace, I shall never behave so as to cast a reflection on the care you have taken in my education. I confess I have given just cause of offence by my want of prudence and experience. I ought not to have listened to what the young man said; and it was my duty to have told you all that passed, but I was ashamed to mention it; and then he behaved so modest and respectful, and seemed to be so melancholy and timorous, that I could not find in my heart to do any thing that should make him miserable and desperate. As for familiarities, I do declare, I never once allowed him the favour of a salute;[7] and as to the few letters that passed between us, they are all in my uncle's hands, and I hope they contain nothing contrary to innocence and honour.—I am still persuaded that he is not what he appears to be: but time will discover—mean while I will endeavour to forget a connexion, which is so displeasing to my family. I have cried without ceasing, and have not tasted any thing

---

Medical treatments like bloodletting and enemas were thought to expel or reduce a harmful surplus of a humor.

6. Welsh. The Latin name for Wales, *Cambria,* derives from the Welsh *Cymru,* meaning "fellow-countrypeople." The names are all typically Welsh, with the exception of Mansel, which likely refers to Francis Mansell (1579–1665), a well-known principal of Jesus College in the 17th century.

7. A kiss.

but tea, since I was hurried away from you; nor did I once close my eyes for three nights running.——My aunt continues to chide me severely when we are by ourselves; but I hope to soften her in time, by humility and submission.—My uncle, who was so dreadfully passionate in the beginning, has been moved by my tears and distress; and is now all tenderness and compassion; and my brother is reconciled to me, on my promise to break off all correspondence with that unfortunate youth: but, notwithstanding all their indulgence, I shall have no peace of mind 'till I know my dear and ever honoured governess has forgiven her poor, disconsolate, forlorn,

Affectionate humble servant,

till death,

Clifton,[8] April 6.   LYDIA MELFORD.

To Miss LÆTITIA WILLIS, at Gloucester.

MY DEAREST LETTY,

I am in such a fright, lest this should not come safe to hand by the conveyance of Jarvis the carrier, that I beg you will write me, on the receipt of it, directing to me, under cover, to Mrs. Winifred Jenkins, my aunt's maid, who is a good girl, and has been so kind to me in my affliction, that I have made her my confidant; as for Jarvis, he was very shy of taking charge of my letter and the little parcel, because his sister Sally had like to have lost her place on my account: indeed I cannot blame the man for his caution; but I have made it worth his while.—My dear companion and bed-fellow,[9] it is a grievous addition to my other misfortunes, that I am deprived of your agreeable company and conversation, at a time when I need so much the comfort of your good humour and good sense; but, I hope, the friendship we contracted at boarding-school, will last for life——I doubt not but on my side it will daily increase and improve, as I gain experience, and learn to know the value of a true friend.—O, my dear Letty! what shall I say about poor Mr. Wilson? I have promised to break off all correspondence, and, if possible, to forget him: but, alas! I begin to perceive that will not be in my power. As it is by no means proper that the picture should remain in my hands, lest it should be the occasion of more mischief, I have sent it to you by this opportunity, begging you will either keep it safe till better times, or

---

8. In the 18th century, a village located on a hill outside the city of Bristol.
9. It was not uncommon for young men or women to sleep in the same bed with a room-mate of the same sex.

return it to Mr. Wilson himself, who, I suppose, will make it his business to see you at the usual place. If he should be low-spirited at my sending back his picture, you may tell him I have no occasion for a picture, while the original continues engraved on my——But no; I would not have you tell him that neither; because there must be an end of our correspondence—I wish he may forget me, for the sake of his own peace; and yet if he should, he must be a barbarous—— But 'tis impossible—poor Wilson cannot be false and inconstant: I beseech him not to write to me, nor attempt to see me for some time; for, considering the resentment and passionate temper of my brother Jery, such an attempt might be attended with consequences which would make us all miserable for life—let us trust to time and the chapter of accidents; or rather to that Providence which will not fail, sooner or later, to reward those that walk in the paths of honour and virtue.—I would offer my love to the young ladies; but it is not fit that any of them should know you have received this letter.—If we go to Bath, I shall send you my simple remarks upon that famous center of polite amusement, and every other place we may chance to visit; and I flatter myself that my dear Miss Willis will be punctual in answering the letters of her affectionate,

Clifton, April 6.   LYDIA MELFORD.

To Dr. LEWIS.

DEAR LEWIS,

I have followed your directions with some success, and might have been upon my legs by this time, had the weather permitted me to use my saddle horse. I rode out upon the Downs[1] last Tuesday, in the forenoon, when the sky, as far as the visible horizon, was without a cloud; but before I had gone a full mile, I was overtaken instantaneously by a storm of rain that wet me to the skin in three minutes— whence it came the devil knows; but it has laid me up (I suppose) for one fortnight. It makes me sick to hear people talk of the fine air upon Clifton-Downs: how can the air be either agreeable or salutary, where the dæmon of vapours descends in a perpetual drizzle? My confinement is the more intolerable, as I am surrounded with domestic vexations.—My niece has had a dangerous fit of illness, occasioned by that cursed incident at Gloucester, which I mentioned in my last.——She is a poor good-natured simpleton, as soft as butter, and as easily melted—not that she's a fool—the girl's parts[2] are

---

1. An area of open limestone chalk hills noted for its picturesque beauty.
2. Abilities, talents, or intellectual qualities.

not despicable, and her education has not been neglected; that is to say, she can write and spell, and speak French, and play upon the harpsichord; then she dances finely, has a good figure, and is very well inclined; but, she's deficient in spirit, and so susceptible—and so tender forsooth!—truly, she has got a languishing eye, and reads romances——Then there's her brother, 'squire Jery, a pert jacka-napes,[3] full of college-petulance and self-conceit; proud as a German count, and as hot and hasty as a Welch mountaineer. As for that fantastical animal, my sister Tabby, you are no stranger to her qual-ifications—I vow to God, she is sometimes so intolerable, that I almost think she's the devil incarnate come to torment me for my sins; and yet I am conscious of no sins that ought to entail such family-plagues upon me—why the devil should not I shake off these torments at once? I an't married to Tabby, thank Heaven! nor did I beget the other two: let them choose another guardian: for my part, I an't in a condition to take care of myself; much less to superintend the conduct of giddy-headed boys and girls. You earnestly desire to know the particulars of our adventure at Gloucester, which are briefly these, and I hope they will go no further:—Liddy had been so long cooped up in a boarding-school, which, next to a nunnery, is the worst kind of seminary that ever was contrived for young women, that she became as inflammable as touch-wood;[4] and going to a play in holiday-time,—'sdeath, I'm ashamed to tell you! she fell in love with one of the actors—a handsome young fellow that goes by the name of Wilson. The rascal soon perceived the impression he had made, and managed matters so as to see her at a house where she went to drink tea with her governess.—This was the beginning of a cor-respondence, which they kept up by means of a jade of a milliner,[5] who made and dressed caps for the girls at the boarding-school. When we arrived at Gloucester, Liddy came to stay at lodgings with her aunt, and Wilson bribed the maid to deliver a letter into her own hands; but it seems Jery had already acquired so much credit with the maid, (by what means he best knows) that she carried the letter to him, and so the whole plot was discovered. The rash boy, without saying a word of the matter to me, went immediately in search of Wilson; and, I suppose, treated him with insolence enough. The theatrical hero was too far gone in romance to brook such usage: he replied in blank verse, and a formal challenge ensued. They agreed to meet early next morning and decide the dispute with sword and pistol. I heard nothing at all of the affair, 'till Mr. Morley came to my bed-side in the morning, and told me he was afraid my nephew was going to fight, as he had been overheard talking very loud

3. A ridiculous or impertinent person.
4. Tinder.
5. Hatmaker.

and vehement with Wilson at the young man's lodgings the night before, and afterwards went and bought powder and ball at a shop in the neighbourhood. I got up immediately, and upon inquiry found he was just gone out. I begged Morley to knock up[6] the mayor, that he might interpose as a magistrate, and in the mean time I hobbled after the squire, whom I saw at a distance walking at a great pace towards the city gate—in spite of all my efforts, I could not come up 'till our two combatants had taken their ground, and were priming their pistols. An old house luckily screened me from their view; so that I rushed upon them at once, before I was perceived. They were both confounded, and attempted to make their escape different ways; but Morley coming up with constables at that instant, took Wilson into custody, and Jery followed him quietly to the mayor's house. All this time I was ignorant of what had passed the preceding day; and neither of the parties would discover a tittle[7] of the matter. The mayor observed that it was great presumption in Wilson, who was a stroller, to proceed to such extremities with a gentleman of family and fortune; and threatened to commit him on the vagrant act.[8]—The young fellow bustled up with great spirit, declaring he was a gentleman, and would be treated as such; but he refused to explain himself further. The master of the company being sent for, and examined, touching the said Wilson, said the young man had engaged[9] with him at Birmingham about six months ago; but never would take his salary; that he had behaved so well in his private character, as to acquire the respect and good-will of all his acquaintance, and that the public owned his merit, as an actor, was altogether extraordinary.——After all, I fancy, he will turn out to be a run-away prentice from London.—The manager offered to bail him for any sum, provided he would give his word and honour that he would keep the peace; but the young gentleman was on his high ropes;[1] and would by no means lay himself under any restrictions: on the other hand, Hopefull was equally obstinate; till at length the mayor declared, that if they both refused to be bound over, he would immediately commit Wilson as a vagrant to hard labour. I own I was much pleased with Jery's behaviour on this occasion: he said, that rather than Mr. Wilson should be treated in such an ignominious manner, he would give his word and honour to prosecute the affair no further while they remained at Gloucester—Wilson thanked him for his generous manner of proceeding, and was discharged.

6. Rouse, mobilize.
7. Explain a tiny bit.
8. Presumably the act of Parliament passed in 1744 that allowed severe punishments for vagrants, beggars, and unlicensed actors. "Stroller": itinerant actor.
9. Taken work.
1. Likely a variant of "on his high horse," i.e., in a haughty frame of mind.

On our return to our lodgings, my nephew explained the whole mystery; and I own I was exceedingly incensed.——Liddy being questioned on the subject, and very severely reproached by that wild-cat my sister Tabby, first swooned away, then dissolving in a flood of tears, confessed all the particulars of the correspondence, at the same time giving up three letters, which was all she had received from her admirer. The last, which Jery intercepted, I send you inclosed, and when you have read it, I dare say you won't wonder at the progress the writer had made in the heart of a simple girl, utterly unacquainted with the characters of mankind. Thinking it was high time to remove her from such a dangerous connexion, I carried her off the very next day to Bristol; but the poor creature was so frightened and fluttered, by our threats and expostulations, that she fell sick the fourth day after our arrival at Clifton, and continued so ill for a whole week, that her life was despaired of. It was not till yesterday that Dr. Rigge[2] declared her out of danger. You cannot imagine what I have suffered, partly from the indiscretion of this poor child, but much more from the fear of losing her entirely. This air is intolerably cold, and the place quite solitary—I never go down to the well without returning low-spirited; for there I meet with half a dozen poor emaciated creatures, with ghostly looks, in the last stage of a consumption, who have made shift to linger through the winter, like so many exotic plants languishing in a hot-house; but, in all appearance, will drop into their graves before the sun has warmth enough to mitigate the rigour of this ungenial spring.—If you think the Bath water will be of any service to me, I will go thither as soon as my niece can bear the motion of the coach.——Tell Barns I am obliged to him for his advice; but don't choose to follow it. If Davis voluntarily offers to give up the farm, the other shall have it; but I will not begin at this time of day to distress my tenants, because they are unfortunate, and cannot make regular payments: I wonder that Barns should think me capable of such oppression—As for Higgins, the fellow is a notorious poacher, to be sure; and an impudent rascal to set his snares in my own paddock; but, I suppose, he thought he had some right (especially in my absence) to partake of what nature seems to have intended for common use—you may threaten him in my name, as much as you please, and if he repeats the offence, let me know it before you have recourse to justice.——I know you are a great sportsman, and oblige many of your friends: I need not tell you to make use of my grounds; but it may be necessary to hint, that I'm more afraid of my fowling piece than of my game. When you can

2. Thomas Rigge (d. 1797), a physician at the Bristol Royal Infirmary from 1767 to 1778; he also practiced medicine at the Hot Well.

spare two or three brace of partidges, send them over by the stage coach, and tell Gwyllim that she forgot to pack up my flannels and wide shoes[3] in the trunk-mail—I shall trouble you as usual, from time to time, 'till at last I suppose you will be tired of corresponding with

Your assured friend,

Clifton, April 17.   M. BRAMBLE.

To Miss LYDIA MELFORD.

Miss Willis has pronounced my doom——you are going away, dear Miss Melford!—you are going to be removed, I know not whither! what shall I do? which way shall I turn for consolation? I know not what I say—all night long have I been tossed in a sea of doubts and fears, uncertainty and distraction, without being able to connect my thoughts, much less to form any consistent plan of conduct—I was even tempted to wish that I had never seen you; or that you had been less amiable, or less compassionate to your poor Wilson; and yet it would be detestable ingratitude in me to form such a wish, considering how much I am indebted to your goodness, and the ineffable pleasure I have derived from your indulgence and approbation— Good God! I never heard your name mentioned without emotion! the most distant prospect of being admitted to your company, filled my whole soul with a kind of pleasing alarm! as the time approached, my heart beat with redoubled force, and every nerve thrilled with a transport of expectation; but, when I found myself actually in your presence;——when I heard you speak;—when I saw you smile; when I beheld your charming eyes turned favourably upon me; my breast was filled with such tumults of delight, as wholly deprived me of the power of utterance, and wrapt me in a delirium of joy!—— encouraged by your sweetness of temper and affability, I ventured to describe the feelings of my heart—even then you did not check my presumption——you pitied my sufferings, and gave me leave to hope——you put a favourable—perhaps too favourable a construction, on my appearance—certain it is, I am no player in love— I speak the language of my own heart; and have no prompter but nature.——Yet there is something in this heart, which I have not yet disclosed—I flattered myself—But, I will not—I must not proceed—Dear Miss Liddy! for Heaven's sake, contrive, if possible,

---

3. Traditional remedies for common symptoms of gout, a medical condition characterized by arthritic attacks. Wide shoes eased swelling of the toes and feet, and flannel wrappings were used to promote sweating (thought to reduce inflammation).

some means of letting me speak to you before you leave Gloucester; otherwise, I know not what will—But I begin to rave again—I will endeavour to bear this trial with fortitude—while I am capable of reflecting upon your tenderness and truth, I surely have no cause to despair—yet I am strangely affected. The sun seems to deny me light—a cloud hangs over me, and there is a dreadful weight upon my spirits! While you stay in this place, I shall continually hover about your lodgings, as the parted soul is said to linger about the grave where its mortal consort lies.—I know, if it is in your power, you will task your humanity—your compassion—shall I add, your affection?—in order to assuage the almost intolerable disquiet that torments the heart of your afflicted,

Gloucester, March 31.   WILSON.

To Sir WATKIN PHILLIPS, of Jesus college, Oxon.

Hot-well, April 18.

DEAR PHILLIPS,

I give Mansel credit for his invention, in propagating the report that I had a quarrel with a mountebank's merry Andrew[4] at Glouces-ter: but I have too much respect for every appendage of wit, to quar-rel even with the lowest buffoonery; and therefore I hope Mansel and I shall always be good friends. I cannot, however, approve of his drowning my poor dog Ponto, on purpose to convert Ovid's pleo-nasm into a punning epitaph.—*deerant quoque Littora Ponto:*[5] for, that he threw him into the Isis,[6] when it was so high and impetuous, with no other view than to kill the fleas, is an excuse that will not hold water—But I leave poor Ponto to his fate, and hope Providence will take care to accommodate Mansel with a drier death.

As there is nothing that can be called company at the Well, I am here in a state of absolute rustication:[7] This, however, gives me lei-sure to observe the singularities in my uncle's character, which seems to have interested your curiosity. The truth is, his disposition and mine, which, like oil and vinegar, repelled one another at first, have now begun to mix by dint of being beat up together. I was once apt

---

4. A professional clown or comedian who would assist an itinerant quack doctor ("moun-tebank") in selling his medicines from a temporary stage.
5. Part of a line from Ovid's *Metamorphosis* (1.292): "There was nothing but the sea, and the sea had no shore." The pun involves *Ponto*, the name of the drowned dog, and *pontus,* Latin for "the sea." "Pleonasm": redundancy.
6. The historical name for the River Thames, which begins slightly upstream of Oxford.
7. To be rusticated meant both to be sent away from Oxford University, usually as punish-ment, and to live in the countryside.

to believe him a complete Cynic;[8] and that nothing but the necessity of his occasions could compel him to get within the pale of society— I am now of another opinion. I think his peevishness arises partly from bodily pain, and partly from a natural excess of mental sensibility; for, I suppose, the mind as well as the body, is in some cases endued with a morbid excess of sensation.

I was t'other day much diverted with a conversation that passed in the Pump-room, betwixt him and the famous Dr. L——n,[9] who is come to ply at the Well for patients. My uncle was complaining of the stink, occasioned by the vast quantity of mud and slime, which the river leaves at low ebb under the windows of the Pump-room. He observed, that the exhalations arising from such a nuisance, could not but be prejudicial to the weak lungs of many consumptive patients, who came to drink the water. The Doctor overhearing this remark, made up to him, and assured him he was mistaken. He said, people in general were so misled by vulgar prejudices, that philosophy was hardly sufficient to undeceive them. Then humming thrice, he assumed a most ridiculous solemnity of aspect, and entered into a learned investigation of the nature of stink. He observed, that stink, or stench, meant no more than a strong impression on the olfactory nerves; and might be applied to substances of the most opposite qualities; that in the Dutch language, *stinken* signified the most agreeable perfume, as well as the most fetid odour, as appears in Van Vloudel's translation of Horace, in that beautiful ode, *Quis multa gracilis*, &c.—The words *liquidis perfusus odoribus*, he translates *van civet & moschata gestinken*: that individuals differed *toto cœlo*[1] in their opinion of smells, which, indeed, was altogether as arbitrary as the opinion of beauty; that the French were pleased with the putrid effluvia of animal food; and so were the Hottentots[2] in Africa, and the Savages in Greenland; and that the Negroes on the coast of Senegal would not touch fish till it was rotten; strong presumptions in favour of what is generally called stink, as those nations are in a state of nature, undebauched by luxury, unseduced by whim and caprice: that he had reason to believe the stercoraceous[3] flavour,

8. Cynics were classical philosophers who, following the example of Diogenes of Sinope (ca. 412–323 B.C.E.), tried to live according to principles of virtue and simplicity. By the 18th century, however, emphasis on perceived negative aspects of cynicism, especially its lack of respect for social authority, led to its contemporary designation of someone who harbors habitual suspicion regarding human motives and actions.
9. Diederich Wessel Linden, a German physician who practiced in England and wrote a number of pieces on the supposed medicinal qualities of spa waters.
1. The whole sky (Latin, literal trans.); i.e., entirely. Joost van den Vondel's Dutch translation of Horace's *Odes* (1.5.1–2) appeared in 1735; Linden's account of the details is inaccurate. The two full lines read in English: "What fair youth, suffused with liquid perfumes, urges you amidst a profusion of roses?"
2. The Khoikhoi people of southern Africa; the term is now considered derogatory.
3. Relating to or consisting of dung or excrement.

condemned by prejudice as a stink, was, in fact, most agreeable to the organs of smelling; for, that every person who pretended to nauseate the smell of another's excretions, snuffed up his own with particular complacency; for the truth of which he appealed to all the ladies and gentlemen then present: he said, the inhabitants of Madrid and Edinburgh found particular satisfaction in breathing their own atmosphere, which was always impregnated with stercoraceous effluvia: that the learned Dr. B—, in his treatise on the Four Digestions,[4] explains in what manner the volatile effluvia from the intestines, stimulate and promote the operations of the animal oeconomy: he affirmed, the last Grand Duke of Tuscany, of the *Medicis* family, who refined upon sensuality with the spirit of a philosopher, was so delighted with that odour, that he caused the essence of ordure to be extracted, and used it as the most delicious perfume: that he himself, (the doctor) when he happened to be low-spirited, or fatigued with business, found immediate relief and uncommon satisfaction from hanging over the stale contents of a close-stool,[5] while his servant stirred it about under his nose; nor was this effect to be wondered at, when we consider that this substance abounds with the self-same volatile salts that are so greedily smelled to by the most delicate invalids, after they have been extracted and sublimed by the chemists.——By this time the company began to hold their noses; but the doctor, without taking the least notice of this signal, proceeded to shew, that many fetid substances were not only agreeable but salutary; such as *assafetida*,[6] and other medicinal gums, resins, roots, and vegetables, over and above burnt feathers, tan-pits, candle-snuffs, &c. In short, he used many learned arguments to persuade his audience out of their senses; and from stench made a transition to *filth*, which he affirmed was also a mistaken idea, in as much as objects so called, were no other than certain modifications of matter, consisting of the same principles that enter into the composition of all created essences, whatever they may be: that in the filthiest production of nature, a philosopher considered nothing but the earth, water, salt, and air of which it was compounded; that, for his own part, he had no more objection to drinking the dirtiest ditch water, than he had to a glass of water from the Hot Well, provided he was assured there was nothing poisonous in the concrete.[7] Then addressing himself to my uncle, "Sir, (said he)

---

4. Edward Barry (1696–1776), created baronet in 1775, was an Irish physician, politician, and author of *A Treatise on the Three Different Digestions and Discharges of the Human Body, and the Diseases of their Principal Organs* (1759).
5. A wooden stool with a hole containing a chamber pot.
6. A strong-smelling resin-like gum made from the dried sap of stems and roots of several herbs native to Afghanistan. It was used frequently in 18th-century Britain to treat spasms and so-called hysterical complaints, such as fainting and shortness of breath.
7. Compound.

you seem to be of a dropsical habit, and probably will soon have a confirmed *ascites*:[8] if I should be present when you are tapped, I will give you a convincing proof of what I assert, by drinking without hesitation the water that comes out of your abdomen."——The ladies made wry faces at this declaration, and my uncle, changing colour, told him he did not desire any such proof of his philosophy: "But I should be glad to know (said he) what makes you think I am of a dropsical habit?" "Sir, I beg pardon, (replied the doctor) I perceive your ancles are swelled, and you seem to have the *facies leucophlegmatica*.[9] Perhaps, indeed, your disorder may be *oedematous*, or gouty, or it may be the *lues venerea*:[1] If you have any reason to flatter yourself it is this last, sir, I will undertake to cure you with three small pills, even if the disease should have attained its utmost inveteracy. Sir, it is an arcanum[2] which I have discovered, and prepared with infinite labour.—Sir, I have lately cured a woman in Bristol—a common prostitute, sir, who had got all the worst symptoms of the disorder; such as *nodi, tophi,* and *gummata, verrucœ, cristœ Galli,* and a *serpiginous* eruption,[3] or rather a pocky itch all over her body.——By that time she had taken the second pill, sir, by Heaven! she was as smooth as my hand, and the third made her as sound and as fresh as a new born infant." "Sir, (cried my uncle peevishly) I have no reason to flatter myself that my disorder comes within the efficacy of your nostrum. But, this patient you talk of, may not be so sound at bottom as you imagine." "I can't possibly be mistaken: (rejoined the philosopher) for I have had communication with her three times—I always ascertain my cures in that manner." At this remark, all the ladies retired to another corner of the room, and some of them began to spit.—As to my uncle, though he was ruffled at first by the doctor's saying he was dropsical, he could not help smiling at this ridiculous confession, and, I suppose, with a view to punish this original, told him there was a wart upon his nose, that looked a little suspicious. "I don't pretend to be a judge of those matters; (said he) but I understand that warts are often produced by the distemper; and that one upon your nose seems to have taken possession of the very keystone of the bridge, which I hope is in no danger of falling."[4] L——n seemed a little confounded at this remark, and assured him it was nothing but a common excrescence of the cuticula, but that the bones were all sound below; for the truth of

8. Abdominal dropsy. "Dropsy" is the old-fashioned term for edema (or oedema), a medical condition characterized by excessive water retention in body cavities beneath the skin.
9. A pale, swollen appearance.
1. Venereal infection.
2. A mysterious, powerful remedy.
3. Hard tumors, gouty deposits, soft tumors, warts, bony ridges, creeping skin disease.
4. Nasal collapse indicates an advanced stage of syphilis.

this assertion he appealed to the touch, desiring he would feel the part. My uncle said it was a matter of such delicacy to meddle with a gentleman's nose, that he declined the office—upon which, the Doctor turning to me, intreated me to do him that favour. I complied with his request, and handled it so roughly, that he sneezed, and the tears ran down his cheeks, to the no small entertainment of the company, and particularly of my uncle, who burst out a-laughing for the first time since I have been with him; and took notice, that the part seemed to be very tender. "Sir, (cried the Doctor) it is naturally a tender part; but to remove all possibility of doubt, I will take off the wart this very night."

So saying, he bowed with great solemnity all round, and retired to his own lodgings, where he applied caustic to the wart; but it spread in such a manner as to produce a considerable inflammation, attended with an enormous swelling; so that when he next appeared, his whole face was overshadowed by this tremendous nozzle; and the rueful eagerness with which he explained this unlucky accident, was ludicrous beyond all description.——I was much pleased with meeting the original of a character, which you and I have often laughed at in description; and what surprizes me very much, I find the features in the picture, which has been drawn for him, rather softened than over-charged.—

As I have something else to say; and this letter has run to an unconscionable length, I shall now give you a little respite, and trouble you again by the very first post. I wish you would take it in your head to retaliate these double strokes upon

Yours always,

J. MELFORD.

To Sir WATKIN PHILLIPS, of Jesus college, Oxon.

Hot Well, April 20.

DEAR KNIGHT,

I now sit down to execute the threat in the tail of my last. The truth is, I am big with the secret, and long to be delivered. It relates to my guardian, who, you know, is at present our principal object in view.

T'other day, I thought I had detected him in such a state of frailty, as would but ill become his years and character. There is a decent sort of a woman, not disagreeable in her person, that comes to the Well, with a poor emaciated child, far gone in a consumption. I had caught my uncle's eyes several times directed to this person, with a very suspicious expression in them, and every time he saw himself observed, he hastily withdrew them, with evident marks of confusion—I resolved to watch him more narrowly, and saw him speaking to her privately in a corner of the walk. At length, going down to the Well one day, I met her half way up the hill to Clifton, and could not help suspecting she was going to our lodgings by appointment, as it was about one o'clock, the hour when my sister and I are generally at the Pump-room.—This notion exciting my curiosity, I returned by a back way, and got unperceived into my own chamber, which is contiguous to my uncle's apartment. Sure enough, the woman was introduced, but not into his bed-chamber; he gave her audience in a parlour; so that I was obliged to shift my station to another room, where, however, there was a small chink in the partition, through which I could perceive what passed.—My uncle, though a little lame, rose up when she came in, and setting a chair for her, desired she would sit down: then he asked if she would take a dish of chocolate, which she declined, with much acknowledgment. After a short pause, he said, in a croaking tone of voice, which confounded me not a little, "Madam, I am truly concerned for your misfortunes; and if this trifle can be of any service to you, I beg you will accept it without ceremony." So saying, he put a bit of paper into her hand, which she opening with great trepidation, exclaimed in an extacy, "Twenty pounds! O, sir!" and sinking down upon a settee, fainted away—Frightened at this fit, and, I suppose, afraid of calling for assistance, lest her situation should give rise to unfavourable conjectures, he ran about the room in distraction, making frightful grimaces; and, at length, had recollection enough to throw a little water in her face; by which application she was brought to herself: but, then her feeling took another turn. She shed a flood of tears, and cried aloud, "I know not who you are: but, sure——worthy sir!—generous sir!—the distress of me and my poor dying child—Oh! if the widow's prayers—if the orphan's tears of gratitude can ought avail—gracious Providence!—Blessings! shower down eternal blessings—" Here she was interrupted by my uncle, who muttered in a voice still more and more discordant, "For Heaven's sake be quiet, madam—consider—the people of the house——'sdeath! can't you—" All this time she was struggling to throw herself on her knees, while he seizing her by the wrists, endeavoured to seat her upon the settee, saying, "Pr'ythee—good now——hold your tongue—" At that instant, who should burst into the room but our aunt Tabby! of all antiquated maidens the most diabolically capricious—Ever prying into other people's affairs, she had seen the woman enter, and followed her to the door, where she stood listening, but probably could hear nothing distinctly, except my uncle's last exclamation; at which she bounced into the parlour in a violent rage, that dyed the tip of her nose of a purple hue,—"Fy upon you, Matt! (cried she) what doings are these, to disgrace your own character, and disparage your family?—" Then, snatching the bank-note out of the stranger's hand, she went on—"How now, twenty pounds!— here is temptation with a witness!——Good-woman, go about your business—Brother, brother, I know not which most to admire; your concupissins,[5] or your extravagance!—" "Good God, (exclaimed the poor woman) shall a worthy gentleman's character suffer for an action, that does honour to humanity?" By this time, uncle's indignation was effectually roused. His face grew pale, his teeth chattered, and his eyes flashed—"Sister, (cried he, in a voice like thunder) I vow to God, your impertinence is exceedingly provoking." With these words, he took her by the hand, and, opening the door of communication, thrust her into the chamber where I stood, so affected by the scene, that the tears ran down my cheeks. Observing these marks of emotion, "I don't wonder (said she) to see you concerned at the backslidings of so near a relation; a man of his years and infirmities: These are fine doings, truly—This is a rare example, set by a guardian, for the benefit of his pupils—Monstrous! incongrous! sophistical!"—I thought it was but an act of justice to set her to rights; and therefore explained the mystery—But she would not be undeceived. "What! (said she) would you go for to offer, for to arguefy me out of my senses? Did'n't I hear him whispering to her to hold her tongue? Did'n't I see her in tears? Did'n't I see him struggling to throw her upon the couch? O filthy! hideous! abominable! Child, child, talk not to me of charity.——Who gives twenty pounds in charity?—But you are a stripling—You know nothing of the world— Besides, charity begins at home—Twenty pounds would buy me a complete suit of flowered silk, trimmings and all—" In short, I quitted the room, my contempt for her, and my respect for her brother, being increased in the same proportion. I have since been informed, that the person, whom my uncle so generously relieved, is the widow of an ensign,[6] who has nothing to depend upon but the pension of fifteen pounds a year. The people of the Well-house give her an excellent character. She lodges in a garret, and works very hard at plainwork,[7] to support her daughter, who is dying of a consumption. I must own, to my shame, I feel a strong inclination to follow my uncle's example, in relieving this poor widow; but, betwixt friends,

5. Concupiscence, i.e., lust.
6. The lowest rank of commissioned infantry officer in the British army.
7. Simple needlework.

I am afraid of being detected in a weakness, that might entail the ridicule of the company upon,

Dear Philips,

yours always,

J. MELFORD.

Direct your next to me at Bath; and remember me to all our fellow-jesuits.[8]

To Dr. LEWIS.

Hot Well, April 20.

I understand your hint. There are mysteries in physick, as well as in religion; which we of the profane have no right to investigate— A man must not presume to use his reason, unless he has studied the categories, and can chop logic by mode and figure[9]—Between friends, I think, every man of tolerable parts ought, at my time of day, to be both physician and lawyer, as far as his own constitution and property are concerned. For my own part, I have had an hospital these fourteen years within myself, and studied my own case with the most painful attention; consequently may be supposed to know something of the matter, although I have not taken regular courses of physiology *et cetera et cetera.*—In short, I have for some time been of opinion, (no offence, dear Doctor) that the sum of all your medical discoveries amounts to this, that the more you study the less you know.—I have read all that has been written on the Hot Wells, and what I can collect from the whole, is, that the water contains nothing but a little salt, and calcarious earth, mixed in such inconsiderable proportion, as can have very little, if any, effect on the animal œconomy.[1] This being the case, I think, the man deserves to be fitted with a cap and bells, who, for such a paltry advantage as this spring affords, sacrifices his precious time, which might be employed in taking more effectual remedies, and exposes himself to the dirt, the stench, the chilling blasts, and perpetual rains, that render this place to me intolerable. If these waters, from a small degree of astringency, are of some service in the *diabetes,* *diarrhœa,* and *night sweats,* when the secretions are too much encreased, must not they do harm in the same proportion, where

8. A nickname for students at Jesus College, Oxford.
9. Terms used in formal logic.
1. Pertaining to the internal organization and management of the components and resources of a body or system. In the 18th century, economy (often still spelled "œconomy") was not yet primarily limited to financial matters. "Calcarious": chalky.

Mrs. Tabitha suspects her brother of incontinency. Courtesy of the Center for Southwest Research, University Libraries, University of New Mexico.

the humours are obstructed, as in the *asthma, scurvy, gout,* and
dropsy?—Now we talk of the *dropsy,* here is a strange, fantastical
oddity, one of your brethren, who harrangues every day in the Pump-
room, as if he was hired to give lectures on all subjects whatsoever—I
know not what to make of him——Sometimes he makes shrewd
remarks; at other times, he talks like the greatest simpleton in
nature—He has read a great deal; but without method or judgment,
and digested nothing. He believes every thing he has read; especially if it has any thing of the marvelous in it; and his conversation
is a surprizing hotch-potch of erudition and extravagance.——He
told me t'other day, with great confidence, that my case was dropsical; or, as he called it, *leucophlegmatic:* A sure sign, that his want of
experience is equal to his presumption; for, you know, there is
nothing analagous to the dropsy in my disorder—I wish those impertinent fellows, with their ricketty understandings, would keep their
advice for those that ask it——*Dropsy,* indeed! Sure I have not lived
to the age of fifty-five, and had such experience of my own disorder,
and consulted you and other eminent physicians, so often, and so
long, to be undeceived by such a—But, without all doubt, the man
is mad; and, therefore, what he says is of no consequence. I had,
yesterday, a visit from Higgins; who came hither under the terror of
your threats, and brought me in a present a brace of hares; which
he owned he took in my ground; and I could not persuade the fellow
that he did wrong, or that I would ever prosecute him for poaching—
I must desire you will wink hard at the practices of this rascallion;
otherwise I shall be plagued with his presents; which cost me more
than they are worth.—If I could wonder at any thing Fitzowen does,
I should be surprized at his assurance, in desiring you to solicit
my vote for him, at the next election for the county: for him, who
opposed me on the like occasion, with the most illiberal competition—
You may tell him civilly, that I beg to be excused. Direct your next
for me at Bath, whither I propose to remove to-morrow; not only on
my own account, but for the sake of my niece, Liddy, who is like to
relapse. The poor creature fell into a fit yesterday, while I was cheapening[2] a pair of spectacles, with a Jew-pedlar.—I am afraid there is
something still lurking in that little heart of her's; which I hope a
change of objects will remove. Let me know what you think of this
half-witted Doctor's impertinent, ridiculous, and absurd notion of
my disorder—So far from being dropsical, I am as lank in the belly
as a grey-hound; and, by measuring my ancle with a pack-thread, I
find the swelling subsides every day—From such doctors, good Lord
deliver us!—I have not yet taken any lodgings in Bath; because there
we can be accommodated at a minute's warning, and I shall choose

2. Bargaining for.

for myself—I need not say your directions for drinking and bathing will be agreeable to,

Dear Lewis,

yours ever,

MAT. BRAMBLE.

P. S. I forgot to tell you, that my right ancle pits,[3] a symptom, as I take it, of its being *œdematous*, not *leucophlegmatic*.

To Miss LETTY WILLIS, at Gloucester.

Hot Well, April 21.

MY DEAR LETTY,

I did not intend to trouble you again, till we should be settled at Bath; but having the occasion of Jarvis, I could not let it slip, especially as I have something extraordinary to communicate—O, my dear companion! What shall I tell you? for several days past there was a Jew-looking man, that plied at the Wells with a box of spectacles; and he always eyed me so earnestly, that I began to be very uneasy. At last, he came to our lodgings at Clifton, and lingered about the door, as if he wanted to speak to somebody——I was seized with an odd kind of fluttering, and begged Win to throw herself in his way: but the poor girl has weak nerves, and was afraid of his beard. My uncle, having occasion for new glasses, called him up stairs, and was trying a pair of spectacles, when the man, advancing to me, said, in a whisper—O gracious! what d'ye think he said?—"I am Wilson!" His features struck me that very moment——it was Wilson, sure enough! but so disguised, that it would have been impossible to know him, if my heart had not assisted in the discovery. I was so surprised, and so frightened, that I fainted away; but soon recovered; and found myself supported by him on the chair, while my uncle was running about the room, with the spectacles on his nose, calling for help. I had no opportunity to speak to him; but our looks were sufficiently expressive. He was payed for his glasses, and went away. Then I told Win who he was, and sent her after him to the Pump-room; where she spoke to him, and begged him in my name to withdraw from the place, that he might not incur the suspicion of my uncle or my brother, if he did not want to see me die of terror and vexation. The poor youth declared, with tears in his eyes,

---

3. To pit is to have the flesh give way easily to the touch and remain indented, a common symptom of edema.

that he had something extraordinary to communicate; and asked, if she would deliver a letter to me: but this she absolutely refused, by my order.—Finding her obstinate in her refusal, he desired she would tell me, that he was no longer a player, but a gentleman; in which character he would very soon avow his passion for me, without fear of censure or reproach—Nay, he even discovered his name and family; which, to my great grief, the simple girl forgot, in the confusion occasioned by her being seen talking to him by my brother; who stopt her on the road, and asked what business she had with that rascally Jew—She pretended she was cheapening a stay hook;[4] but was thrown into such a quandary, that she forgot the most material part of the information; and when she came home, went into an hysteric fit of laughing. This transaction happened three days ago, during which he has not appeared; so that I suppose he is gone. Dear Letty! you see how Fortune takes pleasure in persecuting your poor friend. If you should see him at Gloucester—or if you have seen him, and know his real name and family, pray keep me no longer in suspense—And yet, if he is under no obligation to keep himself longer concealed, and has a real affection for me, I should hope he will, in a little time, declare himself to my relations. Sure, if there is nothing unsuitable in the match, they won't be so cruel as to thwart my inclinations—O what happiness would then be my portion! I can't help indulging the thought, and pleasing my fancy with such agreeable ideas; which, after all, perhaps, will never be realised— But, why should I despair? who knows what will happen?—We set out for Bath to-morrow, and I am almost sorry for it; as I begin to be in love with solitude, and this is a charming romantic place. The air is so pure; the Downs are so agreeable; the furze in full blossom; the ground enamelled with daisies, and primroses, and cowslips; all the trees bursting into leaves, and the hedges already clothed with their vernal livery; the mountains covered with flocks of sheep, and tender bleating wanton lambkins playing, frisking and skipping from side to side; the groves resound with the notes of black-bird, thrush, and linnet; and all night long sweet Philomel[5] pours forth her ravishingly delightful song. Then, for variety, we go down to the *nymph of Bristol spring*, where the company is assembled before dinner; so good-natured, so free, so easy; and there we drink the water so clear, so pure, so mild, so charmingly maukish.[6] There the sun is so chearful and reviving; the weather so soft; the walk so agreeable; the prospect so amusing; and the ships and boats going up and down

---

4. For a corset or other supportive undergarment.
5. The nightingale, whose characteristic mating song is in fact produced only by the male. "Furze": a spiny shrub with yellow flowers, often growing in poor soil; also called gorse.
6. Unpleasant to taste. "*Bristol spring*": probably an allusion to William Whitehead's "A Hymn to the Nymph of Bristol Spring" (1751).

the river, close under the windows of the Pump-room, afford such an enchanting variety of moving pictures, as require a much abler pen than mine to describe. To make this place a perfect paradise to me, nothing is wanting but an agreeable companion and sincere friend; such as my dear miss Willis hath been, and I hope still will be, to her ever faithful

LYDIA MELFORD.

Direct for me, still under cover, to Win; and Jarvis will take care to convey it safe. Adieu.

To Sir WATKIN PHILLIPS, of Jesus college, Oxon.

Bath, April 24.

DEAR PHILLIPS,

You have, indeed, reason to be surprised, that I should have concealed my correspondence with miss Blackerby from you, to whom I disclosed all my other connexions of that nature; but the truth is, I never dreamed of any such commerce, till your last informed me, that it had produced something which could not be much longer concealed. It is a lucky circumstance, however, that her reputation will not suffer any detriment, but rather derive advantage from the discovery; which will prove, at least, that it is not quite so rotten, as most people imagined—For my own part, I declare to you, in all the sincerity of friendship, that, far from having any amorous intercourse with the object in question, I never had the least acquaintance with her person; but, if she is really in the condition you describe, I suspect Mansel to be at the bottom of the whole. His visits to that shrine were no secret; and this attachment, added to some good offices, which you know he has done me, since I left Alma-mater, give me a right to believe him capable of saddling me with this scandal, when my back was turned——Nevertheless, if my name can be of any service to him, he is welcome to make use of it; and if the woman should be abandoned enough to swear his bantling to me, I must beg the favour of you to compound with the parish: I shall pay the penalty without repining;[7] and you will be so good as to draw upon me immediately for the sum required——On this occasion, I act by the advice of my uncle; who says, I shall have good-luck if I pass through life without being obliged to make many more compositions of the same kind. The old gentleman told me last night,

---

7. Complaining. "Bantling": derogatory term for a young child; a brat. "Compound with the parish": to pay the local church district authorities to take over the child's welfare.

with great good-humour, that betwixt the age of twenty and forty, he had been obliged to provide for nine bastards, sworn to him by women whom he never saw—Mr. Bramble's character, which seems to interest you greatly, opens and improves upon me every day.— His singularities afford a rich mine of entertainment: his under-standing, so far as I can judge, is well cultivated: his observations on life are equally just, pertinent, and uncommon. He affects misan-thropy, in order to conceal the sensibility of a heart, which is tender, even to a degree of weakness. This delicacy of feeling, or soreness of the mind, makes him timorous and fearful; but then he is afraid of nothing so much as of dishonour; and although he is exceedingly cautious of giving offence, he will fire at the least hint of insolence or ill-breeding.—Respectable as he is, upon the whole, I can't help being sometimes diverted by his little distresses; which provoke him to let fly the shafts of his satire, keen and penetrating as the arrows of Teucer[8]—Our aunt, Tabitha, acts upon him as a perpet-ual grind-stone—She is, in all respects, a striking contrast to her brother—But I reserve her portrait for another occasion.

Three days ago we came hither from the Hot Well, and took pos-session of the first floor of a lodging-house, on the South Parade; a situation which my uncle chose, for its being near the Bath, and remote from the noise of carriages. He was scarce warm in the lodg-ings when he called for his night cap, his wide shoes, and flannel; and declared himself invested with the gout in his right foot; though, I believe, it had as yet reached no farther than his imagination. It was not long before he had reason to repent his premature decla-ration; for our aunt Tabitha found means to make such a clamour and confusion, before the flannels could be produced from the trunk, that one would have imagined the house was on fire. All this time, uncle sat boiling with impatience, biting his fingers, throwing up his eyes, and muttering ejaculations; at length he burst into a kind of convulsive laugh, after which he hummed a song; and when the hurricane was over, exclaimed, "Blessed be God for all things!" This, however, was but the beginning of his troubles. Mrs. Tabitha's favourite dog Chowder, having paid his compliments to a female turnspit,[9] of his own species, in the kitchen, involved himself in a quarrel with no fewer than five rivals, who set upon him at once, and drove him up stairs to the dining-room door, with hideous noise: there our aunt and her woman, taking arms in his defence, joined the concert; which became truly diabolical. This fray being with dif-ficulty suppressed, by the intervention of our own foot-man and the cook-maid of the house, the 'squire had just opened his mouth,

8. A notable Greek archer in the Trojan War.
9. A small dog trained to turn a cooking spit by walking on a treadmill.

to expostulate with Tabby, when the town-waits,[1] in the passage below, struck up their musick, (if musick it may be called) with such a sudden burst of sound, as made him start and stare, with marks of indignation and disquiet. He had recollection enough to send his servant with some money to silence those noisy intruders; and they were immediately dismissed, though not without some opposition on the part of Tabitha, who thought it but reasonable that he should have more musick for his money. Scarce had he settled this knotty point, when a strange kind of thumping and bouncing was heard right overhead, in the second story, so loud and violent as to shake the whole building. I own I was exceedingly provoked at this new alarm; and before my uncle had time to express himself on the subject, I ran up stairs, to see what was the matter. Finding the room-door open, I entered without ceremony, and perceived an object, which I cannot now recollect without laughing to excess—It was a dancing-master, with his scholar, in the act of teaching. The master was blind of one eye, and lame of one foot, and led about the room his pupil; who seemed to be about the age of three-score, stooped mortally, was tall, raw-boned, hard-favoured, with a woollen night-cap on his head; and he had stript off his coat, that he might be more nimble in his motions—Finding himself intruded upon, by a person he did not know, he forthwith girded himself with a long iron sword, and advancing to me, with a peremptory air, pronounced, in a true Hibernian accent, "Mister What d'ye callum, by my saoul and conscience, I am very glad to sea you, if you are after coming in the way of friendship; and indeed, and indeed now, I believe you are my friend sure enough, gra;[2] though I never had the honour to sea your face before, my dear; for because you come like a friend, without any ceremony at all, at all—" I told him the nature of my visit would not admit of ceremony; that I was come to desire he would make less noise, as there was a sick gentleman below, whom he had no right to disturb with such preposterous doings. "Why, look-ye now; young gentleman, (replied this original) perhaps, upon another occasion, I might shivilly request you to explain the maining of that hard word, *prepasterous:* but there's a time for all things, honey—" So saying, he passed me with great agility, and, running down stairs, found our footman at the dining-room door, of whom he demanded admittance, to pay his respects to the stranger. As the fellow did not think proper to refuse the request of such a formidable figure, he was immediately introduced, and addressed himself to my uncle in these words: "Your humble servant, good sir—I'm not so *prepasterous,* as your son calls it, but I know the

1. Town pipers; often spelled "waites."
2. Darling (Gaelic).

rules of shivility—I'm a poor knight of Ireland, my name is sir Ulic Mackilligut, of the county of Galway; being your fellow-lodger, I'm come to pay my respects, and to welcome you to the South Parade, and to offer my best services to you, and your good lady, and your pretty daughter; and even to the young gentleman your son, though he thinks me a *prepasterous* fellow—You must know I am to have the honour to open a ball next door to-morrow with lady Mac Manus; and being rusted in my dancing, I was refreshing my memory with a little exercise; but if I had known there was a sick person below, by Christ! I would have sooner danced a hornpipe upon my own head, than walk the softest minuet over yours."—My uncle, who was not a little startled at his first appearance, received his compliment with great complacency, insisted upon his being seated, thanked him for the honour of his visit, and reprimanded me for my abrupt expostulation with a gentleman of his rank and character. Thus tutored, I asked pardon of the knight, who, forthwith starting up, embraced me so close, that I could hardly breathe; and assured me, he loved me as his own soul. At length, recollecting his night-cap,[3] he pulled it off in some confusion; and, with his bald-pate uncovered, made a thousand apologies to the ladies, as he retired—At that instant, the Abbey bells began to ring so loud, that we could not hear one another speak; and this peal, as we afterwards learned, was for the honour of Mr. Bullock, an eminent cow-keeper of Tottenham,[4] who had just arrived at Bath, to drink the waters for indigestion. Mr. Bramble had not time to make his remarks upon the agreeable nature of this serenade, before his ears were saluted with another concert that interested him more nearly. Two negroes, belonging to a Creole[5] gentleman, who lodged in the same house, taking their station at a window in the stair-case, about ten feet from our dining-room door, began to practise upon the French-horn; and being in the very first rudiments of execution, produced such discordant sounds, as might have discomposed the organs of an ass——You may guess what effect they had upon the irritable nerves of uncle; who, with the most admirable expression of splenetic surprize in his countenance, sent his man to silence those dreadful blasts, and desire the musicians to practise in some other place, as they had no right to stand there and disturb all the lodgers in the house. Those sable performers, far from taking the hint, and withdrawing, treated the messenger

3. A cloth cap worn at night instead of a wig.
4. Now a suburb of London but still a separate village in the 18th century. "Abbey bells": for a fee, the bells of the Bath Abbey (formally called the Abbey Church of Saint Peter and Saint Paul) were rung to announce new arrivals to town.
5. The 18th-century name for Europeans born in the West Indies; they frequently migrated to Britain with their black slaves. Historians estimate that there were between twenty and thirty thousand black men and women in Britain in the mid-1760s. Slavery was outlawed in Britain in 1772, the year after *Humphry Clinker*'s publication.

with great insolence; bidding him carry his compliments to their master, colonel Rigworm, who would give him a proper answer, and a good drubbing into the bargain; in the mean time they continued their noise, and even endeavoured to make it more disagreeable; laughing between whiles, at the thoughts of being able to torment their betters with impunity. Our 'squire, incensed at the additional insult, immediately dispatched the servant, with his compliments to colonel Rigworm; requesting that he would order his blacks to be quiet, as the noise they made was altogether intolerable—To this message, the Creole colonel replied, that his horns had a right to sound on a common staircase; that there they should play for his diversion; and that those who did not like the noise, might look for lodgings else-where. Mr. Bramble no sooner received this reply, than his eyes began to glisten, his face grew pale, and his teeth chattered. After a moment's pause, he slipt on his shoes, without speaking a word, or seeming to feel any further disturbance from the gout in his toes. Then, snatching his cane, he opened the door and proceeded to the place where the black trumpeters were posted. There, without further hesitation, he began to belabour them both; and exerted himself with such astonishing vigour and agility, that both their heads and horns were broken in a twinkling, and they ran howling down stairs to their master's parlour-door. The 'squire, following them half way, called aloud, that the colonel might hear him, "Go, rascals, and tell your master what I have done; if he thinks himself injured, he knows where to come for satisfaction. As for you, this is but an earnest[6] of what you shall receive, if ever you presume to blow a horn again here, while I stay in the house." So saying, he retired to his apartment, in expectation of hearing from the West Indian; but the colonel prudently declined any farther prosecution of the dispute. My sister Liddy was frighted into a fit, from which she was no sooner recovered, than Mrs. Tabitha began a lecture upon patience; which her brother interrupted with a most significant grin, exclaiming, "True, sister, God increase my patience and your discretion. I wonder (added he) what sort of sonata we are to expect from this overture, in which the devil, that presides over horrid sounds, hath given us such variations of discord—The trampling of porters, the creaking and crashing of trunks, the snarling of curs, the scolding of women, the squeaking and squalling of fiddles and hautboys out of tune, the bouncing of the Irish baronet over-head, and the bursting, belching, and brattling of the French-horns in the passage (not to mention the harmonious peal that still thunders from the Abbey steeple) succeeding one another without interruption, like the different parts of the same concert, have given me such an idea of what

6. An initial payment, i.e., a taste.

a poor invalid has to expect in this temple, dedicated to Silence and
Repose, that I shall certainly shift my quarters to-morrow, and
endeavour to effectuate my retreat before Sir Ulic opens the ball
with my lady Mac Manus; a conjunction that bodes me no good."
This intimation was by no means agreeable to Mrs. Tabitha, whose
ears were not quite so delicate as those of her brother—She said it
would be great folly to move from such agreeable lodgings, the
moment they were comfortably settled. She wondered he should be
such an enemy to musick and mirth. She heard no noise but of his
own making: it was impossible to manage a family in dumb-shew.[7]
He might harp as long as he pleased upon her scolding; but she never
scolded, except for his advantage; but he would never be satisfied,
even tho'f she should sweat blood and water in his service—I have
a great notion that our aunt, who is now declining into the most
desperate state of celibacy, had formed some design upon the heart
of Sir Ulic Mackilligut, which she feared might be frustrated by
our abrupt departure from these lodgings. Her brother, eyeing her
askance, "Pardon me, sister, (said he) I should be a savage, indeed,
were I insensible of my own felicity, in having such a mild, compla-
cent, good-humoured, and considerate companion and house-keeper;
but as I have got a weak head, and my sense of hearing is painfully
acute, before I have recourse to plugs of wool and cotton, I'll try
whether I can't find another lodging, where I shall have more quiet
and less musick." He accordingly dispatched his man upon this service; and next day he found a small house in Milsham-street,[8] which
he hires by the week. Here, at least, we enjoy convenience and quiet
within doors, as much as Tabby's temper will allow; but the 'squire
still complains of flying pains in the stomach and head, for which
he bathes and drinks the waters. He is not so bad, however, but that
he goes in person to the pump, the rooms, and the coffee-houses;
where he picks up continual food for ridicule and satire. If I can
glean any thing for your amusement, either from his observation or
my own, you shall have it freely, though I am afraid it will poorly compensate the trouble of reading these tedious insipid letters of,

Dear Phillips,

yours always,

J. Melford.

7. A part of a play performed in silence.
8. Probably Milsom Street, a fashionable Bath address.

To Dr. LEWIS.

Bath, April 23.

DEAR DOCTOR,

If I did not know that the exercise of your profession has habit-uated you to the hearing of complaints, I should make a conscience of troubling you with my correspondence, which may be truly called *the lamentations of Matthew Bramble*.[9] Yet I cannot help think-ing, I have some right to discharge the overflowings of my spleen[1] upon you, whose province it is to remove those disorders that occasioned it; and let me tell you, it is no small alleviation of my grievances, that I have a sensible friend, to whom I can communi-cate my crusty humours, which, by retention, would grow intoler-ably acrimonious.

You must know, I find nothing but disappointment at Bath; which is so altered, that I can scarce believe it is the same place that I frequented about thirty years ago. Methinks I hear you say, "Altered it is, without all doubt; but then it is altered for the better; a truth which, perhaps, you would own without hesitation, if you yourself was not altered for the worse." The reflection may, for aught I know, be just. The inconveniences which I overlooked in the high-day of health, will naturally strike with exaggerated impression on the irritable nerves of an invalid, surprised by premature old age, and shattered with long-suffering—But, I believe, you will not deny, that this place, which Nature and Providence seem to have intended as a resource from distemper and disquiet, is become the very cen-ter of racket and dissipation. Instead of that peace, tranquility and ease, so necessary to those who labour under bad health, weak nerves, and irregular spirits; here we have nothing but noise, tumult, and hurry; with the fatigue and slavery of maintaining a ceremo-nial, more stiff, formal, and oppressive, than the etiquette of a Ger-man elector.[2] A national hospital it may be; but one would imagine, that none but lunatics are admitted; and, truly, I will give you leave to call me so, if I stay much longer at Bath.—But I shall take another opportunity to explain my sentiments at greater length on this subject—I was impatient to see the boasted improvements in archi-tecture, for which the upper parts of the town have been so much celebrated, and t'other day I made a circuit of all the new build-ings. The Square, though irregular, is, on the whole, pretty well laid out, spacious, open, and airy; and, in my opinion, by far the most

9. An allusion to the book of Lamentations in the Hebrew Bible.
1. Traditionally thought to be the organ that secreted black bile, the melancholy humor.
2. One of the German princes qualified to vote in the election of the Holy Roman Emperor.

wholsome and agreeable situation in Bath, especially the upper side of it; but the avenues to it are mean, dirty, dangerous, and indirect. Its communication with the Baths is through the yard of an inn, where the poor trembling valetudinarian is carried in a chair, betwixt the heels of a double row of horses, wincing under the curry-combs of grooms and postilions,[3] over and above the hazard of being obstructed, or overturned by the carriages which are continually making their exit or their entrance—I suppose after some chairmen shall have been maimed, and a few lives lost by those accidents, the corporation will think, in earnest, about providing a more safe and commodious passage. The Circus is a pretty bauble; contrived for shew, and looks like Vespasian's amphitheatre[4] turned outside in. If we consider it in point of magnificence, the great number of small doors belonging to the separate houses, the inconsiderable height of the different orders, the affected ornaments of the architrave,[5] which are both childish and misplaced, and the areas projecting into the street, surrounded with iron rails, destroy a good part of its effect upon the eye; and, perhaps, we shall find it still more defective, if we view it in the light of convenience. The figure of each separate dwelling house, being the segment of a circle, must spoil the symmetry of the rooms, by contracting them towards the street windows, and leaving a larger sweep in the space behind. If, instead of the areas and iron rails, which seem to be of very little use, there had been a corridore with arcades all round, as in Covent-Garden,[6] the appearance of the whole would have been more magnificent and striking; those arcades would have afforded an agreeable covered walk, and sheltered the poor chairmen and their carriages from the rain, which is here almost perpetual. At present, the chairs stand soaking in the open street, from morning to night, till they become so many boxes of wet leather, for the benefit of the gouty and rheumatic, who are transported in them from place to place. Indeed this is a shocking inconvenience that extends over the whole city; and, I am persuaded, it produces infinite mischief to the delicate and infirm; even the close chairs, contrived for the sick, by standing in the open air, have their frize[7] linings impregnated, like so many spunges, with the moisture of the atmosphere, and those cases of cold vapour

---

3. Servants who rode on the coach horses to aid the coach driver in directing the team. "Valetudinarian": invalid. "Curry-combs": metal-toothed combs for rubbing and cleaning horses.
4. The Colosseum in Rome, the world's largest amphitheater, was begun by the Emperor Vespasion around 70 BCE. "The Circus": three sections of buildings laid out in arcs to form a circle, broken only by three streets that enter the circular middle space. It was designed by John Wood the Elder (1704–1754) and completed by his son in 1764.
5. A molded or decorated band surrounding a panel or opening.
6. A fashionable London locale surrounding a famous theater of the same name.
7. A heavy, napped woolen cloth, usually spelled "frieze." "Close chairs": covered, portable chairs.

must give a charming check to the perspiration of a patient, piping hot from the Bath, with all his pores wide open.

But, to return to the Circus: it is inconvenient from its situation, at so great a distance from all the markets, baths, and places of public entertainment. The only entrance to it, through Gay-street, is so difficult, steep, and slippery, that, in wet weather, it must be exceedingly dangerous, both for those that ride in carriages, and those that walk a-foot; and when the street is covered with snow, as it was for fifteen days successively this very winter, I don't see how any individual could go either up or down, without the most imminent hazard of broken bones. In blowing weather, I am told, most of the houses in this hill are smothered with smoke, forced down the chimneys, by the gusts of wind reverberated from the hill behind, which (I apprehend likewise) must render the atmosphere here more humid and unwholesome than it is in the square below; for the clouds, formed by the constant evaporation from the baths and rivers in the bottom, will, in their ascent this way, be first attracted and detained by the hill that rises close behind the Circus, and load the air with a perpetual succession of vapours: this point, however, may be easily ascertained by means of an hygrometer,[8] or a paper of salt of tartar exposed to the action of the atmosphere. The same artist, who planned the Circus, has likewise projected a Crescent;[9] when that is finished, we shall probably have a Star; and those who are living thirty years hence, may, perhaps, see all the signs of the Zodiac exhibited in architecture at Bath. These, however fantastical, are still designs that denote some ingenuity and knowledge in the architect; but the rage of building has laid hold on such a number of adventurers, that one sees new houses starting up in every out-let and every corner of Bath; contrived without judgment, executed without solidity, and stuck together, with so little regard to plan and propriety, that the different lines of the new rows and buildings interfere with, and intersect one another in every different angle of conjunction. They look like the wreck of streets and squares disjointed by an earthquake, which hath broken the ground into a variety of holes and hillocks; or, as if some Gothic devil had stuffed them altogether in a bag, and left them to stand higgledy piggledy, just as chance directed. What sort of a monster Bath will become in a few years, with those growing excrescences, may be easily conceived: but the want of beauty and proportion is not the worst effect of these new mansions; they are built so slight, with the soft

---

8. Any instrument for measuring humidity.
9. The Royal Crescent, in fact designed by John Wood the Younger (1728–1782), was started in 1767 and completed in 1775. It consists of an unbroken curved row of thirty terraced houses.

crumbling stone found in this neighbourhood, that I should never sleep quietly in one of them, when it blowed (as the sailors say) a cap-full of wind; and, I am persuaded, that my hind,[1] Roger Williams, or any man of equal strength, would be able to push his foot through the strongest part of their walls, without any great exertion of his muscles. All these absurdities arise from the general tide of luxury, which hath overspread the nation, and swept away all, even the very dregs of the people. Every upstart of fortune, harnessed in the trappings of the mode,[2] presents himself at Bath, as in the very focus of observation—Clerks and factors from the East Indies, loaded with the spoil of plundered provinces; planters, negro-drivers, and hucksters, from our American plantations, enriched they know not how; agents, commissaries, and contractors, who have fattened, in two successive wars[3] on the blood of the nation; usurers, brokers, and jobbers of every kind; men of low birth, and no breeding, have found themselves suddenly translated into a state of affluence, unknown to former ages; and no wonder that their brains should be intoxicated with pride, vanity, and presumption. Knowing no other criterion of greatness, but the ostentation of wealth, they discharge their affluence without taste or conduct, through every channel of the most absurd extravagance; and all of them hurry to Bath, because here, without any further qualification, they can mingle with the princes and nobles of the land. Even the wives and daughters of low tradesmen, who, like shovel-nosed sharks, prey upon the blubber of those uncouth whales of fortune, are infected with the same rage of displaying their importance; and the slightest indisposition serves them for a pretext to insist upon being conveyed to Bath, where they may hobble country-dances and cotillons among lordlings, 'squires, counsellors, and clergy. These delicate creatures from Bedfordbury, Butcher-row, Crutched-Friers, and Botolph-lane,[4] cannot breathe in the gross air of the Lower Town, or conform to the vulgar rules of a common lodging-house; the husband, therefore, must provide an entire house, or elegant apartments in the new buildings. Such is the composition of what is called the fashionable company at Bath; where a very inconsiderable proportion of genteel people are lost in a mob of impudent plebeians, who have neither understanding nor judgment, nor the least idea of propriety and decorum; and seem to enjoy nothing so much as an opportunity of insulting their betters.

Thus the number of people, and the number of houses continue to increase; and this will ever be the case, till the streams that swell this irresistible torrent of folly and extravagance, shall either

1. Farm laborer.
2. Current fashion.
3. The War of Austrian Succession (1739–48) and the Seven Years' War (1756–63).
4. Unfashionable, impoverished London neighborhoods.

be exhausted, or turned into other channels, by incidents and events which I do not pretend to foresee. This, I own, is a subject on which I cannot write with any degree of patience; for the mob is a monster I never could abide, either in its head, tail, midriff, or members: I detest the whole of it, as a mass of ignorance, presumption, malice, and brutality; and, in this term of reprobation, I include, without respect of rank, station, or quality, all those of both sexes, who affect its manners, and court its society.

But I have written till my fingers are crampt, and my nausea begins to return—By your advice, I sent to London a few days ago for half a pound of Gengzeng;[5] though I doubt much, whether that which comes from America is equally efficacious with what is brought from the East Indies. Some years ago, a friend of mine paid sixteen guineas for two ounces of it; and, in six months after, it was sold in the same shop for five shillings[6] the pound. In short, we live in a vile world of fraud and sophistication; so that I know nothing of equal value with the genuine friendship of a sensible man; a rare jewel! which I cannot help thinking myself in possession of, while I repeat the old declaration, that I am, as usual,

Dear Lewis,

Your affectionate

M. BRAMBLE.

After having been agitated in a short hurricane, on my first arrival, I have taken a small house in Milsham-street, where I am tolerably well lodged, for five guineas a week. I was yesterday at the Pump-room, and drank about a pint of the water, which seems to agree with my stomach; and to-morrow morning I shall bathe, for the first time; so that in a few posts you may expect farther trouble; mean while, I am glad to find that the inoculation[7] has succeeded so well with poor Joyce, and that her face will be but little marked. If my friend Sir Thomas was a single man, I would not trust such a handsome wench in his family; but as I have recommended her, in a particular manner, to the protection of lady G——,[8] who is one of the best women in the world, she may go thither without hesitation, as soon as she is quite recovered, and fit for service——Let her mother have money to provide her with necessaries, and she may ride behind her brother on Bucks; but you must lay strong injunctions on

---

5. Ginseng.
6. The guinea was a gold coin, the value of which was originally set at twenty shillings (one pound sterling) but was fixed at twenty-one shillings from 1717 to 1816.
7. For treatment of smallpox, approved by the College of Physicians in 1754. It was still a controversial and expensive procedure.
8. Possibly this refers to the fictional Lady Griskin, introduced later in Volume 1.

Jack, to take particular care of the trusty old veteran, who has faithfully earned his present ease, by his past services.

To Miss WILLIS, at Gloucester.

Bath, April 26.

MY DEAREST COMPANION,

The pleasure I received from yours, which came to hand yesterday, is not to be expressed. Love and friendship are, without doubt, charming passions; which absence serves only to heighten and improve. Your kind present of the garnet bracelets, I shall keep as carefully as I preserve my own life; and I beg you will accept, in return, of my heart-housewife,[9] with the tortoise-shell memorandum-book, as a trifling pledge of my unalterable affection.

Bath is to me a new world——All is gayety, good-humour, and diversion. The eye is continually entertained with the splendour of dress and equipage; and the ear with the sound of coaches, chaises, chairs, and other carriages. *The merry bells ring round*,[1] from morn till night. Then we are welcomed by the city-waits in our own lodgings: we have musick in the Pump-room every morning, cotillons every fore-noon in the rooms, balls twice a week, and concerts every other night, besides private assemblies and parties without number—As soon as we were settled in lodgings, we were visited by the Master of the Ceremonies;[2] a pretty little gentleman, so sweet, so fine, so civil, and polite, that in our country he might pass for the prince of Wales; then he talks so charmingly, both in verse and prose, that you would be delighted to hear him discourse; for you must know he is a great writer, and has got five tragedies ready for the stage. He did us the favour to dine with us, by my uncle's invitation; and next day 'squired my aunt and me to every part of Bath; which, to be sure, is an earthly paradise. The Square, the Circus, and the Parades, put you in mind of the sumptuous palaces represented in prints and pictures; and the new buildings, such as Princes-row, Harlequin's-row, Bladud's-row, and twenty other rows, look like so many enchanted castles, raised on hanging terraces.

At eight in the morning, we go in dishabille[3] to the Pump-room; which is crowded like a Welsh fair; and there you see the highest quality, and the lowest trades folks, jostling each other, without

9. A pocket case for needles, pins, thread, and scissors.
1. Quoted from John Milton's "L'Allegro" (1645), in which "the merry bells ring round / and the jocund rebecks [Renaissance fiddles] sound" (lines 93–94).
2. Samuel Derrick (1724–1769), a prodigious writer of Irish birth; he succeeded the celebrated dandy Beau Nash (1674–1761) as master of the ceremonies at Bath.
3. An informal state of dress.

ceremony, hail-fellow well-met. The noise of the musick playing in the gallery, the heat and flavour of such a crowd, and the hum and buz of their conversation, gave me the head-ach and vertigo the first day; but, afterwards, all these things became familiar, and even agreeable.—Right under the Pump-room windows is the King's Bath;[4] a huge cistern, where you see the patients up to their necks in hot water. The ladies wear jackets and petticoats of brown linen, with chip hats,[5] in which they fix their handkerchifs to wipe the sweat from their faces; but, truly, whether it is owing to the steam that surrounds them, or the heat of the water, or the nature of the dress, or to all these causes together, they look so flushed, and so frightful, that I always turn my eyes another way—My aunt, who says every person of fashion should make her appearance in the bath, as well as in the abbey church, contrived a cap with cherry-coloured ribbons to suit her complexion, and obliged Win to attend her yesterday morning in the water. But, really, her eyes were so red, that they made mine water as I viewed her from the Pump-room; and as for poor Win, who wore a hat trimmed with blue, what betwixt her wan complexion and her fear, she looked like the ghost of some pale maiden, who had drowned herself for love. When she came out of the bath, she took assafœtida drops, and was fluttered all day; so that we could hardly keep her from going into hysterics: but her mistress says it will do her good; and poor Win curtsies, with the tears in her eyes. For my part, I content myself with drinking about half a pint of the water every morning.

The pumper, with his wife and servant, attend within a bar; and the glasses, of different sizes, stand ranged in order before them, so you have nothing to do but to point at that which you chuse, and it is filled immediately, hot and sparkling from the pump. It is the only hot water I could ever drink, without being sick—Far from having that effect, it is rather agreeable to the taste, grateful to the stomach, and reviving to the spirits. You cannot imagine what wonderful cures it performs—My uncle began with it the other day; but he made wry faces in drinking, and I'm afraid he will leave it off—The first day we came to Bath, he fell into a violent passion; beat two black-a-moors, and I was afraid he would have fought with their master; but the stranger proved a peaceable man. To be sure, the gout had got into his head, as my aunt observed: but, I believe, his passion drove it away; for he has been remarkably well ever since. It is a thousand pities he should ever be troubled with that ugly distemper; for, when he is free from pain, he is the best-tempered man upon earth; so gentle, so generous, so charitable, that every body loves him; and

4. The largest and most popular of the city's public baths.
5. Hats made of straw or woody fibers.

so good to me, in particular, that I shall never be able to shew the deep sense I have of his tenderness and affection.

Hard by the Pump-room, is a coffee-house for the ladies; but my aunt says, young girls are not admitted, inasmuch as the conversation turns upon politics, scandal, philosophy, and other subjects above our capacity; but we are allowed to accompany them to the booksellers shops, which are charming places of resort; where we read novels, plays, pamphlets, and news-papers, for so small a sub-scription as a crown a quarter; and in these offices of intelligence, (as my brother calls them) all the reports of the day, and all the private transactions of the Bath, are first entered and discussed. From the bookseller's shop, we make a tour through the milliners and toy-men; and commonly stop at Mr. Cill's,[6] the pastry-cook, to take a jelly, a tart, or a small bason of vermicelli. There is, moreover, another place of entertainment on the other side of the water, oppo-site to the Grove; to which the company cross over in a boat—It is called Spring Garden; a sweet retreat, laid out in walks and ponds, and parterres of flowers; and there is a long-room for breakfasting and dancing. As the situation is low and damp, and the season has been remarkably wet, my uncle won't suffer me to go thither, lest I should catch cold: but my aunt says it is all a vulgar prejudice; and, to be sure, a great many gentlemen and ladies of Ireland frequent the place, without seeming to be the worse for it. They say, dancing at Spring Gardens, when the air is moist, is recommended to them as an excellent cure for the rheumatism. I have been twice at the play; where, notwithstanding the excellence of the performers, the gayety of the company, and the decorations of the theatre, which are very fine, I could not help reflecting, with a sigh, upon our poor homely representations at Gloucester—But this, in confidence to my dear Willis—You know my heart, and will excuse its weakness.——

After all, the great scenes of entertainment at Bath, are the two public rooms;[7] where the company meet alternately every evening—They are spacious, lofty, and, when lighted up, appear very strik-ing. They are generally crowded with well-dressed people, who drink tea in separate parties, play at cards, walk, or sit and chat together, just as they are disposed. Twice a-week there is a ball; the expence of which is defrayed by a voluntary subscription among the gentlemen; and every subscriber has three tickets. I was there Friday last with my aunt, under the care of my brother, who is a subscriber; and Sir Ulic Mackilligut recommended his nephew, captain O Donaghan, to

6. Mentioned in Christopher Anstey's *New Bath Guide* (1766). "Toy-men": shopkeepers who sell sporting articles, trinkets, and fancy goods.
7. The two sets of public rooms, to which invitations were not necessary, were located in Terrace Walk.

me as a partner; but Jerry excused himself, by saying I had got the head-ach; and, indeed, it was really so, though I can't imagine how he knew it. The place was so hot, and the smell so different from what we are used to in the country, that I was quite feverish when we came away. Aunt says it is the effect of a vulgar constitution, reared among woods and mountains; and, that as I become accustomed to genteel company, it will wear off.—Sir Ulic was very complaisant, made her a great many high-flown compliments; and, when we retired, handed her with great ceremony to her chair. The captain, I believe, would have done me the same favour; but my brother, seeing him advance, took me under his arm, and wished him good-night. The Captain is a pretty man, to be sure; tall and strait, and well made; with light-grey eyes, and a Roman nose; but there is a certain boldness in his look and manner, that puts one out of countenance—But I am afraid I have put you out of all patience with this long unconnected scrawl; which I shall therefore conclude, with assuring you, that neither Bath nor London, nor all the diversions of life, shall ever be able to efface the idea of my dear Letty, from the heart of her ever affectionate

LYDIA MELFORD.

To Mrs. MARY JONES, at Brambleton-hall.

DEAR MOLLY JONES,

Heaving got a frank,[8] I now return your fever, which I received by Mr. Higgins, at the Hot Well, together with the stockings, which his wife footed for me; but now they are of no survice. No body wears such things in this place—O Molly! you that live in the country have no deception of our doings at Bath. Here is such dressing, and fidling, and dancing, and gadding, and courting, and plotting—O gracious! if God had not given me a good stock of discretion, what a power of things might not I reveal, consarning old mistress and young mistress; Jews with beards, that were no Jews; but handsome Christians, without a hair upon their sin, strolling with spectacles, to get speech of Miss Liddy. But she's a dear sweet soul, as innocent as the child unborn. She has tould me all her inward thoughts, and disclosed her passion for Mr. Wilson; and that's not his name neither; and thof he acted among the player-men, he is meat for their masters; and she has gi'en me her yellow trollopea; which Mrs. Drab, the manty-maker,[9] says will look very well when it is scowred

---

8. A letter could be signed, or franked, by an official in order to be carried free through the British postal system.
9. I.e., mantua-maker; a dressmaker. "Trollopea": or slammerkin; a loose dress or gown.

and smoaked with silfur—You knows as how, yellow fitts my fizzog-
mony.[1] God he knows what havock I shall make among the mail-
sex, when I make my first appearance in this killing collar, with a
full soot of gaze, as good as new, that I bought last Friday of madam
Friponeau, the French mullaner—Dear girl, I have seen all the fine
shews of Bath; the Prades, the Squires, and the Circlis, the Crashit,
the Hottogon, and Bloody Buildings, and Harry King's row;[2] and I
have been twice in the Bath with mistress, and na'r a smoak upon
our backs, hussy——The first time I was mortally afraid, and flus-
tered all day; and afterwards made believe that I had got the heddick;
but mistress said, if I didn't go, I should take a dose of bumtaffy; and
so remembring how it worked Mrs. Gwyllim a pennorth,[3] I chose
rather to go again with her into the Bath, and then I met with an axi-
dent. I dropt my petticoat, and could not get it up from the bottom—
But what did that signify? they mought laff, but they could see
nothing; for I was up to the sin in water. To be sure, it threw me
into such a gumbustion, that I know not what I said, nor what I did,
nor how they got me out, and rapt me in a blanket—Mrs. Tabitha
scoulded a little when we got home; but she knows as I know what's
what—Ah Laud help you!—There is Sir Yury Micligut, of Balna-
clinch, in the cunty of Kalloway—I took down the name from his
gentleman, Mr. O Frizzle, and he has got an estate of fifteen hundred a year—I am sure he is both rich and generous——But you
nose, Molly, I was always famous for keeping secrets; and so he was
very safe in trusting me with his flegm for mistress; which, to be
sure, is very honourable; for Mr. O Frizzle assures me, he values not
her portion a brass varthing[4]—And, indeed, what's poor ten thousand pounds to a Baron Knight of his fortune? and, truly, I told Mr.
O Frizzle, that was all she had to trust to—As for John Thomas,
he's a morass fellor—I vow, I thought he would a fit with Mr. O
Frizzle, because he axed me to dance with him at Spring Garden—
But God he knows I have no thoughts eyther of wan or t'other.

As for house news, the worst is, Chowder has fallen off greatly from
his stomick—He eats nothing but white meats, and not much of that;
and wheezes, and seems to be much bloated. The doctors think he is
threatened with a dropsy—Parson Marrofat, who has got the same
disorder, finds great benefit from the waters; but Chowder seems to

---

1. Physiognomy, i.e., facial features and appearance.
2. Probably Harlequin's Row, so named for its mix of brick and stone facades. "Crashit":
   likely the Royal Crescent. "Hottogon": the Octagon Chapel in Milsom Street, finished
   in 1676, which was a fashionable place of worship. "Bloody Buildings": likely the Bladud
   Buildings, named after Bath's legendary founder and located in Broad Street.
3. I.e., a penny's worth, meaning a very small amount of something.
4. A variation on the proverb "not worth a brass farthing." A farthing was a coin worth one-
   quarter of a British penny. "Flegm": i.e., phlegm, one of the four bodily humors, associated
   with calmness and dispassion.

like them no better than the squire; and mistress says, if his case don't take a favourable turn, she will sartinly carry him to Aberga'nny, to drink goat's-whey—To be sure, the poor dear honymil is lost for want of axercise; for which reason, she intends to give him an airing once a-day upon the Downs, in a post-chaise—I have already made very creditable correxions in this here place; where, to be sure, we have the very squintasense of satiety——Mrs. Patcher, my lady Kilmacullock's woman, and I are sworn sisters. She has shewn me all her secrets, and learned me to wash gaze, and refrash rusty siks and bumbeseens, by boiling them with winegar, chamberlye,[5] and stale beer. My short sack and apron luck as good as new from the shop, and my pumpy-door as fresh as a rose, by the help of turtle-water[6]—But this is all Greek and Latten to you, Molly——If we should come to Aberga'ny, you'll be within a day's ride of us; and then we shall see wan another, please God——If not, remember me in your prayers, as I shall do by you in mine; and take care of my kitten, and give my kind sarvice to Sall; and this is all at present, from your beloved friend and sarvent,

Bath, April 26.   WINIFRED JENKINS.

To Mrs. GWYLLIM, house-keeper at Brambleton-hall.

I am astonished, that Dr. Lewis should take upon him to give away Alderney, without my privity and concurrants—What signi-fies my brother's order? My brother is little better than Noncom-push.[7] He would give away the shirt off his back, and the teeth out of his head; nay, as for that matter, he would have ruinated the family with his ridiculous charities, if it had not been for my four quarters[8]—What between his willfullness and his waste, his trumps, and his frenzy, I lead the life of an indented slave.[9] Alderney gave four gallons a-day, ever since the calf was sent to market. There is so much milk out of my dairy, and the press[1] must stand still: but I won't loose a cheese paring; and the milk shall be made good, if the sarvents should go without butter. If they must needs have but-ter, let them make it of sheeps' milk; but then my wool will suffer

---

5. Urine used in some washing processes to save soap. "Bumbeseens": i.e., bombasine; a twilled or corded dress material.
6. A cosmetic wash containing powdered tortoiseshell. "Short sack": a fashionable dress. "Pumpydoor": i.e., pompadour, or pelisse; a long cloak with slits for the arms.
7. I.e., *non compos mentis*; not of sound mind (Latin).
8. Probably the quarterly returns from an annuity or investment.
9. I.e., indentured slave; someone who has made (voluntarily or under duress) a pledge of labor or service for a certain length of time to pay off debts. "Trumps": blustering or bellowing, like a trumpet.
1. Cheese press, for making fresh cheese.

for want of grace; so that I must be a looser on all sides——Well, patience is like a stout Welsh poney; it bears a great deal, and trots a great way; but it will tire at the long run. Before its long, perhaps I may shew Matt, that I was not born to be the household drudge to my dying day—Gwyn rites from Crickhowel, that the price of flannel is fallen three-farthings an ell; and that's another good penny out of my pocket—When I go to market to sell, my commodity stinks; but when I want to buy the commonest thing, the owner pricks it up under my nose; and it can't be had for love nor money—I think every thing runs cross at Brambleton-hall—You say the gander has broke the eggs; which is a phinumenon I don't understand; for when the fox carried off the old goose last year, he took her place, and hatched the eggs, and partected the goslings like a tender parent—Then you tell me the thunder has soured two barrels of beer in the seller. But how the thunder should get there, when the seller was double-locked, I can't comprehend. Howsomever, I won't have the beer thrown out, till I see it with my own eyes. Perhaps, it will recover—At least it will serve for vinegar to the sarvents. You may leave off the fires in my brother's chamber and mine, as it is unsartain when we return. ——I hope, Gwyllim, you'll take care there is no waste; and have an eye to the maids, and keep them to their spinning. I think they may go very well without beer in hot weather—It serves only to inflame the blood, and set them agog after the men. Water will make them fair, and keep them cool and tamperit. Don't forget to put up in the portmantel, that cums with Williams, along with my riding-habit, hat, and feather, the viol of purl water,[2] and the tincktur for my stomach; being as how I am much troubled with flutterencies. This is all at present, from

Yours,

Bath, April 26.   TABITHA BRAMBLE.

To Dr. LEWIS.

DEAR DICK,

I have done with the waters; therefore your advice comes a day too late—I grant that physick is no mystery of your making. I know it is a mystery in its own nature; and, like other mysteries, requires a strong gulp of faith to make it go down—Two days ago, I went into the King's Bath, by the advice of our friend Ch——,[3] in order to

---

2. A liquor made from beer or ale and bitter herbs, drunk before meals to aid digestion.
3. Rice Charleton (1710–1789), a physician at the Bath General Hospital, wrote several treatises on the spa waters' uses.

clear the strainer of the skin, for the benefit of a free perspiration; and the first object that saluted my eye, was a child full of scrophulous ulcers, carried in the arms of one of the guides, under the very noses of the bathers. I was so shocked at the sight, that I retired immediately with indignation and disgust—Suppose the matter of those ulcers, floating on the water, comes in contact with my skin, when the pores are all open, I would ask you what must be the consequence?——Good Heaven, the very thought makes my blood run cold! we know not what sores may be running into the water while we are bathing, and what sort of matter we may thus imbibe; the king's-evil, the scurvy, the cancer, and the pox; and, no doubt, the heat will render the virus[4] the more volatile and penetrating. To purify myself from all such contamination, I went to the duke of Kingston's private Bath,[5] and there I was almost suffocated for want of free air; the place was so small, and the steam so stifling.

After all, if the intention is no more than to wash the skin, I am convinced that simple element is more effectual than any water impregnated with salt and iron; which, being astringent, will certainly contract the pores, and leave a kind of crust upon the surface of the body. But I am now as much afraid of drinking, as of bathing; for, after a long conversation with the Doctor, about the construction of the pump and the cistern, it is very far from being clear with me, that the patients in the Pumproom don't swallow the scourings of the bathers. I can't help suspecting, that there is, or may be, some regurgitation from the bath into the cistern of the pump. In that case, what a delicate beveridge is every day quaffed by the drinkers; medicated with the sweat, and dirt, and dandriff; and the abominable discharges of various kinds, from twenty different diseased bodies, parboiling in the kettle below. In order to avoid this filthy composition, I had recourse to the spring that supplies the private baths on the Abbey-green; but I at once perceived something extraordinary in the taste and smell; and, upon inquiry, I find that the Roman baths in this quarter, were found covered by an old burying ground, belonging to the Abbey; thro' which, in all probability, the water drains in its passage: so that as we drink the decoction[6] of living bodies at the Pump-room, we swallow the strainings of rotten bones and carcasses at the private bath—I vow to God, the very idea turns my stomach!—Determined, as I am, against any farther use

4. Any agent that causes infectious diseases. (The modern meaning of "virus" as an infectious agent that replicates inside the cells of another organism did not come into usage until the 1890s.) "King's-evil": scrofula; a skin disease of the lymph nodes caused by bacterial infection, especially of the tubercular kind. "Scurvy": a disease caused by vitamin C deficiency, the symptoms of which include bleeding gums and skin spots. "The pox": probably refers to syphilis, though it may mean smallpox as well.
5. A group of small, private baths completed in 1764.
6. Extract.

of the Bath waters, this consideration would give me little disturbance, if I could find any thing more pure, or less pernicious, to
quench my thirst; but, although the natural springs of excellent
water are seen gushing spontaneous on every side, from the hills that
surround us, the inhabitants, in general, make use of well-water, so
impregnated with nitre, or alum, or some other villainous mineral,
that it is equally ungrateful to the taste, and mischievous to the constitution. It must be owned, indeed, that here, in Milsham-street, we
have a precarious and scanty supply from the hill; which is collected in an open bason in the Circus, liable to be defiled with dead
dogs, cats, rats, and every species of nastiness, which the rascally
populace may throw into it, from mere wantonness and brutality.—

Well, there is no nation that drinks so hoggishly as the English——
What passes for wine among us, is not the juice of the grape. It is an
adulterous mixture, brewed up of nauseous ingredients, by dunces,
who are bunglers in the art of poison-making; and yet we, and our
forefathers, are and have been poisoned by this cursed drench, without taste or flavour—The only genuine and wholsome beveridge in
England, is London porter, and Dorchester table-beer; but as for
your ale and your gin, your cyder, and your perry,[7] and all the trashy
family of made wines, I detest them as infernal compositions, contrived for the destruction of the human species.——But what have
I to do with the human species? except a very few friends, I care not
if the whole was——.

Heark ye, Lewis, my misanthropy increases every day—The longer I live, I find the folly and the fraud of mankind grow more and
more intolerable—I wish I had not come from Brambleton-hall;
after having lived in solitude so long, I cannot bear the hurry and
impertinence of the multitude; besides, every thing is sophisticated[8]
in these crowded places. Snares are laid for our lives in every thing
we eat or drink: the very air we breathe, is loaded with contagion.
We cannot even sleep, without risque of infection. I say, infection—
This place is the rendezvous of the diseased—You won't deny, that
many diseases are infectious; even the consumption[9] itself, is highly
infectious. When a person dies of it in Italy, the bed and bedding
are destroyed; the other furniture is exposed to the weather, and
the apartment white-washed, before it is occupied by any other living
soul. You'll allow, that nothing receives infection sooner, or retains it
longer, than blankets, feather-beds, and matrasses—'Sdeath! how
do I know what miserable objects have been stewing in the bed

7. A fermented drink, similar to cider, made from the juice of pears rather than apples.
   "Porter": a dark brown ale. "Dorchester table-beer": a strong beer that was widely distributed and praised.
8. Here used in its older, derogatory sense of altered or tampered with.
9. Tuberculosis of the lungs.

where I now lie!—I wonder, Dick, you did not put me in mind of sending for my own matrasses—But, if I had not been an ass, I should not have needed a remembrancer——There is always some plaguy reflection that rises up in judgment against me, and ruffles my spirits—Therefore, let us change the subject—

I have other reasons for abridging my stay at Bath—You know sister Tabby's complexion—If Mrs. Tabitha Bramble had been of any other race, I should certainly have looked upon her as the most—But, the truth is, she has found means to interest my affection; or, rather, she is beholden to the force of prejudice, commonly called the ties of blood. Well, this amiable maiden has actually commenced a flirting correspondence with an Irish baronet of sixty-five. His name is Sir Ulic Mackilligut. He is said to be much out at elbows;[1] and, I believe, has received false intelligence with respect to her fortune. Be that as it may, the connexion is exceedingly ridiculous, and begins already to excite whispers. For my part, I have no intention to dispute her free-agency; though I shall fall upon some expedient to undeceive her paramour, as to the point which he has principally in view. But I don't think her conduct is a proper example for Liddy, who has also attracted the notice of some coxcombs in the Rooms; and Jerry tells me, he suspects a strapping fellow, the knight's nephew, of some design upon the girl's heart. I shall, therefore, keep a strict eye over her aunt and her, and even shift the scene, if I find the matter grow more serious—You perceive what an agreeable task it must be, to a man of my kidney,[2] to have the cure of such souls as these—But, hold, you shall not have another peevish word (till the next occasion) from

yours,

Bath, April 28.   MATT. BRAMBLE.

To Sir WATKIN PHILLIPS of Jesus college, Oxon.

DEAR KNIGHT,

I think those people are unreasonable, who complain that Bath is a contracted circle, in which the same dull scenes perpetually revolve, without variation—I am, on the contrary, amazed to find so small a place, so crowded with entertainment and variety. London itself can hardly exhibit one species of diversion, to which we have not something analogous at Bath, over and above those singular

---

1. Impoverished or shabby (proverbial), from wearing out one's shirt or jacket at the elbows.
2. Constitution or temperament (proverbial).

advantages that are peculiar to the place. Here, for example, a man has daily opportunities of seeing the most remarkable characters of the community. He sees them in their natural attitudes and true colours; descended from their pedestals, and divested of their formal draperies, undisguised by art and affectation—Here we have ministers of state, judges, generals, bishops, projectors, philosophers, wits, poets, players, *chemists, fiddlers,* and *buffoons.*[3] If he makes any considerable stay in the place, he is sure of meeting with some particular friend, whom he did not expect to see; and to me there is nothing more agreeable, than such casual rencounters—Another entertainment, peculiar to Bath, arises from the general mixture of all degrees assembled in our public rooms, without distinction of rank or fortune. This is what my uncle reprobates, as a monstrous jumble of heterogeneous principles; a vile mob of noise and impertinence, without decency or subordination. But this chaos is to me a source of infinite amusement.

I was extremely diverted, last ball-night, to see the Master of the Ceremonies leading, with great solemnity, to the upper end of the room, an antiquated Abigail,[4] dressed in her lady's cast-clothes; whom he (I suppose) mistook for some countess just arrived at the Bath. The ball was opened by a Scotch lord, with a mulatto heiress from St. Christopher's; and the gay colonel Tinsel danced all the evening with the daughter of an eminent tinman from the borough of Southwark[5]—Yesterday morning, at the Pump-room, I saw a broken-winded Wapping landlady squeeze through a circle of peers, to salute her brandy-merchant, who stood by the window, prop'd upon crutches; and a paralytic attorney of Shoelane, in shuffling up to the bar, kicked the shins of the chancellor of England, while his lordship, in a cut bob,[6] drank a glass of water at the pump. I cannot account for my being pleased with these incidents, any other way than by saying, they are truly ridiculous in their own nature, and serve to heighten the humour in the farce of life, which I am determined to enjoy as long as I can.—

3. From John Dryden's poem *Absalom and Achitophel* (1681). The italicized words apply to Zimri, a satirical portrait of George Villiers, second Duke of Buckingham (1628–1687).
4. A proper name used for any lady's maid, after a character in Francis Beaumont and John Fletcher's comedy *A Scornful Lady* (1616).
5. An inner district of London with a long-standing character for disreputability; home to many of the city's theaters, prisons, and brothels. Saint Christopher Island, also known as Saint Kitts, was a Caribbean British colony in the 18th century. It is now part of an independent country with the island of Nevis. "Tinman": or tinsmith; a maker or repairer of items made of tin and other lightweight metals.
6. A short, uncurled, informal wig. Wapping was an unfashionable section of London. Shoelane, known as a center for journalism near but not in the City of London, would not have been a good address for an 18th-century attorney. "Chancellor": a very high-ranking member of the British government. From 1761 to 1766 the lord chancellor was Robert Henley, Earl of Northington, who also represented the city of Bath in Parliament.

Those follies, that move my uncle's spleen,[7] excite my laughter.
He is as tender as a man without a skin; who cannot bear the slightest
touch without flinching. What tickles another would give him
torment; and yet he has what we may call lucid intervals, when he is
remarkably facetious—Indeed, I never knew a hypochondriac so apt
to be infected with good-humour. He is the most risible misanthrope
I ever met with. A lucky joke, or any ludicrous incident, will set him
a-laughing immoderately, even in one of his most gloomy paroxysms;
and, when the laugh is over, he will curse his own imbecillity. In
conversing with strangers, he betrays no marks of disquiet—He is
splenetic with his familiars only; and not even with them, while they
keep his attention employed; but when his spirits are not exerted
externally, they seem to recoil and prey upon himself——He has
renounced the waters with execration; but he begins to find a more
efficacious, and, certainly, a much more palatable remedy in the
pleasures of society. He has discovered some old friends, among the
invalids of Bath; and, in particular, renewed his acquaintance with
the celebrated James Quin,[8] who certainly did not come here to
drink water. You cannot doubt, but that I had the strongest curiosity
to know this original; and it was gratified by Mr. Bramble, who has
had him twice at our house to dinner.

So far as I am able to judge, Quin's character is rather more
respectable than it has been generally represented. His *bons mots*
are in every witling's mouth; but many of them have a rank flavour,
which one would be apt to think was derived from a natural grossness
of idea. I suspect, however, that justice has not been done the
author, by the collectors of those *Quiniana;* who have let the best of
them slip through their fingers, and only retained such as were suited
to the taste and organs of the multitude. How far he may relax in his
hours of jollity, I cannot pretend to say; but his general conversation
is conducted by the nicest rules of propriety; and Mr. James Quin is,
certainly, one of the best bred men in the kingdom. He is not only a
most agreeable companion; but (as I am credibly informed) a very
honest man; highly susceptible of friendship, warm, steady, and
even generous in his attachments; disdaining flattery, and incapable
of meanness and dissimulation. Were I to judge, however, from
Quin's eye alone, I should take him to be proud, insolent, and cruel.
There is something remarkably severe and forbidding in his aspect;
and, I have been told, he was ever disposed to insult his inferiors
and dependants.——Perhaps that report has influenced my opinion
of his looks——You know we are the fools of prejudice. Howsoever
that may be, I have as yet seen nothing but his favourable side; and

---

7. According to humoral medical theory, the seat of melancholy.
8. English actor of Irish descent (1693–1766) who retired to Bath in 1751.

my uncle, who frequently confers with him in a corner, declares he
is one of the most sensible men he ever knew—He seems to have a
reciprocal regard for old Square-toes,[9] whom he calls by the familiar
name of Matthew, and often reminds of their old tavern-adventures:
on the other hand, Matthew's eyes sparkle whenever Quin makes
his appearance—Let him be never so jarring and discordant, Quin
puts him in tune; and, like treble and bass in the same concert, they
make excellent musick together—T'other day, the conversation turning upon Shakespeare, I could not help saying, with some emotion,
that I would give an hundred guineas to see Mr. Quin act the part
of Falstaff; upon which, turning to me with a smile, "And I would
give a thousand, young gentleman, (said he) that I could gratify your
longing." My uncle and he are perfectly agreed in their estimate of
life; which, Quin says, would stink in his nostrils, if he did not steep
it in claret.

I want to see this phenomenon in his cups; and have almost prevailed upon uncle to give him a small turtle at the Bear.[1] In the mean
time, I must entertain you with an incident, that seems to confirm
the judgment of those two cynic philosophers. I took the liberty to
differ in opinion from Mr. Bramble, when he observed, that the mixture of people in the entertainments of this place was destructive of
all order and urbanity; that it rendered the plebeians insufferably
arrogant and troublesome, and vulgarized the deportment and sentiments of those who moved in the upper spheres of life. He said,
such a preposterous coalition would bring us into contempt with
all our neighbours; and was worse, in fact, than debasing the gold
coin of the nation. I argued, on the contrary, that those plebeians
who discovered such eagerness to imitate the dress and equipage of
their superiors, would likewise, in time, adopt their maxims and their
manners, be polished by their conversation, and refined by their
example; but when I appealed to Mr. Quin, and asked if he did not
think that such an unreserved mixture would improve the whole
mass?—"Yes, (said he) as a plate of marmalade would improve a pan
of sirreverence."[2]

I owned I was not much conversant in high-life, but I had seen
what were called polite assemblies in London and elsewhere; that
those of Bath seemed to be as decent as any; and that, upon the
whole, the individuals that composed it, would not be found deficient
in good manners and decorum. "But let us have recourse to experience, (said I)—Jack Holder, who was intended for a parson, has

9. Square-toed shoes for men were not considered fashionable by the second half of the
   18th century. The nickname may also reflect Matt's use of wide shoes to ease his gout.
1. One of the most luxurious inns of Bath. Turtle soup was a delicacy in 18th-century
   Britain.
2. Human feces.

succeeded to an estate of two thousand a year, by the death of his elder brother. He is now at the Bath, driving about in a phaeton and four, with French horns. He has treated with turtle and claret at all the taverns in Bath and Bristol, till his guests are gorged with good chear: he has bought a dozen suits of fine clothes, by the advice of the Master of the Ceremonies, under whose tuition he has entered himself: he has lost some hundreds at billiards to sharpers, and taken one of the nymphs of Avon-street into keeping; but, finding all these channels insufficient to drain him of his current cash, his counsellor has engaged him to give a general tea-drinking to-morrow at Wilt-shire's room.[3] In order to give it the more eclat, every table is to be furnished with sweet-meats and nosegays; which, however, are not to be touched till notice is given by the ringing of a bell, and then the ladies may help themselves without restriction. This will be no bad way of trying the company's breeding—"

"I will abide by that experiment, (cried my uncle) and if I could find a place to stand secure, without the vortex of the tumult, which I know will ensue, I would certainly go thither and enjoy the scene." Quin proposed that we should take our station in the musick-gallery; and we took his advice. Holder had got thither before us, with his horns perdue;[4] but we were admitted. The tea-drinking passed as usual; and the company having risen from the tables, were saun-tring in groupes, in expectation of the signal for attack, when the bell beginning to ring, they flew with eagerness to the dessert, and the whole place was instantly in commotion. There was nothing but justling, scrambling, pulling, snatching, struggling, scolding, and screaming. The nosegays were torn from one another's hands and bosoms; the glasses and china went to wreck; the tables and floor were strewed with comfits. Some cried; some swore; and the tropes and figures of Billingsgate[5] were used without reserve in all their native zest and flavour; nor were those flowers of rhetoric unattended with significant gesticulation. Some snapped their fingers; some forked them out; some clapped their hands, and some their back-sides; at length, they fairly proceeded to pulling caps, and every thing seemed to presage a general battle; when Holder ordered his horns to sound a charge, with a view to animate the combatants, and inflame the contest; but this manœuvre produced an effect quite contrary to what he expected. It was a note of reproach that roused them to an immediate sense of their disgraceful situation. They were ashamed of their absurd deportment, and suddenly desisted. They gathered

3. One of the two large public rooms in Bath. "Nymphs of Avon-street": a well-known euphemism for the prostitutes who worked near Bath's docks.
4. Concealed.
5. Originally an area in London that housed a famous fish market, the term became syn-onymous with coarse, abusive language.

up their caps, ruffles, and handkerchiefs; and great part of them retired in silent mortification.

Quin laughed at this adventure; but my uncle's delicacy was hurt. He hung his head in manifest chagrin, and seemed to repine at the triumph of his judgment—Indeed, his victory was more complete than he imagined; for, as we afterwards learned, the two amazons who singularized themselves most in the action, did not come from the purlieus of Puddle-dock,[6] but from the courtly neighbourhood of St. James's palace. One was a baroness, and the other, a wealthy knight's dowager[7]—My uncle spoke not a word, till we had made our retreat good to the coffeehouse; where, taking off his hat and wiping his forehead, "I bless God (said he) that Mrs. Tabitha Bramble did not take the field to-day!" "I would pit her for a cool hundred (cried Quin) against the best shake-bag of the whole main."[8] The truth is, nothing could have kept her at home but the accident of her having taken physick before she knew the nature of the entertainment. She has been for some days furbishing up an old suit of black velvet, to make her appearance as Sir Ulic's partner at the next ball.

I have much to say of this amiable kinswoman; but she has not been properly introduced to your acquaintance. She is remarkably civil to Mr. Quin; of whose sarcastic humour she seems to stand in awe; but her caution is no match for her impertinence. "Mr. Gwynn, (said she the other day) I was once vastly entertained with your playing the Ghost of Gimlet at Drury-lane, when you rose up through the stage, with a white face and red eyes, and spoke of *quails upon the frightful porcofine*[9]—Do, pray, spout a little the Ghost of Gimlet." "Madam, (said Quin, with a glance of ineffable disdain) the Ghost of Gimlet is laid, never to rise again—" Insensible of this check, she proceeded: "Well, to be sure, you looked and talked so like a real ghost; and then the cock crowed so natural. I wonder how you could teach him to crow so exact, in the very nick of time; but, I suppose, he's game——An't he game,[1] Mr. Gwynn?" "Dunghill,[2] madam." "Well, dung-hill, or not dunghill, he has got such a clear counter-tenor, that I wish I had such another at Brambleton-hall, to wake the maids of a morning. Do you know where I could find one of his brood?" "Probably in the work-house of St. Giles's parish, madam;

---

6. An area along the River Thames near Blackfriars Bridge.
7. A widow who holds a title or property from her deceased husband.
8. Mainland, i.e., the entire island of Great Britain. "Shake-bag": a gamecock that was excited by shaking it in a bag before releasing it for cockfighting, which was legal in Britain throughout the 18th century.
9. Misquoted from Shakespeare's *Hamlet* (1.5.20), in which the Ghost claims he could tell stories that would make Hamlet's (called "Gimlet" by Tabitha) hair stand on end, "Like quills upon the fretful porpentine [porcupine]."
1. Brave, in cockfighting parlance.
2. Cowardly.

but I protest I know not his particular mew."[3] My uncle, frying with vexation, cried, "Good God, sister, how you talk! I have told you twenty times, that this gentleman's name is not Gwynn.—" "Hoity toity, brother mine, (she replied) no offence, I hope—Gwynn is an honourable name, of true old British extraction——I thought the gentleman had been come of Mrs. Helen Gwynn,[4] who was of his own profession; and if so be that were the case, he might be of king Charles's breed, and have royal blood in his veins—" "No, madam, (answered Quin, with great solemnity) my mother was not a whore of such distinction—True it is, I am sometimes tempted to believe myself of royal descent; for my inclinations are often arbitrary—If I was an absolute prince, at this instant, I belive I should send for the head of your cook in a charger—She has committed felony, on the person of that John Dory; which is mangled in a cruel manner, and even presented without sauce—O *tempora! O mores!*"[5]

This good-humoured sally turned the conversation into a less disagreeable channel—But, lest you should think my scribble as tedious as Mrs. Tabby's clack, I shall not add another word, but that I am as usual

Yours,

Bath, April 30. J. MELFORD.

To Dr. LEWIS.

DEAR LEWIS,

I received your bill upon Wiltshire, which was punctually hon-oured; but as I don't choose to keep so much cash by me, in a com-mon lodging-house, I have deposited 250 *l.* in the bank of Bath, and shall take their bills for it in London, when I leave this place, where the season draws to an end—You must know, that now being a-foot, I am resolved to give Liddy a glimpse of London. She is one of the best hearted creatures I ever knew, and gains upon my affection every day—As for Tabby, I have dropt such hints to the Irish baronet, concerning her fortune, as, I make no doubt, will cool the ardour of his addresses. Then her pride will take the alarm; and the rancour of stale maidenhood being chafed, we shall hear nothing but slander and abuse of Sir Ulic Mackilligut—This rupture, I foresee, will facil-itate our departure from Bath; where, at present, Tabby seems to

---

3. A row of urban stables and the alley or courtyard onto which they opened. Saint Giles is a London neighborhood, infamous in the 18th century for its slum-like conditions.
4. Eleanor "Nell" Gwyn (1650–1687), a popular actress as well as a mistress of Charles II.
5. Oh what times! Oh what customs! (Latin), made famous by the classical orator Cicero (106–43 B.C.E.). "John Dory": a popular variety of fish.

enjoy herself with peculiar satisfaction. For my part, I detest it so much, that I should not have been able to stay so long in the place if I had not discovered some old friends; whose conversation alleviates my disgust—Going to the coffee-house one forenoon, I could not help contemplating the company, with equal surprize and compassion—We consisted of thirteen individuals; seven lamed by the gout, rheumatism, or palsy; three maimed by accident; and the rest either deaf or blind. One hobbled, another hopped, a third dragged his legs after him like a wounded snake, a fourth straddled betwixt a pair of long crutches, like the mummy of a felon hanging in chains; a fifth was bent into a horizontal position, like a mounted telescope, shoved in by a couple of chairmen; and a sixth was the bust of a man, set upright in a wheel machine, which the waiter moved from place to place.

Being struck with some of their faces, I consulted the subscription-book; and, perceiving the names of several old friends, began to consider the groupe with more attention. At length I discovered rear-admiral Balderick, the companion of my youth, whom I had not seen since he was appointed lieutenant of the Severn. He was metamorphosed into an old man, with a wooden leg and a weatherbeaten face; which appeared the more antient from his grey locks, that were truly venerable—Sitting down at the table, where he was reading a news-paper, I gazed at him for some minutes, with a mixture of pleasure and regret, which made my heart gush with tenderness; then, taking him by the hand, "Ah, Sam, (said I) forty years ago I little thought—" I was too much moved to proceed. "An old friend, sure enough! (cried he, squeezing my hand, and surveying me eagerly thro' his glasses) I know the looming of the vessel, though she has been hard strained since we parted; but I can't heave up the name—" The moment I told him who I was, he exclaimed, "Ha! Matt, my old fellow cruizer, still afloat!" And, starting up, hugged me in his arms. His transport, however, boded me no good; for, in saluting me, he thrust the spring of his spectacles into my eye, and, at the same time, set his wooden stump upon my gouty toe; an attack that made me shed tears in sad earnest——After the hurry of our recognition was over, he pointed out two of our common friends in the room: the bust was what remained of colonel Cockril, who had lost the use of his limbs in making an American campaign; and the telescope proved to be my college chum, sir Reginald Bently; who, with his new title, and unexpected inheritance, commenced fox-hunter, without having served his apprenticeship to the mystery; and, in consequence of following the hounds through a river, was seized with an inflammation in his bowels, which has contracted him into his present attitude.

Our former correspondence was forthwith renewed, with the most hearty expressions of mutual good-will; and as we had met so unexpectedly, we agreed to dine together that very day at the tavern.

My friend Quin, being luckily unengaged, obliged us with his company; and, truly, this was the most happy day I have passed these twenty years. You and I, Lewis, having been always together, never tasted friendship in this high goût,[6] contracted from long absence. I cannot express the half of what I felt at this casual meeting of three or four companions, who had been so long separated, and so roughly treated by the storms of life. It was a renovation of youth; a kind of resuscitation of the dead, that realized those interesting dreams, in which we sometimes retrieve our antient friends from the grave. Perhaps my enjoyment was not the less pleasing for being mixed with a strain of melancholy, produced by the remembrance of past scenes, that conjured up the ideas of some endearing connexions, which the hand of Death has actually dissolved.

The spirits and good-humour of the company seemed to triumph over the wreck of their constitutions. They had even philosophy enough to joke upon their own calamities; such is the power of friendship, the sovereign cordial of life—I afterwards found, however, that they were not without their moments, and even hours of disquiet. Each of them apart, in succeeding conferences, expatiated upon his own particular grievances; and they were all malcontents at bottom—Over and above their personal disasters, they thought themselves unfortunate in the lottery of life. Baldrick complained, that all the recompence he had received for his long and hard service, was the half-pay of a rear-admiral. The colonel was mortified to see himself over-topped by upstart generals, some of whom he had once commanded; and, being a man of a liberal turn, could ill put up with a moderate annuity, for which he had sold his commission. As for the baronet, having run himself considerably in debt, on a contested election, he has been obliged to relinquish his seat in parliament, and his seat in the country at the same time, and put his estate to nurse; but his chagrin, which is the effect of his own misconduct, does not affect me half so much as that of the other two; who have acted honourable and distinguished parts on the great theatre, and are now reduced to lead a weary life in this stewpan of idleness and insignificance. They have long left off using the waters, after having experienced their inefficacy. The diversions of the place they are not in a condition to enjoy. How then do they make shift to pass their time? In the forenoon, they crawl out to the Rooms or the coffee-house, where they take a hand at whist, or descant upon the General Advertiser;[7] and their evenings they murder

6. Taste (French); i.e., style.
7. A popular newspaper, consisting mostly of advertisements, which ran from 1744 to 1752. In 1752 it was taken over by its printer, Henry Woodfall (1713–1769) and relaunched as the *Public Advertiser*.

Matthew Bramble recognises some ancient friends. Courtesy of the Center for Southwest Research, University Libraries, University of New Mexico.

in private parties, among peevish invalids, and insipid old women—This is the case with a good number of individuals, whom nature seems to have intended for better purposes.

About a dozen years ago, many decent families, restricted to small fortunes, besides those that came hither on the score of health, were tempted to settle at Bath, where they could then live comfortably, and even make a genteel appearance, at a small expence: but the madness of the times has made the place too hot for them, and they are now obliged to think of other migrations—Some have already fled to the mountains of Wales, and others have retired to Exeter. Thither, no doubt, they will be followed by the flood of luxury and extravagance, which will drive them from place to place to the very Land's End; and there, I suppose, they will be obliged to ship themselves to some other country. Bath is become a mere sink of profligacy and extortion. Every article of house-keeping is raised to an enormous price; a circumstance no longer to be wondered at, when we know that every petty retainer of fortune piques himself upon keeping a table, and thinks 'tis for the honour of his character to wink at the knavery of his servants, who are in a confederacy with the market-people; and, of consequence, pay whatever they demand. Here is now a mushroom of opulence, who pays a cook seventy guineas a week for furnishing him with one meal a day. This portentous frenzy is become so contagious, that the very rabble and refuse of mankind are infected. I have known a negro-driver, from Jamaica, pay over-night to the master of one of the rooms, sixty-five guineas for tea and coffee to the company, and leave Bath next morning, in such obscurity, that not one of his guests had the slightest idea of his person, or even made the least inquiry about his name. Incidents of this kind are frequent; and every day teems with fresh absurdities, which are too gross to make a thinking man merry.—But I feel the spleen creeping on me apace; and therefore will indulge you with a cessation, that you may have no unnecessary cause to curse your correspondence with,

> Dear Dick,
>
> yours ever,

Bath, May 5.   MAT. BRAMBLE.

To Miss LÆTITIA WILLIS, at Gloucester.

MY DEAR LETTY,

I wrote you at great length by the post, the twenty-sixth of last month, to which I refer you for an account of our proceedings at

Bath; and I expect your answer with impatience. But, having this opportunity of a private hand, I send you two dozen of Bath rings;[8] six of the best of which I desire you will keep for yourself, and distribute the rest among the young ladies, our common friends, as you shall think proper——I don't know how you will approve of the mottoes; some of them are not much to my own liking; but I was obliged to take such as I could find ready manufactured—I am vexed, that neither you nor I have received any further information of a certain person—Sure it can't be wilful neglect!—O my dear Willis! I begin to be visited by strange fancies, and to have some melancholy doubts; which, however, it would be ungenerous to harbour without further inquiry—My uncle, who has made me a present of a very fine set of garnets, talks of treating us with a jaunt to London; which, you may imagine, will be highly agreeable: but I like Bath so well, that I hope he won't think of leaving it till the season is quite over; and yet, betwixt friends, something has happened to my aunt, which will probably shorten our stay in this place.

Yesterday, in the forenoon, she went by herself to a breakfasting in one of the rooms; and, in half an hour, returned in great agitation, having Chowder along with her in the chair. I believe some accident must have happened to that unlucky animal, which is the great source of all her troubles. Dear Letty! what a pity it is, that a woman of her years and discretion, should place her affection upon such an ugly, ill-conditioned cur, that snarls and snaps at every body. I asked John Thomas, the footman who attended her, what was the matter? and he did nothing but grin. A famous dog-doctor was sent for, and undertook to cure the patient, provided he might carry him home to his own house; but his mistress would not part with him out of her own sight——She ordered the cook to warm cloths, which she applied to his bowels, with her own hand. She gave up all thoughts of going to the ball in the evening; and when Sir Ulic came to drink tea, refused to be seen; so that he went away to look for another partner. My brother Jery whistles and dances. My uncle sometimes shrugs up his shoulders, and sometimes bursts out a-laughing. My aunt sobs and scolds by turns; and her woman, Win Jinkins, stares and wonders with a foolish face of curiosity; and, for my part, I am as curious as she, but ashamed to ask questions.

Perhaps time will discover the mystery; for if it was any thing that happened in the Rooms, it can't be long concealed—All I know is, that last night at supper, miss Bramble spoke very disdainfully of Sir Ulic Mackilligut, and asked her brother if he intended to keep us sweltering all the summer at Bath? "No, sister Tabitha, (said he, with

8. Decorated souvenir rings.

an arch smile) we shall retreat before the Dog-days[9] begin; though I make no doubt, that with a little temperance and discretion, our constitutions might be kept cool enough all the year, even at Bath." As I don't know the meaning of this insinuation, I won't pretend to make any remarks upon it at present: hereafter, perhaps, I may be able to explain it more to your satisfaction——In the mean time, I beg you will be punctual in your correspondence, and continue to love your ever faithful

Bath, May 6.   Lydia Melford.

To Sir Watkin Phillips, of Jesus college, Oxon.

So then Mrs. Blackerby's affair has proved a false alarm, and I have saved my money? I wish, however, her declaration had not been so premature; for though my being thought capable of making her a mother, might have given me some credit, the reputation of an intrigue with such a cracked pitcher does me no honour at all——In my last I told you I had hopes of seeing Quin, in his hours of elevation at the tavern which is the temple of mirth and good-fellowship; where he, as priest of Comus,[1] utters the inspirations of wit and humour——I have had that satisfaction. I have dined with his club at the Three Tuns,[2] and had the honour to sit him out. At half an hour past eight in the evening, he was carried home with six good bottles of claret under his belt; and it being then Friday, he gave orders, that he should not be disturbed till Sunday at noon—— You must not imagine that this dose had any other effect upon his conversation, but that of making it more extravagantly entertaining—He had lost the use of his limbs, indeed, several hours before we parted, but he retained all his other faculties in perfection; and as he gave vent to every whimsical idea as it rose, I was really astonished at the brilliancy of his thoughts, and the force of his expression. Quin is a real voluptuary in the articles of eating and drinking; and so confirmed an epicure, in the common acceptation of the term, that he cannot put up with ordinary fare. This is a point of such importance with him, that he always takes upon himself the charge of catering; and a man admitted to his mess, is always sure of eating delicate victuals, and drinking excellent wine—He owns himself addicted to the delights of the stomach, and often jokes upon his own sensuality; but there is nothing selfish in this appetite—He

9. The hottest days of the year, from early July to mid-August in Britain. Named after the dog star, Sirius.
1. The Roman god of revelry.
2. A well-known local inn.

finds that good chear unites good company; exhilerates the spirits, opens the heart, banishes all restraint from conversation, and promotes the happiest purposes of social life.—But Mr. James Quin is not a subject to be discussed in the compass of one letter; I shall therefore, at present, leave him to his repose, and call another of a very different complexion.

You desire to have further acquaintance with the person of our aunt, and promise yourself much entertainment from her connexion with Sir Ulic Mackilligut: but in this hope you are baulked already; that connexion is dissolved. The Irish baronet is an old hound, that, finding her carrion, has quitted the scent—I have already told you, that Mrs. Tabitha Bramble is a maiden of forty-five. In her person, she is tall, raw-boned, aukward, flat-chested, and stooping; her complexion is sallow and freckled; her eyes are not grey, but greenish, like those of a cat, and generally inflamed; her hair is of a sandy, or rather dusty hue; her forehead low; her nose long, sharp, and, towards the extremity, always red in cool weather; her lips skinny, her mouth extensive, her teeth straggling and loose, of various colours and conformation; and her long neck shrivelled into a thousand wrinkles—In her temper, she is proud, stiff, vain, imperious, prying, malicious, greedy, and uncharitable. In all likelihood, her natural austerity has been soured by disappointment in love; for her long celibacy is by no means owing to her dislike of matrimony: on the contrary, she has left no stone unturned to avoid the reproachful epithet of old maid.

Before I was born, she had gone such lengths in the way of flirting with a recruiting officer, that her reputation was a little singed. She afterwards made advances to the curate of the parish, who dropped some distant hints about the next presentation to the living,[3] which was in her brother's gift; but finding that was already promised to another, he flew off at a tangent; and Mrs. Tabby, in revenge, found means to deprive him of his cure. Her next lover was lieutenant of a man of war, a relation of the family, who did not understand the refinements of the passion, and expressed no aversion to grapple with cousin Tabby in the way of marriage; but before matters could be properly adjusted, he went out on a cruise, and was killed in an engagement with a French frigate. Our aunt, though baffled so often, did not yet despair—She layed all her snares for Dr. Lewis, who is the *fidus Achates*[4] of my uncle. She even fell sick upon the occasion, and prevailed with Matt to interpose in her behalf with his friend; but the Doctor, being a shy cock, would not be caught with chaff,

3. The income attached to a particular parish in the Anglican Church (Church of England).
4. Aeneas's loyal companion in Virgil's *Aeneid*—hence any faithful friend.

and flatly rejected the proposal: so that Mrs. Tabitha was content to exert her patience once more, after having endeavoured in vain to effect a rupture betwixt the two friends; and now she thinks proper to be very civil to Lewis, who is become necessary to her in the way of his profession.

These, however, are not the only efforts she has made towards a nearer conjunction with our sex. Her fortune was originally no more than a thousand pounds; but she gained an accession of five hundred by the death of a sister, and the lieutenant left her three hundred in his will. These sums she has more than doubled, by living free of all expence, in her brother's house; and dealing in cheese and Welsh flannel, the produce of his flocks and dairy. At present her capital is increased to about four thousand pounds; and her avarice seems to grow every day more and more rapacious: but even this is not so intolerable, as the perverseness of her nature, which keeps the whole family in disquiet and uproar. She is one of those geniuses who find some diabolical enjoyment in being dreaded and detested by their fellow-creatures.

I once told my uncle, I was surprised that a man of his disposition could bear such a domestic plague, when it could be so easily removed—The remark made him sore, because it seemed to tax him with want of resolution—Wrinkling up his nose, and drawing down his eyebrows, "A young fellow, (said he) when he first thrusts his snout into the world, is apt to be surprised at many things, which a man of experience knows to be ordinary and unavoidable—This precious aunt of yours is become insensibly a part of my constitution—Damn her! She's a *noli me tangere*[5] in my flesh, which I cannot bear to be touched or tampered with." I made no reply; but shifted the conversation. He really has an affection for this original; which maintains its ground in defiance of common sense, and in despite of that contempt which he must certainly feel for her character and understanding. Nay, I am convinced, that she has likewise a most virulent attachment to his person; though her love never shews itself but in the shape of discontent; and she persists in tormenting him out of sheer tenderness—The only object within doors upon which she bestows any marks of affection, in the usual stile, is her dog Chowder; a filthy cur from Newfoundland, which she had in a present from the wife of a skipper in Swansey[6]—One would imagine she had distinguished this beast with her favour on account of his ugliness

---

5. Do not touch me (Latin). In the New Testament of the Bible, these are Christ's words to Mary Magdalene after the Resurrection (John 20:17). In medical usage, it became the term for a sensitive ulcer or wart made worse by attempts to cure it.
6. Swansea is a seaport in south Wales. Chowder's name seems to reflect its heritage, because Newfoundland (a British colony in the 18th century) was famous for its fish stew, or chowder.

and ill-nature; if it was not, indeed, an instinctive sympathy between his disposition and her own. Certain it is, she caresses him without ceasing; and even harrasses the family in the service of this cursed animal, which, indeed, has proved the proximate cause of her breach with Sir Ulic Mackilligut.

You must know, she yesterday wanted to steal a march[7] of poor Liddy, and went to breakfast in the Room without any other companion than her dog, in expectation of meeting with the Baronet, who had agreed to dance with her in the evening—Chowder no sooner made his appearance in the Room, than the Master of the Ceremonies, incensed at his presumption, ran up to drive him away, and threatened him with his foot; but the other seemed to despise his authority, and displaying a formidable case of long, white, sharp teeth, kept the puny monarch at bay—While he stood under some trepidation, fronting his antagonist, and bawling to the waiter, Sir Ulic Mackilligut came to his assistance; and seeming ignorant of the connexion between this intruder and his mistress, gave the former such a kick in the jaws, as sent him howling to the door——Mrs. Tabitha, incensed at this outrage, ran after him, squalling in a tone equally disagreeable; while the Baronet followed her on one side, making apologies for his mistake; and Derrick on the other, making remonstrances upon the rules and regulations of the place.

Far from being satisfied with the Knight's excuses, she said she was sure he was no gentleman; and when the Master of the Ceremonies offered to hand her into the chair, she rapped him over the knuckles with her fan. My uncle's footman being still at the door, she and Chowder got into the same vehicle, and were carried off amidst the jokes of the chairmen and other populace——I had been riding out on Clerkendown, and happened to enter just as the *fracas* was over—The Baronet, coming up to me with an affected air of chagrin, recounted the adventure; at which I laughed heartily, and then his countenance cleared up. "My dear soul, (said he) when I saw a sort of a wild baist, snarling with open mouth at the Master of the Ceremonies, like the red cow going to devour Tom Thumb,[8] I could do no less than go to the assistance of the little man; but I never dreamt the baist was one of Mrs. Bramble's attendants——O! if I had, he might have made his breakfast upon Derrick and wellcome—But, you know, my dear friend, how natural it is for us Irishmen to blunder, and to take the wrong sow by the ear—However, I will confess judgment, and cry her mercy; and, 'tis to be hoped, a penitent

---

7. To accomplish something before someone else does it.
8. A tiny man of folktale fame who was the subject of many chapbooks during the early 18th century; he was further popularized in Henry Fielding's plays *Tom Thumb* (1730) and *The Tragedy of Tragedies* (1731).

sinner may be forgiven." I told him, that as the offence was not involuntary of his side, it was to be hoped he would not find her implacable.

But, in truth, all this concern was dissembled. In his approaches of gallantry to Mrs. Tabitha, he had been misled by a mistake of at least six thousand pounds, in the calculation of her fortune; and in this particular he was just undeceived. He, therefore, seized the first opportunity of incurring her displeasure decently, in such a manner as would certainly annihilate the correspondence; and he could not have taken a more effectual method, than that of beating her dog. When he presented himself at our door, to pay his respects to the offended fair, he was refused admittance; and given to understand, that he should never find her at home for the future. She was not so inaccessible to Derrick, who came to demand satisfaction for the insult she had offered to him, even in the verge of his own court. She knew it was convenient to be well with the Master of the Ceremonies, while she continued to frequent the Rooms; and, having heard he was a poet, began to be afraid of making her appearance in a ballad or lampoon.—She therefore made excuses for what she had done, imputing it to the flutter of her spirits; and subscribed handsomely for his poems:[9] so that he was perfectly appeased, and overwhelmed her with a profusion of compliment. He even solicited a reconciliation with Chowder; which, however, the latter declined; and he declared, that if he could find a precedent in the annals of the Bath, which he would carefully examine for that purpose, her favourite should be admitted to the next public breakfasting—But, I believe, she will not expose herself or him to the risque of a second disgrace—Who will supply the place of Mackilligut in her affections, I cannot foresee; but nothing in the shape of man can come amiss. Though she is a violent church-woman, of the most intolerant zeal, I believe in my conscience she would have no objection, at present, to treat on the score of matrimony with an Anabaptist, Quaker, or Jew; and even ratify the treaty, at the expence of her own conversion. But, perhaps, I think too hardly of this kinswoman; who, I must own, is very little beholden to the good opinion of

Yours,

Bath, May 6. J. MELFORD.

---

9. Publishing volumes of poetry by advance subscription was a common practice throughout the 18th century.

To Dr. LEWIS.

You ask me, why I don't take the air a-horseback, during this fine weather?—In which of the avenues of this paradise would you have me take that exercise? Shall I commit myself to the high-roads of London or Bristol, to be stifled with dust, or pressed to death in the midst of post-chaises, flying-machines,[1] waggons, and coal-horses; besides the troops of fine gentlemen that take to the high-way, to shew their horsemanship; and the coaches of fine ladies, who go thither to shew their equipages? Shall I attempt the Downs, and fatigue myself to death in climbing up an eternal ascent, without any hopes of reaching the summit? Know then, I have made divers desperate leaps at those upper regions; but always fell backward into this vapour-pit, exhausted and dispirited by those ineffectual efforts; and here we poor valetudinarians pant and struggle, like so many Chinese gudgeons,[2] gasping in the bottom of a punch-bowl. By Heaven, it is a kind of inchantment! If I do not speedily break the spell, and escape, I may chance to give up the ghost in this nauseous stew of corruption—It was but two nights ago, that I had like to have made my public exit, at a minute's warning. One of my greatest weaknesses is that of suffering myself to be over-ruled by the opinion of people, whose judgment I despise—I own, with shame and confusion of face, that importunity of any kind I cannot resist. This want of courage and constancy is an original flaw in my nature, which you must have often observed with compassion, if not with contempt. I am afraid some of our boasted virtues may be traced up to this defect.——

Without further preamble, I was persuaded to go to a ball, on pur-pose to see Liddy dance a minuet with a young petulant jackanapes, the only son of a wealthy undertaker[3] from London, whose mother lodges in our neighbourhood, and has contracted an acquaintance with Tabby. I sat a couple of long hours, half stifled, in the midst of a noisome crowd; and could not help wondering, that so many hun-dreds of those that rank as rational creatures, could find entertain-ment in seeing a succession of insipid animals, describing[4] the same dull figure for a whole evening, on an area, not much bigger than a taylor's shop-board. If there had been any beauty, grace, activity, mag-nificent dress, or variety of any kind, howsoever absurd, to engage the

---

1. Flying carriages: the generic name for speedy stage coaches. "Post-chaises": fast four-wheeled coaches, pulled by two or four horses, used for carrying mail as well as people.
2. A small fish used for bait.
3. Probably a contractor, although the word is also used in its modern sense of "funeral director" in Bramble's letter of May 29.
4. Tracing an outline of; in this context, dancing.

attention, and amuse the fancy, I should not have been surprised; but there was no such object: it was a tiresome repetition of the same languid, frivolous scene, performed by actors that seemed to sleep in all their motions——The continual swimming of those phantoms before my eyes, gave me a swimming of the head; which was also affected by the fouled air, circulating through such a number of rotten human bellows——I therefore retreated towards the door, and stood in the passage to the next room, talking to my friend Quin; when an end being put to the minuets, the benches were removed to make way for the country-dances; and the multitude rising at once, the whole atmosphere was put in commotion. Then, all of a sudden, came rushing upon me an Egyptian gale,[5] so impregnated with pestilential vapours, that my nerves were overpowered, and I dropt senseless upon the floor.

You may easily conceive what a clamour and confusion this accident must have produced, in such an assembly—I soon recovered, however, and found myself in an easy chair, supported by my own people—Sister Tabby, in her great tenderness, had put me to the torture, squeezing my head under her arm, and stuffing my nose with spirit of hartshorn, till the whole inside was excoriated. I no sooner got home, than I sent for doctor Ch——, who assured me, I needed not be alarmed, for my swooning was entirely occasioned by an accidental impression of fetid effluvia[6] upon nerves of uncommon sensibility. I know not how other people's nerves are constructed; but one would imagine they must be made of very coarse materials, to stand the shock of such a horrid assault. It was, indeed, a compound of *villainous smell's*,[7] in which the most violent stinks, and the most powerful perfumes, contended for the mastery. Imagine to yourself a high exalted essence of mingled odours, arising from putrid gums, imposthumated lungs, sour flatulencies, rank arm-pits, sweating feet, running sores and issues, plasters, ointments, and embrocations, hungary-water, spirit of lavender, assafœtida drops, musk, hartshorn, and sal volatile;[8] besides a thousand frowzy steams, which I could not analyse. Such, O Dick! is the fragrant æther we breathe in the polite assemblies of Bath—Such is the atmosphere I have exchanged for the pure, elastic, animating air of

---

5. Many 18th-century authorities thought that the Egyptian region was the geographical origin of the plague.
6. A noxious emission of tiny particles.
7. Echoes Falstaff's complaint about the bad smell of the laundry basket in which he has been hidden, in Shakespeare's *Merry Wives of Windsor* (3.5.93).
8. Ammonium carbonate: an aromatic solution used to restore fainting victims. "Imposthumated": swollen, ulcerated. "Embrocations": any liquid used for cleansing or soothing a diseased or injured body part. "Hungary-water": a cure-all made from rosemary flowers. "Hartshorn": a water-based solution of ammonia, sometimes made with ground antler.

the Welsh mountains——O *Rus, quando te aspiciam!*[9]—I wonder
what the devil possessed me—

But few words are best: I have taken my resolution—You may well
suppose I don't intend to entertain the company with a second exhibition—I have promised, in an evil hour, to proceed to London, and
that promise shall be performed; but my stay in the metropolis shall
be brief. I have, for the benefit of my health, projected an expedition
to the North, which, I hope, will afford some agreeable pastime. I
have never travelled farther that way than Scarborough; and, I
think, it is a reproach upon me, as a British freeholder, to have lived
so long without making an excursion to the other side of the Tweed.
Besides, I have some relations settled in Yorkshire, to whom it may
not be improper to introduce my nephew and his sister—At present,
I have nothing to add, but that Tabby is happily disentangled from
the Irish Baronet; and that I will not fail to make you acquainted,
from time to time, with the sequel of our adventures: a mark of consideration, which, perhaps, you would willingly dispense with in

Your humble servant,

Bath, May 8.   MATT. BRAMBLE.

To Sir WATKIN PHILLIPS, of Jesus college, Oxon.

DEAR PHILLIPS,

A few days ago we were terribly alarmed by my uncle's fainting at
the ball—He has been ever since cursing his own folly, for going
thither at the request of an impertinent woman. He declares, he
will sooner visit a house infected with the plague, than trust himself in such a nauseous spital for the future, for he swears the accident was occasioned by the stench of the crowd; and that he would
never desire a stronger proof of our being made of very gross materials, than our having withstood the annoyance, by which he was so
much discomposed. For my part, I am very thankful for the coarse-
ness of my organs, being in no danger of ever falling a sacrifice to
the delicacy of my nose. Mr. Bramble is extravagantly delicate in all
his sensations, both of soul and body. I was informed by Dr. Lewis,
that he once fought a duel with an officer of the horse-guards, for
turning a-side to the Park wall, on a necessary occasion, when he
was passing with a lady under his protection.[1] His blood rises at

9. Slightly misquoted from Horace's *Satire* (2.6.60), when the country mouse, now in the
   city, laments "Oh my countryside, when will I see you again?"
1. Since waste fluids were often dumped out of upper-story windows directly onto the
   street below, it was customary for gentlemen to allow women to walk closest to exterior
   walls to avoid being dirtied.

every instance of insolence and cruelty, even where he himself is no way concerned; and ingratitude makes his teeth chatter. On the other hand, the recital of a generous, humane, or grateful action, never fails to draw from him tears of approbation, which he is often greatly distressed to conceal.

Yesterday, one Paunceford[2] gave tea, on particular invitation— This man, after having been long buffetted by adversity, went abroad; and Fortune, resolved to make him amends for her former coyness, set him all at once up to the very ears in affluence. He has now emerged from obscurity, and blazes out in all the tinsel of the times. I don't find that he is charged with any practices that the law deems dishonest, or that his wealth has made him arrogant and inaccessible; on the contrary, he takes great pains to appear affable and gracious. But they say, he is remarkable for shrinking from his former friendships, which were generally too plain and home-spun to appear amidst his present brilliant connexions; and that he seems uneasy at sight of some old benefactors, whom a man of honour would take pleasure to acknowledge—Be that as it may, he had so effectually engaged the company at Bath, that when I went with my uncle to the coffee-house in the evening, there was not a soul in the room but one person, seemingly in years, who sat by the fire, reading one of the papers. Mr. Bramble, taking his station close by him, "There is such a crowd and confusion of chairs in the passage to Simpson's, (said he) that we could hardly get along—I wish those minions of fortune would fall upon more laudable ways of spending their money.—I suppose, sir, you like this kind of entertainment as little as I do?" "I can't say, I have any great relish for such entertainments," answered the other, without taking his eyes off the paper— Mr. Serle, (resumed my uncle) I beg pardon for interrupting you; but I can't resist the curiosity I have to know if you received a card[3] on this occasion?"

The man seemed surprised at this address, and made some pause, as doubtful what answer he should make. "I know my curiosity is impertinent, (added my uncle) but I have a particular reason for asking the favour." "If that be the case, (replied Mr. Serle) I shall gratify you without hesitation, by owning, that I have had no card. But, give me leave, sir, to ask in my turn, what reason you think I have to expect such an invitation from the gentleman who gives tea?" "I have my own reasons; (cried Mr. Bramble, with some emotion) and am convinced, more than ever, that this Paunceford is a contemptible

---

2. A fictional character whose coldness to his former benefactor recalls Smollett's own experiences with one Alexander Campbell, according to Smollett's biographer, Lewis M. Knapp.
3. Invitation.

fellow." "Sir, (said the other, laying down the paper) I have not the
honour to know you; but your discourse is a little mysterious, and
seems to require some explanation. The person you are pleased to
treat so cavalierly, is a gentleman of some consequence in the community; and, for aught you know, I may also have my particular
reasons for defending his character—" "If I was not convinced of
the contrary, (observed the other) I should not have gone so far—"
"Let me tell you, sir, (said the stranger, raising his voice) you have
gone too far, in hazarding such reflections——"

Here he was interrupted by my uncle; who asked peevishly, if he
was Don Quixote[4] enough, at this time of day, to throw down his
gauntlet as champion for a man who had treated him with such
ungrateful neglect. "For my part, (added he) I shall never quarrel with
you again upon this subject; and what I have said now, has been suggested as much by my regard for you, as by my contempt of him—"
Mr. Serle, then pulling off his spectacles, eyed uncle very earnestly,
saying, in a mitigated tone, "Surely I am much obliged——Ah, Mr.
Bramble! I now recollect your features, though I have not seen you
these many years." "We might have been less strangers to one
another, (answered the 'squire) if our correspondence had not been
interrupted, in consequence of a misunderstanding, occasioned by
this very——, but no matter—Mr. Serle, I esteem your character;
and my friendship, such as it is, you may freely command." "The
offer is too agreeable to be declined; (said he) I embrace it very cordially; and, as the first fruits of it, request that you will change this
subject, which, with me, is a matter of peculiar delicacy."

My uncle owned he was in the right, and the discourse took a
more general turn. Mr. Serle passed the evening with us at our lodgings; and appeared to be intelligent, and even entertaining; but
his disposition was rather of a melancholy hue. My uncle says he is
a man of uncommon parts, and unquestioned probity: that his fortune, which was originally small, his been greatly hurt by a romantic spirit of generosity, which he has often displayed, even at the
expence of his discretion, in favour of worthless individuals——
That he had rescued Paunceford from the lowest distress, when he
was bankrupt, both in means and reputation—That he had espoused
his interests with a degree of enthusiasm, broke with several friends,
and even drawn his sword against my uncle, who had particular reasons for questioning the moral character of the said Paunceford:
that, without Serle's countenance and assistance, the other never
could have embraced the opportunity, which has raised him to this

4. The idealistic, fanciful hero of Miguel de Cervantes' comic prose romance (2 vols.,
   1605 and 1615). Smollett published a popular English translation of *Don Quixote* in
   1755, with a revised edition in 1761.

pinnacle of wealth: that Paunceford, in the first transports of his success, had written, from abroad, letters to different correspondents, owning his obligations to Mr. Serle, in the warmest terms of acknowledgment, and declaring he considered himself only as a factor for the occasions[5] of his best friend: that, without doubt, he had made declarations of the same nature to his benefactor himself, though this last was always silent and reserved on the subject; but for some years, those tropes and figures of rhetoric had been disused: that, upon his return to England, he had been lavish in his caresses to Mr. Serle, invited him to his house, and pressed him to make it his own: that he had overwhelmed him with general professions, and affected to express the warmest regard for him, in company of their common acquaintance; so that every body believed his gratitude was as liberal as his fortune; and some went so far as to congratulate Mr. Serle on both.

All this time Paunceford carefully and artfully avoided particular discussions with his old patron, who had too much spirit to drop the most distant hint of balancing the account of obligation: that, nevertheless, a man of his feelings could not but resent this shocking return for all his kindness; and, therefore, he withdrew himself from the connexion, without coming to the least explanation, or speaking a syllable on the subject to any living soul; so that now their correspondence is reduced to a slight salute with the hat, when they chance to meet in any public place; an accident that rarely happens, for their walks lie different ways. Mr. Paunceford lives in a palace, feeds upon dainties, is arrayed in sumptuous apparel, appears in all the pomp of equipage, and passes his time among the nobles of the land. Serle lodges in Stall-street, up two pair of stairs backwards, walks a-foot in a Bath-rug,[6] eats for twelve shillings a-week, and drinks water as a preservative against the gout and gravel——Mark the vicissitude. Paunceford once resided in a garret; where he subsisted upon sheeps'-trotters[7] and cow-heel, from which commons he was translated to the table of Serle, that ever abounded with good-chear; until want of oeconomy and retention, reduced him to a slender annuity in his decline of years, that scarce affords the bare necessaries of life—Paunceford, however, does him the honour to speak of him still, with uncommon regard; and to declare what pleasure it would give him to contribute in any shape to his convenience: "But you know, (he never fails to add) he's a shy kind of a man—And then such a perfect philosopher, that he looks upon all superfluities with the most sovereign contempt."

5. Agent for the transactions.
6. A large piece of wool used as a wrap. Stall-street is in central Bath.
7. The shank and feet of sheep, cooked for cheap food.

Having given you this sketch of 'squire Paunceford, I need not make any comment on his character, but leave it at the mercy of your own reflection; from which, I dare say, it will meet with as little quarter as it has found with

yours always,

Bath, May 10.   J. MELFORD.

To Mrs. MARY JONES, at Brambleton-hall.

DEAR MOLLY,

We are all upon the ving—Hey for London, girl!—Fecks! we have been long enough here; for we're all turned tipsy turvy——Mistress has excarded Sir Ulic for kicking of Chowder; and I have sent O Frizzle away, with a flea in his ear—I've shewn him how little I minded his tinsy and his long tail[8]—A fellor, who would think for to go, for to offer, to take up with a dirty trollop under my nose——I ketched him in the very feet, coming out of the house-maids garret.— But I have gi'en the dirty slut a siserary.[9] O Molly! the sarvants at Bath are devils in garnet—They lite the candle at both ends—Here's nothing but ginketting, and wasting, and thieving, and tricking, and trigging; and then they are never content—They won't suffer the 'squire and mistress to stay any longer; because they have been already above three weeks in the house; and they look for a couple of ginneys a-piece at our going away; and this is a parquisite they expect every month in the season; being as how no family has a right to stay longer than four weeks in the same lodgings; and so the cuck swears, she will pin the dish-clout to mistress's tail; and the house-maid vows, she'll put cowitch[1] in master's bed, if so be he don't discamp without furder ado——I don't blame them for making the most of their market, in the way of vails and parquisites; and I defy the devil to say I am a tail-carrier, or ever brought a poor sarvant into trouble——But then they oft to have some conscience, in vronging those that be sarvants like themselves—For you must no, Molly, I missed three-quarters of blond lace, and a remnant of muslin, and my silver thimble; which was the gift of true love: they were all in my work-basket, that I left upon the table in the sarvants-hall, when mistresses bell rung; but if they had been under lock and kay, 'twould have been all the same; for there are double keys to all the locks in Bath;

8. His long, twisted or braided hair. "Tinsy": tinsel, i.e., cheap flashiness.
9. A severe rebuke or scolding. From the Latin *certiorari*, a writ issued by a superior court.
1. A tropical flowering plant, also known as velvet bean, that causes stinging itchiness on contact. "Pin the dish-clout": pinning a dishcloth to a person's backside was a standard threat by kitchen servants for interfering with their duties.

and they say as how the very teeth an't safe in your head, if you sleep with your mouth open—And so says I to myself, *them things could not go without hands; and so I'll watch their waters:*[2] and so I did with a vitness; for then it was I found Bett consarned with O Frizzle. And as the cuck had thrown her slush at me, because I had taken part with Chowder, when he fit with the turnspit, I resolved to make a clear kitchen, and throw some of her fat into the fire. I ketched the charewoman going out with her load in the morning, before she thought I was up, and brought her to mistress with her whole cargo— Marry, what do'st think she had got in the name of God? Her buckets were foaming full of our best bear, and her lap was stuffed with a cold tongue, part of a buttock of beef, half a turkey, and a swinging lump of butter, and the matter of ten mould kandles, that had scarce ever been lit. The cuck brazened it out, and said it was her rite to rummage the pantry; and she was ready for to go before the mare: that he had been her potticary[3] many years, and would never think of hurting a poor sarvant, for giving away the scraps of the kitchen——I went another way to work with madam Betty, because she had been saucy, and called me skandelus names; and said O Frizzle couldn't abide me, and twenty other odorous falsehoods. I got a varrant from the mare, and her box being sarched by the constable, my things came out sure enuff; besides a full pound of vax candles, and a nite-cap of mistress, that I could sware to on my cruperal oaf[4]—O! then madam Mopstick came upon her merry bones;[5] and as the 'squire wouldn't hare of a pursecution, she scaped a skewering: but the longest day she has to live, she'll remember your

humble sarvant,

Bath, May 15.   WINIFRED JENKINS.

If the hind should come again, before we be gone, pray send me the shift and apron, with the vite gallow manky[6] shoes; which you'll find in my pillowber——Sarvice to Saul—

To Sir WATKIN PHILLIPS, Bar[t].
of Jesus college, Oxon.

You are in the right, dear Phillips; I don't expect regular answers to every letter—I know a college-life is too circumscribed to afford

2. To watch someone's waters was a crude expression meaning to observe someone closely.
3. Apothecary; more than one served as mayor of Bath during the 18th century.
4. Corporal oath; a vow made while touching the Bible.
5. Marrowbones; i.e., knees.
6. White calamanco; a glossy wool fabric.

materials for such quick returns of communication. For my part, I am continually shifting the scene, and surrounded with new objects; some of which are striking enough. I shall therefore conclude my journal for your amusement; and though, in all appearance, it will not treat of very important or interesting particulars, it may prove, perhaps, not altogether uninstructive and unentertaining.

The musick and entertainments of Bath are over for this season; and all our gay birds of passage have taken their flight to Bristol-well, Tunbridge, Brighthelmstone, Scarborough, Harrowgate,[7] &c. Not a soul is seen in this place, but a few broken-winded parsons, waddling like so many crows along the North Parade. There is always a great shew of the clergy at Bath; none of your thin, puny, yellow, hectic figures, exhausted with abstinence and hard study, labouring under the *morbi eruditorum*;[8] but great overgrown dignitaries and rectors, with rubicund noses and gouty ancles, or broad bloated faces, dragging along great swag bellies; the emblems of sloth and indigestion—

Now we are upon the subject of parsons, I must tell you a ludicrous adventure, which was atchieved the other day by Tom Eastgate, whom you may remember on the foundation of Queen's.[9] He had been very assiduous to pin himself upon George Prankley, who was a gentleman-commoner of Christ-church, knowing the said Prankley was heir to a considerable estate, and would have the advowson[1] of a good living, the incumbent of which was very old and infirm. He studied his passions, and flattered them so effectually, as to become his companion and counsellor; and, at last, obtained of him a promise of the presentation, when the living should fall. Prankley, on his uncle's death, quitted Oxford, and made his first appearance in the fashionable world at London; from whence he came lately to Bath, where he has been exhibiting himself among the bucks and gamesters of the place. Eastgate followed him hither; but he should not have quitted him for a moment, at his first emerging into life. He ought to have known he was a fantastic, foolish, fickle fellow, who would forget his college-attachments the moment they ceased appealing to his senses. Tom met with a cold reception from his old friend; and was, moreover, informed, that he had promised the living to another man, who had a vote in the county, where he proposed to offer himself a candidate at the next general election. He now remembered nothing of Eastgate, but the freedoms he had used to take with him, while Tom had quietly stood his butt,[2] with

7. Harrogate; all are popular spa towns. Brighthelmstone is an older name for Brighton.
8. Sicknesses of scholars (Latin).
9. I.e., he held a scholarship from Queen's College, Oxford University.
1. The right to nominate someone to be parish priest. "Gentleman-commoner": student who paid his own bills, in this case at Christ Church, one of the largest colleges at Oxford. Gentleman-commoners paid higher fees than regular students but enjoyed privileges like fancy academic dress and separate dining tables.
2. Remained the target of his jokes.

an eye to the benefice; and those freedoms he began to repeat in common place sarcasms on his person and his cloth, which he uttered in the public coffee-house, for the entertainment of the company. But he was egregiously mistaken in giving his own wit credit for that tameness of Eastgate, which had been entirely owing to prudential considerations. These being now removed, he retorted his repartee with interest, and found no great difficulty in turning the laugh upon the aggressor; who, losing his temper, called him names, and asked, *If he knew whom he talked to?* After much altercation, Prankley, shaking his cane, bid him hold his tongue, otherwise he would dust his cassock for him. "I have no pretensions to such a valet; (said Tom) but if you should do me that office, and overheat yourself, I have here a good oaken towel at your service."

Prankley was equally incensed and confounded at this reply. After a moment's pause, he took him aside towards the window; and, pointing to the clump of firs on Clerken-down, asked in a whisper, if he had spirit enough to meet him there, with a case of pistols, at six o'clock to-morrow morning. Eastgate answered in the affirmative; and, with a steady countenance, assured him, he would not fail to give him the rendezvous at the hour he mentioned. So saying, he retired; and the challenger stayed some time in manifest agitation. In the morning, Eastgate, who knew his man, and had taken his resolution, went to Prankley's lodgings, and roused him by five o'clock—

The 'squire, in all probability, cursed his punctuality in his heart, but he affected to talk big; and having prepared his artillery over-night, they crossed the water at the end of the South Parade. In their progress up the hill, Prankley often eyed the parson, in hopes of perceiving some reluctance in his countenance; but as no such marks appeared, he attempted to intimidate him by word of mouth. "If these flints do their office, (said he) I'll do thy business in a few minutes." "I desire you will do your best; (replied the other) for my part, I come not here to trifle. Our lives are in the hands of God; and one of us already totters on the brink of eternity—" This remark seemed to make some impression upon the 'squire, who changed countenance, and with a faultering accent observed, "That it ill became a clergyman to be concerned in quarrels and blood-shed—" "Your insolence to me (said Eastgate) I should have bore with patience, had not you cast the most infamous reflections upon my order, the honour of which I think myself in duty bound to maintain, even at the expence of my heart's blood; and surely it can be no crime to put out of the world a profligate wretch, without any sense of principle, morality, or religion——" "Thou may'st take away my life, (cried Prankley, in great perturbation) but don't go to murder my character.—What! has't got no conscience?" "My conscience is perfectly quiet (replied the other); and now, sir, we are upon the spot—Take your ground as near as you please; prime your pistol; and the Lord, of his infinite mercy, have compassion upon your miserable soul!"

This ejaculation[3] he pronounced in a loud solemn tone, with his hat off, and his eyes lifted up; then drawing a large horse-pistol, he presented, and put himself in a posture of action. Prankley took his distance, and endeavoured to prime, but his hand shook with such violence, that he found this operation impractible—His antagonist, seeing how it was with him, offered his assistance, and advanced for that purpose; when the poor 'squire, exceedingly alarmed at what he had heard and seen, desired the action might be deferred till next day, as he had not settled his affairs. "I ha'n't made my will (said he); my sisters are not provided for; and I just now recollect an old promise, which my conscience tells me I ought to perform—I'll first convince thee, that I'm not a wretch without principle, and then thou shalt have an opportunity to take my life, which thou seem'st to thirst after so eagerly—"

Eastgate understood the hint; and told him, that one day should break no squares;[4] adding, "God forbid that I should be the means of hindering you from acting the part of an honest man, and a dutiful brother—" By virtue of this cessation, they returned peaceably together. Prankley forthwith made out the presentation of the living, and delivered it to Eastgate, telling him at the same time, he had now settled his affairs, and was ready to attend him to the Fir-grove; but Tom declared he could not think of lifting his hand against the life of so great a benefactor—He did more: when they next met at the coffee-house, he asked pardon of Mr. Prankley, if in his passion he had said any thing to give him offence; and the 'squire was so gracious as to forgive him with a cordial shake of the hand, declaring that he did not like to be at variance with an old college-companion—Next day, however, he left Bath abruptly; and then Eastgate told me all these particulars, not a little pleased with the effects of his own sagacity, by which he has secured a living worth 160 *l. per annum.*

Of my uncle, I have nothing at present to say; but that we set out tomorrow for London *en famille.*[5] He and the ladies, with the maid and Chowder in a coach; I and the man-servant a-horseback. The particulars of our journey you shall have in my next, provided no accident happens to prevent,

Yours ever,

Bath, May 17.   J. MELFORD.

3. A loud assertion.
4. An expression meaning, roughly, do no harm or make no trouble.
5. As a family (French).

To Dr. Lewis.

DEAR DICK,

I shall to-morrow set out for London, where I have bespoke lodgings, at Mrs. Norton's in Golden-square.[6] Although I am no admirer of Bath, I shall leave it with regret; because I must part with some old friends, whom, in all probability, I shall never see again. In the course of coffee-house conversation, I had often heard very extraordinary encomiums passed on the performances of Mr. T——,[7] a gentleman residing in this place, who paints landscapes for his amusement. As I have no great confidence in the taste and judgment of coffee-house connoisseurs, and never received much pleasure from this branch of the art, those general praises made no impression at all on my curiosity; but, at the request of a particular friend, I went yesterday to see the pieces, which had been so warmly commended—I must own I am no judge of painting, though very fond of pictures. I don't imagine that my senses would play me so false, as to betray me into admiration of any thing that was very bad; but, true it is, I have often over-looked capital beauties, in pieces of extraordinary merit.—If I am not totally devoid of taste, however, this young gentleman of Bath is the best landscape-painter now living: I was struck with his performances in such a manner, as I had never been by painting before. His trees not only have a richness of foliage and warmth of colouring, which delights the view; but also a certain magnificence in the disposition, and spirit in the expression, which I cannot describe. His management of the *chiaro oscuro*, or light and shadow, especially gleams of sun-shine, is altogether wonderful, both in the contrivance and execution; and he is so happy in his perspective, and marking his distances at sea, by a progressive series of ships, vessels, capes, and promontories, that I could not help thinking, I had a distant view of thirty leagues upon the back-ground of the picture. If there is any taste for ingenuity left in a degenerate age, fast sinking into barbarism, this artist, I apprehend, will make a capital figure, as soon as his works are known[8]—

Two days ago, I was favoured with a visit by Mr. Fitz-owen; who, with great formality, solicited my vote and interest at the general election. I ought not to have been shocked at the confidence of this man; though it was remarkable, considering what had passed

6. Located north of Piccadilly Circus in London. Smollett lived nearby in 1765 and may have resided with the Nortons. "Bespoke": reserved.
7. Possibly John Taylor (1745–1806), a landscape painter who sometimes signed his paintings "John Taylor of Bath."
8. This praise of T[aylor]'s paintings is similar in tone to other praises of contemporary British painting in the *Critical Review*, which Smollett edited from 1756 to 1763.

between him and me on a former occasion——These visits are mere matter of form, which a candidate makes to every elector; even to those who, he knows, are engaged in the interest of his competitor, lest he should expose himself to the imputation of pride, at a time when it is expected he should appear humble. Indeed, I know nothing so abject as the behaviour of a man canvassing for a seat in parliament——This mean prostration, (to borough-electors, especially) has, I imagine, contributed in a great measure to raise that spirit of insolence among the vulgar; which, like the devil, will be found very difficult to lay.[9] Be that as it may, I was in some confusion at the effrontery of Fitz-owen; but I soon recollected myself, and told him, I had not yet determined for whom I should give my vote, nor whether I should give it for any.—The truth is, I look upon both candidates in the same light; and should think myself a traitor to the constitution of my country, if I voted for either. If every elector would bring the same consideration home to his conscience, we should not have such reason to exclaim against the venality of p——ts.[1] But we are all a pack of venal and corrupted rascals; so lost to all sense of honesty, and all tenderness of character, that, in a little time, I am fully persuaded, nothing will be infamous but virtue and public-spirit.

G. H——,[2] who is really an enthusiast in patriotism, and represented the capital in several successive parliaments, declared to me t'other day, with the tears in his eyes, that he had lived above thirty years in the city of London, and dealt in the way of commerce with all the citizens of note in their turns; but that, as he should answer to God, he had never, in the whole course of his life, found above three or four whom he could call thoroughly honest: a declaration, which was rather mortifying than surprising to me; who have found so few men of worth in the course of my acquaintance, that they serve only as exceptions; which, in the grammarian's phrase, confirm and prove a general canon——I know you will say, G. H—— saw imperfectly through the mist of prejudice, and I am rankled by the spleen—Perhaps, you are partly in the right; for I have perceived that my opinion of mankind, like mercury in the thermometer, rises and falls according to the variations of the weather.

Pray settle accompts with Barnes; take what money of mine is in his hands, and give him acquittance. If you think Davis has stock or credit enough to do justice to the farm, give him a discharge for the rent that is due: this will animate his industry; for I know that nothing is so discouraging to a farmer, as the thoughts of being in

---

9. To lay to rest.
1. Parliaments.
2. George Heathcote (1700–1768), a member of Parliament and lord mayor of London in 1742.

arrears[3] with his landlord. He becomes dispirited, and neglects his labour; and so the farm goes to wreck. Tabby has been clamouring for some days about the lamb's skin, which Williams, the hind,[4] begged of me, when he was last at Bath. Pr'ythee take it back, paying the fellow the full value of it, that I may have some peace in my own house; and let him keep his own counsel, if he means to keep his place—O! I shall never presume to despise or censure any poor man, for suffering himself to be henpecked; conscious how I myself am obliged to truckle to a domestic dæmon; even though (blessed be God) she is not yoked with me for life, in the matrimonial waggon— She has quarrelled with the servants of the house about vails;[5] and such intolerable scolding ensued on both sides, that I have been fain to appease the cook and chamber-maid by stealth. Can't you find some poor gentleman of Wales, to take this precious commodity off the hands of

yours,

Bath, May 19.   M. BRAMBLE.

To Dr. LEWIS.

DOCTER LEWS,

Give me leaf to tell you, methinks you mought employ your talons better, than to encourage servants to pillage their masters—I find by Gwyllim, that Villiams has got my skin; for which he is an impotent rascal. He has not only got my skin, but, moreover, my butter-milk to fatten his pigs; and, I suppose, the next thing he gets, will be my pad to carry his daughter to church and fair: Roger gets this, and Roger gets that; but I'd have you to know, I won't be rogered[6] at this rate by any ragmatical fellow in the kingdom—And I am surprised, docter Lews, you would offer to put my affairs in composition with the refuge and skim of the hearth. I have toiled and moyled to a good purpuss, for the advantage of Matt's family, if I can't safe as much owl as will make me an under petticoat. As for the butter-milk, ne'er a pig in the parish shall thrust his snout in it, with my good-will. There's a famous physician at the Hot Well, that prescribes it to his patience, when the case is consumptive; and the Scots and Irish have begun to drink it already, in such quantities, that there is not

---

3. Behind on rent payments.
4. Shepherd.
5. Occasional bonuses and tips.
6. "To roger" was 18th-century slang for having sexual intercourse with someone, especially a woman. "Pad": either an easy-paced road horse or the soft, stuffed saddle.

a drop left for the hogs in the whole neighbourhood of Bristol. I'll have our butter-milk barrelled up, and sent twice a-week to Aberginny, where it may be sold for a halfpenny the quart; and so Roger may carry his pigs to another market—I hope, Docter, you will not go to put any more such phims in my brother's head, to the prejudice of my pockat; but rather give me some raisins (which hitherto you have not done) to subscribe myself

your humble servant,

Bath, May 19.   Tab. Bramble.

To Sir Watkin Phillips, of Jesus college, Oxon.

Dear Phillips,

Without waiting for your answer to my last, I proceed to give you an account of our journey to London, which has not been wholly barren of adventure. Tuesday last, the 'squire took his place in a hired coach and four, accompanied by his sister and mine, and Mrs. Tabby's maid, Winifrid Jenkins, whose province it was to support Chowder on a cushion in her lap. I could scarce refrain from laughing, when I looked into the vehicle, and saw that animal sitting opposite to my uncle, like any other passenger. The 'squire, ashamed of his situation, blushed to the eyes: and, calling to the postilions to drive on, pulled the glass up in my face. I, and his servant John Thomas, attended them on horseback.

Nothing worth mentioning occured, till we arrived on the edge of Marlborough Downs.[7] There one of the fore horses fell, in going down hill at a round trot; and the postilion behind, endeavouring to stop the carriage, pulled it on one side into a deep rut, where it was fairly overturned. I had rode on about two hundred yards before; but, hearing a loud scream, galloped back and dismounted, to give what assistance was in my power. When I looked into the coach, I could see nothing distinctly, but the nether end of Jenkins, who was kicking her heels and squalling with great vociferation. All of a sudden, my uncle thrust up his bare pate, and bolted through the window, as nimble as a grashopper, having made use of poor Win's posteriors as a step to rise in his ascent—The man (who had likewise quitted his horse) dragged this forlorn damsel, more dead than alive, through the same opening. Then Mr. Bramble, pulling the door off its hinges with a jerk, laid hold on Liddy's arm, and brought her to the light; very much frighted, but little hurt. It fell to my share to deliver our

---

7. A valley of chalk uplands in Wiltshire near the town of Malborough.

aunt Tabitha, who had lost her cap in the struggle; and being rather more than half frantic, with rage and terror, was no bad representation of one of the sister Furies that guard the gates of hell——She expressed no sort of concern for her brother, who ran about in the cold, without his periwig, and worked with the most astonishing agility, in helping to disentangle the horses from the carriage: but she cried, in a tone of distraction, "Chowder! Chowder! my dear Chowder! my poor Chowder is certainly killed!"

This was not the case—Chowder, after having tore my uncle's leg in the confusion of the fall, had retreated under the seat, and from thence the footman drew him by the neck; for which good office, he bit his fingers to the bone. The fellow, who is naturally surly, was so provoked at this assault, that he saluted his ribs with a hearty kick, exclaiming, "Damn the nasty son of a bitch, and them he belongs to!" A benediction, which was by no means lost upon the implacable virago his mistress—Her brother, however, prevailed upon her, to retire into a peasant's house, near the scene of action, where his head and her's were covered, and poor Jenkins had a fit——Our next care was to apply some sticking plaster to the wound in his leg, which exhibited the impression of Chowder's teeth; but he never opened his lips against the delinquent——Mrs. Tabby, alarmed at this scene, "You say nothing, Matt (cried she); but I know your mind—I know the spite you have to that poor unfortunate animal! I know you intend to take his life away!" "You are mistaken, upon my honour! (replied the 'squire, with a sarcastic smile) I should be incapable of harbouring any such cruel design against an object so amiable and inoffensive; even if he had not the happiness to be your favourite."

John Thomas was not so delicate. The fellow, whether really alarmed for his life, or instigated by the desire of revenge, came in, and bluntly demanded, that the dog should be put to death; on the supposition, that if ever he should run mad hereafter, he, who had been bit by him, would be infected—My uncle calmly argued upon the absurdity of his opinion, observing, that he himself was in the same predicament, and would certainly take the precaution he proposed, if he was not sure he ran no risque of infection. Nevertheless, Thomas continued obstinate; and, at length declared, that if the dog was not shot immediately, he himself would be his executioner—— This declaration opened the flood-gates of Tabby's eloquence, which would have shamed the first-rate oratress of Billingsgate. The footman retorted in the same stile; and the 'squire dismissed him from his service, after having prevented me from giving him a good horse-whipping for his insolence.

The coach being adjusted, another difficulty occured—Mrs. Tabitha absolutely refused to enter it again, unless another driver could be found to take the place of the postilion; who, she affirmed, had overturned the carriage from malice aforethought—After much dispute, the man resigned his place to a shabby country fellow, who undertook to go as far as Marlborough, where they could be better provided; and at that place we arrived about one o'clock, without farther impediment. Mrs. Bramble, however, found new matter of offence; which, indeed, she had a particular genius for extracting at will from almost every incident in life. We had scarce entered the room at Marlborough, where we stayed to dine, when she exhibited a formal complaint against the poor fellow who had superseded the postilion. She said, he was such a beggarly rascal, that he had ne'er a shirt to his back; and had the impudence to shock her sight by shewing his bare posteriors, for which act of indelicacy he deserved to be set in the stocks. Mrs. Winifred Jenkins confirmed the assertion, with respect to his nakedness, observing, at the same time, that he had a skin as fair as alabaster.

"This is a heinous offence, indeed, (cried my uncle) let us hear what the fellow has to say in his own vindication." He was accordingly summoned, and made his appearance, which was equally queer and pathetic. He seemed to be about twenty years of age, of a middling size, with bandy legs, stooping shoulders, high forehead, sandy locks, pinking[8] eyes, flat nose, and long chin—but his complexion was of a sickly yellow: his looks denoted famine; and the rags that he wore, could hardly conceal what decency requires to be covered——My uncle, having surveyed him attentively, said, with an ironical expression in his countenance, "An't you ashamed, fellow, to ride postilion without a shirt to cover your backside from the view of the ladies in the coach?" "Yes, I am, an please your noble honour; (answered the man) but necessity has no law, as the saying is——And more than that, it was an accident—My breeches cracked behind, after I had got into the saddle—" "You're an impudent varlet, (cried Mrs. Tabby) for presuming to ride before persons of fashion without a shirt—" "I am so, an please your worthy ladyship; (said he) but I'm a poor Wiltshire lad.—I ha'n't a shirt in the world, that I can call my own, nor a rag of clothes, an please your ladyship, but what you see—I have no friend, nor relation upon earth to help me out—I have had the fever and ague these six months, and spent all I had in the world upon doctors, and to keep soul and body together; and, saving your ladyship's good presence, I han't broke bread these four and twenty hours—"

Mrs. Bramble, turning from him, said, she had never seen such a filthy tatterdemalion, and bid him begone; observing, that he would fill the room full of vermin—Her brother darted a significant glance

8. Peering or blinking.

at her, as she retired with Liddy into another apartment; and then asked the man if he was known to any person in Marlborough?— When he answered, that the landlord of the inn had known him from his infancy; mine host was immediately called, and being interrogated on the subject, declared that the young fellow's name was Humphry Clinker.[9] That he had been a love begotten babe, brought up in the work-house, and put out apprentice by the parish to a country black-smith, who died before the boy's time was out: that he had for some time worked under his ostler, as a helper and extra postilion, till he was taken ill of the ague, which disabled him from getting his bread: that, having sold or pawned every thing he had in the world for his cure and subsistence, he became so miserable and shabby, that he disgraced the stable, and was dismissed; but that he never heard any thing to the prejudice of his character in other respects. "So that the fellow being sick and destitute, (said my uncle) you turned him out to die in the streets." "I pay the poors' rate.[1] (replied the other) and I have no right to maintain idle vagrants, either in sickness or health; besides, such a miserable object would have brought a discredit upon my house—"

"You perceive (said the 'squire, turning to me) our landlord is a Christian of bowels—Who shall presume to censure the morals of the age, when the very publicans[2] exhibit such examples of humanity?—— Heark ye, Clinker, you are a most notorious offender——You stand convicted of sickness, hunger, wretchedness, and want[3]—But, as it does not belong to me to punish criminals, I will only take upon me the task of giving you a word of advice—Get a shirt with all convenient dispatch, that your nakedness may not henceforward give offence to travelling gentlewomen, especially maidens in years—"

So saying, he put a guinea into the hand of the poor fellow, who stood staring at him in silence, with his mouth wide open, till the landlord pushed him out of the room.

In the afternoon, as our aunt stept into the coach, she observed, with some marks of satisfaction, that the postilion, who rode next to her, was not a shabby wretch like the ragamuffin who had drove them into Marlborough. Indeed, the difference was very conspicuous: this

---

9. "Clinker" was an 18th-century slang term for excrement; it may also refer to the coals presumably used by Humphry in his work as a farrier (horseshoer). Furthermore, "to dine with Duke Humphrey" meant to go without dinner (proverbial since the 16th century). Noblemen who could not afford to eat were said to distract themselves during the dinner hour by walking near the tomb of Humphrey, Duke of Gloucester, in Old Saint Paul's Cathedral, which was destroyed in the Great Fire of London in 1666.
1. The tax levied to support poorhouses, where impoverished citizens could go for shelter and employment, albeit at minimal levels of comfort and advantage.
2. Owners or managers of public houses or taverns.
3. An allusion to Jesus' words in the Gospel of Matthew (25:34–36).

Humphry Clinker introduced to the Bramble family. Courtesy of the Center for Southwest Research, University Libraries, University of New Mexico.

was a smart fellow, with a narrow brimmed hat, with gold cording, a cut bob, a decent blue jacket, leather breeches, and a clean linen shirt, puffed above the waist-band. When we arrived at the castle on Spin-hill,[4] where we lay, this new postilion was remarkably assiduous, in bringing in the loose parcels; and, at length, displayed the individual countenance of Humphry Clinker, who had metamorphosed himself in this manner, by relieving from pawn part of his own clothes, with the money he had received from Mr. Bramble.

Howsoever pleased the rest of the company were with such a favourable change in the appearance of this poor creature, it soured on the stomach of Mrs. Tabby, who had not yet digested the affront of his naked skin——She tossed her nose in disdain, saying, she supposed her brother had taken him into favour, because he had insulted her with his obscenity: that a fool and his money were soon parted; but that if Matt intended to take the fellow with him to London, she would not go a foot further that way——My uncle said nothing with his tongue, though his looks were sufficiently expressive; and next morning Clinker did not appear, so that we proceeded without further altercation to Salt-hill,[5] where we proposed to dine—There, the first person that came to the side of the coach, and began to adjust the foot-board, was no other than Humphry Clinker—When I handed out Mrs. Bramble, she eyed him with a furious look, and passed into the house—My uncle was embarrassed, and asked him peevishly, what had brought him hither? The fellow said, his honour had been so good to him, that he had not the heart to part with him; that he would follow him to the world's end, and serve him all the days of his life, without fee or reward—

Mr. Bramble did not know whether to chide or laugh at this declaration——He foresaw much contradiction on the side of Tabby; and, on the other hand, he could not but be pleased with the gratitude of Clinker, as well as with the simplicity of his character—"Suppose I was inclined to take you into my service, (said he) what are your qualifications? what are you good for?" "An please your honour, (answered this original) I can read and write, and do the business of the stable indifferent well—I can dress a horse, and shoe him, and bleed and rowel him;[6] and, as for the practice of sow-gelding, I won't turn my back on e'er a he in the county of Wilts—— Then I can make hog's-puddings and hob-nails,[7] mend kettles, and

4. Speen Hill is in Berkshire, near the town of Speenhamland. It stands approximately halfway on the 115-mile trip from Bath to London.
5. A village on the road to Bath, about halfway between Speenhamland and London.
6. Using a circular piece of leather (or other material), inserted between the flesh and skin of a horse or other animal, to achieve a discharge of built-up fluids.
7. I.e., hobnailed boots: work boots with short, thick-headed nails in their soles for durability. "Hog's-pudding": a type of hearty sausage.

tin saucepans—" Here uncle burst out a-laughing; and enquired, what other accomplishments he was master of—"I know something of single-stick, and psalmody, (proceeded Clinker) I can play upon the Jew's-harp, sing Black-ey'd Susan, Arthur-o'Bradley, and divers other songs; I can dance a Welsh jig, and Nancy Dawson;[8] wrestle a fall with any lad of my inches, when I'm in heart; and, under correction, I can find a hare when your honour wants a bit of game." "Foregad! thou art a complete fellow, (cried my uncle, still laughing) I have a good mind to take thee into my family——Pr'ythee, go and try if thou can'st make peace with my sister—Thou ha'st given her much offence by shewing her thy naked tail."

Clinker accordingly followed us into the room, cap in hand, where, addressing himself to Mrs. Tabitha, "May it please your ladyship's worship (cried he) to pardon and forgive my offences, and, with God's assistance, I shall take care that my tail shall never rise up in judgment against me, to offend your ladyship again——Do, pray, good, sweet, beautiful lady, take compassion on a poor sinner—God bless your noble countenance; I am sure you are too handsome and generous to bear malice—I will serve you on my bended knees, by night and by day, by land and by water; and all for the love and pleasure of serving such an excellent lady—"

This compliment and humiliation had some effect upon Tabby; but she made no reply; and Clinker, taking silence for consent, gave his attendance at dinner. The fellow's natural aukwardness and the flutter of his spirits were productive of repeated blunders in the course of his attendance—At length, he spilt part of a custard upon her right shoulder; and, starting back, trod upon Chowder, who set up a dismal howl——Poor Humphry was so disconcerted at this double mistake, that he dropt the china dish, which broke into a thousand pieces; then, falling down upon his knees, remained in that posture gaping, with a most ludicrous aspect of distress—— Mrs. Bramble flew to the dog, and, snatching him in her arms, presented him to her brother, saying, "This is all a concerted scheme against this unfortunate animal, whose only crime is its regard for me—Here it is: kill it at once; and then you'll be satisfied."

Clinker, hearing these words, and taking them in the literal acceptation, got up in some hurry, and, seizing a knife from the side-board, cried, "Not here, an please your ladyship—It will daub the room— Give him to me, and I'll carry him in the ditch by the roadside—" To this proposal he received no other answer, than a hearty box on the

8. Stage name of Ann Newton (ca. 1728–1767), a London actress who became synonymous with the spirited dances she performed between acts of John Gay's *The Beggar's Opera* (1728) when it ran at Covent Garden Theatre in the late 1750s. "Single-stick": fencing with a short stick or cudgel.

Direful consequences of Clinker's awkwardness. Courtesy of the Center for Southwest Research, University Libraries, University of New Mexico.

ear, that made him stagger to the other side of the room. "What! (said she to her brother) am I to be affronted by every mangy hound that you pick up in the highway? I insist upon your sending this rascallion about his business immediately——" "For God's sake, sister, compose yourself, (said my uncle) and consider, that the poor fellow is innocent of any intention to give you offence—" "Innocent as the babe unborn"—(cried Humphry.) "I see it plainly, (exclaimed this implacable maiden) he acts by your direction; and you are resolved to support him in his impudence—This is a bad return for all the services I have done you; for nursing you in your sickness, managing your family, and keeping you from ruining yourself by your own imprudence——But now you shall part with that rascal or me, upon the spot, without farther loss of time; and the world shall see whether you have more regard for your own flesh and blood, or for a beggarly foundling, taken from the dunghill—"

Mr. Bramble's eyes began to glisten, and his teeth to chatter. "If stated fairly, (said he, raising his voice) the question is, whether I have spirit to shake off an intolerable yoke, by one effort of resolution, or meanness enough to do an act of cruelty and injustice, to gratify the rancour of a capricious woman—Heark ye, Mrs. Tabitha Bramble, I will now propose an alternative in my turn—Either discard your four-footed favourite, or give me leave to bid you eternally adieu—For I am determined, that he and I shall live no longer under the same roof; and now to *dinner with what appetite you may*—"[9] Thunderstruck at this declaration, she sat down in a corner; and, after a pause of some minutes, "Sure I don't understand you, Matt! (said she)" "And yet I spoke in plain English—" answered the 'squire, with a peremptory look. "Sir, (resumed this virago, effectually humbled) it is your prerogative to command, and my duty to obey. I can't dispose of the dog in this place; but if you'll allow him to go in the coach to London, I give you my word, he shall never trouble you again—"

Her brother, entirely disarmed by this mild reply, declared, she could ask him nothing in reason that he would refuse; adding, "I hope, sister, you have never found me deficient in natural affection." Mrs. Tabitha immediately rose, and, throwing her arms about his neck, kissed him on the cheek: he returned her embrace with great emotion. Liddy sobbed, Win Jenkins cackled, Chowder capered, and Clinker skipped about, rubbing his hands for joy of this reconciliation.

Concord being thus restored, we finished our meal with comfort; and in the evening arrived at London, without having met with any other adventure. My aunt seems to be much mended by the hint she

---

9. Quoted from Henry VIII's speech to Cardinal Wolsey after warning him, in Shakespeare's *Henry VIII* (3.2.202–203).

received from her brother. She has been graciously pleased to remove her displeasure from Clinker, who is now retained as a footman; and in a day or two will make his appearance in a new suit of livery; but as he is little acquainted with London, we have taken an occasional valet, whom I intend hereafter to hire as my own servant. We lodge in Golden-square, at the house of one Mrs. Norton, a decent sort of a woman, who takes great pains to make us all easy. My uncle proposes to make a circuit of all the remarkable scenes of this metropolis, for the entertainment of his pupils; but as both you and I are already acquainted with most of those he will visit, and with some others he little dreams of, I shall only communicate what will be in some measure new to your observation. Remember me to our Jesuitical friends, and believe me ever,

Dear knight,

yours affectionately,

London, May 24.   J. MELFORD.

To Dr. LEWIS.

DEAR DOCTOR,

London is literally new to me; new in its streets, houses, and even in its situation; as the Irishman[1] said, "London is now gone out of town." What I left open fields, producing hay and corn, I now find covered with streets, and squares, and palaces, and churches. I am credibly informed, that in the space of seven years, eleven thousand new houses have been built in one quarter of Westminster, exclusive of what is daily added to other parts of this unweildy metropolis. Pimlico and Knightsbridge are now almost joined to Chelsea and Kensington; and if this infatuation continues for half a century, I suppose the whole county of Middlesex will be covered with brick.[2]

It must be allowed, indeed, for the credit of the present age, that London and Westminster are much better paved and lighted than they were formerly. The new streets are spacious, regular, and airy; and the houses generally convenient. The bridge at Blackfriars[3] is a noble monument of taste and public-spirit—I wonder how they stumbled upon a work of such magnificence and utility. But,

---

1. James Bramston (ca. 1694–1744), whose observation in his satirical poem "The Art of Politicks" (1729) is adapted here.
2. The population of metropolitan London grew quickly over the 18th century, from about 575,000 in 1700 to 675,000 in 1750 to 900,000 by 1800.
3. Designed by the Scottish architect Robert Mylne (1733–1811); construction began in 1760.

notwithstanding these improvements, the capital is become an over-grown monster; which, like a dropsical head, will in time leave the body and extremities without nourishment and support. The absurdity will appear in its full force, when we consider, that one sixth part of the natives of this whole extensive kingdom, is crowded within the bills of mortality.[4] What wonder that our villages are depopulated, and our farms in want of day-labourers? The abolition of small farms, is but one cause of the decrease of population. Indeed, the incredible increase of horses and black cattle, to answer the purposes of luxury, requires a prodigious quantity of hay and grass, which are raised and managed without much labour; but a number of hands will always be wanted for the different branches of agriculture, whether the farms be large or small. The tide of luxury has swept all the inhabitants from the open country—The poorest 'squire, as well as the richest peer, must have his house in town, and make a figure with an extraordinary number of domestics. The plough-boys, cowherds, and lower hinds, are debauched and seduced by the appearance and discourse of those coxcombs in livery, when they make their summer excursions. They desert their dirt and drudgery, and swarm up to London, in hopes of getting into service, where they can live luxuriously and wear fine clothes, without being obliged to work; for idleness is natural to man——Great numbers of these, being disappointed in their expectation, become thieves and sharpers; and London being an immense wilderness, in which there is neither watch nor ward of any signification, nor any order or police, affords them lurking-places as well as prey.

There are many causes that contribute to the daily increase of this enormous mass; but they may be all resolved into the grand source of luxury and corruption—About five and twenty years ago, very few, even of the most opulent citizens of London, kept any equipage, or even any servants in livery. Their tables produced nothing but plain boiled and roasted, with a bottle of port and a tankard of beer. At present, every trader in any degree of credit, every broker and attorney, maintains a couple of footmen, a coachman, and postilion. He has his town-house, and his country-house, his coach, and his post-chaise. His wife and daughters appear in the richest stuffs, bespangled with diamonds. They frequent the court, the opera, the theatre, and the masquerade. They hold assemblies at their own houses: they make sumptuous entertainments, and treat with the richest wines of Bourdeaux, Burgundy, and Champagne. The substantial tradesman, who wont to pass his evenings at the ale-house for fourpence half-penny, now spends three shillings at the tavern, while his wife

---

4. I.e., within metropolitan London. The London Company of Parish Clerks began publishing a weekly list of births, deaths, and marriages within the city in 1592.

keeps card-tables at home; she must likewise have fine clothes, her chaise, or pad, with country lodgings, and go three times a-week to public diversions. Every clerk, apprentice, and even waiter of tavern or coffee-house, maintains a gelding by himself, or in partnership, and assumes the air and apparel of a petit maitre[5]——The gayest places of public entertainment are filled with fashionable figures; which, upon inquiry, will be found to be journeymen taylors, serving-men, and abigails, disguised like their betters.

In short, there is no distinction or subordination left——The different departments of life are jumbled together—The hod-carrier, the low mechanic, the tapster, the publican, the shop-keeper, the pettifogger, the citizen, and courtier, *all tread upon the kibes of one another:*[6] actuated by the demons of profligacy and licentiousness, they are seen every where, rambling, riding, rolling, rushing, justling, mixing, bouncing, cracking, and crashing in one vile ferment of stupidity and corruption—All is tumult and hurry; one would imagine they were impelled by some disorder of the brain, that will not suffer them to be at rest. The foot-passengers run along as if they were pursued by bailiffs. The porters and chairmen trot with their burthens. People, who keep their own equipages, drive through the streets at full speed. Even citizens, physicians, and apothecaries, glide in their chariots like lightning. The hackney-coachmen make their horses smoke, and the pavement shakes under them; and I have actually seen a waggon pass through Piccadilly at the hand-gallop. In a word, the whole nation seems to be running out of their wits.

The diversions of the times are not ill suited to the genius of this incongrous monster, called the public. Give it noise, confusion, glare, and glitter; it has no idea of elegance and propriety—What are the amusements at Ranelagh?[7] One half of the company are following one another's tails, in an eternal circle; like so many blind asses in an olive-mill, where they can neither discourse, distinguish, nor be distinguished; while the other half are drinking hot water, under the denomination of tea, till nine or ten o'clock at night, to keep them awake for the rest of the evening. As for the orchestra, the vocal musick especially, it is well for the performers that they cannot be heard distinctly. Vauxhall[8] is a composition of baubles,

---

5. Little master (French); i.e., someone with an excessive interest in appearing fashionable.
6. Alludes to the graveyard scene in Shakespeare's *Hamlet* (5.1.152–153), in which Hamlet observes the crowded burial ground and the equality created by death. "Hod-carrier": carries coal. "Tapster": draws beer for customers at an alehouse. "Pettifogger": derogatory term for a lawyer, especially one who engages in dubious practices.
7. A famous public garden devoted to entertainments, located in Chelsea, just outside of 18th-century London.
8. Another London pleasure garden, situated on the south bank of the Thames. It closed permanently in 1859.

overcharged with paltry ornaments, ill conceived, and poorly executed; without any unity of design, or propriety of disposition. It is
an unnatural assembly of objects, fantastically illuminated in broken masses; seemingly contrived to dazzle the eyes and divert the
imagination of the vulgar—Here a wooden lion, there a stone statue;
in one place, a range of things like coffee-house boxes, covered atop;
in another, a parcel of ale-house benches; in a third, a puppet-shew
representation of a tin cascade; in a fourth, a gloomy cave of a circular form, like a sepulchral vault half lighted; in a fifth, a scanty slip
of grass-plat, that would not afford pasture sufficient for an ass's colt.
The walks, which nature seems to have intended for solitude, shade,
and silence, are filled with crowds of noisy people, sucking up the
nocturnal rheums of an aguish[9] climate; and through these gay scenes,
a few lamps glimmer like so many farthing candles.

When I see a number of well-dressed people, of both sexes, sitting
on the covered benches, exposed to the eyes of the mob; and, which
is worse, to the cold, raw, night-air, devouring sliced beef, and swill-
ing port, and punch, and cyder, I can't help compassionating their
temerity, while I despise their want of taste and decorum; but, when
they course along those damp and gloomy walks, or crowd together
upon the wet gravel, without any other cover than the cope of Heaven,
listening to a song, which one half of them cannot possibly hear, how
can I help supposing they are actually possessed by a spirit, more
absurd and pernicious than any thing we meet with in the precincts
of Bedlam?[1] In all probability, the proprietors of this, and other public gardens of inferior note, in the skirts of the metropolis, are, in
some shape, connected with the faculty of physic, and the company
of undertakers; for, considering that eagerness in the pursuit of what
is called pleasure, which now predominates through every rank and
denomination of life, I am persuaded, that more gouts, rheumatisms,
catarrhs, and consumptions are caught in these nocturnal pastimes,
sub dio,[2] than from all the risques and accidents to which a life of toil
and danger is exposed.

These, and other observations, which I have made in this excursion, will shorten my stay at London, and send me back with a double relish to my solitude and mountains; but I shall return by a
different route from that which brought me to town. I have seen
some old friends, who constantly resided in this virtuous metropolis, but they are so changed in manners and disposition, that we
hardly know or care for one another—In our journey from Bath, my

9. Feverish. "Rheums": watery discharges from a cold.
1. A popular alteration of Bethlem Royal Hospital in London, Europe's oldest continu-
   ously operating psychiatric hospital.
2. Or *sub divo*; under the open sky (Latin).

sister Tabby provoked me into a transport of passion; during which, like a man who has drank himself potvaliant,[3] I talked to her in such a stile of authority and resolution, as produced a most blessed effect. She and her dog have been remarkably quiet and orderly, ever since this expostulation. How long this agreeable calm will last, Heaven above knows—I flatter myself, the exercise of travelling has been of service to my health; a circumstance, which encourages me to proceed in my projected expedition to the North. But I must, in the mean time, for the benefit and amusement of my pupils, explore the depths of this chaos; this mishapen and monstrous capital, without head or tail, members or proportion.

Thomas was so insolent to my sister on the road, that I was obliged to turn him off abruptly, betwixt Chippenham and Marlborough, where our coach was overturned. The fellow was always sullen and selfish; but, if he should return to the country, you may give him a character for honesty and sobriety; and, provided he behaves with proper respect to the family, let him have a couple of guineas in the name of

yours always,

London, May 29.   MATT. BRAMBLE.

To Miss LÆTITIA WILLIS, at Gloucester.

MY DEAR LETTY,

Inexpressible was the pleasure I received from yours of the 25th, which was last night put into my hands by Mrs. Brentwood, the milliner, from Gloucester——I rejoice to hear that my worthy governess is in good health, and, still more, that she no longer retains any displeasure towards her poor Liddy. I am sorry you have lost the society of the agreeable miss Vaughan; but, I hope, you won't have cause much longer to regret the departure of your school companions, as I make no doubt but your parents will, in a little time, bring you into the world, where you are so well qualified to make a distinguished figure. When that is the case, I flatter myself you and I shall meet again, and be happy together; and even improve the friendship which we contracted in our tender years——This at least I can promise—It shall not be for the want of my utmost endeavours, if our intimacy does not continue for life.

About five days ago we arrived in London, after an easy journey from Bath; during which, however, we were overturned, and met

3. I.e., who has gained foolish courage through drunkenness.

with some other little incidents, which had like to have occasioned
a misunderstanding betwixt my uncle and aunt; but now, thank
God, they are happily reconciled: we live in harmony together, and
every day make parties to see the wonders of this vast metropolis,
which, however, I cannot pretend to describe; for I have not as yet
seen one hundredth part of its curiosities, and I am quite in a maze
of admiration.

The cities of London and Westminster are spread out into an
incredible extent. The streets, squares, rows, lanes, and alleys, are
innumerable. Palaces, public buildings, and churches, rise in every
quarter; and, among these last, St. Paul's appears with the most
astonishing preeminence. They say it is not so large as St. Peter's at
Rome; but, for my own part, I can have no idea of any earthly temple more grand and magnificent.

But even these superb objects are not so striking as the crowds of
people that swarm in the streets. I at first imagined, that some great
assembly was just dismissed, and wanted to stand aside till the multitude should pass; but this human tide continues to flow, without
interruption or abatement, from morn till night. Then there is such
an infinity of gay equipages, coaches, chariots, chaises, and other
carriages, continually rolling and shifting before your eyes, that one's
head grows giddy looking at them; and the imagination is quite confounded with splendour and variety. Nor is the prospect by water
less grand and astonishing than that by land: you see three stupendous bridges,[4] joining the opposite banks of a broad, deep, and
rapid river; so vast, so stately, so elegant, that they seem to be the
work of the giants: betwixt them, the whole surface of the Thames
is covered with small vessels, barges, boats, and wherries, passing
to and fro; and below the three bridges, such a prodigious forest of
masts, for miles together, that you would think all the ships in the
universe were here assembled. All that you read of wealth and grandeur, in the Arabian Night's Entertainment, and the Persian Tales,
concerning Bagdad, Diarbekir, Damascus, Ispahan, and Samarkand,[5]
is here realized.

Ranelagh looks like the inchanted palace of a genie, adorned with
the most exquisite performances of painting, carving, and gilding,
enlightened with a thousand golden lamps, that emulate the noon-
day sun; crowded with the great, the rich, the gay, the happy, and the
fair; glittering with cloth of gold and silver, lace, embroidery, and
precious stones. While these exulting sons and daughters of felicity

4. I.e., London, Westminster, and Blackfriars.
5. Baghdad, Diyarbakir, Damascus, Isfahan, and Samarkand are cities in modern-day
Iraq, Turkey, Syria, Iran, and Uzbekistan, respectively. Translations of texts like *One
Thousand and One Nights*, the collection of west and south Asian folktales better
known in English as *Arabian Nights*, were very popular in the 18th century.

tread this round of pleasure, or regale in different parties, and separate lodges, with fine imperial tea and other delicious refreshments, their ears are entertained with the most ravishing delights of musick, both instrumental and vocal. There I heard the famous Tenducci,[6] a thing from Italy—It looks for all the world like a man, though they say it is not. The voice, to be sure, is neither man's nor woman's; but it is more melodious than either; and it warbled so divinely, that, while I listened, I really thought myself in paradise.

At nine o'clock, in a charming moonlight evening, we embarked at Ranelagh for Vauxhall, in a wherry,[7] so light and slender, that we looked like so many fairies sailing in a nut-shell. My uncle, being apprehensive of catching cold upon the water, went round in the coach, and my aunt would have accompanied him, but he would not suffer me to go by water if she went by land; and therefore she favoured us with her company, as she perceived I had a curiosity to make this agreeable voyage——After all, the vessel was sufficiently loaded; for, besides the waterman, there was my brother Jery, and a friend of his, one Mr. Barton, a country gentleman, of a good fortune, who had dined at our house—The pleasure of this little excursion was, however, damped, by my being sadly frighted at our landing; where there was a terrible confusion of wherries, and a crowd of people bawling, and swearing, and quarrelling: nay, a parcel of ugly-looking fellows came running into the water, and laid hold on our boat with great violence, to pull it a-shore; nor would they quit their hold till my brother struck one of them over the head with his cane. But this flutter was fully recompensed by the pleasures of Vauxhall; which I no sooner entered, than I was dazzled and confounded with the variety of beauties that rushed all at once upon my eye. Image to yourself, my dear Letty, a spacious garden, part laid out in delightful walks, bounded with high hedges and trees, and paved with gravel; part exhibiting a wonderful assemblage of the most picturesque and striking objects, pavilions, lodges, groves, grottoes, lawns, temples, and cascades; porticoes, colonades, and rotundos; adorned with pillars, statues, and painting: the whole illuminated with an infinate number of lamps, disposed in different figures of suns, stars, and constellations; the place crowded with the gayest company, ranging through those blissful shades, or supping in different lodges on cold collations,[8] enlivened with mirth, freedom, and

---

6. Giusto Fernando Tenducci (ca. 1736–1790), an Italian soprano (castrato) opera singer and composer who was very popular in England, where he spent much of his career.
7. A light rowing boat.
8. Simple, light meals. "Grottoes": picturesque caves or caverns, in this case artificially constructed. "Cascades": small, human-made waterfalls. "Porticoes": either classical-style columns arranged under a roof, or garden pergolas. "Colonados," or colonnades: regularly spaced columns supporting a flat roof. "Rotundos," or rotundas: circular buildings or rooms, usually with domed roofs.

good-humour, and animated by an excellent band of musick. Among
the vocal performers I had the happiness to hear the celebrated
Mrs.——, whose voice was so loud and so shrill, that it made my
head ake through excess of pleasure.

In about half an hour after we arrived we were joined by my uncle,
who did not seem to relish the place. People of experience and infirmity, my dear Letty, see with very different eyes from those that such
as you and I make use of—Our evening's entertainment was interrupted by an unlucky accident. In one of the remotest walks we
were surprised with a sudden shower, that set the whole company
a-running, and drove us in heaps, one upon another, into the rotunda;
where my uncle, finding himself wet, began to be very peevish and
urgent to be gone. My brother went to look for the coach, and found
it with much difficulty; but as it could not hold us all, Mr. Barton
stayed behind. It was some time before the carriage could be brought
up to the gate, in the confusion, notwithstanding the utmost endeavours of our new footman, Humphry Clinker, who lost his scratch
periwig,[9] and got a broken head in the scuffle. The moment we were
seated, my aunt pulled off my uncle's shoes, and carefully wrapped
his poor feet in her capuchin;[1] then she gave him a mouth-full of
cordial, which she always keeps in her pocket, and his clothes were
shifted as soon as we arrived at lodgings; so that, blessed be God, he
escaped a severe cold, of which he was in great terror.

As for Mr. Barton, I must tell you in confidence, he was a little
particular;[2] but, perhaps, I mistake his complaisance; and I wish I
may, for his sake—You know the condition of my poor heart; which,
in spite of hard usage—And yet I ought not to complain: nor will I,
till farther information.

Besides Ranelagh and Vauxhall, I have been at Mrs. Cornelys'
assembly, which, for the rooms, the company, the dresses, and decorations, surpasses all description; but as I have no great turn for card-
playing, I have not yet entered thoroughly into the spirit of the place:
indeed I am still such a country hoyden,[3] that I could hardly find
patience to be put in a condition to appear, yet I was not above six
hours under the hands of the hair-dresser, who stuffed my head with
as much black wool as would have made a quilted petticoat; and, after
all, it was the smallest head in the assembly, except my aunt's—She,
to be sure, was so particular with her rumpt gown and petticoat, her

9. A short, practical wig, in style after the 1740s.
1. A woman's cloak with a hood, which took its name from the friars whose habit it
   resembled.
2. To pay special attention to someone or something.
3. An awkward or ignorant person. Teresa Cornelys (1723–1797) was an Italian-born
   opera singer who hosted popular assemblies and masquerades at Carlisle House in
   Soho Square during the 1760s.

scanty curls, her lappet-head,[4] deep triple ruffles, and high stays, that every body looked at her with surprise: some whispered, and some tittered; and lady Griskin, by whom we were introduced, flatly told her, she was twenty good years behind the fashion.

Lady Griskin is a person of fashion, to whom we have the honour to be related. She keeps a small rout[5] at her own house, never exceeding ten or a dozen card-tables, but these are frequented by the best company in town—She has been so obliging as to introduce my aunt and me to some of her particular friends of quality, who treat us with the most familiar good-humour: we have once dined with her, and she takes the trouble to direct us in all our motions. I am so happy as to have gained her good-will to such a degree, that she sometimes adjusts my cap with her own hands; and she has given me a kind invitation to stay with her all the winter. This, however, has been cruelly declined by my uncle, who seems to be (I know not how) prejudiced against the good lady; for, whenever my aunt happens to speak in her commendation, I observe that he makes wry faces, though he says nothing.——Perhaps, indeed, these grimaces may be the effect of pain arising from the gout and rheumatism, with which he is sadly distressed—To me, however, he is always good-natured and generous, even beyond my wish. Since we came hither, he has made me a present of a suit of clothes, with trimmings and laces, which cost more money than I shall mention; and Jery, at his desire, has given me my mother's diamond drops, which are ordered to be set a-new; so that it won't be his fault if I do not glitter among the stars of the fourth or fifth magnitude. I wish my weak head may not grow giddy in the midst of all this gallantry and dissipation; though, as yet, I can safely declare, I could gladly give up all these tumultuous pleasures, for country solitude, and a happy retreat with those we love; among whom, my dear Willis will always possess the first place in the breast of her

ever affectionate,

London, May 31.   LYDIA MELFORD.

---

4. A lean cut of ham or beef. "Particular": individualized to the point of eccentricity. "Rumpt": having a bustle, a stuffed pad or wire frame below the waist under a woman's skirt, usually in the back.
5. An evening assembly.

To Sir WATKIN PHILLIPS, of Jesus college, Oxon.

DEAR PHILLIPS,

I send you this letter, franked by our old friend Barton; who is as much altered as it was possible for a man of his kidney to be—Instead of the careless, indolent sloven we knew at Oxford, I found him a busy talkative politician; a petit-maître in his dress, and a ceremonious courtier in his manners. He has not gall enough in his constitution to be enflamed with the rancour of party, so as to deal in scurrilous invectives; but, since he obtained a place, he is become a warm partizan of the ministry,[6] and sees every thing through such an exaggerating medium, as to me, who am happily of no party, is altogether incomprehensible—Without all doubt, the fumes of faction not only disturb the faculty of reason, but also pervert the organs of sense; and I would lay a hundred guineas to ten, that if Barton on one side, and the most conscientious patriot in the opposition on the other, were to draw, upon honour, the picture of the k——or m——,[7] you and I, who are still uninfected, and unbiassed, would find both painters equally distant from the truth. One thing, however, must be allowed for the honour of Barton, he never breaks out into illiberal abuse, far less endeavours, by infamous calumnies, to blast the moral character of any individual on the other side.

Ever since we came hither, he has been remarkably assiduous in his attention to our family; an attention, which, in a man of his indolence and avocations, I should have thought altogether odd, and even unnatural, had not I perceived that my sister Liddy has made some impression upon his heart. I can't say that I have any objection to his trying his fortune in this pursuit: if an opulent estate and a great stock of good-nature are sufficient qualifications in a husband, to render the marriage-state happy for life, she may be happy with Barton; but, I imagine, there is something else required to engage and secure the affection of a woman of sense and delicacy: something which nature has denied our friend—Liddy seems to be of the same opinion. When he addresses himself to her in discourse, she seems to listen with reluctance, and industriously avoids all particular communication; but in proportion to her coyness, our aunt is coming. Mrs. Tabitha goes more than half way to meet his advances; she mistakes, or affects to mistake, the meaning of his courtesy, which is rather formal and fulsome; she returns his compliments with hyperbolical interest, she persecutes him with her

---

6. Supporter of the current government. In this and Jery's next letter from London, Smollett seems purposely to conflate various political events and figures from the era.
7. King or minister.

civilities at table, she appeals to him for ever in conversation, she sighs, and flirts, and ogles, and by her hideous affectation and impertinence, drives the poor courtier to the very extremity of his complaisance: in short, she seems to have undertaken the siege of Barton's heart, and carries on her approaches in such a desperate manner, that I don't know whether he will not be obliged to capitulate. In the mean time, his aversion to this inamorata struggling with his acquired affability, and his natural fear of giving offence, throws him into a kind of distress which is extremely ridiculous.

Two days ago, he persuaded my uncle and me to accompany him to St. James's,[8] where he undertook to make us acquainted with the persons of all the great men in the kingdom; and, indeed, there was a great assemblage of distinguished characters, for it was a high festival at court. Our conductor performed his promise with great punctuality. He pointed out almost every individual of both sexes, and generally introduced them to our notice, with a flourish of panegyrick——Seeing the king approach, "There comes (said he) the most amiable sovereign that ever swayed the sceptre of England; the *deliciæ humani generis*;[9] Augustus, in patronizing merit; Titus Vespasian in generosity; Trajan in beneficence; and Marcus Aurelius, in philosophy." "A very honest kindhearted gentleman (added my uncle); he's too good for the times. A king of England should have a spice of the devil in his composition." Barton, then turning to the duke of C—,[1] proceeded,——"You know the duke; that illustrious hero, who trod rebellion under his feet, and secured us in possession of every thing we ought to hold dear, as Englishmen and Christians. Mark what an eye, how penetrating, yet pacific! what dignity in his mein! what humanity in his aspect——Even malice must own, that he is one of the greatest officers in Christendom." "I think he be (said Mr. Bramble); but who are these young gentlemen that stand beside him?" "Those! (cried our friend) those are his royal nephews; the princes of the blood. Sweet young princes! the sacred pledges of the Protestant line; so spirited, so sensible, so princely—" "Yes; very sensible! very spirited! (said my uncle, interrupting him)

---

8. The palace, situated in Pall Mall just north of Saint James's Park. The most senior royal palace in the United Kingdom, it was partially destroyed by fire in 1809. In 1837 Queen Victoria formalized the move to Buckingham Palace, which has been the royal residence in London ever since.
9. The delight of mankind (Latin); originally said of the Roman emperor Titus by the historian Suetonius. The following emperors were noted for the qualities ascribed to them.
1. William Augustus, Duke of Cumberland (1721–1765), third son of George II (1683–1760) and brother of George III (1738–1820). He was the hero of the battle of Culloden in 1746, helping defeat the rebellion led by Charles Edward Stuart (1720–1788), grandson of the deposed British monarch James II. Cumberland's ruthless suppression of the rebels, known as Jacobites (from the Latin for James), led to his nickname "the Butcher." Smollett published an early poem, "The Tears of Scotland" (1746), lamenting these events (see pp. 359–60 in this volume).

but see the queen! ha, there's the queen![2]—There's the queen! let me see—Let me see——Where are my glasses? ha! there's meaning in that eye——There's sentiment—There's expression—Well, Mr. Barton, what figure do you call next?" The next person he pointed out, was the favourite *yearl*;[3] who stood solitary by one of the windows—"Behold yon northern star, (said he) *Shorn of his beams*——" "What! the Caledonian luminary, that lately blazed so bright in our hemisphere! methinks, at present, it glimmers through a fog;[4] like Saturn without his ring, bleak, and dim, and distant[5]——Ha, there's the other great phœnomenon, the grand pensionary, that weathercock of partiotism that veers about in every point of the political compass, and still feels the wind of popularity in his tail. He too, like a portentous comet, has risen again above the court-horizon; but how long he will continue to ascend, it is not easy to foretel, considering his great eccentricity—Who are those two satellites[6] that attend his motions?" When Barton told him their names, "To their characters (said Mr. Bramble) I am no stranger. One of them, without a drop of red blood in his veins, has a cold intoxicating vapour in his head; and rancour enough in his heart to inoculate and affect a whole nation. The other is (I hear) intended for a share in the ad——n,[7] and the pensionary vouches for his being duly qualified—The only instance I ever heard of his sagacity, was his deserting his former patron, when he found him declining in power, and in disgrace with the people. Without principle, talent, or intelligence, he is ungracious as a hog, greedy as a vulture, and thievish as a jackdaw; but, it must be owned, he is no hypocrite. He pretends to no virtue, and takes no pains to disguise his character—His ministry will be attended with one advantage, no man will be disappointed by his breach of promise, as no mortal ever trusted to his word. I wonder how lord——first discovered this happy genius, and for what purpose lord——has now adopted him: but one would think, that as amber has a power to attract dirt, and straws, and chaff, a minister is

<hr/>

2. Charlotte Sophia (1744–1818), wife of George III.
3. John Stuart, third Earl of Bute (1713–1792), a Scottish nobleman and favorite of George III who served as prime minister from 1762 to 1763. Lacking popular support, he employed Smollett to produce a short-lived pro-government newspaper, *The Briton*, during those years. See pp. 364–66 in this volume.
4. From John Milton's *Paradise Lost* (2nd ed., 1674; 1.594–596), in which Satan's diminished glory is compared to the sun shining through mist. "Caledonian": Scots (Latin).
5. Probably William Pitt, first Earl of Chatham (1708–1778), a career statesman who received an annual pension of £3,000 after leading the House of Commons during the Seven Years' War. Nicknamed "the Great Commoner," he returned to political prominence in 1766–68.
6. Likely the popular politician John Wilkes (1727–1797) and Richard Grenville-Temple, second Earl Temple (1711–1779), both of whom were political allies of Pitt. Wilkes was the editor and chief writer of *The North Briton*, a radical newspaper that opposed Smollett's *Briton*. See pp. 367–69 in this volume.
7. Administration.

endued with the same kind of faculty, to *lick up every knave and blockhead in his way*—"[8] His elogium was interrupted by the arrival of the old duke of N——;[9] who, squeezing into the circle with a busy face of importance, thrust his head into every countenance, as if he had been in search of somebody, to whom he wanted to impart something of great consequence—My uncle, who had been formerly known to him, bowed as he passed; and the duke, seeing himself saluted so respectfully by a well-dressed person, was not slow in returning the courtesy—He even came up, and, taking him cordially by the hand, "My dear friend, Mr. A—,[1] (said he) I am rejoiced to see you—How long have you been come from abroad?—How did you leave our good friends, the Dutch? The king of Prussia don't think of another war, ah?——He's a great king! a great conqueror! a very great conqueror! Your Alexanders and Hannibals were nothing at all to him, sir——Corporals! drummers! dross! mere trash—— Damned trash, heh?—" His grace being by this time out of breath, my uncle took the opportunity to tell him he had not been out of England, that his name was Bramble, and that he had the honour to sit in the last parliament but one of the late king, as representative for the borough of Dymkymraig.[2] "Odso! (cried the duke) I remember you perfectly well, my dear Mr. Bramble——You was always a good and loyal subject——a staunch friend to administration——I made your brother an Irish bishop—" "Pardon me, my lord (said the 'squire) I once had a brother, but he was a captain in the army—" "Ha!" (said his grace) he was so—He was, indeed! But who was the bishop then? Bishop Blackberry——Sure it was bishop Blackberry— Perhaps some relation of yours—" "Very likely, my lord (replied my uncle); the Blackberry is the fruit of the Bramble—But, I believe, the bishop is not a berry of our bush—" "No more he is—No more he is, ha, ha, ha! (exclaimed the duke) there you gave me a scratch, good Mr. Bramble, ha, ha, ha!—Well, I shall be glad to see you at Lincoln's-inn-fields[3]—You know the way——Times are altered. Though I have lost the power, I retain the inclination—Your very humble servant, good Mr. Blackberry—" So saying, he shoved to another corner of the room. "What a fine old gentleman! (cried Mr. Barton) what spirits! what a memory!—He never forgets an old friend." "He does me too much honour, (observed our 'squire) to rank

8. Slightly misquoted from Alexander Pope's satirical poem *The Dunciad* (1st ed., 1728; 3.250), where the line describes the slow progress of the goddess Dulness.
9. Thomas Pelham-Holles, the Duke of Newcastle (1693–1768), a prominent politician who was often ridiculed for his apparent absentmindedness.
1. Possibly John Almon (1737–1805), a journalist and bookseller who published Smollett's biting satire *History and Adventures of an Atom* in late 1768.
2. A fictitious name meaning roughly "I don't speak Welsh."
3. A mansion in the largest public square in London; it was Newcastle's primary residence in the city.

me among the number—Whilst I sat in parliament, I never voted with the ministry but three times, when my conscience told me they were in the right: however, if he still keeps levee,[4] I will carry my nephew thither, that he may see, and learn to avoid the scene; for, I think, an English gentleman never appears to such disadvantage, as at the levee of a minister—Of his grace I shall say nothing at present, but that for thirty years he was the constant and common butt of ridicule and execration. He was generally laughed at as an ape in politics, whose office and influence served only to render his folly the more notorious; and the opposition cursed him, as the indefatigable drudge of a first-mover, who was justly stiled and stigmatized as the father of corruption:[5] but this ridiculous ape, this venal drudge, no sooner lost the places he was so ill qualified to fill, and unfurled the banners of faction, than he was metamorphosed into a pattern of public virtue; the very people who reviled him before, now extolled him to the skies, as a wise, experienced statesman, chief pillar of the Protestant succession, and corner stone of English liberty. I should be glad to know how Mr. Barton reconciles these contradictions, without obliging us to resign all title to the privilege of common sense." "My dear sir, (answered Barton) I don't pretend to justify the extravagations of the multitude; who, I suppose, were as wild in their former censure, as in their present praise: but I shall be very glad to attend you on Thursday next to his grace's levee; where, I'm afraid, we shall not be crowded with company; for, you know, there's a wide difference between his present office of president of the council, and his former post of first lord commissioner of the treasury."[6]

This communicative friend having announced all the remarkable characters of both sexes, that appeared at court, we resolved to adjourn, and retired. At the foot of the stair-case, there was a crowd of laqueys and chairmen, and in the midst of them stood Humphry Clinker, exalted upon a stool, with his hat in one hand, and a paper in the other, in the act of holding forth to the people—Before we could inquire into the meaning of this exhibition, he perceived his master, thrust the paper into his pocket, descended from his elevation, bolted through the crowd, and brought up the carriage to the gate.

My uncle said nothing till we were seated, when, after having looked at me earnestly for some time, he burst out a-laughing, and

4. A reception or assembly held regularly by a person of distinction or importance.
5. Sir Robert Walpole (1676–1745) virtually invented the post of prime minister, which he filled for over twenty years during his long political career. Newcastle served as his secretary of state from 1724 to 1742.
6. The office of the First Lord of the Treasury has since the early 18th century usually been held by the prime minister. Newcastle held this position from 1754 to 1756 and again from 1757 to 1762. He never held the other office mentioned.

asked if I knew upon what subject Clinker was holding forth to the mob——"If (said he) the fellow is turned mountebank, I must turn him out of my service, otherwise he'll make Merry Andrews[7] of us all—" I observed, that, in all probability, he had studied medicine under his master, who was a farrier.

At dinner, the 'squire asked him, if he had ever practised physic? "Yes, an please your honour, (said he) among brute beasts; but I never meddle with rational creatures." "I know not whether you rank in that class the audience you was harranguing in the court at St. James's, but I should be glad to know what kind of powders you was distributing; and whether you had a good sale—" "Sale, sir! (cried Clinker) I hope I shall never be base enough to sell for gold and silver, what freely comes of God's grace. I distributed nothing, an like your honour, but a word of advice to my fellows in servitude and sin." "Advice! concerning what?" "Concerning profane swearing, an please your honour; so horrid and shocking, that it made my hair stand on end." "Nay, if thou can'st cure them of that disease, I shall think thee a wonderful doctor indeed—" "Why not cure them, my good master? the hearts of those poor people are not so stubborn as your honour seems to think——Make them first sensible that you have nothing in view but their good, then they will listen with patience, and easily be convinced of the sin and folly of a practice that affords neither profit nor pleasure—" At this remark, our uncle changed colour, and looked round the company, conscious that his *own withers were not altogether unwrung*.[8] "But, Clinker, (said he) if you should have eloquence enough to persuade the vulgar, to resign those tropes and figures of rhetoric, there will be little or nothing left to distinguish their conversation from that of their betters." "But then your honour knows, their conversation will be void of offence; and, at the day of judgment, there will be no distinction of persons."

Humphry going down stairs to fetch up a bottle of wine, my uncle congratulated his sister upon having such a reformer in the family; when Mrs. Tabitha declared, he was a sober civilized fellow; very respectful, and very industrious; and, she believed, a good Christian into the bargain. One would think, Clinker must really have some very extraordinary talent, to ingratiate himself in this manner with a virago of her character, so fortified against him with prejudice and resentment; but the truth is, since the adventure of Salt-hill, Mrs. Tabby seems to be entirely changed. She has left off scolding the servants, an exercise which was grown habitual, and even seemed necessary to her constitution; and is become so indifferent

---

7. Public clowns. "Mountebank": charlatan or quack doctor.
8. Adapted from Shakespeare's *Hamlet* (3.2.252), where Hamlet proclaims his innocence.

to Chowder, as to part with him in a present to lady Griskin, who proposes to bring the breed of him into fashion. Her ladyship is the widow of sir Timothy Griskin, a distant relation of our family. She enjoys a jointure of five hundred pounds a-year, and makes shift to spend three times that sum. Her character before marriage was a little equivocal; but at present she lives in the *bon ton*,[9] keeps card-tables, gives private suppers to select friends, and is visited by persons of the first fashion—She has been remarkably civil to us all, and cultivates my uncle with the most particular regard; but the more she strokes him, the more his bristles seem to rise—To her compliments he makes very laconic and dry returns—T'other day, she sent us a pottle of fine strawberries, which he did not receive without signs of disgust, muttering from the Æneid, *timeo Danaos et Dona ferentes*.[1] She has twice called for Liddy, of a forenoon, to take an airing in the coach; but Mrs. Tabby was always so alert, (I suppose by his direction) that she never could have the niece without her aunt's company—I have endeavoured to sound Square-toes on this subject; but he carefully avoids all explanation.

I have now, dear Phillips, filled a whole sheet; and if you have read it to an end, I dare say, you are as tired as

Your humble servant,

London, June 2,   J. MELFORD.

To Dr. LEWIS.

Yes. Doctor, I have seen the British Museum; which is a noble collection, and even stupendous, if we consider it was made by a private man, a physician,[2] who was obliged to make his own fortune at the same time: but great as the collection is, it would appear more striking if it was arranged in one spacious saloon, instead of being divided into different apartments, which it does not entirely fill—I could wish the series of medals was connected, and the whole of the animal, vegetable, and mineral kingdoms completed, by adding to each, at the public expence, those articles that are wanting. It would likewise be a great improvement, with respect to the library, if the deficiencies were made up, by purchasing all the books of character

9. Polite or fashionable society (French).
1. I fear the Danaans [Greeks], even those bearing gifts (Latin); a famous warning spoken by the Trojan priest Laocoön in Virgil's epic poem the *Aeneid*, 2.49. "Pottle": a half-gallon container.
2. Sir Hans Sloane (1660–1753), physician, naturalist, and collector, succeeded Sir Isaac Newton (1642–1727) as president of the Royal Society. After Sloane's death, Parliament authorized the purchase of his collection and used it as the nucleus for the British Museum, which opened to the public in 1759.

that are not to be found already in the collection—They might be classed in centuries, according to the dates of their publication, and catalogues printed of them and the manuscripts, for the information of those that want to consult, or compile from such authorities. I could also wish, for the honour of the nation, that there was a complete apparatus for a course of mathematics, mechanics, and experimental philosophy; and a good salary settled upon an able professor, who should give regular lectures on these subjects.

But this is all idle speculation, which will never be reduced to practice—Considering the temper of the times, it is a wonder to see any institution whatsoever established, for the benefit of the public. The spirit of party is risen to a kind of phrenzy, unknown to former ages, or rather degenerated to a total extinction of honesty and candour—You know I have observed, for some time, that the public papers are become the infamous vehicles of the most cruel and perfidious defamation: every rancorous knave——every desperate incendiary, that can afford to spend half a crown or three shillings, may skulk behind the press of a newsmonger, and have a stab at the first character in the kingdom, without running the least hazard of detection or punishment.

I have made acquaintance with a Mr. Barton, whom Jery knew at Oxford; a good sort of a man, though most ridiculously warped in his political principles; but his partiality is the less offensive, as it never appears in the stile of scurrility and abuse. He is a member of parliament, and a retainer to the court; and his whole conversation turns upon the virtues and perfections of the ministers, who are his patrons. T'other day, when he was bedaubing one of those worthies, with the most fulsome praise, I told him I had seen the same nobleman characterised very differently, in one of the daily-papers; indeed, so stigmatized, that if one half of what was said of him was true, he must be not only unfit to rule, but even unfit to live: that those impeachments had been repeated again and again, with the addition of fresh matter; and that as he had taken no steps towards his own vindication, I began to think there was some foundation for the charge. "And pray, sir, (said Mr. Barton) what steps would you have him take?—Suppose he should prosecute the publisher, who screens the anonymous accuser, and bring him to the pillory for a libel; this is so far from being counted a punishment, *in terrorem*,[3] that it will probably make his fortune. The multitude immediately take him into their protection, as a martyr to the cause of defamation, which they have always espoused—They pay his fine, they contribute to the increase of his stock, his shop is crowded with customers, and the sale of his paper rises in proportion to the scandal it contains.

3. For the purpose of terrifying (Latin).

All this time the prosecutor is inveighed against as a tyrant and oppressor, for having chosen to proceed by the way of information, which is deemed a grievance; but if he lays an action for damages, he must prove the damage, and I leave you to judge, whether a gentleman's character may not be brought into contempt, and all his views in life blasted by calumny, without his being able to specify the particulars of the damage he has sustained."

"This spirit of defamation is a kind of heresy, that thrives under persecution. *The liberty of the press* is a term of great efficacy; and, like that of the Protestant religion, has often served the purposes of sedition—A minister, therefore, must arm himself with patience, and bear those attacks without repining—Whatever mischief they may do in other respects, they certainly contribute, in one particular, to the advantage of government; for those defamatory articles have multiplied papers in such a manner, and augmented their sale to such a degree, that the duty upon stamps and advertisements has made a very considerable addition to the revenue."[4] Certain it is, a gentleman's honour is a very delicate subject to be handled by a jury, composed of men, who cannot be supposed remarkable either for sentiment or impartiality—In such a case, indeed, the defendant is tried, not only by his peers, but also by his party; and I really think, that of all patriots, he is the most resolute who exposes himself to such detraction, for the sake of his country—If, from the ignorance or partiality of juries, a gentleman can have no redress from law, for being defamed in a pamphlet or news-paper, I know but one other method of proceeding against the publisher, which is attended with some risque, but has been practised successfully, more than once, in my remembrance—A regiment of horse was represented, in one of the newspapers, as having misbehaved at Dettingen;[5] a captain of that regiment broke the publisher's bones, telling him, at the same time, if he went to law, he should certainly have the like salutation from every officer of the corps. Governor—— took the same satisfaction on the ribs of an author, who traduced him by name in a periodical paper—I know a low fellow of the same class, who, being turned out of Venice for his impudence and scurrility, retired to Lugano, a town of the Grisons, (a free people, God wot)[6] where he found a printing press, from whence he squirted his filth at some respectable characters in the republic, which he had

---

4. The first Stamp Tax in 1712 taxed newspapers, pamphlets, advertisements, and paper. Revised many times over the 18th century, it was always more successful at raising revenues than at controlling the press (its original purpose).

5. Where, in 1743, the Royal Horse Guards were repulsed during the War of the Austrian Succession (1740–48), before the British ultimately won the battle.

6. Knows (archaic). Lugano in fact was not part of Grisons (Graubünden), a region and now a canton of eastern Switzerland.

been obliged to abandon. Some of these, finding him out of the reach of legal chastisement, employed certain useful instruments, such as may be found in all countries, to give him the bastinado;[7] which, being repeated more than once, effectually stopt the current of his abuse.

As for the liberty of the press, like every other privilege, it must be restrained within certain bounds; for if it is carried to a breach of law, religion, and charity, it becomes one of the greatest evils that ever annoyed the community. If the lowest ruffian may stab your good-name with impunity in England, will you be so uncandid as to exclaim against Italy for the practice of common assassination? To what purpose is our property secured, if our moral character is left defenceless? People thus baited, grow desperate; and the despair of being able to preserve one's character, untainted by such vermin, produces a total neglect of fame; so that one of the chief incitements to the practice of virtue is effectually destroyed.

Mr. Barton's last consideration, respecting the stamp-duty, is equally wise and laudable with another maxim which has been long adopted by our financiers, namely, to connive at drunkenness, riot, and dissipation, because they inhance the receipt of the excise; not reflecting, that in providing this temporary convenience, they are destroying the morals, health, and industry of the people——Not-withstanding my contempt for those who flatter a minister, I think there is something still more despicable in flattering a mob. When I see a man of birth, education, and fortune, put himself on a level with the dregs of the people, mingle with low mechanics, feed with them at the same board, and drink with them in the same cup, flat-ter their prejudices, harangue in praise of their virtues, expose them-selves to the belchings of their beer, the fumes of their tobacco, the grossness of their familiarity, and the impertinence of their conversa-tion, I cannot help despising him, as a man guilty of the vilest prosti-tution, in order to effect a purpose equally selfish and illiberal.

I should renounce politics the more willingly, if I could find other topics of conversation discussed with more modesty and candour; but the dæmon of party seems to have usurped every department of life. Even the world of literature and taste is divided into the most virulent factions, which revile, decry, and traduce the works of one another. Yesterday, I went to return an afternoon's visit to a gentle-man of my acquaintance, at whose house I found one of the authors of the present age, who has written with some success[8]—As I had read one or two of his performances, which gave me pleasure, I was

---

7. A blow or beating with a stick or cudgel.
8. Possibly John Shebbeare (1709–1788), a novelist and pamphleteer with whom Smollett quarreled during his time at the *Critical Review*.

glad of this opportunity to know his person; but his discourse and deportment destroyed all the impressions which his writings had made in his favour. He took upon him to decide dogmatically upon every subject, without deigning to shew the least cause for his differing from the general opinions of mankind, as if it had been our duty to acquiese in the *ipse dixit* of this new Pythagoras.[9] He rejudged the characters of all the principal authors, who had died within a century of the present time; and, in this revision, paid no sort of regard to the reputation they had acquired—Milton was harsh and prosaic; Dryden, languid and verbose; Butler and Swift, without humour; Congreve, without wit; and Pope destitute of any sort of poetical merit[1]—As for his cotemporaries, he could not bear to hear one of them mentioned with any degree of applause—They were all dunces, pedants, plagiaries,[2] quacks, and impostors; and you could not name a single performance, but what was tame, stupid, and insipid. It must be owned, that this writer had nothing to charge his conscience with, on the side of flattery; for, I understand, he was never known to praise one line that was written, even by those with whom he lived on terms of good-fellowship. This arrogance and presumption, in depreciating authors, for whose reputation the company may be interested, is such an insult upon the understanding, as I could not bear without wincing.

I desired to know his reasons for decrying some works, which had afforded me uncommon pleasure; and, as demonstration did not seem to be his talent, I dissented from his opinion with great freedom. Having been spoiled by the deference and humility of his hearers, he did not bear contradiction with much temper; and the dispute might have grown warm, had it not been interrupted by the entrance of a rival bard, at whose appearance he always quits the place——They are of different cabals, and have been at open war these twenty years——If the other was dogmatical, this genius was declamatory: he did not discourse, but harangue; and his orations were equally tedious and turgid. He too pronounces *ex cathedra*[3] upon the characters of his cotemporaries; and though he scruples not to deal out praise, even lavishly, to the lowest reptile in Grub street who will either flatter him in private, or mount the public rostrum as his panegyrist, he damns all the other writers of the age, with the utmost insolence and rancour—One is a blunderbuss,

---

9. Greek philosopher and mathematician (ca. 570–ca. 495 B.C.E.) with a loyal, cultish following. "*Ipse dixit*": he, himself, said it (Latin, literal trans.); indicates a dogmatic assertion made solely on the speaker's authority.
1. This list includes the most highly reputed writers of the late 17th and early 18th centuries.
2. Plagiarists.
3. From the chair (Latin); refers to the Roman Catholic doctrine of papal infallibility.

as being a native of Ireland, another, a half-starved louse of literature, from the banks of the Tweed; a third, an ass, because he enjoys
a pension from the government; a fourth, the very angel of dulness;
because he succeeded in a species of writing in which this Aristarchus[4] had failed; a fifth, who presumed to make strictures upon
one of his performances, he holds as a bug in criticism, whose
stench is more offensive than his sting—In short, except himself
and his myrmidons,[5] there is not a man of genius or learning in the
three kingdoms. As for the success of those, who have written
without the pale of this confederacy, he imputes it entirely to want
of taste in the public; not considering, that to the approbation of
that very tasteless public, he himself owes all the consequence he
has in life.

Those originals are not fit for conversation. If they would maintain the advantage they have gained by their writing, they should
never appear but upon paper—For my part, I am shocked to find a
man have sublime ideas in his head, and nothing but illiberal sentiments in his heart—The human soul will be generally found
most defective in the article of candour—I am inclined to think,
no mind was ever wholly exempt from envy; which, perhaps, may
have been implanted, as an instinct essential to our nature. I am
afraid we sometimes palliate this vice, under the specious name of
emulation. I have known a person remarkably generous, humane,
moderate, and apparently self-denying, who could not hear even a
friend commended, without betraying marks of uneasiness; as if
that commendation had implied an odious comparison to his
prejudice, and every wreath of praise added to the other's character, was a garland plucked from his own temples. This is a malig-
nant species of jealousy, of which I stand acquitted in my own
conscience—Whether it is a vice, or an infirmity, I leave you to
inquire.

There is another point, which I would much rather see determined; whether the world was always as contemptible, as it appears
to me at present?—If the morals of mankind have not contracted
an extraordinary degree of depravity, within these thirty years,
then must I be infected with the common vice of old men, *difficilis,
querulus, laudator temporis acti*;[6] or, which is more probable, the
impetuous pursuits and avocations of youth have formerly hindered
me from observing those rotten parts of human nature, which now
appear so offensively to my observation.

---

4. Aristarchus of Samothrace (ca. 220–ca. 143 B.C.E.), a Greek grammarian and critic
famous for criticizing the texts attributed to Homer.
5. Faithful followers or attendants.
6. Peevish, surly, and always praising the days of his youth (Latin); Horace's description of
a typical elderly man in his *Ars Poetica* (1.173).

We have been at court, and change,[7] and every where; and every where we find food for spleen, and subject for ridicule—My new servant, Humphry Clinker, turns out a great original; and Tabby is a changed creature——She has parted with Chowder; and does nothing but smile, like Malvolio in the play[8]——I'll be hanged if she is not acting a part which is not natural to her disposition, for some purpose which I have not yet discovered.

With respect to the characters of mankind, my curiosity is quite satisfied; I have done with the science of men, and must now endeavour to amuse myself with the novelty of things. I am, at present, by a violent effort of the mind, forced from my natural biass; but this power ceasing to act, I shall return to my solitude with redoubled velocity. Every thing I see, and hear, and feel, in this great reservoir of folly, knavery, and sophistication, contributes to inhance the value of a country life, in the sentiments of

yours always,

London, June 2. MAT. BRAMBLE.

To Mrs. MARY JONES, at Brambleton-hall.

DEAR MARY JONES,

Lady Griskin's botler, Mr. Crumb, having got 'squire Barton to frank me a kiver, I would not neglect to let you know how it is with me, and the rest of the family.

I could not rite by John Thomas, for because he went away in a huff, at a minute's warming. He and Chowder could not agree, and so they fitt upon the road, and Chowder bitt his thumb, and he swore he would do him a mischief, and he spoke saucy to mistress, whereby the 'squire turned him off in gudgeon; and by God's providence we picked up another footman, called Umphry Klinker; a good sole as ever broke bread; which shews that a scalded cat may prove a good mouser, and a hound be staunch, thof he has got narro hare on his buttocks; but the proudest nose may be bro't to the grine-stone, by sickness and misfortunes.

O Molly! what shall I say of London? All the towns that ever I beheld in my born-days, are no more than Welsh barrows and crum-lecks[9] to this wonderful sitty! Even Bath itself is but a fillitch, in the

---

7. The Royal Exchange, rebuilt after the Great Fire of 1666, was a stock exchange and housed a fashionable shopping arcade in its upper galleries.
8. In Shakespeare's *Twelfth Night*, the dour steward Malvolio is duped into smiling incessantly, leading others to think he has lost his mind.
9. Cromlechs: prehistoric circles of massive standing stones. "Barrows": burial mounds.

naam of God——One would think there's no end of the streets, but
the land's end. Then there's such a power of people, going hurry
skurry! Such a racket of coxes! Such a noise, and haliballoo! So
many strange sites to be seen! O gracious! my poor Welsh brain has
been spinning like a top ever since I came hither! And I have seen
the Park, and the paleass of Saint Gimses, and the king's and the
queen's magisterial pursing, and the sweet young princes, and the
hillyfents, and pye-bald ass,[1] and all the rest of the royal family.

   Last week I went with mistress to the Tower, to see the crowns and
wild beastis;[2] and there was a monstracious lion, with teeth half a
quarter long; and a gentleman bid me not go near him, if I wasn't a
maid; being as how he would roar, and tear, and play the dickens—
Now I had no mind to go near him; for I cannot abide such dangerous honeymils, not I——but, mistress would go; and the beast kept
such a roaring and bouncing, that I tho't he would have broke his
cage and devoured us all; and the gentleman tittered for sooth; but
I'll go to death upon it, I will, that my lady is as good a firchin, as the
child unborn; and, therefore, either the gentleman told a fib, or
the lion oft to be set in the stocks for bearing false witness again
his neighbour; for the commandment sayeth, *Thou shalt not bear
false witness again thy neighbour.*

   I was afterwards of a party at Sadler's-wells,[3] where I saw such
tumbling and dancing upon ropes and wires, that I was frightened,
and ready to go into a fit—I tho't it was all inchantment; and,
believing myself bewitched, began for to cry——You knows as how
the witches in Wales fly upon broom-sticks; but here was flying
without any broom-stick, or thing in the varsal world[4] and firing of
pistols in the air, and blowing of trumpets, and swinging, and rolling of wheel-barrows upon a wire, (God bless us!) no thicker than a
sewing-thread; that, to be sure, they must deal with the devil!——A
fine gentleman, with a pig's-tail, and a golden sord by his side, came
to comfit me, and offered for to treat me with a pint of wind; but I
would not stay; and so, in going through the dark passage, he began
to shew his cloven futt, and went for to be rude: my fellow-sarvant,
Umpry Klinker, bid him be sivil, and he gave the young man a
dowse in the chops; but, I fackins, Mr. Klinker wa'n't long in his

---

1. Elephants and a zebra were featured attractions at the menagerie in Saint James's Park.
2. As well as the Crown Jewels, the Tower of London, a castle on the north bank of the
   Thames that dates back to the 11th century, featured lions, leopards, and other animals
   drawn from the Royal Menagerie, which was later absorbed into the London Zoo in
   Regent's Park.
3. A music hall opened by Richard Sadler in 1683 in the London borough of Islington. It
   featured somewhat less highbrow entertainment than Vauxhall or Ranelagh Gardens,
   including rope dancers and acrobats.
4. Universal; i.e., in the whole world.

debt——with a good oaken sapling he dusted his doublet, for all his golden cheesetoaster;[5] and, sipping me under his arm, carried me huom, I nose not how, being I was in such a flustration—But, thank God! I'm now vaned from all such vanities; for what are all those rarities and vagaries to the glory that shall be revealed hereafter? O Molly! let not your poor heart be puffed up with vanity.

I had almost forgot to tell you, that I have had my hair cut and pippered, and singed, and bolstered, and buckled, in the newest fashion, by a French freezer—*Parley vow Francey*—*Vee madmansell*[6]——I now carries my head higher than arrow private gentlewoman of Vales. Last night, coming huom from the meeting, I was taken by lamp-light for an iminent poulterer's daughter, a great beauty—But as I was saying, this is all vanity and vexation of spirit—The pleasures of London are no better than sower whey and stale cyder, when compared to the joys of the new Gerusalem.

Dear Mary Jones! An please God when I return, I'll bring you a new cap, with a turkey-shell coom, and a pyehouse sermon, that was preached in the Tabernacle;[7] and I pray of all love, you will mind your vriting and your spilling; for, craving your pardon, Molly, it made me suet to disseyffer your last scrabble, which was delivered by the hind at Bath—O, voman! voman! if thou had'st but the least consumption of what pleasure we scullers have, when we can cunster the crabbidst buck off hand, and spell the ethnitch vords without lucking at the primmer. As for Mr. Klinker, he is qualified to be clerk to a parish—But I'll say no more—Remember me to Saul—poor sole! it goes to my hart to think she don't yet know her letters—But all in God's good time—It shall go hard, but I will bring her the A B C in ginger-bread; and that, you nose, will be learning to her taste.

Mistress says, we are going a long gurney to the North; but go where we will, I shall ever be,

Dear Mary Jones,

yours with true infection,

London, June 3.   WIN. JENKINS

---

5. A fork for toasting cheese; here used ironically to signify a showy sword.
6. An inaccurate transliteration of French, meaning "Do you speak French[?]—Yes, madam." "Freezer": friseur, or hairdresser.
7. Presumably the church built in 1741 for George Whitefield (1714–1770), a Methodist evangelical, in Moorfield. It may also refer to his chapel on Tottenham Court Road, built in 1756 and enlarged in 1759.

To Sir WATKIN PHILLIPS, of Jesus college, Oxon.

DEAR WAT,

I mentioned in my last, my uncle's design of going to the duke of N——'s[8] levee; which design has been executed accordingly. His grace has been so long accustomed to this kind of homage, that though the place he now fills does not imply the tenth part of the influence, which he exerted in his former office, he has given his friends to understand, that they cannot oblige him in any thing more, than in contributing to support the shadow of that power, which he no longer retains in substance; and therefore he has still public days, on which they appear at his levee.

My uncle and I went thither with Mr. Barton, who, being one of the duke's adherents, undertook to be our introducer—The room was pretty well filled with people, in a great variety of dress; but there was no more than one gown and cassock, though I was told his grace had, while he was minister, preferred almost every individual that now filled the bench of bishops in the house of lords; but, in all probability, the gratitude of the clergy is like their charity, which shuns the light—Mr. Barton was immediately accosted by a person, well stricken in years, tall, and rawboned, with a hook-nose, and an arch leer, that indicated, at least, as much cunning as sagacity. Our conductor saluted him, by the name of captain C——, and afterwards informed us he was a man of shrewd parts, whom the government occasionally employed in secret services—But I have had the history of him more at large, from another quartet——He had been, many years ago, concerned in fraudulent practices, as a merchant, in France; and being convicted of some of them, was sent to the gallies, from whence he was delivered by the interest of the late duke of Ormond, to whom he had recommended himself in letter, as his namesake and relation—He was in the sequel, employed by our ministry as a spy; and in the war of 1740, traversed all Spain, as well as France, in the disguise of a capuchin, at the extreme hazard of his life, in as much as the court of Madrid had actually got scent of him, and given orders to apprehend him at St. Sebastian's,[9] from whence he had fortunately retired but a few hours before the order arrived. This and other hair-breadth 'scapes he pleaded so effectually as a merit with the English ministry, that they allowed him a comfortable pension, which he now enjoys in his old age—He has still access to all the ministers, and is said to be consulted by them on many subjects, as a man of uncommon understanding and great

8. Newcastle.
9. Or Donostia; a port city in the Basque country of northern Spain.

experience—He is, in fact, a fellow of some parts, and invincible assurance; and, in his discourse, he assumes such an air of self-sufficiency, as may very well impose upon some of the shallow politicians, who now labour at the helm of administration. But, if he is not belied, this is not the only imposture of which he is guilty—— They say, he is at bottom not only a Roman-catholic, but really a priest; and while he pretends to disclose to our state-pilots all the springs that move the cabinet of Versailles, he is actually picking up intelligence for the service of the French minister——Be that as it may, captain C——entered into conversation with us in the most familiar manner, and treated the duke's character without any ceremony—"This wise-acre (said he) is still a-bed; and, I think, the best thing he can do, is to sleep on till Christmas; for, when he gets up, he does nothing but expose his own folly.—Since Granville was turned out,[1] there has been no minister in this nation worth the meal that whitened his periwig—They are so ignorant, they scarce know a crab from a cauliflower; and then they are such dunces, that there's no making them comprehend the plainest proposition——In the beginning of the war, this poor half-witted creature told me, in a great fright, that thirty thousand French had marched from Acadie to Cape Breton[2]——Where did they find transports? (said I) "Transports! (cried he) I tell you, they marched by land—" By land to the island of Cape Breton? "What! is Cape Breton an island?" Certainly. "Ha! are you sure of that?" When I pointed it out in the map, he examined it earnestly with his spectacles; then, taking me in his arms, "My dear C——! (cried he) you always bring us good news—Egad! I'll go directly, and tell the king that Cape Breton is an island—"

He seemed disposed to entertain us with more anecdotes of this nature, at the expence of his grace, when he was interrupted by the arrival of the Algerine[3] ambassador; a venerable Turk, with a long white beard, attended by his dragoman, or interpreter, and another officer of his household, who had got no stockings to his legs—— Captain C——immediately spoke with an air of authority to a servant in waiting, bidding him go and tell the duke to rise, as there was a great deal of company come, and, among others, the ambassador from Algiers—Then, turning to us, "This poor Turk (said he) notwithstanding his grey beard, is a green-horn——He has been several years resident in London, and still is ignorant of our political

---

1. John Carteret, second Earl Granville (1690–1763), was a long-serving British statesman with a reputation for eccentricity. An early rival of Walpole, he served as secretary of state from 1742 to 1744 and in 1756 declined Newcastle's offer to become prime minister.
2. "Acadie" was the French name for the North American colony that is now the Canadian maritime province of Nova Scotia. Cape Breton Island, which forms its northernmost portion, was ceded by the French to the British under the 1763 Treaty of Paris.
3. Algerian.

Turkish ambassador introduced to the Duke of N———. Courtesy of the Center for Southwest Research, University Libraries, University of New Mexico.

revolutions. This visit is intended for the prime minister of England; but you'll see how this wise duke will receive it as a mark of attachment to his own person—" Certain it is, the duke seemed eager to acknowledge the compliment—A door opening, he suddenly bolted out, with a shaving-cloth under his chin, his face frothed up to the eyes with soap lather; and, running up to the ambassador, grinned hideous in his face—"My dear Mahomet! (said he) God love your long beard, I hope the dey will make you a horse-tail[4] at the next promotion, ha, ha, ha!——Have but a moment's patience, and I'll send to you in a twinkling—" So saying, he retreated into his den, leaving the Turk in some confusion. After a short pause, however, he said something to his interpreter, the meaning of which I had great curiosity to know, as he turned up his eyes while he spoke, expressing astonishment, mixed with devotion——We were gratified by means of the communicative captain C——, who conversed with the dragoman, as an old acquaintance. Ibrahim, the ambassador, who had mistaken his grace for the minister's fool, was no sooner undeceived by the interpreter, than he exlaimed to this effect—"Holy prophet! I don't wonder that this nation prospers, seeing it is governed by the counsel of ideots; a series of men, whom all good mussulmen revere as the organs of immediate inspiration!" Ibrahim was favoured with a particular audience of short duration; after which the duke conducted him to the door, and then returned to diffuse his gracious looks among the crowd of his worshippers.

As Mr. Barton advanced to present me to his grace, it was my fortune to attract his notice, before I was announced—He forthwith met me more than half way, and, seizing me by the hand, "My dear sir Francis![5] (cried he) this is so kind—I vow to Gad! I am so obliged— Such attention to a poor broken minister—Well—Pray when does your excellency set sail?—For God's sake have a care of your health, and eat stewed prunes in the passage—Next to your own precious health, pray, my dear excellency, take care of the Five Nations— Our good friends the Five Nations—The Toryrories, the Maccolmacks, the Out-o'the-ways, the Crickets, and the Kickshaws[6]—Let 'em have plenty of blankets, and stinkubus, and wampum;[7] and

4. Insignia of various ranks of pasha (military commander) throughout the Ottoman Empire.
5. Probably the duke mistakes Jery for Sir Francis Barnard (ca. 1711–1779), governor of New Jersey and then Massachusetts Bay.
6. The original Iroquois League, composed of the Seneca, Mohawk, Cayuga, Oneida, and Onondaga nations living around current-day upstate New York, was joined by the Tuscarora nation in 1722.
7. Traditional sacred shell beads, often used as currency by Europeans for trading with Native Americans. "Blankets": used for trading and often intentionally infected with European diseases like smallpox, against which Native Americans had no natural immunity. "Stinkubus": bad liquor (slang).

your excellency won't fail to scour the kettle, and boil the chain, and bury the tree, and plant the hatchet—Ha, ha, ha!" When he had uttered this rhapsody, with his usual precipitation, Mr. Barton gave him to understand, that I was neither Sir Francis, nor St. Francis, but simply Mr. Melford, nephew to Mr. Bramble; who, stepping forward, made his bow at the same time. "Odso! no more it is Sir Francis—(said this wise statesman) Mr. Melford, I'm glad to see you—I sent you an engineer to fortify your dock—Mr. Bramble—your servant, Mr. Bramble—How d'ye, good Mr. Bramble? Your nephew is a pretty young fellow—Faith and troth, a very pretty fellow!—His father is my old friend—How does he hold it? Still troubled with that damned disorder, ha?" "No, my lord, (replied my uncle) all his troubles are over—He has been dead these fifteen years." "Dead! how—Yes, faith! now I remember: he is dead, sure enough—Well, and how—does the young gentleman stand for Haverford West? or—a—what d'ye—My dear Mr. Milfordhaven,[8] I'll do you all the service in my power—I hope I have some credit left——" My uncle then gave him to understand, that I was still a minor; and that we had no intention to trouble him at present, for any favour whatsoever—"I came hither with my nephew (added he) to pay our respects to your grace; and I may venture to say, that his views and mine are at least as disinterested as those of any individual in this assembly." "My dear Mr. Brambleberry! you do me infinite honour—I shall always rejoice to see you and your hopeful nephew, Mr. Milfordhaven—My credit, such as it is, you may command—I wish we had more friends of your kidney—"

Then, turning to captain C——, "Ha, C——! (said he) what news, C——? How does the world wag? ha!" "The world wags much after the old fashion, my lord (answered the captain): the politicians of London and Westminster have begun again to wag their tongues against your grace; and your short-lived popularity wags like a feather, which the next puff of antiministerial calumny will blow away—" "A pack of rascals (cried the duke)—Tories, Jacobites, rebels; one half of them would wag their heels at Tyburn,[9] if they had their deserts—" So saying, he wheeled about; and, going round the levee, spoke to every individual, with the most courteous familiarity; but he scarce ever opened his mouth without making some blunder, in relation to the person or business of the party with whom he conversed; so that he really looked like a comedian, hired to burlesque the character of a minister—At length, a person of a very prepossessing appearance coming in, his grace ran up, and, hugging him in his

8. Millford Haven and Haverfordwest are both towns in Pembrokeshire, Wales.
9. A village, now part of London, that was notorious as the site of public hangings from the 16th through the 18th centuries.

arms, with the appellation of "My dear Ch——s!" led him forthwith into the inner apartment, or *Sanctum Sanctorum*[1] of this
political temple. "That (said captain C——) is my friend C—T——,[2]
almost the only man of parts who has any concern in the present
administration—Indeed, he would have no concern at all in the
matter, if the ministry did not find it absolutely necessary to make
use of his talents upon some particular occasions—As for the
common business of the nation, it is carried on in a constant rou-
tine by the clerks of the different offices, otherwise the wheels of
government would be wholly stopt amidst the abrupt succession
of ministers, every one more ignorant than his predecessor——I am
thinking what a fine hovel we should be in, if all the clerks of the
treasury, of the secretaries, the war-office, and the admiralty, should
take it in their heads to throw up their places in imitation of the
great pensioner—But, to return to C——T——; he certainly knows
more than all the ministry and all the opposition, if their heads were
laid together, and talks like an angel on a vast variety of subjects—He
would really be a great man, if he had any consistency or stability of
character—Then, it must be owned, he wants courage, otherwise
he would never allow himself to be cowed by the great political
bully,[3] for whose understanding he has justly a very great contempt.
I have seen him as much afraid of that overbearing Hector, as ever
schoolboy was of his pedagogue; and yet this Hector, I shrewdly
suspect, is no more than a craven at bottom—Besides this defect,
C——has another, which he is at too little pains to hide—There's
no faith to be given to his assertions, and no trust to be put in his
promises—However, to give the devil his due, he's very good-natured;
and even friendly, when close urged in the way of solicitation—As
for principle, that's out of the question—In a word, he is a wit and
an orator, extremely entertaining, and he shines very often at the
expence even of those ministers to whom he is a retainer—This is
a mark of great imprudence, by which he has made them all his
enemies, whatever face they may put upon the matter; and sooner
or later he'll have cause to wish he had been able to keep his own
counsel—I have several times cautioned him on this subject; but
'tis all preaching to the desert—His vanity runs away with his discretion—" I could not help thinking the captain himself might have
been the better for some hints of the same nature—His panegyric,
excluding principle and veracity, puts me in mind of a contest I once
over-heard, in the way of altercation, betwixt two apple-women in

---

1. Holy of Holies (Latin); here, Newcastle's private retreat.
2. Charles Townshend (1725–1767), a politician known for his witty speeches in the
   House of Commons.
3. Probably Pitt, who was notorious for bullying his colleagues.

Spring-garden[4]—One of those viragos[5] having hinted something to the prejudice of the other's moral character, her antagonist, setting her hands in her sides, replied—"Speak out, hussy—I scorn your malice—I own I'm both a whore and a thief; and what more have you to say?—Damn you, what more have you to say? bating that, which all the world knows, I challenge you to say black is the white of my eye—" We did not wait for Mr. T—'s coming forth; but after captain C——had characterised all the originals in waiting, we adjourned to a coffee-house, where we had buttered muffins and tea to breakfast, the said captain still favouring us with his company—Nay, my uncle was so diverted with his anecdotes, that he asked him to dinner, and treated him with a fine turbot, to which he did ample justice—That same evening I spent at the tavern with some friends, one of whom let me into C——'s character, which Mr. Bramble no sooner understood, than he expressed some concern for the connexion he had made, and resolved to disengage himself from it without ceremony.

We are become members of the Society for the Encouragement of the Arts,[6] and have assisted at some of their deliberations, which were conducted with equal spirit and sagacity—My uncle is extremely fond of the institution, which will certainly be productive of great advantages to the public, if, from its democratical form, it does not degenerate into cabal and corruption—You are already acquainted with his aversion to the influence of the multitude, which, he affirms, is incompatible with excellence, and subversive of order—Indeed his detestation of the mob has been heightened by fear, ever since he fainted in the room at Bath; and this apprehension has prevented him from going to the Little Theatre in the Hay-market,[7] and other places of entertainment, to which, however, I have had the honour to attend the ladies.

It grates old Square-Toes to reflect, that it is not in his power to enjoy even the most elegant diversions of the capital, without the participation of the vulgar; for they now thrust themselves into all assemblies, from a ridotto at St. James's, to a hop at Rotherhithe.[8]

I have lately seen our old acquaintance Dick Ivy, who we imagined had died of dram-drinking; but he is lately emerged from the Fleet,[9]

---

4. A pleasure garden near Whitehall and Charing Cross.
5. Loud, ill-tempered women.
6. The Society for the Encouragement of Arts, Manufactures, and Commerce was founded in 1754. Granted a royal charter in 1847, it is now the Royal Society of Arts.
7. Small only by comparison to its neighbor, the Opera House, this theater stood near the current site of the Haymarket Theatre.
8. A London sailor's district south of the Thames. "Ridotto": a fashionable gathering featuring music, dancing, and sometimes gambling. "Hop": an informal dancing party.
9. Fleet Prison, at the bottom of Ludgate Hill, where debtors were frequently held. Rebuilt several times over the course of its long history, it was finally torn down in the mid-19th century.

by means of a pamphlet which he wrote and published against the government with some success. The sale of this performance enabled him to appear in clean linen, and he is now going about soliciting subscriptions for his Poems; but his breeches are not yet in the most decent order.

Dick certainly deserves some countenance for his intrepidity and perseverance—It is not in the power of disappointment, nor even of damnation, to drive him to despair—After some unsuccessful essays in the way of poetry, he commenced brandy-merchant, and I believe his whole stock ran out through his own bowels; then he consorted with a milk-woman, who kept a cellar in Petty France:[1] but he could not make his quarters good; he was dislodged and driven up stairs into the kennel by a corporal in the second regiment of footguards—He was afterwards the laureat of Blackfriars,[2] from whence there was a natural transition to the Fleet—As he had formerly miscarried in panegyric, he now turned his thoughts to satire, and really seems to have some talent for abuse. If he can hold out till the meeting of the parliament, and be prepared for another charge, in all probability Dick will mount the pillory, or obtain a pension, in either of which events his fortune will be made—— Mean while he has acquired some degree of consideration with the respectable writers of the age; and as I have subscribed for his works, he did me the favour 'tother night to introduce me to a society of those geniuses; but I found them exceedingly formal and reserved— They seemed afraid and jealous of one another, and sat in a state of mutual repulsion, like so many particles of vapour, each surrounded by its own electrified atmosphere. Dick, who has more vivacity than judgment, tried more than once to enliven the conversation; sometimes making an effort at wit, sometimes letting off a pun, and sometimes discharging a conundrum; nay, at length he started a dispute upon the hackneyed comparison betwixt blank verse and rhyme, and the professors opened with great clamour; but, instead of keeping to the subject, they launched out into tedious dissertations on the poetry of the antients; and one of them, who had been a schoolmaster, displayed his whole knowledge of prosody, gleaned from Disputer and Ruddiman.[3] At last, I ventured to say, I did not see how the subject in question could be at all elucidated by the practice of the antients, who certainly had neither blank verse nor rhyme

---

1. An area of east London, properly called Spitalfields, known for its French emigrant population.
2. A section of central London, near the Thames, notorious for criminal activities in the 18th century.
3. Thomas Ruddiman (1674–1757), a Scottish classicist who published the authoritative textbook *Rudiments of the Latin Tongue* in 1714. Johannes Despauterius (ca. 1480–1520) prepared Latin grammar texts still being used in the 18th century.

in their poems, which were measured by feet, whereas ours are reckoned by the number of syllables—This remark seemed to give umbrage to the pedant, who forthwith involved himself in a cloud of Greek and Latin quotations, which nobody attempted to dispel—A confused hum of insipid observations and comments ensued; and, upon the whole, I never passed a duller evening in my life—Yet, without all doubt, some of them were men of learning, wit, and ingenuity. As they are afraid of making free with one another, they should bring each his butt, or whet-stone, along with him, for the entertainment of the company—My uncle says, he never desires to meet with more than one wit at a time—One wit, like a knuckle of ham in soup, gives a zest and flavour to the dish; but more than one serves only to spoil the pottage——And now I'm afraid I have given you an unconscionable mess, without any flavour at all; for which, I suppose, you will bestow your benedictions upon

your friend,

and servant,

London, June 5.   J. MELFORD.

END OF THE FIRST VOLUME.

Volume II

To Dr. Lewis.

Dear Lewis,

Your fable of the monkey and the pig, is what the Italians call *ben trovata*.[4] but I shall not repeat it to my apothecary, who is a proud Scotchman, very thin skinned, and, for aught I know, may have his degree in his pocket[5]—A right Scotchman has always two strings to his bow, and is *in utrumque paratus*[6]—Certain it is, I have not 'scaped a scouring; but, I believe, by means of that scouring, I have 'scaped something worse, perhaps a tedious fit of the gout or rheumatism; for my appetite began to flagg, and I had certain croakings in the bowels, which boded me no good—Nay, I am not yet quite free of these remembrances, which warn me to be gone from this centre of infection——

What temptation can a man of my turn and temperament have, to live in a place where every corner teems with fresh objects of detestation and disgust? What kind of taste and organs must those people have, who really prefer the adulterate[7] enjoyments of the town to the genuine pleasures of a country retreat? Most people, I know, are originally seduced by vanity, ambition, and childish curiosity; which cannot be gratified, but in the *busy haunts of men*:[8] but, in the course of this gratification, their very organs of sense are perverted, and they become habitually lost to every relish of what is genuine and excellent in it's own nature.

Shall I state the difference between my town grievances, and my country comforts? At Brambleton-hall, I have elbow-room within doors, and breathe a clear, elastic, salutary air——I enjoy refreshing

---

4. Well said (Italian; slightly misspelled).
5. Unlike surgeons and doctors, apothecaries needed only licenses (gained on completion of their apprenticeships) to practice. Ambitious apothecaries could go on to complete medical degrees at universities like Edinburgh and Leyden.
6. Prepared for either (Latin); attributed to Virgil.
7. Adulterated, i.e., impure.
8. In Shakespeare's *Romeo and Juliet* (3.1.53), Benvolio speaks of "the public haunt of men," and the speaker of Milton's "L'Allegro" (line 119) is pleased by "the busy hum of men." Smollett appears to have conflated the two.

sleep, which is never disturbed by horrid noise, nor interrupted, but in a morning, by the sweet twitter of the martlet at my window—I drink the virgin lymph, pure and crystalline as it gushes from the rock, or the sparkling beveridge, home-brewed from malt of my own making; or I indulge with cyder, which my own orchard affords; or with claret of the best growth, imported for my own use, by a correspondent on whose integrity I can depend; my bread is sweet and nourishing, made from my own wheat, ground in my own mill, and baked in my own oven; my table is, in a great measure, furnished from my own ground; my five-year old mutton, fed on the fragrant herbage of the mountains, that might vie with venison in juice and flavour; my delicious veal, fattened with nothing but the mother's milk, that fills the dish with gravy; my poultry from the barn-door, that never knew confinement, but when they were at roost; my rabbits panting from the warren; my game fresh from the moors; my trout and salmon struggling from the stream; oysters from their native banks; and herrings, with other sea-fish, I can eat in four hours after they are taken—My sallads, roots, and pot-herbs, my own garden yields in plenty and perfection; the produce of the natural soil, prepared by moderate cultivation. The same soil affords all the different fruits which England may call her own, so that my desert is every day fresh-gathered from the tree; my dairy flows with nectarious tides of milk and cream, from whence we derive abundance of excellent butter, curds, and cheese; and the refuse fattens my pigs, that are destined for hams and bacon—I go to bed betimes, and rise with the sun—I make shift to pass the hours without weariness or regret, and am not destitute of amusements within doors, when the weather will not permit me to go abroad—I read, and chat, and play at billiards, cards, or back-gammon—Without doors, I superintend my farm, and execute plans of improvement, the effects of which I enjoy with unspeakable delight—Nor do I take less pleasure in seeing my tenants thrive under my auspices, and the poor live comfortably by the employment which I provide——You know I have one or two sensible friends, to whom I can open all my heart; a blessing which, perhaps, I might have sought in vain among the crowded scenes of life: there are a few others of more humble parts, whom I esteem for their integrity; and their conversation I find inoffensive, though not very entertaining. Finally, I live in the midst of honest men, and trusty dependants, who, I flatter myself, have a disinterested attachment to my person—You, yourself, my dear Doctor, can vouch for the truth of these assertions.

Now, mark the contrast at London—I am pent up in frowzy lodgings, where there is not room enough to swing a cat; and I breathe the steams of endless putrefaction; and these would, undoubtedly, produce a pestilence, if they were not qualified by the gross acid of sea-coal,[9] which is itself a pernicious nuisance to lungs of any delicacy of texture: but even this boasted corrector cannot prevent those languid, sallow looks, that distinguish the inhabitants of London from those ruddy swains that lead a country-life——I go to bed after mid-night, jaded and restless from the dissipations of the day—I start every hour from my sleep, at the horrid noise of the watchmen bawling the hour through every street, and thundering at every door; a set of useless fellows, who serve no other purpose but that of disturbing the repose of the inhabitants; and by five o'clock I start out of bed, in consequence of the still more dreadful alarm made by the country carts, and noisy rustics bellowing green pease under my window.[1] If I would drink water, I must quaff the maukish contents of an open aqueduct,[2] exposed to all manner of defilement; or swallow that which comes from the river Thames, impregnated with all the filth of London and Westminster—Human excrement is the least offensive part of the concrete, which is composed of all the drugs, minerals, and poisons, used in mechanics and manufacture, enriched with the putrefying carcases of beasts and men; and mixed with the scourings of all the washtubs, kennels, and common sewers, within the bills of mortality.

This is the agreeable potation, extolled by the Londoners, as the finest water in the universe—As to the intoxicating potion, sold for wine, it is a vile, unpalatable, and pernicious sophistication, balderdashed with cyder, corn-spirit, and the juice of sloes.[3] In an action at law, laid against a carman for having staved a cask of port, it appeared from the evidence of the cooper, that there were not above five gallons of real wine in the whole pipe, which held above a hundred, and even that had been brewed and adulterated by the merchant at Oporto.[4] The bread I eat in London, is a deleterious paste, mixed up with chalk, alum, and bone-ashes; insipid to the taste, and destructive to the constitution. The good people are not ignorant of this adulteration; but they prefer it to wholsome bread, because it is whiter than the meal of corn: thus they sacrifice their taste and their health, and the lives of their tender infants, to a most absurd gratification of a mis-judging eye; and the miller, or the baker, is obliged to poison them and their families, in order to live by his profession.— The same monstrous depravity appears in their veal, which is bleached by repeated bleedings, and other villanous arts, till there

9. Coal brought to London by sea. "Frowzy": dirty, untidy. "Cat": a cat-o'-nine-tails, i.e., a whip.
1. Vegetable sellers who shouted their goods through the streets.
2. The artificial "New River," built 1609–13, supplied London with water from the Chadwell Springs, located between Ware and Hertford.
3. Small, sour fruits of the blackthorn bush. "Balderdashed": made a jumbled mixture of.
4. A Portuguese seaport. Spanish and Portuguese wines were very popular in 18th-century London.

is not a drop of juice left in the body, and the poor animal is paralytic before it dies; so void of all taste, nourishment, and savour, that a man might dine as comfortably on a white fricasee of kidskin gloves, or chip hats from Leghorn.[5]

As they have discharged the natural colour from their bread, their butchers-meat, and poultry, their cutlets, ragouts, fricassees, and sauces of all kinds; so they insist upon having the complexion of their pot-herbs mended, even at the hazard of their lives. Perhaps, you will hardly believe they can be so mad as to boil their greens with brass half-pence, in order to improve their colour; and yet nothing is more true—Indeed, without this improvement in the colour, they have no personal merit. They are produced in an artificial soil, and taste of nothing but the dunghills, from whence they spring. My cabbage, cauliflower, and 'sparagus in the country, are as much superior in flavour to those that are sold in Covent-garden, as my heath-mutton is to that of St. James's-market; which, in fact, is neither lamb nor mutton, but something betwixt the two, gorged in the rank fens of Lincoln and Essex,[6] pale, coarse, and frowzy—As for the pork, it is an abominable carnivorous animal, fed with horse-flesh and distillers grains; and the poultry is all rotten, in consequence of a fever, occasioned by the infamous practice of sewing up the gut, that they may be the sooner fattened in coops, in consequence of this cruel retention.

Of the fish, I need say nothing in this hot weather, but that it comes sixty, seventy, fourscore, and a hundred miles by land-carriage; a circumstance sufficient, without any comment, to turn a Dutchman's stomach,[7] even if his nose was not saluted in every alley with the sweet flavour of *fresh* mackarel, selling by retail—This is not the season for oysters; nevertheless, it may not be amiss to mention, that the right Colchester[8] are kept in slime-pits, occasionally overflowed by the sea; and that the green colour, so much admired by the voluptuaries of this metropolis, is occasioned by the vitriolic scum, which rises on the surface of the stagnant and stinking water—Our rabbits are bred and fed in the poulterer's cellar, where they have neither air nor exercise, consequently they must be firm in flesh, and delicious in flavour; and there is no game to be had for love or money.

It must be owned, that Covent-garden affords some good fruit; which, however, is always engrossed by a few individuals of over

5. The English name for the Italian port city of Livorno. "Fricasse": any dish made from meat that is lightly browned, stewed, and then served in a sauce of its own stock.
6. Counties on England's eastern side.
7. The British associated the Dutch with gluttony.
8. A type of oyster named after the seaside town famous for them.

grown fortune, at an exorbitant price; so that little else than the refuse of the market falls to the share of the community; and that is distributed by such filthy hands, as I cannot look at without loathing. It was but yesterday that I saw a dirty barrow-bunter in the street, cleaning her dusty fruit with her own spittle; and, who knows but some fine lady of St. James's parish might admit into her delicate mouth those very cherries, which had been rolled and moistened between the filthy, and, perhaps, ulcerated chops of a St. Giles's huckster[9]—I need not dwell upon the pallid, contaminated mash, which they call strawberries; soiled and tossed by greasy paws through twenty baskets crusted with dirt; and then presented with the worst milk, thickened with the worst flour, into a bad likeness of cream: but the milk itself should not pass unanalysed, the produce of faded cabbage-leaves and sour draff,[1] lowered with hot water, frothed with bruised snails, carried through the streets in open pails, exposed to foul rinsings, discharged from doors and windows, spittle, snot, and tobacco-quids from foot-passengers, over-flowings from mud-carts, spatterings from coach-wheels, dirt and trash chucked into it by roguish boys for the joke's-sake, the spewings of infants, who have slabbered in the tin-measure, which is thrown back in that condition among the milk, for the benefit of the next customer; and, finally, the vermin that drops from the rags of the nasty drab that vends this precious mixture, under the respectable denomination of milk-maid.

I shall conclude this catalogue of London dainties, with that table-beer, guiltless of hops and malt, vapid and nauseous; much fitter to facilitate the operation of a vomit, than to quench thirst and promote digestion; the tallowy rancid mass, called butter, manufactured with candle-grease and kitchen-stuff; and their fresh eggs, imported from France and Scotland.——Now, all these enormities might be remedied with a very little attention to the article of police, or civil regulation; but the wise patriots of London have taken it into their heads, that all regulation is inconsistent with liberty; and that every man ought to live in his own way, without restraint——Nay, as there is not sense enough left among them, to be discomposed by the nuisances I have mentioned, they may, for aught I care, wallow in the mire of their own pollution.

A companionable man will, undoubtedly, put up with many inconveniences for the sake of enjoying agreeable society. A facetious friend of mine used to say, the wine could not be bad, where the company was agreeable; a maxim which, however, ought to be taken

---

9. Street vendor. "Barrow-bunter": a person employed in pushing a small cart, in this case filled with fruit for sale. Saint Giles is a neighborhood of London long associated with vagrancy.
1. Dregs, i.e., the sediment of a liquid.

cum grano salis:[2] but what is the society of London, that I should be tempted, for its sake, to mortify my senses, and compound with such uncleanness as my soul abhors? All the people I see, are too much engrossed by schemes of interest or ambition, to have any room left for sentiment or friendship—Even in some of my old acquaintance, those schemes and pursuits have obliterated all traces of our former connexion——Conversation is reduced to party-disputes, and illiberal altercation—Social commerce, to formal visits and card-playing—If you pick up a diverting original by accident, it may be dangerous to amuse yourself with his oddities—He is generally a tartar at bottom; a sharper, a spy, or a lunatic. Every person you deal with endeavours to over-reach you in the way of business; you are preyed upon by idle mendicants, who beg in the phrase of borrowing, and live upon the spoils of the stranger—Your tradesmen are without conscience, your friends without affection, and your dependants without fidelity.—

My letter would swell into a treatise, were I to particularize every cause of offence that fills up the measure of my aversion to this, and every other crowded city—Thank Heaven! I am not so far sucked into the vortex, but that I can disengage myself without any great effort of philosophy—From this wild uproar of knavery, folly, and impertinence, I shall fly with double relish to the serenity of retirement, the cordial effusions of unreserved friendship, the hospitality and protection of the rural gods; in a word, the *jucunda oblivia vitæ,*[3] which Horace himself had not taste enough to enjoy.—

I have agreed for a good travelling-coach and four, at a guinea a-day, for three months certain; and next week we intend to begin our journey to the North, hoping still to be with you by the latter end of October——I shall continue to write from every stage where we make any considerable halt, as often as any thing occurs, which I think can afford you the least amusement. In the mean time, I must beg you will superintend the œconomy of Barns, with respect to my hay and corn harvests; assured that my ground produces nothing but what you may freely call your own——On any other terms I should be ashamed to subscribe myself

your unvariable friend,
MATT. BRAMBLE.

London, June 8.

---

2. With a grain of salt (Latin); a proverbial expression meaning "not too seriously."
3. Pleasant obliviousness to life's troubles (Latin); from Horace's *Satires* (2.6.62), in which the country mouse praises rural life over city life.

To Sir WATKIN PHILLIPS, Bar^t.
of Jesus college, Oxon.

DEAR PHILLIPS,

In my last, I mentioned my having spent an evening with a society of authors, who seemed to be jealous and afraid of one another. My uncle was not at all surprised to hear me say I was disappointed in their conversation. "A man may be very entertaining and instructive upon paper, (said he) and exceedingly dull in common discourse. I have observed, that those who shine most in private company, are but secondary stars in the constellation of genius—A small stock of ideas is more easily managed, and sooner displayed, than a great quantity crowded together. There is very seldom any thing extraordinary in the appearance and address of a good writer; whereas a dull author generally distinguishes himself by some oddity or extravagance. For this reason, I fancy, an assembly of Grubs[4] must be very diverting."

My curiosity being excited by this hint, I consulted my friend Dick Ivy, who undertook to gratify it the very next day, which was Sunday last.—He carried me to dine with S——,[5] whom you and I have long known by his writings.—He lives in the skirts of the town, and every Sunday his house is open to all unfortunate brothers of the quill, whom he treats with beef, pudding, and potatoes, port, punch, and Calvert's entire butt beer.[6]—He has fixed upon the first day of the week for the exercise of his hospitality, because some of his guests could not enjoy it on any other, for reasons that I need not explain.[7] I was civilly received in a plain, yet decent habitation, which opened back wards into a very pleasant garden, kept in excellent order; and, indeed, I saw none of the outward signs of authorship, either in the house or the landlord, who is one of those few writers of the age that stand upon their own foundation, without patronage, and above dependence. If there was nothing characteristic in the entertainer, the company made ample amends for his want of singularity.

At two in the afternoon, I found myself one of ten mess-mates seated at table; and, I question, if the whole kingdom could produce such another assemblage of originals. Among their peculiarities, I do not mention those of dress, which may be purely accidental. What struck me were oddities originally produced by affectation, and

---

4. Residents of Grub Street, a London street known for its hack writers and therefore synonymous with anyone who struggled to make a living by freelance writing.
5. Smollett himself.
6. Porter; the Calvert brothers ran a brewery celebrated for its porter. "Skirts of town": i.e., Chelsea, where Smollett resided from 1750 to 1763.
7. Debtors could not be arrested on Sundays.

afterwards confirmed by habit. One of them wore spectacles at dinner, and another, his hat flapped;[8] though (as Ivy told me) the first was noted for having a seaman's eye, when a bailiff was in the wind; and the other was never known to labour under any weakness or defect of vision, except about five years ago, when he was complimented with a couple of black eyes by a player, with whom he had quarrelled in his drink. A third wore a laced stocking, and made use of crutches, because, once in his life, he had been laid up with a broken leg, though no man could leap over a stick with more agility. A fourth had contracted such an antipathy to the country, that he insisted upon sitting with his back towards the window that looked into the garden, and when a dish of cauliflower was set upon the table, he snuffed up volatile salts to keep him from fainting; yet this delicate person was the son of a cottager, born under a hedge, and had many years run wild among asses on a common. A fifth affected distraction—When spoke to, he always answered from the purpose—sometimes he suddenly started up, and rapped out a dreadful oath—sometimes he burst out a-laughing—then he folded his arms, and sighed—and then he hissed like fifty serpents.

At first, I really thought he was mad, and, as he sat near me, began to be under some apprehensions for my own safety, when our landlord, perceiving me alarmed, assured me aloud that I had nothing to fear. "The gentleman (said he) is trying to act a part, for which he is by no means qualified—if he had all the inclination in the world, it is not in his power to be mad. His spirits are too flat to be kindled into frenzy." "'Tis no bad p-p-puff, how-ow-ever (observed a person in a tarnished laced coat): affffected m-madness w-will p-pass for w-wit w-with nine-ninet-teen out of t-twenty."—"And affected stuttering for humour," replied our landlord, "tho', God knows, there is no affinity betwixt them." It seems, this wag, after having made some abortive attempts in plain speaking, had recourse to this defect, by means of which he frequently extorted the laugh of the company, without the least expence of genius; and that imperfection, which he had at first counterfeited, was now become so habitual, that he could not lay it aside.

A certain winking genius, who wore yellow gloves at dinner, had, on his first introduction, taken such offence at S——, because he looked and talked, and ate and drank like any other man, that he spoke contemptuously of his understanding ever after, and never would repeat his visit, until he had exhibited the following proof of his caprice. Wat Wyvil,[9] the poet, having made some unsuccessful

8. With the flaps of his hat pulled down over his face.
9. Probably based on William Woty (ca. 1731–1791), a minor poet to whose verses Smollett had subscribed.

advances towards an intimacy with S—, at last gave him to understand, by a third person, that he had written a poem in his praise, and a satire against his person; that if he would admit him to his house, the first should be immediately sent to press; but that if he persisted in declining his friendship, he would publish the satire without delay. S——replied, that he looked upon Wyvil's panegyrick,[1] as in effect, a species of infamy, and would resent it accordingly with a good cudgel; but if he published the satire, he might deserve his compassion, and had nothing to fear from his revenge. Wyvil having considered the alternative, resolved to mortify S—by printing the panegyrick, for which he received a sound drubbing. Then he swore the peace against the aggressor, who, in order to avoid a prosecution at law, admitted him to his good graces. It was the singularity in S——'s conduct on this occasion, that reconciled him to the yellow-gloved philosopher, who owned he had some genius, and from that period cultivated his acquaintance.

Curious to know upon what subjects the several talents of my fellow-guests were employed, I applied to my communicative friend Dick Ivy, who gave me to understand, that most of them were, or had been, understrappers, or journeymen, to more creditable authors, for whom they translated, collated, and compiled, in the business of book-making; and that all of them had, at different times, laboured in the service of our landlord, though they had now set up for themselves in various departments of literature. Not only their talents, but also their nations and dialects were so various, that our conversation resembled the confusion of tongues at Babel. We had the Irish brogue, the Scotch accent, and foreign idiom, twanged off by the most discordant vociferation; for, as they all spoke together, no man had any chance to be heard, unless he could bawl louder than his fellows. It must be owned, however, there was nothing pedantic in their discourse; they carefully avoided all learned disquisitions, and endeavoured to be facetious; nor did their endeavours always miscarry——some droll repartee passed, and much laughter was excited; and if any individual lost his temper so far as to transgress the bounds of decorum, he was effectually checked by the master of the feast, who exerted a sort of paternal authority over this irritable tribe.

The most learned philosopher of the whole collection, who had been expelled the university for atheism, has made great progress in a refutation of lord Bolingbroke's[2] metaphysical works, which is said to be equally ingenious and orthodox; but, in the mean time, he has been presented to the grand jury as a public nuisance, for having

1. Poem of praise.
2. Henry St. John, first Viscount Bolingbroke (1678–1751), an English politician who published a series of freethinking philosophical texts in the early decades of the 1700s.

blasphemed in an alehouse on the Lord's day. The Scotchman gives lectures on the pronunciation of the English language, which he is now publishing by subscription.

The Irishman is a political writer, and goes by the name of my Lord Potatoe. He wrote a pamphlet in vindication of a minister, hoping his zeal would be rewarded with some place or pension; but finding himself neglected in that quarter, he whispered about, that the pamphlet was written by the minister himself, and he published an answer to his own production. In this, he addressed the author under the title of your *lordship* with such solemnity, that the public swallowed the deceit, and bought up the whole impression. The wise politicians of the metropolis declared they were both masterly performances, and chuckled over the flimsy reveries of an ignorant garretteer, as the profound speculations of a veteran statesman, acquainted with all the secrets of the cabinet. The imposture was detected in the sequel, and our Hibernian pamphleteer retains no part of his assumed importance, but the bare title of my lord, and the upper part of the table at the potatoe-ordinary,[3] in Shoe-lane.

Opposite to me sat a Piedmontese, who had obliged the public with a humorous satire, intituled, *The Balance of the English Poets*, a performance which evinced the great modesty and taste of the author, and, in particular, his intimacy with the elegancies of the English language. The sage, who laboured under the $\alpha\gamma\pi o\phi o\zeta\iota\alpha$[4] or *horror of green fields*, had just finished a treatise on practical agriculture, though, in fact, he had never seen corn[5] growing in his life, and was so ignorant of grain, that our entertainer, in the face of the whole company, made him own, that a plate of hominy was the best rice pudding he had ever eat.

The stutterer had almost finished his travels through Europe and part of Asia, without ever budging beyond the liberties of the King's Bench, except in term-time, with a tipstaff for his companion; and as for little Tim Cropdale, the most facetious member of the whole society, he had happily wound up the catastrophe of a virgin tragedy,[6] from the exhibition of which he promised himself a large fund of profit and reputation. Tim had made shift to live many years by writing novels, at the rate of five pounds a volume; but that branch of

---

3. An ordinary was a place where one could dine for a low fixed price.
4. Fear of the countryside (Greek). This quotation has not been identified.
5. I.e., wheat.
6. An unstaged play. The prison of the King's Bench—at the time, the senior court of common law in England and Wales—was often used for debtors, who were permitted to range within definite bounds ("liberties"). When the court was in session ("term-time"), prisoners would appear for their trials accompanied by a bailiff or "tipstaff," so named for the metal-tipped sticks the official traditionally carried. Smollett was imprisoned in the King's Bench for libel in 1760–61.

business is now engrossed by female authors,[7] who publish merely for the propagation of virtue, with so much ease and spirit, and delicacy, and knowledge of the human heart, and all in the serene tranquillity of high life, that the reader is not only inchanted by their genius, but reformed by their morality.

After dinner, we adjourned into the garden, where, I observed, Mr. S——gave a short separate audience to every individual in a small remote filbert walk, from whence most of them dropt off one after another, without further ceremony; but they were replaced by fresh recruits of the same clan, who came to make an afternoon's visit; and, among other's, a spruce bookseller, called Birkin, who rode his own gelding, and made his appearance in a pair of new jemmy boots,[8] with massy spurs of plate. It was not without reason, that this midwife of the Muses used exercise a-horseback, for he was too fat to walk a-foot, and he underwent some sarcasms from Tim Cropdale, on his unweildy size and inaptitude for motion. Birkin, who took umbrage at this poor author's petulance in presuming to joke upon a man so much richer than himself, told him, he was not so unweildy but that he could move the Marshalsea court[9] for a writ, and even overtake him with it, if he did not very speedily come and settle accounts with him, respecting the expence of publishing his last Ode to the king of Prussia, of which he had sold but three, and one of them was to Whitefield the methodist. Tim affected to receive this intimation with good humour, saying, he expected in a post or two, from Potsdam, a poem of thanks from his Prussian majesty, who knew very well how to pay poets in their own coin; but, in the mean time, he proposed, that Mr. Birkin and he should run three times round the garden for a bowl of punch, to be drank at Ashley's[1] in the evening, and he would run boots against stockings. The bookseller, who valued himself upon his mettle, was persuaded to accept the challenge, and he forthwith resigned his boots to Cropdale, who, when he had put them on, was no bad representation of captain Pisto[2] in the play.

Every thing being adjusted, they started together with great impetuosity, and, in the second round, Birkin had clearly the advantage, *larding the lean earth as he puff'd along.*[3] Cropdale had no mind to

---

7. Popular female novelists of the mid-18th century include Sarah Fielding (1710–1768) and Charlotte Lennox (ca. 1730–1804).
8. Handsome riding boots. "Filbert walk": secluded walk through a garden featuring hazelnut (filbert) trees or shrubs.
9. Located in the prison district of Southwark and primarily dealt with cases of small debts.
1. Ashley's Punch House was located in Fleet Street and claimed to be the original London retailer of punch, a popular drink made of rum or wine and water, sugar, and fruit juices.
2. A character in Shakespeare's *Henry IV*, Part 2, and *Henry V.*
3. Adapted from Prince Hal's description of Falstaff in *Henry IV, Part 1* (2.2.108–109).

contest the victory further; but, in a twinkling, disappeared through
the back-door of the garden, which opened into a private lane, that
had communication with the high road.—The spectators immediately began to hollow, "Stole away!" and Birkin set off in pursuit of
him with great eagerness; but he had not advanced twenty yards in
the lane, when a thorn running into his foot, sent him hopping
back into the garden, roaring with pain, and swearing with vexation.
When he was delivered from this annoyance by the Scotchman, who
had been bred to surgery, he looked about him wildly, exclaiming,
"Sure, the fellow won't be such a rogue as to run clear away with
my boots!" Our landlord, having reconnoitred the shoes he had left,
which, indeed, hardly deserved that name, "Pray, (said he) Mr. Birkin,
wa'n't your boots made of calf-skin?" "Calf-skin or cow-skin, (replied
the other) I'll find a slip of sheep-skin[4] that will do his business—I
lost twenty pounds by his farce, which you persuaded me to buy—I
am out of pocket five pounds by his damn'd ode; and now this
pair of boots, bran new, cost me thirty shillings, as per receipt.—But
this affair of the boots is felony—transportation.—I'll have the dog
indicted at the Old Bailey[5] I will, Mr. S——. I will be reveng'd, even
though I should lose my debt in consequence of his conviction."

Mr. S——said nothing at present, but accommodated him with a
pair of shoes; then ordered his servant to rub him down, and comfort him with a glass of rum-punch, which seemed, in a great measure, to cool the rage of his indignation. "After all, (said our landlord)
this is no more than a humbug in the way of wit, though it deserves
a more respectable epithet, when considered as an effort of invention. Tim, being (I suppose) out of credit with the cordwainer,[6] fell
upon this ingenious expedient to supply the want of shoes, knowing
that Mr. Birkin, who loves humour, would himself relish the joke
upon a little recollection. Cropdale literally lives by his wit, which
he has exercised upon all his friends in their turns. He once borrowed my poney for five or six days to go to Salisbury, and sold him
in Smithfield at his return. This was a joke of such a serious nature,
that, in the first transports of my passion, I had some thoughts of
prosecuting him for horse-stealing; and even when my resentment
had in some measure subsided, as he industriously avoided me, I
vowed, I would take satisfaction on his ribs with the first opportunity.
One day, seeing him at some distance in the street, coming towards
me, I began to prepare my cane for action, and walked in the shadow
of a porter, that he might not perceive me soon enough to make his

4. A court order, which was traditionally written on sheepskin.
5. The Sessions House, or county's central criminal court, on Old Bailey Street, next to
   Newgate Prison.
6. Shoemaker (from the cordovan leather commonly used).

escape; but, in the very instant I had lifted up the instrument of correction, I found Tim Cropdale metamorphosed into a miserable blind wretch, feeling his way with a long stick from post to post, and rolling about two bald unlighted orbs instead of eyes. I was exceedingly shocked at having so narrowly escaped the concern and disgrace that would have attended such a misapplication of vengeance: but, next day, Tim prevailed upon a friend of mine to come and sollicit my forgiveness, and offer his note, payable in six weeks, for the price of the poney.—This gentleman gave me to understand, that the blind man was no other than Cropdale, who having seen me advancing, and guessing my intent, had immediately converted himself into the object aforesaid.—I was so diverted at the ingenuity of the evasion, that I agreed to pardon his offence, refusing his note, however, that I might keep a prosecution for felony hanging over his head, as a security for his future good behaviour—But Timothy would by no means trust himself in my hands till the note was accepted—then he made his appearance at my door as a blind beggar, and imposed in such a manner upon my man, who had been his old acquaintance and pot-companion,[7] that the fellow threw the door in his face, and even threatened to give him the bastinado. Hearing a noise in the hall, I went thither, and immediately recollecting the figure I had passed in the street, accosted him by his own name, to the unspeakable astonishment of the footman."

Birkin declared he loved a joke as well as another; but asked if any of the company could tell where Mr. Cropdale lodged, that he might send him a proposal about restitution, before the boots should be made away with. "I would willingly give him a pair of new shoes, (said he) and half a guinea into the bargain, for the boots, which fitted me like a glove; and I shan't be able to get the fellows of them till the good weather for riding is over." The stuttering wit declared, that the only secret which Cropdale ever kept, was the place of his lodgings; but, he believed, that, during the heats of summer, he commonly took his repose upon a bulk, or indulged himself, in fresco, with one of the kennel-nymphs, under the portico of St. Martin's church.[8] "Pox on him! (cried the bookseller) he might as well have taken my whip and spurs—In that case, he might have been tempted to steal another horse, and then he would have rid to the devil of course."

After coffee, I took my leave of Mr. S——, with proper acknowledgements of his civility, and was extremely well pleased with the

---

7. Drinking partner.
8. Its deep portico attracted homeless people because it provided some shelter. "Bulk": the framework or stall of the front of a shop. "Kennel-nymph": prostitute. A kennel is a gutter or open sewer.

entertainment of the day, though not yet satisfied, with respect to the nature of this connexion, betwixt a man of character in the literary world, and a parcel of authorlings, who, in all probability, would never be able to acquire any degree of reputation by their labours. On this head I interrogated my conductor, Dick Ivy, who answered me to this effect—"One would imagine S——had some view to his own interest, in giving countenance and assistance to those people, whom he knows to be bad men, as well as bad writers; but, if he has any such view, he will find himself disappointed; for if he is so vain as to imagine he can make them subservient to his schemes of profit or ambition, they are cunning enough to make him their property in the mean time. There is not one of the company you have seen to-day (myself excepted) who does not owe him particular obligations.— One of them he bailed out of a spunging-house,[9] and afterwards paid the debt—another he translated into his family, and cloathed, when he was turned out half naked from jail in consequence of an act for the relief of insolvent debtors—a third, who was reduced to a woollen night-cap, and lived upon sheeps trotters, up three pair of stairs backward in Butcher-row,[1] he took into present pay and free quarters, and enabled him to appear as a gentleman, without having the fear of sheriff's officers before his eyes. Those who are in distress he supplies with money when he has it, and with his credit when he is out of cash. When they want business, he either finds employment for them in his own service, or recommends them to booksellers to execute some project he has formed for their subsistence. They are always welcome to his table, (which, though plain, is plentiful) and to his good offices as far as they will go; and when they see occasion, they make use of his name with the most petulant familiarity; nay, they do not even scruple to arrogate to themselves the merit of some of his performances, and have been known to sell their own lucubrations[2] as the produce of his brain. The Scotchman you saw at dinner once personated him at an ale-house in West-Smithfield,[3] and, in the character of S——, had his head broke by a cow-keeper, for having spoke disrespectfully of the Christian religion; but he took the law of him in his own person, and the assailant was fain to give him ten pounds to withdraw his action."

I observed, that all this appearance of liberality on the side of Mr. S——was easily accounted for, on the supposition that they flattered him in private, and engaged his adversaries in public; and yet I was astonished, when I recollected that I often had seen this

9. A house kept by a sheriff, bailiff, or other court officer for the confinement of debtors.
1. A row of tenements located on the Strand, a major road running through central London.
2. Laborious work.
3. A northwest area of London historically known for its meat markets.

writer virulently abused in papers, poems, and pamphlets, and not a pen was drawn in his defence.—"But you will be more astonished (said he) when I assure you, those very guests whom you saw at his table to-day, were the authors of great part of that abuse; and he himself is well aware of their particular favours, for they are all eager to detect and betray one another."—"But this is doing the devil's work for nothing (cried I). What should induce them to revile their benefactor without provocation?" "Envy (answered Dick) is the general incitement; but they are galled by an additional scourge of provocation. S——directs a literary journal,[4] in which their productions are necessarily brought to trial; and though many of them have been treated with such lenity and favour as they little deserved, yet the slightest censure, such as, perhaps, could not be avoided with any pretensions to candour and impartiality, has rankled in the hearts of those authors to such a degree, that they have taken immediate vengeance on the critic in anonymous libels, letters, and lampoons. Indeed, all the writers of the age, good, bad, and indifferent, from the moment he assumed this office, became his enemies, either professed or in petto,[5] except those of his friends who knew they had nothing to fear from his strictures; and he must be a wiser man than me, who can tell what advantage or satisfaction he derives from having brought such a nest of hornets about his ears."

I owned, that was a point which might deserve consideration; but still I expressed a desire to know his real motives for continuing his friendship to a set of rascals equally ungrateful and insignificant.—He said, he did not pretend to assign any reasonable motive; that, if the truth must be told, the man was, in point of conduct, a most incorrigible fool; that, though he pretended to have a knack at hitting off characters, he blundered strangely in the distribution of his favours, which were generally bestowed on the most undeserving of those who had recourse to his assistance; that, indeed, this preference was not so much owing to want of discernment as to want of resolution, for he had not fortitude enough to resist the importunity even of the most worthless; and, as he did not know the value of money, there was very little merit in parting with it so easily; that his pride was gratified in seeing himself courted by such a number of literary dependants; that, probably, he delighted in hearing them expose and traduce one another; and, finally, from their information, he became acquainted with all the transactions of Grubstreet, which he had some thoughts of compiling, for the entertainment of the public.

I could not help suspecting, from Dick's discourse, that he had some particular grudge against S——, upon whose conduct he had

---

4. The *Critical Review*, which Smollett edited from 1756 to 1763.
5. In secret.

put the worst construction it would bear; and, by dint of cross-examination, I found he was not at all satisfied with the character which had been given in the Review of his last performance, though it had been treated civilly, in consequence of the author's application to the critic. By all accounts, S——is not without weakness and caprice; but he is certainly good-humoured and civilized; nor do I find, that there is any thing overbearing, cruel, or implacable in his disposition.

I have dwelt so long upon authors; that you will perhaps suspect I intend to enroll myself among the fraternity; but, if I were actually qualified for the profession, it is at best but a desperate resource against starving, as it affords no provision for old age and infirmity. Salmon, at the age of fourscore, is now in a garret, compiling matter, at a guinea a sheet for a modern historian, who, in point of age, might be his grandchild; and Psalmonazar,[6] after having drudged half a century in the literary mill, in all the simplicity and abstinence of an Asiatic, subsists upon the charity of a few booksellers, just sufficient to keep him from the parish—I think Guy,[7] who was himself a bookseller, ought to have appropriated one wing or ward of his hospital to the use of decayed authors; though, indeed, there is neither hospital, college, nor workhouse, within the bills of mortality, large enough to contain the poor of this society, composed, as it is, from the refuse of every other profession.

I know not whether you will find any amusement in this account of an odd race of mortals, whose constitution had, I own, greatly interested the curiosity of

Yours,

London, June 10.   J. MELFORD.

To Miss LÆTITIA WILLIS, at Gloucester

MY DEAR LETTY,

There is something on my spirits, which I should not venture to communicate by the post, but having the opportunity of Mrs. Brentwood's return, I seize it eagerly, to disburthen my poor heart, which is oppressed with fear and vexation.—O Letty! what a miserable situation it is, to be without a friend to whom one can apply for counsel

---

6. George Psalmanazar (ca. 1679–1763), born in France, passed himself off as a native of Formosa (Taiwan), publishing *A Historical and Geographical Description of Formosa* (1704), which included an invented "Formosan alphabet." He was eventually exposed as a fraud; he later converted to Christianity and made a career as an essayist and hack writer. Thomas Salmon (1679–1767), a writer of histories and travel literature.
7. Thomas Guy (ca. 1645–1724), a bookseller who founded Guy's Hospital in 1722.

and consolation in distress! I hinted in my last, that one Mr. Barton had been very particular in his civilities: I can no longer mistake his meaning—he has formally professed himself my admirer; and, after a thousand assiduities, perceiving I made but a cold return to his addresses, he had recourse to the mediation of lady Griskin, who has acted the part of a very warm advocate in his behalf:—but, my dear Willis, her ladyship over-acts her part—she not only expatiates on the ample fortune, the great connexions, and the unblemished character of Mr. Barton, but she takes the trouble to catechise me; and, two days ago, peremptorily told me, that a girl of my age could not possibly resist so many considerations, if her heart was not pre-engaged.

This insinuation threw me into such a flutter, that she could not but observe my disorder; and, presuming upon the discovery, insisted upon my making her the confidante of my passion. But, although I had not such command of myself as to conceal the emotion of my heart, I am not such a child as to disclose its secrets to a person who would certainly use them to its prejudice. I told her, it was no wonder if I was out of countenance at her introducing a subject of conversation so unsuitable to my years and inexperience; that I believed Mr. Barton was a very worthy gentleman, and I was much obliged to him for his good opinion; but the affections were involuntary, and mine, in particular, had as yet made no concessions in his favour. She shook her head with an air of distrust that made me tremble; and observed, that if my affections were free, they would submit to the decision of prudence, especially when enforced by the authority of those who had a right to direct my conduct. This remark implied a design to interest my uncle or my aunt, perhaps my brother, in behalf of Mr. Barton's passion; and I am sadly afraid that my aunt is already gained over. Yesterday in the forenoon, he had been walking with us in the Park, and stopping in our return at a toy-shop, he presented her with a very fine snuff-box, and me with a gold etuis,[8] which I resolutely refused, till she commanded me to accept it on pain of her displeasure: nevertheless, being still unsatisfied with respect to the propriety of receiving this toy, I signified my doubts to my brother, who said he would consult my uncle on the subject, and seemed to think Mr. Barton had been rather premature in his presents.

What will be the result of this consultation, Heaven knows; but I am afraid it will produce an explanation with Mr. Barton, who will, no doubt, avow his passion, and sollicit their consent to a connexion which my soul abhors; for, my dearest Letty, it is not in my power to love Mr. Barton, even if my heart was untouched by any other tenderness. Not that there is any thing disagreeable about his person,

---

8. A small, often decorative case for needles, cosmetics, and other articles.

but there is a total want of that nameless charm which captivates and controuls the inchanted spirit—at least, he appears to me to have this defect; but if he had all the engaging qualifications which a man can possess, they would be excited in vain against that constancy, which, I flatter myself, is the characteristic of my nature. No, my dear Willis, I may be involved in fresh troubles, and I believe I shall, from the importunities of this gentleman and the violence of my relations; but my heart is incapable of change.

You know, I put no faith in dreams; and yet I have been much disturbed by one that visited me last night.—I thought I was in a church, where a certain person, whom you know, was on the point of being married to my aunt; that the clergyman was Mr. Barton, and that poor forlorn I stood weeping in a corner, half naked, and without shoes or stockings.—Now, I know there is nothing so childish as to be moved by those vain illusions; but, nevertheless, in spite of all my reason, this hath made a strong impression upon my mind, which begins to be very gloomy. Indeed, I have another more substantial cause of affliction—I have some religious scruples, my dear friend, which lie heavy on my conscience.—I was persuaded to go to the Tabernacle, where I heard a discourse that affected me deeply.—I have prayed fervently to be enlightened, but as yet I am not sensible of these inward motions, those operations of grace, which are the signs of a regenerated spirit; and therefore I begin to be in terrible apprehensions about the state of my poor soul. Some of our family have had very uncommon accessions, particularly my aunt and Mrs. Jenkins, who sometimes speak as if they were really inspired; so that I am not like to want for either exhortation or example, to purify my thoughts, and recall them from the vanities of this world, which, indeed, I would willingly resign, if it was in my power; but to make this sacrifice, I must be enabled by such assistance from above as hath not yet been indulged to

Your unfortunate friend,

June 10.   LYDIA MELFORD.

To Sir WATKIN PHILLIPS, of Jesus college, Oxon.

DEAR PHILLIPS,

The moment I received your letter, I began to execute your commission—With the assistance of mine host at the Bull and Gate,[9] I discovered the place to which your fugitive valet had retreated, and

9. A well-known inn in Holborn, in central London.

taxed him with his dishonesty—The fellow was in manifest confusion at sight of me, but he denied the charge with great confidence, till I told him, that if he would give up the watch, which was a family piece, he might keep the money and the clothes, and go to the devil his own way, at his leisure; but if he rejected this proposal, I would deliver him forthwith to the constable, whom I had provided for that purpose, and he would carry him before the justice without further delay. After some hesitation, he desired to speak with me in the next room, where he produced the watch, with all its appendages, and I have delivered it to our landlord, to be sent you by the first safe conveyance——So much for busines.

I shall grow vain, upon your saying you find entertainment in my letters; barren, as they certainly are, of incident and importance, because your amusement must arise, not from the matter, but from the manner, which you know is all my own—Animated, therefore, by the approbation of a person, whose nice taste and consummate judgment I can no longer doubt, I will chearfully proceed with our memoirs—As it is determined we shall set out next week for Yorkshire, I went to-day in the forenoon with my uncle to see a carriage, belonging to a coach-maker in our neighbourhood—Turning down a narrow lane, behind Longacre,[1] we perceived a crowd of people standing at a door; which, it seems, opened into a kind of a methodist meeting, and were informed, that a footman was then holding forth to the congregation within. Curious to see this phœnomenon, we squeezed into the place with much difficulty; and who should this preacher be, but the identical Humphry Clinker. He had finished his sermon, and given out a psalm, the first stave of which he sung with peculiar graces[2]——But if we were astonished to see Clinker in the pulpit, we were altogether confounded at finding all the females of our family among the audience—There was lady Griskin, Mrs. Tabitha Bramble, Mrs. Winifred Jenkins, my sister Liddy, and Mr. Barton, and all of them joined in the psalmody, with strong marks of devotion.

I could hardly keep my gravity on this ludicrous occasion; but old Square-toes was differently affected—The first thing that struck him, was the presumption of his lacquey, whom he commanded to come down, with such an air of authority as Humphry did not think proper to disregard. He descended immediately, and all the people were in commotion. Barton looked exceedingly sheepish, lady Griskin flirted her fan, Mrs. Tabby groaned in spirit, Liddy changed countenance, and Mrs. Jenkins sobbed as if her heart was breaking—My uncle, with a sneer, asked pardon of the ladies, for having interrupted

1. Long Acre Street runs between Saint Martin's Lane and Covent Garden.
2. Musical embellishments.

their devotion, saying, he had particular business with the preacher, whom he ordered to call a hackney-coach. This being immediately brought up to the end of the lane, he handed Liddy into it, and my aunt and I following him, we drove home, without taking any further notice of the rest of the company, who still remained in silent astonishment.

Mr. Bramble, perceiving Liddy in great trepidation, assumed a milder aspect, bidding her be under no concern, for he was not at all displeased at any thing she had done—"I have no objection (said he) to your being religiously inclined; but I don't think my servant is a proper ghostly director, for a devotee of your sex and character—if, in fact, (as I rather believe) your aunt is not the sole conductress of this machine—" Mrs. Tabitha made no answer, but threw up the whites of her eyes, as if in the act of ejaculation—Poor Liddy said she had no right to the title of a devotee; that she thought there was no harm in hearing a pious discourse, even if it came from a footman, especially as her aunt was present; but that if she had erred from ignorance, she hoped he would excuse it, as she could not bear the thoughts of living under his displeasure. The old gentleman, pressing her hand with a tender smile, said she was a good girl, and that he did not believe her capable of doing any thing that could give him the least umbrage or disgust.

When we arrived at our lodgings, he commanded Mr. Clinker to attend him up stairs, and spoke to him in these words—"Since you are called upon by the spirit to preach and to teach, it is high time to lay aside the livery of an earthly master; and, for my part, I am unworthy to have an apostle in my service—" "I hope (said Humphry) I have not failed in my duty to your honour—I should be a vile wretch if I did, considering the misery from which your charity and compassion relieved me—but having an inward admonition of the spirit——" "An admonition of the devil—(cried the 'squire, in a passion) What admonition, you blockhead?—What right has such a fellow as you to set up for a reformer?" "Begging your honour's pardon, (replied Clinker) may not the new light of God's grace shine upon the poor and the ignorant in their humility, as well as upon the wealthy, and the philosopher in all his pride of human learning?" "What you imagine to be the new light of grace, (said his master) I take to be a deceitful vapour, glimmering through a crack in your upper story—In a word, Mr. Clinker, I will have no light in my family but what pays the king's taxes,[3] unless it be the light of reason, which you don't pretend to follow."

"Ah, sir! (cried Humphry) the light of reason, is no more in comparison to the light I mean, than a farthing candle to the sun at

---

3. A tax on windows was established in 1695 and made even more stringent in 1746.

noon—"[4] "Very true, (said uncle) the one will serve to shew you your way, and the other to dazzle and confound your weak brain—Heark-ye, Clinker, you are either an hypocritical knave, or a wrong-headed enthusiast; and, in either case, unfit for my service—If you are a quack in sanctity and devotion, you will find it an easy matter to impose upon silly women, and others of crazed understanding, who will con-tribute lavishly for your support—if you are really seduced by the reveries of a disturbed imagination, the sooner you lose your senses entirely, the better for yourself and the community. In that case, some charitable person might provide you with a dark room and clean straw in Bedlam, where it would not be in your power to infect others with your fanaticism; whereas, if you have just reflection enough left to maintain the character of a chosen vessel in the meetings of the godly, you and your hearers will be misled by a Will-i'the-wisp, from one error into another, till you are plunged into religious frenzy; and then, perhaps, you will hang yourself in despair——" "Which the Lord of his infinite mercy forbid! (exclaimed the affrighted Clinker) It is very possible I may be under the temptation of the devil, who wants to wreck me on the rocks of spiritual pride—Your honour says, I am either a knave or a madman; now, as I'll assure your honour I am no knave, it follows that I must be mad; therefore, I beseech your honour, upon my knees, to take my case into consideration, that means may be used for my recovery—"

The 'squire could not help smiling at the poor fellow's simplicity, and promised to take care of him, provided he would mind the busi-ness of his place, without running after the new-light of methodism: but Mrs. Tabitha took offence at his humility, which she interpreted into poorness of spirit and worldly mindedness—She upbraided him with the want of courage to suffer for conscience sake——She observed, that if he should lose his place for bearing testimony to the truth, Providence would not fail to find him another, perhaps more advantageous; and, declaring that it could not be very agree-able to live in a family where an inquisition was established, retired to another room in great agitation.

My uncle followed her with a significant look, then, turning to the preacher, "You hear what my sister says—If you cannot live with me upon such terms as I have prescribed, the vineyard of methodism lies before you, and she seems very well disposed to reward your labour—" "I would not willingly give offence to any soul upon earth (answered Humphry); her ladyship has been very good to me, ever since we came to London; and surely she has a heart turned for

4. Adapted from Edward Young's "Satire the Last" (98) in his poem *The Universal Passion* (1726).

religious exercises; and both she and lady Criskin sing psalms and hymns like two cherubims——But, at the same time, I'm bound to love and obey your honour—It becometh not such a poor ignorant fellow as me, to hold dispute with gentlemen of rank and learning— As for the matter of knowledge, I am no more than a beast in comparison of your honour; therefore I submit; and, with God's grace, I will follow you to the world's end, if you don't think me too far gone to be out of confinement—"

His master promised to keep him for some time longer on trial; then desired to know in what manner lady Griskin and Mr. Barton came to join their religious society. He told him, that her ladyship was the person who first carried my aunt and sister to the Tabernacle, whither he attended them, and had his devotion kindled by Mr. W——'s[5] preaching: that he was confirmed in this new way, by the preacher's sermons, which he had bought and studied with great attention; that his discourse and prayers had brought over Mrs. Jenkins and the house-maid to the same way of thinking; but as for Mr. Barton, he had never seen him at service before this day, when he came in company with lady Griskin——Humphry, moreover, owned that he had been encouraged to mount the rostrum, by the example and success of a weaver, who was much followed as a powerful minister: that on his first trial, he found himself under such strong impulsions, as made him believe he was certainly moved by the spirit; and that he had assisted in lady Griskin's, and several private houses, at exercises of devotion.

Mr. Bramble was no sooner informed, that her ladyship had acted as the primum mobile of this confederacy, than he concluded she had only made use of Clinker as a tool, subservient to the execution of some design, to the true secret of which he was an utter stranger—He observed, that her ladyship's brain was a perfect mill for projects; and that she and Tabby had certainly engaged in some secret treaty, the nature of which he could not comprehend. I told him I thought it was no difficult matter to perceive the drift of Mrs. Tabitha, which was to ensnare the heart of Barton, and that in all likelihood my lady Griskin acted as her auxiliary: that this supposition would account for their endeavours to convert him to methodism; an event which would occasion a connexion of souls that might be easily improved into a matrimonial union.

My uncle seemed to be much diverted by the thoughts of this scheme's succeeding; but I gave him to understand, that Barton was preengaged: that he had the day before made a present of an etuis to Liddy, which her aunt had obliged her to receive, with a view, no doubt, to countenance her own accepting of a snuff-box at the same

5. George Whitefield; see p. 117, n. 7.

time: that my sister having made me acquainted with this incident, I had desired an explanation of Mr. Barton, who declared his intentions were honourable, and expressed his hope that I would have no objections to his alliance: that I had thanked him for the honour he intended our family; but told him, it would be necessary to consult her uncle and aunt, who were her guardians: and their approbation being obtained, I could have no objection to his proposal; though I was persuaded that no violence would be offered to my sister's inclinations, in a transaction that so nearly interested the happiness of her future life: that he had assured me, he should never think of availing himself of a guardian's authority, unless he could render his addresses agreeable to the young lady herself; and that he would immediately demand permission of Mr. and Miss Bramble, to make Liddy a tender of his hand and fortune.

The 'squire was not insensible to the advantages of such a match, and declared he would promote it with all his influence; but when I took notice that there seemed to be an aversion on the side of Liddy, he said he would sound her on the subject; and if her reluctance was such as would not be easily overcome, he would civilly decline the proposal of Mr. Barton; for he thought that, in the choice of a husband, a young woman ought not to sacrifice the feelings of her heart for any consideration upon earth—"Liddy is not so desperate (said he) as to worship fortune at such an expence." I take it for granted, this whole affair will end in smoke; though there seems to be a storm brewing in the quarter of Mrs. Tabby, who sat with all the sullen dignity of silence at dinner, seemingly pregnant with complaint and expostulation. As she hath certainly marked Barton for her own prey, she cannot possibly favour his suit to Liddy; and therefore I expect something extraordinary will attend his declaring himself my sister's admirer. This declaration will certainly be made in form, as soon as the lover can pick up resolution enough to stand the brunt of Mrs. Tabby's disappointment; for he is, without doubt, aware of her designs upon his person——The particulars of the denouement you shall know in due season: mean while I am

always yours,

London, June 10.   J. Melford.

To Dr. Lewis.

Dear Lewis,

The deceitful calm was of short duration. I am plunged again in a sea of vexation, and the complaints in my stomach and bowels are returned; so that I suppose I shall be disabled from prosecuting the excursion I had planned—What the devil had I to do, to come a plague hunting with a leash of females in my train? Yesterday my precious sister (who, by the bye, has been for some time a professed methodist) came into my apartment, attended by Mr. Barton, and desired an audience with a very stately air—"Brother, (said she) this gentleman has something to propose, which I flatter myself will be the more acceptable, as it will rid you of a troublesome companion." Then Mr. Barton proceeded to this effect—"I am, indeed, extremely ambitious of being allied to your family, Mr. Bramble, and I hope you will see no cause to interpose your authority." "As for authority, (said Tabby, interrupting him with some warmth) I know of none that he has a right to use on this occasion—If I pay him the compliment of making him acquainted with the step I intend to take, it is all he can expect in reason—This is as much as I believe he would do by me, if he intended to change his own situation in life—In a word, brother, I am so sensible of Mr. Barton's extraordinary merit, that I have been prevailed upon to alter my resolution of living a single life, and to put my happiness in his hands, by vesting him with a legal title to my person and fortune, such as they are. The business at present, is to have the writings drawn; and I shall be obliged to you, if you will recommend a lawyer to me for that purpose—"

You may guess what an effect this overture had upon me; who, from the information of my nephew, expected that Barton was to make a formal declaration of his passion for Liddy; I could not help gazing in silent astonishment, alternately at Tabby, and her supposed admirer, which last hung his head in the most aukward confusion for a few minutes, and then retired on pretence of being suddenly seized with a vertigo——Mrs. Tabitha affected much concern, and would have had him make use of a bed in the house; but he insisted upon going home, that he might have recourse to some drops, which he kept for such emergencies, and his innamorata acquiesced—In the mean time I was exceedingly puzzled at this adventure, (though I suspected the truth) and did not know in what manner to demean myself towards Mrs. Tabitha, when Jery came in and told me, he had just seen Mr. Barton alight from his chariot[6] at lady Griskin's door—This incident seemed to threaten a visit from her ladyship, with which we were honoured accordingly, in less than half an hour—"I find (said she) there has been a match of cross purposes among you good folks; and I'm come to set you to rights—" So saying, she presented me with the following billet—

6. A light four-wheeled coach.

"Dear Sir,

I no sooner recollected myself from the extreme confusion I was thrown into, by that unlucky mistake of your sister, than I thought it my duty to assure you, that my devoirs to Mrs. Bramble never exceeded the bounds of ordinary civility; and that my heart is unalterably fixed upon miss Liddy Melford, as I had the honour to declare to her brother, when he questioned me upon that subject—Lady Griskin has been so good as to charge herself, not only with the delivery of this note, but also with the task of undeceiving Mrs. Bramble, for whom I have the most profound respect and veneration, though my affection being otherwise engaged, is no longer in the power of

Sir,

your very humble servant,

RALPH BARTON."

Having cast my eyes over this billet, I told her ladyship, that I would no longer retard the friendly office she had undertaken; and I and Jery forthwith retired into another room. There we soon perceived the conversation grow very warm betwixt the two ladies; and, at length, could distinctly hear certain terms of altercation, which we could no longer delay interrupting, with any regard to decorum. When we entered the scene of contention, we found Liddy had joined the disputants, and stood trembling betwixt them, as if she had been afraid they would have proceeded to something more practical than words——Lady Griskin's face was like the full moon in a storm of wind, glaring, fiery, and portentuous; while Tabby looked grim and ghastly, with an aspect breathing discord and dismay.—Our appearance put a stop to their mutual revilings; but her ladyship turning to me, "Cousin, (said she) I can't help saying I have met with a very ungrateful return from this lady, for the pains I have taken to serve her family—" "My family is much obliged to your ladyship (cried Tabby, with a kind of hysterical giggle); but we have no right to the good offices of such an honourable go-between." "But, for all that, good Mrs. Tabitha Bramble, (resumed the other) I shall be content with the reflection, that virtue is its own reward; and it shall not be my fault, if you continue to make yourself ridiculous—Mr. Bramble, who has no little interest of his own to serve, will, no doubt, contribute all in his power to promote a match betwixt Mr. Barton and his niece, which will be equally honourable and advantageous; and, I dare say, miss Liddy herself will have no objection to a measure so well calculated to make her happy in life——" "I beg your ladyship's pardon, (exclaimed Liddy, with great vivacity) I have nothing but misery to expect from such a measure; and I hope my guardians will have too much compassion, to barter my peace of mind for any consideration of interest or fortune—" "Upon my word, miss Liddy! (said she) you have profited by the example of your good aunt—I comprehend your meaning, and will explain it when I have a proper opportunity——In the mean time, I shall take my leave—Madam, your most obedient, and devoted humble servant," said she, advancing close up to my sister, and curtsying so low, that I thought she intended to squat herself down on the floor—This salutation Tabby returned with equal solemnity; and the expression of the two faces, while they continued in this attitude, would be no bad subject for a pencil like that of the incomparable Hogarth,[7] if any such should ever appear again, in these times of dulness and degeneracy.

Jery accompanied her ladyship to her house, that he might have an opportunity to restore the etuis to Barton, and advise him to give up his suit, which was so disagreeable to his sister, against whom, however, he returned much irritated—Lady Griskin had assured him that Liddy's heart was pre-occupied; and immediately the idea of Wilson recurring to his imagination, his family-pride took the alarm—He denounced vengeance against that adventurer, and was disposed to be very peremptory with his sister; but I desired he would suppress his resentment, until I should have talked with her in private.

The poor girl, when I earnestly pressed her on this head, owned, with a flood of tears, that Wilson had actually come to the Hot Well at Bristol, and even introduced himself into our lodgings as a Jew pedlar; but that nothing had passed betwixt them, further than her begging him to withdraw immediately, if he had any regard for her peace of mind: that he had disappeared accordingly, after having attempted to prevail upon my sister's maid, to deliver a letter; which, however, she refused to receive, though she had consented to carry a message, importing that he was a gentleman of a good family; and that, in a very little time, he would avow his passion in that character—She confessed, that although he had not kept his word in this particular, he was not yet altogether indifferent to her affection; but solemnly promised, she would never carry on any correspondence with him, or any other admirer, for the future, without the privity[8] and approbation of her brother and me.

By this declaration, she made her own peace with Jery; but the hot headed boy is more than ever incensed against Wilson, whom he now considers as an impostor, that harbours some infamous design

---

7. William Hogarth (1697–1764), a prolific and popular artist and engraver, known especially for satirical pictorial series, including *A Rake's Progress* (1735) and *Marriage à-la-mode* (1743–45).
8. Participation, implying consent, in the knowledge of something private or secret.

Altercation between Mrs. Tabitha and Lady Griskin. Courtesy of the Center for Southwest Research, University Libraries, University of New Mexico.

upon the honour of his family—As for Barton, he was not a little mortified to find his present returned, and his addresses so unfavourably received; but he is not a man to be deeply affected by such disappointments; and I know not whether he is not as well pleased with being discarded by Liddy, as he would have been with a permission to prosecute his pretensions, at the risque of being every day exposed to the revenge or machinations of Tabby, who is not to be slighted with impunity.—I had not much time to moralize on these occurrences; for the house was visited by a constable and his gang, with a warrant from justice Buzzard,[9] to search the box of Humphry Clinker, my footman, who was just apprehended as a highway-man—This incident threw the whole family into confusion. My sister scolded the constable for presuming to enter the lodgings of a gentleman on such an errand, without having first asked, and obtained permission; her maid was frightened into fits, and Liddy shed tears of compassion for the unfortunate Clinker, in whose box, however, nothing was found to confirm the suspicion of robbery.

For my own part, I made no doubt of the fellow's being mistaken for some other person, and I went directly to the justice, in order to procure his discharge; but there I found the matter much more serious than I expected—Poor Clinker stood trembling at the bar, surrounded by thief-takers; and at a little distance, a thick, squat fellow, a postilion, his accuser, who had seized him in the street, and swore positively to his person, that the said Clinker had, on the 15th day of March last, on Blackheath,[1] robbed a gentleman in a post-chaise, which he (the postilion) drove—This deposition was sufficient to justify his commitment; and he was sent accordingly to Clerkenwell prison,[2] whither Jery accompanied him in the coach, in order to recommend him properly to the keeper, that he may want for no convenience which the place affords.

The spectators, who assembled to see this highwayman, were sagacious enough to discern something very villanous in his aspect; which (begging their pardon) is the very picture of simplicity; and the justice himself put a very unfavourable construction upon some of his answers, which, he said, savoured of the ambiguity and equivocation of an old offender; but, in my opinion, it would have been more just and humane to impute them to the confusion into which we may suppose a poor country lad to be thrown on such an occasion. I am

---

9. Possibly a caricature of Sir John Hawkins (1719–1789), a well-known magistrate and justice of the peace for Middlesex beginning in 1761.
1. An area known for highwaymen, six miles from London on the road to Canterbury and Dover. "Thief-taker": bounty hunter; thanks to generous rewards, this trade took off in the 18th century.
2. A house of detention on Bowling Green Lane in the Clerkenwell area of London for prisoners awaiting trial.

still persuaded he is innocent; and, in this persuasion, I can do no less than use my utmost endeavours that he may not be oppressed—I shall, to-morrow, send my nephew to wait on the gentleman who was robbed, and beg he will have the humanity to go and see the prisoner; that, in case he should find him quite different from the person of the highwayman, he may bear testimony in his behalf—Howsoever it may fare with Clinker, this cursed affair will be to me productive of intolerable chagrin—I have already caught a dreadful cold, by rushing into the open air from the justice's parlour, where I had been stewing in the crowd; and though I should not be laid up with the gout, as I believe I shall, I must stay at London for some weeks, till this poor devil comes to his trial at Rochester; so that, in all probability, my Northern expedition is blown up.

If you can find any thing in your philosophical budget, to console me in the midst of these distresses and apprehensions, pray let it be communicated to

your unfortunate friend,

London, June 12.   MATT. BRAMBLE.

To Sir WATKIN PHILLIPS, Bart. of Jesus college, Oxon.

DEAR WAT,

The farce is finished, and another piece of a graver cast brought upon the stage.——Our aunt made a desperate attack upon Barton, who had no other way of saving himself, but by leaving her in possession of the field, and avowing his pretensions to Liddy, by whom he has been rejected in his turn.—Lady Griskin acted as his advocate and agent on this occasion, with such zeal as embroiled her with Mrs. Tabitha, and a high scene of altercation passed betwixt these two religionists, which might have come to action, had not my uncle interposed. They are however reconciled, in consequence of an event which hath involved us all in trouble and disquiet. You must know, the poor preacher, Humphry Clinker, is now exercising his ministry among the felons in Clerkenwell prison.—A postilion having sworn a robbery against him, no bail could be taken, and he was committed to jail, notwithstanding all the remonstrances and interest my uncle could make in his behalf.

All things considered, the poor fellow cannot possibly be guilty, and yet, I believe, he runs some risque of being hanged.—Upon his examination, he answered with such hesitation and reserve, as persuaded most of the people, who crowded the place, that he was really a knave, and the justice's remarks confirmed their opinion. Exclusive of my uncle and myself, there was only one person who seemed inclined to favour the culprit.—He was a young man, well dressed, and, from the manner in which he cross-examined the evidence, we took it for granted, that he was a student in one of the inns of court.—He freely checked the justice for some uncharitable inferences he made to the prejudice of the prisoner, and even ventured to dispute with his worship on certain points of law.

My uncle, provoked at the unconnected and dubious answers of Clinker, who seemed in danger of falling a sacrifice to his own simplicity, exclaimed, "In the name of God, if you are innocent, say so." "No, (cried he) God forbid, that I should call myself innocent, while my conscience is burthened with sin." "What then, you did commit this robbery?" resumed his master. "No, sure, (said he) blessed be the Lord, I'm free of that guilt."

Here the justice interposed, observing, that the man seemed inclined to make a discovery by turning king's evidence, and desired the clerk to take his confession; upon which Humphry declared, that he looked upon confession to be a popish fraud, invented by the whore of Babylon.[3] The Templar[4] affirmed, that the poor fellow was *non compos*; and exhorted the justice to discharge him as a lunatic.— —"You know very well, (added he) that the robbery in question was not committed by the prisoner."

The thief-takers grinned at one another; and Mr. Justice Buzzard replied with great emotion, "Mr. Martin, I desire you will mind your own business; I shall convince you one of these days that I understand mine." In short, there was no remedy; the mittimus[5] was made out, and poor Clinker sent to prison in a hackney-coach, guarded by the constable, and accompanied by your humble servant. By the way, I was not a little surprised to hear this retainer to justice bid the prisoner to keep up his spirits, for that he did not at all doubt, but that he would get off for a few weeks confinement.—He said, his worship knew very well that Clinker was innocent of the fact, and that the real highwayman, who robbed the chaise, was no other than that very individual Mr. Martin, who had pleaded so strenuously for honest Humphry.

Confounded at this information, I asked, "Why then is he suffered to go about at his liberty, and this poor innocent fellow treated

---

3. Many Dissenters identified the biblical whore of Babylon (Revelation 17) with the Catholic Church. "Turning king's evidence": when an accused or convicted criminal testifies as a witness for the Crown against his or her associates; cf. turning state's evidence in the United States.
4. The Middle Temple and Inner Temple are two of the legal societies—collectively known as the Inns of Court—that have access to the English bar. Jery assumes that Mr. Martin studies at one of them.
5. A warrant committing a person to custody until his or her next court appearance.

as a malefactor?" "We have exact intelligence of all Mr. Martin's transactions; (said he) but as yet there is not evidence sufficient for his conviction; and as for this young man, the justice could do no less than commit him, as the postilion swore point-blank to his identity." "So if this rascally postilion should persist in the falsity to which he is sworn, (said I) this innocent lad may be brought to the gallows."

The constable observed, that he would have time enough to prepare for his trial, and might prove an *alibi*; or, perhaps, Martin might be apprehended and convicted for another fact; in which case, he might be prevailed upon to take this affair upon himself; or, finally, if these chances should fail, and the evidence stand good against Clinker, the jury might recommend him to mercy, in consideration of his youth, especially if this should appear to be the first fact of which he had been guilty.

Humphry owned, he could not pretend to recollect where he had been on the day when the robbery was committed, much less prove a circumstance of that kind so far back as six months, though he knew he had been sick of the fever and ague, which, however, did not prevent him from going about—then, turning up his eyes, he ejaculated, "The Lord's will be done! if it be my fate to suffer, I hope I shall not disgrace the faith, of which, though unworthy, I make profession."

When I expressed my surprize, that the accuser should persist in charging Clinker, without taking the least notice of the real robber, who stood before him, and to whom, indeed, Humphry bore not the smallest resemblance; the constable (who was himself a thief-taker) gave me to understand, that Mr. Martin was the best qualified for business of all the gentlemen on the road he had ever known; that he had always acted on his own bottom[6] without partner or correspondent, and never went to work, but when he was cool and sober; that his courage and presence of mind never failed him; that his address was genteel, and his behaviour void of all cruelty and insolence; that he never encumbered himself with watches or trinkets, nor even with bank-notes, but always dealt for ready money, and that in the current coin of the kingdom; and that he could disguise himself and his horse in such a manner, that, after the action, it was impossible to recognize either the one or the other—"This great man (said he) has reigned paramount in all the roads within fifty miles of London above fifteen months, and has done more business in that time, than all the rest of the profession put together; for those who pass through his hands are so delicately dealt with, that they have no desire to give him the least disturbance; but for all that, his race is almost run—he is now fluttering about justice, like a moth about a

6. On his own account, from his own resources.

candle—there are so many lime-twigs[7] laid in his way, that I'll bett a cool hundred, he swings before Christmas."

Shall I own to you, that this portrait, drawn by a ruffian, heightened by what I myself had observed in his deportment, has interested me warmly in the fate of poor Martin, whom nature seems to have intended for a useful and honourable member of that community upon which he now preys for subsistence? It seems, he lived some time as a clerk to a timber-merchant, whose daughter Martin having privately married, was discarded, and his wife turned out of doors. She did not long survive her marriage; and Martin, turning fortune-hunter, could not supply his occasions any other way, than by taking to the road, in which he has travelled hitherto with uncommon success.—He pays his respects regularly to Mr. Justice Buzzard, the thief-catcher-general of this metropolis, and sometimes they smoke a pipe together very lovingly, when the conversation generally turns upon the nature of evidence.—The justice has given him fair warning to take care of himself, and he has received his caution in good part.—Hitherto he has baffled all the vigilance, art, and activity of Buzzard and his emissaries, with such conduct as would have done honour to the genius of a Cæsar or a Turenne;[8] but he has one weakness, which has proved fatal to all the heroes of his tribe, namely, an indiscreet devotion to the fair sex, and, in all probability, he will be attacked on this defenceless quarter.

Be that as it may, I saw the body of poor Clinker consigned to the gaoler of Clerkenwell, to whose indulgence I recommended him so effectually, that he received him in the most hospitable manner, though there was a necessity for equipping him with a suit of irons, in which he made a very rueful appearance. The poor creature seemed as much affected by my uncle's kindness, as by his own misfortune. When I assured him, that nothing should be left undone for procuring his enlargement, and making his confinement easy in the mean time, he fell down on his knees, and kissing my hand, which he bathed with his tears, "O 'squire! (cried he, sobbing) what shall I say?—I can't—no, I can't speak—my poor heart is bursting with gratitude to you and my dear—dear—generous—noble benefactor."

I protest, the scene became so pathetic, that I was fain to force myself away, and returned to my uncle, who sent me in the afternoon with a compliment to one Mr. Mead, the person who had been robbed on Blackheath. As I did not find him at home, I left a message, in consequence of which he called at our lodgings this morning, and very humanely agreed to visit the prisoner. By this time, lady Griskin

---

7. Twigs smeared with birdlime (a sticky material made from holly, mistletoe, or other plants) to catch and trap small birds.
8. Henri de la Tour d'Auvergne, Vicomte de Turenne (1611–1675), a highly decorated French general. Julius Caesar (ca. 100–44 B.C.E.), a famous Roman general and politician.

had come to make her formal compliments of condolance to Mrs. Tabitha, on this domestic calamity; and that prudent maiden, whose passion was now cooled, thought proper to receive her ladyship so civilly, that a reconciliation immediately ensued. These two ladies resolved to comfort the poor prisoner in their own persons, and Mr. Mead and I 'squired them to Clerkenwell, my uncle being detained at home by some slight complaints in his stomach and bowels.

The turnkey,[9] who received us at Clerkenwell, looked remarkably sullen; and when we enquired for Clinker, "I don't care, if the devil had him; (said he) here has been nothing but canting and praying since the fellow entered the place.—Rabbit him! the tap will be ruined—we han't sold a cask of beer, nor a dozen of wine, since he paid his garnish[1]—the gentlemen get drunk with nothing but your damned religion.——For my part, I believe as how your man deals with the devil.—Two or three as bold hearts as ever took the air upon Hounslow, have been blubbering all night; and if the fellow an't speedily removed by Habeas Corpus or otherwise, I'll be damn'd if there's a grain of true spirit left within these walls—we shan't have a soul to do credit to the place, or make his exit like a true-born Englishman[2]—damn my eyes! there will be nothing but snivelling in the cart—we shall all die like so many psalm-singing weavers."

In short, we found that Humphry was, at that very instant, haranguing the felons in the chapel; and that the gaoler's wife and daughter, together with my aunt's woman, Win Jenkins, and our house-maid, were among the audience, which we immediately joined. I never saw any thing so strongly picturesque as this congregation of felons clanking their chains, in the midst of whom stood orator Clinker, expatiating, in a transport of fervor, on the torments of hell, denounced in scripture against evil-doers, comprehending murderers, robbers, thieves, and whoremongers. The variety of attention exhibited in the faces of those ragamuffins, formed a groupe that would not have disgraced the pencil of a Raphael.[3] In one, it denoted admiration; in another, doubt; in a third, disdain; in a fourth, contempt; in a fifth, terror; in a sixth, derision; and in a seventh, indignation.—As for Mrs. Winifred Jenkins, she was in tears, overwhelmed with sorrow; but whether for her own sins, or the misfortune of Clinker, I cannot

---

9. Jailer.
1. A fee demanded of a new prisoner by prison inmates, traditionally to pay for a round of drinks.
2. A phrase popularized by Daniel Defoe (ca. 1660–1731) in his satirical poem of the same name from 1701. Hounslow Heath, a large open area southwest of London, was a notorious haunt of highwaymen during the period. "Habeas corpus": a writ or legal action that requires a person under arrest to appear in person before a judge or court. The Habeas Corpus Act of 1679 codified these procedures.
3. One of the great artists of the Italian Renaissance (1483–1520).

pretend to say. The other females seemed to listen with a mixture of wonder and devotion. The gaoler's wife declared he was a saint in trouble, saying, she wished from her heart, there was such another good soul, like him, in every gaol in England.

Mr. Mead, having earnestly surveyed the preacher, declared his appearance was so different from that of the person who robbed him on Black-heath, that he could freely make oath he was not the man: but Humphry himself was by this time pretty well rid of all apprehensions of being hanged; for he had been the night before solemnly tried and acquitted by his fellow-prisoners, some of whom he had already converted to methodism. He now made proper acknowledgements for the honour of our visit, and was permitted to kiss the hands of the ladies, who assured him, he might depend upon their friendship and protection. Lady Griskin, in her great zeal, exhorted his fellow-prisoners to profit by the precious opportunity of having such a saint in bonds among them, and turn over a new leaf for the benefit of their poor souls; and, that her admonition might have the greater effect, she reinforced it with her bounty.

While she and Mrs. Tabby returned in the coach with the two maidservants, I waited on Mr. Mead to the house of justice Buzzard, who, having heard his declaration, said his oath could be of no use at present, but that he would be a material evidence for the prisoner at his trial; so that there seems to be no remedy but patience for poor Clinker; and, indeed, the same virtue, or medicine, will be necessary for us all, the 'squire in particular, who had set his heart upon his excursion to the northward.

While we were visiting honest Humphry in Clerkenwell prison, my uncle received a much more extraordinary visit at his own lodgings. Mr. Martin, of whom I have made such honourable mention, desired permission to pay him his respects, and was admitted accordingly. He told him, that having observed him, at Mr. Buzzard's, a good deal disturbed by what had happened to his servant, he had come to assure him he had nothing to apprehend for Clinker's life; for, if it was possible that any jury could find him guilty upon such evidence, he, Martin himself, would produce in court a person, whose deposition would bring him off clear as the sun at noon.—Sure, the fellow would not be so romantic as to take the robbery upon himself!—He said, the postilion was an infamous fellow, who had been a dabbler in the same profession, and saved his life at the Old Bailey by impeaching his companions; that being now reduced to great poverty, he had made this desperate push, to swear away the life of an innocent man, in hopes of having the reward upon his conviction; but that he would find himself miserably disappointed, for the justice and his myrmidons were determined to admit of no interloper in this branch of business; and that he did not at all doubt but that they would find

Humphry Clinker in prison preaching to the felons. Courtesy of the Center for Southwest Research, University Libraries, University of New Mexico.

matter enough to shop the evidence himself[4] before the next gaol-delivery. He affirmed, that all these circumstances were well known to the justice; and that his severity to Clinker was no other than a hint to his master to make him a present in private, as an acknowledgement of his candour and humanity.

This hint, however, was so unpalatable to Mr. Bramble, that he declared, with great warmth, he would rather confine himself for life to London, which he detested, than be at liberty to leave it to-morrow, in consequence of encouraging corruption in a magistrate. Hearing, however, how favorable Mr. Mead's report had been for the prisoner, he is resolved to take the advice of counsel in what manner to proceed for his immediate enlargement. I make no doubt, but that in a day or two this troublesome business may be discussed; and in this hope we are preparing for our journey. If our endeavours do not miscarry, we shall have taken the field before you hear again from

Yours,

London, June 11.   J. MELFORD.

To Dr. LEWIS.

Thank Heaven! dear Lewis, the clouds are dispersed, and I have now the clearest prospect of my summer campaign, which, I hope, I shall be able to begin to-morrow. I took the advice of counsel, with respect to the case of Clinker, in whose favour a lucky incident has intervened. The fellow who accused him, has had his own battery turned upon himself.—Two days ago, he was apprehended for a robbery on the highway, and committed, on the evidence of an accomplice. Clinker, having moved for a writ of *habeas corpus*, was brought before the lord chief justice, who, in consequence of an affidavit of the gentleman who had been robbed, importing that the said Clinker was not the person who stopped him on the highway, as well as in consideration of the postilion's character and present circumstances, was pleased to order, that my servant should be admitted to bail, and he has been discharged accordingly, to the unspeakable satisfaction of our whole family, to which he has recommended himself in an extraordinary manner, not only by his obliging deportment, but by his talents of preaching, praying, and singing psalms, which he has exercised with such effect, that even Tabby respects him as a chosen vessel. If there was any thing like affectation or hypocrisy in this excess of religion, I would not keep

4. I.e., to imprison the witness against Clinker.

him in my service; but, so far as I can observe, the fellow's character is downright simplicity, warmed with a kind of enthusiasm, which renders him very susceptible of gratitude and attachment to his benefactors.

As he is an excellent horseman, and understands farriery, I have bought a stout gelding for his use, that he may attend us on the road, and have an eye to our cattle, in case the coachman should not mind his business. My nephew, who is to ride his own saddle-horse, has taken; upon trial, a servant just come from abroad with his former master, sir William Strollop, who vouches for his honesty. The fellow, whose name is Dutton, seems to be a petit-maitre.—He has got a smattering of French, bows, and grins, and shrugs, and takes snuff *a la mode de France*,[5] but values himself chiefly upon his skill and dexterity in hair-dressing.—If I am not much deceived by appearance, he is, in all respects, the very contrast of Humphry Clinker.

My sister has made up matters with lady Griskin; though, I must own, I should not have been sorry to see that connexion entirely destroyed: but Tabby is not of a disposition to forgive Barton, who, I understand, is gone to his seat in Berkshire[6] for the summer season. I cannot help suspecting, that in the treaty of peace, which has been lately ratified betwixt those two females, it is stipulated, that her ladyship shall use her best endeavours to provide an agreeable help-mate for our sister Tabitha, who seems to be quite desperate in her matrimonial designs. Perhaps, the match-maker is to have a valuable consideration in the way of brokerage, which she will most certainly deserve, if she can find any man in his senses, who will yoke with Mrs. Bramble from motives of affection or interest.

I find my spirits and my health affect each other reciprocally— that is to say, every thing that discomposes my mind, produces a correspondent disorder in my body; and my bodily complaints are remarkably mitigated by those considerations that dissipate the clouds of mental chagrin.—The imprisonment of Clinker brought on those symptoms which I mentioned in my last, and now they are vanished at his discharge.—It must be owned, indeed, I took some of the tincture of ginseng, prepared according to your prescription, and found it exceedingly grateful to the stomach; but the pain and sickness continued to return, after short intervals, till the anxiety of my mind was entirely removed, and then I found myself perfectly at ease. We have had fair weather these ten days, to the astonishment of the Londoners, who think it portentous. If you enjoy the

---

5. Inhales cured and ground tobacco ("snuff") in the French manner.
6. A county west of London, famous for being the location of Windsor Castle, the longest-occupied royal palace in Europe.

same indulgence in Wales, I hope Barns has got my hay made, and safe cocked,[7] by this time. As we shall be in motion for some weeks, I cannot expect to hear from you as usual; but I shall continue to write from every place at which we make any halt, that you may know our track, in case it should be necessary to communicate any thing to

Your assured friend,

London, June 14. MATT. BRAMBLE.

To Mrs. MARY JONES, at Brambleton-hall, &c.

DEAR MARY,

Having the occasion of my cousin Jenkins of Aberga'ny, I send you, as a token, a turkey-shell comb, a kiple of yards of green ribbon, and a sarment upon the nothingness of good works, which was preached in the Tabernacle; and you will also recieve a horn buck for Saul, whereby she may learn her letters; for I'm much consarned about the state of her poor sole—and what are all the pursuits of this life to the consarns of that immortal part?—What is life but a veil of affliction? O Mary! the whole family have been in such a constipation!—Mr. Clinker has been in trouble, but the gates of hell have not been able to prevail again him.——His virtue is like poor gould, seven times tried in the fire. He was tuck up for a rubbery, and had before gustass Busshard, who made his mittamouse; and the pore youth was sent to prison upon the false oaf of a willian, that wanted to sware his life away for the looker of cain.

The 'squire did all in his power, but could not prevent his being put in chains, and confined among common manufactors, where he stud like an innocent sheep in the midst of wolves and tygers.—Lord knows, what mought have happened to this pyehouse young man, if master had not applied to Apias Korkus, who lives with the ould bailiff, and is, they say, five hundred years ould, (God bless us!) and a congeror: but, if he be, sure I am he don't deal with the devil, otherwise he wouldn't have sought out Mr. Clinker, as he did, in spite of stone walls, iron bolts, and double locks, that flew open at his command; for Ould Scratch[8] has not a greater enemy upon hearth than Mr. Clinker, who is, indeed, a very powerfull labourer in the Lord's vineyard. I do no more than yuse the words of my good lady, who has got the infectual calling; and, I trust, that even myself, though unworthy, shall find grease to be excepted.——Miss

7. Securely stored.
8. Satan.

Liddy has been touch'd to the quick, but is a little timorsome: how-somever, I make no doubt, but she, and all of us, will be brought, by the endeavours of Mr. Clinker, to produce blessed fruit of genera-tion and repentance.——As for master and the young 'squire, they have as yet had narro glimpse of the new light.——I doubt as how their harts are hardened by worldly wisdom, which, as the pyebill faith, is foolishness in the sight of God.

O Mary Jones, pray without seizing for grease to prepare you for the operations of this wonderful instrument, which, I hope, will be exorcised this winter upon you and others at Brambleton-hall.—— To-morrow, we are to set out in a cox and four for Yorkshire; and, I believe, we shall travel that way far, and far, and farther than I can tell; but I shan't go so far as to forget my friends; and Mary Jones will always be remembred as one of them by her

humble sarvant,

London, June 14.   WIN. JENKINS.

To Mrs. GWYLLIM, house-keeper at Brambleton-hall.

MRS. GWILLIM,

I can't help thinking it very strange, that I never had an answer to the letter I wrote you some weeks ago from Bath, concerning the sour bear, the gander, and the maids eating butter, which I won't allow to be wasted.——We are now going upon a long gurney to the north, whereby I desire you will redouble your care and circumflex-ion, that the family may be well manged in our absence; for, you know, you must render accunt, not only to your earthly master, but also to him that is above; and if you are found a good and faithfull sarvant, great will be your reward in haven. I hope there will be twenty stun of cheese ready for market by the time I get huom, and as much owl spun, as will make half a dozen pair of blankets; and that the savings of the butter-milk fetch me a good penny before Martinmass, as the two pigs are to be fed for baking with bitchmast and acrons.[9]

I wrote to doctor Lews for the same porpuss, but he never had the good manners to take the least notice of my letter; for which reason, I shall never favour him with another, though he beshits me on his bended knees. You will do well to keep a watchfull eye over

---

9. The fruit of the beech tree, called mast, and acorns were used as feed for pigs. "Martin-mass": the Feast of Saint Martin (November 11) was traditionally a day for holding fairs and slaughtering livestock for winter.

the hind Villiams, who is one of his amissories, and, I believe, no better than he should be at bottom. God forbid that I should lack christian charity; but charity begins at huom, and sure nothing can be a more charitable work than to rid the family of such vermine. I do suppose, that the brindled cow has been had to the parson's bull, that old Moll has had another litter of pigs, and that Dick is become a mighty mouser. Pray order every thing for the best, and be frugal, and keep the maids to their labour.—If I had a private opportunity, I would send them some hymns to sing instead of profane ballads; but, as I can't, they and you must be contented with the prayers of

Your assured friend,

London, June 14.   T. BRAMBLE.

To Sir WATKIN PHILLIPS, Bar^t.
of Jesus college, Oxon.

DEAR PHILLIPS,

The very day after I wrote my last, Clinker was set at liberty—As Martin had foretold, the accuser was himself committed for a robbery, upon unquestionable evidence. He had been for some time in the snares of the thief-taking society; who, resenting his presumption in attempting to incroach upon their monopoly of impeachment, had him taken up and committed to Newgate, on the deposition of an accomplice, who has been admitted as evidence for the king. The postilion being upon record as an old offender, the chief justice made no scruple of admitting Clinker to bail, when he perused the affidavit of Mr. Mead, importing that the said Clinker was not the person that robbed him on Blackheath; and honest Humphry was discharged— When he came home, he expressed great eagerness to pay his respects to his master, and here his elocution failed him, but his silence was pathetic; he fell down at his feet, and embraced his knees, sheding a flood of tears, which my uncle did not see without emotion—He took snuff in some confusion; and, putting his hand in his pocket, gave him his blessing in something more substantial than words— "Clinker, (said he) I am so well convinced, both of your honesty and courage, that I am resolved to make you my life-guard-man on the highway."

He was accordingly provided with a case of pistols, and a carbine to be slung across his shoulders; and every other preparation being made, we set out last Thursday, at seven in the morning; my uncle, with the three women in the coach; Humphry, well mounted on a black gelding bought for his use; myself a-horseback, attended by my new valet, Mr. Dutton, an exceeding coxcomb, fresh from his travels, whom I have taken upon trial—The fellow wears a solitaire, uses paint, and takes rappee with all the grimace of a French marquis.[1] At present, however, he is in a riding-dress, jack-boots, leather breeches, a scarlet waistcoat, with gold binding, a laced hat, a hanger, a French posting-whip in his hand, and his hair en queue.[2]

Before we had gone nine miles, my horse lost one of his shoes; so that I was obliged to stop at Barnet to have another, while the coach proceeded at an easy pace over the common. About a mile short of Hatfield,[3] the postilions, stopping the carriage, gave notice to Clinker that there were two suspicious fellows a-horse-back, at the end of a lane, who seemed waiting to attack the coach. Humphry forthwith apprised my uncle, declaring he would stand by him to the last drop of his blood; and, unslinging his carbine, prepared for action. The 'squire had pistols in the pockets of the coach, and resolved to make use of them directly; but he was effectually prevented by his female companions, who flung themselves about his neck, and screamed in concert—At that instant, who should come up at a hand-gallop, but Martin, the highway-man, who, advancing to the coach, begged the ladies would compose themselves for a moment; then, desiring Clinker to follow him to the charge, he pulled a pistol out of his bosom, and they rode up together to give battle to the rogues, who, having fired at a great distance, fled across the common. They were in pursuit of the fugitives when I came up, not a little alarmed at the shreiks in the coach, where I found my uncle in a violent rage, without his periwig, struggling to disentangle himself from Tabby and the other two, and swearing with great vociferation. Before I had time to interpose, Martin and Clinker returned from the pursuit, and the former payed his compliments with great politeness, giving us to understand, that the fellows had scampered off, and that he believed they were a couple of raw 'prentices from London. He commended Clinker for his courage, and said, if we would give him leave, he would have the honour to accompany us as far as Stevenage,[4] where he had some business.

The 'squire, having recollected and adjusted himself, was the first to laugh at his own situation; but it was not without difficulty, that Tabby's arms could be untwisted from his neck, Liddy's teeth chattered, and Jenkins was threatened with a fit as usual. I had communicated to my uncle the character of Martin, as it was

---

1. I.e., wears a loose necktie, applies makeup, and takes strong snuff with all the distorted facial expressions of a French nobleman.
2. In a tail or braid. "Hanger": a light sword, still in fashion among the upper classes in England.
3. A residential suburb of London in Hertfordshire.
4. An old Hertfordshire town known for its high-quality coaching inns.

described by the constable, and he was much struck with its singularity—He could not suppose the fellow had any design on our company, which was so numerous and well armed; he therefore thanked him, for the service he had just done them, said he would be glad of his company, and asked him to dine with us at Hatfield. This invitation might not have been agreeable to the ladies, had they known the real profession of our guest, but this was a secret to all, except my uncle and myself—Mrs. Tabitha, however, would by no means consent to proceed with a case of loaded pistols in the coach, and they were forthwith discharged in complaisance to her and the rest of the women.

Being gratified in this particular, she became remarkably good-humoured, and at dinner behaved in the most affable manner to Mr. Martin, with whose polite address and agreeable conversation she seemed to be much taken. After dinner, the landlord accosting me in the yard, asked, with a significant look, if the gentleman that rode the sorrel belonged to our company?—I understood his meaning, but answered, no; that he had come up with us on the common, and helped us to drive away two fellows, that looked like highwaymen—He nodded three times distinctly, as much as to say, he knows his cue. Then he inquired, if one of those men was mounted on a bay mare, and the other on a chesnut gelding with a white streak down his forehead? and being answered in the affirmative, he assured me they had robbed three post-chaises this very morning—I inquired, in my turn, if Mr. Martin was of his acquaintance; and, nodding thrice again, he answered, that *he had seen the gentleman*.

Before we left Hatfield, my uncle, fixing his eyes on Martin with such expression as is more easily conceived than described, asked, if he often travelled that road? and he replied with a look which denoted his understanding the question, that he very seldom did business in that part of the country. In a word, this adventurer favoured us with his company to the neighbourhood of Stevenage, where he took his leave of the coach and me, in very polite terms, and turned off upon a cross-road, that led to a village on the left—At supper, Mrs. Tabby was very full in the praise of Mr. Martin's good-sense and good-breeding, and seemed to regret that she had not a further opportunity to make some experiment upon his affection. In the morning, my uncle was not a little surprised to receive, from the waiter, a billet couched in these words—

"Sir,

"I could easily perceive from your looks, when I had the honour to converse with you at Hatfield, that my character is not unknown to you; and, I dare say, you won't think it strange, that I should be glad to change my present way of life, for any other honest occupation, let it be ever so humble, that will afford me bread in moderation, and sleep in safety—Perhaps you may think I flatter, when I say, that from the moment I was witness to your generous concern in the cause of your servant, I conceived a particular esteem and veneration for your person; and yet what I say is true. I should think myself happy, if I could be admitted into your protection and service, as house-steward, clerk, butler, or bailiff, for either of which places I think myself tolerably well qualified; and, sure I am, I should not be found deficient in gratitude and fidelity—At the same time, I am very sensible how much you must deviate from the common maxims of discretion, even in putting my professions to the trial; but I don't look upon you as a person that thinks in the ordinary stile; and the delicacy of my situation, will, I know, justify this address to a heart warmed with beneficence and compassion—Understanding you are going pretty far north, I shall take an opportunity to throw myself in your way again, before you reach the borders of Scotland; and, I hope, by that time, you will have taken into consideration, the truly distressful case of,

honoured sir,

your very humble,

and devoted servant,

Edward Martin.

The 'squire, having perused this letter, put it into my hand, without saying a syllable; and when I had read it, we looked at each other in silence. From a certain sparkling in his eyes, I discovered there was more in his heart, than he cared to express with his tongue, in favour of poor Martin; and this was precisely my own feeling, which he did not fail to discern, by the same means of communication—"What shall we do (said he) to save this poor sinner from the gallows, and make him a useful member of the commonwealth? and yet the proverb says, Save a thief from the gallows, and he'll cut your throat." I told him, I really believed Martin was capable of giving the proverb the lie; and that I should heartily concur in any step he might take in favour of his sollicitation. We mutually resolved to deliberate upon the subject, and, in the mean time, proceeded on our journey. The roads, having been broke up by the heavy rains in the spring, were so rough, that although we travelled very slowly, the jolting occasioned such pain to my uncle, that he was become exceedingly peevish when we arrived at this place, which lies about eight miles from the post-road, between Wetherby and Boroughbridge.[5]

5. Market towns in West Yorkshire and North Yorkshire, respectively.

Harrigate-water,[6] so celebrated for its efficacy in the scurvy and other distempers, is supplied from a copious spring, in the hollow of a wild common, round which, a good many houses have been built for the convenience of the drinkers, though few of them are inhabited. Most of the company lodge at some distance, in five separate inns, situated in different parts of the common, from whence they go every morning to the well, in their own carriages. The lodgers of each inn form a distinct society, that eat together; and there is a commodious public room, where they breakfast in dishabille, at separate tables, from eight o'clock till eleven, as they chance or chuse to come in— Here also they drink tea in the afternoon, and play at cards or dance in the evening. One custom, however, prevails, which I look upon as a solecism in politeness—The ladies treat with tea in their turns; and even girls of sixteen are not exempted from this shameful imposition——There is a public ball by subscription every night at one of the houses, to which all the company from the others are admitted by tickets; and, indeed, Harrigate treads upon the heels of Bath, in the articles of gaiety and dissipation—with this difference, however, that here we are more sociable and familiar. One of the inns is already full up to the very garrets, having no less than fifty lodgers, and as many servants. Our family does not exceed thirty-six; and I should be sorry to see the number augmented, as our accommodations won't admit of much increase.

At present, the company is more agreeable than one could expect from an accidental assemblage of persons, who are utter strangers to one another—There seems to be a general disposition among us to maintain good-fellowship, and promote the purposes of humanity, in favour of those who come hither on the score of health. I see several faces which we left at Bath, although the majority are of the Northern counties, and many come from Scotland for the benefit of these waters—In such a variety, there must be some originals, among whom Mrs. Tabitha Bramble is not the most inconsiderable—No place where there is such an intercourse between the sexes, can be disagreeable to a lady of her views and temperament—She has had some warm disputes at table, with a lame parson from Northumberland, on the new birth, and the insignificance of moral virtue; and her arguments have been reinforced by an old Scotch lawyer, in a tye periwig, who, though he has lost his teeth, and the use of his limbs, can still wag his tongue with great volubility. He has paid her such fulsome compliments, upon her piety and learning, as seem to have won her heart; and she, in her turn, treats him with such attention as indicates a design upon his person; but, by all accounts,

6. Water from the mineral wells at Harrogate, a spa town in North Yorkshire.

he is too much a fox to be inveigled into any snare that she can lay for his affection.

We do not propose to stay long at Harrigate, though, at present, it is our headquarters, from whence we shall make some excursions, to visit two or three of our rich relations, who are settled in this county.——Pray, remember me to all our friends of Jesus, and allow me to be still

yours affectionately,

Harrigate, June 23.   J. Melford.

To Dr. Lewis.

Dear Doctor,

Considering the tax we pay for turnpikes, the roads of this country constitute a most intolerable grievance. Between Newark[7] and Weatherby, I have suffered more from jolting and swinging than ever I felt in the whole course of my life, although the carriage is remarkably commodious and well hung, and the postilions were very careful in driving. I am now safely housed at the New Inn, at Harrigate, whither I came to satisfy my curiosity, rather than with any view of advantage to my health; and, truly, after having considered all the parts and particulars of the place, I cannot account for the concourse of people one finds here, upon any other principle but that of caprice, which seems to be the character of our nation.

Harrigate is a wild common, bare and bleak, without tree or shrub, or the least signs of cultivation; and the people who come to drink the water, are crowded together in paltry inns, where the few tolerable rooms are monopolized by the friends and favourites of the house, and all the rest of the lodgers are obliged to put up with dirty holes, where there is neither space, air, nor convenience. My apartment is about ten feet square; and when the folding bed is down, there is just room sufficient to pass between it and the fire. One might expect, indeed, that there would be no occasion for a fire at Midsummer; but here the climate is so backward, that an ash tree, which our landlord has planted before my window, is just beginning to put forth its leaves; and I am fain to have my bed warmed every night.

As for the water, which is said to have effected so many surprising cures, I have drank it once, and the first draught has cured me of all desire to repeat the medicine.—Some people say it smells of rotten

7. A market town in Nottinghamshire, on the River Trent.

eggs, and others compare it to the scourings of a foul gun.—It is generally supposed to be strongly impregnated with sulphur; and Dr. Shaw, in his book upon mineral waters, says, he has seen flakes of sulphur floating in the well.—*Pace tanti viri;*[8] I, for my part, have never observed any thing like sulphur, either in or about the well, neither do I find that any brimstone has ever been extracted from the water. As for the smell, if I may be allowed to judge from my own organs, it is exactly that of bilge-water; and the saline taste of it seems to declare that it is nothing else than salt water putrified in the bowels of the earth. I was obliged to hold my nose with one hand, while I advanced the glass to my mouth with the other; and after I had made shift to swallow it, my stomach could hardly retain what it had received.—The only effects it produced were sickness, griping, and insurmountable disgust.——I can hardly mention it without puking.——The world is strangely misled by the affectation of singularity. I cannot help suspecting, that this water owes its reputation in a great measure to its being so strikingly offensive.—On the same kind of analogy, a German doctor has introduced hemlock and other poisons, as specifics, into the *materia medica.*[9]—I am persuaded, that all the cures ascribed to the Harrigate water, would have been as efficaciously, and infinitely more agreeably performed, by the internal and external use of sea-water.[1] Sure I am, this last is much less nauseous to the taste and smell, and much more gentle in its operation as a purge, as well as more extensive in its medical qualities.

Two days ago, we went across the country to visit 'squire Burdock, who married a first cousin of my father, an heiress, who brought him an estate of a thousand a year. This gentleman is a declared opponent of the ministry in parliament; and having an opulent fortune, piques himself upon living in the country, and maintaining *old English hospitality.*——By the bye, this is a phrase very much used by the English themselves, both in words and writing; but I never heard of it out of the island, except by way of irony and sarcasm. What the hospitality of our fore-fathers has been I should be glad to see recorded, rather in the memoirs of strangers who have visited our country, and were the proper objects and judges of such hospitality, than in the discourse and lucubrations of the modern English, who seem to describe it from theory and conjecture. Certain it is, we are generally looked upon by foreigners, as a people totally destitute of

8. With all due respect to the great man (Latin). Peter Shaw (1694–1763), physician to George II and George III, and translator of F. Hoffman's *New Experiments and Observations upon Mineral Waters* (1746).
9. List of substances used in treating diseases (Latin). "German doctor": possibly Anton von Storeck (1731–1803), who wrote a treatise on hemlock reviewed in the *Critical Review.*
1. Smollett published his own treatise on the external uses of water in 1752 (see pp. 361–63).

this virtue; and I never was in any country abroad, where I did not meet with persons of distinction, who complained of having been inhospitably used in Great Britain. A gentleman of France, Italy, or Germany, who has entertained and lodged an Englishman at his house, when he afterwards meets with his guest at London, is asked to dinner at the Saracen's-head, the Turk's-head, the Boar's-head, or the Bear,[2] eats raw beef and butter, drinks execrable port, and is allowed to pay his share of the reckoning.

But to return from this digression, which my feeling for the honour of my country obliged me to make——our Yorkshire cousin has been a mighty fox-hunter *before the Lord*;[3] but now he is too fat and unwieldy to leap ditches and five-bar gates; nevertheless, he still keeps a pack of hounds, which are well exercised; and his huntsman every night entertains him with the adventures of the day's chace, which he recites in a tone and terms that are extremely curious and significant. In the mean time, his broad brawn is scratched by one of his grooms.——This fellow, it seems, having no inclination to curry any beast out of the stable, was at great pains to scollop his nails in such a manner that the blood followed at every stroke.——He was in hopes that he would be dismissed from this disagreeable office, but the event turned out contrary to his expectation.——His master declared he was the best scratcher in the family; and now he will not suffer any other servant to draw a nail upon his carcase.

The 'squire's lady is very proud, without being stiff or inaccessible.——She receives even her inferiors in point of fortune with a kind of arrogant civility; but then she thinks she has a right to treat them with the most ungracious freedoms of speech, and never fails to let them know she is sensible of her own superior affluence.—— In a word, she speaks well of no living soul, and has not one single friend in the world. Her husband hates her mortally; but, although the brute is sometimes so very powerful in him that he will have his own way, he generally truckles to her dominion, and dreads, like a school-boy, the lash of her tongue. On the other hand, she is afraid of provoking him too far, lest he should make some desperate effort to shake off her yoke.—She, therefore, acquiesces in the proofs he daily gives of his attachment to the liberty of an English freeholder, by saying and doing, at his own table, whatever gratifies the brutality of his disposition, or contributes to the ease of his person. The house, though large, is neither elegant nor comfortable.—It looks like a great inn, crowded with travellers, who dine at the landlord's ordinary, where there is a great profusion of victuals and drink, but

2. Pubs and coaching inns in various parts of London.
3. An allusion to Nimrod, the mighty biblical hunter (Genesis 10:8–12).

mine host seems to be misplaced; and I would rather dine upon filberts with a hermit, than feed upon venison with a hog. The footmen
might be aptly compared to the waiters of a tavern, if they were
more serviceable and less rapacious; but they are generally insolent
and inattentive, and so greedy, that, I think, I can dine better, and
for less expence, at the Star and Garter[4] in Pall mall, than at our
cousin's castle in Yorkshire. The 'squire is not only accommodated
with a wife, but he is also blessed with an only son, about two and
twenty, just returned from Italy, a complete fidler and *dillettante*;
and he slips no opportunity of manifesting the most perfect contempt
for his own father.

When we arrived, there was a family of foreigners at the house,
on a visit to this virtuoso, with whom they had been acquainted at
the Spa: it was the count de Melville, with his lady,[5] on their way to
Scotland. Mr. Burdock had met with an accident, in consequence of
which both the count and I would have retired, but the young gentleman and his mother insisted upon our staying dinner; and their
serenity seemed to be so little ruffled by what had happened, that
we complied with their invitation. The 'squire had been brought
home over night in his post-chaise, so terribly belaboured about the
pate,[6] that he seemed to be in a state of stupefaction, and had ever
since remained speechless. A country apothecary, called Grieve,
who lived in a neighbouring village, having been called to his assistance, had let him blood, and applied a poultice to his head, declaring, that he had no fever, nor any other bad symptom but the loss of
speech, if he really had lost that faculty. But the young 'squire said
this practitioner was an *ignorantaccio*, that there was a fracture in
the *cranium*, and that there was a necessity for having him trepanned[7]
without loss of time. His mother, espousing this opinion, had sent
an express to York for a surgeon to perform the operation, and he
was already come with his 'prentice and instruments. Having examined the patient's head, he began to prepare his dressings; though
Grieve still retained his first opinion that there was no fracture, and
was the more confirmed in it as the 'squire had passed the night in
profound sleep, uninterrupted by any catching or convulsion. The
York surgeon said he could not tell whether there was a fracture,
until he should take off the scalp; but, at any rate, the operation
might be of service in giving vent to any blood that might be extrav-
asated, either above or below the *dura mater*. The lady and her son

4. A famous tavern noted for its wine.
5. These are characters from Smollett's earlier novel, *The Adventures of Ferdinand, Count
Fathom* (1753).
6. I.e., with serious head injuries.
7. Literally, to be operated on with a trepan (a bone saw for the skull); figuratively, to be
tricked.

were clear for trying the experiment; and Grieve was dismissed with some marks of contempt, which, perhaps, he owed to the plainness of his appearance. He seemed to be about the middle age, wore his own black hair without any sort of dressing; by his garb, one would have taken him for a quaker, but he had none of the stiffness of that sect, on the contrary, he was very submissive, respectful, and remarkably taciturn.

Leaving the ladies in an apartment by themselves, we adjourned to the patient's chamber, where the dressings and instruments were displayed in order upon a pewter dish. The operator, laying aside his coat and periwig, equipped himself with a night-cap, apron, and sleeves, while his 'prentice and footman, seizing the 'squire's head, began to place it in a proper posture.——But mark what followed.— The patient, bolting upright in the bed, collared each of these assistants with the grasp of Hercules, exclaiming, in a bellowing tone, "I ha'n't lived so long in Yorkshire to be trepanned by such vermin as you;" and leaping on the floor, put on his breeches quietly, to the astonishment of us all. The surgeon still insisted upon the operation, alledging it was now plain that the brain was injured, and desiring the servants to put him into bed again; but no body would venture to execute his orders, or even to interpose: when the 'squire turned him and his assistants out of doors, and threw his apparatus out at the window. Having thus asserted his prerogative, and put on his cloaths with the help of a valet, the count, with my nephew and me, were introduced by his son, and received with his usual stile of rustic civility; then turning to signor Macaroni, with a sarcastic grin, "I tell thee what, Dick, (said he) a man's scull is not to be bored every time his head is broken; and I'll convince thee and thy mother, that I know as many tricks as e'er an old fox in the West Riding."[8]

We afterwards understood he had quarrelled at a public house with an exciseman,[9] whom he challenged to a bout at single stick, in which he had been worsted; and that the shame of this defeat had tied up his tongue. As for madam, she had shewn no concern for his disaster, and now heard of his recovery without emotion.— She had taken some little notice of my sister and niece, though rather with a view to indulge her own petulance, than out of any sentiment of regard to our family.—She said Liddy was a fright, and ordered her woman to adjust her head before dinner; but she would not meddle with Tabby, whose spirit, she soon perceived, was not to be irritated with impunity. At table, she acknowledged me so far as to say she had heard of my father; though she hinted, that he had

8. Administrative district. Yorkshire is broken into three: East, West, and North. "Macaroni": a derogatory name for a young Englishman who returned from travels abroad with European manners and tastes.
9. Tax agent.

disobliged her family by making a poor match in Wales. She was disagreeably familiar in her enquiries about our circumstances; and asked, if I intended to bring up my nephew to the law. I told her, that, as he had an independent fortune, he should follow no profession but that of a country gentleman; and that I was not without hopes of procuring for him a seat in parliament.——"Pray, cousin, (said she) what may his fortune be?" When I answered, that, with what I should be able to give him, he would have better than two thousand a year, she replied, with a disdainful toss of her head, that it would be impossible for him to preserve his independence on such a paltry provision.

Not a little nettled at this arrogant remark, I told her, I had the honour to sit in parliament with her father, when he had little more than half that income; and I believed there was not a more independent and incorruptible member in the house. "Ay; but times are changed, (cried the 'squire)—Country gentlemen now-a-days live after another fashion.—My table alone stands me in a cool thousand a quarter, though I raise my own stock, import my own liquors, and have every thing at the first hand.—True it is, I keep open house, and receive all comers, for the honour of Old England." "If that be the case, (said I) 'tis a wonder you can maintain it at so small an expence; but every private gentleman is not expected to keep a *caravansera*[1] for the accommodation of travellers: indeed, if every individual lived in the same stile, you would not have such a number of guests at your table, of consequence your hospitality would not shine so bright for the glory of the West Riding." The young 'squire, tickled by this ironical observation, exclaimed, "O *che burla!*"[2]—his mother eyed me in silence with a supercilious air; and the father of the feast, taking a bumper of October,[3] "My service to you, cousin Bramble, (said he) I have always heard there was something keen and biting in the air of the Welch mountains."

I was much pleased with the count de Melville, who is sensible, easy, and polite; and the countess is the most amiable woman I ever beheld. In the afternoon they took leave of their entertainers, and the young gentleman, mounting his horse, undertook to conduct their coach through the park, while one of their servants rode round to give notice to the rest, whom they had left at a public house on the road. The moment their backs were turned, the censorious dæmon took possession of our Yorkshire landlady and our sister Tabitha.— The former observed, that the countess was a good sort of a body,

---

1. A type of inn, common in eastern Europe, with a large interior quadrangle for accommodating caravans of travelers.
2. Oh what a joke! (Italian).
3. A large mug of strong autumn ale.

but totally ignorant of good breeding, consequently aukward in her address. The 'squire said he did not pretend to the breeding of any thing but colts; but that the jade would be very handsome, if she was a little more in flesh. "Handsome! (cried Tabby) she has indeed a pair of black eyes without any meaning; but then there is not a good feature in her face." "I know not what you call good features in Wales; (replied our landlord) but they'll pass in Yorkshire." Then turning to Liddy, he added, "What say you, my pretty Redstreak?[4]—what is your opinion of the countess?" "I think, (cried Liddy, with great emotion) she's an angel." Tabby chid her for talking with such freedom in company; and the lady of the house said, in a contemptuous tone, she supposed miss had been brought up at some country boarding-school.

Our conversation was suddenly interrupted by the young gentleman, who galloped into the yard all aghast, exclaiming, that the coach was attacked by a great number of highwaymen. My nephew and I rushing out, found his own and his servant's horse ready saddled in the stable, with pistols in the caps.—We mounted instantly, ordering Clinker and Dutton to follow with all possible expedition; but notwithstanding all the speed we could make, the action was over before we arrived, and the count with his lady, safe lodged at the house of Grieve, who had signalized himself in a very remarkable manner on this occasion. At the turning of a lane, that led to the village where the count's servants remained, a couple of robbers a-horseback suddenly appeared, with their pistols advanced: one kept the coachman in awe, and the other demanded the count's money, while the young 'squire went off at full speed, without ever casting a look behind. The count desiring the thief to withdraw his pistol, as the lady was in great terror, delivered his purse without making the least resistance; but not satisfied with this booty, which was pretty considerable, the rascal insisted upon rifling her of her ear-rings and necklace, and the countess screamed with affright. Her husband, exasperated at the violence with which she was threatened, wrested the pistol out of the fellow's hand, and turning it upon him, snapped it in his face; but the robber knowing there was no charge in it, drew another from his bosom, and in all probability would have killed him on the spot, had not his life been saved by a wonderful interposition. Grieve, the apothecary, chancing to pass that very instant, ran up to the coach, and with a crabstick, which was all the weapon he had, brought the fellow to the ground with the first blow; then seizing his pistol, presented it to his colleague,[5] who fired his piece at random, and fled without further opposition.

4. A common apple used for cider.
5. I.e., aimed it at the second highwayman.

The other was secured by the assistance of the count and the coachman; and his legs being tied under the belly of his own horse, Grieve conducted him to the village, whither also the carriage proceeded. It was with great difficulty the countess could be kept from swooning; but at last she was happily conveyed to the house of the apothecary, who went into the shop to prepare some drops for her, while his wife and daughter administered to her in another apartment.

I found the count standing in the kitchen with the parson of the parish, and expressing much impatience to see his protector, whom as yet he had scarce found time to thank for the essential service he had done him and the countess.—The daughter passing at the same time with a glass of water, monsieur de Melville could not help taking notice of her figure, which was strikingly engaging.—"Ay, (said the parson) she is the prettiest girl, and the best girl in all my parish; and if I could give my son an estate of ten thousand a year, he should have my consent to lay it at her feet. If Mr. Grieve had been as sollicitous about getting money, as he has been in performing all the duties of a primitive Christian, Fy would not have hung so long upon his hands." "What is her name?" said I. "Sixteen years ago (answered the vicar) I christened her by the names of Seraphina Melvilia." "Ha! what! how! (cried the count eagerly) sure, you said Seraphina Melvilia." "I did; (said he) Mr. Grieve told me those were the names of two noble persons abroad, to whom he had been obliged for more than life."

The count, without speaking another syllable, rushed into the parlour, crying, "This is your god-daughter, my dear." Mrs. Grieve, then seizing the countess by the hand, exclaimed with great agitation, "O madam!—O sir!—I am—I am your poor Elinor.——This is my Seraphina Melvilia.——O child! these are the count and countess of Melville, the generous—the glorious benefactors of thy once unhappy parents."

The countess rising from her seat, threw her arms about the neck of the amiable Seraphina, and clasped her to her breast with great tenderness, while she herself was embraced by the weeping mother. This moving scene was completed by the entrance of Grieve himself, who falling on his knees before the count, "Behold (said he) a penitent, who at length can look upon his patron without shrinking." "Ah, Ferdinand! (cried he, raising and folding him in his arms) the play-fellow of my infancy—the companion of my youth!—Is it to you then I am indebted for my life?" "Heaven has heard my prayer, (said the other) and given me an opportunity to prove myself not altogether unworthy of your clemency and protection." He then kissed the hand of the countess, while monsieur de Melville saluted his wife and lovely daughter, and all of us were greatly affected by this pathetic recognition.

In a word, Grieve was no other than Ferdinand count Fathom, whose adventures were printed many years ago. Being a sincere convert to virtue, he had changed his name, that he might elude the enquiries of the count, whose generous allowance he determined to forego, that he might have no dependence but upon his own industry and moderation. He had accordingly settled in this village as a practitioner in surgery and physic, and for some years wrestled with all the miseries of indigence, which, however, he and his wife had borne with the most exemplary resignation. At length, by dint of unwearied attention to the duties of his profession, which he exercised with equal humanity and success, he had acquired a tolerable share of business among the farmers and common people, which enabled him to live in a decent manner. He had been scarce ever seen to smile; was unaffectedly pious; and all the time he could spare from the avocations of his employment he spent in educating his daughter, and in studying for his own improvement.—In short, the adventurer Fathom was, under the name of Grieve, universally respected among the commonalty of this district, as a prodigy of learning and virtue. These particulars I learned from the vicar, when we quitted the room, that they might be under no restraint in their mutual effusions. I make no doubt that Grieve will be pressed to leave off business, and re-unite himself to the count's family; and as the countess seemed extremely fond of his daughter, she will, in all probability, insist upon Seraphina's accompanying her to Scotland.

Having paid our compliments to these noble persons, we returned to the 'squire's, where we expected an invitation to pass the night, which was wet and raw; but, it seems, 'squire Burdock's hospitality reached not so far for the honour of Yorkshire: we therefore departed in the evening, and lay at an inn, where I caught cold.

In hope of riding it down before it could take fast hold on my constitution, I resolved to visit another relation, one Mr. Pimpernel, who lived about a dozen miles from the place where we lodged. Pimpernel being the youngest of four sons, was bred an attorney at Furnival's-inn;[6] but all his elder brothers dying, he got himself called to the bar for the honour of his family, and soon after this preferment, succeeded to his father's estate, which was very considerable. He carried home with him all the knavish chicanery of the lowest pettifogger, together with a wife whom he had purchased of a drayman for twenty pounds; and he soon found means to obtain a *Dedimus*[7] as an acting justice of peace. He is not only a sordid miser in his disposition, but his avarice is mingled with a spirit of despotism,

---

6. An Inn of the Court of Chancery where solicitors ("attorneys") had their offices and frequently their homes.
7. A court order that allows a person who is not a judge to act in place of one. "Drayman": a driver of a low, strong cart without fixed sides.

which is truly diabolical.—He is a brutal husband, an unnatural parent, a harsh master, an oppressive landlord, a litigious neighbour, and a partial magistrate.——Friends he has none; and in point of hospitality and good breeding, our cousin Burdock is a prince in comparison of this ungracious miscreant, whose house is the lively representation of a gaol. Our reception was suitable to the character I have sketched. Had it depended upon the wife, we should have been kindly treated.—She is really a good sort of a woman, in spite of her low original, and well respected in the county; but she has not interest enough in her own house to command a draught of table-beer, far less to bestow any kind of education on her children, who run about, like ragged colts, in a state of nature.—Pox on him! he is such a dirty fellow, that I have not patience to prosecute the subject.

By that time we reached Harrigate, I began to be visited by certain rheumatic symptoms. The Scotch lawyer, Mr. Micklewhimmen, recommended a hot bath of these waters so earnestly, that I was over-persuaded to try the experiment.—He had used it often with success, and always stayed an hour in the bath, which was a tub filled with Harrigate water, heated for the purpose. If I could hardly bear the smell of a single tumbler when cold, you may guess how my nose was regaled by the steams arising from a hot bath of the same fluid. At night, I was conducted into a dark hole on the ground floor, where the tub smoaked and stunk like the pot of Acheron,[8] in one corner, and in another stood a dirty bed provided with thick blankets, in which I was to sweat after coming out of the bath. My heart seemed to die within me when I entered this dismal bagnio,[9] and found my brain assaulted by such insufferable effluvia.—I cursed Micklewhimmen for not considering that my organs were formed on this side of the Tweed;[1] but being ashamed to recoil upon the threshold, I submitted to the process.

After having endured all but real suffocation for above a quarter of an hour in the tub, I was moved to the bed and wrapped in blankets.—There I lay a full hour panting with intolerable heat; but not the least moisture appearing on my skin, I was carried to my own chamber, and passed the night without closing an eye, in such a flutter of spirits as rendered me the most miserable wretch in being. I should certainly have run distracted, if the rarefaction of my blood, occasioned by that Stygian bath,[2] had not burst the vessels, and produced a violent hæmorrhage, which, though dreadful and alarming, removed

8. In Greek mythology, the confluence of the Acheron and Cocytus Rivers in Hades (the underworld).
9. Italianate term for a bath.
1. The river that forms a natural border between Scotland and England.
2. The River Styx, the principal river in Hades.

the horrible disquiet.—I lost two pounds of blood, and more, on this occasion; and find myself still weak and languid; but, I believe, a little exercise will forward my recovery; and therefore I am resolved to set out to-morrow for York, in my way to Scarborough, where I propose to brace up my fibres by sea-bathing, which, I know, is one of your favourite specifics. There is, however, one disease, for which you have found as yet no specific, and that is old age, of which this tedious unconnected epistle is an infallible symptom:—what, therefore, *cannot be cured, must be endured*,[3] by you, as well as by

Yours,

Harrigate, June 26.   Matt. Bramble.

To Sir Watkin Phillips, Bart.
of Jesus college, Oxon.

Dear Knight,

The manner of living at Harrigate was so agreeable to my disposition, that I left the place with some regret—Our aunt Tabby would have probably made some objection to our departing so soon, had not an accident embroiled her with Mr. Micklewhimmen, the Scotch advocate, on whose heart she had been practising, from the second day after our arrival—That original, though seemingly precluded from the use of his limbs, had turned his genius to good account—In short, by dint of groaning, and whining, he had excited the compassion of the company so effectually, that an old lady, who occupied the very best apartment in the house, gave it up for his ease and convenience. When his man led him into the Long Room, all the females were immediately in commotion—One set an elbow-chair; another shook up the cushion; a third brought a stool; and a fourth a pillow, for the accommodation of his feet—Two ladies (of whom Tabby was always one) supported him into the dining-room, and placed him properly at the table; and his taste was indulged with a succession of delicacies, culled by their fair hands. All this attention he repaid with a profusion of compliments and benedictions, which were not the less agreeable for being delivered in the Scottish dialect. As for Mrs. Tabitha, his respects were particularly addressed to her, and he did not fail to mingle them with religious reflections, touching free grace, knowing her biass to methodism, which he also professed upon a calvinistical model.[4]

3. A proverbial phrase dating back to at least the 14th century.
4. John Calvin (1509–1564) was a French theologian whose ideas regarding original sin, predestination, and the centrality of faith as opposed to good works were extremely influential to the course of the Protestant Reformation. The Church of Scotland (known as the Kirk) became strongly Calvinist in the 16th century.

For my part, I could not help thinking this lawyer was not such an invalid as he pretended to be. I observed he ate very heartily three times a-day; and though his bottle was marked *stomachic tincture*, he had recourse to it so often, and seemed to swallow it with such peculiar relish, that I suspected it was not compounded in the apothecary's shop, or the chemist's laboratory. One day, while he was earnest in discourse with Mrs. Tabitha, and his servant had gone out on some occasion or other, I dexterously exchanged the labels, and situation of his bottle and mine; and having tasted his tincture, found it was excellent claret. I forthwith handed it about to some of my neighbours, and it was quite emptied before Mr. Micklewhimmen had occasion to repeat his draught. At length, turning about, he took hold of my bottle, instead of his own, and, filling a large glass, drank to the health of Mrs. Tabitha—It had scarce touched his lips, when he perceived the change which had been put upon him, and was at first a little out of countenance——He seemed to retire within himself, in order to deliberate, and in half a minute his resolution was taken; addressing himself to our quarter, "I give the gentleman cradit for his wit (said he); it was a gude practical joke; but sometimes *hi joci in seria ducunt mala*[5]—I hope for his own sake he has na drank all the liccor; for it was a vara poorful infusion of jallap[6] in Bourdeaux wine; and its possable he may ha ta'en sic a dose as will produce a terrible catastrophe in his ain booels—"

By far the greater part of the contents had fallen to the share of a young clothier from Leeds, who had come to make a figure at Harrigate, and was, in effect a great coxcomb in his way. It was with a view to laugh at his fellow-guests, as well as to mortify the lawyer, that he had emptied the bottle, when it came to his turn, and he had laughed accordingly: but now his mirth gave way to his apprehension— He began to spit, to make wry faces, and writhe himself into various contorsions—"Damn the stuff! (cried he) I thought it had a villanous twang—pah! He that would cozen a Scot, mun get oop betimes, and take Old Scratch for his counsellor—" "In troth mester what d'ye ca'um, (replied the lawyer) your wit has run you into a filthy puddle—I'm truly consarned for your waeful case—The best advice I can give you, in sic a delemma, is to send an express to Rippon[7] for doctor Waugh, without delay, and, in the mean time, swallow all the oil and butter you can find in the hoose, to defend your poor stomach and intastins from the villication of the particles of the jallap, which is vara violent, even when taken in moderation."

5. These jokes will lead to serious consequences (Latin); misquoted from Horace's *Ars Poetica* (451–52).
6. A purgative drug obtained from the roots of tuberous plants.
7. A cathedral city and market town about eleven miles from Harrogate; usually spelled "Ripon."

The poor clothier's torments had already begun: he retired, roaring with pain, to his own chamber; the oil was swallowed, and the doctor sent for; but before he arrived, the miserable patient had made such discharges upwards and downwards, that nothing remained to give him further offence; and this double evacuation, was produced by imagination alone; for what he had drank was genuine wine of Bourdeaux, which the lawyer had brought from Scotland for his own private use. The clothier, finding the joke turn out so expensive and disagreeable, quitted the house next morning, leaving the triumph to Micklewhimmen, who enjoyed it internally, without any outward signs of exultation—on the contrary, he affected to pity the young man for what he had suffered; and acquired fresh credit from this shew of moderation.

It was about the middle of the night, which succeeded this adventure, that the vent of the kitchen chimney being foul, the soot took fire, and the alarm was given in a dreadful manner—Every body leaped naked[8] out of bed, and in a minute the whole house was filled with cries and confusion—There were two stairs in the house, and to these we naturally ran; but they were both so blocked up, by the people pressing one upon another, that it seemed impossible to pass, without throwing down and trampling upon the women. In the midst of this anarchy, Mr. Micklewhimmen, with a leathern portmanteau on his back, came running as nimble as a buck along the passage; and Tabby, in her under-petticoat, endeavouring to hook him under the arm, that she might escape through his protection, he very fairly pushed her down, crying, "Na, na, gude faith, charity begins at hame!" Without paying the least respect to the shrieks and intreaties of his female friends, he charged through the midst of the crowd, overturning every thing that opposed him; and actually fought his way to the bottom of the stair-case—By this time Clinker had found a ladder, by which he entered the window of my uncle's chamber, where our family was assembled, and proposed that we should make our exit successively by that conveyance. The 'squire exhorted his sister to begin the descent; but, before she could resolve, her woman, Mrs. Winifred Jenkins, in a transport of terror, threw herself out at the window upon the ladder, while Humphry dropped upon the ground, that he might receive her in her descent——This maiden was just as she had started out of bed, the moon shone very bright, and a fresh breeze of wind blowing, none of Mrs. Winifred's beauties could possibly escape the view of the fortunate Clinker, whose heart was not able to withstand the united force of so many charms; at least, I am much mistaken, if he has not been her humble slave

8. In 18th-century usage, "naked" frequently meant wearing only an undergarment.

from that moment—He received her in his arms, and, giving her his coat to protect her from the weather, ascended again with admirable dexterity.

At that instant, the landlord of the house called out with an audible voice, that the fire was extinguished, and the ladies had nothing further to fear: this was a welcome note to the audience, and produced an immediate effect; the shrieking ceased, and a confused sound of expostulation ensued. I conducted Mrs. Tabitha and my sister to their own chamber, where Liddy fainted away; but was soon brought to herself. Then I went to offer my services to the other ladies, who might want assistance—They were all scudding through the passage to their several apartments; and as the thoroughfair was lighted by two lamps, I had a pretty good observation of them in their transit; but as most of them were naked to the smock, and all their heads shrouded in huge night-caps, I could not distinguish one face from another, though I recognized some of their voices— These were generally plaintive; some wept, some scolded, and some prayed—I lifted up one poor old gentlewoman, who had been overturned and sore bruised by a multitude of feet; and this was also the case with the lame parson from Northumberland, whom Micklewhimmen had in his passage overthrown, though not with impunity, for the cripple, in falling, gave him such a good pelt on the head with his crutch, that the blood followed.

As for this lawyer, he waited below till the hurly burly was over, and then stole softly to his own chamber, from whence he did not venture to make a second sally till eleven in the forenoon, when he was led into the Public Room by his own servant and another assistant, groaning most woefully, with a bloody napkin round his head. But things were greatly altered—The selfish brutality of his behaviour on the stairs had steeled their hearts against all his arts and address——Not a soul offered to accommodate him with chair, cushion, or footstool; so that he was obliged to sit down on a hard wooden bench—In that position, he looked around with a rueful aspect, and, bowing very low, said in a whining tone, "Your most humble servant, ladies—Fire is a dreadful calamity—" "Fire purifies gold, and it tries friendship," cried Mrs. Tabitha, bridling. "Yea, madam (replied Micklewhimmen); and it trieth discretion also—" "If discretion consists in forsaking a friend in adversity, you are eminently possessed of that virtue," resumed our aunt—"Na, madam, (rejoined the advocate) well I wot, I cannot claim any merit from the mode of my retreat—Ye'll please to observe ladies, there are twa independent principles that actuate our nature—One is instinct, which we have in common with the brute creation, and the other is reason— Noo, in certain great emergencies, when the faculty of reason is suspended, instinct taks the lead, and when this predominates, having no affinity with reason, it pays no sort of regard to its connections; it only operates for the preservation of the individual, and that by the most expeditious and effectual means; therefore, begging your pardon, ladies, I'm no accountable in *foro conscientiæ*,[9] for what I did, while under the influence of this irresistible pooer."

Here my uncle interposing, "I should be glad to know, (said he) whether it was instinct that prompted you to retreat with bag and baggage; for, I think, you had a portmanteau on your shoulder—" The lawyer answered, without hesitation, "Gif I might tell my mind freely, withoot incuring the suspicion of presumption, I should think it was something superior to either reason or instinct which suggested that measure, and this on a twafald accoont: in the first place, the portmanteau contained the writings of a worthy nobleman's estate; and their being burnt would have occasioned a loss that could not be repaired; secondly, my good angel seems to have laid the portmantle on my shoulders, by way of defence, to sustain the violence of a most inhuman blow, from the crutch of a reverend clergyman; which, even in spite of that medium, hath wounded me sorely, even unto the pericranium."[1] "By your own doctrine, (cried the parson, who chanced to be present) I am not accountable for the blow, which was the effect of instinct." "I crave your pardon, reverend sir, (said the other) instinct never acts but for the preservation of the individual; but your preservation was out of the case——you had already received the damage, and therefore the blow must be imputed to revenge, which is a sinful passion, that ill becomes any Christian, especially a protestant divine; and let me tell you, most reverend doctor, gin I had a mind to plea, the law would hauld my libel relevant." "Why, the damage is pretty equal on both sides (cried the parson); your head is broke, and my crutch is snapt in the middle—Now, if you will repair the one, I will be at the expence of curing the other."

This sally raised the laugh against Micklewhimmen, who began to look grave; when my uncle, in order to change the discouse, observed, that instinct had been very kind to him in another respect; for it had restored to him the use of his limbs, which, in his exit, he had moved with surprising agility.——He replied, that it was the nature of fear to brace up the nerves; and mentioned some surprising feats of strength and activity performed by persons under the impulse of terror; but he complained, that in his own particular, the effects had ceased when the cause was taken away—The 'squire said, he would lay a tea-drinking on his head, that he should dance a Scotch measure, without making a false step; and the advocate grinning, called

9. In conscience's forum (Latin).
1. The fibrous membrane covering the skull's external surface.

for the piper—A fiddler being at hand, this original started up, with his bloody napkin over his black tye-periwig, and acquitted himself in such a manner as exerted the mirth of the whole company; but he could not regain the good graces of Mrs. Tabby, who did not understand the principle of instinct; and the lawyer did not think it worth his while to proceed to further demonstration.

From Harrigate, we came hither, by the way of York, and here we shall tarry some days, as my uncle and Tabitha are both resolved to make use of the waters. Scarborough, though a paltry town, is romantic from its situation along a cliff that over-hangs the sea. The harbour is formed by a small elbow of land that runs out as a natural mole, directly opposite to the town; and on that side is the castle, which stands very high, of considerable extent, and, before the invention of gun-powder, was counted impregnable. At the other end of Scarborough are two public rooms for the use of the company, who resort to this place in the summer, to drink the waters and bathe in the sea; and the diversions are pretty much on the same footing here as at Bath. The Spa is a little way beyond the town, on this side, under a cliff, within a few paces of the sea, and thither the drinkers go every morning in dishabille; but the descent is by a great number of steps, which invalids find very inconvenient. Betwixt the well and the harbour, the bathing machines are ranged along the beach, with all their proper utensils and attendants——You have never seen one of these machines—Image to yourself a small, snug, wooden chamber, fixed upon a wheel-carriage, having a door at each end, and on each side a little window above, a bench below—The bather, ascending into this apartment by wooden steps, shuts himself in, and begins to undress, while the attendant yokes a horse to the end next the sea, and draws the carriage forwards, till the surface of the water is on a level with the floor of the dressing-room, then he moves and fixes the horse to the other end—The person within, being stripped, opens the door to the seaward, where he finds the guide ready, and plunges headlong into the water——After having bathed, he re-ascends into the apartment, by the steps which had been shifted for that purpose, and puts on his clothes at his leisure, while the carriage is drawn back again upon the dry land; so that he has nothing further to do, but to open the door, and come down as he went up—Should he be so weak or ill as to require a servant to put off and on his clothes, there is room enough in the apartment for half a dozen people. The guides who attend the ladies in the water, are of their own sex, and they and the female bathers have a dress of flannel for the sea; nay, they are provided with other conveniences for the support of decorum. A certain number of the machines are fitted with tilts, that project from the sea-ward ends of them, so as to screen the bathers from the view of all persons whatsoever—The beach is admirably adapted for this practice, the descent being gently gradual, and the sand soft as velvet; but then the machines can be used only at a certain time of the tide, which varies every day; so that sometimes the bathers are obliged to rise very early in the morning——For my part, I love swimming as an exercise, and can enjoy it at all times of the tide, without the formality of an apparatus— You and I have often plunged together into the Isis; but the sea is a much more noble bath, for health as well as pleasure. You cannot conceive what a flow of spirits it gives, and how it braces every sinew of the human frame. Were I to enumerate half the diseases which are every day cured by sea-bathing, you might justly say you had received a treatise, instead of a letter, from

your affectionate friend

and servant,

Scarborough, July 1.   J. MELFORD.

To Dr. LEWIS.

I have not found all the benefit I expected at Scarborough, where I have been these eight days—From Harrigate we came hither by the way of York, where we stayed only one day to visit the Castle, the Minster, and the Assembly-room. The first, which was heretofore a fortress, is now converted to a prison, and is the best, in all respects, I ever saw at home or abroad—It stands in a high situation, extremely well ventilated; and has a spacious area within the walls, for the health and convenience of all the prisoners, except those whom it is necessary to secure in close confinement——Even these last have all the comforts that the nature of their situation can admit. Here the assizes are held, in a range of buildings erected for that purpose.

As for the Minster, I know not how to distinguish it, except by its great size and the height of its spire, from those other antient churches in different parts of the kingdom, which used to be called monuments of Gothic architecture; but it is now agreed, that this stile is Saracen rather than Gothic;[2] and, I suppose, it was first imported into England from Spain, great part of which was under the dominion of the Moors. Those British architects, who adopted this stile, don't seem to have considered the propriety of their adoption. The climate of the country, possessed by the Moors or Saracens, both in Africa and Spain, was so exceedingly hot and dry, that

---

2. Matt echoes the famous English architect Sir Christopher Wren (1632–1723) in his erroneous use of "Saracen" to describe the lighter Gothic mode of architecture.

those who built places of worship for the multitude, employed their talents in contriving edifices that should be cool; and, for this purpose, nothing could be better adopted than those buildings; vast, narrow, dark, and lofty, impervious to the sun-beams, and having little communication with the scorched external atmosphere; but ever affording a refreshing coolness, like subterranean cellars in the heats of summer, or natural caverns in the bowels of huge mountains. But nothing could be more preposterous, than to imitate such a mode of architecture in a country like England, where the climate is cold, and the air eternally loaded with vapours; and where, of consequence, the builder's intention should be to keep the people dry and warm—For my part, I never entered the Abbey church at Bath but once, and the moment I stept over the threshold, I found myself chilled to the very marrow of my bones—When we consider, that in our churches, in general, we breathe a gross stagnated air, surcharged with damps from vaults, tombs, and charnel-houses, may we not term them so many magazines of rheums, created for the benefit of the medical faculty? and safely aver, that more bodies are lost, than souls saved, by going to church, in the winter especially, which may be said to engross eight months in the year. I should be glad to know, what offence it would give to tender consciences, if the house of God was made more comfortable, or less dangerous to the health of valetudinarians; and whether it would not be an encouragement to piety, as well as the salvation of many lives, if the place of worship was well floored, wainscotted, warmed, and ventilated, and its area kept sacred from the pollution of the dead. The practice of burying in churches was the effect of ignorant superstition, influenced by knavish priests, who pretended that the devil could have no power over the defunct, if he was interred in holy ground; and this, indeed, is the only reason that can be given for consecrating all cemeteries, even at this day.

The external appearance of an old cathedral cannot be but displeasing to the eye of every man, who has any idea of propriety and proportion, even though he may be ignorant of architecture as a science; and the long slender spire puts one in mind of a criminal impaled, with a sharp stake rising up through his shoulder—These towers, or steeples, were likewise borrowed from the Mahometans;[3] who, having no bells, used such minarets for the purpose of calling the people to prayers—They may be of further use, however, for making observations and signals; but I would vote for their being distinct from the body of the church, because they serve only to make the pile more barbarous, or Saracenical.

3. A formerly common term for followers of Mohammad, i.e., Muslims.

There is nothing of this Arabic architecture in the Assembly Room, which seems to me to have been built upon a design of Palladio, and might be converted into an elegant place of worship; but it is indifferently contrived for that sort of idolatry which is performed in it at present: the grandeur of the fane[4] gives a diminutive effect to the little painted divinities that are adored in it, and the company, on a ball-night, must look like an assembly of fantastic fairies, revelling by moon-light among the columns of a Grecian temple.

Scarborough seems to be falling off, in point of reputation—— All these places (Bath excepted) have their vogue, and then the fashion changes—I am persuaded, there are fifty spaws in England as efficacious and salutary as that of Scarborough, though they have not yet risen to fame; and, perhaps, never will, unless some medical encomiast[5] should find an interest in displaying their virtues to the public view——Be that as it may, recourse will always be had to this place for the convenience of sea-bathing, while this practice prevails; but it were to be wished, they would make the beach more accessible to invalids.

I have here met with my old acquaintance, H——t,[6] whom you have often heard me mention as one of the most original characters upon earth——I first knew him at Venice, and afterwards saw him in different parts of Italy, where he was well known by the nick-name of Cavallo Bianco, from his appearing always mounted on a pale horse, like Death in the Revelations. You must remember the account I once gave you of a curious dispute he had at Constantinople, with a couple of Turks, in defence of the Christian religion; a dispute from which he acquired the epithet of Demonstrator[7]—The truth is, H——owns no religion but that of nature; but, on this occasion, he was stimulated to shew his parts, for the honour of his country—Some years ago, being in the Campidoglio[8] at Rome, he made up to the bust of Jupiter, and, bowing very low, exclaimed in the Italian language, "I hope, sir, if ever you get your head above water again, you will remember that I paid my respects to you in your adversity." This sally was reported to the cardinal Camerlengo, and by him laid before pope Benedict XIV.[9] who could not help

---

4. The temple.
5. Eulogist.
6. Colonel William Hewett (1693–1766), a well-known traveler.
7. According to contemporary sources, while in a dispute with some Turks concerning the Islamic view of heaven, Hewett argued that Christian men were better qualified to enjoy its traditional beautiful virginal companions than either their Jewish or Islamic counterparts. Apparently he then demonstrated this supposed qualification by presenting his uncircumcised penis as evidence. Constantinople is the Roman name for the ancient city now known as Istanbul, located in modern-day Turkey.
8. One of the classical hills of Rome and a popular stop for visitors.
9. A scholarly pope (1740–58) who enjoyed good relations with Protestants. "Camerlengo": title for the cardinal in charge of the Holy See's property.

laughing at the extravagance of the address, and said to the cardinal, "Those English heretics think they have a right to go to the devil in their own way."

Indeed H—— was the only Englishman I ever knew, who had resolution enough to live in his own way, in the midst of foreigners; for, neither in dress, diet, customs, or conversation, did he deviate one tittle from the manner in which he had been brought up. About twelve years ago, he began a Giro or circuit, which he thus performed—At Naples, where he fixed his head-quarters, he embarked for Marseilles, from whence he travelled with a Voiturin[1] to Antibes—There he took his passage to Genoa and Lerici; from which last place he proceeded, by the way of Cambratina, to Pisa and Florence—After having halted some time in this metropolis, he set out with a Vetturino for Rome, where he reposed himself a few weeks, and then continued his route for Naples, in order to wait for the next opportunity of embarkation—After having twelve times described this circle, he lately flew off at a tangent to visit some trees at his country-house in England, which he had planted above twenty years ago, after the plan of the double colonnade in the piazza of St. Peter's at Rome[2]——He came hither to Scarborough, to pay his respects to his noble friend and former pupil, the M— of G——,[3] and, forgetting that he is now turned of seventy, sacrificed so liberally to Bacchus, that next day he was seized with a fit of the apoplexy, which has a little impaired his memory; but he retains all the oddity of his character in perfection, and is going back to Italy, by the way of Geneva, that he may have a conference with his friend Voltaire,[4] about giving the last blow to the Christian superstition—He intends to take shipping here for Holland or Hamburgh; for it is a matter of great indifference to him at what part of the continent he first lands.

When he was going abroad the last time, he took his passage in a ship bound for Leghorn, and his baggage was actually embarked. In going down the river by water, he was by mistake put on board of another vessel under sail; and, upon inquiry, understood she was bound to Petersburgh[5]—"Petersburgh, —Petersburgh—(said he) I don't care if I go along with you." He forthwith struck a bargain with the captain; bought a couple of shirts of the mate, and was safe conveyed to the court of Muscovy,[6] from whence he travelled

---

1. French carriage driver.
2. Saint Peter's Basilica, a late-Renaissance Catholic church in Vatican City, located within Rome.
3. The Marquis of Granby, John Manners (1721–1770).
4. François Marie Arouet (1694–1778), a famous French philosopher and writer.
5. Saint Petersburg, Russia.
6. An old-fashioned name for Moscow, now the capital city of Russia.

by land to receive his baggage at Leghorn——He is now more likely than ever to execute a whim of the same nature; and I will hold any wager, that as he cannot be supposed to live much longer, according to the course of nature, his exit will be as odd as his life has been extravagant.[7]

But, to return from one humorist to another; you must know I have received benefit, both from the chalybeate[8] and the sea, and would have used them longer, had not a most ridiculous adventure, by making me the town-talk, obliged me to leave the place; for I can't bear the thoughts of affording a spectacle to the multitude—— Yesterday morning, at six o'clock, I went down to the bathing-place, attended by my servant Clinker, who waited on the beach as usual— The wind blowing from the north, and the weather being hazy, the water proved so chill, that when I rose from my first plunge, I could not help sobbing and bawling out, from the effects of the cold. Clinker, who heard me cry, and saw me indistinctly a good way without the guide, buffeting the waves, took it for granted I was drowning, and rushing into the sea, clothes and all, overturned the guide in his hurry to save his master. I had swam out a few strokes, when hearing a noise, I turned about and saw Clinker, already up to his neck, advancing towards me, with all the wildness of terror in his aspect—Afraid he would get out of his depth, I made haste to meet him, when, all of a sudden, he seized me by one ear, and dragged me bellowing with pain upon the dry beach, to the astonishment of all the people, men, women, and children there assembled.

I was so exasperated by the pain of my ear, and the disgrace of being exposed in such an attitude, that, in the first transport, I struck him down; then, running back into the sea, took shelter in the machine where my clothes had been deposited. I soon recollected myself so far as to do justice to the poor fellow, who, in great simplicity of heart, had acted from motives of fidelity and affection— Opening the door of the machine, which was immediately drawn on shore, I saw him standing by the wheel, dropping like a water-work, and trembling from head to foot; partly from cold, and partly from the dread of having offended his master—I made my acknowledgments

7. This gentleman crossed the sea to France, visited and conferred with Mr. de Voltaire at Fernay, resumed his old circuit at Genoa, and died in 1767, at the house of Vanini in Florence. Being taken with a suppression of urine, he resolved, in imitation of Pomponius Atticus, to take himself off by abstinence; and this resolution he executed like an ancient Roman. He saw company to the last, cracked his jokes, conversed freely, and entertained his guests with music. On the third day of his fast, he found himself entirely freed of his complaint; but refused taking sustenance. He said the most disagreeable part of the voyage was past, and he should be a cursed fool indeed, to put about ship, when he was just entering the harbour. In these sentiments he persisted, without any marks of affectation, and thus finished his course with such ease and serenity, as would have done honour to the firmest Stoic of antiquity [Smollett's note].
8. A mineral spring impregnated with salts of iron.

for the blow he had received, assured him I was not angry, and insisted upon his going home immediately, to shift his clothes; a command which he could hardly find in his heart to execute, so well disposed was he to furnish the mob with further entertainment at my expence. Clinker's intention was laudable without all doubt, but, nevertheless, I am a sufferer by his simplicity—I have had a burning-heat, and a strange buzzing noise in that ear, ever since it was so roughly treated; and I cannot walk the street without being pointed at, as the monster that was hauled naked a-shore upon the beach—Well, I affirm that folly is often more provoking than knavery, aye and more mischievous too; and whether a man had not better choose a sensible rogue, than an honest simpleton for his servant, is no matter of doubt with

yours,

Scarborough, July 4.   MATT. BRAMBLE.

To Sir WATKIN PHILLIPS, Bar^t.
of Jesus college, Oxon.

DEAR WATT,

We made a precipitate retreat from Scarborough, owing to the excessive delicacy of our 'squire, who cannot bear the thoughts of being *prætereuntium digito monstratus*.[9]

One morning, while he was bathing in the sea, his man Clinker took it in his head that his master was in danger of drowning; and, in this conceit, plunging into the water, he lugged him out naked on the beach, and almost pulled off his ear in the operation. You may guess how this atchievement was relished by Mr. Bramble, who is impatient, irascible, and has the most extravagant ideas of decency and decorum in the œconomy of his own person—In the first ebullition[1] of his choler, he knocked Clinker down with his fist; but he afterwards made him amends for this outrage, and, in order to avoid the further notice of the people, among whom this incident had made him remarkable, he resolved to leave Scarborough next day.

We set out accordingly over the moors, by the way of Whitby, and began our journey betimes, in hopes of reaching Stockton that night; but in this hope we were disappointed—In the afternoon, crossing a deep gutter, made by a torrent, the coach was so hard strained, that one of the irons, which connect the frame, snapt, and the leather sling

9. Pointed at by the fingers of passers-by (Latin); adapted from Horace's *Carmina* (4.3.22).
1. Overflowing, boiling up.

on the same side, cracked in the middle—The shock was so great, that my sister Liddy struck her head against Mrs. Tabitha's nose with such violence that the blood flowed; and Win Jenkins was darted through a small window, in that part of the carriage next the horses, where she stuck like a bawd[2] in the pillory, till she was released by the hand of Mr. Bramble. We were eight miles distant from any place where we could be supplied with chaises, and it was impossible to proceed with the coach, until the damage should be repaired—In this dilemma, we discovered a blacksmith's forge on the edge of a small common, about half a mile from the scene of our disaster, and thither the postilions made shift to draw the carriage slowly, while the company walked a-foot; but we found the black-smith had been dead some days; and his wife, who had been lately delivered, was deprived of her senses, under the care of a nurse, hired by the parish. We were exceedingly mortified at this disappointment, which, however, was surmounted by the help of Humphry Clinker, who is a surprising compound of genius and simplicity. Finding the tools of the defunct, together with some coals in the smithy, he unscrewed the damaged iron in a twinkling, and, kindling a fire, united the broken pieces with equal dexterity and dispatch—While he was at work upon this operation, the poor woman in the straw,[3] struck with the well-known sound of the hammer and anvil, started up, and, notwithstanding all the nurse's efforts, came running into the smithy, where, throwing her arms about Clinker's neck, "Ah, Jacob! (cried she) how could you leave me in such a condition?"

This incident was too pathetic to occasion mirth——it brought tears into the eyes of all present. The poor widow was put to bed again; and we did not leave the village without doing something for her benefit—Even Tabitha's charity was awakened on this occasion. As for the tenderhearted Humphry Clinker, he hammered the iron and wept at the same time—But his ingenuity was not confined to his own province of farrier and black-smith—it was necessary to join the leather sling, which had been broke; and this service he likewise performed, by means of a broken awl, which he new-pointed and ground, a little hemp, which he spun into lingels, and a few tacks[4] which he made for the purpose—Upon the whole, we were in a condition to proceed in little more than one hour; but even this delay obliged us to pass the night at Cisborough—Next day we crossed the Tees at Stockton, which is a neat agreeable town; and there we resolved to dine, with purpose to lie at Durham.

2. A prostitute.
3. I.e., the woman who just gave birth.
4. Short, sharp, flat-headed nails. "Awl": a pointed instrument for poking small holes in leather. "Lingels": waxed threads used by shoemakers and harness makers.

Whom should we meet in the yard, when we alighted, but Martin the adventurer? Having handed out the ladies, and conducted them into an apartment, where he payed his compliments to Mrs. Tabby, with his usual address, he begged leave to speak to my uncle in another room; and there, in some confusion, he made an apology for having taken the liberty to trouble him with a letter at Stevenage. He expressed his hope, that Mr. Bramble had bestowed some consideration on his unhappy case, and repeated his desire of being taken into his service.

My uncle, calling me into the room, told him, that we were both very well inclined to rescue him from a way of life that was equally dangerous and dishonourable; and that he should have no scruples in trusting to his gratitude and fidelity, if he had any employment for him, which he thought would suit his qualifications and his circumstances; but that all the departments he had mentioned in his letter, were filled up by persons of whose conduct he had no reason to complain; of consequence he could not, without injustice, deprive any one of them of his bread—Nevertheless, he declared himself ready to assist him in any feasible project, either with his purse or credit.

Martin seemed deeply touched at this declaration—The tear started in his eye, while he said, in a faultering accent—"Worthy sir— your generosity oppresses me—I never dreamed of troubling you for any pecuniary assistance—indeed I have no occasion—I have been so lucky at billiards and betting in different places, at Buxton, Harrigate, Scarborough, and Newcastle races, that my stock in ready-money amounts to three hundred pounds, which I would willingly employ, in prosecuting some honest scheme of life; but my friend, justice Buzzard, has set so many springs for my life, that I am under the necessity of either retiring immediately to a remote part of the country, where I can enjoy the protection of some generous patron, or of quitting the kingdom altogether——It is upon this alternative that I now beg leave to ask your advice—I have had information of all your route, since I had the honour to see you at Stevenage; and, supposing you would come this way from Scarborough, I came hither last night from Darlington, to pay you my respects."

"It would be no difficult matter to provide you with an asylum in the country (replied my uncle); but a life of indolence and obscurity would not suit with your active and enterprizing disposition—I would therefore advise you to try your fortune in the East Indies— I will give you a letter to a friend in London, who will recommend you to the direction, for a commission in the company's service;[5] and if

5. That of the East India Company. Originally granted a royal charter in 1600 to explore and trade in the East Indies, it became a British joint-stock company in 1707, and by the mid-18th century it was flourishing financially and militarily.

that cannot be obtained, you will at least be received as a volunteer—
in which case, you may pay for your passage, and I shall undertake
to procure you such credentials, that you will not be long without
a commission."

Martin embraced the proposal with great eagerness; it was therefore resolved, that he should sell his horse, and take a passage by sea
for London, to execute the project without delay—In the mean time
he accompanied us to Durham, where we took up our quarters for
the night—Here, being furnished with letters from my uncle, he
took his leave of us, with strong symptoms of gratitude and attachment, and set out for Sunderland, in order to embark in the first
collier, bound for the river Thames. He had not been gone half an
hour, when we were joined by another character, which promised
something extraordinary—A tall, meagre figure, answering, with
his horse, the description of Don Quixote mounted on Rozinante,
appeared in the twilight at the inn door, while my aunt and Liddy
stood at a window in the dining-room—He wore a coat, the cloth of
which had once been scarlet, trimmed with Brandenburgs,[6] now
totally deprived of their metal, and he had holster-caps and housing
of the same stuff and same antiquity. Perceiving ladies at the window above, he endeavoured to dismount with the most graceful air
he could assume; but the ostler neglecting to hold the stirrup when
he wheeled off his right foot, and stood with his whole weight on the
other, the girth unfortunately gave way, the saddle turned, down
came the cavalier to the ground, and his hat and periwig falling off,
displayed a head-piece of various colours, patched and plaistered in
a woeful condition—The ladies, at the window above, shrieked with
affright, on the supposition that the stranger had received some
notable damage in his fall; but the greatest injury he had sustained
arose from the dishonour of his descent, aggravated by the disgrace
of exposing the condition of his cranium; for certain plebeians that
were about the door, laughed aloud, in the belief that the captain had
got either a scald head,[7] or a broken head, both equally opprobrious.

He forthwith leaped up in a fury, and snatching one of his pistols,
threatened to put the ostler to death, when another squall from the
women checked his resentment. He then bowed to the window, while
he kissed the butt-end of his pistol, which he replaced; adjusted his
wig in great confusion, and led his horse into the stable—By this
time I had come to the door, and could not help gazing at the strange
figure that presented itself to my view—He would have measured
above six feet in height, had he stood upright; but he stooped very
much; was very narrow in the shoulders, and very thick in the

---

6. Brightly colored ornamental facings on officer's coats.
7. I.e., a scalp infection, such as ringworm.

First appearance of the gallant Lismahago. Courtesy of the Center for Southwest Research, University Libraries, University of New Mexico.

calves of his legs, which were cased in black spatterdashes[8]—As for his thighs, they were long and slender, like those of a grasshopper; his face was, at least, half a yard in length, brown and shrivelled, with projecting cheek-bones, little grey eyes on the greenish hue, a large hook-nose, a pointed chin, a mouth from ear to ear, very ill furnished with teeth, and a high, narrow fore-head, well furrowed with wrinkles. His horse was exactly in the stile of its rider; a resurrection of dry bones, which (as we afterwards learned) he valued exceedingly, as the only present he had ever received in his life.

Having seen this favourite steed properly accommodated in the stable, he sent up his compliments to the ladies, begging permission to thank them in person for the marks of concern they had shewn at his disaster in the court-yard—As the 'squire said they could not decently decline his visit, he was shewn up stairs, and paid his respects in the Scotch dialect, with much formality—"Laddies, (said he) perhaps ye may be scandaleezed at the appearance my heed made, when it was uncovered by accident; but I can assure you, the condition you saw it in, is neither the effects of disease, nor of drunkenness; but an honest scar received in the service of my country." He then gave us to understand, that having been wounded at Ticonderoga,[9] in America, a party of Indians rifled him, scalped him, broke his scull with the blow of a tomahawk, and left him for dead on the field of battle; but that being afterwards found with signs of life, he had been cured in the French hospital, though the loss of substance could not be repaired; so that the scull was left naked in several places, and these he covered with patches.

There is no hold by which an Englishman is sooner taken than that of compassion—We were immediately interested in behalf of this veteran—Even Tabby's heart was melted; but our pity was warmed with indignation, when we learned, that in the course of two sanguinary wars, he had been wounded, maimed, mutilated, taken, and enslaved, without ever having attained a higher rank than that of lieutenant——My uncle's eyes gleamed, and his nether lip quivered, while he exclaimed, "I vow to God, sir, your case is a reproach to the service—The injustice you have met with is so flagrant——" "I must crave your pardon, sir, (cried the other, interrupting him) I complain of no injustice—I purchased an ensigncy thirty years ago; and, in the course of service, rose to be a lieutenant, according to my seniority—" "But in such a length of time, (resumed the 'squire) you must have seen a great many young officers put over your head—" "Nevertheless, (said he) I have no cause to murmur—They

8. Long leggings to prevent trousers or stockings from being muddied, especially when horseback riding.
9. Presumably a reference to the 1758 battle of Carillon, in which sixteen thousand British troops failed to take Fort Ticonderoga from the French in what is now upstate New York.

bought their preferment with their money—I had no money to carry to market—that was my misfortune; but no body was to blame—" "What! no friend to advance a sum of money?" (said Mr. Bramble) "Perhaps, I might have borrowed money for the purchase of a company (answered the other); but that loan must have been refunded; and I did not chuse to incumber myself with a debt of a thousand pounds, to be payed from an income of ten shillings a-day." "So you have spent the best part of your life, (cried Mr. Bramble) your youth, your blood, and your constitution, amidst the dangers, the difficulties, the horrors and hardships of war, for the consideration of three or four shillings a-day—a consideration—" "Sir, (replied the Scot, with great warmth) you are the man that does me injustice, if you say or think I have been actuated by any such paultry consideration——I am a gentleman; and entered the service as other gentlemen do, with such hopes and sentiments as honourable ambition inspires— If I have not been lucky in the lottery of life, so neither do I think myself unfortunate—I owe no man a farthing; I can always command a clean shirt, a mutton-chop, and a truss of straw; and when I die, I shall leave effects sufficient to defray the expence of my burial."

My uncle assured him, he had no intention to give him the least offence, by the observations he had made; but, on the contrary, spoke from a sentiment of friendly regard to his interest—The lieutenant thanked him with a stiffness of civility, which nettled our old gentleman, who perceived that his moderation was all affected; for, whatsoever his tongue might declare, his whole appearance denoted dissatisfaction—In short, without pretending to judge of his military merit, I think I may affirm, that this Caledonian is a self-conceited pedant, aukward, rude, and disputacious—He has had the benefit of a school-education, seems to have read a good number of books, his memory is tenacious, and he pretends to speak several different languages; but he is so addicted to wrangling, that he will cavil at the clearest truths, and, in the pride of argumentation, attempt to reconcile contradictions——Whether his address and qualifications are really of that stamp which is agreeable to the taste of our aunt, Mrs. Tabitha, or that indefatigable maiden is determined to shoot at every sort of game, certain it is she has begun to practise upon the heart of the lieutenant, who favoured us with his company to supper.

I have many other things to say of this man of war, which I shall communicate in a post or two; mean while, it is but reasonable that you should be indulged with some respite from those weary lucubrations of

yours,

Newcastle upon Tyne, July 10.   J. MELFORD.

To Sir WATKIN PHILLIPS, Bar[t].
of Jesus college, Oxon.

DEAR PHILLIPS,

In my last I treated you with a high flavoured dish, in the character of the Scotch lieutenant, and I must present him once more for your entertainment. It was our fortune to feed upon him the best part of three days; and I do not doubt that he will start again in our way before we shall have finished our northern excursion. The day after our meeting with him at Durham proved so tempestuous that we did not choose to proceed on our journey; and my uncle persuaded him to stay till the weather should clear up, giving him, at the same time, a general invitation to our mess. The man has certainly gathered a whole budget of shrewd observations, but he brings them forth in such an ungracious manner as would be extremely disgusting, if it was not marked by that characteristic oddity which never fails to attract the attention.—He and Mr. Bramble discoursed, and even disputed, on different subjects in war, policy, the belles lettres, law, and metaphysics; and sometimes they were warmed into such altercation as seemed to threaten an abrupt dissolution of their society; but Mr. Bramble set a guard over his own irascibilty, the more vigilantly as the officer was his guest; and when, in spite of all his efforts, he began to wax warm, the other prudently cooled in the same proportion.

Mrs. Tabitha chancing to accost her brother by the familiar diminutive of Matt, "Pray, sir, (said the lieutenant) is your name Matthias?" You must know, it is one of our uncle's foibles to be ashamed of his name Matthew, because it is puritanical; and this question chagrined him so much, that he answered, "No, by G—d!" in a very abrupt tone of displeasure.—The Scot took umbrage at the manner of his reply, and bristling up, "If I had known (said he) that you did not care to tell your name, I should not have asked the question—The leddy called you Matt, and I naturally thought it was Matthias——perhaps, it may be Methuselah, or Metrodorus, or Metellus, or Mathurinus, or Malthinnus, or Matamoros, or——"
"No, (cried my uncle laughing) it is neither of those, captain:—my name is Matthew Bramble, at your service.—The truth is, I have a foolish pique at the name of Matthew, because it savours of those canting hypocrites, who, in Cromwell's time, christened all their children by names taken from the scripture."——"A foolish pique indeed, (cried Mrs. Tabby) and even sinful, to fall out with your name because it is taken from holy writ.—I would have you to know, you was called after great-uncle Matthew ap Madoc ap Meredith, esquire, of Llanwysthin, in Montgomeryshire, justice of the *quorum*,

and *crusty ruttleorum*,[1] a gentleman of great worth and property, descended in a strait line, by the female side, from Llewellyn, prince of Wales."[2]

This genealogical anecdote seemed to make some impression upon the North-Briton, who bowed very low to the descendants of Llewellyn, and observed that he himself had the honour of a scriptural nomination. The lady expressing a desire of knowing his address, he said, he designed himself Lieutenant Obadiah Lismahago; and, in order to assist her memory, he presented her with a slip of paper inscribed with these three words, which she repeated with great emphasis, declaring, it was one of the most noble and sonorous names she had ever heard. He observed, that Obadiah was an adventitious appellation, derived from his great-grandfather, who had been one of the original covenanters; but Lismahago was the family surname, taken from a place in Scotland so called.[3] He likewise dropped some hints about the antiquity of his pedigree, adding, with a smile of self-denial, *Sed genus et proavos, et quæ non fecimus ipsi, vix ea nostra voco*,[4] which quotation he explained in deference to the ladies; and Mrs. Tabitha did not fail to compliment him on his modesty in waving the merit of his ancestry, adding, that it was the less necessary to him, as he had such a considerable fund of his own. She now began to glew herself to his favour with the grossest adulation.—She expatiated upon the antiquity and virtues of the Scottish nation, upon their valour, probity, learning, and politeness.—She even descended to encomiums on his own personal address, his gallantry, good sense, and erudition.—She appealed to her brother, whether the captain was not very image of our cousin governor Griffith.—She discovered a surprising eagerness to know the particulars of his life, and asked a thousand questions concerning his atchievements in war; all which Mr. Lismahago answered with a sort of jesuitical[5] reserve, affecting a reluctance to satisfy her curiosity on a subject that concerned his own exploits.

By dint of her interrogations, however, we learned, that he and ensign Murphy had made their escape from the French hospital at Montreal, and taken to the woods, in hope of reaching some

1. Tabitha's version of *custus rotulorum*, Latin for the principal justice of the peace of a county. "Justice of the Quorum": a justice whose presence is required to allow a trial to proceed.
2. Llywelyn the Great (ca. 1172–1240), Prince of Gwynedd in north Wales, who, beginning in 1216, effectively ruled the entire country. His line remained royal until Edward I of England conquered Wales in 1283.
3. Lesmahagow is a small town about twenty miles southeast of Glasgow. "Covenanters": originally those who signed the National Covenant in 1638 to uphold Presbyterianism in Scotland against Charles I's reforms. Many adopted biblical names; Obadiah means "servant of Yahweh [God]."
4. But as to race, ancestors, and those things which we did not do ourselves, I can hardly call those our own (Latin); adapted from Ovid's *Metamorphoses* (13.140).
5. Having the character ascribed to Jesuits by their detractors, i.e., deceitful, equivocal.

English settlement; but mistaking their route, they fell in with a party of Miamis, who earn them away in captivity. The intention of these Indians was to give one of them as an adopted son to a venerable sachem,[6] who had lost his own in the course of the war, and to sacrifice the other according to the custom of the country. Murphy, as being the younger and handsomer of the two, was designed to fill the place of the deceased, not only as the son of the sachem, but as the spouse of a beautiful squaw, to whom his predecessor had been betrothed; but in passing through the different whigwhams or villages of the Miamis, poor Murphy was so mangled by the women and children, who have the privilege of torturing all prisoners in their passage, that, by the time they arrived at the place of the sachem's residence, he was rendered altogether unfit for the purposes of marriage: it was determined therefore, in the assembly of the warriors, that ensign Murphy should be brought to the stake, and that the lady should be given to lieutenant Lismahago, who had likewise received his share of torments, though they had not produced emasculation.—A joint of one finger had been cut, or rather sawed off with a rusty knife; one of his great toes was crushed into a mash betwixt two stones; some of his teeth were drawn, or dug out with a crooked nail; splintered reeds had been thrust up his nostrils and other tender parts; and the calves of his legs had been blown up with mines of gunpowder dug in the flesh with the sharp point of the tomahawk.

The Indians themselves allowed that Murphy died with great heroism, singing, as his death song, the *Drimmendoo*,[7] in concert with Mr. Lismahago, who was present at the solemnity. After the warriors and the matrons had made a hearty meal upon the muscular flesh which they pared from the victim, and had applied a great variety of tortures, which he bore without flinching, an old lady, with a sharp knife, scooped out one of his eyes, and put a burning coal in the socket. The pain of this operation was so exquisite that he could not help bellowing, upon which the audience raised a shout of exultation, and one of the warriors stealing behind him, gave him the *coup de grace*[8] with a hatchet.

Lismahago's bride, the squaw Squinkinacoosta, distinguished herself on this occasion.——She shewed a great superiority of genius in the tortures which she contrived and executed with her own hands.—She vied with the stoutest warrior in eating the flesh of the sacrifice; and after all the other females were fuddled with

6. The chief of a tribe.
7. An old Irish folk song titled "Drynaun dhun" (Dear Black Cow). The title was applied to several melodies in Ireland and Scotland and was also adapted as a Jacobite song.
8. The final blow (French).

dram-drinking, she was not so intoxicated but that she was able to play the game of the platter[9] with the conjuring sachem, and afterwards go through the ceremony of her own wedding, which was consummated that same evening. The captain had lived very happily with this accomplished squaw for two years, during which she bore him a son, who is now the representative of his mother's tribe; but, at length, to his unspeakable grief, she had died of a fever, occasioned by eating too much raw bear, which they had killed in a hunting excursion.

By this time, Mr. Lismahago was elected sachem, acknowledged first warrior of the Badger tribe, and dignified with the name or epithet of Occacanastaogarora, which signifies *nimble as a weasel;* but all these advantages and honours he was obliged to resign, in consequence of being exchanged for the orator of the community, who had been taken prisoner by the Indians that were in alliance with the English. At the peace, he had sold out upon half-pay,[1] and was returned to Britain, with a view to pass the rest of his life in his own country, where he hoped to find some retreat where his slender finances would afford him a decent subsistence. Such are the outlines of Mr. Lismahago's history, to which Tabitha *did seriously incline her ear;*—indeed, she seemed to be taken with the same charms that captivated the heart of Desdemona, who loved the Moor *for the dangers he had past.*[2]

The description of poor Murphy's sufferings, which threw my sister Liddy into a swoon, extracted some sighs from the breast of Mrs. Tabby: when she understood he had been rendered unfit for marriage, she began to spit, and ejaculated, "Jesus, what cruel barbarians!" and she made wry faces at the lady's nuptial repast; but she was eagerly curious to know the particulars of her marriage-dress; whether she wore high-breasted stays or boddice, a robe of silk or velvet, and laces of Mechlin or minionette[3]—she supposed, as they were connected with the French, she used rouge, and had her hair dressed in the Parisian fashion. The captain would have declined giving a categorical explanation of all these particulars, observing, in general, that the Indians were too tenacious of their own customs to adopt the modes of any nation whatsoever: he said, moreover, that neither the simplicity of their manners, nor the commerce of their country, would admit of those articles of luxury which are deemed magnificence in Europe; and that they were too virtuous

9. Presumably a game of chance played by shaking bones on a plate, as described in Thomas Hutchinson's *History of the Colony and Province of Massachusetts's Bay* (1764).
1. I.e., sold his military commission in exchange for a pension worth half his original salary.
2. Adapted from Shakespeare's *Othello* (1.3.145–50), in which Desdemona is said to have listened so carefully to Othello's tales of his past adventures that she fell in love with him.
3. A type of lace. Mechelen is a city in Belgium known for its fine lace.

and sensible to encourage the introduction of any fashion which might help to render them corrupt and effeminate.

These observations served only to inflame her desire of knowing the particulars about which she had enquired; and, with all his evasion, he could not help discovering the following circumstances—that his princess had neither shoes, stockings, shift, nor any kind of linen—that her bridal dress consisted of a petticoat of red bays,[4] and a fringed blanket, fastened about her shoulders with a copper skewer; but of ornaments she had great plenty.—Her hair was curiously plaited, and interwoven with bobbins of human bone—one eye-lid was painted green, and the other yellow; the cheeks were blue, the lips white, the teeth red, and there was a black list drawn down the middle of the forehead as far as the tip of the nose—a couple of gaudy parrot's feathers were stuck through the division of the nostrils—there was a blue stone set in the chin—her ear-rings consisted of two pieces of hickory, of the size and shape of drumsticks—her arms and legs were adorned with bracelets of wampum—her breast glittered with numerous strings of glass beads—she wore a curious pouch, or pocket, of woven grass, elegantly painted with various colours—about her neck was hung the fresh scalp of a Mohawk warrior, whom her deceased lover had lately slain in battle—and, finally, she was anointed from head to foot with bear's grease, which sent forth a most agreeable odour.

One would imagine that these paraphernalia would not have been much admired by a modern fine lady; but Mrs. Tabitha was resolved to approve of all the captain's connexions.—She wished, indeed, the squaw had been better provided with linen; but she owned there was much taste and fancy in her ornaments; she made no doubt, therefore, that madam Squinkinacoosta was a young lady of good sense and rare accomplishments, and a good christian at bottom. Then she asked whether his consort had been high-church or low-church, presbyterian or anabaptist, or had been favoured with any glimmering of the new light of the gospel? When he confessed that she and her whole nation were utter strangers to the christian faith, she gazed at him with signs of astonishment, and Humphry Clinker, who chanced to be in the room, uttered a hollow groan.

After some pause, "In the name of God, captain Lismahago, (cried she) what religion do they profess?" "As to religion, madam, (answered the lieutenant) it is among those Indians a matter of great simplicity—they never heard of any Alliance between Church and State.[5]—They, in general, worship two contending principles; one

---

4. A soft woolen material, usually spelled "baize."
5. Probably an allusion to William Warburton's *Alliance between Church and State: or the Necessity and Equity of an Established Religion and a Test Law demonstrated* (1736).

the Fountain of all Good, the other the source of evil.—The common people there, as in other countries, run into the absurdities of superstition; but sensible men pay adoration to a Supreme Being, who created and sustains the universe." "O! what pity, (exclaimed the pious Tabby) that some holy man has not been inspired to go and convert these poor heathens!"

The lieutenant told her, that while he resided among them, two French missionaries arrived, in order to convert them to the catholic religion; but when they talked of mysteries and revelations, which they could neither explain nor authenticate, and called in the evidence of miracles which they believed upon hearsay; when they taught, that the Supreme Creator of Heaven and Earth had allowed his only Son, his own equal in power and glory, to enter the bowels of a woman, to be born as a human creature, to be insulted, flagellated, and even executed as a malefactor; when they pretended to create God himself, to swallow, digest, revive, and multiply him *ad infinitum*, by the help of a little flour and water[6] the Indians were shocked at the impiety of their presumption.—They were examined by the assembly of the sachems, who desired them to prove the divinity of their mission by some miracle.—They answered, that it was not in their power.——"If you were really sent by Heaven for our conversion, (said one of the sachems) you would certainly have some supernatural endowments, at least you would have the gift of tongues, in order to explain your doctrine to the different nations among which you are employed; but you are so ignorant of our language, that you cannot express yourselves even on the most trifling subjects."

In a word, the assembly were convinced of their being cheats, and even suspected them of being spies:—they ordered them a bag of Indian corn a-piece, and appointed a guide to conduct them to the frontiers; but the missionaries having more zeal than discretion, refused to quit the vineyard.—They persisted in saying mass, in preaching, baptizing, and squabbling with the conjurers, or priests of the country, till they had thrown the whole community into confusion.—Then the assembly proceeded to try them as impious impostors, who represented the Almighty as a trifling, weak, capricious being, and pretended to make, unmake, and reproduce him at pleasure: they were, therefore, convicted of blasphemy and sedition, and condemned to the stake, where they died singing *Salve regina*,[7] in a rapture of joy, for the crown of martyrdom which they had thus obtained.

6. Referring to the Catholic rite of the Eucharist, also called Holy Communion, in which celebrants eat unleavened bread and drink wine that represents (or, according to the doctrine of transubstantiation, is said to become) the body and blood of Jesus Christ.
7. A medieval hymn to the Virgin Mary.

In the course of this conversation, lieutenant Lismahago dropt some hints by which it appeared he himself was a free-thinker. Our aunt seemed to be startled at certain sarcasms he threw out against the creed of saint Athanasius.[8]—He dwelt much upon the words, *reason, philosophy,* and *contradiction in terms*—he bid defiance to the eternity of hell-fire; and even threw such squibs at the immortality of the soul, as singed a little the whiskers of Mrs. Tabitha's faith; for, by this time, she began to look upon Lismahago as a prodigy of learning and sagacity.—In short, he could be no longer insensible to the advances she made towards his affection; and although there was something repulsive in his nature, he overcame it so far as to make some return to her civilities.—Perhaps, he thought it would be no bad scheme, in a superannuated lieutenant on half-pay, to effect a conjunction with an old maid, who, in all probability, had fortune enough to keep him easy and comfortable in the fag-end of his days.— An ogling correspondence forthwith commenced between this amiable pair of originals.—He began to sweeten the natural acidity of his discourse with the treacle of compliment and commendation.— He from time to time offered her snuff, of which he himself took great quantities, and even made her a present of a purse of silk grass, woven by the hands of the amiable Squinkinacoosta, who had used it as a shot-pouch in her hunting-expeditions.

From Doncaster northwards, all the windows of all the inns are scrawled with doggrel rhimes,[9] in abuse of the Scotch nation; and what surprised me very much, I did not perceive one line written in the way of recrimination—Curious to hear what Lismahago would say on this subject, I pointed out to him a very scurrilous epigram against his countrymen, which was engraved on one of the windows of the parlour where we sat.——He read it with the most starched composure; and when I asked his opinion of the poetry, "It is vara terse and vara poignant; (said he) but with the help of a wat dish-clout, it might be rendered more clear and parspicous.—I marvel much that some modern wit has not published a collection of these essays under the title of the *Glazier's Triumph over Sawney the Scot*—— I'm persuaded it would be a vara agreable offering to the patriots of London and Westminster." When I expressed some surprize that the natives of Scotland, who travel this way, had not broke all the windows upon the road, "With submission, (replied the lieutenant) that were but shailow policy—it would only serve to make the satire more cutting and severe; and, I think, it is much better to let it stand in the window, than have it presented in the reckoning."

---

8. An ancient Christian creed, often erroneously attributed to Saint Athanasius, affirming Christ's divinity.
9. Satirical verses.

My uncle's jaws began to quiver with indignation.——He said, the scribblers of such infamous stuff deserved to be scourged at the cart's tail for disgracing their country with such monuments of malice and stupidity.—"These vermin (said he) do not consider, that they are affording their fellow-subjects, whom they abuse, continual matter of self-gratulation, as well as the means of executing the most manly vengeance that can be taken for such low, illiberal attacks. For my part, I admire the philosophic forbearance of the Scots, as much as I despise the insolence of those wretched libellers, which is akin to the arrogance of the village cock, who never crows but upon his own dunghill." The captain, with an affectation of candour, observed, that men of illiberal minds were produced in every soil; that in supposing those were the sentiments of the English in general, he should pay too great a compliment to his own country, which was not of consequence enough to attract the envy of such a flourishing and powerful people.

Mrs. Tabby broke forth again in praise of his moderation, and declared that Scotland was the soil which produced every virtue under heaven.—When Lismahago took his leave for the night, she asked her brother if the captain was not the prettiest gentleman he had ever seen; and whether there was not something wonderfully engaging in his aspect?—Mr. Bramble having eyed her some time in silence, "Sister, (said he) the lieutenant is, for aught I know, an honest man, and a good officer—he has a considerable share of understanding, and a title to more encouragement than he seems to have met with in life; but I cannot, with a safe conscience, affirm, that he is the prettiest gentleman I ever saw; neither can I discern any engaging charm in his countenance, which, I vow to Gad, is, on the contrary, very hard-favoured and forbidding."

I have endeavoured to ingratiate myself with this North-Briton, who is really a curiosity; but he has been very shy of my conversation ever since I laughed at his asserting that the English tongue was spoke with more propriety at Edinburgh than at London. Looking at me with a double squeeze of souring in his aspect, "If the old definition be true, (said he) that risibility is the distinguishing characteristic of a rational creature, the English are the most distinguished for rationality of any people I ever knew." I owned, that the English were easily struck with any thing that appeared ludicrous, and apt to laugh accordingly; but it did not follow, that, because they were more given to laughter, they had more rationality than their neighbours: I said, such an inference would be an injury to the Scots, who were by no means defective in rationality, though generally supposed little subject to the impressions of humour.

The captain answered, that this supposition must have been deduced either from their conversation or their compositions, of which the English could not possibly judge with precision, as they did not understand the dialect used by the Scots in common discourse, as well as in their works of humour. When I desired to know what those works of humour were, he mentioned a considerable number of pieces, which he insisted were equal in point of humour to any thing extant in any language dead or living.——He, in particular, recommended a collection of detached poems, in two small volumes, intituled, *The Ever-green*,[1] and the works of Allan Ramsay, which I intend to provide myself with at Edinburgh.—He observed, that a North-Briton is seen to a disadvantage in an English company, because he speaks in a dialect that they can't relish, and in a phraseology which they don't understand.—He therefore finds himself under a restraint, which is a great enemy to wit and humour.— These are faculties which never appear in full lustre, but when the mind is perfectly at ease, and, as an excellent writer says, enjoys her elbow-room.[2]

He proceeded to explain his assertion that the English language was spoken with greater propriety at Edinburgh than in London.—He said, what we generally called the Scottish dialect was, in fact, true, genuine old English, with a mixture of some French terms and idioms, adopted in a long intercourse betwixt the French and Scotch nations;[3] that the modern English, from affectation and false refinement, had weakened, and even corrupted their language, by throwing out the guttural sounds, altering the pronunciation and the quantity, and disusing many words and terms of great significance. In consequence of these innovations, the works of our best poets, such as Chaucer, Spenser, and even Shakespeare, were become, in many parts, unintelligible to the natives of South-Britain, whereas the Scots, who retain the antient language, understand them without the help of a glossary. "For instance, (said he) how have your commentators been puzzled by the following expression in the *Tempest*— *He's gentle, and not fearful*;[4] as if it was a paralogism[5] to say, that being gentle, he must of course be courageous: but the truth is, one of the original meanings, if not the sole meaning, of that word was, *noble, high-minded*; and to this day, a Scotch woman, in the situation of the young lady in the *Tempest*, would express herself nearly in the same terms—Don't provoke him; for being gentle, that is, *high*

1. *The Evergreen*, an anthology of Scots poems first assembled and published by the poet Allan Ramsay (1686–1758) in Edinburgh in 1724.
2. From the poem "A Day" (1761), by the writer and physician John Armstrong (1709–1779).
3. The longstanding friendly relationship between Scotland and France, known in the former as "the Auld Alliance," dates from a treaty signed in 1295 to oppose Edward I of England.
4. From Shakespeare's *The Tempest* (1.2.468), in which Miranda pleads for Ferdinand's life.
5. Contradiction.

spirited, he won't tamely bear an insult. Spenser, in the very first stanza of his Fairy Queen, says,

> 'A gentle knight was pricking on the plain;'

which knight, far from being tame and fearful, was so stout that

> 'Nothing did he dread, but ever was ydrad.'[6]

To prove that we had impaired the energy of our language by false refinement, he mentioned the following words, which, though widely different in signification, are pronounced exactly in the same manner—*wright, write, right, rite*; but among the Scots, these words are as different in pronunciation, as they are in meaning and orthography; and this is the case with many others which he mentioned by way of illustration.——He, moreover, took notice, that we had (for what reason he could never learn) altered the sound of our vowels from that which is retained by all the nations in Europe; an alteration which rendered the language extremely difficult to foreigners, and made it almost impracticable to lay down general rules for orthography and pronunciation. Besides, the vowels were no longer simple sounds in the mouth of an Englishman, who pronounced both i and u as diphthongs.[7] Finally, he affirmed, that we mumbled our speech with our lips and teeth, and ran the words together without pause or distinction, in such a manner, that a foreigner, though he understood English tolerably well, was often obliged to have recourse to a Scotchman to explain what a native of England had said in his own language.

The truth of this remark was confirmed by Mr. Bramble from his own experience; but he accounted for it on another principle.——He said, the same observation would hold in all languages; that a Swiss talking French was more easily understood than a Parisian, by a foreigner who had not made himself master of the language; because every language had its peculiar recitative,[8] and it would always require more pains, attention, and practice, to acquire both the words and the music, than to learn the words only; and yet no body would deny, that the one was imperfect without the other: he therefore apprehended, that the Scotchman and the Swiss were better understood by learners, because they spoke the words only, without the music, which they could not rehearse. One would imagine this check might have damped the North-Briton; but it served only to agitate his humour for disputation.——He said, if every nation had its own recitative or music, the Scots had theirs, and the

---

6. From *The Faerie Queene* (lines 1.1.1 and 1.1.19). Edmund Spenser (ca. 1552–1599) published the first two parts of his famous allegorical poem in 1590 and 1596.
7. A vowel sound in which a single syllable is given two successive qualities.
8. An operatic term denoting sung speech.

Scotchman who had not yet acquired the cadence of the English, would naturally use his own in speaking their language; therefore, if he was better understood than the native, his recitative must be more intelligible than that of the English; of consequence, the dialect of the Scots had an advantage over that of their fellow-subjects, and this was another strong presumption that the modern English had corrupted their language in the article of pronunciation.

The lieutenant was, by this time, become so polemical, that every time he opened his mouth out flew a paradox, which he maintained with all the enthusiasm of altercation; but all his paradoxes savoured strong of a partiality for his own country. He undertook to prove that poverty was a blessing to a nation; that oatmeal was preferable to wheat-flour; and that the worship of Cloacina,[9] in temples which admitted both sexes, and every rank of votaries promiscuously, was a filthy species of idolatry that outraged every idea of delicacy and decorum. I did not so much wonder at his broaching these doctrines, as at the arguments, equally whimsical and ingenious, which he adduced in support of them.

In fine, lieutenant Lismahago is a curiosity which I have not yet sufficiently perused; and therefore I shall be sorry when we lose his company, though, God knows, there is nothing very amiable in his manner or disposition.—As he goes directly to the south-west division of Scotland, and we proceed in the road to Berwick, we shall part to-morrow at a place called Felton-bridge,[1] and, I dare say, this separation will be very grievous to our aunt Mrs. Tabitha, unless she has received some flattering assurance of his meeting her again. If I fail in my purpose of entertaining you with these unimportant occurrences, they will at least serve as exercises of patience, for which you are indebted to

Yours always,

Morpeth, July 13. J. MELFORD.

To Dr. LEWIS.

DEAR DOCTOR,

I have now reached the northern extremity of England, and see, close to my chamber-window, the Tweed gliding through the arches of that bridge which connects this suburb to the town of Berwick.— Yorkshire you have seen, and therefore I shall say nothing of that

9. The cleanser (Latin); a surname for the Roman goddess Venus. It is invoked here as a euphemism for using the bathroom.
1. A bridge crossing the Rover Coquet at the town of Felton.

opulent province. The city of Durham appears like a confused heap of stones and brick, accumulated so as to cover a mountain, round which a river winds its brawling course. The streets are generally narrow, dark, and unpleasant, and many of them almost impassible in consequence of their declivity. The cathedral is a huge gloomy pile; but the clergy are well lodged——The bishop lives in a princely manner—the golden prebends keep plentiful tables—and, I am told, there is some good sociable company in the place; but the country, when viewed from the top of Gateshead Fell,[2] which extends to Newcastle, exhibits the highest scene of cultivation that ever I beheld. As for Newcastle, it lies mostly in a bottom, on the banks of the Tyne, and makes an appearance still more disagreeable than that of Durham; but it is rendered populous and rich by industry and commerce; and the country lying on both sides the river, above the town, yields a delightful prospect of agriculture and plantation. Morpeth and Alnwick are neat, pretty towns, and this last is famous for the castle which has belonged so many ages to the noble house of Piercy, earls of Northumberland.—It is, doubtless, a large edifice, containing a great number of apartments, and stands in a commanding situation; but the strength of it seems to have consisted not so much in its site, or the manner in which it is fortified, as in the valour of its defendants.

Our adventures since we left Scarborough, are scarce worth reciting; and yet I must make you acquainted with my sister Tabby's progress in husband-hunting, after her disappointments at Bath and London. She had actually begun to practise upon a certain adventurer, who was in fact a highwayman by profession; but he had been used to snares much more dangerous than any she could lay, and escaped accordingly.—Then she opened her batteries upon an old weather-beaten Scotch lieutenant, called Lismahago, who joined us at Durham, and is, I think, one of the most singular personages I ever encountered.—His manner is as harsh as his countenance; but his peculiar turn of thinking, and his pack of knowledge made up of the remnants of rarities, rendered his conversation desirable, in spite of his pedantry and ungracious address.—I have often met with a crab-apple in a hedge, which I have been tempted to eat for its flavour, even while I was disgusted by its austerity. The spirit of contradiction is naturally so strong in Lismahago, that I believe in my conscience he has rummaged, and read, and studied with indefatigable attention, in order to qualify himself to refute established maxims, and thus raise trophies for the gratification of polemical pride.—Such is the asperity of his self-conceit, that he will not even

2. A parish that rises to Beacon Hill, noted for its extensive views. "Prebends": cathedral administrators.

acquiesce in a transient compliment made to his own individual in particular, or to his country in general.

When I observed, that he must have read a vast number of books to be able to discourse on such a variety of subjects, he declared he had read little or nothing, and asked how he should find books among the woods of America, where he had spent the greatest part of his life. My nephew remarking that the Scots in general were famous for their learning, he denied the imputation, and defied him to prove it from their works.—"The Scots (said he) have a slight tincture of letters, with which they make a parade among people who are more illiterate than themselves; but they may be said to float on the surface of science, and they have made very small advances in the useful arts." "At least, (cried Tabby) all the world allows that the Scots behaved gloriously in fighting and conquering the savages of America." "I can assure you, madam, you have been misinformed; (replied the lieutenant) in that continent the Scots did nothing more than their duty, nor was there one corps in his majesty's service that distinguished itself more than another.—Those who affected to extol the Scots for superior merit, were no friends to that nation."

Though he himself made free with his countrymen, he would not suffer any other person to glance a sarcasm at them with impunity. One of the company chancing to mention lord B——'s inglorious peace,[3] the lieutenant immediately took up the cudgels in his lordship's favour; and argued very strenuously to prove that it was the most honourable and advantageous peace that England had ever made since the foundation of the monarchy.—Nay, between friends, he offered such reasons on this subject, that I was really confounded, if not convinced.—He would not allow that the Scots abounded above their proportion in the army and navy of Great-Britain, or that the English had any reason to say his countrymen had met with extraordinary encouragement in the service.—"When a South and North-Briton (said he) are competitors for a place or commission, which is in the disposal of an English minister or an English general, it would be absurd to suppose that the preference will not be given to the native of England, who has so many advantages over his rival.—First and foremost, he has in his favour that laudable partiality, which, Mr. Addison says, never fails to cleave to the heart of an Englishman;[4] secondly, he has more powerful connexions, and

---

3. The Peace of Paris (February 10, 1763) ended the Seven Years' War. Although Britain gained Canada and Florida in the peace negotiations, the treaty was controversial largely because of the unpopularity of Lord Bute, who aided the negotiations.
4. Joseph Addison (1672–1719), a prolific writer best remembered for *The Spectator*, a daily periodical he wrote with Richard Steele (1672–1729) from 1711 to 1712. The reference here may be specifically to *Spectator* 69 (May 19, 1711), in which Addison writes of "the secret Satisfaction" he takes as "an Englishman" at seeing merchants and traders from around the world gather to do business at London's Royal Exchange.

a greater share of parliamentary interest, by which those contests are generally decided; and lastly, he has a greater command of money to smooth the way to his success. For my own part, (said he) I know no Scotch officer, who has risen in the army above the rank of a sub-altern,[5] without purchasing every degree of preferment either with money or recruits; but I know many gentlemen of that country, who, for want of money and interest, have grown grey in the rank of lieuten-ants; whereas very few instances of this ill fortune are to be found among the natives of South-Britain.—Not that I would insinuate that my countrymen have the least reason to complain.—Preferment in the service, like success in any other branch of traffic, will natu-rally favour those who have the greatest stock of cash and credit, merit and capacity being supposed equal on all sides."

But the most hardy of all this original's positions were these:— That commerce would, sooner or later, prove the ruin of every nation, where it flourishes to any extent—that the parliament was the rotten part of the British constitution—that the liberty of the press was a national evil—and that the boasted institution of juries, as managed in England, was productive of shameful perjury and flagrant injustice. He observed, that traffick was an enemy to all the liberal passions of the soul, founded on the thirst of lucre, a sordid disposition to take advantage of the necessities of our fellow-creatures.——He affirmed, the nature of commerce was such, that it could not be fixed or perpetuated, but, having flowed to a certain height, would immediately begin to ebb, and so continue till the channels should be left almost dry; but there was no instance of the tide's rising a second time to any considerable influx in the same nation. Mean while the sudden affluence occasioned by trade, forced open all the sluices of luxury and overflowed the land with every species of profligacy and corruption; a total pravity[6] of man-ners would ensue, and this must be attended with bankruptcy and ruin. He observed of the parliament, that the practice of buying bor-oughs, and canvassing for votes, was an avowed system of venality, already established on the ruins of principle, integrity, faith, and good order, in consequence of which the elected and the elector, and, in short, the whole body of the people, were equally and univer-sally contaminated and corrupted. He affirmed, that of a parliament thus constituted, the crown would always have influence enough to secure a great majority in its dependence, from the great number of posts, places, and pensions it had to bestow; that such a parliament would (as it had already done) lengthen the term of its sitting and authority, whenever the prince should think it for his interest to

---

5. A commissioned officer below the rank of captain.
6. Depravity.

continue the representatives; for, without doubt, they had the same right to protract their authority *ad infinitum*, as they had to extend it from three to seven years.—With a parliament, therefore, dependent upon the crown, devoted to the prince, and supported by a standing army, garbled and modelled for the purpose, any king of England may, and probably some ambitious sovereign will, totally overthrow all the bulwarks of the constitution; for it is not to be supposed that a prince of a high spirit will tamely submit to be thwarted in all his measures, abused and insulted by a populace of unbridled ferocity, when he has it in his power to crush all opposition under his feet with the concurrence of the legislature. He said, he should always consider the liberty of the press as a national evil, while it enabled the vilest reptile to soil the lustre of the most shining merit, and furnished the most infamous incendiary with the means of disturbing the peace and destroying the good order of the community. He owned, however, that, under due restrictions, it would be a valuable privilege; but affirmed, that at present there was no law in England sufficient to restrain it within proper bounds.

With respect to juries, he expressed himself to this effect:—— Juries are generally composed of illiterate plebeians, apt to be mistaken, easily misled, and open to sinister influence; for if either of the parties to be tried, can gain over one of the twelve jurors, he has secured the verdict in his favour; the juryman thus brought over will, in despight of all evidence and conviction, generally hold out till his fellows are fatigued, and harrassed, and starved into concurrence; in which case the verdict is unjust, and the jurors are all perjured: but cases will often occur, when the jurors are really divided in opinion, and each side is convinced in opposition to the other; but no verdict will be received, unless they are unanimous, and they are all bound, not only in conscience, but by oath, to judge and declare according to their conviction.—What then will be the consequence?—They must either starve in company, or one side must sacrifice their conscience to their convenience, and join in a verdict which they believe to be false. This absurdity is avoided in Sweden, where a bare majority is sufficient; and in Scotland, where two thirds of the jury are required to concur in the verdict.[7]

You must not imagine that all these deductions were made on his part, without contradiction on mine.—No—the truth is, I found myself piqued in point of honour, at his pretending to be so much wiser than his neighbours.—I questioned all his assertions, started innumerable objections, argued and wrangled with uncommon perseverance, and grew very warm, and even violent, in the debate.— Sometimes he was puzzled, and once or twice, I think, fairly refuted;

---

7. In fact, Scottish law required only a bare majority.

but from those falls he rose again, like Antæus,[8] with redoubled vigour, till at length I was tired, exhausted, and really did not know how to proceed, when luckily he dropped a hint, by which he discovered he had been bred to the law; a confession which enabled me to retire from the dispute with a good grace, as it could not be supposed that a man like me, who had been bred to nothing, should be able to cope with a veteran in his own profession. I believe, however, that I shall for some time continue to chew the cud of reflection upon many observations which this original discharged.

Whether our sister Tabby was really struck with his conversation, or is resolved to throw at every thing she meets in the shape of a man, till she can fasten the matrimonial noose, certain it is, she has taken desperate strides towards the affection of Lismahago, who cannot be said to have met her half way, tho' he does not seem altogether insensible to her civilities.—She insinuated more than once how happy we should be to have his company through that part of Scotland which we proposed to visit, till at length he plainly told us, that his road was totally different from that which we intended to take; that, for his part, his company would be of very little service to us in our progress, as he was utterly unacquainted with the country, which he had left in his early youth; consequently, he could neither direct us in our inquiries, nor introduce us to any family of distinction. He said, he was stimulated by an irresistible impulse to revisit the *paternus lar, or patria domus,*[9] though he expected little satisfaction, inasmuch as he understood that his nephew, the present possessor, was but ill qualified to support the honour of the family.—He assured us, however, as we design to return by the west road, that he will watch our motions, and endeavour to pay his respects to us at Dumfries.——Accordingly he took his leave of us at a place half way betwixt Morpeth and Alnwick, and pranced away in great state, mounted on a tall, meagre, raw-boned, shambling grey gelding, without e'er a tooth in his head, the very counter-part of the rider; and, indeed, the appearance of the two was so picturesque, that I would give twenty guineas to have them tolerably represented on canvas.

Northumberland is a fine county, extending to the Tweed, which is a pleasant pastoral stream; but you will be surprised when I tell you that the English side of that river is neither so well cultivated nor so populous as the other.—The farms are thinly scattered, the lands uninclosed, and scarce a gentleman's seat is to be seen in some miles from the Tweed; whereas the Scots are advanced in crowds to the very brink of the river, so that you may reckon above

8. In Greek mythology, a giant who was invincible as long as he could touch the earth.
9. The paternal hearth or paternal home (Latin).

thirty good houses, in the compass of a few miles, belonging to proprietors whose ancestors had fortified castles in the same situations, a circumstance that shews what dangerous neighbours the Scots must have formerly been to the northern counties of England.

Our domestic œconomy continues on the old footing.—My sister Tabby still adheres to methodism, and had the benefit of a sermon at Wesley's meeting in Newcastle;[1] but I believe the passion of love has in some measure abated the fervour of devotion both in her and her woman, Mrs. Jenkins, about whose good graces there has been a violent contest betwixt my nephew's valet, Mr. Dutton, and my man, Humphry Clinker.—Jery has been obliged to interpose his authority to keep the peace; and to him I have left the discussion of that important affair, which had like to have kindled the flames of discord in the family of

Yours always,

Tweedmouth, July 15.   Matt. Bramble.

To Sir Watkin Phillips, Bar^t. at Oxon.

Dear Wat,

In my two last you had so much of Lismahago, that I suppose you are glad he is gone off the stage for the present.—I must now descend to domestic occurrences.—Love, it seems, is resolved to assert his dominion over all the females of our family.—After having practised upon poor Liddy's heart, and played strange vagaries with our aunt Mrs. Tabitha, he began to run riot in the affections of her woman Mrs. Winifred Jenkins, whom I have had occasion to mention more than once in the course of our memoirs. Nature intended Jenkins for something very different from the character of her mistress; yet custom and habit have effected a wonderful resemblance betwixt them in many particulars. Win, to be sure, is much younger and more agreeable in her person; she is likewise tenderhearted and benevolent, qualities for which her mistress is by no means remarkable, no more than she is for being of a timorous disposition, and much subject to fits of the mother, which are the infirmities of Win's constitution: but then she seems to have adopted Mrs. Tabby's manner with her cast cloaths.—She dresses and endeavours to look like her mistress, although her own looks are much more engaging.——She enters into her scheme of œconomy, learns her phrases, repeats her remarks, imitates her stile in scolding the

---

1. John Wesley, Methodism's founder, preached in Newcastle in May 1766, when Smollett may have heard him.

inferior servants, and, finally, subscribes implicitly to her system of devotion—This, indeed, she found the more agreeable, as it was in a great measure introduced and confirmed by the ministry of Clinker, with whose personal merit she seems to have been struck ever since he exhibited the pattern of his naked skin at Marlborough.

Nevertheless, though Humphry had this double hank[2] upon her inclinations, and exerted all his power to maintain the conquest he had made, he found it impossible to guard it on the side of vanity, where poor Win was as frail as any female in the kingdom. In short, my rascal Dutton professed himself her admirer, and, by dint of his outlandish qualifications, threw his rival Clinker out of the saddle of her heart. Humphry may be compared to an English pudding, composed of good wholesome flour and suet, and Dutton to a syllabub[3] or iced froth, which, though agreeable to the taste, has nothing solid or substantial. The traitor not only dazzled her with his second-hand finery, but he fawned, and flattered, and cringed—he taught her to take rappee, and presented her with a snuff-box of *papier maché*[4]—he supplied her with a powder for her teeth—he mended her complexion, and he dressed her hair in the Paris fashion—he undertook to be her French master and her dancing-master, as well as friseur, and thus imperceptibly wound himself into her good graces. Clinker perceived the progress he had made, and repined in secret.—He attempted to open her eyes in the way of exhortation, and finding it produced no effect had recourse to prayer. At Newcastle, while he attended Mrs. Tabby to the methodist meeting, his rival accompanied Mrs. Jenkins to the play. He was dressed in a silk coat, made at Paris for his former master, with a tawdry waistcoat of tarnished brocade; he wore his hair in a great bag with a huge solitaire[5] and a long sword dangled from his thigh. The lady was all of a flutter with faded lutestring, washed gauze, and ribbons three times refreshed; but she was most remarkable for the frisure of her head, which rose, like a pyramid, seven inches above the scalp, and her face was primed and patched from the chin up to the eyes; nay, the gallant himself had spared neither red nor white in improving the nature of his own complexion. In this attire, they walked together through the high street to the theatre, and as they passed for players ready dressed for acting, they reached it unmolested; but as it was still light when they returned, and by that time the people had got information of their real character and condition, they hissed

2. Nautical term for a fastening ring or shackle.
3. A whipped cream dessert, typically flavored with wine or sherry. "Suet": the hard white fat on the kidneys and loins of livestock.
4. Stiffened paper that can be molded into different forms. "Rappee": strong snuff made from dark, pungent tobacco leaves.
5. A small silken pouch, fastened with a single diamond or other precious stone, to contain the back hair of a wig.

and hooted all the way, and Mrs. Jenkins was all bespattered with dirt, as well as insulted with the opprobrious name of *painted Jeza-bel*,[6] so that her fright and mortification threw her into an hysteric fit the moment she came home.

Clinker was so incensed at Dutton, whom he considered as the cause of her disgrace, that he upbraided him severely for having turned the poor young woman's brain. The other affected to treat him with contempt, and mistaking his forbearance for want of courage, threatened to horsewhip him into good manners. Humphry then came to me, humbly beging I would give him leave to chastise my servant for his insolence—"He has challenged me to fight him at sword's point; (said he) but I might as well challenge him to make a horse-shoe, or a plough-iron; for I know no more of the one than he does of the other.—Besides, it doth not become servants to use those weapons, or to claim the privilege of gentlemen to kill one another when they fall out; moreover, I would not have his blood upon my conscience for ten thousand times the profit or satisfaction I should get by his death; but if your honour won't be angry, I'll engage to gee en a good drubbing, that, may hap, will do 'en service, and I'll take care it shall do 'en no harm." I said, I had no objection to what he proposed, provided he could manage matters so as not to be found the aggressor, in case Dutton should prosecute him for an assault and battery.

Thus licensed, he retired; and that same evening easily provoked his rival to strike the first blow, which Clinker returned with such interest that he was obliged to call for quarter, declaring, at the same time, that he would exact severe and bloody satisfaction the moment we should pass the border, when he could run him through the body without fear of the consequence.——This scene passed in presence of lieutenant Lismahago, who encouraged Clinker to hazard a thrust of cold iron with his antagonist. "Cold iron (cried Humphry) I shall never use against the life of any human creature; but I am so far from being afraid of his cold iron, that I shall use nothing in my defence but a good cudgel, which shall always be at his service." In the mean time, the fair cause of this contest, Mrs. Winifred Jenkins, seemed overwhelmed with affliction, and Mr. Clinker acted much on the reserve, though he did not presume to find fault with her conduct.

The dispute between the two rivals was soon brought to a very unexpected issue. Among our fellow-lodgers at Berwick,[7] was a couple

6. In the Bible, the scheming wife of Ahab (2 Kings 9:30–37), who puts on makeup (paints her face) to appear even more seductive. Her name became synonymous with an evil or wanton female.
7. Possibly an error, but since Tweedmouth (the site of Matt's previous letter) and Berwick are nearly contiguous, it seems more likely that the former, smaller town has simply been subsumed by the latter here.

from London, bound to Edinburgh, on the voyage of matrimony. The female was the daughter and heiress of a pawn-broker deceased, who had given her guardians the slip, and put herself under the tuition of a tall Hibernian, who had conducted her thus far in quest of a clergyman to unite them in marriage, without the formalities required by the law of England.[8] I know not how the lover had behaved on the road, so as to decline in the favour of his innamorata; but, in all probability, Dutton perceived a coldness on her side, which encouraged him to whisper, it was a pity she should have cast her affections upon a taylor, which he affirmed the Irishman to be. This discovery completed her disgust, of which my man taking the advantage, began to recommend himself to her good graces, and the smooth-tongued rascal found no difficulty to insinuate himself into the place of her heart, from which the other had been discarded— Their resolution was immediately taken. In the morning, before day, while poor Teague lay snoring a-bed, his indefatigable rival ordered a post-chaise, and set out with the lady for Coldstream, a few miles up the Tweed, where there was a parson who dealt in this branch of commerce, and there they were noosed, before the Irishman ever dreamt of the matter. But when he got up at six o'clock, and found the bird was flown, he made such a noise as alarmed the whole house. One of the first persons he encountered, was the postilion returned from Coldstream, where he had been witness to the marriage, and over and above an handsome gratuity, had received a bride's favour,[9] which he now wore in his cap—When the forsaken lover understood they were actually married, and set out for London; and that Dutton had discovered to the lady, that he (the Hibernian) was a taylor, he had like to have run distracted. He tore the ribbon from the fellow's cap, and beat it about his ears. He swore he would pursue him to the gates of hell, and ordered a post-chaise and four to be got ready as soon as possible; but, recollecting that his finances would not admit of this way of travelling, he was obliged to countermand this order.

For my part, I knew nothing at all of what had happened, till the postilion brought me the keys of my trunk and portmanteau, which he had received from Dutton, who sent me his respects, hoping I would excuse him for his abrupt departure, as it was a step upon which his fortune depended—Before I had time to make my uncle

8. The Marriage Act of 1753 required that marriage banns (proclamations) be publicly announced or that a marriage license be obtained in advance of any wedding, which had to take place in a church (Jews and Quakers were excepted). The act did not apply in Scotland. "Hibernian": Irishman.
9. A decorative piece of lace or ribbon, designed to be removed from the bride's clothing and presented to well-wishers at the wedding.

acquainted with this event, the Irishman burst into my chamber, without any introduction, exclaiming,—"By my soul, your sarvant has robbed me of five thousand pounds, and I'll have satisfaction, if I should be hanged tomorrow.—" When I asked him who he was, "My name (said he) is Master Macloughlin—but it should be Leighlin Oneale, for I am come from Ter-Owen the Great;[1] and so I am as good a gentleman as any in Ireland; and that rogue, your sarvant, said I was a taylor, which was as big a lie as if he had called me the pope—I'm a man of fortune, and have spent all I had; and so being in distress, Mr. Coshgrave, the fashioner in Shuffolk-street,[2] tuck me out, and made me his own private shecretary: by the same token, I was the last he bailed; for his friends obliged him to tie himself up, that he would bail no more above ten pounds; for why, becaase as how, he could not refuse any body that asked, and therefore in time would have robbed himself of his whole fortune, and, if he had lived long at that rate, must have died bankrupt very soon—and so I made my addresses to Miss Skinner, a young lady of five thousand pounds fortune, who agreed to take me for better nor worse; and, to be sure, this day would have put me in possession, if it had not been for that rogue, your sarvant, who came like a tief, and stole away my property, and made her believe I was a taylor; and that she was going to marry the ninth part of a man: but the devil burn my soul, if ever I catch him on the mountains of Tulloghobegly, if I don't shew him that I'm nine times as good a man as he, or e'er a bug of his country."[3]

When he had rung out his first alarm, I told him I was sorry he had allowed himself to be so jockied; but it was no business of mine; and that the fellow who robbed him of his bride, had likewise robbed me of my servant—"Didn't I tell you then, (cried he,) that Rogue was his true Christian name.—Oh if I had but one fair trust with him upon the sod, I'd give him lave to brag all the rest of his life."

My uncle hearing the noise, came in, and being informed of this adventure, began to comfort Mr. Oneale for the lady's elopement; observing that he seemed to have had a lucky escape, that it was better she should elope before, than after marriage—The Hibernian was of a very different opinion. He said, "If he had been once married, she might have eloped as soon as she pleased; he would have taken care that she should not have carried her fortune along

---

1. Presumably a reference to Owen Roe O'Neill (1590–1649), a famous soldier from the O'Neill dynasty of Ulster.
2. Suffolk Street, a fashionable London street near Pall Mall.
3. "The ninth part of a man" is an allusion to the proverb "Nine tailors make a man." The mountains of Tulloghobegly presumably refer to those of County Tyrone in what is now Northern Ireland, near the bally (townland) of Tullagh Beg. "Bug": an Irish nickname for the English, who were said to have introduced insects to Ireland.

with her—Ah (said he) she's a Judas Iscariot, and has betrayed me
with a kiss; and, like Judas, she carried the bag,[4] and has not left me
money enough to bear my expences back to London; and so as I'm
come to this pass, and the rogue that was the occasion of it has left
you without a sarvant, you may put me in his place; and by Jasus, it
is the best thing you can do.—" I begged to be excused, declaring I
could put up with any inconvenience, rather than treat as a footman the descendant of Tir-Owen the Great. I advised him to return
to his friend, Mr. Cosgrave, and take his passage from Newcastle
by sea, towards which I made him a small present, and he retired,
seemingly resigned to his evil fortune. I have taken upon trial a
Scotchman, called Archy M'Alpin, an old soldier, whose last master,
a colonel, lately died at Berwick. The fellow is old and withered; but
he has been recommended to me for his fidelity, by Mrs. Humphreys,
a very good sort of a woman, who keeps the inn at Tweedmouth,
and is much respected by all the travellers on this road.

Clinker, without doubt, thinks himself happy in the removal of
a dangerous rival, and he is too good a Christian, to repine at
Dutton's success. Even Mrs. Jenkins will have reason to congratulate
herself upon this event, when she cooly reflects upon the matter;
for, howsoever she was forced from her poise for a season, by snares
laid for her vanity, Humphrey is certainly the north-star to which
the needle of her affection would have pointed at the long run. At
present, the same vanity is exceedingly mortified, upon finding herself abandoned by her new admirer, in favour of another innamorata. She received the news with a violent burst of laughter, which
soon brought on a fit of crying; and this gave the finishing blow to
the patience of her mistress, which had held out beyond all expectation. She now opened all those floodgates of reprehension, which
had been shut so long. She not only reproached her with her levity
and indiscretion, but attacked her on the score of religion, declaring roundly that she was in a state of apostacy and reprobation; and
finally, threatened to send her a-packing at this extremity of the kingdom. All the family interceded for poor Winifrid, not even excepting
her slighted swain, Mr. Clinker, who, on his knees, implored and
obtained her pardon.

There was, however, another consideration that gave Mrs. Tabitha
some disturbance. At Newcastle, the servants had been informed
by some wag, that there was nothing to eat in Scotland, but *oat-meal*
and sheep's-heads; and Lieutenant Lismahago being consulted,
what he said served rather to confirm than to refute the report. Our
aunt being apprised of this circumstance, very gravely advised her

---

4. In the New Testament, Judas Iscariot betrays Jesus to the Romans with a kiss. According to the account in the Gospel of John (13:29), Judas was the disciples' treasurer and
   therefore carried their moneybag.

brother to provide a sumpter horse[5] with store of hams, tongues, bread, biscuit, and other articles for our subsistence, in the course of our peregrination, and Mr. Bramble as gravely replied, that he would take the hint into consideration: but, finding no such provision was made, she now revived the proposal, observing that there was a tolerable market at Berwick, where we might be supplied; and that my man's horse would serve as a beast of burthen—The 'squire, shrugging up his shoulders, eyed her askance with a look of ineffable contempt; and, after some pause, "Sister, (said he) I can hardly persuade myself you are serious." She was so little acquainted with the geography of the island, that she imagined we could not go to Scotland but by sea; and, after we had passed through the town of Berwick, when he told her we were upon Scottish ground, she could hardly believe the assertion—If the truth must be told, the South Britons in general are woefully ignorant in this particular. What, between want of curiosity, and traditional sarcasms, the effect of ancient animosity, the people at the other end of the island know as little of Scotland as of Japan.

If I had never been in Wales, I should have been more struck with the manifest difference in appearance betwixt the peasants and commonalty on different sides of the Tweed. The boors of Northumberland are lusty fellows, fresh complexioned, cleanly, and well cloathed; but the labourers in Scotland are generally lank, lean, hard-featured, sallow, soiled, and shabby, and their little pinched blue caps have a beggarly effect. The cattle are much in the same stile with their drivers, meagre, stunted, and ill equipt. When I talked to my uncle on this subject, he said, "Though all the Scottish hinds would not bear to be compared with those of the rich counties of South Britain, they would stand very well in competition with the peasants of France, Italy, and Savoy—not to mention the mountaineers of Wales, and the redshanks[6] of Ireland."

We entered Scotland by a frightful moor of sixteen miles, which promises very little for the interior parts of the kingdom; but the prospect mended as we advanced. Passing through Dunbar, which is a neat little town, situated on the sea-side, we lay at a country inn, where our entertainment far exceeded our expectation; but for this we cannot give the Scots credit, as the landlord is a native of England. Yesterday we dined at Haddington, which has been a place of some consideration, but is now gone to decay; and in the evening arrived at this metropolis[7] of which I can say very little. It is very romantic, from its situation on the declivity of a hill, having a fortified castle

5. Pack horse.
6. An allusion to the reddened legs of kilt-wearing Celts.
7. I.e., the city of Edinburgh.

at the top, and a royal palace at the bottom. The first thing that strikes the nose of a stranger, shall be nameless;[8] but what first strikes the eye, is the unconscionable height of the houses, which generally rise to five, six, seven, and eight stories, and, in some places, (as I am assured) to twelve. This manner of building, attended with number-less inconveniences, must have been originally owing to want of room. Certain it is, the town seems to be full of people: but their looks, their language, and their customs, are so different from ours, that I can hardly believe myself in Great-Britain.

The inn at which we put up, (if it may be so called) was so filthy and disagreeable in all respects, that my uncle began to fret, and his gouty symptoms to recur—Recollecting, however, that he had a let-ter of recommendation to one Mr. Mitchelson,[9] a lawyer, he sent it by his servant, with a compliment, importing that he would wait upon him next day in person; but that gentleman visited us imme-diately, and insisted upon our going to his own house, until he could provide lodgings for our accommodation. We gladly accepted of his invitation, and repaired to his house, where we were treated with equal elegance and hospitality, to the utter confusion of our aunt, whose prejudices, though beginning to give way, were not yet entirely removed. Today, by the assistance of our friend, we are set-tled in convenient lodgings, up four pair of stairs, in the High-street, the fourth story being, in this city, reckoned more genteel than the first. The air is, in all probability, the better; but it requires good lungs to breathe it at this distance above the surface of the earth.— While I do remain above it, whether higher or lower, provided I breathe at all,

I shall ever be,

dear Phillips, yours,

July 18.   J. MELFORD.

To Dr. LEWIS.

DEAR LEWIS,

That part of Scotland contiguous to Berwick, nature seems to have intended as a barrier between two hostile nations. It is a brown desert of considerable extent, that produces nothing but heath and

---

8. The smell of raw sewage, which was dumped into the streets, and coal smoke combined to give Edinburgh its nickname of "Auld Reekie."
9. Samuel Mitchelson (d. 1788), an attorney and friend of Smollett's. As a writer to the signet, he could prepare royal writs and charters bearing the signet (seal) of the Court of Session, the supreme civil court.

fern; and what rendered it the more dreary when we passed, there was a thick fog that hindered us from seeing above twenty yards from the carriage—My sister began to make wry faces, and use her smelling-bottle; Liddy looked blank, and Mrs. Jenkins dejected; but in a few hours these clouds were dissipated; the sea appeared upon our right, and on the left the mountains retired a little, leaving an agreeable plain betwixt them and the beach; but, what surprised us all, this plain, to the extent of several miles, was covered with as fine wheat as ever I saw in the most fertile parts of South Britain—— This plentiful crop is raised in the open field, without any inclosure, or other manure than the alga marina, or sea-weed, which abounds on this coast; a circumstance which shews that the soil and climate are favourable; but that agriculture in this country is not yet brought to that perfection which it has attained in England. Inclosures would not only keep the grounds warm, and the several fields distinct, but would also protect the crop from the high winds, which are so frequent in this part of the island.

Dunbar is well situated for trade, and has a curious bason, where ships of small burthen may be perfectly secure; but there is little appearance of business in the place—From thence, all the way to Edinburgh, there is a continual succession of fine seats, belonging to noblemen and gentlemen; and as each is surrounded by its own parks and plantation, they produce a very pleasing effect in a country which lies otherwise open and exposed. At Dunbar there is a noble park, with a lodge, belonging to the Duke of Roxburgh, where Oliver Cromwell had his head-quarters, when Lesley,[1] at the head of a Scotch army, took possession of the mountains in the neighbourhood, and hampered him in such a manner, that he would have been obliged to embark and get away by sea, had not the fanaticism of the enemy forfeited the advantage which they had obtained by their general's conduct—Their ministers, by exhortation, prayer, assurance, and prophecy, instigated them to go down and slay the Philistines in Gilgal,[2] and they quitted their ground accordingly, notwithstanding all that Lesley could do to restrain the madness of their enthusiasm——When Oliver saw them in motion, he exclaimed, "Praised be the Lord, he hath delivered them into the hands of his servant!" and ordered his troops to sing a psalm of thanksgiving, while they advanced in order to the plain, where the Scots were routed with great slaughter.

1. When the Scottish government declared loyalty to Charles II and Oliver Cromwell (1599–1658) invaded Scotland, David Leslie, Lord Newark (ca. 1600–1682), commanded the Scottish troops.
2. An allusion to 1 Samuel 13. Newark was apparently pressured to relinquish his army's superior geographical position by overconfident Kirk ministers.

In the neighbourhood of Haddington, there is a gentleman's house, in the building of which, and the improvements about it, he is said to have expended forty thousand pounds: but I cannot say I was much pleased with either the architecture or the situation; though it has in front a pastoral stream, the banks of which are laid out in a very agreeable manner. I intended to pay my respects to lord Elibank,[3] whom I had the honour to know at London many years ago. He lives in this part of Lothian;[4] but was gone to the North, on a visit—You have often heard me mention this nobleman, whom I have long revered for his humanity and universal intelligence, over and above the entertainment arising from the originality of his character—At Musselburgh, however, I had the good-fortune to drink tea with my old friend Mr. Cardonel; and at his house I met with Dr. C——,[5] the parson of the parish, whose humour and conversation inflamed me with a desire of being better acquainted with his person—I am not at all surprised that these Scots make their way in every quarter of the globe.

This place is but four miles from Edinburgh, towards which we proceeded along the sea-shore, upon a firm bottom of smooth sand, which the tide had left uncovered in its retreat——Edinburgh, from this avenue, is not seen to much advantage—We had only an imperfect view of the Castle[6] and upper parts of the town, which varied incessantly according to the inflexions of the road, and exhibited the appearance of detached spires and turrets, belonging to some magnificent edifice in ruins. The palace of Holyrood house stands on the left, as you enter the Canongate[7]—This is a street continued from hence to the gate called Nether Bow, which is now taken away;[8] so that there is no interruption for a long mile, from the bottom to the top of the hill on which the Castle stands in a most imperial situation——Considering its fine pavement, its width, and the lofty houses on each side, this would be undoubtedly one of the

3. Patrick Murray, fifth Baron Elibank (1703–1778), was an attorney and an intelligent patron of the arts. "Gentleman's house": probably Amisfield, formerly the seat of Colonel Francis Charteris (1675–1732), a notorious profligate.
4. A traditional region of Scotland comprising West Lothian, Midlothian, and East Lothian.
5. Alexander Carlyle (1722–1805), a clergyman in Musselburgh, a suburb of Edinburgh. A good friend and correspondent of Smollett's, he left vivid portraits of him and other Edinburgh literati in his posthumously published *Autobiography* (1860). Mansfeldt de Cardonnel, a customs commissioner for Scotland.
6. The earliest remaining structures of Edinburgh Castle date from the 12th century, but the site appears to have been occupied since at least the 7th century, when the city was supposedly founded by Edwin, king of Northumbria, after whom it is named.
7. The easternmost section of Edinburgh's "Royal Mile," named after the Augustinian clergy (canons) who founded Holyrood Abbey. Holyrood Palace (formally the Palace of Holyroodhouse), originally the site of an abbey founded by King David I in 1128, developed from a guesthouse attached to the abbey. It became an official royal residence under James V of Scotland in 1529.
8. The Netherbow gate was removed in 1764.

noblest streets in Europe, if an ugly mass of mean buildings, called the Lucken-Booths, had not thrust itself, by what accident I know not, into the middle of the way, like Middle-Row in Holborn.[9] The city stands upon two hills, and the bottom between them; and, with all its defects, may very well pass for the capital of a moderate kingdom—It is full of people, and continually resounds with the noise of coaches and other carriages, for luxury as well as commerce. As far as I can perceive, here is no want of provisions—The beef and mutton are as delicate here as in Wales; the sea affords plenty of good fish; the bread is remarkably fine; and the water is excellent, though I'm afraid not in sufficient quantity to answer all the purposes of cleanliness and convenience; articles in which, it must be allowed, our fellow-subjects are a little defective—The water is brought in leaden pipes from a mountain in the neighbourhood, to a cistern on the Castle-hill, from whence it is distributed to public conduits in different parts of the city—From these it is carried in barrels, on the backs of male and female porters, up two, three, four, five, six, seven, and eight pair of stairs, for the use of particular families—Every story is a complete house, occupied by a separate family; and the stair being common to them all, is generally left in a very filthy condition; a man must tread with great circumspection to get safe housed with unpolluted shoes—Nothing can form a stronger contrast, than the difference betwixt the outside and inside of the door; for the good-women of this metropolis are remarkably nice[1] in the ornaments and propriety of their apartments, as if they were resolved to transfer the imputation from the individual to the public. You are no stranger to their method of discharging all their impurities from their windows, at a certain hour of the night, as the custom is in Spain, Portugal, and some parts of France and Italy—A practice to which I can by no means be reconciled; for notwithstanding all the care that is taken by their scavengers to remove this nuisance every morning by break of day, enough still remains to offend the eyes, as well as other organs of those whom use has not hardened against all delicacy of sensation.

The inhabitants seem insensible to these impressions, and are apt to imagine the disgust that we avow is little better than affectation; but they ought to have some compassion for strangers, who have not been used to this kind of sufferance; and consider, whether it may not be worth while to take some pains to vindicate themselves from the reproach that, on this account, they bear among their

9. A block of homes that protruded into Gray's Inn Lane in Holborn, an area of central London, until they were removed in 1868. Lucken-Booths were a row of houses, with shops on the first floors, in the High Street near St. Giles's Cathedral. They were removed in 1817.
1. Careful, fastidious.

neighbours. As to the surprising height of their houses, it is absurd in many respects; but in one particular light I cannot view it without horror; that is, the dreadful situation of all the families above, in case the common stair-case should be rendered impassable by a fire in the lower stories—In order to prevent the shocking consequences that must attend such an accident, it would be a right measure to open doors of communication from one house to another, on every story, by which the people might fly from such a terrible visitation. In all parts of the world, we see the force of habit prevailing over all the dictates of convenience and sagacity—All the people of business at Edinburgh, and even the genteel company, may be seen standing in crowds every day, from one to two in the afternoon, in the open street, at a place where formerly stood a market-cross, which (by the bye) was a curious piece of Gothic architecture, still to be seen in lord Sommerville's[2] garden in this neighbourhood—I say, the people stand in the open street from the force of custom, rather than move a few yards to an Exchange that stands empty on one side, or to the Parliament-close on the other, which is a noble square, adorned with a fine equestrian statue of king Charles II.—The company thus assembled, are entertained with a variety of tunes, played upon a set of bells, fixed in a steeple hard by—As these bells are well-toned, and the musician, who has a salary from the city, for playing upon them with keys, is no bad performer, the entertainment is really agreeable, and very striking to the ears of a stranger.

The public inns of Edinburgh, are still worse than those of London; but by means of a worthy gentleman, to whom I was recommended, we have got decent lodgings in the house of a widow gentlewoman, of the name of Lockhart;[3] and here I shall stay until I have seen every thing that is remarkable in and about this capital. I now begin to feel the good effects of exercise——I eat like a farmer, sleep from mid-night till eight in the morning without interruption, and enjoy a constant tide of spirits, equally distant from inanition and excess; but whatever ebbs or flows my constitution may undergo, my heart will still declare that I am,

Dear Lewis,

Your affectionate friend and servant,

Edr. July 18.   MATT. BRAMBLE.

---

2. James Somerville, fourteenth Lord Somerville (1727–1796). "Market-cross": when the ancient Mercat Cross of Edinburgh was removed in 1756, the pillar (but not the fifteen-foot tower) was moved to the nearby Somerville estate.
3. According to Edinburgh tax records, a Mrs. Lockhart lived on High Street until 1769.

To Mrs. MARY JONES, at Brambleton-hall.

DEAR MARY,

The 'squire has been so kind as to rap my bit of nonsense under the kiver of his own sheet—O, Mary Jones! Mary Jones! I have had trials and trembulation. God help me! I have been a vixen and a griffin these many days—Sattin has had power to temp me in the shape of van Ditton, the young 'squire's wally de shamble;[4] but by God's grease he did not purvail—I thoft as how, there was no arm in going to a play at Newcastle, with my hair dressed in the Parish fashion; and as for the trifle of paint, he said as how my complexion wanted rouch, and so I let him put it on with a little Spanish owl;[5] but a mischievous mob of colliers, and such promiscous ribble rabble, that could bare no smut but their own, attacked us in the street, and called me hoar and *painted Issabel*, and splashed my close, and spoiled me a complete set of blond lace triple ruffles, not a pin the worse for the ware—They cost me seven good sillings, to lady Griskin's woman at London.

When I axed Mr. Clinker what they meant by calling me Issabel, he put the byebill into my hand, and I read of van Issabel a painted harlot, that vas thrown out of a vindore, and the dogs came and licked her blood—But I am no harlot; and, with God's blessing, no dog shall have my poor blood to lick: marry, Heaven forbid, amen! As for Ditton, after all his courting, and his compliment, he stole away an Irishman's bride, and took a French leave of me and his master; but I vally not his going a farting; but I have had hanger on his account—Mistriss scoulded like mad; thof I have the comfit that all the family took my part, and even Mr. Clinker pleaded for me on his bended knee; thof, God he knows, he had raisins enuff to complain; but he's a good sole, abounding with Christian meekness, and one day will meet with his reward.

And now, dear Mary, we have got to Haddingborrough, among the Scots, who are civil enuff for our money, thof I don't speak their lingo—But they should not go for to impose upon foreigners; for the bills in their houses say, they have different easements to let; and behold there is nurro geaks[6] in the whole kingdom, nor any thing for poor sarvants, but a barrel with a pair of tongs thrown a-cross; and all the chairs in the family are emptied into this here barrel once a-day; and at ten o'clock at night the whole cargo is flung out of a back windore that looks into some street or lane, and the maid calls *gardy loo*[7] to the passengers, which signifies *Lord have mercy upon you!*

4. I.e., valet de chambre; a personal servant.
5. I.e., Spanish wool; wool impregnated with a red dye.
6. Not a single jakes (outhouse).
7. From *gardez l'eau* (French); "look out for the water."

and this is done every night in every house in Haddingborrough; so you may guess, Mary Jones, what a sweet savour comes from such a number of profuming pans; but they say it is wholsome, and, truly, I believe it is; for being in the vapours, and thinking of Issabel and Mr. Clinker, I was going into a fit of astericks, when this fiff, saving your presence, took me by the nose so powerfully that I sneezed three times, and found myself wonderfully refreshed; and this to be sure is the raisin why there are no fits in Haddingborrough.

I was likewise made believe, that there was nothing to be had but *oat-meal* and *seeps-heads*; but if I hadn't been a fool, I mought have known there could be no heads without kerkasses——This very blessed day I dined upon a delicate leg of Velsh mutton and cullyflower; and as for the oat-meal, I leave that to the sarvants of the country, which are pore drudges, many of them without shoes or stockings—Mr. Clinker tells me here is a great call of the gospel; but I wish, I wish some of our family be not fallen off from the rite way—O, if I was given to tail-baring, I have my own secrets to discover——There has been a deal of huggling and flurtation betwixt mistress and an ould Scots officer, called Kismycago. He looks for all the orld like the scarecrow that our gardener set up to frite away the sparrows; and what will come of it, the Lord nows; but come what will, it shall never be said that I menchioned a syllabub of the matter—Remember me kindly to Saul and the kitten——I hope they got the horn-buck, and will put it to a good yuse, which is the constant prayer of,

Dear Molly,

your loving friend,

Addingborough, July 18.   WIN. JENKINS.

To Sir WATKIN PHILLIPS, Bar^t.
of Jesus college, Oxon.

DEAR PHILLIPS,

If I stay much longer at Edinburgh, I shall be changed into a downright Caledonian—My uncle observes, that I have already acquired something of the country accent. The people here are so social and attentive in their civilities to strangers, that I am insensibly sucked into the channel of their manners and customs, although they are in fact much more different from ours than you can imagine—That difference, however, which struck me very much at my first arrival, I now hardly perceive, and my ear is perfectly reconciled to the

Scotch accent, which I find even agreeable in the mouth of a pretty woman—It is a sort of Doric dialect,[8] which gives an idea of amiable simplicity——You cannot imagine how we have been caressed and feasted in the *good town of Edinburgh*, of which we are become free denizens and guild brothers, by the special favour of the magistracy.

I had a whimsical commission from Bath, to a citizen of this metropolis—Quin, understanding our intention to visit Edinburgh, pulled out a guinea, and desired the favour I would drink it at a tavern, with a particular friend and bottle-companion of his, one Mr. R—C—,[9] a lawyer of this city—I charged myself with the commission, and, taking the guinea, "You see (said I) I have pocketed your bounty." "Yes (replied Quin, laughing); and a head-ake into the bargain, if you drink fair." I made use of this introduction to Mr. C——, who received me with open arms, and gave me the rendezvous, according to the cartel. He had provided a company of jolly fellows, among whom I found myself extremely happy; and did Mr. C——and Quin all the justice in my power; but, alas, I was no more than a tiro[1] among a troop of veterans, who had compassion upon my youth, and conveyed me home in the morning, by what means I know not—Quin was mistaken, however, as to the headake; the claret was too good to treat me so roughly.

While Mr. Bramble holds conferences with the graver literati of the place, and our females are entertained at visits by the Scotch ladies, who are the best and kindest creatures upon earth, I pass my time among the bucks of Edinburgh; who, with a great share of spirit and vivacity, have a certain shrewdness and self-command that is not often found among their neighbours, in the high-day of youth and exultation——Not a hint escapes a Scotchman that can be interpreted into offence by any individual in the company; and national reflections are never heard—In this particular, I must own, we are both unjust and ungrateful to the Scots; for, as far as I am able to judge, they have a real esteem for the natives of South-Britain; and never mention our country, but with expressions of regard—Nevertheless, they are far from being servile imitators of our modes and fashionable vices. All their customs and regulations of public and private œconomy, of business and diversion, are in their own stile. This remarkably predominates in their looks, their dress, and manner, their music, and even their cookery. Our 'squire

8. A rustic linguistic variation. Debate continues as to whether Scots (sometimes called Lowland Scots to distinguish it from Scottish Gaelic, the Celtic language spoken by in most of the western Highlands and Hebrides) is a dialect of Standard English or a separate language.
9. Robert Cullen (d. 1810) was an attorney and later a judge.
1. Tyro: a novice.

declares, that he knows not another people upon earth, so strongly marked with a national character—Now we are upon the article of cookery, I must own, some of their dishes are savoury, and even delicate; but I am not yet Scotchman enough to relish their singed sheep's-head and haggice, which were provided at our request, one day at Mr. Mitchelson's, where we dined—The first put me in mind of the history of Congo,[2] in which I had read of negros' heads sold publickly in the markets; the last, being a mess of minced lights, livers, suet, oat-meal, onions, and pepper, inclosed in a sheep's stomach, had a very sudden effect upon mine, and the delicate Mrs. Tabby changed colour; when the cause of our disgust was instantaneously removed at the nod of our entertainer. The Scots, in general, are attached to this composition, with a sort of national fondness, as well as to their oat-meal bread; which is presented at every table, in thin triangular cakes, baked upon a plate of iron, called a girdle; and these, many of the natives, even in the higher ranks of life, prefer to wheaten-bread, which they have here in perfection—You know we used to vex poor Murray of Baliol-college,[3] by asking, if there was really no fruit but turnips in Scotland?——Sure enough, I have seen turnips make their appearance, not as a desert, but by way of *hors d'oeuvres,* or whets, as radishes are served up betwixt more substantial dishes in France and Italy; but it must be observed, that the turnips of this country are as much superior in sweetness, delicacy, and flavour, to those of England, as a musk-melon[4] is to the stock of a common cabbage. They are small and conical, of a yellowish colour, with a very thin skin; and, over and above their agreeable taste, are valuable for their antiscorbutic[5] quality—As to the fruit now in season, such as cherries, gooseberries, and currants, there is no want of them at Edinburgh; and in the gardens of some gentlemen, who live in this neighbourhood, there is now a very favourable appearance of apricots, peaches, nectarines, and even grapes: nay, I have seen a very fine shew of pine-apples within a few miles of this metropolis. Indeed, we have no reason to be surprised at these particulars, when we consider how little difference there is, in fact, betwixt this climate and that of London.

All the remarkable places in the city and its avenues, for ten miles around, we have visited, much to our satisfaction. In the Castle are some royal apartments, where the sovereign occasionally resided; and here are carefully preserved the regalia of the kingdom, consisting

---

2. Probably a reference to William Snelgrave's *A New Account of Some Parts of Guinea and the Slave Trade* (1734).
3. Perhaps a reference to Gideon Murray, the younger brother of Lord Elibank. Murray was a student at Balliol College, Oxford, from 1729 to 1736.
4. A yellow or green melon with raised networks of markings on its skin—i.e., a cantaloupe.
5. Effective at preventing scurvy.

of a crown, said to be of great value, a sceptre, and a sword of state, adorned with jewels—Of these symbols of sovereignty, the people are exceedingly jealous—A report being spread, during the sitting of the union-parliament,[6] that they were removed to London, such a tumult arose, that the lord commissioner would have been torn in pieces, if he had not produced them for the satisfaction of the populace.

The palace of Holyrood-house is an elegant piece of architecture, but sunk in an obscure, and, as I take it, unwholesome bottom, where one would imagine it had been placed on purpose to be concealed. The apartments are lofty, but unfurnished; and as for the pictures of the Scottish kings, from Fergus I. to king William, they are paultry daubings, mostly by the same hand,[7] painted either from the imagination, or porters hired to sit for the purpose. All the diversions of London we enjoy at Edinburgh, in a small compass. Here is a well-conducted concert, in which several gentlemen perform on different instruments—The Scots are all musicians—Every man you meet plays on the flute, the violin, or violoncello; and there is one nobleman,[8] whose compositions are universally admired—Our company of actors is very tolerable; and a subscription is now on foot for building a new theatre;[9] but their assemblies please me above all other public exhibitions.

We have been at the hunters ball,[1] where I was really astonished to see such a number of fine women—The English, who have never crossed the Tweed, imagine erroneously, that the Scotch ladies are not remarkable for personal attractions; but, I can declare with a safe conscience, I never saw so many handsome females together, as were assembled on this occasion. At the Leith races,[2] the best company comes hither from the remoter provinces; so that, I suppose, we had all the beauty of the kingdom concentrated as it were into one focus; which was, indeed, so vehement, that my heart could hardly resist its power—Between friends, it has sustained some damage from the bright eyes of the charming miss R——n,[3] whom I had the honour to dance with at the ball—The countess of Melvile attracted all

6. A reference to the Scottish parliament that met in 1706–07 to pass the Act of Union between England and Scotland. Scotland subsequently gave up its own parliament (in favor of forty-five seats in the newly expanded British Parliament in Westminster) until 1999, when it met again following the 1998 Scotland Act.
7. Jacob de Wet (1640–1697), a Dutch painter. In 1684, he contracted to paint 110 portraits of Scottish monarchs in two years.
8. Likely Thomas Erskine, sixth Earl of Kellie (1732–1781), an accomplished violinist, composer, and conductor. Weekly concerts were a well-known feature of Edinburgh social life through most of the 18th century.
9. Edinburgh's Theatre Royal formally opened in December 1769.
1. Presumably the annual ball given by the Caledonian Hunt, a society of Scottish nobility and gentry who supported field sports.
2. Horse races were held annually since the mid-17th century in the historic port of Leith: about two miles north of central Edinburgh.
3. Probably Cecilia Renton, although possibly her sister Eleanora. The former married Smollett's nephew, Alexander Telfer.

eyes, and the admiration of all present—She was accompanied by the agreeable miss Grieve, who made many conquests; nor did my sister Liddy pass unnoticed in the assembly—She is become a toast at Edinburgh, by the name of the Fair Cambrian, and has already been the occasion of much wine-shed; but the poor girl met with an accident at the ball, which has given us great disturbance.

A young gentleman, the express image of that rascal Wilson, went up to ask her to dance a minuet; and his sudden appearance shocked her so much, that she fainted away—I call Wilson a rascal, because, if he had been really a gentleman, with honourable intentions, he would have, ere now, appeared in his own character—I must own, my blood boils with indignation when I think of that fellow's presumption; and Heaven confound me if I don't—But I won't be so womanish as to rail—Time will, perhaps, furnish occasion—Thank God, the cause of Liddy's disorder remains a secret. The lady directress of the ball, thinking she was overcome by the heat of the place, had her conveyed to another room, where she soon recovered so well, as to return and join in the country-dances, in which the Scotch lasses acquit themselves with such spirit and agility, as put their partners to the height of their mettle—I believe our aunt, Mrs. Tabitha, had entertained hopes of being able to do some execution among the cavaliers at this assembly——She had been several days in consultation with milliners and mantua-makers, preparing for the occasion, at which she made her appearance in a full suit of damask, so thick and heavy, that the sight of it alone, at this season of the year, was sufficient to draw drops of sweat from any man of ordinary imagination—She danced one minuet with our friend, Mr. Mitchelson, who favoured her so far, in the spirit of hospitality and politeness; and she was called out a second time by the young laird of Ballymawhawple,[4] who, coming in by accident, could not readily find any other partner; but as the first was a married man, and the second payed no particular homage to her charms, which were also over-looked by the rest of the company, she became dissatisfied and censorious—At supper, she observed that the Scotch gentlemen made a very good figure, when they were a little improved by travelling; and therefore it was pity they did not all take the benefit of going abroad—She said the women were aukward, masculine creatures; that, in dancing, they lifted their legs like so many colts; that they had no idea of graceful motion, and put on their clothes in a frightful manner; but if the truth must be told, Tabby herself was the most ridiculous figure, and the worst dressed of the whole assembly—The neglect of the male sex rendered her malcontent and

4. A comic Irish name, since many Irish place names begin with "Bally." A laird was a landed proprietor and should not be confused with a lord, i.e., a member of the nobility.

peevish; she now found fault with every thing at Edinburgh, and teized her brother to leave the place, when she was suddenly reconciled to it on a religious consideration——There is a sect of fanaticks, who have separated themselves from the established kirk, under the name of Seceders[5]—They acknowledge no earthly head of the church, reject lay-patronage, and maintain the methodist doctrines of the new birth, the new light, the efficacy of grace, the insufficiency of works, and the operations of the spirit. Mrs. Tabitha, attended by Humphry Clinker, was introduced to one of their conventicles,[6] where they both received much edification; and she has had the good fortune to come acquainted with a pious Christian, called Mr. Moffat, who is very powerful in prayer, and often assists her in private exercises of devotion.

I never saw such a concourse of genteel company at any races in England, as appeared on the course of Leith—Hard by, in the fields called the Links, the citizens of Edinburgh divert themselves at a game called golf,[7] in which they use a curious kind of bats, tipt with horn, and small elastic balls of leather, stuffed with feathers, rather less than tennis balls, but of a much harder consistence—This they strike with such force and dexterity from one hole to another, that they will fly to an incredible distance. Of this diversion the Scots are so fond, that when the weather will permit, you may see a multitude of all ranks, from the senator of justice to the lowest tradesmen, mingled together in their shirts, and following the balls with the utmost eagerness—Among others, I was shewn one particular set of golfers, the youngest of whom was turned of fourscore—— They were all gentlemen of independent fortunes, who had amused themselves with this pastime for the best part of a century, without having ever felt the least alarm from sickness or disgust; and they never went to bed, without having each the best part of a gallon of claret in his belly. Such uninterrupted exercise, cooperating with the keen air from the sea, must, without all doubt, keep the appetite always on edge, and steel the constitution against all the common attacks of distemper.

The Leith races gave occasion to another entertainment of a very singular nature—There is at Edinburgh a society or corporation of errand-boys, called cawdies, who ply in the streets at night with paper lanthorns, and are very serviceable in carrying messages— These fellows, though shabby in their appearance, and rudely familiar in their address, are wonderfully acute, and so noted for fidelity, that there is no instance of a cawdy's having betrayed his

---

5. A sect that left the Kirk in the 1730s.
6. Nonconformist religious meetings.
7. Invented in Scotland and dating back to at least the mid-15th century. The Honourable Company of Edinburgh Golfers was established in 1744.

trust—Such is their intelligence, that they know, not only every individual of the place, but also every stranger, by that time he has been four and twenty hours in Edinburgh; and no transaction, even the most private, can escape their notice—They are particularly famous for their dexterity in executing one of the functions of Mercury;[8] though, for my own part, I never employed them in this department of business—Had I occasion for any service of this nature, my own man Archy M'Alpine, is as well qualified as e'er a cawdie in Edinburgh; and I am much mistaken, if he has not been heretofore of their fraternity. Be that as it may, they resolved to give a dinner and a ball at Leith, to which they formally invited all the young noblemen and gentlemen that were at the races; and this invitation was reinforced by an assurance that all the celebrated ladies of pleasure would grace the entertainment with their company.—I received a card on this occasion, and went thither with half a dozen of my acquaintance.—In a large hall the cloth was laid on a long range of tables joined together, and here the company seated themselves, to the number of about fourscore, lords, and lairds, and other gentlemen, courtezans and cawdies mingled together, as the slaves and their masters were in the time of the Saturnalia[9] in ancient Rome.—The toastmaster, who sat at the upper end, was one Cawdie Fraser, a veteran pimp, distinguished for his humour and sagacity, well known and much respected in his profession by all the guests, male and female, that were here assembled.—He had bespoke the dinner and the wine: he had taken care that all his brethren should appear in decent apparel and clean linen; and he himself wore a periwig with three tails, in honour of the festival—I assure you the banquet was both elegant and plentiful, and seasoned with a thousand sallies, that promoted a general spirit of mirth and good humour.—After the desert, Mr. Fraser proposed the following toasts, which I don't pretend to explain.—"The best in Christendom."—"Gibb's contract."—"The beggar's bennison."[1] —"King and kirk."—"Great-Britain and Ireland."——Then, filling a bumper, and turning to me, "Mester Malford, (said he) may a' unkindness cease betwixt John Bull and his sister Moggy."[2]—The next person he singled out, was a nobleman who had been long abroad.—"Ma lord, (cried Fraser) here is a bumper to a' those noblemen who have

---

8. The classical deity Mercury, god of commerce and communication, occasionally acted as a procurer of women (i.e., a pimp) for other gods.
9. A Roman festival in honor of the god Saturn, celebrated between December 17 and 23, in which social hierarchies were overturned, e.g., masters served meals to their slaves.
1. Drinking toasts. The first stands for "To the best cunt in Christendom," and the third is "May your prick and your purse never fail you." It was not unusual for 18th-century carousers to mix patriotic and obscene toasts.
2. A variant of Maggie, short for Margaret. Peg, another nickname for Margaret, was commonly used to refer to Scotland. John Bull was the name for a stereotypical Englishman.

virtue enough to spend their rents in their ain countray."—He afterwards addressed himself to a member of parliament in these words:— "Mester—I'm sure ye'll ha' nae objection to my drinking, Disgrace and dule to ilka Scot, that sells his conscience and his vote."—He discharged a third sarcasm at a person very gaily dressed, who had risen from small beginnings, and made a considerable fortune at play.—Filling his glass, and calling him by name, "Lang life (said he) to the wylie loon that gangs a-field with a toom poke at his lunzie,[3] and comes hame with a sackful of siller."——All these toasts being received with loud bursts of applause, Mr. Fraser called for pint glasses, and filled his own to the brim: then standing up, and all his brethren following his example, "Ma lords and gentlemen (cried he), here is a cup of thanks for the great and undeserved honour you have done your poor errand-boys this day."—So saying, he and they drank off their glasses in a trice, and, quitting their seats, took their station each behind one of the other guests;—exclaiming, "Noo we're your honours cawdies again."

The nobleman who had bore the first brunt of Mr. Fraser's satire, objected to his abdication. He said, as the company was assembled by invitation from the cawdies, he expected they were to be entertained at their expence. "By no means, my lord, (cried Fraser) I wad na be guilty of sic presumption for the wide warld—I never affronted a gentleman since I was born; and sure at this age, I wonnot offer an indignity to sic an honourable convention." "Well, (said his Lordship) as you have expended some wit, you have a right to save your money. You have given me good counsel, and I take it in good part. As you have voluntarily quitted your seat, I will take your place with the leave of the good company, and think myself happy to be hailed, *Father of the Feast.*" He was forthwith elected into the chair, and complimented in a bumper in his new character.

The claret continued to circulate without interruption, till the glasses seemed to dance upon the table, and this, perhaps, was a hint to the ladies to call for music—At eight in the evening the ball began in another apartment: at midnight we went to supper; but it was broad day before I found the way to my lodgings; and, no doubt, his Lordship had a swinging bill to discharge.

In short, I have lived so riotously for some weeks, that my uncle begins to be alarmed on the score of my constitution, and very seriously observes, that all his own infirmities are owing to such excesses indulged in his youth—Mrs. Tabitha says it would be more for the advantage of my soul as well as body, if, instead of frequenting these scenes of debauchery, I would accompany Mr. Moffat and her to hear a sermon of the reverend Mr. M'Corkindale.—Clinker often

---

3. With an empty purse at his side.

exhorts me, with a groan, to take care of my precious health; and even Archy M'Alpine, when he happens to be overtaken,[4] (which is oftener the case than I could wish) reads me a long lecture upon temperance and sobriety; and is so very wise and sententious, that, if I could provide him with a professor's chair, I would willingly give up the benefit of his admonitions and service together; for I was tutor-sick at alma mater.

I am not, however, so much engrossed by the gaieties of Edinburgh, but that I find time to make parties in the family way.—We have not only seen all the villas and villages within ten miles of the capital, but we have also crossed the Firth, which is an arm of the sea seven miles broad, that divides Lothian from the shire, or, as the Scots call it, the *kingdom of Fife*.[5] There is a number of large open sea-boats that ply on this passage from Leith to Kinghorn, which is a borough on the other side. In one of these our whole family embarked three days ago, excepting my sister, who, being exceedingly fearful of the water, was left to the care of Mrs. Mitchelson. We had an easy and quick passage into Fife, where we visited a number of poor towns on the sea-side, including St. Andrew's, which is the skeleton of a venerable city; but we were much better pleased with some noble and elegant seats and castles, of which there is a great number in that part of Scotland. Yesterday we took boat again on our return to Leith, with fair wind and agreeable weather; but we had not advanced half-way when the sky was suddenly overcast, and the wind changing, blew directly in our teeth; so that we were obliged to turn, or tack the rest of the way. In a word, the gale increased to a storm of wind and rain, attended with such a fog, that we could not see the town of Leith, to which we were bound, nor even the castle of Edinburgh, notwithstanding its high situation. It is not to be doubted but that we were all alarmed on this occasion. And at the same time, most of the passengers were seized with a nausea that produced violent retchings. My aunt desired her brother to order the boatmen to put back to Kinghorn, and this expedient he actually proposed; but they assured him there was no danger. Mrs. Tabitha finding them obstinate, began to scold, and insisted upon my uncle's exerting his authority as a justice of the peace. Sick and peevish as he was, he could not help laughing at this wise proposal, telling her, that his commission did not extend so far, and, if it did, he should let the people take their own way; for he thought it would be great presumption in him to direct them in the exercise of their own profession. Mrs. Winifred Jenkins made a general clearance with the assistance of Mr. Humphrey Clinker, who joined her both in prayer

---

4. Drunk.
5. A historic county on Scotland's eastern shore, between the firths of Forth and Tay.

and ejaculation.—As he took it for granted that we should not be long in this world, he offered some spiritual consolation to Mrs. Tabitha, who rejected it with great disgust, bidding him keep his sermons for those who had leisure to hear such nonsense.—My uncle sat, recollected in himself, without speaking; my man Archy had recourse to a brandy-bottle, with which he made so free, that I imagined he had sworn to die of drinking any thing rather than sea-water: but the brandy had no more effect upon him in the way of intoxication, than if it had been sea water in good earnest.—As for myself, I was too much engrossed by the sickness at my stomach, to think of any thing else.—Meanwhile the sea swelled mountains high, the boat pitched with such violence, as if it had been going to pieces; the cordage rattled, the wind roared; the lightning flashed, the thunder bellowed, and the rain descended in a deluge— Every time the vessel was put about, we ship'd a sea that drenched us all to the skin.—When, by dint of turning, we thought to have cleared the pier head, we were driven to leeward, and then the boatmen themselves began to fear that the tide would fail before we should fetch up our lee-way: the next trip, however, brought us into smooth water, and we were safely landed on the quay, about one o'clock in the afternoon.—"To be sure (cried Tabby, when she found herself on *terra firma*,) we must all have perished, if we had not been the particular care of Providence."—"Yes, (replied my uncle) but I am much of the honest highlander's mind—after he had made such a passage as this: his friend told him he was much indebted to Providence;— "Certainly, (said Donald) but, by my saul, mon, I'se ne'er trouble Providence again, so long as the brig of Stirling stands."——You must know the brig, or bridge of Stirling, stands above twenty miles up the river Forth, of which this is the outlet—I don't find that our 'squire has suffered in his health from this adventure; but poor Liddy is in a peaking way—I'm afraid this unfortunate girl is uneasy in her mind; and this apprehension distracts me, for she is really an amiable creature.

We shall set out to-morrow or next day for Stirling and Glasgow; and we propose to penetrate a little way into the Highlands, before we turn our course to the southward—In the mean time, commend me to all our friends round Carfax, and believe me to be, ever yours,

Edinburgh, Aug. 8.   J. MELFORD.

END OF THE SECOND VOLUME.

Volume III

To Dr. LEWIS.

I should be very ungrateful, dear Lewis, if I did not find myself disposed to think and speak favourably of this people, among whom I have met with more kindness, hospitality, and rational entertainment, in a few weeks, than ever I received in any other country during the whole course of my life.—Perhaps, the gratitude excited by these benefits may interfere with the impartiality of my remarks; for a man is as apt to be prepossessed by particular favours as to be prejudiced by private motives of disgust. If I am partial, there is, at least, some merit in my conversion from illiberal prejudices which had grown up with my constitution.

The first impressions which an Englishman receives in this country, will not contribute to the removal of his prejudices; because he refers every thing he sees to a comparison with the same articles in his own country; and this comparison is unfavourable to Scotland in all its exteriors, such as the face of the country in respect to cultivation, the appearance of the bulk of the people, and the language of conversation in general.—I am not so far convinced by Mr. Lismahago's arguments, but that I think the Scots would do well, for their own sakes, to adopt the English idioms and pronunciation; those of them especially, who are resolved to push their fortunes in South-Britain.——I know, by experience, how easily an Englishman is influenced by the ear, and how apt he is to laugh, when he hears his own language spoken with a foreign or provincial accent.—I have known a member of the house of commons speak with great energy and precision, without being able to engage attention, because his observations were made in the Scotch dialect, which (no offence to lieutenant Lismahago) certainly gives a clownish air even to sentiments of the greatest dignity and decorum.—I have declared my opinion on this head to some of the most sensible men of this country, observing, at the same time, that if they would employ a few natives of England to teach the pronunciation of our vernacular tongue, in twenty years there would be no difference, in point of dialect, between the youth of Edinburgh and of London.

The civil regulations of this kingdom and metropolis are taken from very different models from those of England, except in a few particular establishments, the necessary consequences of the union.[6]—Their college of justice is a bench of great dignity, filled with judges of character and ability.—I have heard some causes tried before this venerable tribunal; and was very much pleased with the pleadings of their advocates, who are by no means deficient either in argument or elocution. The Scottish legislation is founded, in a great measure, on the civil law;[7] consequently, their proceedings vary from those of the English tribunals; but, I think, they have the advantage of us in their method of examining witnesses apart, and in the constitution of their jury,[8] by which they certainly avoid the evil which I mentioned in my last from Lismahago's observation.

The university of Edinburgh[9] is supplied with excellent professors in all the sciences; and the medical school, in particular, is famous all over Europe.—The students of this art have the best opportunity of learning it to perfection, in all its branches, as there are different courses for the *theory of medicine*, and the *practice of medicine*; for *anatomy, chemistry, botany*, and the *materia medica*, over and above those of mathematics and experimental philosophy; and all these are given by men of distinguished talents. What renders this part of education still more complete, is the advantage of attending the infirmary,[1] which is the best instituted charitable foundation that I ever knew. Now we are talking of charities, here are several hospitals, exceedingly well endowed, and maintained under admirable regulations; and these are not only useful, but ornamental to the city. Among these, I shall only mention the general work-house, in which all the poor, not otherwise provided for, are employed, according to their different abilities, with such judgment and effect, that they nearly maintain themselves by their labour, and there is not a beggar to be seen within the precincts of this metropolis. It was Glasgow that set the example of this establishment, about thirty years ago.—Even the kirk of Scotland, so long reproached with fanatacism and canting, abounds at present with ministers celebrated for their learning, and respectable for their moderation.—I have heard their sermons with equal astonishment and pleasure.—The good people of Edinburgh no longer think dirt and cobwebs essential to the house of God.—Some of their churches have admitted such ornaments as would have excited sedition, even in England, a little more than a

6. The Act of Union between England and Scotland was ratified on January 16, 1707.
7. Roman law (rather than common law) was the basis for most Scottish jurisprudence.
8. Defendants could select their fifteen jury members from a pool of forty-five. Witnesses were often examined in private and their testimonies then read aloud in court.
9. Founded in 1583.
1. The Royal Infirmary, founded in 1736.

century ago; and psalmody is here practised and taught by a professor from the cathedral of Durham:[2]—I should not be surprised, in a few years, to hear it accompanied with an organ.

Edinburgh is a hot bed of genius.——I have had the good fortune to be made acquainted with many authors of the first distinction; such as the two Humes, Robertson, Smith, Wallace, Blair, Ferguson, Wilkie,[3] &c. and I have found them all as agreeable in conversation as they are instructive and entertaining in their writings. These acquaintances I owe to the friendship of Dr. Carlyle, who wants nothing but inclination to figure with the rest upon paper. The magistracy of Edinburgh is changed every year by election, and seems to be very well adapted both for state and authority.—The lord provost is equal in dignity to the *lord mayor of London*; and the *four bailies* are equivalent to the rank of aldermen.—There is a *dean of guild*, who takes cognizance of mercantile affairs; a treasurer; a town-clerk; and the council is composed of deacons, one of whom is returned every year, in rotation, as representative of every company of artificers or handicraftsmen. Though this city, from the nature of its situation, can never be made either very convenient or very cleanly, it has, nevertheless, an air of magnificence that commands respect.—The castle is an instance of the sublime in scite and architecture.—Its fortifications are kept in good order, and there is always in it a garrison of regular soldiers, which is relieved every year; but it is incapable of sustaining a siege carried on according to the modern operations of war.——The castle hill, which extends from the outward gate to the upper end of the high-street, is used as a public walk for the citizens, and commands a prospect, equally extensive and delightful, over the county of Fife, on the other side of the Frith, and all along the sea-coast, which is covered with a succession of towns that would seem to indicate a considerable share of commerce; but, if the truth must be told, these towns have been falling to decay ever since the union, by which the Scots were in a great measure deprived of their trade with France.— The palace of Holyrood-house is a jewel in architecture, thrust into a hollow where it cannot be seen; a situation which was certainly not chosen by the ingenious architect, who must have been confined to the scite of the old palace, which was a convent. Edinburgh is considerably extended on the south side, where there are divers little elegant squares built in the English manner; and the citizens have

---

2. Probably Cornforth Gilson, a professional musician who arrived in Edinburgh in 1753.
3. William Wilkie (1721–1772), a poet and educator. David Hume (1711–1776), philosopher, critic, and historian. John Home (pronounced "Hume") (1722–1808), playwright. Dr. William Robertson (1721–1793), prominent historian, educator, and churchman. Adam Smith (1723–1790), philosopher, critic, and economist. Dr. Robert Wallace (1697–1771), churchman and author. Hugh Blair (1718–1800), churchman, critic, and rhetorician. Adam Ferguson (1723–1816), philosopher and historian.

planned some improvements on the north, which, when put in execution, will add greatly to the beauty and convenience of this capital.

The sea-port is Leith, a flourishing town, about a mile from the city, in the harbour of which I have seen above one hundred ships lying all together. You must know, I had the curiosity to cross the Frith in a passage-boat, and stayed two days in Fife, which is remarkably fruitful in corn, and exhibits a surprising number of fine seats, elegantly built, and magnificently furnished. There is an incredible number of noble houses in every part of Scotland that I have seen.— Dalkeith, Pinkie, Yester, and lord Hopton's,[4] all of them within four or five miles of Edinburgh, are princely palaces, in every one of which a sovereign might reside at his ease.—I suppose the Scots affect these monuments of grandeur.—If I may be allowed to mingle censure with my remarks upon a people I revere, I must observe, that their weak side seems to be vanity.—I am afraid that even their hospitality is not quite free of ostentation.—I think I have discovered among them uncommon pains taken to display their fine linen, of which, indeed, they have great plenty, their furniture, plate, house-keeping, and variety of wines, in which article, it must be owned, they are profuse, if not prodigal.—A burgher of Edinburgh, not content to vie with a citizen of London, who has ten times his fortune, must excel him in the expence as well as elegance of his entertainments.

Though the villas of the Scotch nobility and gentry have generally an air of grandeur and state, I think their gardens and parks are not comparable to those of England; a circumstance the more remarkable, as I was told by the ingenious Mr. Philip Miller of Chelsea,[5] that almost all the gardeners of South-Britain were natives of Scotland. The verdure of this country is not equal to that of England.—The pleasure-grounds are, in my opinion, not so well laid out according to the *genius loci*;[6] nor are the lawns, and walks, and hedges kept in such delicate order.—The trees are planted in prudish rows, which have not such an agreeable natural effect, as when they are thrown into irregular groupes, with intervening glades; and the firs, which they generally raise around their houses, look dull and funereal in the summer season.——I must confess, indeed, that they yield serviceable timber, and good shelter against the northern blasts; that they grow and thrive in the most barren soil, and continually perspire a fine balsam of turpentine, which must render the air very salutary and sanative to lungs of a tender texture.

---

4. Hopetoun House was built by Charles Hope (1681–1742), the first Earl of Hopetoun. Dalkeith Palace was the seat of the Duke of Buccleugh. Pinkie House was a country home of the Marquess of Tweeddale, and Yester House was their family seat. "Frith," above, is an alternate spelling of "Firth," the Scots word for their coastal estraries and inlets.
5. Botanist and chief gardener of the Botanic Gardens at Chelsea from 1722 to 1767.
6. Spirit of the place (Latin).

Tabby and I have been both frightened in our return by sea from the coast of Fife.——She was afraid of drowning, and I of catching cold, in consequence of being drenched with sea-water; but my fears, as well as her's, have been happily disappointed.——She is now in perfect health; I wish I could say the same of Liddy.——Something uncommon is the matter with that poor child; her colour fades, her appetite fails, and her spirits flag.——She is become moping and melancholy, and is often found in tears.——Her brother suspects internal uneasiness on account of Wilson, and denounces vengeance against that adventurer.——She was, it seems, strongly affected at the ball by the sudden appearance of one Mr. Gordon, who strongly resembles the said Wilson; but I am rather suspicious that she caught cold by being overheated with dancing.—I have consulted Dr. Gregory, an eminent physician of an amiable character, who advises the highland air, and the use of goat-milk whey,[7] which, surely, cannot have a bad effect upon a patient who was born and bred among the mountains of Wales.—The doctor's opinion is the more agreeable, as we shall find those remedies in the very place which I proposed as the utmost extent of our expedition—I mean the borders of Argyle.

Mr. Smollett,[8] one of the judges of the commissary court, which is now sitting, has very kindly insisted upon our lodging at his country-house, on the banks of Lough-Lomond, about fourteen miles beyond Glasgow. For this last city we shall set out in two days, and take Stirling in our way, well provided with recommendations from our friends at Edinburgh, whom, I protest, I shall leave with much regret. I am so far from thinking it any hardship to live in this country, that, if I was obliged to lead a town life, Edinburgh would certainly be the headquarters of

Yours always,

Edr. August 8.   MATT. BRAMBLE.

To Sir WATKIN PHILLIPS, Bar^t.
of Jesus college, Oxon.

DEAR KNIGHT,

I am now little short of the *Ultima Thule*,[9] if this appellation properly belongs to the Orkneys or Hebrides. These last are now lying

---

7. The watery liquid of milk after it has curdled. John Gregory (1724–1773), physician and author who taught at both Aberdeen and Edinburgh.
8. James Smollett, the author's cousin.
9. The name given by the classical historian Polybius (ca. 200–ca. 118 B.C.E) to the northernmost land, which he believed lay six days' sail beyond Britain.

before me, to the amount of some hundreds, scattered up and down the Deucalidonian sea,[1] affording the most picturesque and romantic prospect I ever beheld——I write this letter in a gentleman's house, near the town of Inverary, which may be deemed the capital of the West Highlands, famous for nothing so much as for the stately castle begun, and actually covered in by the late duke of Argyle, at a prodigious expence—Whether it will ever be completely finished is a question[2]——

But, to take things in order.——We left Edinburgh ten days ago; and the further North we proceed, we find Mrs. Tabitha the less manageable; so that her inclinations are not of the nature of the loadstone; they point not towards the pole. What made her leave Edinburgh with reluctance at last, if we may believe her own assertions, was a dispute which she left unfinished with Mr. Moffat, touching the eternity of hell torments. That gentleman, as he advanced in years, began to be sceptical on this head, till, at length, he declared open war against the common acceptation of the word *eternal*. He is now persuaded, that *eternal* signifies no more than an indefinite number of years; and that the most enormous sinner may be quit for *nine millions, nine hundred thousand, nine hundred and ninety-nine years of hell-fire*; which term or period, as he very well observes, forms but an inconsiderable drop, as it were, in the ocean of eternity—For this mitigation he contends, as a system agreeable to the ideas of goodness and mercy, which we annex to the supreme Being—Our aunt seemed willing to adopt this doctrine in favour of the wicked; but he hinted, that no person whatever was so righteous as to be exempted entirely from punishment in a future state; and that the most pious Christian upon earth might think himself very happy to get off for a fast of seven or eight thousand years in the midst of fire and brimstone. Mrs. Tabitha revolted at this dogma, which filled her at once with horror and indignation— She had recourse to the opinion of Humphry Clinker, who roundly declared it was the popish doctrine of purgatory, and quoted scripture in defence of the *fire everlasting, prepared for the devil and his angels*—The reverend mester Mackcorkendale, and all the theologists and saints of that persuasion were consulted, and some of them had doubts about the matter; which doubts and scruples had begun to infect our aunt, when we took our departure from Edinburgh.

We passed through Linlithgow, where there was an elegant royal palace, which is now gone to decay, as well as the town itself—This too is pretty much the case with Stirling, though it still boasts of a fine old castle, in which the kings of Scotland were wont to reside

---

1. A play on *Caledonian* and *Deucalion's flood*. Deucalion was a mythical king of Thessaly who supposedly saw the entire world flooded during his reign.
2. Inverary Castle, seat of the Duke of Argyll, was finally completed in 1789.

in their minority—But Glasgow is the pride of Scotland, and, indeed, it might very well pass for an elegant and flourishing city in any part of Christendom. There we had the good fortune to be received into the house of Mr. Moore,[3] an eminent surgeon, to whom we were recommended by one of our friends at Edinburgh; and, truly, he could not have done us more essential service—Mr. Moore is a merry facetious companion, sensible and shrewd, with a considerable fund of humour; and his wife an agreeable woman, well bred, kind, and obliging—Kindness, which I take to be the essence of good-nature and humanity, is the distinguishing characteristic of the Scotch ladies in their own country—Our landlord shewed us every thing, and introduced us to all the world at Glasgow; where, through his recommendation, we were complimented with the freedom of the town. Considering the trade and opulence of this place, it cannot but abound with gaiety and diversions——Here is a great number of young fellows that rival the youth of the capital in spirit and expence; and I was soon convinced, that all the female beauties of Scotland were not assembled at the hunters ball in Edinburgh—The town of Glasgow flourishes in learning, as well as in commerce—Here is an university, with professors in all the different branches of science, liberally endowed, and judiciously chosen—It was vacation time when I passed, so that I could not entirely satisfy my curiosity; but their mode of education is certainly preferable to ours in some respects—The students are not left to the private instruction of tutors; but taught in public schools or classes, each science by its particular professor or regent.

My uncle is in raptures with Glasgow—He not only visited all the manufactures of the place, but made excursions all round, to Hamilton, Paisley, Renfrew, and every other place within a dozen miles, where there was any thing remarkable to be seen in art or nature. I believe the exercise, occasioned by these jaunts, was of service to my sister Liddy, whose appetite and spirits begin to revive—Mrs. Tabitha displayed her attractions as usual, and actually believed she had entangled one Mr. Maclellan, a rich inkle-manufacturer,[4] in her snares; but when matters came to an explanation, it appeared that his attachment was altogether spiritual, founded upon an intercourse of devotion, at the meeting of Mr. John Wesley;[5] who, in the course of his evangelical mission, had come hither in person—At length, we set out for the banks of Lough-Lomond, passing through the little borough of Dumbarton, or (as my uncle will have it) Dunbritton,

3. John Moore (1729–1802) was apprenticed to the same surgeon as Smollett, and they remained friends and correspondents. Eventually, Moore was able to give up practicing medicine and became a traveler and novelist. He also edited Smollett's *Works* (1797).
4. A maker of linen tape.
5. Wesley visited Glasgow a number of times and may have met Smollett there in June 1766.

where there is a castle, more curious than any thing of the kind I had ever seen—It is honoured with a particular description by the elegant Buchannan, as an *arx inexpugnabilis*,[6] and, indeed, it must have been impregnable by the antient manner of besieging. It is a rock of considerable extent, rising with a double top, in an angle formed by the confluence of two rivers, the Clyde and the Leven; perpendicular and inaccessible on all sides, except in one place where the entrance is fortified; and there is no rising-ground in the neighbourhood from whence it could be damaged by any kind of battery.

From Dumbarton, the West Highlands appear in the form of huge, dusky mountains, piled one over another; but this prospect is not at all surprising to a native of Glamorgan—We have fixed our head-quarters at Cameron, a very neat country-house belonging to commissary Smollett, where we found every sort of accommodation we could desire—It is situated like a Druid's temple, in a grove of oak, close by the side of Lough-Lomond, which is a surprising body of pure transparent water, unfathomably deep in many places, six or seven miles broad, four and twenty miles in length, displaying above twenty green islands, covered with wood; some of them cultivated for corn, and many of them stocked with red deer—They belong to different gentlemen, whose seats are scattered along the banks of the lake, which are agreeably romantic beyond all conception. My uncle and I have left the women at Cameron, as Mrs. Tabitha would by no means trust herself again upon the water, and to come hither it was necessary to cross a small inlet of the sea, in an open ferry-boat——This country appears more and more wild and savage the further we advance; and the people are as different from the Lowland Scots, in their looks, garb, and language, as the mountaineers of Brecknock are from the inhabitants of Herefordshire.[7]

When the Lowlanders want to drink a chearupping-cup, they go to the public house, called the Change-house, and call for a chopine[8] of two-penny, which is a thin, yeasty beverage, made of malt; not quite so strong as the table-beer of England—This is brought in a pewter stoop, shaped like a skittle[9] from whence it is emptied into a quaff; that is, a curious cup made of different pieces of wood, such as box and ebony, cut into little staves, joined alternately, and secured with delicate hoops, having two ears or handles—It holds about a gill,[1] is sometimes tipt round the mouth with silver, and has

---

6. Unassailable fortress (Latin). George Buchanan (1506–1582), an accomplished Latin scholar, was tutor to Mary, Queen of Scots, and James VI.
7. A western English county that borders Wales. Brecknockshire is located in central Wales.
8. A half-pint measure used in Scotland.
9. A small bowling pin used in the game of skittles, from which bowling originated.
1. A quarter pint.

a plate of the same metal at bottom, with the landlord's cypher engraved—The Highlanders, on the contrary, despise this liquor, and regale themselves with whisky; a malt spirit, as strong as geneva,[2] which they swallow in great quantities, without any signs of inebriation. They are used to it from the cradle, and find it an excellent preservative against the winter cold, which must be extreme on these mountains—I am told that it is given with great success to infants, as a cordial in the confluent smallpox[3] when the erruption seems to flag, and the symptoms grow unfavourable—The Highlanders are used to eat much more animal food than falls to the share of their neighbours in the Low-country—They delight in hunting; have plenty of deer and other game, with a great number of sheep, goats, and black-cattle running wild, which they scruple not to kill as venison, without being at much pains to ascertain the property.

Inverary is but a poor town, though it stands immediately under the protection of the duke of Argyle, who is a mighty prince in this part of Scotland. The peasants live in wretched cabins, and seem very poor; but the gentlemen are tolerably well lodged, and so loving to strangers, that a man runs some risque of his life from their hospitality—It must be observed that the poor Highlanders are now seen to disadvantage—They have been not only disarmed by act of parliament; but also deprived of their antient garb,[4] which was both graceful and convenient; and what is a greater hardship still, they are compelled to wear breeches; a restraint which they cannot bear with any degree of patience: indeed, the majority wear them, not in the proper place, but on poles or long staves over their shoulders—— They are even debared the use of their striped stuff, called Tartane, which was their own manufacture, prized by them above all the velvets, brocards, and tissues of Europe and Asia. They now lounge along in loose great coats, of coarse russet, equally mean and cumbersome, and betray manifest marks of dejection—Certain it is, the government could not have taken a more effectual method to break their national spirit.

We have had princely sport in hunting the stag on these mountains—These are the lonely hills of Morven, where Fingal and his heroes enjoyed the same pastime: I feel an enthusiastic pleasure when I survey the brown heath that Ossian wont to tread; and hear the wind whistle through the bending grass——When I enter our

2. A liquor made in Holland from wheat and flavored with juniper berries. The British version bears the shortened name gin.
3. An infectious disease, eradicated in the 1970s but responsible for nearly half a million deaths annually in Europe in the later 18th century. Smallpox was characterized by a heavy pustular rash that frequently left survivors with severe scarring.
4. After the defeat of the (largely Scottish) Jacobite force at Culloden in 1746, the British Parliament passed acts that prohibited wearing kilts, forced the Highlanders to disarm, and effectively dismantled their clan organization.

landlord's hall, I look for the suspended harp of that divine bard, and listen in hopes of hearing the aerial sound of his respected spirit—The Poems of Ossian[5] are in every mouth—A famous antiquarian of this country, the laird of Mackfarlane,[6] at whose house we dined a few days ago, can repeat them all in the original Gaelick, which has a great affinity to the Welch, not only in the general sound, but also in a great number of radical words; and I make no doubt but that they are both sprung from the same origin. I was not a little surprised, when asking a Highlander one day, if he knew where we should find any game? he replied, *"hu niel Sassenagh,"* which signifies *No English:* the very same answer I should have received from a Welchman, and almost in the same words. The Highlanders have no other name for the people of the Low-country, but Sassenagh, or Saxons; a strong presumption, that the Lowland Scots and the English are derived from the same stock——The peasants of these hills strongly resemble those of Wales in their looks, their manners, and habitations; every thing I see, and hear, and feel, seems Welch——The mountains, vales, and streams; the air and climate; the beef, mutton, and game, are all Welch—It must be owned, however, that this people are better provided than we in some articles— They have plenty of red deer and roebuck, which are fat and delicious at this season of the year—Their sea teems with amazing quantities of the finest fish in the world; and they find means to procure very good claret at a very small expence.

Our landlord is a man of consequence in this part of the country; a cadet from the family of Argyle, and hereditary captain of one of his castles[7]—His name, in plain English, is Dougal Campbell; but as there is a great number of the same appellation, they are distinguished (like the Welch) by patronimics; and as I have known an antient Briton called Madoc ap-Morgan, ap-Jenkin, ap-Jones, our Highland chief designs himself Dou'l Mac-amish mac-'oul ich-ian, signifying Dougal, the son of James, the son of Dougal, the son of John—He has traveled in the course of his education, and is disposed to make certain alterations in his domestic œconomy; but he finds it impossible to abolish the antient customs of the family; some of which are ludicrous enough—His piper, for example, who is an hereditary officer of the household, will not part with the least particle of his privileges——He has a right to wear the kilt, or

5. A body of epic poetry, including *Fingal* (1761) and *Temora* (1763), published by James Macpherson (1736–1796). Presented by Macpherson as the work of an ancient Scottish bard, their questionable authenticity caused considerable controversy, especially in light of their immense popularity.
6. Walter Macfarlane (d. 1767), a Scottish antiquary.
7. Possibly Dunstaffnage Castle, on Scotland's western coast. Its staff has long included a hereditary captain responsible for the castle's upkeep and defense.

antient Highland dress, with the purse, pistol, and durk—a broad yellow ribbon, fixed to the chanter-pipe, is thrown over his shoulder, and trails along the ground, while he performs the function of his minstrelsy; and this, I suppose, is analogous to the pennon or flag which was formerly carried before every knight in battle—— He plays before the laird every Sunday in his way to the kirk, which he circles three times, performing the family march, which implies defiance to all the enemies of the clan; and every morning he plays a full hour by the clock, in the great hall, marching backwards and forwards all the time, with a solemn pace, attended by the laird's kinsmen, who seem much delighted with the music—In this exercise, he indulges them with a variety of pibrachs or airs, suited to the different passions, which he would either excite or assuage.

Mr. Campbell himself, who performs very well on the violin, has an invincible antipathy to the sound of the Highland bag-pipe, which sings in the nose with a most alarming twang, and, indeed, is quite intolerable to ears of common sensibility, when aggravated by the echo of a vaulted hall—He therefore begged the piper would have some mercy upon him, and dispense with this part of the morning service— —A consultation of the clan being held on this occasion, it was unanimously agreed, that the laird's request could not be granted without a dangerous encroachment upon the customs of the family— The piper declared, he could not give up for a moment the privilege he derived from his ancestors; nor would the laird's relations forego an entertainment which they valued above all others—There was no remedy; Mr. Campbell, being obliged to acquiesce, is fain to stop his ears with cotton; to fortify his head with three or four nightcaps, and every morning retire into the penetralia[8] of his habitation, in order to avoid this diurnal annoyance. When the music ceases, he produces himself at an open window that looks into the courtyard, which is by this time filled with a crowd of his vassals and dependents, who worship his first appearance, by uncovering their heads, and bowing to the earth with the most humble prostration. As all these people have something to communicate in the way of proposal, complaint, or petition, they wait patiently till the laird comes forth, and, following him in his walks, are favoured each with a short audience in his turn. Two days ago, he dispatched above an hundred different sollicitors, in walking with us to the house of a neighbouring gentleman, where we dined by invitation. Our landlord's house-keeping is equally rough and hospitable, and savours much of the simplicity of ancient times: the great hall, paved with flat stones, is about forty-five feet by twenty-two, and serves not only for a dining-room, but also for a bed-chamber to gentlemen-dependents and

8. Inner rooms.

hangers-on of the family. At night, half a dozen occasional beds are ranged on each side along the wall. These are made of fresh heath, pulled up by the roots, and disposed in such a manner as to make a very agreeable couch, where they lie, without any other covering than the plaid—My uncle and I were indulged with separate chambers and down beds, which we begged to exchange for a layer of heath; and indeed I never slept so much to my satisfaction. It was not only soft and elastic, but the plant, being in flower, diffused an agreeable fragrance, which is wonderfully refreshing and restorative.

Yesterday we were invited to the funeral of an old lady, the grandmother of a gentleman in this neighbourhood, and found ourselves in the midst of fifty people, who were regaled with a sumptuous feast, accompanied by the music of a dozen pipers. In short, this meeting had all the air of a grand festival; and the guests did such honour to the entertainment, that many of them could not stand when we were reminded of the business on which we had met. The company forthwith taking horse, rode in a very irregular cavalcade to the place of interment, a church, at the distance of two long miles from the castle. On our arrival, however, we found we had committed a small oversight, in leaving the corpse behind;[9] so that we were obliged to wheel about, and met the old gentlewoman half way, carried upon poles by the nearest relations of her family, and attended by the *coronach*, composed of a multitude of old hags, who tore their hair, beat their breasts, and howled most hideously. At the grave, the orator, or *senachie*, pronounced the panegyric of the defunct, every period being confirmed by a yell of the *coronach*. The body was committed to the earth, the pipers playing a pibroch[1] all the time; and all the company standing uncovered. The ceremony was closed with the discharge of pistols; then we returned to the castle, resumed the bottle, and by midnight there was not a sober person in the family, the females excepted. The 'squire and I were, with some difficulty, permitted to retire with our landlord in the evening; but our entertainer was a little chagrined at our retreat; and afterwards seemed to think it a disparagement to his family, that not above a hundred gallons of whisky had been drank upon such a solemn occasion. This morning we got up by four, to hunt the roebuck, and, in an half an hour, found breakfast ready served in the hall. The hunters consisted of Sir George Colquhoun[2] and me, as strangers, (my uncle not chusing to be of the party) of the *laird in person, the*

9. An oft-repeated anecdote of Scottish funerals. Most of the funerary traditions described here had become obsolete by the 1760s.
1. A musical piece for bagpipes consisting of a theme and variations. It can be martial or (as here) funereal.
2. Of Tilliquhoun; an officer in the Dutch service.

laird's brother, the laird's brother's son, the laird's sister's son, the laird's father's brother's son, and all their *foster brothers,* who are counted parcel of the family: but we were attended by an infinite number of *Gaellys,* or ragged Highlanders, without shoes or stockings.

The following articles formed our morning's repast: one kit of boiled eggs; a second, full of butter; a third, full of cream; an entire cheese, made of goat's milk; a large earthen pot full of honey; the best part of a ham; a cold venison pasty; a bushel of oat meal, made in thin cakes and bannocks, with a small wheaten loaf in the middle for the strangers; a large stone bottle full of whisky, another of brandy, and a kilderkin³ of ale. There was a laddle chained to the cream kit, with curious wooden bickers⁴ to be filled from this reservoir. The spirits were drank out of a silver quaff, and the ale out of horns: great justice was done to the collation by the guests in general; one of them in particular ate above two dozen of hard eggs, with a proportionable quantity of bread, butter, and honey; nor was one drop of liquor left upon the board. Finally, a large roll of tobacco was presented by way of desert, and every individual took a comfortable quid, to prevent the bad effects of the morning air. We had a fine chace over the mountains, after a roebuck, which we killed, and I got home time enough to drink tea with Mrs. Campbell and our 'squire. To-morrow we shall set out on our return for Cameron. We propose to cross the Frith of Clyde, and take the towns of Greenock and Port-Glasgow in our way. This circuit being finished, we shall turn our faces to the south, and follow the sun with augmented velocity, in order to enjoy the rest of the autumn in England, where Boreas⁵ is not quite so biting as he begins already to be on the tops of these northern hills. But our progress from place to place shall continue to be specified in these detached journals of,

yours always,

Argyleshire, Septr. 3.   J. MELFORD.

To Dr. LEWIS.

DEAR DICK,

About a fortnight is now elapsed, since we left the capital of Scotland, directing our course towards Stirling, where we lay—The castle of this place is such another as that of Edinburgh, and affords a surprising prospect of the windings of the river Forth, which are so

---

3. A sixteen-gallon cask. "Bannocks": flat, oval, usually unleavened bread.
4. Bowls or dishes, often used for drinking.
5. Greek name for the northern wind.

extraordinary, that the distance from hence to Alloa by land, is but four miles, and by water it is twenty-four. Alloa is a neat thriving town, that depends in a great measure on the commerce of Glasgow, the merchants of which send hither tobacco and other articles, to be deposited in warehouses for exportation from the Frith of Forth. In our way hither we visited a flourishing iron-work, where, instead of burning wood, they use coal, which they have the art of clearing in such a manner as frees it from the sulphur, that would otherwise render the metal too brittle for working. Excellent coal is found in almost every part of Scotland.

The soil of this district produces scarce any other grain but oats and barley; perhaps because it is poorly cultivated, and almost altogether uninclosed. The few inclosures they have consist of paultry walls of loose stones gathered from the fields, which indeed they cover, as if they had been scattered on purpose. When I expressed my surprize that the peasants did not disencumber their grounds of these stones; a gentleman, well aquainted with the theory as well as practice of farming, assured me that the stones, far from being prejudicial, were serviceable to the crop. This philosopher had ordered a field of his own to be cleared, manured and sown with barley, and the produce was more scanty than before. He caused the stones to be replaced, and next year the crop was as good as ever. The stones were removed a second time, and the harvest failed; they were again brought back, and the ground retrieved its fertility. The same experiment has been tried in different parts of Scotland with the same success—Astonished at this information, I desired to know in what manner he accounted for this strange phenomenon; and he said there were three ways in which the stones might be serviceable. They might possibly restrain an excess in the perspiration of the earth, analogous to colliquative sweats,[6] by which the human body is sometimes wasted and consumed. They might act as so many fences to protect the tender blade from the piercing winds of the spring; or, by multiplying the reflexion of the sun, they might increase the warmth, so as to mitigate the natural chilness of the soil and climate—But, surely this excessive perspiration might be more effectually checked by different kinds of manure, such as ashes, lime, chalk, or marl,[7] of which last it seems there are many pits in this kingdom: as for the warmth, it would be much more equally obtained by inclosures; one half of the ground which is now covered, would be retrieved; the cultivation would require less labour; and the ploughs, harrows, and horses, would not suffer half the damage which they now sustain.

6. A disease characterized by profuse sweating.
7. Soil consisting of clay and lime.

These north-western parts are by no means fertile in corn. The ground is naturally barren and moorish. The peasants are poorly lodged, meagre in their looks, mean in their apparel, and remarkably dirty. This last reproach they might easily wash off, by means of those lakes, rivers, and rivulets of pure water, with which they are so liberally supplied by nature. Agriculture cannot be expected to flourish where the farms are small, the leases short, and the husbandman begins upon a rack rent,[8] without a sufficient stock to answer the purposes of improvement. The granaries of Scotland are the banks of the Tweed, the counties of East and Mid-Lothian, the Carse of Gowrie,[9] in Perthshire, equal in fertility to any part of England, and some tracts in Aberdeenshire and Murray, where I am told the harvest is more early than in Northumberland, although they lie above two degrees farther north. I have a strong curiosity to visit many places beyond the Forth and the Tay, such as Perth, Dundee, Montrose, and Aberdeen, which are towns equally elegant and thriving; but the season is too far advanced, to admit of this addition to my original plan.

I am so far happy as to have seen Glasgow, which, to the best of my recollection and judgment, is one of the prettiest towns in Europe; and, without all doubt, it is one of the most flourishing in Great Britain. In short, it is a perfect bee-hive in point of industry. It stands partly on a gentle declivity; but the greatest part of it is in a plain, watered by the river Clyde. The streets are straight, open, airy, and well paved; and the houses lofty and well built of hewn stone. At the upper end of the town, there is a venerable cathedral, that may be compared with York minster or Westminster; and, about the middle of the descent from this to the Cross, is the college,[1] a respectable pile of building, with all manner of accommodation for the professors and students, including an elegant library, and an observatory well provided with astronomical instruments. The number of inhabitants is said to amount to thirty thousand; and marks of opulence and independency appear in every quarter of this commercial city, which, however, is not without its inconveniences and defects. The water of their public pumps is generally hard and brackish, an imperfection the less excusable, as the river Clyde runs by their doors, in the lower part of the town; and there are rivulets and springs above the cathedral, sufficient to fill a large reservoir with excellent water, which might be thence distributed to all the different parts of the city. It is of more consequence to consult the health of the inhabitants in this article, than to employ so much attention in beautifying their town

8. Excessive or extortionate rent.
9. The low alluvial land along the north side of the River Tay between Perth and Dundee.
1. The University of Glasgow, founded in 1451. Glasgow Cathedral, supposedly built on the burial site of Saint Mungo, was consecrated in 1197 and completed in 1450.

with new streets, squares, and churches. Another defect, not so easily remedied, is the shallowness of the river, which will not float vessels of any burthen within ten or twelve miles of the city; so that the merchants are obliged to load and unload their ships at Greenock and Port-Glasgow, situated about fourteen miles nearer the mouth of the Frith, where it is about two miles broad.

The people of Glasgow have a noble spirit of enterprise—Mr. Moore, a surgeon, to whom I was recommended from Edinburgh, introduced me to all the principal merchants of the place. Here I became acquainted with Mr. Cochran,[2] who may be stiled one of the sages of this kingdom. He was first magistrate at the time of the last rebellion. I sat as member when he was examined in the house of commons; upon which occasion Mr. P——[3] observed he had never heard such a sensible evidence given at that bar—I was also introduced to Dr. John Gordon,[4] patriot of a truly Roman spirit, who is the father of the linen manufacture in this place, and was the great promoter of the city workhouse, infirmary, and other works of public utility. Had he lived in ancient Rome, he would have been honoured with a statue at the public expence. I moreover conversed with one Mr. G—ssf—d,[5] whom I take to be one of the greatest merchants in Europe. In the last war, he is said to have had at one time five and twenty ships, with their cargoes, his own property, and to have traded for above half a million sterling a year. The last war was a fortunate period for the commerce of Glasgow—The merchants, considering that their ships bound for America, launching out at once into the Atlantic by the north of Ireland, pursued a track very little frequented by privateers, resolved to insure one another, and saved a very considerable sum by this resolution, as few or none of their ships were taken——You must know I have a sort of national attachment to this part of Scotland—The great church dedicated to St. Mongah, the river Clyde, and other particulars that smack of our Welch language and customs, contribute to flatter me with the notion, that these people are the descendants of the Britons, who once possessed this country. Without all question, this was a Cumbrian kingdom: its capital was Dumbarton (a corruption of Dumbritton) which still exists as a royal borough, at the influx of the Clyde and Leven, ten miles below Glasgow. The same neighbourhood gave birth to St. Patrick, the apostle of Ireland, at a place where there is

2. Andrew Cochrane (ca. 1692–1777), provost (mayor) of Glasgow in 1744–45 and 1748–50. He successfully sought compensation from Parliament for funds he was forced to give the Jacobites as they retreated during the 1745–46 rebellion.
3. Either William Pitt or Henry Pelham (1694–1754), both prominent politicians during the period of the hearing on Glasgow's losses.
4. The surgeon to whom Smollett was apprenticed during the 1730s.
5. John Glassford (1715–1783), prominent tobacco merchant and one of the founders of the Glasgow Chamber of Commerce.

still a church and village, which retain his name. Hard by are some vestiges of the famous Roman wall, built in the reign of Antonine,[6] from the Clyde to the Forth, and fortified with castles, to restrain the incursions of the Scots or Caledonians, who inhabited the West-Highlands. In a line parallel to this wall, the merchants of Glasgow have determined to make a navigable canal betwixt the two Friths, which will be of incredible advantage to their commerce, in transporting merchandize from one side of the island to the other.[7]

From Glasgow we travelled along the Clyde, which is a delightful stream, adorned on both sides with villas, towns, and villages. Here is no want of groves, and meadows, and corn-fields interspersed; but on this side of Glasgow, there is little other grain than oats and barley; the first are much better, the last much worse, than those of the same species in England. I wonder, there is so little rye, which is a grain that will thrive in almost any soil; and it is still more surprising, that the cultivation of potatoes should be so much neglected in the Highlands, where the poor people have not meal enough to supply them with bread through the winter. On the other side of the river are the towns of Paisley and Renfrew. The first, from an inconsiderable village, is become one of the most flourishing places of the kingdom, enriched by the linen, cambrick, flowered lawn, and silk manufactures. It was formerly noted for a rich monastery of the monks of Clugny, who wrote the famous *Scoti-Chronicon*, called *The Black Book of Paisley*.[8] The old abbey still remains, converted into a dwelling-house, belonging to the earl of Dundonald.[9] Renfrew is a pretty town, on the banks of Clyde, capital of the shire, which was heretofore the patrimony of the Stuart family, and gave the title of baron to the king's eldest son, which is still assumed by the prince of Wales.

The Clyde we left a little on our left-hand at Dunbritton, where it widens into an æstuary or frith, being augmented by the influx of the Leven. On this spot stands the castle formerly called Alcluyd, washed by these two rivers on all sides, except a narrow isthmus, which at every spring-tide is overflowed. The whole is a great curiosity, from the quality and form of the rock, as well as from the nature of its situation—We now crossed the water of Leven, which, though nothing near so considerable as the Clyde, is much more transparent, pastoral, and delightful. This charming stream is the outlet of Lough-Lomond, and through a tract of four miles pursues

6. Antoninus Pius (86–161), emperor of Rome from 138 to 161.
7. The Forth-Clyde canal was begun in 1768 and completed in 1790.
8. The book contains a manuscript of the *Scotichronicon*, a continuation by Walter Bower (ca. 1385–1449), abbot of Inchcolm Abbey in the Firth of Forth, of an original Scottish history chronicle by John of Fordun (ca. 1360–ca. 1384). The copy in question belonged to Cluny monks who acquired the Abbey of Paisley in 1614.
9. Thomas Cochrane, eighth Earl of Dundonald (1691–1778).

its winding course, murmuring over a bed of pebbles, till it joins the Frith at Dunbritton. A very little above its source, on the lake, stands the house of Cameron, belonging to Mr. Smollett, so embosomed in an oak wood, that we did not see it till we were within fifty yards of the door. I have seen the Lago di Carda, Albano, De Vico, Bolsena, and Geneva,[1] and, upon my honour, I prefer Lough-Lomond to them all; a preference which is certainly owing to the verdant islands that seem to float upon its surface, affording the most inchanting objects of repose to the excursive view. Nor are the banks destitute of beauties, which even partake of the sublime. On this side they display a sweet variety of woodland, corn-field, and pasture, with several agreeable villas emerging as it were out of the lake, till, at some distance, the prospect terminates in huge mountains covered with heath, which being in the bloom, affords a very rich covering of purple. Every thing here is romantic beyond imagination. This country is justly stiled the Arcadia of Scotland; and I don't doubt but it may vie with Arcadia in every thing but climate.—I am sure it excels it in verdure, wood, and water.—What say you to a natural bason of pure water, near thirty miles long, and in some places seven miles broad, and in many above a hundred fathom deep, having four and twenty habitable islands, some of them stocked with deer, and all of them covered with wood; containing immense quantities of delicious fish, salmon, pike, trout, perch, flounders, eels, and powans, the last a delicate kind of fresh-water herring peculiar to this lake; and finally communicating with the sea, by sending off the Leven, through which all those species (except the powan) make their exit and entrance occasionally?

Inclosed I send you the copy of a little ode to this river, by Dr. Smollett,[2] who was born on the banks of it, within two miles of the place where I am now writing.—It is at least picturesque and accurately descriptive, if it has no other merit.—There is an idea of truth in an agreeable landscape taken from nature, which pleases me more than the gayest fiction which the most luxuriant fancy can display.

I have other remarks to make; but as my paper is full, I must reserve them till the next occasion. I shall only observe at present, that I am determined to penetrate at least forty miles into the Highlands, which now appear like a vast fantastic vision in the clouds, inviting the approach of

Yours always,

Cameron, Aug. 28.   MATT. BRAMBLE.

---

1. One of the largest lakes in Europe, on the border between Switzerland and France. The other lakes are in Italy.
2. Smollett here takes the opportunity to present this poem about his birthplace.

ODE to LEVEN-WATER.

On Leven's banks, while free to rove,
And tune the rural pipe to love;
I envied not the happiest swain
That ever trod th' Arcadian plain.

Pure stream! in whose transparent wave
My youthful limbs I wont to lave;
No torrents stain thy limpid source;
No rocks impede thy dimpling course,
That sweetly warbles oe'r its bed,
With white, round, polish'd pebbles spread;
While, lightly pois'd, the scaly brood
In myriads cleave thy crystal flood;
The springing trout in speckled pride;
The salmon, monarch of the tide;
The ruthless pike, intent on war;
The silver eel, and motled par.[3]
Devolving from thy parent lake,
A charming maze thy waters make,
By bow'rs of birch, and groves of pine,
And hedges flow'r'd with eglantine.

Still on thy banks so gayly green,
May num'rous herds and flocks be seen,
And lasses chanting o'er the pail,
And shepherd's piping in the dale,
And ancient faith that knows no guile,
And industry imbrown'd with toil,
And hearts resolv'd, and hands prepar'd,
The blessings they enjoy to guard.

To Dr. LEWIS.

DEAR DOCTOR,

If I was disposed to be critical, I should say this house of Cameron is too near the lake, which approaches, on one side, to within
six or seven yards of the window. It might have been placed in a
higher site, which would have afforded a more extensive prospect

---

3. The par is a small fish, not unlike the smelt, which it rivals in delicacy and flavor [Smol-
lett's note].

and a drier atmosphere; but this imperfection is not chargeable on
the present proprietor, who purchased it ready built, rather than be
at the trouble of repairing his own family house of Bonhill, which
stands two miles from hence on the Leven, so surrounded with
plantation, that it used to be known by the name of the Mavis (or
thrush) Nest. Above that house is a romantic glen or clift of a mountain, covered with hanging woods, having at bottom a stream of fine
water that forms a number of cascades in its descent to join the
Leven; so that the scene is quite enchanting. A captain of a man of
war, who had made the circuit of the globe with Mr. Anson, being
conducted to this glen, exclaimed, "Juan Fernandez,[4] by God!"

Indeed, this country would be a perfect paradise, if it was not, like
Wales, cursed with a weeping climate, owing to the same causes in
both, the neighbourhood of high mountains, and a westerly situation, exposed to the vapours of the Atlantic ocean. This air, however,
notwithstanding its humidity, is so healthy, that the natives are scarce
ever visited by any other disease than the small-pox, and certain
cutaneous[5] evils, which are the effects of dirty living, the great and
general reproach of the commonalty of this kingdom. Here are a
great many living monuments of longevity; and among the rest a
person, whom I treat with singular respect, as a venerable druid,[6]
who has lived near ninety years, without pain or sickness, among
oaks of his own planting.—He was once proprietor of these lands;
but being of a projecting spirit, some of his schemes miscarried,
and he was obliged to part with his possession, which hath shifted
hands two or three times since that period; but every succeeding
proprietor hath done every thing in his power, to make his old age
easy and comfortable. He has a sufficiency to procure the necessaries of life; and he and his old woman resided in a small convenient
farmhouse, having a little garden which he cultivates with his own
hands. This ancient couple live in great health, peace, and harmony, and, knowing no wants, enjoy the perfection of content. Mr.
Smollet calls him the admiral, because he insists upon steering his
pleasure-boat upon the lake; and he spends most of his time in
ranging through the woods, which he declares he enjoys as much as
if they were still his own property—I asked him the other day, if he
was never sick, and he answered, Yes; he had a slight fever the year
before the union. If he was not deaf, I should take much pleasure in

---

4. The Juan Fernández Islands form a small group of islands in the South Pacific. "Captain": likely Robert Mann (d. 1762), a member of Anson's expedition and later Smollett's
friend. Admiral George Anson (1697–1762) refitted his remaining ships there in 1741
during his circumnavigation of the globe.
5. On the skin's surface.
6. Donald Govan, who had once owned Cameron House, and was nicknamed "The Old
Admiral."

his conversation; for he is very intelligent, and his memory is surprisingly retentive—These are the happy effects of temperance, exercise, and good nature—Notwithstanding all his innocence, however, he was the cause of great perturbation to my man Clinker, whose natural superstition has been much injured, by the histories of witches, fairies, ghosts, and goblins, which he has heard in this country—On the evening after our arrival, Humphry strolled into the wood, in the course of his meditation, and all at once the admiral stood before him, under the shadow of a spreading oak. Though the fellow is far from being timorous in cases that are not supposed preternatural, he could not stand the sight of this apparition, but ran into the kitchen, with his hair standing on end, staring wildly, and deprived of utterance. Mrs. Jenkins, seeing him in this condition, screamed aloud, "Lord have mercy upon us, he has seen something!" Mrs. Tabitha was alarmed, and the whole house in confusion. When he was recruited with a dram, I desired him to explain the meaning of all this agitation; and, with some reluctance, he owned he had seen a spirit, in the shape of an old man with a white beard, a black cap, and a plaid night gown. He was undeceived by the admiral in person, who, coming in at this juncture, appeared to be a creature of real flesh and blood.

Do you know how we fare in this Scottish paradise? We make free with our landlord's mutton, which is excellent, his poultry-yard, his garden, his dairy, and his cellar, which are all well stored. We have delicious salmon, pike, trout, perch, par, &c. at the door, for the taking. The Frith of Clyde, on the other side of the hill, supplies us with mullet, red and grey, cod, mackarel, whiting, and a variety of sea-fish, including the finest fresh herrings I ever tasted. We have sweet, juicy beef, and tolerable veal, with delicate bread from the little town of Dunbritton; and plenty of partridge, growse, heath-cock, and other game in presents.

We have been visited by all the gentlemen in the neighbourhood, and they have entertained us at their houses, not barely with hospitality, but with such marks of cordial affection, as one would wish to find among near relations, after an absence of many years.

I told you, in my last, I had projected an excursion to the Highlands, which project I have now happily executed, under the auspices of Sir George Colquhoun, a colonel in the Dutch service, who offered himself as our conductor on this occasion. Leaving our women at Cameron, to the care and inspection of Lady H———C———,[7] we set out on horseback for Inverary, the county town of Argyle, and dined on the road with the Laird of Macfarlane, the

7. Lady Helen Colquhoun (1717–1791), wife of Sir James Colquhoun.

greatest genealogist I ever knew in any country, and perfectly acquainted with all the antiquities of Scotland.

The Duke of Argyle has an old castle at Inverary, where he resides when he is in Scotland; and hard by is the shell of a noble Gothic palace, built by the last duke, which, when finished, will be a great ornament to this part of the Highlands. As for Inverary, it is a place of very little importance.

This country is amazingly wild, especially towards the mountains, which are heaped upon the backs of one another, making a most stupendous appearance of savage nature, with hardly any signs of cultivation, or even of population. All is sublimity, silence, and solitude. The people live together in glens or bottoms, where they are sheltered from the cold and storms of winter: but there is a margin of plain ground spread along the sea side, which is well inhabited and improved by the arts of husbandry; and this I take to be one of the most agreeable tracts of the whole island; the sea not only keeps it warm, and supplies it with fish, but affords one of the most ravishing prospects in the whole world; I mean the appearance of the Hebrides, or Western Islands, to the number of three hundred, scattered as far as the eye can reach, in the most agreeable confusion. As the soil and climate of the Highlands are but ill adapted to the cultivation of corn, the people apply themselves chiefly to the breeding and feeding of black cattle, which turn to good account. Those animals run wild all the winter, without any shelter or subsistence, but what they can find among the heath. When the snow lies so deep and hard, that they cannot penetrate to the roots of the grass, they make a diurnal progress, guided by a sure instinct, to the sea-side at low water, where they feed on the *alga marina*[8] and other plants that grow upon the beach.

Perhaps this branch of husbandry,[9] which requires very little attendance and labour, is one of the principal causes of that idleness and want of industry, which distinguishes these mountaineers in their own country—When they come forth into the world, they become as diligent and alert as any people upon earth. They are undoubtedly a very distinct species from their fellow-subjects of the Lowlands, against whom they indulge an ancient spirit of animosity; and this difference is very discernible even among persons of family and education. The Lowlanders are generally cool and circumspect, the Highlanders fiery and ferocious: but this violence of their passions serves only to inflame the zeal of their devotion to strangers, which is truly enthusiastic.

We proceeded about twenty miles beyond Inverary, to the house of a gentleman, a friend of our conductor, where we stayed a few

8. Seaweed. "Diurnal": daily.
9. Agriculture and farming.

days, and were feasted in such a manner, that I began to dread the consequence to my constitution.

Notwithstanding the solitude that prevails among these mountains, there is no want of people in the Highlands. I am credibly informed that the duke of Argyle can assemble five thousand men in arms, of his own clan and surname, which is Campbell; and there is besides a tribe of the same appellation, whose chief is the Earl of Breadalbine.[1] The Macdonalds are as numerous, and remarkably warlike: the Camerons, M'Leods, Frasers, Grants, M'Kenzies, M'Kays, M'Phersons, M'Intoshes, are powerful clans; so that if all the Highlanders, including the inhabitants of the Isles, were united, they could bring into the field an army of forty thousand fighting men, capabable of undertaking the most dangerous enterprize. We have lived to see four thousand of them, without discipline, throw the whole kingdom of Great Britain into confusion. They attacked and defeated two armies of regular troops, accustomed to service. They penetrated into the centre of England; and afterwards marched back with deliberation, in the face of two other armies, through an enemy's country, where every precaution was taken to cut off their retreat.[2] I know not any other people in Europe, who, without the use or knowledge of arms, will attack regular forces sword in hand, if their chief will head them in battle. When disciplined, they cannot fail of being excellent soldiers. They do not walk like the generality of mankind, but trot and bounce like deer, as if they moved upon springs. They greatly excel the Lowlanders in all the exercises that require agility; they are incredibly abstemious, and patient of hunger and fatigue; so steeled against the weather, that in travelling, even when the ground is covered with snow, they never look for a house, or any other shelter but their plaid, in which they wrap themselves up, and go to sleep under the cope[3] of heaven. Such people, in quality of soldiers, must be invincible, when the business is to perform quick marches in a difficult country, to strike sudden strokes, beat up the enemy's quarters, harrass their cavalry, and perform expeditions without the formality of magazines, baggage, forage, and artillery. The chieftainship of the Highlanders is a very dangerous influence operating at the extremity of the island, where the eyes and hands of government cannot be supposed to see and act with precision and vigour. In order to break the force of clanship, administration has always practised the political maxim,

---

1. John Campbell, third Earl of Breadalbane (1696–1782).
2. The 1745 Jacobite Rebellion, led by Prince Charles Edward Stewart (known to his supporters as Bonnie Prince Charlie), began in June 1745 and ended with the battle of Culloden in April 1746. The Jacobites penetrated England as far as Derby before retreating.
3. Cloak or canopy; here, sky.

Divide et impera.[4] The legislature hath not only disarmed these mountaineers, but also deprived them of their ancient garb, which contributed in a great measure to keep up their military spirit; and their slavish tenures are all dissolved by act of parliament; so that they are at present as free and independent of their chiefs, as the law can make them: but the original attachment still remains, and is founded on something prior to the *feudal system*, about which the writers of this age have made such a pother, as if it was a new discovery, like the *Copernican system*.[5] Every peculiarity of policy, custom, and even temperament, is affectedly traced to this origin, as if the feudal constitution had not been common to almost all the natives of Europe. For my part, I expect to see the use of trunk-hose and buttered ale ascribed to the influence of the *feudal system*. The connection between the clans and their chiefs is, without all doubt, patriarchal. It is founded on hereditary regard and affection, cherished through a long succession of ages. The clan consider the chief as their father, they bear his name, they believe themselves descended from his family, and they obey him as their lord, with all the ardour of filial love and veneration; while he, on his part, exerts a paternal authority, commanding, chastising, rewarding, protecting, and maintaining them as his own children. If the legislature would entirely destroy this connection, it must compel the Highlanders to change their habitation and their names. Even this experiment has been formerly tried without success—In the reign of James VI. a battle was fought within a few short miles of this place, between two clans, the M'Gregors and the Colquhouns, in which the latter were defeated: the Laird of M'Gregor made such a barbarous use of his victory, that he was forfeited and outlawed by act of parliament: his lands were given to the family of Montrose, and his clan were obliged to change their name. They obeyed so far, as to call themselves severally Campbell, Graham, or Drummond, the surnames of the families of Argyle, Montrose, and Perth, that they might enjoy the protection of those houses; but they still added M'Gregor to their new appellation; and as their chief was deprived of his estate, they robbed and plundered for his subsistence.—Mr. Cameron of Lochiel, the chief of that clan, whose father was attainted for having been concerned in the last rebellion, returning from France in obedience to a proclamation and act of parliament,[6] passed at the beginning of the late war, payed a visit to his own country, and hired a farm in the neighbourhood of

---

4. Divide and conquer (Latin).
5. Nicolaus Copernicus (1473–1543) argued, in defiance of Church doctrine, that the earth revolved around the sun.
6. Presumably the Militia Act of 1757, which among other provisions created Highland regiments that fought for Britain in the Seven Years' War and after. Mr. Cameron was probably Charles, the third son of Donald Cameron. The elder Cameron took a leading Jacobite role in 1745–46 and died in exile.

his father's house, which had been burnt to the ground. The clan, though ruined and scattered, no sooner heard of his arrival than they flocked to him from all quarters, to welcome his return, and in a few days stocked his farm with seven hundred black cattle, which they had saved in the general wreck of their affairs: but their beloved chief, who was a promising youth, did not live to enjoy the fruits of their fidelity and attachment.

The most effectual method I know to weaken, and at length destroy this influence, is to employ the commonalty in such a manner as to give them a taste of property and independence—In vain the government grants them advantageous leases on the forfeited estates, if they have no property to prosecute the means of improvement—The sea is an inexhaustible fund of riches; but the fishery cannot be carried on without vessels, casks, salt, lines, nets, and other tackle. I conversed with a sensible man of this country, who, from a real spirit of patriotism, had set up a fishery on the coast, and a manufacture of coarse linen, for the employment of the poor Highlanders. Cod is here in such plenty, that he told me he had seen seven hundred taken on one line, at one hawl—It must be observed, however, that the line was of immense length, and had two thousand hooks, baited with muscles; but the fish was so superior to the cod caught on the banks of New-foundland, that his correspondent at Lisbon sold them immediately at his own price, although Lent was just over when they arrived, and the people might be supposed quite cloyed with this kind of diet—His linen manufacture was likewise in a prosperous way, when the late war intervening, all his best hands were pressed into the service.

It cannot be expected, that the gentlemen of this country should execute commercial schemes to render their vassals independent; nor, indeed, are such schemes suited to their way of life and inclination; but a company of merchants might, with proper management, turn to good account a fishery established in this part of Scotland——Our people have a strange itch to colonize America, when the uncultivated parts of our own island might be settled to greater advantage.

After having rambled through the mountains and glens of Argyle, we visited the adjacent islands of Ila, Jura, Mull, and Icolmkill.[7] In the first, we saw the remains of a castle, built in a lake, where Macdonald, lord or king of the isles, formerly resided.[8] Jura is famous for having given birth to one Mackcrain,[9] who lived one hundred and eighty years in one house, and died in the reign of Charles the

---

7. Islands of the Inner Hebrides, off Scotland's western coast "Ila": Islay.
8. Finlaggan Castle was the former seat of the powerful Clan Donald on the island of Islay.
9. Gillour Mack Crain or Mackirain, who was featured in the travel writer Martin Martin's *Description of the Western Islands of Scotland* (1703).

Second. Mull affords several bays, where there is safe anchorage; in one of which, the Florida, a ship of the Spanish armada, was blown up by one of Mr. Smollett's ancestors—About forty years ago, John duke of Argyle[1] is said to have consulted the Spanish registers, by which it appeared, that this ship had the military chest on board—He employed experienced divers to examine the wreck; and they found the hull of the vessel still entire, but so covered with sand, that they could not make their way between decks; however, they picked up several pieces of plate, that were scattered about in the bay, and a couple of fine brass cannon.

Icolmkill, or Iona, is a small island which St. Columba chose for his habitation[2]—It was respected for its sanctity, and college or seminary of ecclesiastics—Part of its church is still standing, with the tombs of several Scottish, Irish, and Danish sovereigns, who were here interred—These islanders are very bold and dexterous watermen, consequently the better adapted to the fishery: in their manners they are less savage and impetuous than their countrymen on the continent; and they speak the Erse or Gaelick[3] in its greatest purity. Having sent round our horses by land, we embarked in the district of Cowal, for Greenock, which is a neat little town, on the other side of the Frith, with a curious harbour, formed by three stone jetties, carried out a good way into the sea——Newport-Glasgow is such another place, about two miles higher up—Both have a face of business and plenty, and are supported entirely by the shipping of Glasgow, of which I counted sixty large vessels in these harbours—Taking boat again at Newport, we were in less than an hour landed on the other side, within two short miles of our head-quarters, where we found our women in good health and spirits—They had been two days before joined by Mr. Smollett and his lady, to whom we have such obligations as I cannot mention, even to you, without blushing.

To-morrow we shall bid adieu to the Scotch Arcadia, and begin our progress to the southward, taking our way by Lanerk and Nithsdale, to the west borders of England. I have received so much advantage and satisfaction from this tour, that if my health suffers no revolution in the winter, I believe I shall be tempted to undertake another expedition to the Northern extremity of Caithness,[4] unencumbered by those impediments which now clog the heels of,

yours,

Cameron, Sept. 6.   MATT. BRAMBLE.

---

1. John Campbell, second Duke of Argyle (1678–1743).
2. An early center of Celtic Christianity, starting in the 6th century.
3. A Celtic language spoken also in Ireland; usually spelled "Gaelic."
4. The county at the extreme northeast corner of Scotland, overlooking the Orkney islands. Lanerk, above, is usually spelled "Lanark."

To Miss LÆTITIA WILLIS, at Gloucester.

MY DEAREST LETTY,

Never did poor prisoner long for deliverance, more than I have longed for an opportunity to disburthen my cares into your friendly bosom; and the occasion which now presents itself, is little less than miraculous—Honest Saunders Macawly, the travelling Scotchman, who goes every year to Wales, is now at Glasgow, buying goods, and coming to pay his respects to our family, has undertaken to deliver this letter into your own hand—We have been six weeks in Scotland, and seen the principal towns of the kingdom, where we have been treated with great civility—The people are very courteous; and the country being exceedingly romantic, suits my turn and inclinations—I contracted some friendships at Edinburgh, which is a large and lofty city, full of gay company; and, in particular, commenced an intimate correspondence with one miss R—t—n,[5] an amiable young lady of my own age, whose charms seemed to soften, and even to subdue the stubborn heart of my brother Jery; but he no sooner left the place than he relapsed into his former insensibility——I feel, however, that this indifference is not the family-constitution—I never admitted but one idea of love, and that has taken such root in my heart, as to be equally proof against all the pulls of discretion, and the frosts of neglect.

Dear Letty! I had an alarming adventure at the hunters ball in Edinburgh—While I sat discoursing with a friend in a corner, all at once the very image of Wilson stood before me, dressed exactly as he was in the character of Aimwell![6] It was one Mr. Gordon, whom I had not seen before—Shocked at the sudden apparition, I fainted away, and threw the whole assembly in confusion——However, the cause of my disorder remained a secret to every body but my brother, who was likewise struck with the resemblance, and scolded after we came home—I am very sensible of Jery's affection, and know he spoke as well with a view to my own interest and happiness, as in regard to the honour of the family; but I cannot bear to have my wounds probed severely—I was not so much affected by the censure he passed upon my own indiscretion, as with the reflection he made on the conduct of Wilson—He observed, that if he was really the gentleman he pretended to be, and harboured nothing but honourable designs, he would have vindicated his pretensions in

5. Either Cecilia or Eleanora Renton, as previously mentioned by Jery in his August 8 letter from Edinburgh.
6. One of the heroes of George Farquahar's *The Beaux' Stratagem* (1707), the play presented at Gloucester.

the face of day—This remark made a deep impression upon my mind——I endeavoured to conceal my thoughts; and this endeavour had a bad effect upon my health and spirits; so it was thought necessary that I should go to the Highlands, and drink the goat-milk-whey.

We went accordingly to Lough-Lomond, one of the most enchanting spots in the whole world; and what with this remedy, which I had every morning fresh from the mountains, and the pure air, and chearful company, I have recovered my flesh and appetite; though there is something still at bottom, which it is not in the power of air, exercise, company, or medicine to remove——These incidents would not touch me so nearly, if I had a sensible confidant to sympathize with my affliction, and comfort me with wholesome advice—I have nothing of this kind, except Win Jenkins, who is really a good body in the main, but very ill qualified for such an office—The poor creature is weak in her nerves, as well as in her understanding; otherwise I might have known the true name and character of that unfortunate youth—But why do I call him unfortunate? perhaps the epithet is more applicable to me for having listened to the false professions of——But, hold! I have as yet no right, and sure I have no inclination to believe any thing to the prejudice of his honour—In that reflection I shall still exert my patience—As for Mrs. Jenkins, she herself is really an object of compassion—Between vanity, methodism, and love, her head is almost turned. I should have more regard for her, however, if she had been more constant in the object of her affection; but, truly, she aimed at conquest, and flirted at the same time with my uncle's footman, Humphry Clinker, who is really a deserving young man, and one Dutton, my brother's valet de chambre, a debauched fellow; who, leaving Win in the lurch, ran away with another man's bride at Berwick.

My dear Willis, I am truly ashamed of my own sex——We complain of advantages which the men take of our youth, inexperience, sensibility, and all that; but I have seen enough to believe, that our sex in general make it their business to ensnare the other; and for this purpose, employ arts which are by no means to be justified—— In point of constancy, they certainly have nothing to reproach the male part of the creation—My poor aunt, without any regard to her years and imperfections, has gone to market with her charms in every place where she thought she had the least chance to dispose of her person, which, however, hangs still heavy on her hands—I am afraid she has used even religion as a decoy, though it has not answered her expectation—She has been praying, preaching, and catechising among the methodists, with whom this country abounds; and pretends to have such manifestations and revelations, as even Clinker himself can hardly believe, though the poor fellow is half crazy with enthusiasm. As for Jenkins, she affects to take all her mistress's reveries for gospel—She has also her heart-heavings and motions of the spirit; and God forgive me if I think uncharitably, but all this seems to me to be downright hypocrisy and deceit—Perhaps, indeed, the poor girl imposes on herself—She is generally in a flutter, and is much subject to vapours—Since we came to Scotland, she has seen apparitions, and pretends to prophesy——If I could put faith in all these supernatural visitations, I should think myself abandoned of grace; for I have neither seen, heard, nor felt any thing of this nature, although I endeavour to discharge the duties of religion with all the sincerity, zeal, and devotion, that is in the power of,

Dear Letty,

your ever affectionate,

Glasgow, Sept. 7.   LYDIA MELFORD.

We are so far on our return to Brambleton-hall; and I would fain hope we shall take Gloucester in our way, in which case I shall have the inexpressible pleasure of embracing my dear Willis—Pray remember me to my worthy governess.

To Mrs. MARY JONES, at Brambleton-hall.

DEAR MARY,

Sunders Macully, the Scotchman, who pushes directly for Vails, has promised to give it you into your own hand, and therefore I would not miss the oportunity to let you now as I am still in the land of the living; and yet I have been on the brink of the other world since I sent you my last letter.—We went by sea to another kingdom called Fife, and coming back, had like to have gone to pot in a storm.—What between the frite and sickness, I thought I should have brought my heart up; even Mr. Clinker was not his own man for eight and forty hours after we got ashore.—It was well for some folks that we scaped drownding; for mistress was very frexious, and seemed but indifferently prepared for a change; but, thank God, she was soon put in a better frame by the private exaltations of the reverend Mr. Macrocodile.—We afterwards churned to Starling and Grascow, which are a kiple of handsome towns; and then we went to a gentleman's house at Loff-Loming, which is a wonderful sea of fresh water, with a power of hylands in the midst on't.—They say as how it has got n'er a bottom, and was made by a musician; and, truly, I believe it; for it is not in the coarse of nature.—It has got *waves without wind, fish without fins, and a floating hyland;*[7] and one of them is a crutch-yard, where the dead are buried; and always before the person dies, a bell rings of itself to give warning.

O Mary! this is the land of congyration—The bell knolled when we were there—I saw lights, and heard lamentations.—The gentleman, our landlord, has got another house, which he was fain to quit, on account of a mischievious ghost, that would not suffer people to lie in their beds.—The fairies dwell in a hole of Kairmann, a mounting hard by; and they steal away the good women that are in the straw,[8] if so be as how there a'n't a horshoe nailed to the door: and I was shewn an ould vitch, called Elspath Ringavey, with a red petticoat, bleared eyes, and a mould of grey bristles on her sin.—That she mought do me no harm, I crossed her hand with a taster,[9] and bid her tell my fortune; and she told me such things—descriving Mr. Clinker to a hair—but it shall ne'er be said, that I minchioned a word of the matter.—As I was troubled with fits, she advised me to bathe in the loff, which was holy water; and so I went in the morning to a private place along with the house-maid, and we bathed in our birthday soot,[1] after the fashion of the country; and behold, whilst we dabbled in the loff, sir Gorge Coon started up with a gun; but we clapt our hands to our faces, and passed by him to the place where we had left our smocks—A civil gentleman would have turned his head another way.—My comfit is, he new not which was which; and, as the saying is, *all cats in the dark are grey.*—Whilst we stayed at Loff-Loming, he and our two squires went three or four days churning among the wild men of the mountings; a parcel of selvidges that lie in caves among the rocks, devour young children, speak Velch, but the vords are different. Our ladies would not part with Mr. Clinker, because he is so stout, and so pyehouse, that he fears neither man nor devils, if so be as they don't take him by surprise.— Indeed, he was once so flurried by an operition, that he had like to have sounded.—He made believe as if it had been the ould edmiral; but the ould edmiral could not have made his air to stand on end, and his teeth to shatter; but he said so in prudence, that the ladies mought not be affear'd. Miss Liddy has been puny, and like to go into a decline—I doubt her pore art is too tinder—but the got's-fey has sat her on her legs again.—You nows got's-fey is mother's milk to a Velchvoman. As for mistress, blessed be God, she ails nothing.—Her stomick is good, and she improves in grease and godliness; but, for

---

7. A series of local legends about Loch Lomond.
8. In labor. Kairmann is presumably a reference to Ptarmigan, the western shoulder of Ben Lomond, which rises 2,398 feet beside Loch Lomond.
9. Tester: a colloquial term for a sixpenny coin, worth half a shilling.
1. An early usage of the modern meaning of the expression: to be naked. Previously, it referred to the extravagant costumes worn at court on a sovereign's birthday.

all that, she may have infections like other people, and I believe, she wouldn't be sorry to be called *your ladyship*, whenever sir George thinks proper to ax the question.—But, for my part, whatever I may see or hear, not a praticle shall ever pass the lips of,

Dear Molly,

Your loving friend,

Grasco, Sept. 7.   Win. Jenkins.

Remember me, as usual, to Sall.—We are now coming home, though not the nearest road.——I do suppose, I shall find the kitten a fine boar at my return.

To Sir Watkin Phillips, Bar^t. at Oxon.

Dear Knight,

Once more I tread upon English ground, which I like not the worse for the six weeks' ramble I have made among the woods and mountains of Caledonia; no offence to the *land of cakes, where bannocks grow upon straw.*[2] I never saw my uncle in such health and spirits as he now enjoys. Liddy is perfectly recovered; and Mrs. Tabitha has no reason to complain. Nevertheless, I believe, she was, till yesterday, inclined to give the whole Scotch nation to the devil, as a pack of insensible brutes, upon whom her accomplishments had been displayed in vain.—At every place where we halted, did she mount the stage, and flourished her rusty arms, without being able to make one conquest. One of her last essays was against the heart of sir George Colquhoun, with whom she fought all the weapons more than twice over.—She was grave and gay by turns—she moralized and methodized—she laughed, and romped, and danced, and sung, and sighed, and ogled, and lisped, and fluttered, and flattered—but all was preaching to the desart—The baronet, being a well-bred man, carried his civilities as far as she could in conscience expect, and, if evil tongues are to be believed, some degrees farther; but he was too much a veteran in gallantry, as well as in war, to fall into any ambuscade that she could lay for his affection.— While we were absent in the Highlands, she practised also upon the laird of Ladrishmore, and even gave him the rendezvous in the wood of Drumscailloch;[3] but the laird had such a reverend care of

---

2. Scotland was known for its oat bread or oat cake. The italics suggest this is a quotation, but it has not been precisely identified.
3. Apparently, Jery conflates several place names here. Ledrishmore Wood is by Loch Lomond.

his own reputation, that he came attended with the parson of the parish, and nothing passed but spiritual communication.——After all these miscarriages, our aunt suddenly recollected lieutenant Lismahago, whom, ever since our first arrival at Edinburgh, she seemed to have utterly forgot, but now she expressed her hopes of seeing him at Dumfries, according to his promise.

We set out from Glasgow by the way of Lanerk, the county-town of Clydesdale, in the neighbourhood of which, the whole river Clyde, rushing down a steep rock, forms a very noble and stupendous cascade. Next day we were obliged to halt in a small borough, until the carriage, which had received some damage, should be repaired; and here we met with an incident which warmly interested the benevolent spirit of Mr. Bramble.—As we stood at the window of an inn that fronted the public prison, a person arrived on horseback, genteelly, tho' plainly, dressed in a blue frock, with his own hair cut short, and a gold-laced hat upon his head.— Alighting, and giving his horse to the landlord, he advanced to an old man who was at work in paving the street, and accosted him in these words: "This is hard work for such an old man as you."—So saying, he took the instrument out of his hand, and began to thump the pavement.—After a few strokes, "Have you never a son (said he) to ease you of this labour?" "Yes, an please your honour, (replied the senior) I have three hopeful lads, but, at present, they are out of the way." "Honour not me (cried the stranger); it more becomes me to honour your grey hairs.—Where are those sons you talk of?" The ancient paviour[4] said, his eldest son was a captain in the East-Indies; and the youngest had lately inlisted as a soldier, in hopes of prospering like his brother. The gentleman desiring to know what was become of the second, he wiped his eyes, and owned, he had taken upon him his old father's debts, for which he was now in the prison hard by.

The traveller made three quick steps towards the jail, then turning short, "Tell me, (said he) has that unnatural captain sent you nothing to relieve your distresses?" "Call him not unnatural (replied the other); God's blessing be upon him! he sent me a great deal of money; but I made a bad use of it; I lost it by being security for a gentleman that was my landlord[5] and was stript of all I had in the world besides." At that instant a young man, thrusting out his head and neck between two iron bars in the prison-window, exclaimed, "Father! father! if my brother William is in life, that's he!" "I am!—I am!—(cried the stranger, clasping the old man in his arms, and

4. Someone who lays paving stones.
5. I.e., he put up collateral to help his landlord qualify for a loan on which he subsequently defaulted.

shedding a flood of tears)—I am your son Willy, sure enough!" Before the father, who was quite confounded, could make any return to this tenderness, a decent old woman bolting out from the door of a poor habitation, cried, "Where is my bairn? where is my dear Willy?"— The captain no sooner beheld her, than he quitted his father, and ran into her embrace.[6]

I can assure you, my uncle, who saw and heard every thing that passed, was as much moved as any one of the parties concerned in this pathetic[7] recognition—He sobbed, and wept, and clapped his hands, and hollowed, and finally ran down into the street. By this time, the captain had retired with his parents, and all the inhabitants of the place were assembled at the door.—Mr. Bramble, nevertheless, pressed thro' the crowd, and entering the house, "Captain, (said he) I beg the favour of your acquaintance—I would have travelled a hundred miles to see this affecting scene; and I shall think myself happy, if you and your parents will dine with me at the public house." The captain thanked him for his kind invitation, which, he said, he would accept with pleasure; but, in the mean time, he could not think of eating or drinking, while his poor brother was in trouble.—He forthwith deposited a sum equal to the debt in the hands of the magistrate, who ventured to set his brother at liberty without farther process; and then the whole family repaired to the inn with my uncle, attended by the crowd, the individuals of which shook their townsman by the hand, while he returned their caresses without the least sign of pride or affectation.

This honest favourite of fortune, whose name was Brown, told my uncle, that he had been bred a weaver, and, about eighteen years ago, had, from a spirit of idleness and dissipation, enlisted as a soldier in the service of the East-India company; that, in the course of duty, he had the good fortune to attract the notice and approbation of lord Clive, who preferred[8] him from one step to another, till he attained the rank of captain and pay-master to the regiment, in which capacities he had honestly amassed above twelve thousand pounds, and, at the peace, resigned his commission.—He had sent several remittances to his father, who received the first only, consisting of one hundred pounds; the second had fallen into the hands of a bankrupt; and the third had been consigned to a gentleman of Scotland, who died before it arrived; so that it still remained to be accounted for by his executors. He now presented the old man with fifty pounds for his present occasions, over and above bank notes

---

6. According to Robert Anderson's *Works of the British Poets* (1794), this story is based on the actual experiences of Martin White of the village of Milton.
7. Emotionally stirring.
8. Promoted. Robert Clive, first Baron Clive (1725–1774), was the British military officer who led the East India Company to establish supremacy in Bengal in the later 1750s.

for one hundred, which he had deposited for his brother's release.—
He brought along with him a deed ready executed, by which he
settled a perpetuity[9] of fourscore pounds upon his parents, to be
inherited by their other two sons after their decease.—He promised
to purchase a commission for his youngest brother; to take the
other as his own partner in a manufacture which he intended to set
up, to give employment and bread to the industrious; and to give
five hundred pounds, by way of dower, to his sister, who had married a farmer in low circumstances.—Finally, he gave fifty pounds to
the poor of the town where he was born, and feasted all the inhabitants without exception.

My uncle was so charmed with the character of captain Brown,
that he drank his health three times successively at dinner.—He
said, he was proud of his acquaintance; that he was an honour to his
country, and had in some measure redeemed human nature from the
reproach of pride, selfishness, and ingratitude.—For my part, I was
as much pleased with the modesty as with the filial virtue of this
honest soldier, who assumed no merit from his success, and said very
little of his own transactions, though the answers he made to our
inquiries were equally sensible and laconic. Mrs. Tabitha behaved
very graciously to him until she understood that he was going to
make a tender of his hand to a person of low estate, who had been his
sweet-heart while he worked as a journeyman weaver.—Our aunt
was no sooner made acquainted with this design, than she starched
up her behaviour with a double proportion of reserve; and when the
company broke up, she observed, with a toss of her nose, that Brown
was a civil fellow enough, considering the lowness of his origin; but
that Fortune, though she had mended his circumstances, was incapable to raise his ideas, which were still humble and plebeian.

On the day that succeeded this adventure, we went some miles
out of our road to see Drumlanrig, a seat belonging to the duke of
Queensberry,[1] which appears like a magnificent palace erected by
magic, in the midst of a wilderness.—It is indeed a princely mansion, with suitable parks and plantations, rendered still more striking by the nakedness of the surrounding country, which is one of
the wildest tracts in all Scotland.—This wildness, however, is different from that of the Highlands; for here the mountains, instead
of heath, are covered with a fine green swarth, affording pasture to
innumerable flocks of sheep. But the fleeces of this country, called
Nithsdale, are not comparable to the wool of Galloway, which is
said to equal that of Salisbury plain. Having passed the night at the
castle of Drumlanrig, by invitation from the duke himself, who is

9. Annual income.
1. Drumlanrig, seat of the Duke of Queensberry—who at the time was Charles Douglas
   (1698–1778)—was built in the late 17th century.

one of the best men that ever breathed, we prosecuted our journey to Dumfries, a very elegant trading town near the borders of England, where we found plenty of good provision and excellent wine, at very reasonable prices, and the accommodation as good in all respects as in any part of South-Britain.—If I was confined to Scotland for life, I would chuse Dumfries as the place of my residence. Here we made enquiries about captain Lismahago, of whom hearing no tidings, we proceeded, by the Solway Frith, to Carlisle. You must know, that the Solway sands, upon which travellers pass at low water, are exceedingly dangerous, because, as the tide makes, they become quick[2] in different places, and the flood rushes in so impetuously, that passengers are often overtaken by the sea, and perish.

In crossing these treacherous Syrtes[3] with a guide, we perceived a drowned horse, which Humphry Clinker, after due inspection, declared to be the very identical beast which Mr. Lismahago rode when he parted with us at Felton-bridge[4] in Northumberland. This information, which seemed to intimate that our friend the lieutenant had shared the fate of his horse, affected us all, and above all our aunt Tabitha, who shed salt tears, and obliged Clinker to pull a few hairs out of the dead horse's tail; to be worn in a ring as a remembrance of his master: but her grief and ours was not of long duration; for one of the first persons we saw in Carlisle, was the lieutenant *in propria persona*,[5] bargaining with a horse-dealer for another steed, in the yard of the inn where we alighted.—Mrs. Bramble was the first that perceived him, and screamed as if she had seen a ghost; and, truly, at a proper time and place, he might very well have passed for an inhabitant of another world; for he was more meagre and grim than before—We received him the more cordially for having supposed he had been drowned; and he was not deficient in expressions of satisfaction at this meeting.—He told us, he had enquired for us at Dumfries, and been informed by a travelling merchant from Glasgow, that we had resolved to return by the way of Coldstream.—He said, that in passing the sands without a guide, his horse had knocked up;[6] and he himself must have perished, if he had not been providentially relieved by a return post-chaise.—He moreover gave us to understand, that his scheme of settling in his own country having miscarried, he was so far on his way to London, with a view to embark for North-America, where he intended to pass the rest of his days among his old friends the Miamis, and amuse himself in finishing the education of the son he had by his beloved Squinkinacoosta.

2. Like quicksand.
3. Quicksands off the northern African coast.
4. A 15th-century bridge that crosses the River Coquet about one hour south of the Scottish border.
5. In his own person (Latin).
6. Died.

This project was by no means agreeable to our good aunt, who expatiated upon the fatigues and dangers that would attend such a long voyage by sea, and afterwards such a tedious journey by land— She enlarged particularly on the risque he would run, with respect to the concerns of his precious soul, among savages who had not yet received the glad tidings of salvation; and she hinted that his abandoning Great-Britain might, perhaps, prove fatal to the inclinations of some deserving person, whom he was qualified to make happy for life. My uncle, who is really a Don Quixote in generosity, understanding that Lismahago's real reason for leaving Scotland was the impossibility of subsisting in it with any decency upon the wretched provision of a subaltern's half-pay, began to be warmly interested on the side of compassion.—He thought it very hard, that a gentleman who had served his country with honour, should be driven by necessity to spend his old age, among the refuse of mankind, in such a remote part of the world.—He discoursed with me upon the subject; observing, that he would willingly offer the lieutenant an asylum[7] at Brambleton-hall, if he did not foresee that his singularities and humour of contradiction would render him an intolerable house-mate, though his conversation at some times might be both instructive and entertaining; but, as there seemed to be something particular in his attention to Mrs, Tabitha, he and I agreed in opinion, that this intercourse[8] should be encouraged, and improved, if possible, into a matrimonial union; in which case there would be a comfortable provision for both; and they might be settled in a house of their own, so that Mr. Bramble should have no more of their company than he desired.

In pursuance of this design, Lismahago has been invited to pass the winter at Brambleton-hall, as it will be time enough to execute his American project in the spring.—He has taken time to consider of this proposal; mean while, he will keep us company as far as we travel in the road to Bristol, where he has hopes of getting a passage for America. I make no doubt but that he will postpone his voyage, and prosecute his addresses to a happy consummation; and sure, if it produces any fruit, it must be of a very peculiar flavour. As the weather continues favourable, I believe, we shall take the Peak of Derbyshire and Buxton Wells in our way.—At any rate, from the first place where we make any stay, you shall hear again from

Yours always,

Carlisle, Sept. 12.   J. MELFORD.

7. A place of refuge.
8. Communication.

To Dr. LEWIS.

DEAR DOCTOR,

The peasantry of Scotland are certainly on a poor footing all over the kingdom; and yet they look better, and are better cloathed than those of the same rank in Burgundy, and many other places of France and Italy; nay, I will venture to say they are better fed, notwithstanding the boasted wine of these foreign countries. The country people of North-Britain live chiefly on oat-meal, and milk, cheese, butter, and some garden-stuff, with now and then a pickled-herring, by way of delicacy; but flesh-meat they seldom or never taste; nor any kind of strong liquor, except two-penny,[9] at times of uncommon festivity—Their breakfast is a kind of hasty pudding, of oat-meal or pease-meal, eaten with milk. They have commonly pottage to dinner, composed of cale or cole, leeks, barley or big,[1] and butter; and this is reinforced with bread and cheese, made of skimmed-milk—At night they sup on sowens or flummery[2] of oat-meal—In a scarcity of oats, they use the meal of barley and pease, which is both nourishing and palatable. Some of them have potatoes; and you find parsnips in every peasant's garden—They are cloathed with a coarse kind of russet[3] of their own making, which is both decent and warm—They dwell in poor huts, built of loose stones and turf, without any mortar, having a fire-place or hearth in the middle, generally made of an old mill-stone, and a hole at top to let out the smoke.

These people, however, are content, and wonderfully sagacious—All of them read the Bible, and are even qualified to dispute upon the articles of their faith; which, in those parts I have seen, is entirely Presbyterian. I am told, that the inhabitants of Aberdeen-shire are still more acute. I once knew a Scotch gentleman at London, who had declared war against this part of his countrymen; and swore that the impudence and knavery of the Scots, in that quarter, had brought a reproach upon the whole nation.

The river Clyde, above Glasgow, is quite pastoral; and the banks of it are every where adorned with fine villas. From the sea to its source, we may reckon the seats of many families of the first rank, such as the duke of Argyle at Roseneath, the earl of Bute in the isle of that name, the earl of Glencairn at Finlayston, lord Blantyre at Areskine, the dutchess of Douglas at Bothwell, duke Hamilton at Hamilton, the duke of Douglas at Douglas, and the earl of Hyndford

---

9. A kind of cheap ale.
1. A hardy Scottish variety of barley, usually spelled "bigge."
2. Here, a synonym for "sowens"—starchy matter extracted from bran or oat husks; it is also the name for a creamy dessert.
3. Homespun cloth.

at Carmichael. Hamilton is a noble palace, magnificently furnished; and hard by is the village of that name, one of the neatest
little towns I have seen in any country. The old castle of Douglas
being burned to the ground by accident, the late duke[4] resolved, as
head of the first family in Scotland, to have the largest house in the
kingdom, and ordered a plan for this purpose; but there was only
one wing of it finished when he died. It is to be hoped that his
nephew, who is now in possession of his great fortune, will complete the design of his predecessor—Clydesdale is in general populous and rich, containing a great number of gentlemen, who are
independent in their fortune; but it produces more cattle than corn—
This is also the case with Tweedale, through part of which we passed,
and Nidsdale, which is generally rough, wild, and mountainous—
These hills are covered with sheep; and this is the small delicious
mutton, so much preferable to that of the London-market. As their
feeding costs so little, the sheep are not killed till five years old,
when their flesh, juices, and flavour, are in perfection; but their
fleeces are much damaged by the tar, with which they are smeared
to preserve them from the rot in winter, during which they run
wild night and day, and thousands are lost under huge wreaths of
snow——'Tis pity the farmers cannot contrive some means to shelter this useful animal from the inclemencies of a rigorous climate,
especially from the perpetual rains, which are more prejudicial than
the greatest extremity of cold weather.

On the little river Nid, is situated the castle of Drumlanrig,
one of the noblest seats in Great-Britain, belonging to the duke of
Queensberry; one of those few noblemen whose goodness of heart
does honour to human-nature—I shall not pretend to enter into a
description of this palace, which is really an instance of the sublime in magnificence, as well as in situation, and puts one in mind
of the beautiful city of Palmyra,[5] rising like a vision in the midst of
the wilderness. His grace keeps open house, and lives with great
splendour—He did us the honour to receive us with great courtesy,
and detain us all night, together with above twenty other guests,
with all their servants and horses, to a very considerable number—
The dutchess was equally gracious, and took our ladies under her
immediate protection. The longer I live, I see more reason to believe
that prejudices of education are never wholly eradicated, even
when they are discovered to be erroneous and absurd. Such habits
of thinking as interest the grand passions, cleave to the human
heart in such a manner, that though an effort of reason may force
them from their hold for a moment, this violence no sooner ceases,

4. Archibald Douglas, first Duke of Douglas (1694–1761).
5. An ancient city, famed for its beauty, which was located in present-day Syria.

than they resume their grasp with an encreased elasticity and adhesion.

I am led into this reflection, by what passed at the duke's table after supper. The conversation turned upon the vulgar notions of spirits and omens, that prevail among the commonalty of North-Britain, and all the company agreed, that nothing could be more ridiculous. One gentleman, however, told a remarkable story of himself, by way of speculation—"Being on a party of hunting in the North, (said he) I resolved to visit an old friend, whom I had not seen for twenty years—So long he had been retired and sequestered from all his acquaintance, and lived in a moping melancholy way, much afflicted with lowness of spirits, occasioned by the death of his wife, whom he had loved with uncommon affection. As he resided in a remote part of the country, and we were five gentlemen with as many servants, we carried some provision with us from the next market town, lest we should find him unprepared for our reception. The roads being bad, we did not arrive at the house till two o'clock in the afternoon; and were agreeably surprised to find a very good dinner ready in the kitchen, and the cloth laid with six covers. My friend himself appeared in his best apparel at the gate, and received us with open arms, telling me he had been expecting us these two hours—Astonished at this declaration, I asked who had given him intelligence of our coming? and he smiled without making any other reply—However, presuming upon our former intimacy, I afterwards insisted upon knowing; and he told me, very gravely, he had seen me in a vision of the second sight[6]—Nay, he called in the evidence of his steward, who solemnly declared, that his master had the day before apprised him of my coming, with four other strangers, and ordered him to provide accordingly; in consequence of which intimation, he had prepared the dinner which we were now eating; and laid the covers according to the number foretold." The incident we all owned to be remarkable, and I endeavoured to account for it by natural means. I observed, that as the gentleman was of a visionary turn, the casual idea, or remembrance of his old friend, might suggest those circumstances, which accident had for once realized; but that in all probability he had seen many visions of the same kind, which were never verified. None of the company directly dissented from my opinion; but from the objections that were hinted, I could plainly perceive, that the majority were persuaded there was something more extraordinary in the case.

Another gentleman of the company, addressing himself to me, "Without all doubt, (said he) a diseased imagination is very apt to

---

6. Spontaneous precognition or "remote viewing," belief in which was widespread in the Highlands.

produce visions; but we must find some other method to account for something of this kind, that happened within these eight days in my neighbourhood——A gentleman of a good family, who cannot be deemed a visionary in any sense of the word, was near his own gate, in the twilight, visited by his grandfather, who has been dead these fifteen years—The spectre was mounted seemingly on the very horse he used to ride, with an angry and terrible countenance, and said something, which his grandson, in the confusion of his fear, could not understand. But this was not all—He lifted up a huge horse-whip, and applied it with great violence to his back and shoulders, on which I saw the impression with my own eyes. The apparition was afterwards seen by the sexton of the parish, hovering about the tomb where his body lies interred; as the man declared to several persons in the village, before he knew what had happened to the gentleman—Nay, he actually came to me as a justice of the peace, in order to make oath of these particulars, which, however, I declined administering. As for the grandson of the defunct, he is a sober, sensible, worldly-minded fellow, too intent upon schemes of interest to give into reveries. He would have willingly concealed the affair; but he bawled out in the first transport of his fear, and, running into the house, exposed his back and his sconce[7] to the whole family; so that there was no denying it in the sequel. It is now the common discourse of the country, that this appearance and behaviour of the old man's spirit, portends some great calamity to the family, and the good woman has actually taken to her bed in this apprehension."

Though I did not pretend to explain this mystery, I said, I did not at all doubt, but it would one day appear to be a deception; and, in all probability, a scheme executed by some enemy of the person who had sustained the assault; but still the gentleman insisted upon the clearness of the evidence, and the concurrence of testimony, by which two creditable witnesses, without any communication one with another, affirmed the appearance of the same man, with whose person they were both well acquainted—From Drumlanrig we pursued the course of the Nid to Dumfries, which stands several miles above the place where the river falls into the sea; and is, after Glasgow, the handsomest town I have seen in Scotland—The inhabitants, indeed, seem to have proposed that city as their model; not only in beautifying their town and regulating its police, but also in prosecuting their schemes of commerce and manufacture, by which they are grown rich and opulent.

We re-entered England, by the way of Carlisle, where we accidentally met with our friend Lismahago, whom we had in vain inquired

7. Head or skull.

after at Dumfries and other places—It would seem that the captain, like the prophets of old, is but little honoured in his own country, which he has now renounced for ever—He gave me the following particulars of his visit to his native soil—In his way to the place of his nativity, he learned that his nephew had married the daughter of a burgeois, who directed a weaving manufacture, and had gone into partnership with his father-in-law: chagrined with this information, he had arrived at the gate in the twilight, where he heard the sound of treddles[8] in the great hall, which had exasperated him to such a degree, that he had like to have lost his senses: while he was thus transported with indignation, his nephew chanced to come forth, when, being no longer master of his passion, he cried, "Degenerate rascall you have made my father's house a den of thieves;" and at the same time chastised him with his horse-whip; then, riding round the adjoining village, he had visited the burying-ground of his ancestors by moon-light; and, having paid his respects to their *manes*,[9] travelled all night to another part of the country——Finding the head of his family in such a disgraceful situation, all his own friends dead or removed from the places of their former residence, and the expence of living encreased to double of what it had been, when he first left his native country, he had bid it an eternal adieu,[1] and was determined to seek for repose among the forests of America.

I was no longer at a loss to account for the apparition, which had been described at Drumlanrig; and when I repeated the story to the lieutenant, he was much pleased to think his resentment had been so much more effectual than he intended; and he owned, he might at such an hour, and in such an equipage, very well pass for the ghost of his father, whom he was said greatly to resemble——Between friends, I fancy Lismahago will find a retreat without going so far as the wigwams of the Miamis. My sister Tabby is making continual advances to him, in the way of affection; and, if I may trust to appearances, the captain is disposed to take opportunity by the forelock.[2] For my part, I intend to encourage this correspondence, and shall be glad to see them united—In that case, we shall find a way to settle them comfortably in our own neighbourhood. I, and my servants, will get rid of a very troublesome and tyrannic gouvernante; and I shall have the benefit of Lismahago's conversation, without being obliged to take more of his company than I desire;

---

8. Usually spelled "treadles," the rocking levers used to work machines by foot; here, the reference is to the weaving machines themselves. "Burgeois": an obsolete spelling of *bourgeois*, which at the time meant a shopkeeper or merchant.
9. Spirits (Latin).
1. Farewell (French).
2. To seize the opportunity (proverbial).

for though an olla[3] is a high-flavoured dish, I could not bear to dine upon it every day of my life.

I am much pleased with Manchester, which is one of the most agreeable and flourishing towns in Great-Britain; and I perceive that this is the place which hath animated the spirit, and suggested the chief manufactures of Glasgow. We propose to visit Chatsworth, the Peak, and Buxton,[4] from which last place we shall proceed directly homewards, though by easy journies. If the season has been as favourable in Wales as in the North, your harvest is happily finished; and we have nothing left to think of but our October, of which let Barns be properly reminded. You will find me much better in flesh than I was at our parting; and this short separation has given a new edge to those sentiments of friendship with which I always have been, and ever shall be,

yours,

Manchester, Sept. 15.   MATT. BRAMBLE.

To Mrs. GWYLLIM, house-keeper at Brambleton-hall.

MRS. GWILLIM,

It has pleased Providence to bring us safe back to England, and partake us in many pearls by land and water, in particular the *Devil's Harse a pike*, and *Hoyden's Hole*,[5] which hath got no bottom; and, as we are drawing huomwards, it may be proper to uprise you, that Brambleton-hall may be in a condition to receive us, after this long gurney to the islands of Scotland. By the first of next month you may begin to make constant fires in my brother's chamber and mine; and burn a fagget every day in the yellow damask room: have the tester and curtains dusted, and the fatherbed and matrosses well haired, because, perhaps, with the blissing of haven, they may be yoosed on some occasion. Let the ould hogsheads be well skewred and seasoned for bear, as Mat is resolved to have his seller choak fool.

If the house was mine, I would turn over a new leaf——I don't see why the sarvants of Wales should'n't drink fair water, and eat

---

3. A dish made from a variety meats and vegetables cooked in a clay pot. "Gouvernante": female chaperone.
4. An ancient spa town that had become a fashionable resort along the lines of Bath. Chatsworth House was the seat of the Dukes of Devonshire. The Peak refers to a hilly district in Derbyshire.
5. Perhaps Elden Hole, a geographical feature of the Peak District near Castleton. "Devil's Arse" refers to Peak Cavern in Darbyshire, England, which earned its nickname because of the evocative noises made by echoes of draining water.

hot cakes and barley cale, as they do in Scotland, without troubling the botcher above once a quarter—I hope you keep accunt of Roger's purseeding in reverence to the butter-milk. I expect my dew when I come huom, without baiting an ass,[6] I'll assure you.—As you must have layed a great many more eggs than would be eaten, I do suppose there is a power of turks, chickings, and guzzling about the house; and a brave kergo of cheese ready for market; and that the owl has been sent to Crickhowel, saving what the maids spun in the family.

Pray let the whole house and furniture have a thorough cleaning from top to bottom, for the honour of Wales; and let Roger search into, and make a general clearance of the slit holes which the maids have in secret;[7] for I know they are much given to sloth and uncleanness. I hope you have worked a reformation among them, as I exhorted you in my last, and set their hearts upon better things than they can find in junkitting and caterwauling with the fellows of the country.

As for Win Jenkins, she has undergone a perfect metamurphysis, and is become a new creeter from the ammunition of Humphrey Clinker, our new footman, a pious young man, who has laboured exceedingly, that she may bring forth fruits of repentance. I make no doubt but he will take the same pains with that pert hussey Mary Jones, and all of you; and that he may have power given to penetrate and instill his goodness, even into your most inward parts, is the fervent prayer of

your friend in the spirit,

Septr. 18.   TAB. BRAMBLE.

To Dr. LEWIS.

DEAR LEWIS,

Lismahago is more paradoxical than ever.—The late gulp he had of his native air, seems to have blown fresh spirit into all his polemical faculties. I congratulated him the other day on the present flourishing state of his country, observing that the Scots were now in a fair way to wipe off the national reproach of poverty, and expressing my satisfaction at the happy effects of the union, so conspicuous in the improvement of their agriculture, commerce, manufactures, and manners—The lieutenant, screwing up his features into a look of dissent and disgust, commented on my remarks to

6. To bate an ace: to abate some little things (proverbial).
7. Tabitha apparently wants Roger to check the girls' mattresses for concealed pockets.

this effect—"Those who reproach a nation for its poverty, when it is not owing to the profligacy or vice of the people, deserve no answer. The Lacedæmonians[8] were poorer than the Scots, when they took the lead among all the free states of Greece, and were esteemed above them all for their valour and their virtue. The most respectable heroes of ancient Rome, such as Fabricius, Cincinnatus, and Regulus, were poorer than the poorest freeholder in Scotland; and there are at this day individuals in North-Britain, one of whom can produce more gold and silver than the whole republic of Rome could raise at those times when her public virtue shone with unrivalled lustre; and poverty was so far from being a reproach, that it added fresh laurels to her fame, because it indicated a noble contempt of wealth, which was proof against all the arts of corruption—If poverty be a subject for reproach, it follows that wealth is the object of esteem and veneration—In that case, there are Jews and others in Amsterdam and London, enriched by usury, peculation, and different species of fraud and extortion, who are more estimable than the most virtuous and illustrious members of the community. An absurdity which no man in his senses will offer to maintain.—Riches are certainly no proof of merit: nay they are often (if not most commonly) acquired by persons of sordid minds and mean talents: nor do they give any intrinsic worth to the possessor; but, on the contrary, tend to pervert his understanding, and render his morals more depraved. But, granting that poverty were really matter of reproach, it cannot be justly imputed to Scotland. No country is poor that can supply its inhabitants with the necessaries of life, and even afford articles for exportation. Scotland is rich in natural advantages: it produces every species of provision in abundance, vast herds of cattle and flocks of sheep, with a great number of horses; prodigious quantities of wool and flax, with plenty of copse wood, and in some parts large forests of timber. The earth is still more rich below than above the surface. It yields inexhaustible stores of coal, free-stone, marble, lead, iron, copper, and silver, with some gold. The sea abounds with excellent fish, and salt to cure them for exportation; and there are creeks and harbours round the whole kingdom, for the convenience and security of navigation. The face of the country displays a surprising number of cities, towns, villas, and villages, swarming with people; and there seems to be no want of art, industry, government, and police: such a kingdom can never be called poor, in any sense of the word, though there may be many others more powerful and opulent. But the proper use of those advantages, and the present prosperity of the Scots, you seem to derive from the union of the two kingdoms!"

8. Spartans.

I said, I supposed he would not deny that the appearance of the country was much mended; that the people lived better, had more trade, and a greater quantity of money circulating since the union, than before. "I may safely admit these premises, (answered the lieutenant) without subscribing to your inference. The difference you mention, I should take to be the natural progress of improvement—Since that period, other nations, such as the Swedes, the Danes, and in particular the French, have greatly increased in commerce, without any such cause assigned. Before the union, there was a remarkable spirit of trade among the Scots, as appeared in the case of their Darien company,[9] in which they had embarked no less than four hundred thousand pounds sterling; and in the flourishing state of the maritime towns in Fife, and on the eastern coast, enriched by their trade with France, which failed in consequence of the union. The only solid commercial advantage reaped from that measure, was the privilege of trading to the English plantations; yet, excepting Glasgow and Dumfries, I don't know any other Scotch towns concerned in that traffick. In other respects, I conceive the Scots were losers by the union.—They lost the independency of their state, the greatest prop of national spirit; they lost their parliament, and their courts of justice were subjected to the revision and supremacy of an English tribunal."

"Softly, captain, (cried I) you cannot be said to have lost your own parliament, while you are represented in that of Great-Britain." "True, (said he, with a sarcastic grin) in debates of national competition, the sixteen peers and forty-five commoners of Scotland, must make a formidable figure in the scale, against the whole English legislature." "Be that as it may, (I observed) while I had the honour to sit in the lower house, the Scotch members had always the majority on their side." "I understand you, Sir, (said he) they generally side with the majority; so much the worse for their constituents. But even this evil is not the worst they have sustained by the union. Their trade has been saddled with grievous impositions, and every article of living severely taxed, to pay the interest of enormous debts, contracted by the English, in support of measures and connections in which the Scots had no interest nor concern." I begged he would at least allow, that by the union the Scots were admitted to all the privileges and immunities of English subjects; by which means multitudes of them were provided for in the army and navy, and got fortunes in different parts of England, and its dominions. "All these, (said he) become English subjects to all intents and purposes, and are in a great measure lost to their mother-country. The spirit of

9. Founded in 1695 as the Company of Scotland Trading to Africa and the Indies, it established a colony in Panama that had to be abandoned due to lack of financial support, rampart disease, and Spanish military opposition.

rambling and adventure has been always peculiar to the natives of Scotland. If they had not met with encouragement in England, they would have served and settled, as formerly, in other countries, such as Muscovy, Sweden, Denmark, Poland, Germany, France, Piedmont, and Italy, in all which nations their descendents continue to flourish even at this day."

By this time my patience began to fail, and I exclaimed, "For God's sake, what has England got by this union which, you say, has been so productive of misfortune to the Scots." "Great and manifold are the advantages which England derives from the union (said Lismahago, in a solemn tone). First and foremost, the settlement of the protestant succession, a point which the English ministry drove with such eagerness, that no stone was left unturned, to cajole and bribe a few leading men, to cram the union down the throats of the Scottish nation, who were surprisingly reverse[1] to the expedient. They gained by it a considerable addition of territory, extending their dominion to the sea on all sides of the island, thereby shutting up all back-doors against the enterprizes of their enemies. They got an accession of above a million of useful subjects, constituting a never-failing nursery of seamen, soldiers, labourers, and mechanics; a most valuable acquisition to a trading country, exposed to foreign wars, and obliged to maintain a number of settlements in all the four quarters of the globe. In the course of seven years, during the last war, Scotland furnished the English army and navy with seventy thousand men, over and above those who migrated to their colonies, or mingled with them at home in the civil departments of life. This was a very considerable and seasonable supply to a nation, whose people had been for many years decreasing in number, and whose lands and manufactures were actually suffering for want of hands. I need not remind you of the hackneyed maxim, that, to a nation in such circumstances, a supply of industrious people is a supply of wealth; nor repeat an observation, which is now received as an eternal truth, even among the English themselves, that the Scots who settle in South Britain are remarkably sober, orderly, and industrious."

I allowed the truth of this remark, adding, that by their industry, œconomy, and circumspection, many of them in England, as well as in her colonies, amassed large fortunes, with which they returned to their own country, and this was so much lost to South-Britain.——"Give me leave, sir, (said he) to assure you, that in your fact you are mistaken, and in your deduction, erroneous.—Not one in two hundred that leave Scotland ever returns to settle in his own country; and the few that do return, carry thither nothing that can

1. Averse.

possibly diminish the stock of South-Britain; for none of their treasure stagnates in Scotland—There is a continual circulation, like that
of the blood in the human body, and England is the heart, to which
all the streams which it distributes are refunded and returned: nay,
in consequence of that luxury which our connexion with England
hath greatly encouraged, if not introduced, all the produce of our
lands, and all the profits of our trade, are engrossed by the natives
of South-Britain; for you will find that the exchange between the
two kingdoms is always against Scotland; and that she retains neither gold nor silver sufficient for her own circulation.—The Scots,
not content with their own manufactures and produce, which would
very well answer all necessary occasions, seem to vie with each other
in purchasing superfluities from England; such as broad-cloth, velvets, stuffs, silks, lace, furs, jewels, furniture of all sorts, sugar, rum,
tea, chocolate, and coffee; in a word, not only every mode of the most
extravagant luxury, but even many articles of convenience, which
they might find as good, and much cheaper in their own country.
For all these particulars, I conceive, England may touch[2] about one
million sterling a-year.—I don't pretend to make an exact calculation; perhaps, it may be something less, and, perhaps, a great deal
more.—The annual revenue arising from all the private estates of
Scotland cannot fall short of a million sterling; and, I should imagine, their trade will amount to as much more.—I know, the linen
manufacture alone returns near half a million, exclusive of the home-
consumption of that article.—If, therefore, North-Britain pays a
balance of a million annually to England, I insist upon it, that country is more valuable to her in the way of commerce, than any colony
in her possession, over and above the other advantages which I have
specified: therefore, they are no friends, either to England or to
truth, who affect to depreciate the northern part of the united
kingdom."

I must own, I was at first a little nettled to find myself schooled
in so many particulars.——Though I did not receive all his assertions as gospel, I was not prepared to refute them; and I cannot
help now acquiescing in his remarks so far as to think, that the contempt for Scotland, which prevails too much on this side the Tweed, is
founded on prejudice and error.——After some recollection, "Well,
captain, (said I) you have argued stoutly for the importance of
your own country: for my part, I have such a regard for our fellow-
subjects of North-Britain, that I shall be glad to see the day, when
your peasants can afford to give all their oats to their cattle, hogs,
and poultry, and indulge themselves with good wheaten loaves,

2. Earn.

instead of such poor, unpalatable, and inflammatory diet." Here again I brought myself into a premunire[3] with the disputaceous Caledonian. He said, he hoped he should never see the common people lifted out of that sphere for which they were intended by nature and the course of things; that they might have some reason to complain of their bread, if it were mixed, like that of Norway, with sawdust and fish-bones; but that oatmeal was, he apprehended, as nourishing and salutary as wheat-flour, and the Scots in general thought it at least as savoury.—He affirmed, that a mouse, which, in the article of self-preservation, might be supposed to act from infallible instinct, would always prefer oats to wheat, as appeared from experience; for, in a place where there was a parcel of each, that animal had never begun to feed upon the latter till all the oats were consumed: for their nutritive quality, he appealed to the hale, robust constitutions of the people who lived chiefly upon oatmeal; and, instead of being inflammatory, he asserted, that it was a cooling sub-acid, balsamic and mucilaginous;[4] insomuch, that in all inflammatory distempers, recourse was had to water-gruel, and flummery made of oatmeal.

"At least, (said I) give me leave to wish them such a degree of commerce as may enable them to follow their own inclinations."——— "Heaven forbid! (cried this philosopher) Woe be to that nation, where the multitude is at liberty to follow their own inclinations! Commerce is undoubtedly a blessing, while restrained within its proper channels; but a glut of wealth brings along with it a glut of evils: it brings false taste, false appetite, false wants, profusion, venality, contempt of order, engendering a spirit of licentiousness, insolence, and faction, that keeps the community in continual ferment, and in time destroys all the distinctions of civil society; so that universal anarchy and uproar must ensue. Will any sensible man affirm, that the national advantages of opulence are to be sought on these terms?" "No, sure; but I am one of those who think, that, by proper regulations, commerce may produce every national benefit, without the allay of such concomitant evils."

So much for the dogmata of my friend Lismahago, whom I describe the more circumstantially, as I firmly believe he will set up his rest in Monmouthshire. Yesterday, while I was alone with him, he asked, in some confusion, if I should have any objection to the success of a gentleman and a soldier, provided he should be so fortunate as to engage my sister's affection. I answered, without hesitation, that my sister was old enough to judge for herself; and that I should be very

---

3. Originally a particular kind of legal writ, but generalized to mean an argumentative difficulty or predicament.
4. Moist, sticky.

far from disapproving any resolution she might take in his favour.—
His eyes sparkled at this declaration. He declared, he should think
himself the happiest man on earth to be connected with my family;
and that he should never be weary of giving me proofs of his gratitude and attachment. I suppose Tabby and he are already agreed; in
which case, we shall have a wedding at Brambleton-hall, and you
shall give away the bride.—It is the least thing you can do, by way
of atonement for your former cruelty to that poor love-sick maiden,
who has been so long a thorn in the side of

Yours,

Sept. 20.   MATT. BRAMBLE.

We have been at Buxton; but, as I did not much relish either the
company or the accommodations, and had no occasion for the water,
we stayed but two nights in the place.

To Sir WATKIN PHILLIPS, Bar[t]. at Oxon.

DEAR WAT,

Adventures begin to thicken as we advance to the southward.—
Lismahago has now professed himself the admirer of our aunt, and
carries on his addresses under the sanction of her brother's approbation; so that we shall certainly have a wedding by Christmas. I
should be glad you was present at the nuptials, to help me to throw
the stocking,[5] and perform other ceremonies peculiar to that occasion——I am sure it will be productive of some diversion; and,
truly, it would be worth your while to come across the country on
purpose to see two such original figures in bed together, with their
laced night-caps; he, the emblem of good chear, and she, the picture of good nature. All this agreeable prospect was clouded, and
had well nigh vanished entirely, in consequence of a late misunderstanding between the future brothers-in-law, which, however, is
now happily removed.

A few days ago, my uncle and I, going to visit a relation, met with
lord Oxmington at his house, who asked us to dine with him next
day, and we accepted the invitation.—Accordingly, leaving our women
under the care of captain Lismahago, at the inn where we had lodged
the preceding night, in a little town, about a mile from his lordship's
dwelling, we went at the hour appointed, and had a fashionable meal
served up with much ostentation to a company of about a dozen

---

5. A custom according to which the bride's stocking was thrown among the wedding
   guests; the person it hit was said to be next in line for marriage.

persons, none of whom we had ever seen before.—His lordship is much more remarkable for his pride and caprice, than for his hospitality and understanding; and, indeed, it appeared, that he considered his guests merely as objects to shine upon, so as to reflect the lustre of his own magnificence.—There was much state, but no courtesy; and a great deal of compliment without any conversation.— Before the desert was removed, our noble entertainer proposed three general toasts; then calling for a glass of wine, and bowing all round, wished us a good afternoon. This was the signal for the company to break up, and they obeyed it immediately, all except our 'squire, who was greatly shocked at the manner of this dismission.—He changed countenance, bit his lip in silence, but still kept his seat, so that his lordship found himself obliged to give us another hint, by saying, he should be glad to see us another time. "There is no time like the present time (cried Mr. Bramble); your lordship has not yet drank a bumper to *the best in Christendom*." "I'll drink no more bumpers to-day (answered our landlord); and I am sorry to see you have drank too many.—Order the gentleman's carriage to the gate."—So saying, he rose and retired abruptly; our 'squire starting up at the same time, laying his hand upon his sword, and eying him with a most ferocious aspect. The master having vanished in this manner, our uncle bad one of the servants to see what was to pay; and the fellow answering, "This is no inn," "I cry you mercy, (cried the other) I perceive it is not; if it were, the landlord would be more civil.—There's a guinea, however; take it, and tell your lord, that I shall not leave the country till I have had an opportunity to thank him in person for his politeness and hospitality."

We then walked down stairs through a double range of lacqueys, and getting into the chaise, proceeded homewards. Perceiving the 'squire much ruffled, I ventured to disapprove of his resentment, observing, that as lord Oxmington was well known to have his brain very ill timbered, a sensible man should rather laugh, than be angry at his ridiculous want of breeding.—Mr. Bramble took umbrage at my presuming to be wiser than he upon this occasion; and told me, that as he had always thought for himself in every occurrence in life, he would still use the same privilege, with my good leave.

When we returned to our inn, he closeted Lismahago; and having explained his grievance, desired that gentleman to go and demand satisfaction of lord Oxmington in his name.—The lieutenant charged himself with this commission, and immediately set out a horseback[6] for his lordship's house, attended, at his own request, by my man Archy Macalpine, who had been used to military service;

6. I.e., on horseback.

and truly, if Macalpine had been mounted upon an ass, this couple might have passed for the knight of La Mancha and his 'squire Panza.[7] It was not till after some demur that Lismahago obtained a private audience, at which he formally defied his lordship to single combat, in the name of Mr. Bramble, and desired him to appoint the time and place. Lord Oxmington was so confounded at this unexpected message, that he could not, for some time, make any articulate reply; but stood staring at the lieutenant with manifest marks of perturbation. At length, ringing a bell with great vehemence, he exclaimed, "What! a commoner send a challenge to a peer of the realm!—Privilege! privilege!—Here's a person brings me a challenge from the Welshman that dined at my table—An impudent fellow!—My wine is not yet out of his head."

The whole house was immediately in commotion.—Macalpine made a soldierly retreat with the two horses; but the captain was suddenly surrounded and disarmed by the footmen, whom a French valet de chambre headed in this exploit; his sword was passed through a close-stool,[8] and his person through the horse-pond.—In this plight he returned to the inn, half mad with his disgrace.—So violent was the rage of his indignation, that he mistook its object.— He wanted to quarrel with Mr. Bramble; he said, he had been dishonoured on his account, and he looked for reparation at his hands.—My uncle's back was up in a moment; and he desired him to explain his pretensions.—"Either compel lord Oxmington to give me satisfaction, (cried he) or give it me in your own person." "The latter part of the alternative is the most easy and expeditious (replied the 'squire, starting up): if you are disposed for a walk, I'll attend you this moment."

Here they were interrupted by Mrs. Tabby, who had overheard all that passed.——She now burst into the room, and running betwixt them, in great agitation, "Is this your regard for me, (said she to the lieutenant) to seek the life of my brother?" Lismahago, who seemed to grow cool as my uncle grew hot, assured her he had a very great respect for Mr. Bramble, but he had still more for his own honour, which had suffered pollution; but if that could be once purified, he should have no further cause of dissatisfaction.——The 'squire said, he should have thought it incumbent upon him to vindicate the lieutenant's honour; but, as he had now carved for himself, he might swallow and digest it as well as he could[9]——In a word, what betwixt the mediation of Mrs. Tabitha, the recollection of the captain, who perceived he had gone too far, and the remonstrances

7. Don Quixote and his squire, Sancho Panza.
8. Was stuck into the contents of a chamber pot, a serious insult.
9. He who creates a given situation must then resolve it for himself (proverbial).

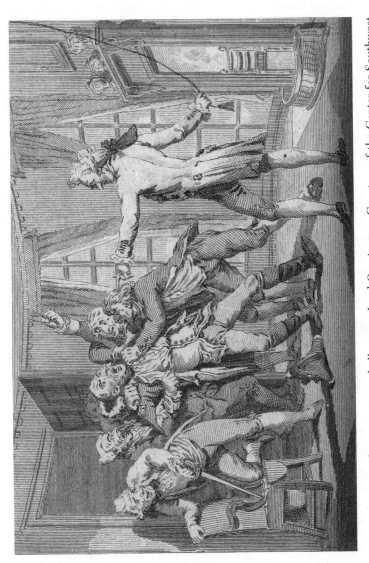

Lieutenant Lismahago carries a challenge to Lord Oxmington. Courtesy of the Center for Southwest Research, University Libraries, University of New Mexico.

of your humble servant, who joined them at this juncture, those two originals were perfectly reconciled; and then we proceeded to deliberate upon the means of taking vengeance for the insults they had received from the petulant peer; for, until that aim should be accomplished, Mr. Bramble swore, with great emphasis, that he would not leave the inn where we now lodged, even if he should pass his Christmas on the spot.

In consequence of our deliberations, we next day, in the forenoon, proceeded in a body to his lordship's house, all of us, with our servants, including the coachman, mounted a-horseback, with our pistols loaded and ready primed.—Thus prepared for action, we paraded solemnly and slowly before his lordship's gate, which we passed three times in such a manner, that he could not but see us, and suspect the cause of our appearance.—After dinner we returned, and performed the same cavalcade, which was again repeated the morning following; but we had no occasion to persist in these manœuvres.—— About noon, we were visited by the gentleman, at whose house we had first seen lord Oxmington.—He now came to make apologies in the name of his lordship, who declared he had no intention to give offence to my uncle, in practising what had been always the custom of his house; and that as for the indignities which had been put upon the officer, they were offered without his lordship's knowledge, at the instigation of his valet de chambre.—"If that be the case, (said my uncle, in a peremptory tone) I shall be contented with lord Oxmington's personal excuses; and I hope my friend will be satisfied with his lordship's turning that insolent rascal out of his service."—"Sir, (cried Lismahago) I must insist upon taking personal vengeance for the personal injuries I have sustained."

After some debate, the affair was adjusted in this manner.—— His lordship, meeting us at our friend's house, declared he was sorry for what had happened; and that he had no intention to give umbrage.—The valet de chambre asked pardon of the lieutenant upon his knees, when Lismahago, to the astonishment of all present, gave him a violent kick on the face, which laid him on his back, exclaiming in a furious tone, "*Oui je te pardonne, gens foutre.*"[1]

Such was the fortunate issue of this perilous adventure, which threatened abundance of vexation to our family; for the 'squire is one of those who will sacrifice both life and fortune, rather than leave what they conceive to be the least speck or blemish upon their honour and reputation. His lordship had no sooner pronounced his apology, with a very bad grace, than he went away in some

---

1. Yes I pardon you, you scoundrel (French). The final insult is a phoneticized rendering of *jean-foutre*, an obscene term of abuse denoting someone who is incompetent or morally suspect.

disorder, and, I dare say, he will never invite another Welchman to his table.

We forthwith quitted the field of this atchievement, in order to prosecute our journey; but we follow no determinate course.——We make small deviations, to see the remarkable towns, villas, and curiosities on each side of our route; so that we advance by slow steps towards the borders of Monmouthshire: but in the midst of these irregular motions, there is no abberration nor eccentricity in that affection with which I am, dear Wat,

Yours always,

Sept. 28.   J. MELFORD.

To Dr. LEWIS.

DEAR DICK,

At what time of life may a man think himself exempted from the necessity of sacrificing his repose to the punctilios[2] of a contempt-ible world? I have been engaged in a ridiculous adventure, which I shall recount at meeting; and this, I hope, will not be much longer delayed, as we have now performed almost all our visits, and seen every thing that I think has any right to retard us in our journey homewards——A few days ago, understanding by accident, that my old friend Baynard was in the country, I would not pass so near his habitation without paying him a visit, though our correspondence had been interrupted for a long course of years.

I felt myself very sensibly affected by the ideas of our past inti-macy, as we approached the place where we had spent so many happy days together; but when we arrived at the house, I could not recognize any one of those objects, which had been so deeply impressed upon my remembrance—The tall oaks that shaded the avenue, had been cut down, and the iron gates at the end of it removed, together with the high wall that surrounded the court yard. The house itself, which was formerly a convent of Cistercian monks,[3] had a venerable appearance; and along the front that looked into the garden, was a stone gallery, which afforded me many an agree-able walk, when I was disposed to be contemplative—Now the old front is covered with a screen of modern architecture; so that all without is Grecian, and all within Gothic—As for the garden, which was well stocked with the best fruit which England could produce,

2. Fine details, especially of conduct.
3. An ancient order under the rule of Saint Benedict.

there is not now the least vestage remaining of trees, walls, or hedges——Nothing appears but a naked circus of loose sand, with a dry bason and a leaden triton in the middle.

You must know, that Baynard, at his father's death, had a clear estate of fifteen hundred pounds a-year, and was in other respects extremely well qualified to make a respectable figure in the common-wealth; but, what with some excesses of youth, and the expence of a contested election, he in a few years found himself encumbered with a debt of ten thousand pounds, which he resolved to discharge by means of a prudent marriage—He accordingly married a miss Thom-son, whose fortune amounted to double the sum that he owed—She was the daughter of a citizen, who had failed in trade; but her for-tune came by an uncle, who died in the East-Indies—Her own par-ents being dead, she lived with a maiden aunt, who had superintended her education; and, in all appearance, was well enough qualified for the usual purposes of the married state—Her virtues, however, stood rather upon a negative, than a positive foundation—She was neither proud, insolent, nor capricious, nor given to scandal, nor addicted to gaming, nor inclined to gallantry—She could read, and write, and dance, and sing, and play upon the harpsichord, and smatter French, and take a hand at whist and ombre; but even these accomplishments she possessed by halves—She excelled in noth-ing. Her conversation was flat, her stile mean, and her expression embarrassed—In a word, her character was totally insipid. Her per-son was not disagreeable; but there was nothing graceful in her address, nor engaging in her manners; and she was so ill qualified to do the honours of the house, that when she sat at the head of the table, one was always looking for the mistress of the family in some other place.

Baynard had flattered himself, that it would be no difficult matter to mould such a subject after his own fashion, and that she would chearfully enter into his views, which were wholly turned to domes-tic happiness. He proposed to reside always in the country, of which he was fond to a degree of enthusiasm, to cultivate his estate, which was very improvable; to enjoy the exercise of rural diversions; to maintain an intimacy of correspondence with some friends that were settled in his neighbourhood; to keep a comfortable house, without suffering his expence to exceed the limits of his income; and to find pleasure and employment for his wife in the management and avoca-tions of her own family——This, however, was a visionary scheme, which he never was able to realize. His wife was as ignorant as a new-born babe of every thing that related to the conduct of a fam-ily; and she had no idea of a country life—Her understanding did not reach so far as to comprehend the first principles of discretion; and, indeed, if her capacity had been better than it was, her natural

indolence would not have permitted her to abandon a certain rou-
tine, to which she had been habituated. She had not taste enough
to relish any rational enjoyment; but her ruling passion was vanity,
not that species which arises from self-conceit of superior accomplishments, but that which is of a bastard and idiot nature, excited
by shew and ostentation, which implies not even the least consciousness of any personal merit.

The nuptial peal of noise and nonsense being rung out in all
the usual changes, Mr. Baynard thought it high time to make her
acquainted with the particulars of the plan which he had projected——He told her that his fortune, though sufficient to afford
all the comforts of life, was not ample enough to command all the
superfluities of pomp and pageantry, which, indeed, were equally
absurd and intolerable—He therefore hoped she would have no
objection to their leaving London in the spring, when he would
take the opportunity to dismiss some unnecessary domestics, whom
he had hired for the occasion of their marriage—She heard him in
silence, and after some pause, "So, (said she) I am to be buried in
the country!" He was so confounded at this reply, that he could not
speak for some minutes: at length he told her, he was much mortified to find he had proposed any thing that was disagreeable to her
ideas—"I am sure (added he) I meant nothing more than to lay
down a comfortable plan of living within the bounds of our fortune, which is but moderate." "Sir, (said she) you are the best judge
of your own affairs—My fortune, I know, does not exceed twenty
thousand pounds——Yet, even with that pittance, I might have had
a husband who would not have begrudged me a house in London—"
"Good God! my dear, (cried poor Baynard, in the utmost agitation)
you don't think me so sordid—I only hinted what I thought—But, I
don't pretend to impose—" "Yes, sir, (resumed the lady) it is your
prerogative to command, and my duty to obey—"

So saying, she burst into tears and retired to her chamber, where
she was joined by her aunt—He endeavoured to recollect himself,
and act with vigour of mind on this occasion; but was betrayed by
the tenderness of his nature, which was the greatest defect of his
constitution. He found the aunt in tears, and the niece in a fit,
which held her the best part of eight hours, at the expiration of
which, she began to talk incoherently about *death* and her *dear husband*, who had sat by her all this time, and now pressed her hand to
his lips, in a transport of grief and penitence for the offence he had
given—From thence forward, he carefully avoided mentioning the
country; and they continued to be sucked deeper and deeper into
the vortex of extravagance and dissipation, leading what is called a
fashionable life in town—About the latter end of July, however,
Mrs. Baynard, in order to exhibit a proof of conjugal obedience,

desired of her own accord, that they might pay a visit to his country house, as there was no company left in London. He would have excused himself from this excursion, which was no part of the œconomical plan he had proposed; but she insisted upon making this sacrifice to his taste and prejudices, and away they went with such an equipage as astonished the whole country—All that remained of the season was engrossed by receiving and returning visits in the neighbourhood; and, in this intercourse, it was discovered that sir John Chickwell had a house-steward and one footman in livery more than the complement of Mr. Baynard's household. This remark was made by the aunt at table, and assented to by the husband, who observed that sir John Chickwell might very well afford to keep more servants than were found in the family of a man who had not half his fortune. Mrs. Baynard ate no supper that evening; but was seized with a violent fit, which completed her triumph over the spirit of her consort. The two supernumerary servants were added—The family plate was sold for old silver, and a new service procured; fashionable furniture was provided, and the whole house turned topsy turvy.

At their return to London, in the beginning of winter, he, with a heavy heart, communicated these particulars to me in confidence. Before his marriage, he had introduced me to the lady as his particular friend; and I now offered in that character, to lay before her the necessity of reforming her œconomy, if she had any regard to the interest of her own family, or complaisance for the inclinations of her husband—But Baynard declined my offer, on the supposition that his wife's nerves were too delicate to bear expostulation; and that it would only serve to overwhelm her with such distress as would make himself miserable.

Baynard is a man of spirit, and had she proved a termagant,[4] he would have known how to deal with her; but, either by accident or instinct, she fastened upon the weak side of his soul, and held it so fast, that he has been in subjection ever since—I afterwards advised him to carry her abroad to France or Italy, where he might gratify her vanity for half the expence it cost him in England; and this advice he followed accordingly—She was agreeably flattered with the idea of seeing and knowing foreign parts, and foreign fashions; of being presented to sovereigns, and living familiarly with princes. She forthwith seized the hint which I had thrown out on purpose, and even pressed Mr. Baynard to hasten his departure; so that in a few weeks they crossed the sea to France, with a moderate train, still including the aunt; who was her bosom counsellor, and abetted her in all her opposition to her husband's will——Since that period, I have had

4. A scolding, shrewish woman (pejorative).

little or no opportunity to renew our former correspondence—All that I knew of his transactions, amounted to no more than that after an absence of two years, they returned so little improved in œconomy, that they launched out into new oceans of extravagance, which, at length, obliged him to mortgage his estate—By this time she had bore him three children, of which the last only survives, a puny boy of twelve or thirteen, who will be ruined in his education by the indulgence of his mother.

As for Baynard, neither his own good sense, nor the dread of indigence,[5] nor the consideration of his children, has been of force sufficient to stimulate him into the resolution of breaking at once the shameful spell by which he seems enchanted——With a taste capable of the most refined enjoyment, a heart glowing with all the warmth of friendship and humanity, and a disposition strongly turned to the more rational pleasures of a retired and country life, he is hurried about in a perpetual tumult, amidst a mob of beings pleased with rattles, baubles, and gewgaws, so void of sense and distinction, that even the most acute philosophy would find it a very hard task to discover for what wise purpose of providence they were created— Friendship is not to be found; nor can the amusements for which he sighs be enjoyed within the rotation of absurdity, to which he is doomed for life. He has long resigned all views of improving his fortune by management and attention to the exercise of husbandry, in which he delighted; and as to domestic happiness, not the least glimpse of hope remains to amuse his imagination. Thus blasted in all his prospects, he could not fail to be overwhelmed with melancholy and chagrin, which have preyed upon his health and spirits in such a manner, that he is now threatened with a consumption.

I have given you a sketch of the man, whom the other day I went to visit—At the gate we found a great number of powdered lacquies,[6] but no civility—After we had sat a considerable time in the coach, we were told, that Mr. Baynard had rode out, and that his lady was dressing; but we were introduced to a parlour, so very fine and delicate, that in all appearance it was designed to be seen only, not inhabited. The chairs and couches were carved, gilt, and covered with rich damask, so smooth and slick, that they looked as if they had never been sat upon. There was no carpet on the floor; but the boards were rubbed and waxed in such a manner, that we could not walk, but were obliged to slide along them; and as for the stove, it was too bright and polished to be polluted with sea-coal, or stained by the smoke of any gross material fire—When we had remained above half an hour sacrificing to the inhospitable powers in this

5. Poverty.
6. Footmen, servants.

temple of cold reception,[7] my friend Baynard arrived, and understanding we were in the house, made his appearance, so meagre, yellow, and dejected, that I really should not have known him, had I met with him in any other place——Running up to me, with great eagerness, he strained me in his embrace, and his heart was so full, that for some minutes he could not speak—Having saluted us all round, he perceived our uncomfortable situation, and conducting us into another apartment, which had fire in the chimney, called for chocolate—— Then, withdrawing, he returned with a compliment from his wife, and, in the mean time, presented his son Harry, a shambling, blear-eyed boy, in the habit of a hussar;[8] very rude, forward, and impertinent—His father would have sent him to a boarding-school, but his mamma and aunt would not hear of his lying out of the house; so that there was a clergyman engaged as his tutor in the family.

As it was but just turned of twelve, and the whole house was in commotion to prepare a formal entertainment, I foresaw it would be late before we dined, and proposed a walk to Mr. Baynard, that we might converse together freely. In the course of this perambulation, when I expressed some surprise that he had returned so soon from Italy, he gave me to understand, that his going abroad had not at all answered the purpose, for which he left England; that although the expence of living was not so great in Italy as at home, respect being had to the same rank of life in both countries, it had been found necessary for him to lift himself above his usual stile, that he might be on some footing with the counts, marquises, and cavalieres, with whom he kept company——He was obliged to hire a great number of servants, to take off a great variety of rich cloaths, and to keep a sumptuous table for the fashionable scorocconi[9] of the country; who, without a consideration of this kind, would not have payed any attention to an untitled foreigner, let his family or fortune be ever so respectable—Besides, Mrs. Baynard was continually surrounded by a train of expensive loungers, under the denominations of language-masters, musicians, painters, and ciceroni;[1] and had actually fallen into the disease of buying pictures and antiques upon her own judgment, which was far from being infallible—At length she met with an affront, which gave her a disgust to Italy, and drove her back to England with some precipitation. By means of frequenting the dutchess of B——'s conversazione,[2] while her grace was at Rome, Mrs. Baynard became acquainted with all the

7. The italics suggest this is a quotation, but it has not been traced.
8. A member of Hungarian light cavalry. To be dressed like a hussar came to stand for anyone wearing a striking or flamboyant uniform.
9. A misspelling of the Italian word for "freeloaders."
1. Guides to local antiquities (Italian).
2. An evening assembly for social amusement. The woman in question has tentatively been identified as Gertrude Russell, Duchess of Bedford.

fashionable people of that city, and was admitted to their assemblies without scruple—Thus favoured, she conceived too great an idea of her own importance, and when the duchess left Rome, resolved to have a conversazione that should leave the Romans no room to regret her grace's departure. She provided hands for a musical entertainment, and sent biglietti[3] of invitation to every person of distinction; but not one Roman of the female sex appeared at her assembly—She was that night seized with a violent fit, and kept her bed three days, at the expiration of which she declared that the air of Italy would be the ruin of her constitution. In order to prevent this catastrophe, she was speedily removed to Geneva, from whence they returned to England by the way of Lyons and Paris. By the time they arrived at Calais, she had purchased such a quantity of silks, stuffs, and laces, that it was necessary to hire a vessel to smuggle them over, and this vessel was taken by a custom-house cutter;[4] so that they lost the whole cargo, which had cost them above eight hundred pounds.

It now appeared, that her travels had produced no effect upon her, but that of making her more expensive and fantastic than ever:—She affected to lead the fashion, not only in point of female dress, but in every article of taste and connoisseurship. She made a drawing of the new facade to the house in the country; she pulled up the trees, and pulled down the walls of the garden, so as to let in the easterly wind, which Mr. Baynard's ancestors had been at great pains to exclude. To shew her taste in laying out ground, she seized into her own hand a farm of two hundred acres, about a mile from the house, which she parcelled out into walks and shrubberies, having a great bason in the middle, into which she poured a whole stream that turned two mills, and afforded the best trout in the country. The bottom of the bason, however, was so ill secured, that it would not hold the water which strained through the earth, and made a bog of the whole plantation: in a word, the ground which formerly payed him one hundred and fifty pounds a year, now cost him two hundred pounds a year to keep it in tolerable order, over and above the first expence of trees, shrubs, flowers, turf, and gravel. There was not an inch of garden ground left about the house, nor a tree that produced fruit of any kind; nor did he raise a truss of hay, or a bushel of oats for his horses, nor had he a single cow to afford milk for his tea; far less did he ever dream of feeding his own mutton, pigs, and poultry: every article of house-keeping, even the most inconsiderable, was brought from the next market town, at the distance of five miles, and thither they sent a courier every morning to fetch hot rolls for breakfast. In short, Baynard fairly owned that he spent

3. Tickets or notes.
4. A small ship staffed by government customs officers, who controlled imports and exports and could levy taxes and penalties accordingly.

double his income, and that in a few years he should be obliged to sell his estate for the payment of his creditors. He said his wife had such delicate nerves, and such imbecillity[5] of spirit, that she could neither bear remonstrance, be it ever so gentle, nor practise any scheme of retrenchment, even if she perceived the necessity of such a measure. He had therefore ceased struggling against the stream, and endeavoured to reconcile himself to ruin, by reflecting that his child at least, would inherit his mother's fortune, which was secured to him by the contract of marriage.

The detail which he gave me of his affairs, filled me at once with grief and indignation. I inveighed bitterly against the indiscretion of his wife, and reproached him with his unmanly acquiescence under the absurd tyranny which she exerted. I exhorted him to recollect his resolution, and make one effectual effort to disengage himself from a thraldom, equally shameful and pernicious. I offered him all the assistance in my power. I undertook to regulate his affairs, and even to bring about a reformation in his family, if he would only authorise me to execute the plan I should form for his advantage. I was so affected by the subject, that I could not help mingling tears with my remonstrances, and Baynard was so penetrated with these marks of my affection, that he lost all power of utterance. He pressed me to his breast with great emotion, and wept in silence. At length he exclaimed, "Friendship is undoubtedly the most precious balm of life! Your words, dear Bramble, have in a great measure recalled me from an abyss of despondence, in which I have been long overwhelmed—I will, upon honour, make you acquainted with a distinct state of my affairs, and, as far as I am able to go, will follow the course you prescribe. But there are certain lengths which my nature——The truth is, there are tender connexions, of which a bachelor has no idea—Shall I own my weakness? I cannot bear the thoughts of making that woman uneasy—" "And yet, (cried I) she has seen you unhappy for a series of years—unhappy from her misconduct, without ever shewing the least inclination to alleviate your distress—" "Nevertheless (said he) I am persuaded she loves me with the most warm affection; but these are incongruities in the composition of the human mind which I hold to be inexplicable."

I was shocked at his infatuation, and changed the subject, after we had agreed to maintain a close correspondence for the future—He then gave me to understand, that he had two neighbours, who, like himself, were driven by their wives at full speed, in the high road to bankruptcy and ruin. All the three husbands were of dispositions

---

5. Weakness.

very different from each other, and, according to this variation, their consorts were admirably suited to the purpose of keeping them all three in subjection. The views of the ladies were exactly the same. They vied in grandeur, that is, in ostentation, with the wife of Sir Charles Chickwell,[6] who had four times their fortune; and she again piqued herself upon making an equal figure with a neighbouring peeress, whose revenue trebled her own. Here then was the fable of the frog and the ox,[7] realized in four different instances within the same county: one large fortune, and three moderate estates, in a fair way of being burst by the inflation of female vanity; and in three of these instances, three different forms of female tyranny were exercised. Mr. Baynard was subjugated by practising upon the tenderness of his nature. Mr. Milksan, being of a timorous disposition, truckled to the insolence of a termagant. Mr. Sowerby, who was of a temper neither to be moved by fits, nor driven by menaces, had the fortune to be fitted with a helpmate, who assailed him with the weapons of irony and satire; sometimes sneering in the way of compliment; sometimes throwing out sarcastic comparisons, implying reproaches upon his want of taste, spirit, and generosity: by which means she stimulated his passions from one act of extravagance to another, just as the circumstances of her vanity required.

All these three ladies have at this time the same number of horses, carriages, and servants in and out of livery; the same variety of dress; the same quantity of plate and china; the like ornaments in furniture; and in their entertainments they endeavour to exceed one another in the variety, delicacy, and expence of their dishes. I believe it will be found upon enquiry, that nineteen out of twenty, who are ruined by extravagance, fall a sacrifice to the ridiculous pride and vanity of silly women, whose parts are held in contempt by the very men whom they pillage and enslave. Thank heaven, Dick, that among all the follies and weaknesses of human nature, I have not yet fallen into that of matrimony.

After Baynard and I had discussed all these matters at leisure, we returned towards the house, and met Jery with our two women, who had come forth to take the air, as the lady of the mansion had not yet made her appearance. In short, Mrs. Baynard did not produce herself, till about a quarter of an hour before dinner was upon the table. Then her husband brought her into the parlour, accompanied by her aunt and son, and she received us with a coldness of reserve sufficient to freeze the very soul of hospitality. Though she knew I had been the intimate friend of her husband, and had often

6. Referred to earlier as Sir John Chickwell.
7. An animal fable, attributed to the classical author Aesop, in which a frog tries to inflate itself to the size of an ox.

seen me with him in London, she shewed no marks of recognition or regard, when I addressed myself to her in the most friendly terms of salutation. She did not even express the common complement of, *I am glad to see you*; or, *I hope you have enjoyed your health since we had the pleasure of seeing you*; or some such words of course: nor did she once open her mouth in the way of welcome to my sister and my niece: but sat in silence like a statue, with an aspect of insensibility. Her aunt, the model upon which she had been formed, was indeed the very essence of insipid formality: but the boy was very pert and impudent, and prated without ceasing.

At dinner, the lady maintained the same ungracious indifference, never speaking but in whispers to her aunt; and as to the repast, it was made up of a parcel of kickshaws,[8] contrived by a French cook, without one substantial article adapted to the satisfaction of an English appetite. The pottage[9] was little better than bread soaked in dishwashings, lukewarm. The ragouts looked as if they had been once eaten and half digested: the fricassees were involved in a nasty yellow poultice; and the rotis were scorched and stinking, for the honour of the fumet.[1] The desert consisted of faded fruit and iced froth, a good emblem of our landlady's character; the table-beer was sour, the water foul, and the wine vapid; but there was a parade of plate and china, and a powdered lacquey stood behind every chair, except those of the master and mistress of the house, who were served by two valets dressed like gentlemen. We dined in a large old Gothic parlour, which was formerly the hall. It was now paved with marble, and, notwithstanding the fire, which had been kindled about an hour, struck me with such a chill sensation, that when I entered it the teeth chattered in my jaws—In short, every thing was cold, comfortless, and disgusting, except the looks of my friend Baynard, which declared the warmth of his affection and humanity.

After dinner we withdrew into another apartment, where the boy began to be impertinently troublesome to my niece Liddy. He wanted a play-fellow, forsooth; and would have romped with her, had she encouraged his advances—He was even so impudent as to snatch a kiss, at which she changed countenance, and seemed uneasy; and though his father checked him for the rudeness of his behaviour, he became so outrageous as to thrust his hand in her

---

8. Fancy but insubstantial dishes of food, derived from the French phrase *quelque chose* (something). "Repast": a light meal.
9. A thick soup.
1. The smell of game or other meat that is well aged. "Ragouts": stews of meat or fowl cut into small pieces and prepared with spices or sauces. "Fricassees": similar to ragouts. "Poultice": a soft mass of material that is pressed to the body as a treatment for injury or infection. "Rotis": roast meat.

bosom: an insult to which she did not tamely submit, though one of the mildest creatures upon earth. Her eyes sparkling with resentment, she started up, and lent him such a box in the ear, as sent him staggering to the other side of the room.

"Miss Melford, (cried his father) you have treated him with the utmost propriety—I am only sorry that the impertinence of any child of mine should have occasioned this exertion of your spirit, which I cannot but applaud and admire." His wife was so far from assenting to the candour of his apology, that she rose from table, and, taking her son by the hand, "Come, child, (said she) your father cannot abide you." So saying, she retired with this hopeful youth, and was followed by her gouvernante: but neither the one nor the other deigned to take the least notice of the company.

Baynard was exceedingly disconcerted; but I perceived his uneasiness was tinctured with resentment, and derived a good omen from this discovery. I ordered the horses to be put to the carriage, and, though he made some efforts to detain us all night, I insisted upon leaving the house immediately; but, before I went away, I took an opportunity of speaking to him again in private. I said every thing I could recollect, to animate his endeavours in shaking off those shameful trammels. I made no scruple to declare, that his wife was unworthy of that tender complaisance which he had shewn for her foibles: that she was dead to all the genuine sentiments of conjugal affection; insensible of her own honour and interest, and seemingly destitute of common sense and reflection. I conjured him to remember what he owed to his father's house, to his own reputation, and to his family, including even this unreasonable woman herself, who was driving on blindly to her own destruction. I advised him to form a plan for retrenching superfluous expence, and try to convince the aunt of the necessity for such a reformation, that she might gradually prepare her niece for its execution; and I exhorted him to turn that disagreeable piece of formality out of the house, if he should find her averse to his proposal.

Here he interrupted me with a sigh, observing that such a step would undoubtedly be fatal to Mrs. Baynard—"I shall lose all patience, (cried I), to hear you talk so weakly—Mrs. Baynard's fits will never hurt her constitution. I believe in my conscience they are all affected: I am sure she has no feeling for your distresses; and, when you are ruined, she will appear to have no feeling for her own." Finally, I took his word and honour, that he would make an effort, such as I had advised; that he would form a plan of œconomy, and, if he found it impracticable without my assistance, he would come to Bath in the winter, where I promised to give him the meeting, and contribute all in my power to the retrieval of his affairs—With this mutual engagement we parted; and I shall think myself supremely happy, if, by my means, a worthy man, whom I love and esteem, can be saved from misery, disgrace, and despair.

I have only one friend more to visit in this part of the country, but he is of a complexion very different from that of Baynard. You have heard me mention Sir Thomas Bullford, whom I knew in Italy. He is now become a country gentleman; but, being disabled by the gout from enjoying any amusement abroad, he entertains himself within doors, by keeping open house for all comers, and playing upon the oddities and humours of his company: but he himself is generally the greatest original at his table. He is very good-humoured, talks much, and laughs without ceasing. I am told that all the use he makes of his understanding at present, is to excite mirth, by exhibiting his guests in ludicrous attitudes. I know not how far we may furnish him with entertainment of this kind, but I am resolved to beat up[2] his quarters, partly with a view to laugh with the knight himself, and partly to pay my respects to his lady, a good-natured sensible woman, with whom he lives upon very easy terms, although she has not had the good fortune to bring him an heir to his estate.

And now, dear Dick, I must tell you for your comfort, that you are the only man upon earth to whom I would presume to send such a long-winded epistle, which I could not find in my heart to curtail, because the subject interested the warmest passions of my heart; neither will I make any other apology to a correspondent who has been so long accustomed to the impertinence of

Sept. 30.   MATT. BRAMBLE.

To Sir WATKIN PHILLIPS, Bar^t. at Oxon.

DEAR KNIGHT,

I believe, there is something mischievious in my disposition, for nothing diverts me so much as to see certain characters tormented with false terrors.——We last night lodged at the house of sir Thomas Bullford, an old friend of my uncle, a jolly fellow, of moderate intellects, who, in spite of the gout, which hath lamed him, is resolved to be merry to the last; and mirth he has a particular knack in extracting from his guests, let their humour be never so caustic or refractory.—Besides our company, there was in the house a fat-headed justice of the peace, called Frogmore, and a country practitioner in surgery, who seemed to be our landlord's chief companion and confidant.—We found the knight sitting on a couch, with his crutches by his side, and his feet supported on cushions; but he

---

2. To investigate, from hunting jargon for scouring woodlands to rouse game for shooting.

received us with a hearty welcome, and seemed greatly rejoiced at our arrival.—After tea, we were entertained with a sonata on the harpsichord by lady Bullford, who sung and played to admiration; but sir Thomas seemed to be a little asinine in the article of ears, though he affected to be in raptures, and begged his wife to favour us with an *arietta*[3] of her own composing.—This *arietta*, however, she no sooner began to perform, than he and the justice fell asleep; but the moment she ceased playing, the knight waked snorting, and exclaimed, "O *cara*![4] what d'ye think, gentlemen? Will you talk any more of your Pargolesi and your Corelli?"[5]—At the same time, he thrust his tongue in one cheek, and leered with one eye at the doctor and me, who sat on his left hand.—He concluded the pantomime with a loud laugh, which he could command at all times extempore.[6]— Notwithstanding his disorder, he did not do penance at supper,[7] nor did he ever refuse his glass when the toast went round, but rather encouraged a quick circulation, both by precept and example.

I soon perceived the doctor had made himself very necessary to the baronet.—He was the whetstone of his wit, the butt of his satire, and his operator in certain experiments of humour, which were occasionally tried upon strangers.—Justice Frogmore was an excellent subject for this species of philosophy; sleek and corpulent, solemn and shallow, he had studied Burn[8] with uncommon application, but he studied nothing so much as the art of living (that is, eating) well.—This fat buck had often afforded good sport to our landlord; and he was frequently started with tolerable success, in the course of this evening; but the baronet's appetite for ridicule seemed to be chiefly excited by the appearance, address, and conversation of Lismahago, whom he attempted in all the different modes of exposition; but he put me in mind of a contest that I once saw betwixt a young hound and an old hedge-hog—The dog turned him over and over, and bounced, and barked, and mumbled; but as often as he attempted to bite, he felt a prickle in his jaws, and recoiled in manifest confusion:—The captain, when left to himself, will not fail to turn his ludicrous side to the company, but if any man attempts to force him into that attitude, he becomes stubborn as a mule, and unmanageable as an elephant unbroke.

Divers tolerable jokes were cracked upon the justice, who ate a most unconscionable supper, and, among other things, a large plate

3. A little musical piece for voice and piano.
4. O beloved (Italian).
5. Giovanni Battista Pergolesi (1710–1736) and Arcangelo Corelli (1653–1713) were popular Italian composers.
6. Spontaneously; without preparation.
7. I.e., did not deny himself food.
8. Richard Burn (1709–1785) wrote *The Justice of the Peace and Parish* (1755), the standard work of reference for country magistrates of the period.

of broiled mushrooms, which he had no sooner swallowed than the doctor observed, with great gravity, that they were of the kind called *champignons*,[9] which in some constitutions had a poisonous effect.—Mr. Frogmore, startled at this remark, asked, in some confusion, why he had not been so kind as to give him that notice sooner.—He answered, that he took it for granted, by his eating them so heartily, that he was used to the dish; but as he seemed to be under some apprehension, he prescribed a bumper of plague water,[1] which the justice drank off immediately, and retired to rest, not without marks of terror and disquiet.

At midnight we were shewn to our different chambers, and in half an hour, I was fast asleep in bed; but about three o'clock in the morning I was waked with a dismal cry of *Fire!* and starting up, ran to the window in my shirt.—The night was dark and stormy; and a number of people half-dressed ran backwards and forwards thro' the court-yard, with links and lanthorns,[2] seemingly in the utmost hurry and trepidation.—Slipping on my cloaths in a twinkling, I ran down stairs, and, upon inquiry, found the fire was confined to a back-stair, which led to a detached apartment where Lismahago lay.——By this time, the lieutenant was alarmed by bawling at his window, which was in the second story, but he could not find his cloaths in the dark, and his room-door was locked on the outside.—— The servants called to him, that the house had been robbed; that, without all doubt, the villains had taken away his cloaths, fastened the door, and set the house on fire, for the stair-case was in flames.— In this dilemma the poor lieutenant ran about the room naked like a squirrel in a cage, popping out his head at the window between whiles, and imploring assistance.—At length, the knight in person was brought out in his chair, attended by my uncle and all the family, including our aunt Tabitha, who screamed, and cried, and tore her hair, as if she had been distracted.—Sir Thomas had already ordered his people to bring a long ladder, which was applied to the captain's window, and now he exorted him earnestly to descend.— There was no need of much rhetoric to persuade Lismahago, who forthwith made his exit by the window, roaring all the time to the people below to hold fast the ladder.

Notwithstanding the gravity of the occasion, it was impossible to behold this scene without being seized with an inclination to laugh. The rueful aspect of the lieutenant in his shirt, with a quilted night-cap fastened under his chin, and his long lank limbs and posteriors exposed to the wind, made a very picturesque appearance, when

9. Mushrooms (French).
1. An infusion of herbs and roots in wine, supposed to protect against infection.
2. With torches and lanterns.

illumined by the links and torches which the servants held up to light him in his descent.—All the company stood round the ladder, except the knight, who sat in his chair, exclaiming from time to time, "Lord have mercy upon us!—save the gentleman's life!—mind your footing, dear captain!—softly!—stand fast!—clasp the ladder with both hands!—there!—well done, my dear boy!—O bravo!—an old soldier for ever!—bring a blanket——bring a warm blanket to comfort his poor carcase——warm the bed in the green room—— give me your hand, dear captain—I'm rejoiced to see thee safe and sound with all my heart." Lismahago was received at the foot of the ladder by his innamorata[3] who snatching a blanket from one of the maids, wrapped it about his body; two men-servants took him under the arms, and a female conducted him to the green room, still accompanied by Mrs. Tabitha, who saw him fairly put to bed.— During this whole transaction, he spoke not a syllable, but looked exceeding grim, sometimes at one, sometimes at another of the spectators, who now adjourned in a body to the parlour where we had supped, every one surveying another with marks of astonishment and curiosity.

The knight being seated in an easy chair, seized my uncle by the hand, and bursting into a long and loud laugh, "Matt, (cried he) crown me with oak, or ivy, or laurel, or parsley, or what you will, and acknowledge this to be a *coup de maitre*[4] in the way of waggery—ha, ha, ha!—Such a *camisicata, scagliata, beffata!*—O, *che roba!*[5]—O, what a subject!——O, what *caricatura!*—O, for a Rosa, a Rembrandt, a Schalken![6]—Zooks,[7] I'll give a hundred guineas to have it painted!——what a fine descent from the cross, or ascent to the gallows!—what lights and shadows!—what a groupe below!—what expression above!—what an aspect!—did you mind the aspect?—ha, ha, ha!—and the limbs, and the muscles—every toe denoted terror!—ha, ha, ha!——then the blanket!—O, what *costume!* St. Andrew! St. Lazarus! St. Barrabas![8]—ha, ha, ha!" "After all then, (cried Mr. Bramble very gravely) this was no more than a false alarm.—We have been frightened out of our beds, and almost out of our senses, for the joke's sake." "Ay, and such a joke! (cried our landlord) such a farce! such a *denouement!* such a catastrophe!"

---

3. Female romantic partner.
4. Masterstroke (Latin).
5. Such a trick, what a prank, what a fool! Oh, what a business! (nonstandard Italian).
6. Salvator Rosa (1615–1673), Rembrandt van Rijn (1606–1669), and Godfried Schalken (1643–1706) were celebrated European painters.
7. Contraction of *God's hooks,* i.e., the nails used to crucify Christ, used as an exclamation.
8. Possibly a reference to the biblical Barabbas, the criminal freed instead of Christ in the Gospels of the New Testament. Saint Andrew and Saint Lazarus were early Christian martyrs and therefore well-known subjects of dramatic, evocative paintings.

"Have a little patience (replied our 'squire); we are not yet come to the catastrophe; and pray God it may not turn out a tragedy instead of a farce.——The captain is one of those saturnine[9] subjects, who have no idea of humour.—He never laughs in his own person; nor can he bear that other people should laugh at his expence—Besides, if the subject had been properly chosen, the joke was too severe in all conscience." "'Sdeath![1] (cried the knight) I could not have bated him an ace had he been my own father; and as for the subject, such another does not present itself once in half a century." Here Mrs. Tabitha interposing, and bridling up, declared, she did not see that Mr. Lismahago was a fitter subject for ridicule than the knight himself; and that she was very much afraid, he would very soon find he had mistaken his man.——The baronet was a good deal disconcerted by this intimation, saying, that he must be a Goth and a barbarian, if he did not enter into the spirit of such a happy and humorous contrivance.—He begged, however, that Mr. Bramble and his sister would bring him to reason; and this request was reinforced by lady Bullford, who did not fail to read the baronet a lecture upon his indiscretion, which lecture he received with submission on one side of his face, and a leer upon the other.

We now went to bed for the second time; and before I got up, my uncle had visited Lismahago in the green room, and used such arguments with him, that when we met in the parlour he seemed to be quite appeased.—He received the knight's apology with a good grace, and even professed himself pleased at finding he had contributed to the diversion of the company.——Sir Thomas shook him by the hand, laughing heartily; and then desired a pinch of snuff, in token of perfect reconciliation—The lieutenant, putting his hand in his waistcoat pocket, pulled out, instead of his own Scotch mull,[2] a very fine gold snuff box, which he no sooner perceived than he said, "Here is a small mistake." "No mistake at all (cried the baronet): a fair exchange is no robbery.—Oblige me so far, captain, as to let me keep your mull as a memorial." "Sir, (said the lieutenant) the mull is much at your service; but this machine I can by no means retain.—It looks like compounding a sort of felony in the code of honour.—Besides, I don't know but there may be another joke in this conveyance; and I don't find myself disposed to be brought upon the stage again.——I won't presume to make free with your pockets, but I beg you will put it up again with your own hand."——So saying, with a certain austerity of aspect, he presented the snuff-box to the knight, who received it in some confusion, and restored

<hr />

9. Gloomy.
1. A contraction of *God's death,* used as an exclamation.
2. A snuff box with a milling mechanism for grinding tobacco powder.

the mull, which he would by no means keep, except on the terms of exchange.

This transaction was like to give a grave cast to the conversation, when my uncle took notice that Mr. Justice Frogmore had not made his appearance either at the night-alarm, or now at the general rendezvous. The baronet hearing Frogmore mentioned, "Odso![3] (cried he) I had forgot the justice.—Pr'ythee, doctor, go and bring him out of his kennel."—Then laughing till his sides were well shaken, he said he would shew the captain, that he was not the only person of the drama exhibited for the entertainment of the company. As to the night-scene, it could not affect the justice, who had been purposely lodged in the farther end of the house, remote from the noise, and lulled with a dose of opium into the bargain. In a few minutes, Mr. Justice was led into the parlour in his night-cap and loose morning gown, rolling his head from side to side, and groaning piteously all the way.—"Jesu! neighbour Frogmore, (exclaimed the baronet) what is the matter?—you look as if you was not a man for this world.——Set him down softly on the couch——poor gentleman!—Lord have mercy upon us!—What makes him so pale, and yellow, and bloated?" "Oh, sir Thomas! (cried the justice) I doubt[4] 'tis all over with me——Those mushrooms I ate at your table have done my business——ah! oh! hey!" "Now the Lord forbid! (said the other)—what! man, have a good heart.—How does thy stomach feel?—hah?"

To this interrogation he made no reply, but throwing aside his night gown, discovered that his waistcoat would not meet upon his belly by five good inches at least. "Heaven protect us all! (cried sir Thomas)—what a melancholy spectacle!—never did I see a man so suddenly swelled, but when he was either just dead, or just dying.——Doctor, can'st thou do nothing for this poor object?" "I don't think the case is quite desperate (said the surgeon), but I would advise Mr. Frogmore to settle his affairs with all expedition; the parson may come and pray by him, while I prepare a glyster and an emetic draught."[5] The justice, rolling his languid eyes, ejaculated with great fervency, "Lord, have mercy upon us! Christ, have mercy upon us!"——Then he begged the surgeon, in the name of God, to dispatch—"As for my worldly affairs, (said he) they are all settled but one mortgage, which must be left to my heirs—but my poor soul! my poor soul! what will become of my poor soul?—miserable sinner that I am!" "Nay, pr'ythee, my dear boy, compose thyself

---

3. A mild oath or expression of surprise. It is a variation of *gadso,* which in turn stands for *God's own* at the start of an oath.
4. I suspect.
5. A drink to induce vomiting. "Glyster": enema.

(resumed the knight); consider the mercy of heaven is infinite; thou can'st not have any sins of a very deep dye on thy conscience, or the devil's in't." "Name not the devil (exclaimed the terrified Frogmore), I have more sins to answer for than the world dreams of.—Ah! friend, I have been sly—sly—damn'd sly!——Send for the parson without loss of time, and put me to bed, for I am posting to eternity."—— He was accordingly raised from the couch, and supported by two servants, who led him back to his room; but before he quitted the parlour, he intreated the good company to assist him with their prayers.—He added, "Take warning by me, who am suddenly cut off in my prime, like a flower of the field; and God forgive you, sir Thomas, for suffering such poisonous trash to be eaten at your table."

He was no sooner removed out of hearing, than the baronet abandoned himself to a violent fit of laughing, in which he was joined by the greatest part of the company; but we could hardly prevent the good lady from going to undeceive the patient, by discovering, that while he slept his waistcoat had been straitened by the contrivance of the surgeon; and that the disorder in his stomach and bowels was occasioned by some antimonial wine,[6] which he had taken over night, under the denomination of plague-water.——She seemed to think that his apprehension might put an end to his life: the knight swore he was no such chicken, but a tough old rogue, that would live long enough to plague all his neighbours.—Upon enquiry, we found his character did not intitle him to much compassion or respect, and therefore we let our landlord's humour take its course.—A glyster was actually administered by an old woman of the family, who had been sir Thomas's nurse, and the patient took a draught made with oxymel of squills[7] to forward the operation of the antimonial wine, which had been retarded by the opiate of the preceding night. He was visited by the vicar, who read prayers, and began to take an account of the state of his soul, when those medicines produced their effect; so that the parson was obliged to hold his nose while he poured forth spiritual consolation from his mouth. The same expedient was used by the knight and me, who, with the doctor, entered the chamber at this juncture, and found Frogmore enthroned on an easing-chair,[8] under the pressure of a double evacuation. The short intervals betwixt every heave he employed in crying for mercy, confessing his sins, or asking the vicar's opinion of his case; and the vicar answered, in a solemn snuffling tone, that heightened the

6. Wine treated with a compound of antimony (a toxic crystalline element) to produce emetic effects.
7. A medicinal syrup of vinegar, honey, and a variety of seaside onion.
8. A piece of furniture enclosing a chamber pot for ease of use and privacy, especially at night.

ridicule of the scene. The emetic having done its office, the doctor interfered, and ordered the patient to be put in bed again. When he examined the *egista*,[9] and felt his pulse, he declared that much of the virus was discharged, and, giving him a composing draught, assured him he had good hopes of his recovery.—This welcome hint he received with the tears of joy in his eyes, protesting, that if he should recover, he would always think himself indebted for his life to the great skill and tenderness of his doctor, whose hand he squeezed with great fervor; and thus he was left to his repose.

We were pressed to stay dinner, that we might be witnesses of his resuscitation; but my uncle insisted upon our departing before noon, that we might reach this town before it should be dark.—In the mean time, lady Bullford conducted us into the garden to see a fish-pond just finished, which Mr. Bramble censured as being too near the parlour, where the knight now sat by himself, dozing in an elbow-chair after the fatigues of his morning atchievement.——In this situation he reclind, with his feet wrapped in flannel, and supported in a line with his body, when the door flying open with a violent shock, lieutenant Lismahago rushed into the room with horror in his looks, exclaiming, "A mad dog! a mad dog!" and throwing up the window sash, leaped into the garden.—Sir Thomas, waked by this tremendous exclamation, started up, and forgetting his gout, followed the lieutenant's example by a kind of instinctive impulse.—He not only bolted thro' the window like an arrow from a bow, but ran up to his middle in the pond before he gave the least sign of recollection. Then the captain began to bawl, "Lord, have mercy upon us!—pray, take care of the gentleman!—for God's sake, mind your footing, my dear boy!—get warm blankets—comfort his poor carcase—warm the bed in the green room."

Lady Bullford was thunder-struck at this phænomenon, and the rest of the company gazed in silent astonishment, while the servants hastened to assist their master, who suffered himself to be carried back into the parlour without speaking a word.——Being instantly accommodated with dry clothes and flannels, comforted with a cordial, and replaced *in statu quo*, one of the maids was ordered to chafe his lower extremities, an operation in consequence of which his senses seemed to return and his good humour to revive.—As we had followed him into the room, he looked at every individual in his turn, with a certain ludicrous expression in his countenance, but fixed his eye in particular upon Lismahago, who presented him with a pinch of snuff, and when he took it in silence, "Sir Thomas Bullford, (said he) I am much obliged to you for all

9. The excreted matter.

your favours, and some of them I have endeavoured to repay in your own coin." "Give me thy hand (cried the baronet); thou hast indeed payed me *Scot and lot*;[1] and even left a balance in my hands, for which, in presence of this company, I promise to be accountable."—So saying, he laughed very heartily, and even seemed to enjoy the retaliation which had been exacted at his own expence; but lady Bullford looked very grave; and in all probability thought the lieutenant had carried his resentment too far, considering that her husband was valetudinary—but, according to the proverb, *he that will play at bowls must expect to meet with rubbers.*[2]

I have seen a tame bear, very diverting when properly managed, become a very dangerous wild beast when teized for the entertainment of the spectators.—As for Lismahago, he seemed to think the fright and the cold bath would have a good effect upon his patient's constitution; but the doctor hinted some apprehension that the gouty matter might, by such a sudden shock, be repelled from the extremities and thrown upon some of the more vital parts of the machine.—I should be very sorry to see this prognostic verified upon our facetious landlord, who told Mrs. Tabitha at parting, that he hoped she would remember him in the distribution of the bride's favours, as he had taken so much pains to put the captain's parts and mettle to the proof.——After all, I am afraid our 'squire will appear to be the greatest sufferer by the baronet's wit; for his constitution is by no means calculated for night-alarms.—He has yawned and shivered all day, and gone to bed without supper; so that, as we have got into good quarters, I imagine we shall make a halt to-morrow; in which case, you will have at least one day's respite from the persecution of

Oct. 3.   J. MELFORD.

To Mrs. MARY JONES, at Brambleton-hall.

DEAR MARY JONES,

Miss Liddy is so good as to unclose me in a kiver as fur as Gloster, and the carrier will bring it to hand—God send us all safe to Monmouthshire, for I'm quite jaded with rambling—'Tis a true saying, *live and learn*—O woman, what chuckling and changing have I seen!—Well, there's nothing sartain in this world——Who would have thought that mistriss, after all the pains taken for the good of

---

1. Paid completely (proverbial), from the Old English *sceot* (payment).
2. If you play the game, you must take your chances (proverbial). "Bowls": a popular form of lawn bowling. "Rubbers": single, and therefore decisive, games in series.

her prusias sole, would go for to throw away her poor body? that she would cast the heys of infection upon such a carryingcrow as Lashmihago! as old as Matthewsullin, as dry as a red herring, and as pore as a starved veeze!—O, Molly! hadst thou seen him come down the ladder, in a shirt so scanty, that it could not kiver his nakedness!—The young 'squire called him Dunquickset; but he looked for all the world like Cradoc-ap Morgan, the ould tinker, that suffered at Abergany for steeling of kettle—Then he's a profane scuffle, and, as Mr. Clinker says, no better than an impfiddle, continually playing upon the pyebill and the newburth—I doubt he has as little manners as money; for he can't say a civil word, much more make me a present of a pair of gloves for good-will; but he looks as if he wanted to be very forewood and familiar—O! that ever a gentlewoman of years and discretion should tare her air, and cry and disporridge herself for such a nubjack! as the song goes—

> "I vow she would fain have a burd
> That bids such a price for an owl."[3]

but, for sartain, he must have dealt with some Scotch musician to bring her to this pass——As for me, I put my trust in the Lord; and I have got a slice of witch elm sowed in the gathers of my under petticoat;[4] and Mr. Clinker assures me, that by the new light of grease, I may deify the devil and all his works—But I nose what I nose—If mistriss should take up with Lashmyhago, this is no sarvice for me—Thank God, there's no want of places; and if it wan't for wan thing, I would——but, no matter—Madam Baynar's woman has twenty good pounds a-year and parquisites; and dresses like a parson of distinkson——I dined with her and the valley de shambles, with bags and golden jackets; but there was nothing kimfit-table to eat, being as how they live upon board, and having nothing but a piss of could cuddling tart and some blamangey,[5] I was tuck with the cullick, and a murcy it was that mistriss had her viol of assings in the cox. But, as I was saying, I think for sartain this match will go forewood; for things are come to a creesus; and I have seen with my own hays, such smuggling——But I scorn for to exclose the secrets of the family; and if it wance comes to marrying, who nose but the frolick may go round—I believes as how, Miss Liddy would have no reversion if her swan would appear; and you would be surprised, Molly, to receive a bride's fever from your humble sarvant—but this

---

3. Byron Gassman has identified similar lines in the song "Directions for Damosels," which appears in *A Book of Roxburghe Ballads* (1884), a collection of mostly 17th-century English ballads first published by John Payne Collier (1789–1883).
4. In Wales, witch hazel or witch elm twigs were believed to have beneficial properties.
5. I.e., blancmange, a sweet, white pudding. "Could cuddling tart": probably a pie made with coddle, an Irish stew of bacon, sausage, and vegetables.

is all suppository, dear girl; and I have sullenly promised to Mr. Clinker, that neither man, woman, nor child, shall no that arrow said a civil thing to me in the way of infection—I hopes to drink your health at Brambleton-hall, in a horn of October, before the month be out—Pray let my bed be turned once a-day, and the windore opened, while the weather is dry; and burn a few billets with some brush in the footman's garret, and see their mattrash be dry as a bone; for both our gentlemen have got a sad could by lying in damp shits at sir Tummas Ballfart's. No more at present, but my sarvice to Saul and the rest of our fellow-sarvents, being,

Dear Mary Jones,

always yours,

Oct. 4.   WIN. JENKINS.

To Miss LÆTITIA WILLIS, at Gloucester.

MY DEAR LETTY,

This method of writing to you from time to time, without any hopes of an answer, affords me, I own, some ease and satisfaction in the midst of my disquiet, as it in some degree lightens the burthen of affliction; but it is at best a very imperfect enjoyment of friendship, because it admits of no return of confidence and good counsel—I would give the whole world to have your company for a single day—I am heartily tired of this itinerant way of life—I am quite dizzy with a perpetual succession of objects—Besides it is impossible to travel such a length of way, without being exposed to inconveniences, dangers, and disagreeable accidents, which prove very grievous to a poor creature of weak nerves like me, and make me pay very dear for the gratification of my curiosity.

Nature never intended me for the busy world——I long for repose and solitude, where I can enjoy that disinterested friendship which is not to be found among crouds, and indulge those pleasing reveries that shun the hurry and tumult of fashionable society— Unexperienced as I am in the commerce of life, I have seen enough to give me a disgust to the generality of those who carry it on— There is such malice, treachery, and dissimulation, even among professed friends and intimate companions, as cannot fail to strike a virtuous mind with horror; and when Vice quits the stage for a moment, her place is immediately occupied by Folly, which is often too serious to excite any thing but compassion—Perhaps I ought to be silent on the foibles of my poor aunt; but with you, my dear Willis, I have no secrets; and, truly, her weaknesses are such as cannot be concealed. Since the first moment we arrived at Bath, she has been employed constantly in spreading nets for the other sex; and, at length, she has caught a superannuated lieutenant, who is in a fair way to make her change her name—My uncle and my brother seem to have no objection to this extraordinary match, which, I make no doubt, will afford abundance of matter of conversation and mirth; for my part, I am too sensible of my own weaknesses, to be diverted with those of other people——At present, I have something at heart that employs my whole attention, and keeps my mind in the utmost terror and suspence.

Yesterday in the forenoon, as I stood with my brother at the parlour window of an inn, where we had lodged, a person passed a-horse-back, whom (gracious Heaven!) I instantly discovered to be Wilson! He wore a white riding-coat, with the cape buttoned up to his chin; looked remarkably pale, and passed at a round trot, without seeming to observe us——Indeed, he could not see us; for there was a blind that concealed us from the view. You may guess how I was affected at this apparition—The light forsook my eyes; and I was seized with such a palpitation and trembling, that I could not stand. I sat down upon a couch, and strove to compose myself, that my brother might not perceive my agitation; but it was impossible to escape his prying eyes—He had observed the object that alarmed me; and, doubtless, knew him at the first glance—He now looked at me with a stern countenance; then he ran out into the street, to see what road the unfortunate horseman had taken—He afterwards dispatched his man for further intelligence, and seemed to meditate some violent design. My uncle, being out of order, we remained another night at the inn; and all day long Jery acted the part of an indefatigable spy upon my conduct—He watched my very looks with such eagerness of attention, as if he would have penetrated into the utmost recesses of my heart—This may be owing to his regard for my honour, if it is not the effect of his own pride; but he is so hot, and violent, and unrelenting, that the sight of him alone throws me into a flutter; and really it will not be in my power to afford him any share of my affection, if he persists in persecuting me at this rate. I am afraid he has formed some scheme of vengeance, which will make me completely wretched! I am afraid he suspects some collusion from this appearance of Wilson.——Good God! did he really appear? or was it only a phantom, a pale spectre to apprise me of his death?

O Letty, what shall I do?—where shall I turn for advice and consolation?—shall I implore the protection of my uncle, who has been always kind and compassionate.—This must be my last resource.—I dread the thoughts of making him uneasy; and would rather suffer a thousand deaths than live the cause of dissension in the family.—I cannot perceive the meaning of Wilson's coming hither:—perhaps, he was in quest of us, in order to disclose his real name and situation:—but wherefore pass without staying to make the least inquiry?—My dear Willis, I am lost in conjecture.—I have not closed an eye since I saw him.—All night long have I been tossed about from one imagination to another.—The reflection finds no resting place.—I have prayed, and sighed, and wept plentifully.—— If this terrible suspence continues much longer, I shall have another fit of illness, and then the whole family will be in confusion.—If it was consistent with the wise purposes of Providence, would I were in my grave.—But it is my duty to be resigned.—My dearest Letty, excuse my weakness—excuse these blots—my tears fall so fast that I cannot keep the paper dry—yet I ought to consider that I have as yet no cause to despair——but I am such a faint-hearted timorous creature!

Thank God, my uncle is much better than he was yesterday.—He is resolved to pursue our journey strait to Wales.—I hope we shall take Gloucester in our way—that hope chears my poor heart—I shall once more embrace my best beloved Willis, and pour all my griefs into her friendly bosom.——O heaven! is it possible that such happiness is reserved for

The dejected and forlorn

Oct. 4.   LYDIA MELFORD.

To Sir WATKIN PHILLIPS, Bar^t.
of Jesus college, Oxon.

DEAR WATKIN,

I yesterday met with an incident which I believe you will own to be very surprising—As I stood with Liddy at the window of the inn where we had lodged, who should pass by but Wilson a-horse-back!—I could not be mistaken in the person, for I had a full view of him as he advanced; I plainly perceived by my sister's confusion that she recognized him at the same time. I was equally astonished and incensed at his appearance, which I could not but interpret into an insult, or something worse. I ran out at the gate, and, seeing him turn the corner of the street, I dispatched my servant to observe his motions, but the fellow was too late to bring me that satisfaction. He told me, however, that there was an inn, called the Red Lion, at that end of the town, where he supposed the horseman had alighted, but that he would not enquire without further orders. I sent him back immediately to know what strangers were in the house, and he returned with a report that there was one Mr. Wilson lately arrived. In consequence of this information I charged him with a note directed to that gentleman, desiring him to meet me in half an hour in a certain field at the town's end, with a case of pistols, in order to decide the difference which could not be determined at our last rencounter: but I did not think proper to subscribe the billet.[6] My man assured me he had delivered it into his own hand; and, that having read it, he declared he would wait upon the gentleman at the place and time appointed.

M'Alpine being an old soldier, and luckily sober at the time, I entrusted him with my secret. I ordered him to be within call, and, having given him a letter to be delivered to my uncle in case of accident, I repaired to the rendezvous, which was an inclosed field at a little distance from the highway. I found my antagonist had already taken his ground, wrapped in a dark horseman's coat, with a laced hat flapped over his eyes; but what was my astonishment, when, throwing off this wrapper, he appeared to be a person whom I had never seen before! He had one pistol stuck in a leather belt, and another in his hand ready for action, and, advancing a few steps, called to know if I was ready—I answered, "No," and desired a parley; upon which he turned the muzzle of his piece towards the earth; then replaced it in his belt, and met me half way—When I assured him he was not the man I expected to meet, he said, *it might be so:* that he had received a slip of paper directed to Mr. Wilson, requesting him to come hither; and that as there was no other in the place of that name, he naturally concluded the note was intended for him, and him only—I then gave him to understand, that I had been injured by a person who assumed that name, which person I had actually seen within the hour, passing through the street on horseback; that hearing there was a Mr. Wilson at the Red Lion, I took it for granted he was the man, and in that belief had writ the billet; and I expressed my surprize, that he, who was a stranger to me and my concerns, should give me such a rendezvous, without taking the trouble to demand a previous explanation—He replied, that there was no other of his name in the whole county; that no such horseman had alighted at the Red Lion since nine o'clock, when he arrived—that having had the honour to serve his majesty, he thought he could not decently decline any invitation of this kind, from what quarter soever it might come; and that if any explanation was necessary, it did not belong to him to demand it, but to the gentleman who summoned him into the field—Vexed as I was at this adventure, I could not help admiring the coolness of this officer, whose open countenance prepossessed me in his favour.—He

6. Sign the letter.

seemed to be turned of forty; wore his own short black hair, which curled naturally about his ears, and was very plain in his apparel— When I begged pardon for the trouble I had given him, he received my apology with great good humour.—He told me that he lived about ten miles off, at a small farm-house, which would afford me tolerable lodging, if I would come and take the diversion of hunting with him for a few weeks; in which case we might, perhaps, find out the man who had given me offence—I thanked him very sincerely for his courteous offer, which, I told him, I was not at liberty to accept at present, on account of my being engaged in a family partie; and so we parted, with mutual professions of good will and esteem.

Now tell me, dear knight, what am I to make of this singular adventure?—Am I to suppose that the horseman I saw was really a thing of flesh and blood, or a bubble that vanished into air?—or must I imagine Liddy knows more of the matter than she chuses to disclose?—If I thought her capable of carrying on any clandestine correspondence with such a fellow, I should at once discard all tenderness, and forget that she was connected with me by the ties of blood—But how is it possible that a girl of her simplicity and inexperience, should maintain such an intercourse, surrounded, as she is with so many eyes, destitute of all opportunity, and shifting quarters every day of her life!—Besides, she has solemnly promised— No—I can't think the girl so base—so insensible to the honour of her family.—What disturbs me chiefly, is the impression which these occurrences seem to make upon her spirits—These are the symptoms from which I conclude that the rascal has still a hold on her affection—surely I have a right to call him a rascal, and to conclude that his designs are infamous—But it shall be my fault if he does not one day repent his presumption——I confess I cannot think, much less write on this subject, with any degree of temper or patience; I shall therefore conclude with telling you, that we hope to be in Wales by the latter end of the month: but before that period you will probably hear again from

your affectionate

Oct. 4.   J. MELFORD.

To Sir WATKIN PHILLIPS, Bar^t. at Oxon.

DEAR PHILLIPS,

When I wrote you by last post, I did not imagine I should be tempted to trouble you again so soon: but I now sit down with a heart so full that it cannot contain itself; though I am under such agitation

of spirits, that you are to expect neither method or connexion in this
address—We have been this day within a hair's breadth of losing
honest Matthew Bramble, in consequence of a cursed accident,
which I will endeavour to explain.—In crossing the country to get
into the post road, it was necessary to ford a river, and we that were
a-horseback passed without any danger or difficulty; but a great
quantity of rain having fallen last night and this morning, there
was such an accumulation of water, that a mill-head gave way, just
as the coach was passing under it, and the flood rushed down with
such impetuosity, as first floated, and then fairly overturned the
carriage in the middle of the stream—Lismahago and I, and the two
servants, alighting instantaneously, ran into the river to give all
the assistance in our power.—Our aunt, Mrs. Tabitha, who had the
good fortune to be uppermost, was already half way out of the coach
window, when her lover approaching, disengaged her entirely; but,
whether his foot slipt, or the burthen was too great, they fell over
head and ears in each other's arms. He endeavoured more than once
to get up, and even to disentangle himself from her embrace, but she
hung about his neck like a mill-stone[7] (no bad emblem of matrimony,) and if my man had not proved a staunch auxiliary, those two
lovers would in all probability have gone hand in hand to the shades
below—For my part, I was too much engaged to take any cognizance of their distress.—I snatched out my sister by the hair of the
head, and, dragging her to the bank, recollected that my uncle had
not yet appeared—Rushing again into the stream, I met Clinker
hauling ashore Mrs. Jenkins, who looked like a mermaid with her
hair dishevelled about her ears; but, when I asked if his master was
safe, he forthwith shook her from him, and she must have gone to
pot,[8] if a miller had not seasonably come to her relief.—As for Humphrey, he flew like lightning to the coach, that was by this time filled
with water, and, diving into it, brought up the poor 'squire, to all
appearance, deprived of life—It is not in my power to describe what
I felt at this melancholy spectacle—it was such an agony as baffles
all description! The faithful Clinker, taking him up in his arms, as
if he had been an infant of six months, carried him ashore, howling
most piteously all the way, and I followed him in a transport of grief
and consternation—When he was laid upon the grass, and turned
from side to side, a great quantity of water ran out at his mouth, then
he opened his eyes, and fetched a deep sigh—Clinker perceiving
these signs of life, immediately tied up his arm with a garter, and,
pulling out a horse-fleam,[9] let him blood in the farrier stile.—At first

7. A burden (proverbial). Millstones are heavy circular stones used to grind grain.
8. Gone to ruin (proverbial).
9. A lancet for bleeding horses.

a few drops only issued from the orifice; but the limb being chafed, in a little time the blood began to flow in a continued stream, and he uttered some incoherent words, which were the most welcome sounds that ever saluted my ear. There was a country inn hard by, the landlord of which had by this time come with his people to give their assistance.—Thither my uncle being carried, was undressed and put to bed, wrapped in warm blankets; but having been moved too soon, he fainted away, and once more lay without sense or motion, notwithstanding all the efforts of Clinker and the landlord, who bathed his temples with Hungary water,[1] and held a smelling-bottle to his nose. As I had heard of the efficacy of salt in such cases, I ordered all that was in the house to be laid under his head and body; and whether this application had the desired effect, or nature of herself prevailed, he, in less than a quarter of an hour, began to breathe regularly, and soon retrieved his recollection, to the unspeakable joy of all the by-standers. As for Clinker, his brain seemed to be affected.—He laughed, and wept, and danced about in such a distracted manner, that the landlord very judiciously conveyed him out of the room. My uncle, seeing me dropping wet, comprehended the whole of what had happened, and asked if all the company was safe?—Being answered in the affirmative, he insisted upon my putting on dry clothes; and, having swallowed a little warm wine, desired he might be left to his repose. Before I went to shift myself, I inquired about the rest of the family—I found Mrs. Tabitha still delirious from her fright, discharging very copiously the water she had swallowed. She was supported by the captain, distilling drops from his uncurled periwig, so lank and so dank, that he looked like father Thames without his sedges, embracing Isis, while she cascaded in his urn.[2] Mrs. Jenkins was present also, in a loose bed-gown, without either cap or handkerchief; but she seemed to be as little *compos mentis*[3] as her mistress, and acted so many cross purposes in the course of her attendance, that, between the two, Lismahago had occasion for all his philosophy. As for Liddy, I thought the poor girl would have actually lost her senses. The good-woman of the house had shifted her linen, and put her into bed; but she was seized with the idea that her uncle had perished, and in this persuasion made a dismal out-cry; nor did she pay the least regard to what I said, when I solemnly assured her he was safe. Mr. Bramble hearing the noise, and being informed of her apprehension, desired she might be brought into his chamber; and she

1. A perfumed solution made of brandy infused with various herbs.
2. The Rivers Thames and Isis converge at Oxford; personified images of them were iconic during the 18th century.
3. Of sound mind (Latin).

no sooner received this intimation, than she ran thither half naked, with the wildest expression of eagerness in her countenance— Seeing the 'squire sitting up in the bed, she sprung forwards, and, throwing her arms about his neck, exclaimed in a most pathetic tone, "Are you—Are you indeed my uncle—My dear uncle!—My best friend! My father!—Are you really living? or is it an illusion of my poor brain!" Honest Matthew was so much affected, that he could not help shedding tears, while he kissed her forehead, saying, "My dear Liddy, I hope I shall live long enough to shew how sensible I am of your affection—But your spirits are fluttered, child—You want rest—Go to bed and compose yourself—" "Well, I will (she replied)— but still methinks this cannot be real—The coach was full of water—My uncle was under us all—Gracious God!—You was[4] under water—How did you get out?—tell me that? or I shall think this is all a deception—" "In what manner I was brought out, I know as little as you do, my dear (said the 'squire); and, truly, that is a circumstance of which I want to be informed." I would have given him a detail of the whole adventure, but he would not hear me until I should change my clothes; so that I had only time to tell him, that he owed his life to the courage and fidelity of Clinker; and having given him this hint, I conducted my sister to her own chamber.

This accident happened about three o'clock in the afternoon, and in little more than an hour the hurricane was all over; but as the carriage was found to be so much damaged, that it could not proceed without considerable repairs, a blacksmith and wheelwright were immediately sent for to the next market-town, and we congratulated ourselves upon being housed at an inn, which, though remote from the post-road, afforded exceeding good lodging. The women being pretty well composed, and the men all a-foot, my uncle sent for his servant, and, in the presence of Lismahago and me, accosted him in these words—"So, Clinker, I find you are resolved I shan't die by water—As you have fished me up from the bottom at your own risque, you are at least entitled to all the money that was in my pocket, and there it is—" So saying, he presented him with a purse containing thirty guineas, and a ring nearly of the same value— "God forbid! (cried Clinker) your honour shall excuse me—I am a poor fellow; but I have a heart—O! if your honour did but know how I rejoice to see—Blessed be his holy name, that made me the humble instrument—But as for the lucre of gain, I renounce it—I have done no more than my duty—No more than I would have done for the most worthless of my fellow-creatures—No more than I would have done for captain Lismahago, or Archy Macalpine, or any sinner upon earth—But for your worship, I would go through fire as

4. Commonly used this way in the 18th century; now deemed ungrammatical.

well as water——" "I do believe it, Humphry (said the 'squire); but as you think it was your duty to save my life at the hazard of your own, I think it is mine to express the sense I have of your extraordinary fidelity and attachment—I insist upon your receiving this small token of my gratitude; but don't imagine that I look upon this as an adequate recompence for the service you have done me—I have determined to settle thirty pounds a-year upon you for life; and I desire these gentlemen will bear witness to this my intention, of which I have a memorandum in my pocket-book." "Lord make me thankful for all these mercies! (cried Clinker, sobbing) I have been a poor bankrupt from the beginning—your honour's goodness found me, when I was—naked—when I was—sick and forlorn— —I understand your honour's looks—I would not give offence—but my heart is very full—and if your worship won't give me leave to speak,—I must vent it in prayers to heaven for my benefactor." When he quitted the room, Lismahago said, he should have a much better opinion of his honesty, if he did not whine and cant so abominably; but that he had always observed those weeping and praying fellows were hypocrites at bottom. Mr. Bramble made no reply to this sarcastic remark, proceeding from the lieutenant's resentment of Clinker's having, in pure simplicity of heart, ranked him with M'Alpine and the sinners of the earth.——The landlord being called to receive some orders about the beds, told the 'squire that his house was very much at his service, but he was sure he should not have the honour to lodge him and his company. He gave us to understand that his master, who lived hard by, would not suffer us to be at a public house, when there was accommodation for us at his own; and that, if he had not dined abroad in the neighbourhood he would have undoubtedly come to offer his services at our first arrival. He then launched out in praise of that gentleman, whom he had served as butler, representing him as a perfect miracle of goodness and generosity. He said he was a person of great learning, and allowed to be the best farmer in the country:—that he had a lady who was as much beloved as himself, and an only son, a very hopeful young gentleman, just recovered from a dangerous fever, which had like to have proved fatal to the whole family; for, if the son had died, he was sure the parents would not have survived their loss—He had not yet finished the encomium of Mr. Dennison, when this gentleman arrived in a post-chaise, and his appearance seemed to justify all that had been said in his favour. He is pretty well advanced in years, but hale, robust, and florid,[5] with an ingenuous countenance, expressive of good sense and humanity. Having condoled[6] with us

5. Ruddy, healthy.
6. Sympathized.

on the accident which had happened, he said he was come to conduct us to his habitation, where we should be less incommoded
than at such a paultry inn, and expressed his hope that the ladies
would not be the worse for going thither in his carriage, as the distance was not above a quarter of a mile. My uncle having made a
proper return to this courteous exhibition, eyed him attentively,
and then asked if he had not been at Oxford, a commoner of
Queen's college? When Mr. Dennison answered, "Yes," with some
marks of surprise—"Look at me then (said our 'squire) and let us
see if you can recollect the features of an old friend, whom you
have not seen these forty years."——The gentleman, taking him by
the hand, and gazing at him earnestly,—"I protest, (cried he,) I do
think I recal the idea of Matthew Loyd of Glamorganshire, who
was student of Jesus." "Well remembered, my dear friend, Charles
Dennison, (exclaimed my uncle, pressing him to his breast), I am
that very identical Matthew Loyd of Glamorgan." Clinker, who had
just entered the room with some coals for the fire, no sooner heard
these words, than, throwing down the scuttle on the toes of Lismahago, he began to caper as if he was mad, crying—"Matthew Loyd
of Glamorgan!—O Providence!—Matthew Loyd of Glamorgan!"——
Then, clasping my uncle's knees, he went on in this manner—
—"Your worship must forgive me—Matthew Loyd of Glamorgan!—O
Lord, Sir!—I can't contain myself!—I shall lose my senses—" "Nay,
thou hast lost them already, I believe, (said the 'squire, peevishly)
prithee Clinker be quiet——What is the matter?"——Humphry,
fumbling in his bosom, pulled out an old wooden snuffbox, which
he presented in great trepidation to his master, who, opening it
immediately, perceived a small cornelian[7] seal, and two scraps of
paper—At sight of these articles he started, and changed colour,
and, casting his eye upon the inscriptions—"Ha!—how!—what!—
where (cried he) is the person here named?" Clinker, knocking his
own breast, could hardly pronounce these words—"Here—here—
here is Matthew Loyd, as the certificate sheweth—Humphry Clinker was the name of the farrier that took me 'prentice"—"And who
gave you these tokens,"—said my uncle, hastily—"My poor mother
on her death-bed"—replied the other—"And who was your mother?"
"Dorothy Twyford, an please your honour, heretofore barkeeper
at the Angel at Chippenham."[8]—"And why were not these tokens
produced before?" "My mother told me she had wrote to Glamorganshire, at the time of my birth, but had no answer; and that afterwards, when she made enquiry, there was no such person in that
county." "And so in consequence of my changing my name and

7. A semitransparent quartz.
8. A coaching inn in Wiltshire.

going abroad at that very time, thy poor mother and thou have been left to want and misery—I am really shocked at the consequence of my own folly."—Then, laying his hand on Clinker's head, he added, "Stand forth, Matthew Loyd—You see, gentlemen, how the sins of my youth rise up in judgment against me—Here is my direction written with my own hand, and a seal which I left at the woman's request; and this is a certificate of the child's baptism, signed by the curate of the parish." The company were not a little surprised at this discovery, upon which Mr. Dennison facetiously congratulated both the father and the son: for my part, I shook my new-found cousin heartily by the hand, and Lismahago complimented him with the tears in his eyes, for he had been hopping about the room, swearing in broad Scotch, and bellowing with the pain occasioned by the fall of the coal-scuttle upon his foot. He had even vowed to drive the *saul* out of the body of that mad rascal: but, perceiving the unexpected turn which things had taken, he wished him joy of his good fortune, observing that it went very near his heart, as he was like to be a great toe out of pocket by the discovery—Mr. Dennison now desired to know for what reason my uncle had changed the name by which he knew him at Oxford, and our 'squire satisfied him, by answering to this effect.—"I took my mother's name, which was Loyd, as heir to her lands in Glamorganshire; but, when I came of age, I sold that property, in order to clear my paternal estate, and resumed my real name; so that I am now Matthew Bramble of Brambleton-hall in Monmouthshire, at your service; and this is my nephew, Jeremy Melford of Belfield, in the county of Glamorgan." At that instant the ladies entering the room, he presented Mrs. Tabitha as his sister, and Liddy as his niece. The old gentleman saluted them very cordially, and seemed struck with the appearance of my sister, whom he could not help surveying with a mixture of complacency and surprize——"Sister, (said my uncle) there is a poor relation that recommends himself to your good graces—The quondam Humphry Clinker is metamorphosed into Matthew Loyd; and claims the honour of being your carnal kinsman—in short, the rogue proves to be a crab of my own planting[9] in the days of hot blood and unrestrained libertinism." Clinker had by this time dropt upon one knee, by the side of Mrs. Tabitha, who, eyeing him askance, and flirting her fan with marks of agitation, thought proper, after some conflict, to hold out her hand for him to kiss, saying, with a demure aspect, "Brother, you have been very wicked: but I hope you'll live to see the folly of your ways—I am very sorry to say the young man, whom you have this day acknowledged, has

---

9. An allusion to the proverbial saying, Plant a crab [apple] tree where you will, it will never bear pippins [i.e., sweet apples]. "Quondam": former.

more grace and religion, by the gift of God, than you with all your
profane learning, and repeated opportunity—I do think he has got
the trick of the eye, and the tip of the nose of my uncle Loyd of
Flluydwellyn; and as for the long chin, it is the very moral[1] of the
governor's—Brother, as you have changed his name pray change his
dress also; that livery doth not become any person that hath got our
blood in his veins."—Liddy seemed much pleased with this acquisition to the family.—She took him by the hand, declaring she should
always be proud to own her connexion with a virtuous young man,
who had given so many proofs of his gratitude and affection to her
uncle.—Mrs. Winifred Jenkins, extremely fluttered between her
surprize at this discovery, and the apprehension of losing her sweet-
heart, exclaimed in a giggling tone,—"I wish you joy, Mr. Clinker—
Floyd—I would say—hi, hi, hi!—you'll be so proud you won't look at
your poor fellow servants, oh, oh, oh!" Honest Clinker owned, he was
overjoyed at his good fortune, which was greater than he deserved—
"But wherefore should I be proud? (said he) a poor object conceived
in sin, and brought forth in iniquity, nursed in a parish work-house,
and bred in a smithy—Whenever I seem proud, Mrs. Jenkins, I beg
of you to put me in mind of the condition I was in, when I first saw
you between Chippenham and Marlborough."

When this momentous affair was discussed to the satisfaction of
all parties concerned, the weather being dry, the ladies declined the
carriage; so that we walked all together to Mr. Dennison's house,
where we found the tea ready prepared by his lady, an amiable
matron, who received us with all the benevolence of hospitality.—
The house is old fashioned and irregular, but lodgeable and commodious. To the south it has the river in front, at the distance of a
hundred paces; and on the north, there is a rising ground, covered
with an agreeable plantation; the greens and walks are kept in the
nicest order, and all is rural and romantic. I have not yet seen the
young gentleman, who is on a visit to a friend in the neighbourhood,
from whose house he is not expected 'till to-morrow.

In the mean time, as there is a man going to the next market-town
with letters for the post, I take this opportunity to send you the history
of this day, which has been remarkably full of adventures; and you will
own I give you them like a beef-steak at Dolly's,[2] *hot* and *hot*, without
ceremony and parade, just as they come from the recollection of

Yours,

J. Melford.[3]

1. Likeness.
2. A tavern in London famous for its meats served hot and in quick succession.
3. This is the only undated letter in the novel; based on internal evidence it can safely be
dated October 6.

To Dr. Lewis.

DEAR DICK,

Since the last trouble I gave you, I have met with a variety of incidents, some of them of a singular nature, which I reserve as a fund for conversation; but there are others so interesting, that they will not keep *in petto*[4] till meeting.

Know then, it was a thousand pounds to a sixpence, that you should now be executing my will, instead of perusing my letter! Two days ago, our coach was overturned in the midst of a rapid river, where my life was saved with the utmost difficulty, by the courage, activity, and presence of mind of my servant Humphry Clinker—But this is not the most surprising circumstance of the adventure—The said Humphry Clinker proves to be Matthew Loyd, natural son of one Matthew Loyd of Glamorgan, if you know any such person—You see, Doctor, that notwithstanding all your philosophy, it is not without some reason that we Welchmen ascribe such energy to the force of blood—But we shall discuss this point on some future occasion.

This is not the only discovery which I made in consequence of our disaster—We happened to be wrecked upon a friendly shore—The lord of the manor is no other than Charles Dennison, our fellow-rake at Oxford—We are now happily housed with that gentleman, who has really attained to that pitch of rural felicity, at which I have been aspiring these twenty years in vain. He is blessed with a consort, whose disposition is suited to his own in all respects; tender, generous, and benevolent—She, moreover, possesses an uncommon share of understanding, fortitude, and discretion, and is admirably qualified to be his companion, confidant, counsellor, and coadjutrix.[5] These excellent persons have an only son, about nineteen years of age, just such a youth as they could have wished that Heaven would bestow to fill up the measure of their enjoyment—In a word, they know no other allay to their happines, but their apprehension and anxiety about the life and concerns of this beloved object.

Our old friend, who had the misfortune to be a second brother, was bred to the law, and even called to the bar; but he did not find himself qualified to shine in that province, and had very little inclination for his profession—He disobliged his father, by marrying for love, without any consideration of fortune; so that he had little or nothing to depend upon for some years but his practice, which afforded him a bare subsistence; and the prospect of an increasing

---

4. In the breast (Latin); i.e., undisclosed, secret.
5. Female partner in making decisions and judgments.

family, began to give him disturbance and disquiet. In the mean time, his father dying, was succeeded by his elder brother, a fox-hunter and a sot, who neglected his affairs, insulted and oppressed his servants, and in a few years had well nigh ruined the estate, when he was happily carried off by a fever, the immediate consequence of a debauch.[6] Charles, with the approbation of his wife, immediately determined to quit business, and retire into the country, although this resolution was strenuously and zealously opposed by every individual, whom he consulted on the subject. Those who had tried the experiment, assured him that he could not pretend to breathe in the country for less than the double of what his estate produced; that, in order to be upon the footing of a gentleman, he would be obliged to keep horses, hounds, carriages, with a suitable number of servants, and maintain an elegant table for the entertainment of his neighbours; that farming was a mystery, known only to those who had been bred up to it from the cradle, the success of it depending not only upon skill and industry, but also upon such attention and œconomy as no gentleman could be supposed to give or practise; accordingly, every attempt made by gentlemen miscarried, and not a few had been ruined by their prosecution of agriculture—Nay, they affirmed that he would find it cheaper to buy hay and oats for his cattle, and to go to market for poultry, eggs, kitchen herbs, and roots, and every the most inconsiderable article of house-keeping, than to have those articles produced on his own ground.

These objections did not deter Mr. Dennison, because they were chiefly founded on the supposition, that he would be obliged to lead a life of extravagance and dissipation, which he and his consort equally detested, despised, and determined to avoid—The objects he had in view, were health of body, peace of mind, and the private satisfaction of domestic quiet, unallayed by actual want, and uninterrupted by the fears of indigence—He was very moderate in his estimate of the necessaries, and even of the comforts of life—He required nothing but wholesome air, pure water, agreeable exercise, plain diet, convenient lodging, and decent apparel. He reflected, that if a peasant without education, or any great share of natural sagacity, could maintain a large family, and even become opulent upon a farm, for which he payed an annual rent of two or three hundred pounds to the landlord, surely he himself might hope for some success from his industry, having no rent to pay, but, on the contrary, three or four hundred pounds a-year to receive—He considered, that the earth was an indulgent mother, that yielded her fruits to all her children without distinction. He had studied the theory of agriculture with a degree of eagerness and delight; and he

6. An uninhibited spree, here of drinking. "Sot": drunkard.

could not conceive there was any mystery in the practice, but what he should be able to disclose by dint of care and application. With respect to houshold expence, he entered into a minute detail and investigation, by which he perceived the assertions of his friends were altogether erroneous—He found he should save sixty pounds a-year in the single article of house-rent, and as much more in pocket-money and contingencies; that even butcher's-meat was twenty per cent cheaper in the country than in London; but that poultry, and almost every other circumstance of house-keeping, might be had for less than one half of what they cost in town; besides, a considerable saving on the side of dress, in being delivered from the oppressive imposition of ridiculous modes, invented by ignorance, and adopted by folly.

As to the danger of vying with the rich in pomp and equipage, it never gave him the least disturbance. He was now turned of forty, and, having lived half that time in the busy scenes of life, was well skilled in the science of mankind. There cannot be in nature a more contemptible figure than that of a man, who with five hundred a year presumes to rival in expence a neighbour who possesses five times that income—His ostentation, far from concealing, serves only to discover his indigence, and render his vanity the more shocking; for it attracts the eyes of censure, and excites the spirit of inquiry. There is not a family in the county, nor a servant in his own house, nor a farmer in the parish, but what knows the utmost farthing that his lands produce, and all these behold him with scorn or compassion. I am surprised that these reflections do not occur to persons in this unhappy dilemma, and produce a salutary effect; but the truth is, of all the passions incident to human nature, vanity is that which most effectually perverts the faculties of the understanding; nay, it sometimes becomes so incredibly depraved, as to aspire at infamy, and find pleasure in bearing the stigmas of reproach.

I have now given you a sketch of the character and situation of Mr. Dennison, when he came down to take possession of this estate; but as the messenger, who carries the letters to the next town is just setting off, I shall reserve what further I have to say on this subject, till the next post, when you shall certainly hear from

Yours always,

Oct. 8. MATT. BRAMBLE.

To Dr. Lewis.

Once more, dear doctor, I resume the pen for your amusement.—It was on the morning after our arrival that, walking out with my friend, Mr. Dennison, I could not help breaking forth into the warmest expressions of applause at the beauty of the scene, which is really inchanting; and I signified, in particular, how much I was pleased with the disposition of some detached groves, that afforded at once shelter and ornament to his habitation.

"When I took possession of these lands, about two and twenty years ago, (said he) there was not a tree standing within a mile of the house, except those of an old neglected orchard, which produced nothing but leaves and moss.—It was in the gloomy month of November, when I arrived, and found the house in such a condition, that it might have been justly stiled the *tower of desolation*.[7]— The court-yard was covered with nettles and docks, and the garden exhibited such a rank plantation of weeds as I had never seen before;—the window-shutters were falling in pieces;——the sashes broken;——and owls and jack-daws had taken possession of the chimnies.—The prospect within was still more dreary.—All was dark, and damp, and dirty beyond description;—the rain penetrated in several parts of the roof;—in some apartments the very floors had given way;—the hangings were parted from the walls, and shaking in mouldy remnants;—the glasses were dropping out of their frames;—the family-pictures were covered with dust;—and all the chairs and tables worm-eaten and crazy.——There was not a bed in the house that could be used, except one old-fashioned machine, with a high gill tester, and fringed curtains of yellow mohair, which had been, for aught I know, two centuries in the family.—In short, there was no furniture but the utensils of the kitchen; and the cellar afforded nothing but a few empty butts and barrels, that stunk so abominably, that I would not suffer any body to enter it until I had flashed a considerable quantity of gunpowder to qualify the foul air within.

"An old cottager and his wife, who were hired to lie in the house, had left it with precipitation, alledging, among other causes of retreat, that they could not sleep for frightful noises, and that my poor brother certainly walked after his death.—In a word, the house appeared uninhabitable; the barn, stable, and out-houses were in ruins; all the fences broken down, and the fields lying waste.

---

7. There are echoes here of passages from both the Bible (Ezekiel 29:10; 2 Samuel 22:51) and *Paradise Lost* (1.180–181).

"The farmer who kept the key never dreamed I had any intention to live upon the spot.—He rented a farm of sixty pounds, and his lease was just expiring.—He had formed a scheme of being appointed bailiff to the estate, and of converting the house and the adjacent grounds to his own use.—A hint of his intention I received from the curate at my first arrival; I therefore did not pay much regard to what he said by way of discouraging me from coming to settle in the country; but I was a little startled when he gave me warning that he should quit the farm at the expiration of his lease, unless I would abate considerably in the rent.

"At this period I accidentally became acquainted with a person, whose friendship laid the foundation of all my prosperity. In the next market-town, I chanced to dine at an inn with a Mr. Wilson, who was lately come to settle in the neighbourhood.—He had been lieutenant of a man of war; but quitted the sea in some disgust, and married the only daughter of farmer Bland, who lives in this parish, and has acquired a good fortune in the way of husbandry,—Wilson is one of the best natured men I ever knew; brave, frank, obliging, and ingenuous.—He liked my conversation, I was charmed with his liberal manner; an acquaintance immediately commenced, and this was soon improved into a friendship without reserve.—There are characters which, like similar particles of matter, strongly attract each other.—He forthwith introduced me to his father-in-law, farmer Bland, who was well acquainted with every acre of my estate, of consequence well qualified to advise me on this occasion.—Finding I was inclined to embrace a country life, and even to amuse myself with the occupations of farming, he approved of my design—He gave me to understand that all my farms were under-lett; that the estate was capable of great improvement; that there was plenty of chalk in the neighbourhood; and that my own ground produced excellent marle[8] for manure.—With respect to the farm, which was like to fall into my hands, he said he would willingly take it at the present rent; but at the same time owned, that if I would expend two hundred pounds in enclosure,[9] it would be worth more than double the sum.

"Thus encouraged, I began the execution of my scheme without further delay, and plunged into a sea of expence, though I had no fund in reserve, and the whole produce of the estate did not exceed three hundred pounds a year.—In one week, my house was made weather tight, and thoroughly cleansed from top to bottom; then it was well ventilated by throwing all the doors and windows open,

8. A mix of clay and calcium carbonate that improves the texture of light or sandy soil. "Under-lett": leased for less than the going rate.
9. Marking off the property's boundaries.

and making blazing fires of wood in every chimney from the kitchen to the garrets.—The floors were repaired, the sashes new glazed, and out of the old furniture of the whole house, I made shift to fit up a parlour and three chambers in a plain yet decent manner.—The court-yard was cleared of weeds and rubbish, and my friend Wilson charged himself with the dressing of the garden; bricklayers were set at work upon the barn and stable; and labourers engaged to restore the fences, and begin the work of hedging and ditching, under the direction of farmer Bland, at whose recommendation I hired a careful hind[1] to lie in the house, and keep constant fires in the apartments.

"Having taken these measures, I returned to London, where I forthwith sold off my houshold-furniture, and, in three weeks from my first visit, brought my wife hither to keep her Christmas.——Considering the gloomy season of the year, the dreariness of the place, and the decayed aspect of our habitation, I was afraid that her resolution would sink under the sudden transition from a town-life to such a melancholy state of rustication; but I was agreeably disappointed.——She found the reality less uncomfortable than the picture I had drawn.——By this time, indeed, things were mended in appearance.—The out-houses had risen out of their ruins; the pigeon-house was rebuilt, and replenished by Wilson, who also put my garden in decent order, and provided a good stock of poultry, which made an agreeable figure in my yard; and the house, on the whole, looked like the habitation of human creatures.—Farmer Bland spared me a milch-cow[2] for my family, and an ordinary saddle-horse for my servant to go to market at the next town.—I hired a country lad for a footman; the hind's daughter was my house-maid, and my wife had brought a cook-maid from London.

"Such was my family when I began house-keeping in this place, with three hundred pounds in my pocket, raised from the sale of my superfluous furniture—I knew we should find occupation enough through the day to employ our time; but I dreaded the long winter evenings; yet for these too we found a remedy.——The curate,[3] who was a single man, soon became so naturalized to the family, that he generally lay in the house; and his company was equally agreeable and useful.—He was a modest man, a good scholar, and perfectly well qualified to instruct me in such country matters as I wanted to know.—Mr. Wilson brought his wife to see us, and she became so fond of Mrs. Dennison, that she said she was never so happy as when she enjoyed the benefit of her conversation.—She was then a fine

1. Household servant.
2. A cow bred or kept for milking
3. Parish priest.

buxom country lass, exceedingly docile, and as good-natured as her husband Jack Wilson; so that a friendship ensued among the women, which hath continued to this day.

"As for Jack, he hath been my constant companion, counsellor, and commissary.[4]—I would not for a hundred pounds you should leave my house without seeing him.——Jack is an universal genius—his talents are really astonishing—He is an excellent carpenter, joiner, and turner,[5] and a cunning artist in iron and brass.—He not only superintended my œconomy, but also presided over my pastimes.—He taught me to brew beer, to make cyder, perry, mead, usquebaugh, and plague-water; to cook several outlandish delicacies, such as *ollas, pepper-pots, pillaws, corys, chabobs*, and *stufatas*[6]—He understands all manner of games from chess down to chuck-farthing, sings a good song, plays upon the violin, and dances a hornpipe[7] with surprising agility.—He and I walked, and rode, and hunted, and fished together, without minding the vicissitudes of the weather; and I am persuaded, that in a raw, moist climate, like this of England, continual exercise is as necessary as food to the preservation of the individual.—In the course of two and twenty years, there has not been one hour's interruption or abatement in the friendship subsisting between Wilson's family and mine; and, what is a rare instance of good fortune, that friendship is continued to our children.—His son and mine are nearly of the same age and the same disposition; they have been bred up together at the same school and college, and love each other with the warmest affection.

"By Wilson's means, I likewise formed an acquaintance with a sensible physician, who lives in the next market-town; and his sister, an agreeable old maiden, passed the Christmas holidays at our house.—Mean while I began my farming with great eagerness, and that very winter planted these groves that please you so much.—As for the neighbouring gentry, I had no trouble from that quarter during my first campaign; they were all gone to town before I settled in the country; and by the summer I had taken measures to defend myself from their attacks.—When a gay equipage came to my gates, I was never at home; those who visited me in a modest

---

4. Someone commissioned to act as a representative.
5. Someone skilled at using a lathe. "Joiner": a woodworker who does lighter or more ornamental work than a carpenter.
6. Stews (from the Italian). "Usquebaugh": usually whiskey, but here may mean a drink composed of brandy, licorice, dried fruits, and spices because whiskey requires distillation (unlike the other drinks listed). "Pepper-pots": West Indian dishes that include red peppers and other spices cooked with meat and fish. "Pillaws": or pilaus; South Asian dishes consisting of rice cooked with spices and usually meats. "Corys": probably curries, highly spiced East Indian dishes of rice with various meats, vegetables, or seafoods served over it. "Chabobs": kabobs, meats and vegetables broiled on skewers.
7. A general term for a variety of vigorous dances associated with sailors. "Chuck-farthing": a game that involves attempting to toss a small coin into a hole in the ground.

way, I received; and according to the remarks I made on their characters and conversation, either rejected their advances, or returned
their civility.—I was in general despised among the fashionable
company, as a low fellow, both in breeding and circumstances; nevertheless, I found a few individuals of moderate fortune, who gladly
adopted my stile of living; and many others would have acceded to
our society, had they not been prevented by the pride, envy, and
ambition of their wives and daughters.—Those, in times of luxury
and dissipation, are the rocks upon which all the small estates in
the country are wrecked.

"I reserved in my own hands, some acres of ground adjacent to
the house, for making experiments in agriculture, according to the
directions of Lyle, Tull, Hart, Duhamel,[8] and others who have written on this subject; and qualified their theory with the practical
observations of farmer Bland, who was my great master in the art of
husbandry.——In short, I became enamoured of a country life; and
my success greatly exceeded my expectation.——I drained bogs,
burned heath, grubbed up furze and fern; I planted copse and wil-
lows where nothing else would grow; I gradually inclosed all my
farms, and made such improvements, that my estate now yields me
clear twelve hundred pounds a year.—All this time my wife and I
have enjoyed uninterrupted health, and a regular flow of spirits,
except on a very few occasions, when our chearfulness was invaded
by such accidents as are inseparable from the condition of life.—I
lost two children in their infancy, by the small-pox, so that I have
one son only, in whom all our hopes are centred.—He went yesterday to visit a friend, with whom he has stayed all night, but he will
be here to dinner.—I shall this day have the pleasure of presenting
him to you and your family; and I flatter myself you will find him
not altogether unworthy of our affection.

"The truth is, either I am blinded by the partiality of a parent, or
he is a boy of a very amiable character; and yet his conduct has
given us unspeakable disquiet.—You must know, we had projected
a match between him and a gentleman's daughter in the next
county, who will in all probability be heiress of a considerable fortune; but, it seems, he had a personal disgust to the alliance.—He
was then at Cambridge, and tried to gain time on various pretences;
but being pressed in letters by his mother and me to give a definitive answer, he fairly gave his tutor the slip, and disappeared about
eight months ago.—Before he took this rash step, he wrote me a

8. Henri Louis Duhamel du Monceau (1700–1781) wrote *The Elements of Agriculture*
(trans. 1764). Edward Lisle (ca. 1667–1772) was the author of *Observations in Husbandry* (1756). Jethro Tull (1674–1714) was a pioneer in the modernization of farming
who invented several agricultural machines and wrote *Horseshoeing Husbandry* (1731).
Walter Harte (1709–1774) wrote *Essays on Husbandry* (1764).

letter, explaining his objections to the match, and declaring, that he would keep himself concealed until he should understand that his parents would dispense with his contracting an engagement that must make him miserable for life, and he prescribed the form of advertising in a certain newspaper, by which he might be apprized of our sentiments on this subject.

"You may easily conceive how much we were alarmed and afflicted by this elopement, which he had made without dropping the least hint to his companion Charles Wilson, who belonged to the same college.—We resolved to punish him with the appearance of neglect, in hopes that he would return of his own accord; but he maintained his purpose till the young lady chose a partner for herself; then he produced himself, and made his peace by the mediation of Wilson.— Suppose we should unite our families by joining him with your niece, who is one of the most lovely creatures I ever beheld.—My wife is already as fond of her as if she were her own child, and I have a pre-sentiment that my son will be captivated by her at first sight." "Noth-ing could be more agreeable to all our family (said I) than such an alliance; but, my dear friend, candour obliges me to tell you, that I am afraid Liddy's heart is not wholly disengaged——there is a cursed obstacle——" "You mean the young stroller at Gloucester (said he)—You are surprised that I should know this circumstance; but you will be more surprised when I tell you that stroller is no other than my son George Dennison—That was the character he assumed in his eclipse." "I am, indeed, astonished and overjoyed, (cried I) and shall be happy beyond expression to see your proposal take effect."

He then gave me to understand that the young gentleman, at his emerging from concealment, had disclosed his passion for Miss Melford, the niece of Mr. Bramble of Monmouthshire. Though Mr. Dennison little dreamed that this was his old friend Matthew Loyd, he nevertheless furnished his son with proper credentials, and he had been at Bath, London, and many other places in quest of us, to make himself and his pretensions known.—The bad success of his enquiry had such an effect upon his spirits, that immediately at his return he was seized with a dangerous fever, which overwhelmed his parents with terror and affliction; but he was now happily recov-ered, though still weak and disconsolate. My nephew joining us in our walk, I informed him of these circumstances, with which he was wonderfully pleased. He declared he would promote the match to the utmost of his power, and that he longed to embrace young Mr. Dennison as his friend and brother.—Mean while, the father went to desire his wife to communicate this discovery gradually to Liddy, that her delicate nerves might not suffer too sudden a shock; and I imparted the particulars to my sister Tabby, who expressed some surprize, not altogether unmixed, I believe, with an emotion of envy; for, though she could have no objection to an alliance at once so honourable and advantageous, she hesitated in giving her consent, on pretence of the youth and inexperience of the parties: at length, however, she acquiesced, in consequence of having consulted with captain Lismahago.

Mr. Dennison took care to be in the way when his son arrived at the gate, and, without giving him time or opportunity to make any enquiry about the strangers, brought him up stairs to be presented to Mr. Loyd and his family—The first person he saw, when he entered the room, was Liddy, who, notwithstanding all her preparation, stood trembling in the utmost confusion—At sight of this object he was fixed motionless to the floor, and, gazing at her with the utmost eagerness of astonishment, exclaimed, "Sacred heaven! what is this!—ha! wherefore—." Here his speech failing, he stood straining his eyes, in the most emphatic silence—"George (said his father) this is my friend Mr. Loyd." Roused at this intimation, he turned and received my salute, when I said, "Young gentleman, if you had trusted me with your secret at our last meeting, we should have parted upon better terms." Before he could make any answer, Jery came round and stood before him with open arms.—At first, he started and changed colour; but after a short pause, he rushed into his embrace, and they hugged one another as if they had been intimate friends from their infancy: then he payed his respects to Mrs. Tabitha, and advancing to Liddy, "Is it possible, (cried he) that my senses do not play me false!—that I see Miss Melford under my father's roof—that I am permitted to speak to her without giving offence—and that her relations have honoured me with their countenance and protection." Liddy blushed, and trembled, and faultered—"To be sure, sir, (said she) it is a very surprising circumstance——a great—a providential——I really know not what I say—but I beg you will think I have said what's agreeable."

Mrs. Dennison interposing said, "Compose yourselves, my dear children.—Your mutual happiness shall be our peculiar care." The son going up to his mother, kissed one hand; my niece bathed the other with her tears; and the good old lady pressed them both in their turns to her breast.—The lovers were too much affected to get rid of their embarrassment for one day; but the scene was much enlivened by the arrival of Jack Wilson, who brought, as usual, some game of his own killing——His honest countenance was a good letter of recommendation.—I received him like a dear friend after a long separation; and I could not help wondering to see him shake Jery by the hand as an old acquaintance.——They had, indeed, been acquainted some days, in consequence of a diverting incident, which I shall explain at meeting.—That same night a consultation was held upon the concerns of the lovers, when the match was formally agreed to, and all the marriage-articles were settled without the least dispute.—My nephew and I promised to make Liddy's fortune five thousand pounds. Mr. Dennison declared, he would make over one half of his estate immediately to his son, and that his daughter-in-law should be secured in a jointure[9] of four hundred.—Tabby proposed, that, considering their youth, they should undergo one year at least of probation before the indissoluble knot should be tied; but the young gentleman being very impatient and importunate, and the scheme implying that the young couple should live in the house, under the wings of his parents, we resolved to make them happy without further delay.

As the law requires that the parties should be some weeks resident in the parish,[1] we shall stay here till the ceremony is performed.——Mr. Lismahago requests that he may take the benefit of the same occasion; so that next Sunday the banns will be published for all four together.—I doubt, I shall not be able to pass my Christmas with you at Brambleton-hall.—Indeed, I am so agreeably situated in this place, that I have no desire to shift my quarters; and I foresee, that when the day of separation comes, there will be abundance of sorrow on all sides.—In the mean time, we must make the most of those blessings which Heaven bestows.—Considering how you are tethered by your profession, I cannot hope to see you so far from home; yet the distance does not exceed a summer-day's journey, and Charles Dennison, who desires to be remembered to you, would be rejoiced to see his old compotator;[2] but as I am now stationary, I expect regular answers to the epistles of

Yours invariably,

Oct. 11.   MATT BRAMBLE.

To Sir WATKIN PHILLIPS, Bar[t]. at Oxon.

DEAR WAT,

Every day is now big with incident and discovery——Young Mr. Dennison proves to be no other than that identical person whom I have execrated so long, under the name of Wilson—He had eloped from college at Cambridge, to avoid a match that he detested, and

---

9. An estate or property legally settled on a woman upon her marriage that would still be owned by her after her husband's death. "Make over": sign over or grant.
1. In fact, even after the Marriage Act of 1753, only one member of the couple needed to be a resident of the parish in which the marriage was to take place.
2. Drinking companion.

acted in different parts of the country as a stroller,[3] until the lady in question made choice of a husband for herself; then he returned to his father, and disclosed his passion for Liddy, which met with the approbation of his parents, though the father little imagined that Mr. Bramble was his old companion Matthew Loyd. The young gentleman, being impowered to make honourable proposals to my uncle and me, had been in search of us all over England, without effect; and he it was whom I had seen pass on horseback by the window of the inn, where I stood with my sister, but he little dreamed that we were in the house—As for the real Mr. Wilson, whom I called forth to combat, by mistake, he is the neighbour and intimate friend of old Mr. Dennison, and this connexion had suggested to the son the idea of taking that name while he remained in obscurity.

You may easily conceive what pleasure I must have felt on discovering that the honour of our family was in no danger from the conduct of a sister, whom I love with uncommon affection; that, instead of debasing her sentiments and views to a wretched stroller, she had really captivated the heart of a gentleman, her equal in rank and superior in fortune; and that, as his parents approved of his attachment, I was on the eve of acquiring a brother-in-law so worthy of my friendship and esteem. George Dennison is, without all question, one of the most accomplished young fellows in England. His person is at once elegant and manly, and his understanding highly cultivated. Tho' his spirit is lofty, his heart is kind; and his manner so engaging, as to command veneration and love, even from malice and indifference. When I weigh my own character with his, I am ashamed to find myself so light in the balance; but the comparison excites no envy—I propose him as a model for imitation—I have endeavoured to recommend myself to his friendship, and hope I have already found a place in his affection. I am, however, mortified to reflect what flagrant injustice we every day commit, and what absurd judgment we form, in viewing objects through the falsifying medium of prejudice and passion. Had you asked me a few days ago, the picture of Wilson the player, I should have drawn a portrait very unlike the real person and character of George Dennison— Without all doubt, the greatest advantage acquired in travelling and perusing mankind in the original, is that of dispelling those shameful clouds that darken the faculties of the mind, preventing it from judging with candour and precision.

The real Wilson is a great original, and the best tempered, companionable man I ever knew—I question if ever he was angry or low-spirited in his life. He makes no pretensions to letters; but he is an adept in every thing else that can be either useful or entertaining.

3. Wanderer, vagrant, or itinerant performer.

Among other qualifications, he is a complete sportsman, and counted the best shot in the county. He and Dennison, and Lismahago and I, attended by Clinker, went a-shooting yesterday, and made great havock among the partridges—To-morrow we shall take the field against the wood-cocks and snipes. In the evening we dance and sing, or play at commerce, loo, and quadrille.[4]

Mr. Dennison is an elegant poet, and has written some detached pieces on the subject of his passion for Liddy, which must be very flattering to the vanity of a young woman—Perhaps he is one of the greatest theatrical geniuses that ever appeared. He sometimes entertains us with reciting favourite speeches from our best plays. We are resolved to convert the great hall into a theatre, and get up the *Beaux Stratagem* without delay—I think I shall make no contemptible figure in the character of *Scrub*; and Lismahago will be very great in *Captain Gibbet*[5]—Wilson undertakes to entertain the country people with *Harlequin Skeleton*,[6] for which he has got a jacket ready painted with his own hand.

Our society is really enchanting. Even the severity of Lismahago relaxes, and the vinegar of Mrs. Tabby is remarkably dulcified,[7] ever since it was agreed that she should take precedency of her niece in being first noosed: for, you must know, the day is fixed for Liddy's marriage; and the banns for both couples have been already once published in the parish church. The Captain earnestly begged that one trouble might serve for all, and Tabitha assented with a vile affectation of reluctance. Her inamorato, who came hither very slenderly equipt, has sent for his baggage to London, which, in all probability, will not arrive in time for the wedding; but it is of no great consequence, as every thing is to be transacted with the utmost privacy—Meanwhile, directions are given for making out the contracts of marriage, which are very favourable for both females; Liddy will be secured in a good jointure; and her aunt will remain mistress of her own fortune, except one half of the interest, which her husband shall have a right to enjoy for his natural life: I think this is as little in conscience as can be done for a man who yokes with such a partner for life.

These expectants seem to be so happy, that if Mr. Dennison had an agreeable daughter, I believe I should be for making the third couple in this country dance. The humour seems to be infectious; for Clinker, alias Loyd, has a month's mind[8] to play the fool, in the

---

4. Popular 18th-century card games.
5. Scrub is a servant and Captain Gibbet a highwayman in Farquhar's play.
6. The subtitle of a popular comic play, *The Royal Chace; or Merlin's Cave* (1739), by Edward Philips.
7. Sweetened.
8. A strong inclination. A proverbial expression derived from the Catholic tradition of saying mass for a deceased person one month after her or his death.

same fashion, with Mrs. Winifred Jenkins. He has even sounded me on the subject; but I have given him no encouragement to prosecute this scheme—I told him I thought he might do better, as there was no engagement nor promise subsisting; that I did not know what designs my uncle might have formed for his advantage; but I was of opinion, that he should not, at present, run the risque of disobliging him by any premature application of this nature——Honest Humphry protested he would suffer death sooner than do or say any thing that should give offence to the 'squire: but he owned he had a kindness for the young woman, and had reason to think she looked upon him with a favourable eye; that he considered this mutual manifestation of good will, as an engagement understood, which ought to be binding to the conscience of an honest man; and he hoped the 'squire and I would be of the same opinion, when we should be at leisure to bestow any thought about the matter—I believe he is in the right; and we shall find time to take his case into consideration—You see we are fixed for some weeks at least, and as you have had a long respite, I hope you will begin immediately to discharge the arrears due to

Your affectionate,

Oct. 14.   J. MELFORD.

To Miss LÆTITIA WILLIS, at Gloucester.

MY DEAR, DEAR LETTY,

Never did I sit down to write in such agitation as I now feel—In the course of a few days, we have met with a number of incidents so wonderful and interesting, that all my ideas are thrown into confusion and perplexity—You must not expect either method or coherence in what I am going to relate—my dearest Willis. Since my last, the aspect of affairs is totally changed!—and so changed!—but, I would fain give you a regular detail—In passing a river, about eight days ago, our coach was overturned, and some of us narrowly escaped with life—My uncle had well nigh perished—O Heaven, I cannot reflect upon that circumstance without horror—I should have lost my best friend, my father and protector, but for the resolution and activity of his servant Humphry Clinker, whom Providence really seems to have placed near him for the necessity of this occasion.—I would not be thought superstitious; but surely he acted from a stronger impulse than common fidelity—Was it not the voice of nature that loudly called upon him to save the life of his own father? for, O Letty, it was discovered that Humphry Clinker was my uncle's natural son.

Almost at the same instant, a gentleman, who came to offer us his assistance, and invite us to his house, turned out to be a very old friend of Mr. Bramble—His name is Mr. Dennison, one of the worthiest men living; and his lady is a perfect saint upon earth. They have an only son—who do you think is this only son?—O Letty!—O gracious heaven! how my heart palpitates, when I tell you that this only son of Mr. Dennison, is that very identical youth who, under the name of Wilson, has made such ravage in my heart!—Yes, my dear friend! Wilson and I are now lodged in the same house, and converse together freely—His father approves of his sentiments in my favour; his mother loves me with all the tenderness of a parent; my uncle, my aunt, and my brother, no longer oppose my inclinations—On the contrary, they have agreed to make us happy without delay; and in three weeks or a month, if no unforeseen accident intervenes, your friend Lydia Melford, will have changed her name and condition—I say, if no accident *intervenes*, because such a torrent of success makes me tremble!—I wish there may not be something treacherous in this sudden reconciliation of fortune—I have no merit—I have no title to such felicity! Far from enjoying the prospect that lies before me, my mind is harrassed with a continued tumult, made up of hopes and wishes, doubts and apprehensions—I can neither eat nor sleep, and my spirits are in perpetual flutter.—I more than ever feel that vacancy in my heart, which your presence alone can fill.—The mind, in every disquiet, seeks to repose itself on the bosom of a friend; and this is such a trial as I really know not how to support without your company and counsel—I must therefore, dear Letty, put your friendship to the test—I must beg you will come and do the last offices of maidenhood[9] to your companion Lydia Melford.

This letter goes inclosed in one to our worthy governess, from Mrs. Dennison, entreating her to interpose with your mamma, that you may be allowed to favour us with your company on this occasion; and I flatter myself that no material objection can be made to our request—The distance from hence to Gloucester, does not exceed one hundred miles, and the roads are good.—Mr. Clinker, alias Loyd, shall be sent over to attend your motions—If you step into the post-chaise, with your maid Betty Barker, at seven in the morning, you will arrive by four in the afternoon at the half-way house, where there is good accommodation. There you shall be met by my brother and myself, who will next day conduct you to this place, where, I am sure, you will find yourself perfectly at your ease in the midst of an agreeable society.—Dear Letty, I will take

9. Lydia is asking her friend to come help her prepare for her wedding.

no refusal—if you have any friendship—any humanity—you will come.—I desire that immediate application may be made to your mamma; and that the moment her permission is obtained, you will apprise

Your ever faithful,

Oct. 14.   LYDIA MELFORD.

To Mrs. JERMYN, at her house in Gloucester.

DEAR MADAM,

Though I was not so fortunate as to be favoured with an answer to the letter with which I troubled you in the spring, I still flatter myself that you retain some regard for me and my concerns. I am sure the care and tenderness with which I was treated, under your roof and tuition, demand the warmest returns of gratitude and affection on my part, and these sentiments, I hope, I shall cherish to my dying day—At present, I think it my duty to make you acquainted with the happy issue of that indiscretion by which I incurred your displeasure.—Ah! madam, the slighted Wilson is metamorphosed into George Dennison, only son and heir of a gentleman, whose character is second to none in England, as you may understand upon inquiry. My guardians, my brother and I, are now in his house; and an immediate union of the two families is to take place in the persons of the young gentleman and your poor Lydia Melford.— You will easily conceive how embarrassing this situation must be to a young inexperienced creature like me, of weak nerves and strong apprehensions; and how much the presence of a friend and confidante would encourage and support me on this occasion. You know, that of all the young ladies, Miss Willis was she that possessed the greatest share of my confidence and affection; and, therefore, I fervently wish to have the happiness of her company at this interesting crisis.

Mrs. Dennison, who is the object of universal love and esteem, has, at my request, written to you on this subject, and I now beg leave to reinforce her sollicitation.—My dear Mrs. Jermyn! my ever honoured governess! let me conjure you by that fondness which once distinguished your favourite Liddy! by that benevolence of heart which disposes you to promote the happiness of your fellow-creatures in general! lend a favourable ear to my petition, and use your influence with Letty's mamma, that my most earnest desire may be gratified. Should I be indulged in this particular, I will engage to return her safe, and even to accompany her to Glocester, where, if you will give me leave, I will present to you, under another name,

Dear madam,

Your most affectionate

humble servant,

and penitent,

Oct. 14.   LYDIA MELFORD.

To Mrs. MARY JONES, at Brambleton-hall.

O MARY JONES! MARY JONES!

I have met with so many axidents, suprisals, and terrifications, that I am in a parfeck fantigo, and believe I shall never be my own self again. Last week I was dragged out of a river like a drowned rat, and lost a bran-new night-cap, with a sulfur stay-hook, that cost me a good half-a-crown, and an odd shoe of green gallow monkey; besides wetting my cloaths and taring my smuck, and an ugly gash made in the back part of my thy, by the stump of a tree—To be sure Mr. Clinker tuck me out of the cox; but he left me on my back in the water, to go to the 'squire; and I mought have had a watry grave, if a millar had not brought me to the dry land—But, O! what choppings and changes girl—The player man that came after miss Liddy, and frightened me with a beard at Bristol Well, is now matthewmurphy'd into a fine young gentleman, son and hare of 'squire Dollison—We are all together in the same house, and all parties have agreed to the match, and in a fortnite the surrymony will be preformed.

But this is not the only wedding we are to have—Mistriss is resolved to have the same frolick, in the naam of God! Last Sunday in the parish crutch, if my own ars may be trusted, the clerk called the banes of marridge betwixt Opaniah Lashmeheygo, and Tapitha Brample, spinster; he mought as well have called her inkle-weaver, for she never spun and hank of yarn in her life—Young 'squire Dollison and miss Liddy make the second kipple; and there might have been a turd, but times are changed with Mr. Clinker—O, Molly! what do'st think? Mr. Clinker is found to be a pye-blow of our own 'squire, and his rite naam is Mr. Mattew Loyd (thof God he nose how that can be); and he is now out of livery, and wares ruffles—but I new him when he was out at elbows, and had not a rag to kiver his pistereroes; so he need not hold his head so high—He is for sartain very umble and compleasant, and purtests as how he has the same regard as before; but that he is no longer his own master, and cannot portend to marry without the 'squire's consent—He says we must wait with patience, and trust to Providence, and such nonsense—But if so be as how his regard be the same, why stand shilly shally? Why not strike while the iron is hot, and speak to the 'squire without loss of time?—What subjection can the 'squire make to our coming together?—Thof my father wan't a gentleman, my mother was an honest woman—I did'n't come on the wrong side of the blanket, girl—My parents were marred according to the rights of holy mother crutch, in the face of men and angles—Mark that, Mary Jones.

Mr. Clinker (Loyd I would say) had best look to his tackle—There be other chaps in the market, as the saying is——What would he say if I should except the soot and sarvice of the young 'squire's valley? Mr. Machappy is a gentleman born, and has been abroad in the wars—He has a world of buck laming, and speaks French, and Ditch, and Scotch, and all manner of outlandish lingos; to be sure he's a little the worse for the ware, and is much given to drink; but then he's good-tempered in his liquor, and a prudent woman mought wind him about her finger—But I have no thoughts of him, I'll assure you——I scorn for to do, or to say, or to think any thing that mought give unbreech to Mr. Loyd, without furder occasion—But then I have such vapours, Molly—I sit and cry by myself, and take ass of etida, and smill to burnt fathers, and kindalsnuffs; and I pray constantly for grease, that I may have a glimpse of the new-light, to shew me the way through this wretched veil of tares—And yet, I want for nothing in this family of love, where every sole is so kind and so courteous, that wan would think they are so many saints in haven. Dear Molly, I recommend myself to your prayers, being, with my sarvice to Saul,

your ever loving,

and discounselled friend,

Octr. 14.   WIN. JENKINS.

To Dr. LEWIS.

DEAR DICK,

You cannot imagine what pleasure I have in seeing your hand-writing, after such a long cessation on your side of our correspondence—Yet, Heaven knows, I have often seen your hand-writing with disgust—I mean, when it appeared in abbreviations of apothecary's Latin—I like your hint of making interest for the reversion of the collector's place, for Mr. Lismahago, who is much pleased with the scheme, and presents you with his compliments and best thanks for thinking so kind of his concerns—The man seems to mend, upon further acquaintance. That harsh reserve, which formed a disagreeable husk about his character, begins to peel off in the course of our communication——I have great hopes that he and Tabby will be as happily paired as any two draught animals[1] in the kingdom; and I make no doubt but that he will prove a valuable acquisition to our little society, in the article of conversation, by the fireside in winter.

Your objection to my passing this season of the year at such a distance from home, would have more weight if I did not find myself perfectly at my ease where I am; and my health so much improved, that I am disposed to bid defiance to gout and rheumatism.—I begin to think I have put myself on the superannuated list too soon, and absurdly sought for health in the retreats of laziness—I am persuaded that all valetudinarians are too sedentary, too regular, and too cautious——We should sometimes increase the motion of the machine, to *unclog the wheels of life;*[2] and now and then take a plunge amidst the waves of excess, in order to case-harden the constitution. I have even found a change of company as necessary as a change of air, to promote a vigorous circulation of the spirits, which is the very essence and criterion of good health.

Since my last, I have been performing the duties of friendship, that required a great deal of exercise, from which I hope to derive some benefit—Understanding, by the greatest accident in the world, that Mr. Baynard's wife was dangerously ill of a pleuritic fever,[3] I borrowed Dennison's post-chaise, and went a-cross the country to his habitation, attended only by Loyd (quondam Clinker) on horseback.—As the distance is not above thirty miles, I arrived about four in the afternoon, and meeting the physician at the door, was informed that his patient had just expired.—I was instantly seized with a violent emotion, but it was not grief.—The family being in confusion, I ran up stairs into the chamber, where, indeed, they were all assembled—The aunt stood wringing her hands in a kind of stupefaction of sorrow, but my friend acted all the extravagancies of affliction——He held the body in his arms, and poured forth such a lamentation, that one would have thought he had lost the most amiable consort and valuable companion upon earth.

---

1. Strong working animals used to pull loaded carts, plows, and other implements.
2. An allusion to, or possibly a misquotation of, *The Art of Preserving Health* (1744), a poem by Smollett's friend John Armstrong. The original line is "unloads the wheels of life" (2.261).
3. A fever caused by inflammation of the pleura (lung membranes) associated with respiratory illnesses.

Affection may certainly exist independent of esteem; nay, the same object may be lovely in one respect, and detestable in another—The mind has a surprising faculty of accommodating, and even attaching itself, in such a manner, by dint of use, to things that are in their own nature disagreeable, and even pernicious, that it cannot bear to be delivered from them without reluctance and regret. Baynard was so absorbed in his delirium, that he did not perceive me when I entered, and desired one of the women to conduct the aunt into her own chamber.—At the same time I begged the tutor to withdraw the boy, who stood gaping in a corner, very little affected with the distress of the scene.—These steps being taken, I waited till the first violence of my friend's transport was abated, then disengaged him gently from the melancholy object, and led him by the hand into another apartment; though he struggled so hard, that I was obliged to have recourse to the assistance of his valet de chambre.——In a few minutes, however, he recollected himself, and folding me in his arms, "This (cried he) is a friendly office, indeed!——I know not how you came hither; but, I think, Heaven sent you to prevent my going distracted.—O Matthew! I have lost my dear Harriet!—my poor, gentle, tender creature, that loved me with such warmth and purity of affection—my constant companion of twenty years!—She's gone—she's gone for ever!—Heaven and earth! where is she?—— Death shall not part us!"

So saying, he started up, and could hardly be with-held from returning to the scene we had quitted—You will perceive it would have been very absurd for me to argue with a man that talked so madly.—On all such occasions, the first torrent of passion must be allowed to subside gradually.—I endeavoured to beguile his attention by starting little hints and insinuating other objects of discourse imperceptibly; and being exceedingly pleased in my own mind at this event, I exerted myself with such an extraordinary flow of spirits as was attended with success.——In a few hours, he was calm enough to hear reason, and even to own that Heaven could not have interposed more effectually to rescue him from disgrace and ruin.—That he might not, however, relapse into weaknesses for want of company, I passed the night in his chamber, in a little tent bed[4] brought thither on purpose; and well it was I took this precaution, for he started up in bed several times, and would have played the fool, if I had not been present.

Next day he was in a condition to talk of business, and vested me with full authority over his household, which I began to exercise without loss of time, tho' not before he knew and approved of the scheme I had projected for his advantage.—He would have quitted

4. Cot.

the house immediately; but this retreat I opposed.——Far from encouraging a temporary disgust, which might degenerate into an habitual aversion, I resolved, if possible, to attach him more than ever to his Household Gods.[5]—I gave directions for the funeral to be as private as was consistent with decency; I wrote to London, that an inventory and estimate might be made of the furniture and effects in his town-house, and gave notice to the landlord, that Mr. Baynard should quit the premises at Lady-day;[6] I set a person at work to take account of every thing in the country-house, including horses, carriages, and harness; I settled the young gentleman at a boarding-school, kept by a clergyman in the neighbourhood, and thither he went without reluctance, as soon as he knew that he was to be troubled no more with his tutor, whom we dismissed.—The aunt continued very sullen, and never appeared at table, though Mr. Baynard payed his respects to her every day in her own chamber; there also she held conferences with the waiting-women and other servants of the family: but, the moment her niece was interred, she went away in a post-chaise prepared for that purpose: she did not leave the house, however, without giving Mr. Baynard to understand, that the wardrobe of her niece was the perquisite of her woman; accordingly that worthless drab received all the clothes, laces, and linen of her deceased mistress, to the value of five hundred pounds, at a moderate computation.

The next step I took was to disband that legion of supernumerary domestics,[7] who had preyed so long upon the vitals of my friend: a parcel of idle drones, so intolerably insolent, that they even treated their own master with the most contemptuous neglect. They had been generally hired by his wife, according to the recommendation of her woman, and these were the only patrons to whom they payed the least deference. I had therefore uncommon satisfaction in clearing the house of those vermin. The woman of the deceased, and a chambermaid, a valet de chambre, a butler, a French cook, a master gardener, two footmen, and a coachman, I payed off, and turned out of the house immediately, paying to each a month's wages in lieu of warning. Those whom I retained, consisted of a female cook, who had been assistant to the Frenchman, a house maid, an old lacquey, a postilion, and under-gardener. Thus I removed at once a huge mountain of expence and care from the shoulders of my friend, who could hardly believe the evidence of his own senses, when he

5. The particular gods worshiped by each Roman household; at the time, an informal expression referring to the essentials of domestic life.
6. A day kept by some Christians to memorialize events in the life of the Virgin Mary. There are only two in the Anglican Church's calendar: the Purification (February 2) and the Annunciation (March 25). The latter, also traditionally a day for renewing or canceling leases in Britain, is clearly meant here.
7. Unnecessary household servants.

found himself so suddenly and so effectually relieved. His heart, however, was still subject to vibrations of tenderness, which returned at certain intervals, extorting sighs, and tears, and exclamations of grief and impatience: but these fits grew every day less violent and less frequent, 'till at length his reason obtained a complete victory over the infirmities of his nature.

Upon an accurate inquiry into the state of his affairs, I find his debts amount to twenty thousand pounds, for eighteen thousand pounds of which sum his estate is mortgaged; and as he pays five per cent. interest, and some of his farms are unoccupied, he does not receive above two hundred pounds a year clear from his lands, over and above the interest of his wife's fortune, which produced eight hundred pounds annually. For lightening this heavy burthen, I devised the following expedient.—His wife's jewels, together with his superfluous plate and furniture in both houses, his horses and carriages, which are already advertised to be sold by auction, will, according to the estimate, produce two thousand five hundred pounds in ready money, with which the debt will be immediately reduced to eighteen thousand pounds—I have undertaken to find him ten thousand pounds at four per cent. by which means he will save one hundred a-year in the article of interest, and perhaps we shall be able to borrow the other eight thousand on the same terms. According to his own scheme of a country life, he says he can live comfortably for three hundred pounds a year; but, as he has a son to educate, we will allow him five hundred; then there will be an accumulating fund of seven hundred a-year, principal and interest, to pay off the incumbrance; and, I think, we may modestly add three hundred, on the presumption of new-leasing and improving the vacant farms: so that, in a couple of years, I suppose there will be above a thousand a-year appropriated to liquidate a debt of sixteen thousand.

We forthwith began to class and set apart the articles designed for sale, under the direction of an upholder[8] from London; and, that nobody in the house might be idle, commenced our reformation without doors, as well as within. With Baynard's good leave, I ordered the gardner to turn the rivulet into its old channel, to refresh the fainting Naiads,[9] who had so long languished among mouldring roots, withered leaves, and dry pebbles.—The shrubbery is condemned to extirpation; and the pleasure-ground will be restored to its original use of corn-field and pasture.—Orders are given for rebuilding the walls of the garden at the back of the house, and for planting clumps of firs, intermingled with beech and chesnut, at the

---

8. A dealer in small, often secondhand goods.
9. In classical mythology, these were nymphs of the rivers and streams.

east end, which is now quite exposed to the surly blasts that come from that quarter. All these works being actually begun, and the house and auction left to the care and management of a reputable attorney, I brought Baynard along with me in the chaise, and made him acquainted with Dennison, whose goodness of heart would not fail to engage his esteem and affection.—He is indeed charmed with our society in general, and declares that he never saw the theory of true pleasure reduced to practice before.—I really believe it would not be an easy task to find such a number of individuals assembled under one roof, more happy than we are at present.

I must tell you, however, in confidence, I suspect Tabby of tergiversation.[1]—I have been so long accustomed to that original, that I know all the caprices of her heart, and can often perceive her designs while they are yet in embrio—She attached herself to Lismahago for no other reason but that she despaired of making a more agreeable conquest.—At present, if I am not much mistaken in my observation, she would gladly convert the widowhood of Baynard to her own advantage.—Since he arrived, she has behaved very coldly to the captain, and strove to fasten on the other's heart, with the hooks of over-strained civility.—These must be the instinctive efforts of her constitution, rather than the effects of any deliberate design; for matters are carried to such a length with the lieutenant, that she could not retract with any regard to conscience or reputation. Besides, she will meet with nothing but indifference or aversion on the side of Baynard, who has too much sense to think of such a partner at any time, and too much delicacy to admit a thought of any such connexion at the present juncture—Meanwhile, I have prevailed upon her to let him have four thousand pounds at four per cent, towards paying off his mortgage. Young Dennison has agreed that Liddy's fortune shall be appropriated to the same purpose, on the same terms.—His father will sell out three thousand pounds stock for his accommodation.—Farmer Bland has, at the desire of Wilson, undertaken for two thousand; and I must make an effort to advance what further will be required to take my friend out of the hands of the Philistines.[2] He is so pleased with the improvements made on this estate, which is all cultivated like a garden, that he has entered himself as a pupil in farming to Mr. Dennison, and resolved to attach himself wholly to the practice of husbandry.

Every thing is now prepared for our double wedding. The marriage-articles for both couples are drawn and executed; and the ceremony only waits until the parties shall have been resident in the parish the

1. Equivocation; second thoughts.
2. Those lacking cultural or aesthetic refinement (pejorative), from the ancient Philistia people of the eastern Mediterranean coast.

term prescribed by law. Young Dennison betrays some symptoms of impatience; but, Lismahago bears this necessary delay with the temper of a philosopher.—You must know, the captain does not stand altogether on the foundation of personal merit. Besides his half-pay, amounting to two and forty pounds a year, this indefatigable œconomist has amassed eight hundred pounds, which he has secured in the funds. This sum arises partly from his pay's running up while he remained among the Indians; partly from what he received as a consideration for the difference between his full appointment and the half-pay, to which he is now restricted; and partly from the profits of a little traffic he drove in peltry,[3] during his sachemship among the Miamis.

Liddy's fears and perplexities have been much assuaged by the company of one Miss Willis, who had been her intimate companion at the boarding-school. Her parents had been earnestly sollicited to allow her making this friendly visit on such an extraordinary occasion; and two days ago she arrived with her mother, who did not chuse that she should come without a proper gouvernante. The young lady is very sprightly, handsome, and agreeable, and the mother a mighty good sort of a woman; so that their coming adds considerably to our enjoyment. But we shall have a third couple yoked in the matrimonial chain. Mr. Clinker Loyd has made humble remonstrance, through the canal of my nephew, setting forth the sincere love and affection mutually subsisting between him and Mrs. Winifred Jenkins, and praying my consent to their coming together for life. I would have wished that Mr. Clinker had kept out of this scrape; but as the nymph's happiness is at stake, and she has had already some fits in the way of despondence, I, in order to prevent any tragical catastrophe, have given him leave to play the fool, in imitation of his betters; and I suppose we shall in time have a whole litter of his progeny at Brambleton-hall. The fellow is stout and lusty, very sober and conscientious; and the wench seems to be as great an enthusiast in love as in religion.

I wish you would think of employing him some other way, that the parish may not be overstocked—you know he has been bred a farrier, consequently belongs to the faculty; and as he is very docile, I make no doubt but, with your good instruction, he may be, in a little time, qualified to act as a Welsh apothecary. Tabby, who never did a favour with a good grace, has consented, with great reluctance, to this match. Perhaps it hurts her pride, as she now considers Clinker in the light of a relation; but, I believe, her objections are of a more selfish nature. She declares she cannot think of retaining the wife of Matthew Loyd in the character of a servant; and she

---

3. Trade in animal furs and skins.

foresees, that on such an occasion the woman will expect some gratification for her past services. As for Clinker, exclusive of other considerations, he is so trusty, brave, affectionate, and alert, and I owe him such personal obligations, that he merits more than all the indulgence that can possibly be shewn him, by

yours,

Oct. 26.   Matt. Bramble.

To Sir Watkin Phillips, Bar[t]. at Oxon.

Dear Knight,

The fatal knots are now tied. The comedy is near a close; and the curtain is ready to drop: but, the latter scenes of this act I shall recapitulate in order.—About a fortnight ago, my uncle made an excursion across the country, and brought hither a particular friend, one Mr. Baynard, who has just lost his wife, and was for some time disconsolate, though by all accounts he had much more cause for joy than for sorrow at this event.—His countenance, however, clears up apace; and he appears to be a person of rare accomplishments.— But, we have received another still more agreeable reinforcement to our company, by the arrival of Miss Willis from Glocester. She was Liddy's bosom friend at boarding-school, and being earnestly sollicited to assist at the nuptials, her mother was so obliging as to grant my sister's request, and even to come with her in person. Liddy, accompanied by George Dennison and me, gave them the meeting half-way, and next day conducted them hither in safety. Miss Willis is a charming girl, and, in point of disposition, an agreeable contrast to my sister, who is rather too grave and sentimental for my turn of mind.—The other is gay, frank, a little giddy, and always good-humoured. She has, moreover, a genteel fortune, is well born, and remarkably handsome.—Ah Phillips! if these qualities were permanent—if her humour would never change, nor her beauties decay, what efforts would I not make—But these are idle reflections—my destiny must one day be fulfilled.

At present we pass the time as agreeably as we can.—We have got up several farces, which afforded unspeakable entertainment by the effects they produced among the country people, who are admitted to all our exhibitions.—Two nights ago, Jack Wilson acquired great applause in Harlequin Skeleton, and Lismahago surprized us all in the character of Pierot.[4]—His long lank sides, and strong

---

4. I.e., Pierrot; a stock character, often Harlequin's rival, in French pantomime or Italian farce.

marked features, were all peculiarly adapted to his part.——He appeared with a ludicrous stare, from which he had discharged all meaning: he adopted the impressions of fear and amazement so naturally, that many of the audience were infected by his looks; but when the skeleton held him in chace his horror became most divertingly picturesque, and seemed to endow him with such præter-natural agility as confounded all the spectators. It was a lively representation of Death in pursuit of Consumption, and had such an effect upon the commonalty, that some of them shrieked aloud, and others ran out of the hall in the utmost consternation.

This is not the only instance in which the lieutenant has lately excited our wonder. His temper, which had been soured and shrivelled by disappointment and chagrin, is now swelled out, and smoothed like a raisin in plum-porridge. From being reserved and punctilious, he is become easy and obliging. He cracks jokes, laughs and banters, with the most facetious familiarity; and, in a word, enters into all our schemes of merriment and pastime—The other day his baggage arrived in the waggon from London, contained in two large trunks and a long deal box not unlike a coffin. The trunks were filled with his wardrobe, which he displayed for the entertainment of the company, and he freely owned, that it consisted chiefly of the *opima spolia*[5] taken in battle. What he selected for his wedding suit, was a tarnished white cloth faced with blue velvet, embroidered with silver; but, he valued himself most upon a tyeperiwig,[6] in which he had made his first appearance as a lawyer above thirty years ago. This machine had been in buckle[7] ever since, and now all the servants in the family were employed to frizz it out for the occasion, which was yesterday celebrated at the parish church. George Dennison and his bride were distinguished by nothing extraordinary in their apparel. His eyes lightened with eagerness and joy, and she trembled with coyness and confusion. My uncle gave her away, and her friend Willis supported her during the ceremony.

But my aunt and her paramour took the pas,[8] and formed, indeed, such a pair of originals, as, I believe, all England could not parallel. She was dressed in the stile of 1739; and the day being cold, put on a manteel[9] of green velvet laced with gold: but this was taken off by the bridegroom, who threw over her shoulders a fur cloak of American sables, valued at fourscore guineas, a present equally agreeable

---

5. The spoils taken from the enemy's general when slain by the commander of the army himself. Usually the order of words in this phrase is reversed.
6. A wig worn by university graduates, in which the hair was drawn back to form a lock hanging down at the back and tied low with a black ribbon.
7. Kept in a curled state.
8. A step, especially in a dance.
9. A loose cloak or cape.

and unexpected. Thus accoutred, she was led up to the altar by Mr. Dennison, who did the office of her father: Lismahago advanced in the military step with his French coat reaching no farther than the middle of his thigh, his campaign wig that surpasses all description, and a languishing leer upon his countenance, in which there seemed to be something arch and ironical. The ring, which he put upon her finger, he had concealed till the moment it was used. He now produced it with an air of self-complacency. It was a curious antique, set with rose diamonds: he told us afterwards, it had been in his family two hundred years, and was a present from his grandmother. These circumstances agreeably flattered the pride of our aunt Tabitha, which had already found uncommon gratification in the captain's generosity; for he had, in the morning, presented my uncle with a fine bear's skin, and a Spanish fowling-piece, and me with a case of pistols curiously mounted with silver. At the same time he gave Mrs. Jenkins an Indian purse, made of silk grass, containing twenty crown pieces. You must know, this young lady, with the assistance of Mr. Loyd, formed the third couple who yesterday sacrificed to Hymen.[1] I wrote to you in my last, that he had recourse to my mediation, which I employed successfully with my uncle; but Mrs. Tabitha held out 'till the love-sick Jenkins had two fits of the mother;[2] then she relented, and those two cooing turtles were caged for life—Our aunt made an effort of generosity in furnishing the bride with her superfluities of clothes and linen, and her example was followed by my sister; nor did Mr. Bramble and I neglect her on this occasion. It was, indeed, a day of peace offering—Mr. Dennison insisted upon Liddy's accepting two bank notes of one hundred pounds each, as pocket-money; and his lady gave her a diamond necklace of double that value. There was, besides, a mutual exchange of tokens among the individuals of the two families thus happily united.

As George Dennison and his partner were judged improper objects of mirth, Jack Wilson had resolved to execute some jokes on Lismahago, and after supper began to ply him with bumpers,[3] when the ladies had retired; but the captain perceiving his drift, begged for quarter, alledging that the adventure, in which he had engaged, was a very serious matter; and that it would be more the part of a good Christian to pray that he might be strengthened, than to impede his endeavours to finish the adventure.—He was spared accordingly, and permitted to ascend the nuptial couch with all his senses about him.—There he and his consort sat in state, like

1. The Greek god of weddings.
2. Presumably, an emotional spell or attack.
3. Large cups or tankards, usually filled with beer or ale.

Saturn and Cybele, while the benediction-posset[4] was drank; and a cake being broken over the head of Mrs. Tabitha Lismahago, the fragments were distributed among the bystanders, according to the custom of the antient Britons, on the supposition that every person who ate of this hallowed cake, should that night have a vision of the man or woman whom Heaven designed should be his or her wedded mate.

The weight of Wilson's waggery fell upon honest Humphry and his spouse, who were bedded in an upper room, with the usual ceremony of throwing the stocking.—This being performed, and the company withdrawn, a sort of catter-wauling ensued, when Jack found means to introduce a real cat shod with walnut-shells, which galloping along the boards, made such a dreadful noise as effectually discomposed our lovers.——Winifred screamed aloud, and shrunk under the bed-cloaths.—Mr. Loyd, believing that Satan was come to buffet him *in propria persona*,[5] laid aside all carnal thoughts, and began to pray aloud with great fervency.—At length, the poor animal, being more afraid than either, leaped into the bed, and meauled with the most piteous exclamation.—Loyd, thus informed of the nature of the annoyance, rose and set the door wide open, so that this troublesome visitant retreated with great expedition; then securing himself, by means of a double bolt, from a second intrusion, he was left to enjoy his good fortune without further disturbance.

If one may judge from the looks of the parties, they are all very well satisfied with what has passed.—George Dennison and his wife are too delicate to exhibit any strong-marked signs of their mutual satisfaction, but their eyes are sufficiently expressive.—Mrs. Tabitha Lismahago is rather fulsome in signifying her approbation of the captain's love; while his deportment is the very pink of gallantry.— He sighs, and ogles, and languishes at this amiable object; he kisses her hand, mutters ejaculations of rapture, and sings tender airs; and, no doubt, laughs internally at her folly in believing him sincere.— In order to shew how little his vigour was impaired by the fatigues of the preceding day, he this morning danced a Highland sarabrand over a naked back-sword, and leaped so high, that I believe he would make no contemptible figure as a vaulter at Sadler's Wells.[6]—Mr. Matthew Loyd, when asked how he relishes his bargain, throws up his eyes, crying, "For what we have received, Lord make us thankful: amen."——His helpmate giggles, and holds her hand before her

---

4. A traditional drink made of hot milk curdled with ale or wine and flavored with spices. The Roman god Saturn, associated with melancholy, is considered the father of the other deities. Cybele, the goddess of plenty, is considered the mother.
5. In his own person (Latin).
6. A dance theater in Clerkenwell, London, infamous in the 18th century for its tawdry shows. "Sarabande": a vigorous dance in triple meter, usually associated with Spain and Latin America. "Back-sword": a blade with only one cutting edge.

The marriage of Lieutenant Lismahago and Mrs. Tabitha &c. Courtesy of the Center for Southwest Research, University Libraries, University of New Mexico.

eyes, affecting to be ashamed of having been in bed with a man.—
Thus all these widgeons[7] enjoy the novelty of their situation; but,
perhaps their note will be changed, when they are better acquainted
with the nature of the decoy.

As Mrs. Willis cannot be persuaded to stay, and Liddy is engaged
by promise to accompany her daughter back to Gloucester, I fancy
there will be a general migration from hence, and that most of us
will spend the Christmas holidays at Bath; in which case, I shall
certainly find an opportunity to beat up your quarters.—By this
time, I suppose, you are sick of *alma mater*, and even ready to execute that scheme of peregrination, which was last year concerted
between you and

Your affectionate

Nov. 8.   J. MELFORD.

To Dr. LEWIS.

DEAR DOCTOR,

My niece Liddy is now happily settled for life; and captain Lismahago has taken Tabby off my hands; so that I have nothing further
to do, but to comfort my friend Baynard, and provide for my son
Loyd, who is also fairly joined to Mrs. Winifred Jenkins.—You are
an excellent genius at hints.—Dr. Arbuthnot was but a type[8] of Dr.
Lewis in that respect.——What you observe of the vestry-clerk[9]
deserves consideration.—I make no doubt but Matthew Loyd is
well enough qualified for the office; but, at present, you must find
room for him in the house.——His incorruptible honesty and indefatigable care will be serviceable in superintending the œconomy of
my farm; tho' I don't mean that he shall interfere with Barns, of
whom I have no cause to complain.—I am just returned with Baynard, from a second trip to his house, where every thing is regulated
to his satisfaction.—He could not, however, review the apartments
without tears and lamentation, so that he is not yet in a condition
to be left alone; therefore I will not part with him till the spring,
when he intends to plunge into the avocations of husbandry, which
will at once employ and amuse his attention.—Charles Dennison
has promised to stay with him a fortnight, to set him fairly afloat in
his improvements; and Jack Wilson will see him from time to time;

---

7. Wild ducks; here, fools and simpletons.
8. Forerunner. John Arbuthnot (1667–1735) was a well-respected Scottish physician who
   reportedly also gave many authors hints for their works.
9. Clerk or secretary of the local parish vestry, or council of the congregation.

besides, he has a few friends in the country, whom his new plan of life will not exclude from his society.—In less than a year, I make no doubt, but he will find himself perfectly at ease both in his mind and body, for the one had dangerously affected the other; and I shall enjoy the exquisite pleasure of seeing my friend rescued from misery and contempt.

Mrs. Willis being determined to return with her daughter, in a few days, to Gloucester, our plan has undergone some alteration.— Jery has persuaded his brother-in-law to carry his wife to Bath; and I believe his parents will accompany him thither.—For my part, I have no intention to take that route.—It must be something very extraordinary that will induce me to revisit either Bath or London.——My sister and her husband, Baynard and I, will take leave of them at Gloucester, and make the best of our way to Brambleton-hall, where I desire you will prepare a good chine[1] and turkey for our Christmas dinner.——You must also employ your medical skill in defending me from the attacks of the gout, that I may be in good case to receive the rest of our company, who promise to visit us in their return from the Bath.——As I have laid in a considerable stock of health, it is to be hoped you will not have much trouble with me in the way of physic,[2] but I intend to work you on the side of exercise.—I have got an excellent fowling-piece from Mr. Lisma-hago, who is a keen sportsman, and we shall take the heath in all weathers.—That this scheme of life may be prosecuted the more effectually, I intend to renounce all sedentary amusements, partic-ularly that of writing long letters; a resolution, which, had I taken it sooner, might have saved you the trouble which you have lately taken in reading the tedious epistles of

Nov. 20.   MATT. BRAMBLE.

To Mrs. GWYLLIM, at Brambleton-hall.

GOOD MRS. GWILLIM,

Heaven, for wise porpuses, hath ordained that I should change my name and citation in life, so that I am not to be considered any more as manger of my brother's family; but as I cannot surrender up my stewardship till I have settled with you and Williams, I desire you will get your accunts ready for inspection, as we are coming home without further delay.——My spouse, the captain, being sub-ject to rummaticks, I beg you will take great care to have the blew

---

1. A portion of meat or fowl consisting of the backbone and adjoining meat.
2. Medicine.

chamber, up two pair of stairs, well warmed for his reception.—Let the sashes be secured, the crevices stopt, the carpets laid, and the beds well tousled.—Mrs. Loyd, late Jenkins, being married to a relation of the family, cannot remain in the capacity of a sarvant; therefore, I wish you would cast about for some creditable body to be with me in her room—If she can spin, and is mistress of plain-work, so much the better—but she must not expect extravagant wages—having a family of my own, I must be more occumenical than ever. No more at present, but rests

Your loving friend,

Nov. 20.   TAB. LISMAHAGO.

To Mrs. MARY JONES, at Brambleton-hall.

MRS. JONES,

Providinch hath bin pleased to make great halteration in the pasture of our affairs.——We were yesterday three kiple chined, by the grease of God, in the holy bands of mattermoney, and I now subscrive myself Loyd at your sarvice.—All the parish allowed that young 'squire Dallison and his bride was a comely pear for to see.—As for madam Lashmiheygo, you nose her picklearities—her head, to be sure, was fintastical; and her spouse had rapt her with a long marokin furze cloak from the land of the selvidges, thof they say it is of immense bally.—The captain himself had a huge hassock of air, with three tails, and a tumtawdry coat, boddered with sulfur.—Wan said he was a monkey-bank; and the ould bottler swore he was the born imich of Titidall.[3]——For my part, I says nothing, being as how the captain has done the handsome thing by me.—Mr. Loyd was dressed in a lite frog, and checket with gould binding; and thof he don't enter in caparison with great folks of quality, yet he has got as good blood in his veins as arrow privet 'squire in the county; and then his pursing is far from contentible.—Your humble sarvant had on a plain pea-green tabby sack, with my Runnela cap,[4] ruff toupee, and side curls.—They said, I was the very moral of lady Rickmanstone, but not so pale—that may well be, for her layship is my elder by seven good years and more.—Now, Mrs. Mary, our satiety is to suppurate—Mr. Millfart goes to Bath along with the Dallisons, and the rest of us push home to Wales, to pass our Chrishmarsh at

---

3. Probably the devil Titivil, a character in medieval mystery plays. "Monkey bank": mountebank; see n. 4, p. 22
4. I.e., Ranelagh cap: a piece of gauze folded diagonally and tied under the chin, named after the fashionable park in London.

Brampleton hall.—As our apartment is to be the yallow pepper, in the thurd story, pray carry my things thither.——Present my cumpliments to Mrs. Gwyllim, and I hope she and I will live upon dissent terms of civility.—Being, by God's blessing, removed to a higher spear, you'll excuse my being familiar with the lower sarvents of the family; but, as I trust you'll behave respectful, and keep a proper distance, you may always depend upon the good will and purtection of

Yours,

Nov. 20.   W. Loyd.

FINIS.

BACKGROUNDS AND CONTEXTS

TOBIAS SMOLLETT

The Tears of Scotland. Written in the Year 1746 (1746)†

Mourn, hapless Caledonia, mourn
Thy banish'd peace, thy laurels torn!
Thy sons, for valour long renown'd,
Lie slaughter'd on their native ground;
5   Thy hospitable roofs no more
Invite the stranger to the door;
In smoky ruins sunk they lie,
The monuments of cruelty.

The wretched owner sees afar
10 His all become the prey of war;
Bethinks him of his babes and wife,
Then smites his breast and curses life.
Thy swains are famish'd on the rocks,
Where once they fed their wanton flocks:
15 Thy ravish'd virgins shriek in vain;
Thy infants perish on the plain.

What boots it then in every clime,
Through the wild spreading waste of time,
Thy martial glory, crown'd with praise,
20 Still shone with undiminish'd blaze?
Thy tow'ring spirit now is broke,
Thy neck is bended to the yoke.
What foreign arms could never quell,
By civil rage and rancour fell.

25 The rural pipe and merry lay
No more shall cheer the happy day:
No social scenes of gay delight
Beguile the dreary winter night.
No strains but those of sorrow flow,
30 And nought be heard but sounds of woe,

---

† Smollett's first published work, *The Tears of Scotland* was written in the aftermath of the news of the crushing Jacobite defeat at Culloden on April 16, 1746. Its deployment of an unreservedly sentimental vocabulary seems to register the depth of Smollett's feelings at the time. Subsequently, Smollett would publish two well-received satirical poems, "Advice" and "Reproof," before turning almost exclusively to prose. The text here is taken from *The Poetical Works of Tobias Smollett, M.D.* (London: Cooke, n.d.).

While the pale phantoms of the slain
Glide nightly o'er the silent plain.

O baneful cause, Oh! fatal morn,
Accursed to ages yet unborn!
35 The sons against their father stood,
The parent shed his children's blood.
Yet, when the rage of battle ceas'd,
The victor's soul was not appeas'd:
The naked and forlorn must feel
40 Devouring flames, and murd'ring steel!

The pious mother, doom'd to death,
Forsaken wanders o'er the heath,
The bleak wind whistles round her head,
Her helpless orphans cry for bread;
45 Bereft of shelter, food and friend,
She views the shades of night descend:
And stretch'd beneath the inclement skies,
Weeps o'er her tender babe, and dies.

While the warm blood bedews my veins,
50 And unimpair'd remembrance reigns,
Resentment of my country's fate,
Within my filial breast shall beat;
And, spite of her insulting foe,
My sympathizing verse shall flow:
55 "Mourn, hapless Caledonia, mourn
Thy banish'd peace, thy laurels torn."

TOBIAS SMOLLETT

From An Essay on the External Uses of Water, in a Letter to Dr. ****, with Particular Remarks upon the present Method of using the Mineral Waters at Bath in Somersetshire, and Plan for rendering them more safe, agreeable, and efficacious (1752)[†]

Sir,

Since our last conversation, I have been endeavouring to collect and digest my thoughts, touching the external use of Mineral Waters, as comprehended in the three several articles of *Pumping, Bathing,* and *Fomentation*; but in the course of my reflections, I find the subject cannot be properly discussed within the limits of a small occasional Pamphlet; and, with regard to a compleat system, I have neither time nor opportunity to confirm by experiments, the particular notions I entertain concerning the efficacy of those Waters: Nevertheless, I shall, in compliance with your request, commit to the Public, these opinions, singular as they are, with the reasons on which they are built, in hope that they will prove serviceable hints to those who are better qualified than myself, for prosecuting useful inquiries in the medical world.

* * *

I have known the most sordid and inveterate *scrophulous* and *scorbutic* ulcers cured by the aspersion[1] of common Well-water, which to the taste and smell exhibited no signs of mineral impregnation; but, at first, derived its reputation from the superstition of the people, by whom, in times of ignorance, it had been dedicated to one of the saints of the Roman kalendar. Such cures are undoubtedly performed by the coldness, pressure, and moisture of those waters: the first communicates a spring to the decayed or diseased solids, by which the vessels are enabled to propel their contents, and renew

---

[†] At nearly fifty pages, Smollett's only published medical treatise made a sizable addition to the thriving mid-18th-century market for pamphlets and occasional pieces. Smollett would subsequently write and edit many volumes of prose nonfiction, including his popular *Complete History of England* (1757–58) and the even more ambitious *Present State of All Nations* (1760–68). But his abiding interests in individual mental and physical health are clear from the fact that many of the subjects discussed in this early pamphlet reappear—albeit through the filter of Matt Bramble's idiosyncrasies—in *Humphry Clinker*'s scenes of taking the waters at Bath and elsewhere. The pamphlet assumes the form of a letter, whose addressee has not been identified. The text here is taken from a facsimile edition of the original.

1. Sprinkling or showering. "Scrophulous and scorbutic": caused by tuberculosis and scurvy, respectively. The former refers to swollen neck glands.

the circulation, which had been impeded; the pressure supports the weakened sides of the capillaries or fine lymphatics[2] against the increased momentum of the juices thus set in motion, helping, at the same time, to restrain the *fungous* excrescences, in determining that præternatural *Incrementum*[3] in a lateral direction, by which a re-union of the fibres is effected; and the moisture deterges the ulcer, by washing away the *acrid* matter, which would otherwise *corrode* the parts, and consequently obstruct the cure.

*   *   *

The warm Bath conduces to the restoration of health, by rendring the rigid fibres more pliable and supple; by washing away those unctuous and *acrid* impurities, which are apt to obstruct the pores, corrode the nerves and disorder the perspiration; by enlarging the opening of the cuticular strainer,[4] and inviting the fluids towards the surface; by reviving the natural heat, and causing an *Oscillatory* motion, which will restore to parts that are cold, insensible and contracted, their former warmth, functions and flexibility: and in a languid circulation, proceeding from a *Viscidity* of the juices, the warm bath will be serviceable by increasing the velocity of the blood, which is agitated and attenuated by the rarefaction[5] of the heat within, and the pressure of the Water without the vessels.

From these effects of the warm Bath, it must be salutary in *paralytic Disorders, contracted Sinews, spasmodic Affections* of the *Nerves, hypochondriachal* and *hysterical Cases*, Obstructions of the *Menses, Haemorrhoids* and *Perspiration*; the Scurvy, venereal Distemper, and all diseases, the causes of which are to be discharged through the *Emunctories*[6] of the skin; accordingly there is often an amazing quantity of foul humours, expelled into the *Bath* from this outlet.

*   *   *

[In the complex at Bath], [d]iseased persons of all ages, sexes, and conditions, are promiscuously admitted into an open Bath, which affords little or no shelter from the inclemencies of the weather, such as wind, rain, hail, and snow: for, by the peculiar sagacity of the learned in that place, the bathing time is limited to the most severe season of the year. This being the case, it may reasonably be supposed, that many of the fair sex are withheld by modesty from going into the Bath, where they must not only mingle with male

2. Vessels that contain or convey lymphatic fluids.
3. Unnatural growth.
4. The outermost layer of epidermis.
5. The process of making something less dense.
6. Pores.

patients, to whose persons and complaints they are utter strangers; but, likewise, be exposed in a very mortifying point of view, to the eyes of all the company, in the Pump-room, as well as to those of the footmen and common people, whose curiosity leads them to look over the walls of the Bath: some may be apprehensive of being tainted with infectious distempers; or disgusted with the nauseating appearance of the filth, which, being washed from the bodies of the patients, is left sticking to the sides of the place.

Although the king's and queen's Baths[7] have been known to contain five-and-forty patients at one time, the number of guides does not exceed half a dozen of each sex; so that if any of those Bathers who are unattended should be seized with a sudden *Vertigo*, fit, or other accident, they might lose their lives for want of proper assistance. But, granting no such accident should happen, some of them, on retiring from the Bath, must, from this defect in point of attendance, remain in the wet bathing dress, until their constitutions are greatly endangered. This inconvenience is rendered more grievous by the nature of that dress, which, being made of canvas, grows cold and clammy in a moment, and clings to the surface of the body with a most hazardous adhesion. If they should escape the consequences of both these risques, they may still be subject to another, in being obliged to wait in a cold slip for their respective chairs, which cannot always be brought to them in proper time, because the passage is frequently blocked up. After all, they are carried to their lodgings, while their pores are open from the effects of the Bath, in paultry chairs made of slight cross bars of wood, fastened together with girth web,[8] covered with bays, and, for the most part, destitute of lining: these machines, by standing in the street till called for, are often rendered so damp by the weather, that the Bathers cannot use them without imminent hazard of their lives.

* * *

7. The largest and most popular pools in the complex.
8. An encircling band.

TOBIAS SMOLLETT

From The Briton 1 (May 29, 1762)†

"*Ego semper ea mente fui, ut, quæ utilia æquaque viderentur, con-*
silia de republica afferrem: quad quidem hoc præsertim tempore
facturus sum: in quo si concordiam, adjecta contentione & fastidio,
inter nos confirmabimus, & ipsi incolmes erimus, & alios vel invitos
conservare poterimus."

—Cicero[1]

The Briton thinks it unnecessary to produce himself amidst the
parade of pompous professions, which serve only to excite idle curiosity, and raise expectations which may be attended with disappointment. Neither will he make any apology for thus appearing to
the public view, without the ceremony of a formal introduction: his
intention is not to alarm, but appease; not to puzzle, but explain;
not to inflame, but to allay. His design is that which ought to be the
aim, and is the undoubted privilege of every Briton, to speak his
opinion freely, and offer his advice with decency and candour, on
every subject that concerns the community, of which he is a member; to watch the exertions of power and prerogative; to observe the
tides of popular commotion; to detect the falsehood of malice; to
expose and refute the insinuations of calumny; to pluck the mask of
patriotism from the front of faction, and the torch of discord from
the hand of sedition.

To a merely speculative politician, it will appear scarce credible,
that there should be the least occasion for a task of this nature, at a
period when the Throne is filled with such exalted virtue, as the
poisonous breath of envy cannot taint, as all the tongues of slander
cannot charge with blemish or infirmity: at a period when the councils of the Sovereign are shared among the natural counsellors of
the Crown, a set of noblemen whose abilities are unquestionable,
whose probity is unimpeached: at a period when the administration
is conducted with such integrity as defies reproach; with such vigour
and success as, one would think, might silence the most inveterate
malice: at a period when the whole kingdom echoes with the sound

---

† In the wake of Lord Bute's ongoing unpopularity, Smollett agreed to write a progovern-
ment weekly paper. *The Briton* was published in small folio, costing two pence-
halfpenny for each four-leafed number, the first of which appeared on May 29, 1762.
The text here is taken from a facsimile edition of the original.
1. "I have always intended to produce policies for the republic that would seem fair and
useful; I will do so especially at this time when if we can establish harmony among us,
having cast off discord and disdain, we will both be safe ourselves and be able to save
others despite themselves." Byron Gassman's translation from the Latin, modified by
the editor. According to Gassman, these lines have not been located, despite Smollett's
attribution of them to Cicero, the Roman orator.

of triumph and festivity; and the consummation of national happiness depends, in an especial manner, upon the continuation of national concord.

But as the sun that ripens the peach, and renovates all nature, is also known to exalt the poison of the viper, and hatch every species of vermin that annoys mankind; so extraordinary merit, while it adorns and sustains the common weal, has the particular faculty of generating and inflaming the virulence of envy and all her rancorous attendants.

I was led to this reflection by perusing the last number of a weekly paper, called the Monitor;[2] a paper so devoid of all merit in the execution, that the author, conscious of his own unimportance and incapacity, seems to have had recourse, in despair, to the only expedient which he thought would give him any chance for engaging the attention of the public; to insinuation against the Th—ne, and abuse on the M—y.[3]

* * *

But as there is no slander so bare-faced, as not to produce some effect, and no argument so frail, as not to persuade some well-meaning individuals, whom it may be worth while to undeceive; I shall take the trouble to examine the particulars of his honest essay, and, I doubt not, shall be able to convict the author, not barely of fallacy, but of fraud, not of a weakness only, but of wickedness also.

* * *

In any court of judicature,[4] a general charge, unsupported by evidence, is answered and refuted by general negation. Even where there is a suspicion of guilt, unless that guilt is made manifest by circumstantial proof, the culprit is of course acquitted. Shall the privilege granted to the meanest subject, be refused to the Prince? Shall we upon your unfounded insinuations condemn our So—n,[5] against whom your inventive malice has not been able to collect the least grounds for suspicion? or, would you deprive him of the prerogative, which every prince and every private man enjoys, of forming friendships, of rewarding services, of distinguishing merit? Have you exhibited any specimens of his weakness, of his tyranny, of his having given himself up implicitly to the pernicious counsels of any favourite? Have you adduced one circumstance to render it

2. Issue 357 of *The Monitor*, one of many small-circulation periodicals of its day, is the issue Smollett appears to have in mind; it argued against private interests in government, and strongly suggested that Bute in particular could not be trusted.
3. Throne and monarchy, respectively.
4. Justice.
5. Sovereign.

probable, that any individual has crept into his favour by the vile arts of flattery and vicious complaisance, or to prove, that any favourite has maintained his influence, by discouraging patriotism, rejecting merit, planting the throne with spies, excluding truth from the Royal ear, and sacrificing the good of the public to his own private advantage? If no such circumstances are to be found—if on the contrary our Sovereign's character is in all respects so amiable as to encourage the affection of every one not blasted with envy, not inflamed with rancour: if his heart benevolently sympathises with all children of distress: if his hand is liberally opened to every appearance of merit: if his sole aim is to augment and secure the happiness of his people with the independence of his crown; and he has invariably pursued that aim with prudence, dignity, and resolution: if he has communicated his councils and diffused his confidence among the nobles of the land; among men distinguished by their virtue, capacity and experience, without partiality of favour, without distinction of party: if the person whose character you have defamed and traduced by implication, under the odious title of *favourite*, be a nobleman of unblemished integrity, who attached himself to his Sovereign in his tender years, who helped to form his young mind to virtue, who infused into his heart the principles of a patriot king,[6] directing him to pursuits which were truly royal; if he has ever scorned, and taught his Prince to scorn the vile arts of a sycophant; if, in the execution of his office, he hath ever avoided the least appearance of usurpation, and stood forth among the other servants of the crown, the open steady counsellor of his Sovereign; undisturbed by prejudice, undismayed by clamour.—If all these suppositions are true; and that they are literally true your own heart will declare; what character must you maintain in the opinion of all good men; let me add, in your own opinion? the character of a desperate incendiary, perhaps the partisan and tool of disappointed ambition, endeavouring to depreciate one of the best princes that ever reigned, to defame one of the most upright ministers that ever lived; to embroil a virtuous prince with an affectionate people; to clog the wheels of government at a juncture which is truly critical; and finally, to ruin that commonwealth, which it could not rule.

(To be continued.)

---

6. This phrase was popularized by Bolingbroke in his *On the Idea of a Patriot King* (1749). Smollett is of course alluding to John Stuart, Earl of Bute (1713–1792), who joined the royal household in 1750 and quickly became George III's mentor and closest adviser.

JOHN WILKES

From The North Briton 2 (June 12, 1762)†

"Malé se res habit, cùm, quad VIRTUTE effici debit, intentatur
PECUNIA."

—Cicero[1]

I cannot conceal the joy I feel as a North Briton, and I heartily congratulate my dear countrymen on our having at length accomplished
the great, long-sought and universally national object of all our
wishes, the planting a *Scotsman* at the head of the *English* treasury. I
was indeed before very well pleased with the conduct of the two
other gentlemen at that board, who are likewise natives of our
country; but then they were obliged to serve under a noble Duke of
a peculiar cast,[2] whose views were most evidently neither to enrich
himself, nor to aggrandize us. My joy and exultation are now complete, for I have lived to see my countryman, the Earl of BUTE,
adorned with the most noble order of the *Garter*[3] (which hath been
given to *us* with so sparing a hand, and only for the most brilliant
national services), and presiding over the finances of this kingdom.
This is the post which the prime minister hath generally kept for
himself, and is of the first importance in this country. It must ever be
so in times of war, and above all in this wide-extended but glorious
war, when nearly the sum of twenty millions, will be this year raised
on the subject; though, I thank heaven, but a *fortieth* part of it will be
paid by us. This, I must confess, is matter of still greater triumph to
me; for the poor pittance we pay to the support of the Public, does
not give us even the most distant claim to the disposition of whole,
much less to the most important department of the state, our share
of the legislature being much to our advantage settled at about a
thirteenth, not a *fortieth*.[4] It is clearly then merit, superior to all the
English nobility, which hath raised the Earl of BUTE to the first dig-
nities, and to the power of disposing of so great public treasure.

---

† Smollett and Wilkes were on friendly terms before the latter founded *The North Briton* as
an antigovernment paper supposedly written by a partisan and scheming Scot. Its satirical tone proved highly popular with English readers, and it continued publication long
after Smollett's own venture folded. *The North Briton* 45 contained such vicious attacks
on King George III that Wilkes was charged with libel and briefly imprisoned in the
Tower of London. The text here is corrected from a facsimile edition of the original.
1. From Cicero's *De Officiis* (2.6): "For things are in a bad way, when what should be
achieved by merit, is attempted by money." Editor's translation (from the Latin), with
assistance from Andy Hahn and Brett D. Wilson.
2. The Duke of Newcastle. "Two other gentlemen": Gilbert Elliot and James Oswald.
3. Founded in 1348, the Most Noble Order of the Garter is one of the most illustrious
honors in Britain.
4. According to the terms of the 1707 Act of Union, Scotland was represented in the British Parliament by sixteen Lords and forty-five Members of Parliament (MPs).

Another circumstance must make this event peculiarly grateful to us. The Earl of Bute has no *hereditary* right to a seat in parliament, nor is he elected by the free voice of the people: no; he is chosen by the *opulent* and *independent* nobility of Scotland; and when the commons have such various marks of favour and affection shewn to them, it must be a satisfaction to so many *free* and *loyal* nobles to see the object of their choice thus honoured, for all his public toils and *private services*. Our *ancient kingdom* therefore cannot but be satisfied, and by every tie of gratitude, as well as duty, must *now* be fiercely attached to the government. The most suspicious can have no doubt concerning us for the future, in case of a rebellion's springing up in any other country; which to me seems *highly improbable*.

The wisdom of this measure hath been decried by shallow politicians, because two great rebellions from *Scotland* have within a few years disturbed the tranquility of this island, and shook the thrones of two of the mildest and best sovereigns who ever governed a happy people. Nothing can be more weak or frivolous than this objection. * * * I never shall be brought to believe that *rebellion* is natural to any part of *Scotland*, as the plague is said to be to Egypt; *but* certainly in some parts this wicked spirit has been kept up with much art; and the late most unnatural rebellion was carefully nursed by Scotsmen, till it became the most accursed fiend we ever saw, which all the united plagues of Egypt could never equal. I cannot but say, the peculiar baseness and perfidy of my countrymen at that time struck me: for while the *English* were so gallantly fighting for the liberties of Europe, and indeed of mankind, they were called back to deal out halters and gibbets to their fellow subjects of *Scotland*, who were forging chains for both nations; and, worse than the infamous Cappadocians[5] of old, not only refused the liberty they might enjoy themselves, but endeavoured to entail their vassalage and slavery on the whole island.

＊　　＊　　＊

I am happy to find that the *English* are not so sparing and penurious toward us both of money and praise, as they used to be. We are certainly grown into fashion. The most rude of our bards are admired; and I know some choice wits here, who have thrown aside *Shakespeare*, and taken up *Fingal*, charmed with the variety of character, and richness of imagery.

＊　　＊　　＊

5. An ancient people, known for their warlike spirit, who occupied what is now central Turkey.

There are only two other persons I have to recommend to his lordship. I must say a word of the poor BRITON: He deserves something—I will not name what—for sacrificing, at the shrine of BUTE, grammar, conscience, and common sense, for his lordship's *glorification*: I will borrow only one word from the BRITON. Do not I too deserve something for reading every week the flimsy publications from so weak a head?

JOHANN WILHELM von ARCHENHOLZ

From A Picture of England: Containing
a Description of the Laws, Customs,
and Manners of England (1789)†

* * *

Thirty years ago it was difficult to ascertain whether London or Paris was the larger city. Since, however, they have prescribed certain bounds to the latter, which they are not allowed to exceed, and this wise regulation has not yet been adopted in the metropolis of England, which every day receives a new increase of buildings, it cannot now be doubted that the English have the misfortune to possess a capital infinitely more extensive than the French. That which adds not a little to its magnitude, is the great number of large villages, which serve as country houses; and which being incorporated as it were with the suburbs of the town, form with it a monstrous aggregate, to which there are neither limits nor regulations. No less than forty-three thousand new houses were built, between 1762 and 1779.

* * *

For these twenty years past, an actual emigration has taken place from the eastern parts of London toward the western; thousands have left the former, where they do not erect new buildings, for the latter, where the most fertile fields and most agreeable gardens are daily metamorphosed into houses and streets.

---

† In this travel book written in the decade following *Humphry Clinker*, Archenholz—an officer in the Prussian army and later a well-known historian—takes advantage of his outsider's perspective to provide a relatively objective portrait of Britain at the turn of the 19th century. Archenholz's descriptions of London and Westminster as deeply divided, socioeconomically as well as politically, seem to reflect another facet of the social disorder that *Humphry Clinker*'s Bramble identifies all around him in the city. The text here is taken from volume 1, chapter 4, of the English translation from the French (London: Edward Jeffrey, 1789). Thanks to Lee Kahan for suggesting this text's inclusion.

The city, especially the houses along the banks of the Thames, is composed of old ruins: the streets are narrow, obscure, and badly paved: it is the residence of the seamen, of the workmen employed in ship-building, and of a great part of the Jews who reside in London. The contrast betwixt that and the western parts of the metropolis is astonishing: the houses there are almost all new, and of an excellent construction; the squares are magnificent; the streets are built in straight lines, and perfectly well lighted: no city in Europe is better paved. If London were equally well built, no place in the whole world would be comparable to it.

It is a singular circumstance, and one that no traveller has ever remarked, that the western division of London, which is in extent more than half the capital, and which is entirely separated from the city, has not as yet received any name. When the citizens speak of any particular part of it, they content themselves with mentioning the name of the street; and when they talk of the whole, they term it *the other end of the town*. Foreigners and geographers do wrong in calling this prodigious assemblage of streets and squares Westminster: that district does not form a tenth of it; all the rest of it is included in that of Middlesex.

*   *   *

During the fire in 1666, thirty thousand four hundred houses, eighty seven churches, and twenty-six hospitals in the city were consumed by the flames. Of this terrible devastation no trace now remains; but as every person was anxious to rebuild his dwelling house, necessity made them neglect to make the buildings either regular or convenient. From thence proceed the number of ill-formed masses of brick and mortar, dark, and without taste; the crooked and narrow streets, and the obscure situation of the churches and other public edifices: faults which have been carefully avoided in the western part of the capital.

The churches eastward of Temple Bar[1] are heaped upon one another; they have all been rebuilt on their ancient foundations; and one would imagine, from their number, that London was formerly composed of chapels and convents. West of Temple Bar, on the other hand, they are very few: the zeal to lodge themselves seems more to have influenced the inhabitants, than the desire to erect places of worship for the Deity: in some parts, there are six thousand habits to one parish church.

The shops are open by eight o'clock every morning in the city; all is then in motion, everybody is at work; while on the other hand, at

---

1. The place where Fleet Street in the City of London becomes the Strand, Westminster. During the 18th century it was marked by a monumental gate designed by the famous English architect Christopher Wren (1632–1723).

the court end of the town, the streets are empty, the houses shut, and even the very domestics are asleep; the sound of coaches is not heard, and one seems to walk about in a place that has been deserted. This difference, which extends to eating and drinking, amusements, dress, and manner of expression, occasions a kind of hatred between the inhabitants of each. Those in the city charge the people who live at the west end of the town with luxury, idleness, effeminacy, and an attachment to French fashions; while the others speak of a citizen as a dull, fat animal, who places all his merits in his strong box.

But it is more especially when the lord mayor, sheriffs and common council have an audience at St. James's, to present a petition, or compliment his majesty on some great event, that the courtiers attempt to ridicule them. One may easily imagine that a simple tradesman, totally unacquainted with the modes and customs of a court, will not be able to acquit himself on such solemn occasions with the ease of a courtier who has made *etiquette* his chief and his only study, and who looks upon it as the most interesting and the most useful of all accomplishments.

This antipathy is so notorious, that it is mentioned in ballads, noticed on the stage, and is not forgotten even in the parliament itself. In Italy, they would arm themselves with poignards, and spill each other's blood on a similar occasion; but so far from being attended with fatal consequences in England, it serves only to banish the spleen of the nation.

The English nobility generally live three quarters of the year in the country. This ancient custom of staying but a short time in the capital, is the reason why there are so few magnificent mansions in London. It is observed, however, that the metropolis having lately acquired more attractions, people of distinction now reside there longer than they were wont to do: however, they still look on their country seats as their principal habitations.

* * *

CRITICISM

Early Reviews and Criticism

The Critical Review†

Though novels have long since been divested of that extravagance which characterised the earlier productions in Romance, they have, nevertheless, continued, in the hands of meaner writers, to be distinguished by a similarity of fable, which, notwithstanding it is of a different cast, and less unnatural than the former, is still no less unfit for affording agreeable entertainment. From the wild excursions of fancy, invention is brought home to range through the probable occurrences of life; but, however, it may have improved in point of credibility, it is certainly too often deficient with regard to variety of adventure. With many, an adherence to simplicity has produced the effects of dulness; and, with most, too close an imitation of their predecessors has excluded the pleasure of novelty.

The celebrated author of this production is one of those few writers who have discovered an original genius. His novels are not more distinguished for the natural management of the fable, and a fertility of interesting incidents, than for a strong, lively, and picturesque description of characters. The same vigour of imagination that animates his other works, is conspicuous in the present, where we are entertained with a variety of scenes and characters almost unanticipated. Those, in particular, of Mr. Bramble, Mrs. Tabitha Bramble, and lieutenant Lismahago, are painted with the highest touches of discriminating humour and expression. As to Humphry Clinker, he is only to be considered as the nominal hero of the work.

The inimitable descriptions of life, which we have already observed to be so remarkable in our author's works, receive, if possible, an additional force from the epistolary manner, in which this novel is written; which is farther enhanced by the contrast that arises from the general alternate insertion of the letters of the several correspondents.

* * *

† From *The Critical Review* 32 (August 1771): 81–88.

The letters from Mr. Bramble, and Mr. Melford, his nephew, upon their expedition to North Britain, contain so many interesting observations, that they must not only gratify every reader of curiosity, but also tend to correct many wrong notions concerning that part of the island. We would willingly give an account of many of the particulars related of Edinburgh and its inhabitants, but as our readers are probably less acquainted with the manners of the people farther North, we shall extract the representation which is given of the oeconomy in the house of a Highland gentleman.

* * *

We should deprive our readers of a prospect of, perhaps, one of the most beautiful rural scenes that exists in nature, did we not produce the account of the water of Leven, with Dr. Smollett's description of it, in an highly poetical ode. We find, from another passage in the work, that Lough Lomond, from whence the river Leven issues, is a body of pure transparent water, unfathomably deep in many places, six or seven miles broad, and four and twenty miles in length, displaying above twenty green islands, covered with wood; some of them cultivated for corn, and many of them stocked with red deer.

* * *

Instead of visionary scenes and persons, the usual subjects of romance, we are frequently presented with many uncommon anecdotes, and curious exhibitions of real life, described in such a manner as to afford a pleasure even superior to what arises from the portraits of fancy. We are every where entertained with the narration or description of something interesting and extraordinary, calculated at once to amuse the imagination, and release the understanding from prejudice. Upon the whole, the various merit of this production might raise to eminence a writer of inferior reputation to that of its celebrated author; and we should have indulged ourselves in extracting more copiously from it, were we not certain that the original must come into the hands of all such as are readers of taste, by whom we may venture to affirm it will be ranked among the most entertaining performances of the kind.

Gentleman's Magazine[†]

This work is by no means a novel or romance, of which Humphry Clinker is the hero; Humphry makes almost as inconsiderable a

† From *Gentleman's Magazine* 41 (July 1771): 317.

figure in this work as the dog does in the history of Tobit:[1] nor is it indeed principally a narrative of events, but rather a miscellany containing dissertations on various subjects, exhibitions of character, and descriptions of places. Many of the characters are drawn with a free but a masterly hand; in some particulars perhaps they are exaggerated, but are not therefore the less entertaining or instructive: Some appear to be pictures of particular persons, but others of human nature, represented indeed in individuals peculiarly distinguished, but drawn rather from imagination than life. Some, however, are as extravagant as the fancies of Calot,[2] but though they do not less deviate from nature, their irregularities discover the same vivacity and spirit.

In this part of the work consists its principal excellence, and its principal defect is the want of events. The whole story might be told in a few pages, and the author has been so parsimonious of his invention, that he has twice overturned a coach, and twice introduced a fire, to exhibit a scene of ridiculous distress, by setting women on their heads, and making some of his dramatic characters descend from a window by a ladder, as they rose out of bed.

It is by no means deficient in sentiment, and it abounds with satire that is equally sprightly and just. It has, however, blemishes, which would be less regretted where there was less to commend. In the celebrated treatise on the art of sinking in poetry, under the article stile, the incomparable author considers one, which on account of the source whence it is derived, he calls the prurient; there is another stile, which, with respect to its source, may justly be termed the *stercoraceous*. The stercoraceous stile would certainly have found a place in the art of sinking, if had been then to be found in any author not wholly contemptible. But it was not then in being; its original author was Swift, the only writer who had ever made nastiness the vehicle of wit: since his time they have frequently been confounded, and by those who could not distinguish better, the nastiness has been mistaken for the wit: Swift therefore has been imitated in this particular by those who could imitate him in nothing else; and others have, under the sanction of Swift, taken the liberty to be filthy, who were under no necessity to seek occasions for wit in an hospital or a jakes.

The stile of this work is frequently *stercoraceous*, and sometimes it is also *prurient*. The *prurient* however is as harmless as the *stercoraceous*, as it tends much more to chill than to inflame every imagination, except perhaps those of the thieves and bunters in Broad

1. The book of Tobit (or Tobias), part of the Catholic scriptural canon but considered apocryphal by Protestants, features a dog that accompanies the protagonist's son on his journeys.
2. Jacques Callot (ca. 1592–1635) was a French artist who specialized in vivid etchings of both courtly and provincial life.

St. Giles's, to whom the coarsest terms being familiar, they convey sensual ideas without the antidote of disgust.

Among other parts of this work which might have been spared, is the description of several places both in England and Scotland that are well known...

London Magazine[†]

Dr. Smollet's reputation is so justly established, particularly in the walk of novel-writing, that very little need be said to recommend the present performance to the public. Yet, though we have read it with much satisfaction, we cannot pretend to say it is wholly without imperfections: the title is certainly an improper one, because Humphrey [sic] Clinker is one of the least considerable in the whole catalogue of persons; there is besides, no great contrivance in the plan, nor any thing extremely interesting in the incidents. The characters, however, are marked with all that strength of colouring, for which Smollet's pencil is deservedly celebrated; and the reader is either continually entertained with some whimsical relation, or what is still better, instructed with some original remarks upon men and things, that do honour to the good-sense and humanity of the author.

The chief characters of this novel are, Mr. Bramble, a Welch batchellor of great benevolence and extensive understanding: He has a sister, an old maid, the very reverse of himself in the amiable particulars we have mentioned, together with a niece and a nephew both under age, to whom he is guardian. Having a desire for a journey into Scotland, he goes from Bath to London, and thence northwards accompanied by this family and their domestics. Previous to the tour, Miss Melford, his niece, discovers a prepossession for a strolling player, which nearly involves her brother in a duel, and excites the displeasure of her uncle and aunt; but promising never more to hold the smallest intercourse with Mr. Wilson, the actor, she is forgiven, and our travellers proceed in as much harmony as the irascibility of Mrs. Tabitha Bramble will admit, who is generally miserable herself, or endeavoring to make others miserable. On the road, this virago quarrelling with one of the servants, Humphrey Clinker, a poor country fellow, pickt up in a stable-yard, is engaged through necessity in his room; and though at first strongly disliked by the old maid, becomes a remarkable favourite in consequence of being a very warm methodist. The description of Scarborough, Harrowgate, and the various places through which the family pass in their way to Scotland, as well as in their return constitutes from

† From *London Magazine* 40 (June 1771): 317.

this period the chief part of the expedition, and the whole is concluded by a marriage between Miss Melford and Mr. Wilson, who
turns out a gentleman of fortune; with another marriage between
Mr. Tabitha and one Lismahago, a Scotch lieutenant on half pay, a
very extraordinary personage; and a third between Tabitha's woman,
Winifred Jenkins, and Humphrey Clinker, who proves in the catastrophe a natural son to Mr. Bramble.

From these materials the reader will see, that much of the dreadful dangers, the surprizing escapes, the deep distresses, and the
romantic passions which characterize our modern novel-writers, is
not to be expected in this performance; in fact, it is something
greatly preferable to a novel; it is a pleasing, yet an important lesson
on life; and that part of it which describes the Scotch nation, is
at once calculated to entertain the most gay, and to give the most
serious a very useful fund of information.

Monthly Review[†]

Some modern wits appear to have entertained a notion that there is
but one kind of *indecency* in writing; and that, provided they exhibit
nothing of a lascivious nature, they may freely paint, with their
pencils dipt in the most odious materials that can possibly be raked
together for the most filthy and disgusting colouring.—These nasty
geniuses seem to follow their great leader, Swift, only in his obscene
and dirty walks. The present Writer, nevertheless, has humour and
wit, as well as grossness and ill nature.—But we need not enlarge
on his literary character, which is well known to the public. Roderick Random and Peregrine Pickle have long been numbered with
the best of our English romances. His present work, however, is not
equal to these; but it is superior to his Ferdinand Fathom, and perhaps equal to the Adventures of an Atom.

WALTER SCOTT

[Tobias Smollett][‡]

The very ingenious scheme of describing the various effects produced upon different members of the same family by the same
objects, was not original, though it has been supposed to be so.

† From *Monthly Review* 45 (1771): 152.
‡ From Walter Scott, "Prefatory Memoir" to Smollett's *The Expedition of Humphry Clinker*
  (London: Ballantyne, 1821), xxix–xlii.

Anstey,[1] the facetious author of the *New Bath Guide*, had employed it six or seven years before *Humphry Clinker* appeared. But Anstey's diverting satire was but a light sketch, compared to the finished and elaborate manner in which Smollett has, in the first place, identified his characters, and then fitted them with language, sentiments, and powers of observation, in exact correspondence with their talents, temper, condition, and disposition. The portrait of Matthew Bramble, in which Smollett described his own peculiarities, using towards himself the same rigid anatomy which he exercised upon others, is unequalled in the line of fictitious composition. It is peculiarly striking to observe, how often, in admiring the shrewd and sound sense, active benevolence, and honourable sentiments combined in Matthew, we lose sight of the humorous peculiarities of his character, and with what effect they are suddenly recalled to our remembrance, just at the time and in the manner when we least expect them. All shrewish old maids, and simple waiting-women, which shall hereafter be drawn, must be contented with the praise of approaching in merit to Mrs Tabitha Bramble, and Winifred Jenkins. The peculiarities of the hot-headed young Oxonian, and the girlish romance of his sister, are admirably contrasted with the sense, and pettish half-playful misanthropy of their uncle; and Humphry Clinker (who by the way resembles Strap,[2] supposing that excellent person to have a turn towards methodism) is, as far as he goes, equally delightful. Captain Lismahago was probably no violent caricature, allowing for the manners of the time. We can remember a good and gallant officer who was said to have been his prototype, but believe the opinion was only entertained from the striking resemblance which he bore in externals to the doughty captain.

When *Humphry Clinker* appeared in London, the popular odium against the Scotch nation, which Wilkes and Churchill[3] had excited, was not yet appeased, and Smollet had enemies amongst the periodical critics, who failed not to charge him with undue partiality to his own country. They observed, maliciously, but not untruly, that the cynicism of Matthew Bramble becomes gradually softened as he journies northward, and that he who equally detested Bath and London, becomes wonderfully reconciled to walled cities and the hum of men, when he finds himself an inhabitant of the northern metropolis. It is not worth defending so excellent a work against so

---

1. Christopher Anstey (1724–1805), poet and writer best known for his satirical epistolary poem *The New Bath Guide, or Memoirs of the Blunderhead Family* (1766).
2. The servant and traveling companion of the titular character in Smollett's first novel, *The Adventures of Roderick Random* (1748).
3. Charles Churchill (1732–1764) worked with Wilkes on *The North Briton* and also wrote a number of popular and provocative satirical poems, including *The Prophecy of Famine: A Scots Pastoral* (1763).

weak an objection. The author was a dying man, and his thoughts were turned towards the scenes of youthful gaiety and the abode of early friends, with a fond partiality, which, had they been even less deserving of his attachment, would have been not only pardonable, but praiseworthy.

* * *

In leaving Smollett's personal for his literary character, it is impossible not to consider the latter as contrasted with that of his eminent contemporary, Fielding.[4] It is true, that such comparisons, though recommended by the example of Plutarch,[5] are not in general the best mode of estimating individual merit. But in the present case, the history, accomplishments, talents, pursuits, and, unfortunately, the fates of these two great authors, are so closely allied, that it is scarce possible to name the one without exciting recollections of the other. Fielding and Smollett were both born in the highest rank of society, both educated to learned professions, yet both obliged to follow miscellaneous literature as the means of subsistence. Both were confined, during their lives, by the narrowness of their circumstances,—both united a humorous cynicism with generosity and good nature,—both died of the diseases incident to a sedentary life, and to literary labour,—and both drew their last breath in a foreign land, to which they retreated under the adverse circumstances of a decayed constitution, and an exhausted fortune.

Their studies were no less similar than their lives. They both wrote for the stage, and neither of them successfully. They both meddled in politics; they both wrote travels, in which they shewed that their good humour was wasted under the sufferings of their disease; and, to conclude, they were both so eminently successful as novelists, that no other English author of that class has a right to be mentioned in the same breath with Fielding and Smollett.

* * *

In the comic part of their writings, we have already said, Fielding is pre-eminent in grave irony, a Cervantic species of pleasantry, in which Smollett is not equally successful. On the other hand, the Scotchman, (notwithstanding the general opinion denies that quality to his countrymen,) excels in broad and ludicrous humour. His

4. Henry Fielding, author of such well-regarded comic novels as *The History of the Adventures of Joseph Andrews* (1742) and *The History of Tom Jones, Foundling* (1749) as well as many plays and nonfiction pieces. In *Habbakkuk Hilding* (1752), an anonymous pamphlet generally attributed to Smollett, Fielding is grossly attacked and accused of plagiarizing Smollett.
5. Plutarch (ca. 46–120 C.E.), Greek historian and author of *Parallel Lives*, a series of comparative biographies.

fancy seems to run riot in accumulating ridiculous circumstances one upon another, to the utter destruction of all power of gravity; and perhaps no books ever written have excited such peals of inextinguishable laughter as those of Smollett. The descriptions which affect us thus powerfully, border sometimes upon what is called farce or caricature; but if it be the highest praise of pathetic composition that it draws forth tears, why should it not be esteemed the greatest excellence of the ludicrous that it compels laughter? The one tribute is at least as genuine an expression of natural feeling as the other; and he who can read the calamities of Trunnion and Hatchway, when run away with by their mettled steeds, or the inimitable absurdities of the feast of the ancients, without a good hearty burst of honest laughter, must be well qualified to look sad and gentleman-like with Lord Chesterfield or Master Stephen.[6]

Upon the whole, the genius of Smollett may be said to resemble that of Rubens.[7] His pictures are often deficient in grace; sometimes coarse, and even vulgar in conception; deficient too in keeping, and in the due subordination of parts to each other; and intimating too much carelessness on the part of the artist. But these faults are redeemed by such richness and brilliancy of colours; such a profusion of imagination—now bodying forth the grand and terrible—now the natural, the easy, and the ludicrous; there is so much of life, action, and bustle, in every groupe he has painted; so much force and individuality of character, that we readily grant to Smollett an equal rank with his great rival Fielding, while we place both far above any of their successors in the same line of fictitious composition.

6. Not identified. Trunnion and Hatchway are comic characters in Smollett's *The Adventures of Peregrine Pickle* (1751). Philip Dormer Stanhope, fourth Earl of Chesterfield (1694–1773), wrote letters of advice to his son that were published in 1774.
7. Peter Paul Rubens (1577–1640), a Flemish painter noted for the lushness and vitality of his portraits.

Contemporary Criticism

ERIC ROTHSTEIN

Scotophilia and *Humphry Clinker*: The Politics of Beggary, Bugs, and Buttocks[†]

Many scholars have commented on Horace Walpole's words about *Humphry Clinker*: 'a party novel, written by the profligate hireling Smollett, to vindicate the Scots and cry down juries.'[1] Behind Walpole's hyperbole lies fact: Smollett's attempt to wean the English from their inveterate animus against his native land. Habitual scorn had turned into active hatred, fanned by party writers opposed to the court, during the years of Lord Bute's influence, the earlier 1760s. This concentrated attack, I propose, established an agenda for the irenic *Humphry Clinker* (1771) by setting forth a number of topics, charges against the Scots, which Smollett tried to annul or, if possible, to turn to his own persuasive advantage. I am led to this general hypothesis by joining two facts. The first, from the novel itself, sticks in the memory of every reader. When the titular hero comes upon the scene, he is so ragged that his buttocks show through his clothes, thus amusing Jery, entrancing Winifred, and outraging Tabby. He has also been ill and hungry, 'his looks denote famine,' and Tabby sums him up as 'a filthy tatterdemalion . . . [who will] fill the room full of vermin,' a 'mangy hound' (Jery, 24 May).[2] The second fact

---

† From *University of Toronto Quarterly* 52.2 (Fall 1982): 63–78. Reprinted with permission from University of Toronto Press (www.utpjournals.com).

1. Horace Walpole, *Memoirs of the Reign of King George the Third*, ed. Sir Denis Le Marchant, re-ed. G.F. Russell Barker (1894; rpt Freeport, NY: Books for Libraries Press 1970), IV, 218. Walpole's remark has stimulated several responses, the fullest of which is Wolfgang Franke, 'Smollett's *Humphry Clinker* as a "Party Novel",' *Studies in Scottish Literature*, 9 (1971/2), 97–106. Franke mentions eighteenth-century anti-Scots feeling and makes a number of points about *Humphry Clinker*'s Scotophilia, for example that the picture of Scotland is descriptive in the novel and far more nearly complete than the narrative giving a picture of England; he also discusses shifting attitudes towards Lismahago. The political attitudes expressed in *Humphry Clinker* and their relation to Smollett's party writings are taken up by Byron Gassman, 'The Briton and Humphry Clinker,' *Studies in English Literature 1500–1900*, 3 (1963), 397–414.
2. Since at the time of writing no standard edition of *Humphry Clinker* has been published, I have given references to the letters only by author and date. The text for my citations is the Riverside edition edited by André Parreaux (Boston: Houghton Mifflin 1968).

does not stick in the memories of present-day readers but, I suggest, stuck at least in the unconscious memories of readers in Smollett's day. It is that, although Humphry is of English birth, the anti-Scots propaganda of the 1760s made bare buttocks, beggarliness, mange, and filth standard accusations against 'North Britons.'

Some of these accusations, of course, predated the Bute years and even predated the Jacobite Rebellion of 1745, after which, according to Sir Charles Hanbury Williams, the cowardly Scots ran joyfully home 'To beggary, Oatmeal, and Itch.'[3] The itch itself is probably why in the middle of the previous century John Cleveland called Scotland a 'scabbie Land.'[4] From at least as far back as the mid-1670s (in Rochester's 'Tunbridge Wells,' line 113) it had the name 'the Scotch fiddle,' from the bow-like action of the scratching hand or finger. Slightly later in Thomas Durfey's play *The Royalists* (1682) is mentioned Sawny Scrubbam, 'a red-haired *Scotchman*, that will engage upon his honour to give the Itch to a whole Army; and to that degree, that in a short time they shall scratch themselves to Death' (p 48). In domestic animals this itch was called the 'mange,' as Johnson's *Dictionary* and the OED note; hence Tabby's 'mangy hound.' Her vermin may well also be related to the mange, for by the early eighteenth century microscopic vermin were blamed for such itches. Dr Richard Mead had told the Royal Society in 1703 of an Italian physician's inference that subcutaneous mites, fast-moving on the surface of the skin and fast-breeding, caused or at least spread the itch.[5] Entries under 'itch' in Johnson's *Dictionary* (1755) and Rees's edition of Chambers's *Cyclopaedia* (vol II, 1779) show that this theory remained current in the time of *Humphry Clinker*. Beggary and filth, far less specific libels, are equally endemic in anti-Scots literature from before the start of Smollett's literary career.

The charge of bare buttocks, however, is quite specific, and probably originated with Highland dress, the wearing of which was outlawed after the 45.[6] The influx of Scots with Bute at the accession of George III in 1760 meant that the Highland lover 'Trotting with

---

3. 'The Highlanders Flight,' in Williams's *Works*, ed Horace Walpole (London 1822), II, 68–9.

4. 'The Scots Apostasie' (1647?), in *The Poems of John Cleveland*, ed Brian Morris and Eleanor Withington (Oxford: Clarendon Press 1967), pp 67–8.

5. The letter, 'from Dr. Bonomo to Signior Redi,' appears in *The Philosophical Transactions of the Royal Society*, no. 283.

6. Dr Johnson's comments on Scotsmen's breeches as a novelty appear in *Johnsonian Miscellanies*, ed George Birkbeck Hill (Oxford: Clarendon Press 1897), II, 169. John Hill Burton, *History of Scotland from the Revolution to the Extinction of the Last Jacobite Insurrection* (London 1853), has a valuable discussion of Highland costume, II, 374–82, in which he remarks that a blanket or belted plaid was the only covering worn by 'the humbler people' day and night—the separable kilt was itself an eighteenth-century invention—and later recounts the rage and suspicion of the 'Black Watch,' camped in London in May 1740 as loyal soldiers of George II, at 'the sarcasm and practical jokes to which their costume was so very apt to expose them' (II, 388).

his buttocks bare,' according to John Hall-Stevenson in 1761, began to be clad as an Englishman and to cover a nakedness which anti-Scots writers were glad to attribute to poverty.[7] As seen by Hugh Dalrymple in *Rodondo; or, the State Jugglers* (1763),

> bare a–s'd *Caledonian* Rogues
> Forsook their Oatmeal, Plaids, and Brogues;
> And over *Berwick Bridge* came flocking,
> For *Galligaskin*, Shoe and Stocking.   (P 2)

In a salacious, mock-Ossianic account of this influx, *Gisbal, an Hyperborean Tale*, Bute himself is joined by Scots like '*Heth*, whose skin was spotted like a Lizard, and *Eber*, of *Posteriors* that disdained the *Use of Breeches*' (2nd ed, 1762, p 11). Charles Churchill preferred to depict the Scots at home, sometimes successful ones who 'By lyes prophetic heap up riches, / And boast the luxury of breeches,' and sometimes ones in domestic peace, like the Highland lass in *The Prophecy of Famine* (1763), who '*scratch'd* her lover into rest.'[8] Print-makers delighted in joining naked buttocks and the itch in their prints, particularly in pictures showing the southward migration of kilted or blanketed Highlanders along roads thoughtfully provided with 'scrubbing posts' for the relief of the itch in transit. Satiric versi-fiers, perhaps punning anatomically, complained that 'Our Manners now we all must change-a, / Talk ERSE and get the SC-TT-SH Mange-a,' or be forced into a new pattern of 'a *good subject*,' that is 'A man with a bare backside, and a lover of the itch.' It is no wonder that a mock-petition in a collection called *The Scots Scourge* begs 'that it may be death to mention itch, . . . bare posteriors, . . . or any thing else that makes the Scotch ridiculous.'[9] In the appropriate volume of the British Museum catalogue of satiric prints and drawings I count some nine prints from 1762 and 1763 alone showing Scots with bare buttocks—one of them, no. 3910, incidentally a direct attack on Smollett—and another two from later in the sixties; I count some twenty prints dur-ing the sixties showing the Scots suffering from the itch.[1] Even Smol-lett's *Critical Review*, discussing Churchill's *Rosciad* in March 1761 (vol 11, p 209), refers to itching Scots, and shortly thereafter, in December 1761, found itself in a dispute with Hall-Stevenson about the 'buttocks bare' of his Highland lover (p 461).

---

7. *The Works of John Hall-Stevenson*, Esq. (London 1795), I, 52.

8. *The Poetical Works of Charles Churchill*, ed Douglas Grant (Oxford: Clarendon Press 1956), pp 68 (*The Ghost* 1.137–8), 203 (*The Prophecy of Famine* 293).

9. *The British Antidote to Caledonian Poison* and *The Scots Scourge: or, Pridden's Supple-ment to the British Antidote to Caledonian Poison*, undated London publications of ca. 1762–3, collected satirical verses and prints of the Bute period. The two volumes of each held about fifty prints reduced to duodecimo size for cheap, broad consumption. My quotations are from BA, II, 10; SS, 1,34, II, 61.

1. That is vol 4 of *Catalogue of Prints and Drawings in the British Museum, Division I. Political and Personal Satires*, ed. Frederic George Stephens (London 1883).

Ideally I should like to be able to say that bare posteriors in the 1760s were as exclusively related to Scots as the sentence from *The Scots Scourge* just above implies. Perhaps that is so; I do not know, though I can suggest that two apparent counterexamples, if anything, show that the identification of buttocks and Scots went beyond a simple reference to beggary and Highland dress. One seeming exception is in the prints that depict Britannia bared for a flogging, the other in the poems (and a few prints) that punningly celebrate 'the Queen's ass,' the satiric name given to a zebra presented to the royal family. Both Britannia and the Queen are on view because of the Scots: the former is 'stripped naked and bound to the whipping-post, while a Scotchman is scourging her mercilessly with thistles';[2] the latter (the Princess Dowager) was reputed to strip herself to enjoy a much-caricatured sexual liaison with Bute. Still other prints, showing Bute's own hindquarters available for kissing by job-seekers and sycophants, continued a pictorial tradition favoured by enemies of Walpole and his 'golden rump'—Bute as the new Great Man, the new potential tyrant—but of course reinforced the association of ideas between Scots and buttocks.

That association of ideas continued throughout the 1760s, the Scots buttock thereby outlasting the Scots Bute. The *Gentleman's Magazine* in 1765 reprinted 'On the Sheriffs Waiting on His Majesty,' a poem which presents Londoners terrified by '*Scotland*'s Highland-rebel sons, / Bare without breeches, cash, or guns' (vol 35, p 528). Three years later (vol 38, p 335) the same periodical quoted the anonymous 'The Expostulator' (1768) in which 'Caledonian clans' are said to be 'chaf'd with breeches.' The incongruity of decorously clad Scotsmen also struck the writers of the *Political Register*, no. 18 (September 1768), who saw Scots soldiers 'from rags or nakedness [to] have jumped suddenly into breeches and laced regimentals' (p 150). No wonder the Scots detachments from the army who dispersed a Wilkite mob in May 1768 were scornfully called 'the Blanket-Arse Regim^t.'[3] Less military is the combination of itch and buttocks in 'Hints for a Political Print. Written in November, 1767,' which tells us that Scots writers 'may be itched out to the life with one hand grasping a pen, the other rivetted in their respective posteriors. Your southern writers are apt to rub their foreheads in the agony of composition; but with Scotchmen, the seat of inspiration lies in a lower place, which, while the furor is upon them, they lacerate without mercy.'[4] Year after year, then, the image of the bare-bottomed, vermin-ridden, mangy Scot was brought to public attention, right

2. Thomas Wright, *Caricature History of the Georges* (London [1868]), p 285.
3. Stephens, *Catalogue*, print 4328.
4. 'Hints for a Political Print. Written in November, 1767,' in *The New Foundling Hospital for Wit*, new ed. (London 1784), IV, 87–92.

till the time when Smollett left Great Britain forever, in 1768. The evidence leads, I think, to an exceptionally strong inference that in writing his Scotophile novel Smollett recalled this image—how, after so many repetitions, could he have forgotten it?—and deliberately evoked it in our initial view of the young Englishman who is his eponymous hero.

Within the text Smollett draws attention to this composite image through his usual means of analogy. The incident that brings Humphry in touch with the Bramble party, two or three paragraphs in Jery's letter of 24 May before Tabby has her maidenly eyes shocked by bare posteriors, involves the coach's overturning. On peering in, Jery 'could see nothing distinctly, but the nether end of Jenkins,' which then serves Bramble as a step to use in getting out the window; Bramble appears wigless—'my uncle thrust up his bald pate'—so as to repeat, comically, the shape of an upside-down buttock. Tabby's fear of Clinker's supposed vermin has analogues, still in the same letter, in two other kinds of contagion, the fear of rabies claimed by Clinker's predecessor, the footman John, from the bite of Tabby's dog Chowder, and the publican's fear that his house would lose credit by having someone as shabby as Clinker for an ostler's helper. Clinker's own 'sickness, hunger, wretchedness, and want,' as Bramble puts it, of course has its partial analogue in Bramble's ailments and the imagined pangs of rabies. These analogues would make Clinker's raggedness, sickness, and 'naked tail' hard to forget even if the reader were not also put on the alert quite naturally when the titular character of a novel first appears. I might add that Smollett's interest in calling attention to the 'naked tail' specifically, not simply to nakedness, does not recur till the events at Bullford's (Jery, 3 October) bring the Scot Lismahago down a ladder on a windy night, 'posteriors' in view; and the linkage of that letter and the one about Clinker is suggested by a reappearance of the 'mad dog' theme as part of the same episode, related to us a few paragraphs later.

One can make a reasonable guess about Smollett's intentions here, in terms of what I have called a 'negative agenda.' The barrage of Scotophobe verses and prints during the 1760s, all in support of what Henry Fox in 1762 called 'a national prejudice which is inveterate & universal,' gave him a body of topics to be taken up and offensive strategies to counter; he also had a sceptical if not hostile audience, aware of his Scots nationality and his previous services for Bute and the Scots party.[5] In this episode he takes up the topic

---

5. Fox is quoted by M. Dorothy George, *English Political Caricature to 1792* (Oxford: Clarendon Press 1959), p. 120; she mentions, pp 123–4, the zebra and the itch, and her chapter 'Pitt, Bute, and George III' (with accompanying illustrations) makes clear how violent and aggressive the anti-government, anti-Scots satire of the period was.

of the bare-bottomed, verminous, beggarly Scot, and transfers the stereotypical image to a Wiltshire postilion, thus freeing the Scots. Moreover, he reverses the value of the image by showing how easily one can fall into distress, how easily one can be cured of it, and how desirable the cured man is. Smollett invalidates the rhetoric of disgust by putting it in Tabby's pharisaical mouth (and making her, besides, an analogue of the publican who has turned the sick, destitute Clinker 'out to die in the streets'). He turns scornful laughter into sympathy and benign condescension as Clinker's good qualities are balanced against more dubious ones, like naïveté, awkwardness, and being a jack-of-all-trades. In the rest of the narrative, then, he continues using analogues to defuse and diffuse the negative connotations of nakedness and poverty. Among these analogues are some that associate nakedness with the egalitarian state of being human, and others that associate poverty with humane charity, in short the very values that Scotophobes abandon.

Further evidence that the baring of Humphry Clinker has this bearing on *Humphry Clinker* is that other Scotophobe charges also have their echoes in Smollett's beggarly hero. Superstition or 'second sight' reappears as Methodism, the more pointedly so as Clinker's Whitefieldian version of Methodism has—as the novel makes clear—a theology with close affinities to Scots Calvinism. 'Second sight,' an inexplicable gift that descends on perhaps otherwise undistinguished men and women, also has affinities with the Methodists' stress on mysterious grace, election, visionary powers, non-logical knowledge, and spiritual equality. Another anti-Scots accusation, that those who bustled in after Bute were usurpers of Englishmen's goods, takes the form of Clinker's developing a hold in employment, religion, affection, wedlock, and kinship to the travellers; he begins by displacing both a postilion and the dog Chowder, whom Bramble expels from the party largely on his account. From servitude and repression Clinker emerges to share what otherwise would have passed wholly, one supposes, to the Melford children. The charge of Scots backwardness, finally, turns into Humphry's ingenuous simpleness. Each of these three themes—superstition and 'second sight,' usurpation, and backwardness—later appears in the novel in direct relation to the Scots, whether Lismahago, the Bramble party's travelling experiences in Scotland, or both. By that time the embodiment of the themes in Clinker has demonstrated that they are neither exclusively Scottish nor always negative in connotation.

Humphry Clinker's role in 'his' novel goes beyond his being an agent for Scotophilia, and Smollett counters Scotophobia with methods that do not follow the paradigm which we have been examining. One may take, for example, the common charge that Scots were disloyal to England and cosy with the French. To this Smollett responds by showing us the loyalty of Lismahago, who 'in the course of two sanguinary wars . . . had been wounded, maimed, mutilated, taken, and enslaved, without ever having attained a higher rank than that of lieutenant' (Jery, 10 July). We are left to recall that it was in fighting the French that Lismahago has suffered, with a little jogging of our memories through Tabby's query (Jery, 13 July) whether the squaw Squinkinacoosta's wedding dress was in the Parisian fashion inasmuch as the Indians 'were connected with the French.' Once he has established this beachhead, Smollett turns to Humphry to extend it. The next two letters (Bramble, 15 July; Jery, 18 July) deal with the frenchified valet Dutton, who primps the willing Winifred à la mode de Paris before decamping—or, as Win puts it (18 July), taking 'a French leave of me and his master'—with an heiress. Honest Humphry battles this Dutton so as to focus the novel's anti-Scots feeling just after the case for Scots loyalty has been put quietly through Lismahago's scars, mental and physical, and just before the travellers cross into Scotland and Jery replaces Dutton with a Scots servant, 'an old soldier . . . recommended to me for his fidelity' (Jery, 18 July; one might note that Bramble's letter of the same date, directly after Jery's in the book, tells of a Scots army under Alexander Leslie, loyal to Charles I, which fought the canting usurper Cromwell). Smollett's mode of countering the charge of Scots disloyalty differs from the paradigm discussed earlier; the difference suggests that one might learn most about the effects of a 'negative agenda' in *Humphry Clinker* by looking at other Scotophobe charges and the specific strategies they elicit, still involving diffusion, analogy, and perhaps revaluation.

It should be said that Smollett's negative agenda does not include one mass of anti-Scots material of the early 1760s, the attacks proper to the political situation under Bute. He almost completely ignores charges of bribery, the accusation of adultery between Bute and the Princess Dowager, furor about the excise bill, claims of royal despotism, and denunciation of the peace treaty of 1763 as exactly the sort of sell-out to be expected from a Scot, that is, a francophile and Jacobite who despised England. By the time of *Humphry Clinker* these issues were dead, the events of a shelved play acted before a still-present backdrop. In that backdrop were the Scotophobe prejudices that Smollett counters, and they can be separated from the more ephemeral excitements of politics in reading, for example, the leading anti-Bute organ, the *North Briton*. People did keep reading that journal when the political situation it reflected had passed. The continuing furor over Wilkes and *North Briton* no. 45, which went on with varying degrees of to-do throughout the 1760s, guaranteed an audience for reprints, and stimulated two sets of continuations by other men—Brooke and Bingley—into or during the late sixties. In 1768, the year Smollett left England, anti-Scots feeling had especially focused on the Wilkite cause, with some harassment of Scots in the streets by 'Wilkes and Liberty!' mobs and with the trials in August of three Scots soldiers for having killed a man during the Wilkite riots and the consequent 'Massacre of St George's Fields' (10 May, 1768). That too presumably guaranteed the *North Briton*'s sardonic Scotophobia a continuing audience.

In the *North Briton* appear charges we have already discussed, like Scots poverty. 'In our disputes with the English,' writes a Scots persona in no. 4, 'there hath always been one subject, our *poverty*, with which they have *illiberally* and *falsely* reproached us.'[6] Then there is Scots superstition, to an example of which another Scots persona, 'B. MacStuart,' refers in no. 7: 'I mean the gift of *second sight*, which, tho' laughed at by every sensible man of every other nation, we all believe to be possessed in an eminent degree by many of our countrymen, and to be found among us in the highest perfection, where there are no traces of common sense, nor the first principles of any science.' Scots are usurpers too, according to the *North Briton*. No. 26 satirizes them in two verses by Churchill's companion Robert Lloyd, one about poetry, the other about politics, in both of which Scots hope to replace Englishmen and to have—in Lloyd's words—the THISTLE choak the ROSE.'[7] He provides a dream vision in which the thistle, a reigning favourite, brings the '*brier* and *bramble*' and the rest of a '*scrubby, prickly* throng' to court with him, while turning out of power the rose and the laurel. This is a theme too in no. 41, where 'Macdonald' declares in London, 'Sir, we have as geud a right to this country as yoursels; and let me tell you, Sir, there is nae such thing as an *Englishman*, and I hope shortly the very name will be annihilated.' In addition to their usurping greed, their superstition, and their poverty, the Scots of the *North Briton* display selfishness ('a true *Scot* never opposes his own interest,' no. 34 announces), a fondness for their outlandish jargon, and a meanness or 'oeconomy' (a subject to which no. 42 is wholly devoted, because economy was 'the *Shibboleth* of the whole *Scottish* faction'). Add to this that they are 'restless and turbulent' francophiles and one can see why they 'have justly rendered the very name of *Scot* hateful to every true *Englishman*' (no. 44). This body of accusations, to be found (with some different emphases) in collections like *The Scots Scourge* and *The British Antidote to Caledonian Poison*, would have set a basic 'negative agenda' for a pro-Scots *Humphry Clinker*.

6. My citations are from the collected edition of the *North Briton* (Dublin 1764).
7. The poets whom Lloyd singles out, 'bonny RAMSAY,' Macpherson, and 'JACKY HOME,' 'With new-got pension, neat and clear, / Three hundred *English* pounds a year,' are all commended in *Humphry Clinker* (Jery, 13 July, 3 September; Bramble, 8 August).

Neither outlandish jargon nor 'oeconomy' marks Clinker himself but both appear among the non-Scottish Celts in the Bramble party: I am thinking of Win's and Tabby's misspellings, some of which represent Welsh pronunciations, and of Tabby's obsession that the house be kept orderly, the subject of every letter to her correspondent, the housekeeper Mrs Gwyllim. Let Bramble give a cow to 'Morgan's widow' (2 April) and Tabby flies into a rage:

> What between his willfullness and his waste, his trumps, and his frenzy, I lead the life of an indented slave. Alderney gave four gallons a-day, ever since the calf was sent to market. There is so much milk out of my dairy, and the press must stand still: but I won't loose a cheese paring; and the milk shall be made good, if the sarvents should go without butter. If they needs must have butter, let them make it of sheeps' milk; but then my wool must suffer for want of grace; so that I must be a looser on all sides . . . Gwyn rites from Crickhowel, that the price of flannel is fallen three-farthings an ell; and that's another good penny out of my pocket—When I go to the market to sell, my commodity stinks; but when I want to buy the commonest thing, the owner pricks it up under my nose; and it can't be had for love nor money—(26 April)

The last line of her last letter (20 November) announces that her new maid must not expect high wages: 'having a family of my own, I must be more oecumenical than ever.' Only Win's letter of 20 November comes after this of Tabby's, and that, like her others, of course exhibits her bizarre English, as unreformed by travel as is her erstwhile mistress's niggardliness. These two allegedly Scots traits, then, are displaced into two ridiculous non-Scots who exhibit them in every letter, but surrounded by other Celts (Welsh) who do not.[8]

Smollett deals with the two traits quite differently. He first revalues the depredations upon English English by making Win's letters both funny and revelatory, so as to change our contempt to something more kindly. Next he confronts us with Scots dialect itself in the mouths of the lawyer Micklewhimmen and of Lismahago (about whom, more later), and has Lismahago, Jery, and Bramble all discuss 'the Scotch dialect' openly. Lismahago defends it, of course, as 'true, genuine old English' (Jery, 13 July), an argument from a patriotic

---

8. A caricature history of Celtic type figures, Irish, Welsh, and Scots, in the drama is provided by J. O. Bartley, *Teague, Shenkin, and Sawney* (Cork: Cork University Press 1954), where parallels between the treatment of these ethnic types are plain. The lack of anti-Welsh animus which Bartley notes explains why Smollett found it easy to use Welsh figures in *Humphry Clinker* to transpose and lull English animus against the Scots who paralleled the Welsh in various respects. For Win's English, see W. Arthur Boggs—the author of ten or more articles on the subject—on 'Dialectal Ingenuity in *Humphry Clinker*,' *Papers on Language and Literature*, 1 (1965), 327–37.

quixotism which makes one discount it but which is presented at
some length so as to erode the reader's prejudice simply by showing
the subject amenable to rational discussion. After that the superiority of the South British over the North British dialect ceases being
dogma. Jery begins the last letter of volume II (8 August) by writing
that he has 'already acquired something of the country accent . . .
[M]y ear is perfectly reconciled to the Scotch accent, which I find
even agreeable in the mouth of a pretty woman—It is a sort of Doric
dialect, which gives an idea of amiable simplicity.' The first letter of
volume III, also 8 August, concludes the subject, as Bramble tells
Dr Lewis of his 'conversion from illiberal prejudices which had
grown up with my constitution,' prejudices which make Englishmen
laugh at the Scots accent and the 'clownish air' it gives 'even to sentiments of the greatest dignity and decorum.' (Bramble's 'clownish'
is Jery's 'Doric'; cf in Johnson's *Dictionary*, s.v. 'clownishness,' the
citation from Dryden, 'Even his Dorick dialect has an incomparable
sweetness in its *clownishness*.')

Thus the scorn attached to a Scots accent, a remediable blemish
with its own rights and charms, dissipates; and dissipates in a way
that—in emphasizing the simple and pristine—underlines the truth
about the other, more serious charge that Scots practice miserly
'oeconomy.' Far from being the sort of peremptory meanness seen in
Tabby, 'oeconomy' in *Humphry Clinker* more properly has to do with
simplicity, a frugality that comes from an agrarian way of life rather
than avarice. Smollett does not take up 'oeconomy' directly in relation to his Scots, but he uses the pervasive theme of luxury and its
evils to nudge readers towards treating the economical man as
opposite not to the generous one but to the modish spendthrift.
With Bramble as his hyperbolic spokesman Smollett uses one kind
of prejudice—the broad though not universal consensus disapproving 'luxury'—to help dispel another, that Scots are stingy.[9] Scots
hospitality, therefore, recurs throughout the travellers' journey
through Scotland, but always with the forthright simplicity which
Englishmen could be counted on to approve. Any modern reader
can see Scotophilia at work here, but to see the full force of the
argument, I believe, one needs to recall its anti-Bute, anti-Scots
beginnings and to understand its place in the strategies I have been
outlining.

Suspicious as Smollett's contemporaries may have been—as Horace Walpole we know was—of Scotophile propaganda from a veteran pro-Bute publicist, they had to be eased into tolerance. The

9. 'Luxury' and the consensus about it have been most fully treated by John Sekora, *Luxury: The Concept in Western Thought, Eden to Smollett* (Baltimore: Johns Hopkins
University Press 1977).

persuasive motifs of *Humphry Clinker* stay largely clandestine, and when possible are absorbed into thematics that have nothing directly to do with Scots. Bramble's visiting the Baynards and Dennisons, for example, enacts a lesson about 'oeconomy' and its saving powers which reinforces a general attitude tangent to arguments about Scotland (3 September, 8 October). From the superstitious creed of Methodism come the principles of brotherhood, grace, rebirth, new light, and the operation of the spirit by which a non-Scot, Bramble himself, attains healing and both recognizes and rectifies the sins of his past. And I have already indicated how bare buttocks, usurpation, and the mangling of the language appear thematically *in bono* as well as *in malo* so as to reinforce basic attitudes not pointedly pro-Scots. These attitudes, however, if accepted, ban a Scotophobia founded on the reasons and pseudo-reasons current in the 1760s.

Smollett himself, so recently a partisan apologist, conducts his argument under a shawl of objectivity. He treats the Scots very much as an outsider, even going so far as to specify via Jery (10 June) that he, Smollett, lives in London, not Scotland, and that he fills the bellies of 'all unfortunate brothers of the quill' not with oatmeal and haggis but with those hearty English staples, 'beef, pudding, and potatoes, port, punch, and Calvert's entire butt beer'—not only was Calvert's butt porter a favourite London drink, but Nicolson Calvert, MP, the brewer's brother, was a prominent Wilkite.[1] Equally important, Smollett banks his old satirical fires, an act of peace which is at least as likely to be a rhetorical ploy as a mark of real mellowing. An angry Scot like the author of Smollett's *Travels through France and Italy* (1766) or *The History and Adventures of an Atom* (1769) would set a bad example in *Humphry Clinker*, where ripe acceptance, good humour, and charity allow, among other things, 'a' unkindness [to] cease betwixt John Bull and his sister Moggy' (Jery, 8 August).

Within this context Lismahago's discourses and the actions of the travellers' Scots hosts appear to be no more than parts of a humane pattern, wise and shrewd, humorous and compassionate. My hypothesis, that for Smollett the Scots motif may have been the figure in the carpet as well as a marking in the tartan, involves a shift in traditional emphasis which is not mandated by *Humphry*

1. As a signpost in the print shows, Calvert's entire butt beer is the drink exalted by Hogarth in his *Beer Street* (1751); Goldsmith praises it as a lower-class favourite in the *Citizen of the World*, no. 30 (1760), and, in October of the same year, in the *British Magazine*, Nicolson Calvert had been recently in the news for proposing in 1765 that the powers of the attorney-general be curtailed; as MP for Tewksbury he was a violent and extremely candid Whig. Smollett might have chosen a different brewer, for brewers were by no means united in party allegiance, as Peter Mathias proves in *The Brewing Industry in England 1700–1830* (Cambridge: Cambridge University Press 1959), pp. 334–6.

Clinker. It is, however, quite compatible with the text, and explains elements of the novel which have been ignored as mere travelogue or staffage. I can illustrate this more fully in the treatment of Lismahago, the Scot whose social integration the novel portrays. Elsewhere I have suggested that Lismahago

> is elaborately anticipated by two Celts dear to Tabby, Sir Ulic [Mackilligut] and Mr. Micklewhimmen [Jery, 24 April, 6 May; Jery, 1 July]. These men, a dubious knight and a deceitful lawyer with a wounded head, lead naturally to battle-scarred, disputatious Lismahago. His maimed body and grievances about pay and promotion repeat what the crippled admiral and colonel have shown and told us at Bath. His freethinking and chauvinism appear in Bramble's portrait, six days before Lismahago shows up, of the whimsical deist H[ewe]t, who has performed a 'Giro or circuit' of Europe, but 'neither in dress, diet, customs, or conversation, did he deviate one tittle from the manner in which he had been brought up' (4 July).[2]

In sketching these anticipations of Lismahago I limited myself to formal arrangements and treated the lieutenant himself as an adjunct to the theme of Bramble's cure. My hypothesis here calls for elaborating and somewhat modifying that earlier treatment. The English military men and the Englishman Hewet anticipate and thus normalize some of Lismahago's appearance and conduct, particularly by being brought into the narrative as old friends of Bramble's. More important is Lismahago's relationship with his fellow Scot Micklewhimmen, from whom Smollett at once associates and differentiates him.

Micklewhimmen is not a friend of Bramble's, to whom he gives nearly fatal medical advice at Harrogate (Bramble, 26 June). Rather he is a repository of traits odious to anti-Scots: as a usurper Micklewhimmen abuses the kindness of English women by feigning illness to get 'the very best apartment in the house' and 'a succession of delicacies' at table; he speaks 'the Scottish dialect'; he professes 'methodism . . . upon a calvinistic model'; he drinks 'genuine wine of Bourdeaux . . . brought from Scotland' where the enemy across the water was a trading partner; his cunning makes a clothier exclaim 'He that would cozen a Scot, mun get oop betimes, and take Old Scratch for his counsellor'; and his overweening self-interest is

---

2. *Systems of Order and Inquiry in Later Eighteenth-Century Fiction* (Berkeley and Los Angeles: University of California Press 1975), p. 130. That book contains, pp. 109–53, a long discussion of *Humphry Clinker* which does not develop the hypothesis set forth in this article but does establish the complexity and commonness of the analogical procedures I ascribe to Smollett here. Eighteenth-century readers, the book argues by citing contemporary theory and practice both, were trained to read analogically. They would have been exceptionally alert to the kinds of argument mentioned in this paper.

discovered when he tramples on women and invalids to escape from a fire, crying 'Na, na, gude faith, charity begins at hame!' He is not poor, bug-ridden, or bare-buttocked, but he is grasping enough to seize 'bag and baggage' as he dashes from the burning house, and to win a wagered 'tea-drinking' he casts off his pretended infirmity and grinningly 'dance[s] a Scotch measure.' From Smollett's decision to risk so bald a caricature in the first Scot we meet, one can infer correctly that by the time he has brought the travellers to Harrogate he has already muted the specific association between Scots and some of these traits. As we have seen, he does so through the Bramble party in the matters of dialect, grasping, and religious zeal; in the matters of usurpation and self-interest he has shown us a London in which English politicians, judges, and critics have taken unmerited positions of authority. French fashions among the fashionable English and an alleged French spy (and convicted swindler) who entertains Bramble and Jery at the duke's levee (Jery, 5 June) ensure that francophilia is not limited to Scots. By the time the party gets to Harrogate, Smollett has freed himself to use Micklewhimmen as a guarantee of his own lack of blind Scots chauvinism, the same purpose for which he earlier used snide comments about Bute, a Scots apothecary, and a Scots accent (Jery, 2 June; Bramble, 8 June; Jery, 10 June). The guarantee, in turn, is needed just before Lismahago arrives in Scarborough, the travellers' last stop before they go north of the Tweed to receive—as we do—a great dose of elixir of Scotophilia. Smollett must make us ready to swallow the dose without our recognizing him, heretofore determinedly hidden, as the wielder of the spoon.

His agent, Lismahago, shares Micklewhimmen's accent and ingenious modes of disputation, for 'he had been bred to the law' (Bramble, 15 July). Lismahago does not, though, have truck with the French, whom he has fought. He never spouts religious cant or supports rustic superstitions, and he shows no mercenary interest, very much the opposite. The two Scots are linked adventitiously by their wounded heads—Micklewhimmen's in his own service, Lismahago's in that of his country—and their being wooed by Tabby, but these analogies are neither lasting nor contributory to Scotophobe prejudices. As soon as he can, moreover, Smollett also drops the Scots accent for Lismahago, at precisely the point in Jery's letter of 13 July in which the lieutenant boasts of its merits. As to the disputations, in subject and meatiness Lismahago's differ from the sophistical self-interest of Micklewhimmen's. Jery first stands amazed at Lismahago's 'arguments, equally whimsical and ingenious' (13 July), but his wiser uncle (15 July) confesses 'that I shall for some time, continue to chew the cud of reflection upon many observations which this original discharged.' When Lismahago reappears on the party's return to England, he 'is more paradoxical than ever,' so we are told, but in fact Smollett—or Bramble—allows him to speak at great, persuasive length, almost always getting the last word and 'a little nettl[ing Bramble] to find myself schooled in so many particulars' (20 September). In short, Smollett tries to sustain an appearance of objectivity toward Scots by linking Lismahago to the damaging Micklewhimmen, and then he erodes that linkage as rapidly as he can, thereby bringing the reader to respect a man established as a stereotypical Scot. The trip through Scotland, which offers a respite from Lismahago and enhances his country, helps in this process. I propose that all these manœuvres are not meant to convince us that Lismahago speaks the truth about dialect, the union between England and Scotland, oatmeal, commerce, or politics. They are meant to muffle and to push aside our prejudices on these subjects, an affective and attitudinal rather than a cognitive purpose.

Once the Scotophobe litany has been brought into the open by the arguments between Lismahago and Bramble, Smollett can give it the *coup de grâce*. He does so by renewing it in the context of two episodes in which the honour of Lismahago the man is tested. One of these (Jery, 28 September) has to do with his fiery temper at the insult to him and Bramble from Lord Oxmington. (At the time of the lord's first rudeness Bramble is, interestingly enough, in the process of proposing a Scots toast, to 'the best in Christendom,' which is first quoted in Jery's letter from Edinburgh of 8 August.) The other episode (Jery, 3 October) has to do with Lismahago's paying Squire Bullford '*Scot and lot*' for the practical joke of calling 'Fire!' and making him descend a ladder by torchlight; here the fire alarm, the descent by ladder, and an associated prank involving a dose of cathartic all repeat elements of the encounter with Micklewhimmen earlier in the book. This repetition calls quietly to our attention that the anti-Scots charges that coagulate around Micklewhimmen have dissipated. Francophilia? The Oxmington episode has included the insulting of Lismahago by a French *valet de chambre* who is forced to kneel for the lieutenant's pardon, granted in French, 'Oui, je te pardonne, gens foutre,' along with 'a violent kick on the face.' Usurpation? Lismahago, through his merits, has won his way to the affections of Bramble and Jery as well as having made the easy conquest of Tabby. Self-interested grasping? Lismahago gravely turns down Bulford's condescendingly given gold snuff box; and he is even cleared, late in the novel (Bramble, 26 October), from the imputation of having courted Tabby for her money, since, as we learn, 'this indefatigable oeconomist' has supplemented his £42 a year of half pay with investments of 'eight hundred pounds, which he has secured in the funds.' This is in itself enough to answer the charge of poverty, a state which anyhow would have been honourable in the case of Lismahago, maltreated as he was by the army; but it might raise the charge of 'oeconomy' if Smollett had not interlaced this exposition of Lismahago's qualities with the Baynard and Dennison episodes in favour of economic prudence.

As to the motif of Scots buttocks, the sight of the lieutenant's 'long lank limbs and posteriors' as he clambers down the ladder is now divorced from Highland dress, except that the blanket with which Lismahago is wrapped on his descent reminds one very faintly of the poor 'Blanket-Arse' Scot. 'Lankness' only distantly suggests poverty, and superstition is equally vaguely suggested by Bullford's delighted references to popish and zealous paintings: 'O, what *caricatura!*—O, for a Rosa, a Rembrandt, a Schalken! . . . what a fine descent from the cross, or ascent to the gallows!—what lights and shadows!—what a groupe below! . . . O, what *costume*! St. Andrew! St. Lazarus! St. Barrabas!—ha, ha, ha!' Scotophobia surely prompts the combination of the Scots' patron saint with the names of Lazarus (associated with ragged dress and bodily sores—Luke 16; John 11) and Barabbas, the seditious usurper of the freedom properly Christ's (Mark 15; Luke 23). But these allusions are oblique and not malicious; moreover, they are blunted against the emphatically non-Scots exoticism of numerous Italian phrases in Bullford's full speech and the foreign painters' names. Still another charge, that of restless turbulence, is turned aside by having Lismahago's fury at Oxmington seconded by Bramble (and Oxmington's rancour twice referred to the Welsh, not the Scots) and by portraying Lismahago's coolness over Bullford's vulgar prank, which he then pays back precisely in Bullford's own coin. Finally, in the first paragraph of the first letter after the Bullford episode ends Win (4 October) exculpates Lismahago from the anti-Scots charge of superstition by accusing him as 'no better than an impfiddle, continually playing upon the pyebill and the new-burth,' as an enchanter of Tabby through the arts of 'some Scotch musician,' and perhaps as a devil whose works Win will 'deify' through 'a slice of witch elm sowed in the gathers of my under petticoat' (a remedy she gets from Humphry). If one keeps the negative agenda in mind, incidents and comments such as these, which otherwise seem arbitrary, make sense in a whole.

Eventually, adjustments to the Scotophile motif in *Humphry Clinker* come with Lismahago's loss of dourness as the Scot, the Englishmen, and the Welsh travellers compose a family at last. By that time, though, the argument from the negative agenda has worked and, helped by the ongoing analogy with Bramble, one accepts Lismahago as a person rather than either a clump of alleged Scots qualities—some of them, like francophilia, present in their emphatic absence—or an 'original,' such as Bramble and Jery at first insist he is. The success of the line of largely clandestine argument I have been tracing results in the evaporation of the preset categories on which the argument has had to dwell. Like Bramble's accusations against parts of his own body, so with those of Briton against Briton: their truth depends on one's insisting on their being true. Smollett strikes, wisely and well, at the desire for that insistence. The facile system of order based on prejudice gives way to a far more flexible and comprehensive kind of ordering based on knowing the strengths and limits of analogical understanding. In that way Bramble can pass from his lists of symptoms and the English reader can pass from his dog-eared *North Briton*, and both can be healed.

JOHN ZOMCHICK

Social Class, Character, and Narrative Strategy in *Humphry Clinker*†

Tobias Smollett's *Humphry Clinker* has been the subject of both formalist and contextual commentary. Eric Rothstein, for example, has argued persuasively and at length that the novel is carefully constructed upon the repetition of analogous structures, which not only give unity to the work but also prepare the reader for the romance and comic devices of closure that otherwise would seem contrived.[1] Other studies—preeminent by virtue of its exhaustiveness is John Sekora's *Luxury*—have placed Smollett's last novel in its historical context in order to discuss the political and social elements in the work.[2] In the reading that follows, however, I want to connect the novel's formal elements and its historical context in order to show that *Humphry Clinker* arrives at a solution to the breakdown of traditional, deferential relations between two social

† From *Eighteenth-Century Life* 10.3 (1986): 172–85. Copyright © 1986, Duke University Press. All rights reserved. Republished by permission of the copyright holder, Duke University Press. www.dukeupress.edu.
1. Eric Rothstein, *Systems of Order and Inquiry in Later Eighteenth-Century Fiction* (Berkeley: Univ. of California, 1975), pp. 109–53. For other studies relevant to my own treatment, see William Park, "Fathers and Sons—*Humphry Clinker*," *Literature and Psychology* 16 (1966): 166–74 and Robert Folkenflik, "Self and Society: Comic Union in *Humphry Clinker*," *Philological Quarterly* 53 (1974): 195-204.
2. John Sekora, *Luxury: The Concept in Western Thought, Eden to Smollett* (Baltimore: Johns Hopkins Univ., 1977). See also Byron Gassman, "The *Briton* and *Humphry Clinker*," *Studies in English Literature* 3 (1963): 397-414, and Eric Rothstein, "Scotophilia and *Humphry Clinker*. The Politics of Beggary, Bugs and Buttocks," *University of Toronto Quarterly* 52 (1982): 63-78.

orders by delivering specific suggestions for reform in a powerful wish-fulfillment narrative.

Humphry Clinker's need for solutions to social problems is expressed in the wishes and anxieties of individual characters, who—despite their individuality—appear as points of eruption of specific class characteristics and conflicts into the narrative. Another way of putting this is to say that the novel's wishes and anxieties are bound to the fortunes of its characters: to a provincial, valetudinarian landholder who lives from his estate; and a destitute, vagabond, jack-of-all-trades bastard who lives more by his good-nature than by his wits. The illnesses that afflict these characters (Matt Bramble's constipation, Humphry Clinker's fever) demand the reading of the social back into the physical and temperamental, and the reciprocal influences of the characters with their illnesses suggest the potential effects of one social group upon the other at a transitional moment for the formation of class in pre-industrial England. Torpor among the elites is dispelled by plebeian energy reduced to a safe level.

Before naming the problems that the narrative seeks to solve and master through and in the fortunes of its characters, one further question remains to be asked: what stake does the narrative have in its representations, so that it aspires to a solution to the problems generated by the act of representation itself? Suggestions toward an answer to this question can be found in recent theoretical speculation on the ideological contributions and functions of fictions.[3] According to these theories, narrative provides a more or less coherent view of social experience in a manner analogous to that in which the psychoanalytic concept "dream work" provides a more or less coherent version of individual, psychic material, which in an unintegrated and unrevised state threatens coherence, stability, and continuity of a consciously elaborated personal identity. Ideology limits narrative form and content. According to Frederic Jameson, such limits appear as "strategies of containment": organizational strategies that enable the author to present the problems of his imagined world in a coherent and manageable way (pp. 49–58).

Smollett's strategies of containment in *Humphry Clinker* often take the form of a nostalgic invocation of a golden, patriarchal age. As John Sekora correctly points out, Smollett invokes "the world of inherited rights . . . where the laws of nature and the laws of tradition are regarded as synonymous, and where social position fixes one's

---

3. See, for example, Pierre Macherey, *A Theory of Literary Production*, trans. Geoffrey Wall (London: Routledge & Kegan Paul, 1978), esp, pp. 82-84; Terry Eagleton, *Criticism and Ideology: A Study in Marxist Literary Theory* (London: Verso Books, 1978), pp. 89-92; and Frederic Jameson, *The Political Unconscious: Narrative as a Socially Symbolic Act* (Ithaca: Cornell Univ., 1981), pp. 58-68.

activities and aspirations."[4] Such a strategy, founded on stasis, ill accords with the dynamic and fluid demands of the novel.[5] It can only ever be a gesture, an obvious wish for conditions to be other than they are, simpler and more manageable, immune from the historical processes of change. In fact, the invocation of a golden age is predicated upon its absence, upon strife and competition in a society where hierarchical organization no longer operates as a totalizing system but has been weakened by the homogenizing effect of increased opportunities for consumption and the employment of leisure time. Smollett's invocation of a static world signals the dominance of a dynamic one in which class interests and antagonisms have made a return to the past utterly fantastic and purely formal in a fictional sense.

The problems and energies, then, that *Humphry Clinker* attempts to resolve and manage are such as arise from emerging class conflicts in a developing market society. Although the England represented in *Humphry Clinker* is by and large still pre-industrial, Smollett captures the disruptive effects of economic and social change in the conflict between emergent and traditional groups. Even if these groups lack a fully articulated class consciousness, they function as coherent class actors within the fictional economy of the text. Smollett's appropriation of these groups should be read as a response to a perception of general weakening in structures of deference and hence a decline in stability and continuity.

Before turning to *Humphry Clinker*, I want to offer some reasons why a modified class model is a fruitful means of examining this—and other—eighteenth-century novels even if one admits that classes themselves were neither as minutely articulated nor as centrally featured as they would become in later novels. Eric Hobsbawm provides a partial answer to this reservation in his assertion that the traditional antagonisms between higher and lower orders in precapitalist or pre-industrial societies show that "the absence of class consciousness does not imply the absence of classes and class conflict."[6] Whether such conflicts take the form of food riots, riots against the Tyburn Surgeons, threatening anonymous letters, or alternative cultural practices, they involve the interests or the traditional practices of one group over against another. When the novel

---

4. Sekora, p. 286. See also Michael Rosenblum, "Smollett as Conservative Satirist," *ELH* 42 (1975): 556–79, for a similar evaluation.

5. "The novel took shape precisely at the point when epic distance was disintegrating, when both the world and man were assuming a degree of comic familiarity, when the object of artistic representation was being degraded to the level of a contemporary reality that was inconclusive and fluid." (M. M. Bakhtin, "Epic and the Novel," in his *The Dialogic Imagination*, ed. Michael Holquist, trans. Caryl Emerson and Michael Holquist [Austin: Univ. of Texas, 1981], p. 39).

6. Eric Hobsbawm, "Class Consciousness in History," in *Aspects of History and Class Consciousness*, ed. István Mészáros (London: Routledge & Kegan Paul, 1971), p. 11.

represents conflict, it does two things: it reproduces the discourse of a specific historical moment and it contributes to the formation of the class consciousness that grows out of the ever-deepening lines of conflict themselves.

Conflict, then, or the gradual awareness of the organization of economic, social, and political practices for or against the particular rank one occupies in a society or the particular way one chooses to organize—or would choose to organize were such power available—is the matrix of class itself. E. P. Thompson writes that "class eventuates as men and women *live* their productive relations, and as they *experience* their determinate situations, within 'the *ensemble* of the productive relations,' with their inherited culture and expectations, and as they handle these experiences in cultural ways."[7] Thompson reminds us that class is a dynamic event, one that continually develops in conjunction with complex productive, social, cultural, and political forces. It follows that class consciousness itself is being made and remade, itself is adapting to external and internal forces as well as prompting such forces to adapt to its changes. The study of class in the eighteenth-century novel, then, should not be undertaken in order to ascertain the degree to which social groups are accorded representation as classes in themselves or for themselves; rather, the point is to examine the strategies, defenses, accommodations, and repressions that the clash of privileged and nonprivileged groups produces. The stakes in such a clash are no less than social dominance, which is transformed often into fulfillment of individual desire. In the novel, this dominance is reproduced most frequently as a universalizing of the practices and interests of a single group.

Both E. P. Thompson and Raymond Williams have argued for the importance of cultural practices in the contest for social dominance. The former writes that "ruling-class control in the eighteenth century was located primarily in a cultural hegemony, and only secondarily in an expression of economic or physical (military) power."[8] The latter states that

> A new class is always a source of emergent cultural practice, but while it is still, as a class, relatively subordinate, this is always likely to be incomplete. . . . To the degree that it emerges, and especially to the degree that it is oppositional rather than alternative, incorporation significantly begins.[9]

---

7. E. P. Thompson, "Eighteenth-Century English Society: Class Struggle without Class?" *Social History* 3 (1978): 150.
8. E. P. Thompson, "Patrician Society, Plebeian Culture," *Journal of Social History* 7 (1974): 387.
9. Raymond Williams, *Marxism and Literature* (Oxford: Oxford Univ., 1977), p. 124.

It bears repeating that the novel plays a significant part in any conflict over cultural practices, not least in the manner in which it reproduces and transforms cultural and social practices themselves so that individual destinies appear subject to the inexorable logic of those practices in narrative. Success or failure, happiness or misery, attraction or aversion are the valences and repulsions of the social models elaborated in the novel.

It should be clear that evidence of class conflict in the eighteenth-century novel does not lie waiting to be discovered in some archive or record office. Rather, such evidence must be recreated from the narrative strategies employed to master forces that threaten authority and stability. Even in *Humphry Clinker*, a work in which the explicitly polemical passages push politics into the foreground, the narrative's relation to class conflict and class relations—specifically the way it works to contain the dangerous disorder of the lower class and rejuvenate the enfeebled representative of the ruling class—can be found only by looking away from the obvious polemic. In the words of Frederic Jameson, fictional texts reveal their full political and social import only with "the restoration or artificial reconstruction of the voice to which they were initially opposed, a voice . . . marginalized, its own utterances scattered to the winds, or reappropriated, . . . by the hegemonic culture" (p. 85). Jameson asserts that evidence of social and political struggle can be found in narrative utterances that have undergone a kind of social repression and transformation. He sees narrative as a semantic battlefield over which the critic ranges in order to recreate the battle, identify the combatants, explain the strategies, and analyze the outcomes. At the end of its narrative, *Humphry Clinker* represses the strident voice of an emergent culture—as embodied in the mob—through solutions that transform social relations into more manageable personal or familial ones, and it brings Matt Bramble back to health through the nostrums of immersion (magic) and purpose (work).[1]

Smollett's novel, however, is not merely a repressed text awaiting the textual analyst who can give it the symptomatic reading necessary to free it from repeating its social repressions. Just as it is involved in social conflict, so too narrative form participates in the creation of that which Raymond Williams has called "structures of feeling," or new and constantly evolving cultural practices. Williams' concept offers a healthy check to allegorical abstractions by emphasizing the materiality of all cultural practices, including the novel:

> the actual alternative to the received and produced fixed forms [of social experience and individual consciousness] is not silence: not the absence, the unconscious, which bourgeois

1. Folkenflik notes that "work" is an important value in the novel (p. 199).

culture has mythicized. It is a kind of feeling and thinking
which is indeed social and material, but each in an embry-
onic phase before it can become fully articulate and defined
exchange. (p. 131)

Thus, the evidence of social struggle is not only in the unsaid or in
absence, but in the actual events and figures represented in the novel,
especially in the ironic laughter directed at Matt Bramble himself.[2]
Humphry Clinker is rife with alternative voices that speak loudly and
clearly to the reader. Its efforts to silence or incorporate the voices of
the mob or Win Jenkins or Edward Martin cannot entirely eradicate
the new kinds of social and material thinking and feeling that the
novel represents in a memorable, substantial manner.

The Expedition of Humphry Clinker introduces the reader to a society in need of tradition to direct and stabilize the consequences of
its energetic expansion. The initial confusion in the Bramble family
arises from the attentions paid to Lydia by Mr. Wilson, whose rank
"did not entitle him to much deference" according to Jery and who
is probably "a run-away prentice from London" according to Matt
Bramble [14, 19].[3] That he turns out to be the son of one of Bramble's
old friends foreshadows the social confusion that makes deference impracticable and that makes romance conventions the way in
which the narrative resolves erotic and social entanglements. Above
all else, however, the novel's confusion and instability evoke a discourse of order and continuity from Matt Bramble and his nephew
Jery Melford. Although these two men speak, as it were, in genera-
tionally and constitutionally differentiated dialects, they both
speak a language of tradition and continuity. Theirs are the narrative's dominant voices, punctuated and counterpointed by the humorous, eccentric, or willful voices of their female companions. The
title of the novel, however, calls attention to neither of these two
men but to a third, who can appear as yet only as a bastard whose
utterances are relayed through the letters of the peculiar Bramble
family. Furthermore, the title suggests a man on a voyage of discovery or perhaps conquest. The object of this particular expedition
and of the narrative is to find a place for "a poor object conceived in

2. Sekora's assertion that "as a freeholder and country gentleman" Bramble "is placed in a
   relatively disinterested political position, untainted by the selfish motives of professional politicians, courtiers, merchants, and financiers" (p. 220), should be subjected to
   the kind of dialogic analysis that finds parody and travesty to be important weapons
   against authority. See Bakhtin, esp. p. 21.
3. Tobias Smollett, *The Expedition of Humphry Clinker*, ed. Angus Ross (Harmondsworth:
   Penguin, 1967) JM, Apr. 2, p. 36, and MB, Apr, 17, p. 41. All ref. are to this edn. and
   will appear parenthetically in the text. [Page numbers in square brackets refer to this
   Norton Critical Edition.]

sin, and brought forth in iniquity, nursed in a parish workhouse, and bred in a smithy" (JM, Oct. 5[?], p. 360) [323]. It is the pedigree that Clinker wears around his neck, however, that finally ties him to "a gentleman of great worth and property, descended in a strait line, by the female side, from Llewllyn, prince of Wales," according to Tabitha Bramble (JM, July 13, p. 227) [404]. One object of the narrative, then, is to incorporate the vigor and difference of Clinker into the system of Bramble and Melford: in other words, to legitimize the bastard without giving him a voice of his own, a voice that might at some point claim the right to speak its own narrative.

The text's resolution of Clinker's troublesome status, which entails the resolution of the contradiction between social stability and economic expansion, is what Frederic Jameson calls the "ideological act" in which the narrative "invent[s] imaginary or formal 'solutions' to irresolvable social contradictions" (p. 79). At the outset of the journey, the man who (we must assume) finances the expedition, dispenses charity, and censures contemporary social mores, is both "hard to . . . move" (MB, April 2, p. 33) [11] and possessed of "nerves of uncommon sensibility," which make him "extravagantly delicate in all his sensations, both of soul and body" (MB, May 8, p. 96 [72]; JM, May 10, p. 97 [73]). Having been exposed to "*a compound of villainous smells*" emanating from mixed company at a Bath assembly, the valetudinarian "drop[s] senseless upon the floor." Bramble's health and bodily conditions reveal that internal and external forces are organized to maximize his sense of control and minimize the extent to which that organization is vulnerable to adventitious and historical developments. His experience tells him, however, that extrinsic events will impinge upon his delicate nerves, and that sheer, dogged opposition will not secure him from their harmful effects.

As a man who lives not only from the income of his estates, but also from his devotion to the principles of a benevolent and independent individualism, Bramble stands in the novel as a sign of an older tradition's increasing difficulties in reproducing both itself and its values. Not only has he remained unmarried and, so it seems at first, childless, but his complaints about his niece and nephew suggest resentment of generation itself. To be sure, Bramble's occasional misanthropy protects his otherwise generous nature from being imposed upon; moreover, it is a conventional part of his character. But his misanthropy and the fear that his generosity is tainted by weakness show that the tradition Bramble represents has lost certainty, a loss that precedes by little a loss of authority:

> One of my greatest weaknesses is that of suffering myself to be over-ruled by the opinion of people, whose judgment I despise—I

own, with shame and confusion of face, that importunity of any kind I cannot resist. . . . I am afraid some of our boasted virtues may be traced up to this defect.

(MB, May 8, p. 95) [71]

For Bramble, there is a lurking contradiction between independence and benevolence, between being impervious to all importunities and being linked to a wide acquaintance through ties of social necessity. In moments of frustration or anger he states that his wards can find other guardians and his sister another cohabitant. He would deny the necessity of connections. For similar reasons the novelist gives Bramble friends who are amenable to his suggestions or who are capable of being swayed by him once other, deleterious influences have been removed, as is the case with Baynard. For Bramble, to enter into negotiations is to risk losing values altogether, but to refrain from negotiating social intercourse is to abdicate the responsibility to determine social relations.

Bramble's fierce independence is part of his "originality," and as such it becomes a necessary component of the narrative's representation of preferred social relations. The character of the benevolent misanthrope can be revealed only through private actions: in public his scorn for humankind must be foremost. The public character all but denies the value of public experience, while the private character gratifies sensibility as long as it is exercised between one individual and another, and only when the chance for a successful exercise is great. Thus, charity becomes one way of sharing with another, who stands in for society, while still remaining in control of a situation where the roles of giver and receiver are well-defined. Bramble becomes enraged with his sister when she discovers him giving charity to the poor woman with the consumptive child because Tabitha has redefined the roles in a way which makes Bramble a driver in the trade that he spends much time excoriating. Her misinterpretation destroys Matt's fantasy that public actions can be transformed into private ones.

Much of the humor of *Humphry Clinker* comes at Bramble's expense as time and again his efforts to control his emotions, his entourage, or his environment go awry. The laughter is one way that the novelist can make his character's minor failures seem inconsequential, less a decline in mastery than the inevitable outcome of events that are beyond anyone's mastery. Society—as well as its individuals—is in motion. Matt Bramble does entertain the degenerative theory of history, but he realizes that such a perspective arises from changes in motion that affect perception: "the impetuous pursuits and avocations of youth have formerly hindered me from observing those rotten parts of human nature, which now appear so offensively to my observation" (MB, June 2, p. 138) [114]. None-theless, change is real and relative, and the narrative works to pro-vide its chief character and its readers with the security of control. The best way to accomplish this security is to allow them to partici-pate in the world, to claim a directive part in it. As Bramble begins to find proper venues for the exercise of his mastery, the reader—who feels superior to Bramble at whom laughter is directed—begins to be assured that social forces can respond to individual manipulation.

In order that his mastery may seem plausible, Bramble himself is given an interest in improvement, that best outcome of change. Although he cherishes the political and social ideals of a static Harringtonian republicanism, he also rejoices at the sight of mate-rial advances in agriculture and even in certain handicrafts. If Bramble were a rank primitivist or one among those whom Hume calls "men of severe morals [who] blame even the most innocent luxury," there would be mere atavism rather than contradiction in his voice.[4] Smollett, however, has created a complex character, criss-crossed by regressive and progressive ideals. His internal con-tradictions arise from the undesirable social effects of the mechan-ical improvements that he supports. While travelling in Scotland (where social conditions limit the bad effects of improvement, as I shall discuss below), he speaks with pleasure of a "flourishing iron-work, where, instead of burning wood, they use coal, which they have the art of clearing in such a manner as frees it from sulphur" (MB, Aug. 28, p. 281) [251]. He also observes that "agriculture can-not be expected to flourish where the farms are small, the leases short, and the husbandman begins upon a rack rent, without a suf-ficient stock to answer the purposes of improvement" (MB, Aug. 28, p. 283) [252]. Although Bramble delights in modernization and improvement, he refuses to accept that innovation is often incom-patible with social stability and continuity.

The deleterious effects of economic expansion upon social rela-tions are most evident in England. In Bath, Matt Bramble has been disturbed and disgusted by the "impudent plebeians, who have nei-ther understanding nor judgment, nor the least idea of propriety and decorum; and seem to enjoy nothing so much as an opportu-nity of insulting their betters" (MB, Apr. 23, p. 66) [43]. In Lon-don he decries luxury, which has obliterated "distinction or subordination" (MB, May 20, p. 119) [96]. The luxury that money buys becomes the explanation (it is part of Bramble's republicanism) for all the reprehensible social changes that he witnesses. Luxury,

4. David Hume, "Of Refinement in the Arts," *Essays Moral, Political and Literary* (Oxford: Oxford Univ., 1963), p. 276.

however, is also an older concept easily applied to the phenomenon of a new mass-culture of tea-rooms and cheap clothing, which has become less responsive to the kinds of personal relations upon which patriarchal patterns of deference depend. The march of improvement (Bramble values science) and the influx of money (the means of his charity) may be inevitable; however, a highly personalized social organization, opposed to the social collectivity of the mob, limits the harmful effects of change by checking the development of mass social phenomena, whether these be social classes or popular entertainment.

As Bramble nears Scotland, however, discussions of luxury all but disappear from his letters. By representing Scotland as a place of rustic simplicity and the home of an orderly people, the novel suggests that a return to less commerce-ridden times (and thus an earlier stage of national development) is one remedy for the breakdown in subordination. But the temporary turn away from England is also a temporary turn away from the complex and less tractable social problems that the text represents as prevailing among the South Britons. Because of its more primitive stage of economic development and the survival of "patriarchal" affiliations, Scotland is a nation at the threshhold of modernity. (Indeed, Bramble even recommends that the South Britons think of colonizing it rather than America, though he is aware that improvements would make the "vassals independent" [MB, Sept. 6, p. 294]) [262]. Because of its transitional status, Scotland does not suffer from the South's problems; rather, it serves as a model for an imaginary solution to the social dislocations accompanying development.

The juxtaposition of conditions in the two countries reveals the blueprint, then, for a utopian *and* practical remedy to the South's problems. Even though the travellers find Scotland more congenial than the South, the North still receives it share of criticism from the party. The criticism, however, never really touches the Caledonian inhabitants. As Jery writes, the Scots "are so social and attentive in their civilities to strangers" (JM, Aug. 8, p. 258) [228] and "kindness, . . . the essence of good-nature and humanity, is the distinguishing characteristic of the Scotch ladies in their own country" (JM, Sept. 3, p. 274) [244]. In essence, the people of Scotland treat one another either without regard for station or with the deference due strangers or superiors. Impudence seems as yet unknown to them. The solution takes place at the level of the individual, and is taken over into the entire social fabric.

One of the narrative's strategies of containment becomes clear at this point: the individual is endowed with the appropriate moral nature, which will enable him or her to resist the disorder of a world of things and at the same time prevent an identification with

others in a similar station over against those in a better one. This
narrative strategy is manifested in Bramble's description of Scotland's chief city. Although Edinburgh is every bit as dirty as Bath or
London, the filth has far different consequences in each country. In
Bath, Bramble worries about drinking others' bodily discharges; in
London, he sees "a dirty barrow bunter . . . cleaning her dusty fruit
with her own spittle" from "filthy, and, perhaps, ulcerated chops,"
and imagines some fine lady partaking of this repast (MB, June 8,
p. 153) [131]. In Edinburgh, on the other hand, the public filth does
not enter the private space nor threaten the health and welfare of
the polite observer. The common stairs of the houses there are

> generally left in a very filthy condition; a man must tread with
> great circumspection to get safe housed with unpolluted shoes—
> Nothing can form a stronger contrast, than the difference
> betwixt the outside and inside of the door; the good-women of
> this metropolis are remarkably nice in the ornaments and pro-
> priety of their apartments, as if they were resolved to transfer
> the imputation from the individual to the public.
>
> (MB, July 18, p. 254) [225]

In England, pollution passes from the commonalty into the very
bodies of their betters, thereby threatening an already precarious
constitution. Scotland offers a double protection against this kind
of contamination. On the one hand, the filth does not travel through
the person; the person passes through it with impunity to all but his
shoes. On the other hand, the corruption is dissociated from the
people, who are paragons of order within their own private spheres.
Society is parcelled into orderly households and the threat of contagion is dispersed. That we see the "good-women of the metropolis"
at home rather than at an assembly or ridotto contributes in no small
way to the sanitary and—ultimately—moral superiority of the Scottish commonfolk.

The Scots enjoy this internalized sense of order amidst ordure in
part because the society itself is represented as an "order based"
one.[5] A possible way of eliminating the contradiction between the
desire for material improvement and the need for social stability is
to endow those most likely to be affected by the change—both the
elite and the lower orders—with a strong tradition that establishes
a symbiotic, if unequal, relation between orders. Dougald Campbell, a laird who has travelled and acquired a cultured taste, no

5. See R. S. Neale, *Class in English History, 1680-1850* (Oxford: Basil Blackwell, 1981),
   pp. 84-99, for a discussion of "order-based" societies with special reference to the work
   of Peter Laslett and for Neale's own estimation of the social structure of eighteenth-
   century England.

longer enjoys the music of the bagpipe. Although he wishes to dismiss the clan piper, he cannot do so "without a dangerous encroachment upon the custom of the family" (JM, Sept. 3, p. 278) [248]. Similarly, the Highland clansmen are fiercely loyal to their chieftains despite the government's attempt to destroy the clans themselves. For better or worse, tradition limits the damage that might be done by improvement, especially as it enjoins reciprocal rights and duties accepted by both laird and piper, chieftain and clansman. Even Matt Bramble, however, recognizes that some traditions cannot or should not survive. His idea for facilitating the breaking-up of the clans—"to employ the commonalty in such a manner as to give them a taste of property and independence" (MB, Sept. 6, p. 293) [262]—replaces a feudal mentality with a petty-landholding one. Such a suggestion has the obvious—if utopian—advantage of a direct shift of allegiance (from laird to mortgage-holder or rent collector) without the disadvantage of producing a propertyless horde that descends upon the cities and threatens the life, liberty, and property of the citizens.

Although the representation of Scotland reveals the full character of Bramble's concerns in its function as a partial solution to some of the problems raised in the first part of the trip through England, the "Scottish solution" does not survive the second portage across the Tweed. On the return trip, however, subjects other than "this incongruous monster, called *the public*" (MB, May 20, p. 120) [96] occupy the thoughts of the correspondents. As the narrative directs its attention to the working out of the erotic fortunes of the principal characters (including the resolution of Matt Bramble's erotic history), it also creates a familial solution to the intractable social problems that it has sought to abandon. The familial solution works primarily by enlisting excess energies (chiefly identified as erotic) under the banner of the domestic household. Tabitha's lust, Lydia's romance, and Win's vitality are bound to their husbands. Even the episode that receives most attention after the return to England—Baynard's impoverishment—has a direct relation to marriage. Baynard has made a marriage in which the erotic energies have been displaced into luxurious consumption, a proclivity that wastes Baynard's fortune and destroys his authority.[6]

Although the ultimate solution is familial, the novel puts forth at least one alternative resolution of the contradiction between energy and stability. Before the Bramble party had reached Scotland and

---

6. It is worth noting here that whereas all the female correspondents marry, the male correspondents do not. If female nature suffers from the association with vanity, expense, and disorder, then it stands to reason that it must be contained in some way. Matt Bramble's bound condition is more tolerable than the unbound exuberance of the women.

the final pairings had been settled, they encountered the highway-man Martin. This man, "whom nature seems to have intended for a useful and honourable member of the community" (JM, June 11, p. 182) [158], is a representative of the new forces that cannot be channeled into old conduits and for which new conduits do not yet exist. After a series of personal misfortunes, Martin finally "tak[es] to the road . . . with uncommon success." After helping to vindicate Clinker of the charge of robbery and later helping him drive off two highwaymen from the party, Martin appeals to Matt Bramble for help to escape the life of the road and its sure, if delayed, end. Having no employment for Martin on his estates, Bramble strikes upon another idea:

> "It would be no difficult matter to provide you with an asylum in the country (replied my uncle); but a life of indolence and obscurity would not suit with your active and enterprising dis-position—I would therefore advise you to try your fortune in the East Indies. . . ."   (JM, July 10, p. 222) [194]

And off Mr. Martin goes, the enterprise that led him to highway robbery now enlisted by the imperial project. No longer will he threaten innocent travellers.

Martin's voluntary transportation saves a "useful and honour-able" man from Tyburn, but it does not solve the problem of class relations. Although Martin escapes from England aided by Bram-ble's beneficence, the novel has made it quite clear in the person of the ungrateful Paunceford—who avoids paying his debt to a former benefactor—that the obligation of gratitude is too weak to preserve subordination. Bramble, by giving Martin his ticket to a possible fortune, also risks creating his hated mushroom nabob and devo-tee to luxury. Almost as if the novelist himself is aware of the risk of placing Martin in the dubious shadow of Paunceford, he introduces the character of Captain Brown. Brown is a Scot who has worked his way through the ranks and to a fortune in the East Indies. His return, however, gives Bramble only joy because Brown uses his new colonial wealth to fulfill his obligations to his father and fam-ily. If Martin is placed, as it were, between Paunceford and Brown, it becomes apparent that family plays a crucial role in determining whether or not one's wealth will be put toward undermining or sup-porting patriarchal and order-based relations.

Although Brown may be a later incarnation of Martin, the narra-tive never fully resolves the doubt about Martin's fidelity. (The latter man's wife is dead, so he—like Paunceford—seems to have no fam-ily.) The narrative, then, still needs to create a working, pacific, and fixed relationship between the old order and the new energy within England itself. It does so by generating the son of Matt Bramble, "a love begotten babe," who makes his appearance sick, hungry, and dressed in "rags . . . that could hardly conceal what decency requires to be covered" (JM, May 24, pp. 113, 112) [87]. What begins quite clearly as a class relation—especially for Tabitha—takes on the characteristics of a family relation by the end of the novel and reinscribes the new social forces in a traditional patriarchal mode.

Humphry Clinker stands as a near-perfect amalgam of the old and the new. He has blood-ties to the old order, but he is not full-blooded. (That he carries the name of Bramble's mother, a name that Bramble rejects in favor of his patronymic, emphasizes this difference.) He is deferential, but there are also hints of radical Christian equality in his methodism. He is strong, affectionate, and educated in a useful occupation, as he demonstrates when he repairs single-handedly the party's broken coach. And finally, even though Clinker is twice-transformed, once when he changes into livery and again when he changes out of it, his basic nature does not change: unlike Roderick Random or Tom Jones he is not to the manor born and does not aspire to occupy it. His ambitions and his tastes are as modest as his faith and loyalty are unwavering. No, Humphry Clinker will never be a squire; his function is to stabilize the *idea* of the squirearchy as it appears in the novel. Clinker is clear about class distinctions. He compromises his methodism at Matt Bramble's ultimatum that active proselytizing is incompatible with service, and he tells his master that "it becometh not such a poor ignorant fellow as [him], to hold dispute with gentlemen of rank and learning" (JM, June 10, p. 172) [148]. Later he asks Jery for permission to answer his valet's challenge with fists rather than swords, for "it doth not become servants to use those weapons, or to claim the privilege of gentlemen to kill one another when they fall out" (JM, July 18, p. 246) [217]. Humphry seems quite at home in his natural place in the order of things.

Nowhere is the "natural" quality of Clinker's social relationships clearer than in his rescue of Matt Bramble from the inundated coach. The flood of water released when "a mill-head gave way," released by natural forces working on the society's productive forces, indicates the danger of unharnessed energy and the inadequacy of existing channels designed to carry off that energy safely. At this moment in the narrative, Bramble needs Clinker in order to survive the force of the flood's "impetuosity." Clinker does not fail him: "The faithful Clinker [the then helpless Jery Melford writes], taking him [Bramble] up in his arms, as if he had been an infant of six months, carried him ashore, howling most piteously all the way, and I followed him in a transport of grief and consternation" (JM, Oct. 6 [?], pp. 353-54) [317]. Clinker's rescue of Bramble makes him at first glance a kind of *pius Aeneas*, except that any suggestion that

Clinker will go on to found an empire has been repressed in favor of service to the already-existing social formation. *Pius Aeneas* proves to be *fidus Achates*. The incident signals purgation, rejuvenation, and the proof of generative power that has been absent until this moment. All responses and relations in this action are revealed to be natural and inevitable. As the child is father to the man, so this love-born babe restores life to his feeble father. When Bramble writes about the event to his correspondent in Wales and tells him that he has learned that Clinker is his own son, he comments that "it is not without some reason that we Welchmen ascribe such energy to the force of blood" (MB, Oct. 8, p. 361) [324]. It is the energy of the blood that is the hope for countervailing the other, unbound natural and social energies in the text. And what is more, with the surprizing discovery of relation where no relation was to be expected, the narrative suggests that the Bramble/Clinker or the master/servant relation is a natural one. Class relations are naturalized into family relations. Or, as Clarissa says, "the world is but one great family": once this relation is rediscovered, internecine conflicts will end.

If the paternity of Clinker raises the spectre of an oedipal struggle sometime in the future (and this oedipal struggle could be read as a displacement of the class struggle, given the double relationship of Clinker and Bramble), the novel takes care to eliminate that possibility quickly and finally. Clinker-Loyd finds a place on the paternal estate under the eye of a provident father who will "provide for [his] son" by securing him a sinecure as a vestry clerk. Even the father's choice of occupation suggests that Clinker will be removed from the enthusiastic disturbances of lower-class methodism and placed within the established Anglican institution. By the end of the novel, then, Matt Bramble is justified in feeling stronger and in control, a feeling which may explain in part why he has only slight anxieties over "a whole litter of . . . progeny" issuing from the coupling of his natural son and Win Jenkins (MB, Oct. 26, p. 387) [347].

The comic resolution of the novel is especially appropriate for its ideological project. The traditional lower order in the form of Clinker-Loyd is reabsorbed into a paternalist Utopia, taking with it the more threatening person of Winifred Jenkins, who dares to dress like her betters.[7] Smollett's last novel attains comic harmony at various points, not least when it brings together the bastard son of a battlefield kite and a count's son, who once were fierce

---

7. Smollett gets in one last swipe at the lower orders by having Win Jenkins-Loyd adopt a haughty attitude toward her correspondent Mary Jones, thereby suggesting the natural depravity of the lower orders and predicting a way of preventing the formation of class solidarity.

opponents. The spurious Count Fathom, now Grieve (a name which sounds like the noble and quixotic hero of another one of Smollett's novels and gives forth at the same time the air of penitence and sorrow), rescues Count Melville and his Lady from death at the hands of highwaymen. All is in order in this world where plebeian resentment learns its lesson and is transformed into selfless gratitude in order that even the outcast and the bastard may have a fine and private place in the order of things.

Were it not for Winifred Jenkins' final letter, *Humphry Clinker* would seem to be a novel that ended on a note of social consensus. The reader would be left with the impression of a conflict having been waged among persons of similar status or at least with common interests. Yet Bramble's fears and Jenkins' undiminished ambition are real, even more real perhaps than their solutions. A split between the representation of social forces and the resolution of the problems caused by the clash of such forces inheres in the novel itself. The representation of the former is almost present to the senses: in any event the illusion of materiality is great. Because of the burden of this materiality, the less material and more imaginary solution is all the more necessary and crucial. Underlying the comic resolution is a belief that something should be done, a doubt that anything ever will, and a lingering hope that old answers will solve new problems.

And yet *Humphry Clinker*, like Matt Bramble himself, does not look backwards only. With its emphasis upon a patriarchal context for individualism and its narrative control of the kinds of representations accorded to different social groups, it engages in issues that have current relevance and it proffers ideological solutions that remain basically unchanged, if not unchallenged. In *The Eighteenth Brumaire of Louis Bonaparte*, Marx writes the following about the small peasant proprietors in nineteenth-century France: "They cannot represent themselves; they must be represented. Their representative must appear simultaneously as their master, as an authority over them, an unrestricted governmental power that protects them from the other classes and sends them rain and sunshine from above."[8] Smollett's narrative labors to manage social fears and individual ambitions by absorbing them into a system of patriarchal benevolence—represented in and by Matt Bramble—in order to lift the storm clouds of conflict and thereby show that all are engaged in the same project of seeding the national ground for a prosperity that somehow benefits all as long as the hand on the plow remains steady and unchallenged.

---

8. In *Surveys from Exile*, Political Writings, Vol. 2, ed. David Fernbach (New York: Vintage, 1974), p. 239.

ROBERT MAYER

History, *Humphry Clinker*, and the Novel[†]

Smollett's fictional narratives often seem to be texts at odds with themselves. A large literature has grown up around the question of what they are—satires, picaresque tales, and romances being among the most popular, but by no means the only, candidates.[1] For some critics the application of one or more of these generic labels to Smollett's narratives amounts to an assertion that those texts ought not to be considered novels.[2] Critics have also decried the "methodlessness" of Smollett's fiction, and such complaints have often been another way of commenting on the multiform character of his texts.[3] An exception is generally made, however, for *The Expedition of Humphry Clinker*. Robert Folkenflik finds in Smollett's last fiction not "a high-spirited hodge-podge" but a "sense of unity in variety."[4] Scholars have offered various explanations for the greater coherence of *Humphry Clinker*, some of which are discussed below. In what follows I argue that the key to the structural superiority of *Humphry Clinker*, as compared with Smollett's other fictions, is a historical argument about the United Kingdom that is enacted within the text. I also contend that Smollett's use of history in his last fictional narrative—both in the historical argument and in the implicit definition of the novel found in the frame of *Humphry Clinker*—is what makes Smollett's last

---

† From *Eighteenth-Century Fiction* 4.3 (1992): 239–55. Reprinted by permission of *Eighteenth-Century Fiction*. www.humanities.mcmaster.ca/~ecf.

1. See, for example, Sheridan Baker, "*Humphry Clinker* as Comic Romance," *Papers of the Michigan Academy of Science, Arts, and Letters* 46 (1961), 645–54; David K. Jeffrey, "*Roderick Random*: The Form and Structure of a Romance," *Revue Belge de Philologie et d'Histoire* 58 (1980), 604–14; Ronald Paulson, *Satire and the Novel in Eighteenth-Century England* (New Haven: Yale University Press, 1967), pp. 165–218; G. S. Rousseau, "Smollett and the Picaresque: Some Questions about a Label," *Studies in Burke and His Time* 12 (1970–71), 1886–1904; and Robert D. Spector, *Tobias George Smollett* (Boston: G.K. Hall, 1989).

2. Ronald Paulson argues that the "unmodified satiric conventions" found in *Roderick Random* are at odds with "the realistic world of the post-Richardsonian novel" (pp. 176–79). See also Alan McKillop, *The Early Masters of English Fiction* (Lawrence: University of Kansas Press, 1956), p. 151; and Jeffrey, p. 614.

3. H. W. Hodges, ed., *Roderick Random* by Tobias Smollett (London: Dent, 1927), p. xiii; see also A. R. Humphreys, "Fielding and Smollett," in *From Dryden to Johnson: Volume 4 of The Pelican Guide to English Literature*, ed. Boris Ford (Harmondsworth: Penguin, 1957), p. 314.

4. Robert Folkenflik, "Self and Society: Comic Union in *Humphry Clinker*," *Philological Quarterly* 53 (1974), 204. Others who have asserted the unity of the work include Robert Gorham Davis, ed., *The Expedition of Humphry Clinker* (New York: Holt, Rinehart and Winston, 1967), pp. v–xxiii; and B. L. Reid, "Smollett's Healing Journey," *Virginia Quarterly Review* 41 (1965), 549–70.

work his most "novelistic" achievement and his one indisputably canonical novel.[5]

That Smollett had history on his mind when he wrote *Humphry Clinker* is not a new idea. Louis Martz argued that *Humphry Clinker* was "an adaptation to novel-form of the topical and historical interests" of Smollett's various historiographical efforts, and many critics have discussed the political or historical theme in the text.[6] Robert Gorham Davis showed that "in *Humphry Clinker*, the movement through time is also a movement through space, a movement from England into Scotland and back into England again, a movement of reconciliation which ends . . . with symbolic intermarriages of Welsh, Scotch, and English."[7] What I now want to demonstrate is that, while Davis and other like-minded critics have been correct in linking the greater unity of *Humphry Clinker* to its political theme, they have not gone far enough; they have failed to discuss the underlying historical argument in the text that ultimately explains both the superior structural unity of Smollett's last narrative and its greater importance in the canon of eighteenth-century English novels.

Ever since the work appeared in 1771, critics have argued that the text was used by Smollett as a means of denigrating England and praising Scotland; Martz asserted that many important aspects of both the form and the content of *Humphry Clinker* result from Smollett's use of the work as "a vehicle for a denunciation of England."[8] Although the narrative ends in a spirit of reconciliation, much of *Humphry Clinker* seems to constitute a scathing attack upon English society and a celebration of life in Scotland.[9] Matthew Bramble's

5. By "history," I mean historiography or historical writing, not historical events; by "historical argument" and "historical vision," I mean a line of reasoning or a set of insights about the evolution of the British nation. I assume, here and elsewhere, even though I recognize the problematic character of my assumption, that "fiction" and "history" are fundamentally different forms of discourse, that the latter is distinguished from the former by "its being submitted as a whole to the control of evidence." See Arnaldo Momigliano, "The Rhetoric of History and the History of Rhetoric: On Hayden White's Tropes," in *Comparative Criticism: A Yearbook*, ed. E. S. Shaffer (Cambridge: Cambridge University Press, 1981), pp. 267–68. I use the word "novelistic" to suggest that *Humphry Clinker*, of all of Smollett's fictions, is his most fully novel-like achievement. I substantiate this claim in the latter half of the essay by considering the text in light of several definitions of the novel, showing how an appreciation of Smollett's use of history in this text helps us to see why *Humphry Clinker* is Smollett's best approximation of the form.

6. Louis L. Martz, *The Later Career of Tobias Smollett* (1942; reprinted Hamden, CT: Archon, 1967), pp. 11, 13–16. Sekora finds in Smollett's various histories a "political history of luxury" and the source for his later writings on luxury—that "capital crime against British civilization"—including *Humphry Clinker*. Sekora argues that Smollett's final work "is a highly political novel, one of the most politically charged of the century" (pp. 136, 219).

7. Davis, ed., p. xix.

8. Fred W. Boege, *Smollett's Reputation as a Novelist* (Princeton: Princeton University Press, 1947), p. 30; Martz, p. 129.

9. Critics who have argued that the novel concludes in such a spirit include Davis, pp. ix, xxi; Folkenflik, p. 204; and Reid, p. 550.

famous description of Bath typifies the overall view of England that emerges from his letters and those of his fellow travellers, at least before the final section of the novel, when the wanderers return to England.[1] In addition to being an attack upon England, *Humphry Clinker* is also a panegyric on Scotland. Although Bramble has almost nothing good to say about Bath, he tells his friend, physician, and correspondent, Dr Lewis, that "Edinburgh is considerably extended on the south side, where there are divers little elegant squares built in the English manner; and the citizens have planned some improvements in the north, which, when put in execution, will add greatly to the beauty and convenience of this capital" (p. 234) [240]. Bramble praises the Scottish city as "a hot-bed of genius," one in which such institutions as the infirmary and the workhouse ensure a healthy social atmosphere (pp. 232–34) [240]. There is a negative side to Bramble's representation of Edinburgh and of Scotland in general, but on balance it is not inaccurate to see the letters of the first English section and the Scottish section of *Humphry Clinker* as an attack on the southern kingdom predicated on the view that Scotland embodies an ideal which England falls miserably short of achieving.

At least one critic has argued, however, that the real split in the book is not between England and Scotland, but between city and country or even between new and old. The well-ordered country estate is a social ideal that dominates the final English section of the book, and the projection of this ideal involves, to some extent at least, a rejection of modernity in eighteenth-century Britain.[2] The opposition of England and Scotland may be said to mediate these more fundamental antagonisms. Scotland is, after all, a more pastoral society than England; its cities are smaller and closer to the towns and estates of the countryside. Glasgow is seen by Bramble as "a perfect bee-hive in point of industry . . . [which] stands partly on a gentle declivity . . . in a plain, watered by the river Clyde" (p. 246) [252]; he might well be speaking of a country house. Scotland is also preferred because the old ways have been preserved and honoured there much more faithfully than in England. The "Ode to Leven-Water" that Bramble sends to Dr Lewis evokes an "Arcadian" Scotland, one dominated by an "ancient faith that knows no guile" (pp. 249–50) [256]. Scotland and England are represented as being at different stages of development, and at times it seems that England's "progress" has been her ruination.

---

1. See *The Expedition of Humphry Clinker*, ed. with introduction, Lewis M. Knapp, revised, Paul-Gabriel Boucé (Oxford: Oxford University Press, 1984), pp. 34–38. References are to this edition. [Page numbers in squares brackets refer to this Norton Critical Edition.]
2. John F. Sena, "Ancient Designs and Modern Folly: Architecture in *The Expedition of Humphry Clinker*," *Harvard Library Bulletin* 27 (1979), 113.

Why then the final English section of the narrative and its harmonious conclusion to the journey, which involves not only Bramble's return to his own well-ordered country seat but also the return of his wards to Bath? Bramble's apparent reconciliation to England and to Bath can be explained by the fact that the views of the other letter-writers are different from those of Bramble. Jery considers Bath society "as decent as any" and thinks "the individuals that composed it, would not be found deficient in good manners and decorum" elsewhere; Liddy sees it as "an earthly paradise" and avers that "the new buildings . . . look like so many enchanted castles" (pp. 51, 39) [57, 45]. It is perhaps not surprising, therefore, that the young people return to Bath, while their uncle returns to his home in Wales. But the various correspondents are not as far apart as they sometimes appear to be, and the return of Bramble's wards to Bath seems to have his blessing (p. 351) [354].

Smollett's use of the epistolary technique ensures that no one perspective in the narrative is definitive. As each letter-writer's viewpoint is a necessarily restricted one, a unifying perspective is required, one that encompasses the perceptions of the five correspondents. Ultimately the reader has to make sense of it all: "the multiplicity of concrete—but limited—aspects must 'coalesce' in the reader's imagination."[3] Nevertheless, something like a common perspective does begin to emerge within the narrative towards the end of the journey as the five letter-writers—previously so much at odds with one another—achieve a kind of harmony. Tabitha Bramble, Matthew's sister, marries Lismahago, a Scottish former officer in the British army. A principal source of Tabitha's conflict with her brother—her husband-hunting—is thereby removed. Win Jenkins, formerly Tabitha's maid, marries Matthew Bramble's former servant, Clinker, who turns out to be Bramble's natural son; the servants thus move up the social ladder, closer to the Brambles. Wilson, the apparently shiftless young man who claims to be in love with Liddy, turns out to be the son of Bramble's friends, Mr and Mrs Denison—the exemplars in the text of a happy rural existence—and the young man wins Liddy's hand. Jery exclaims "our society is really enchanting," and Bramble sings the praises of society in general: "a change of company [is] as necessary as a change of air, to promote a vigorous circulation of spirits, which is the very essence and criterion of good health" (pp. 333, 339) [336, 342]. At the novel's end, then, an emerging harmonious order is projected in which the characters,

3. Wolfgang Iser, *The Implied Reader: Patterns of Communication in Prose Fiction from Bunyan to Beckett* (Baltimore: John Hopkins University Press, 1974), p. 71; see also R. D. S. Jack, "Appearance and Reality in *Humphry Clinker*," in *Smollett: Author of the First Distinction*, ed. Alan Bold (Totowa, NJ: Barnes and Noble, 1982), pp. 212–13.

whose differences have been thoroughly aired in the letters, will be able to live and prosper together.

This increasingly felicitous personal order is linked in important ways to the public realm, which is apparently dominated by the antagonisms of England and Scotland, new and old, city and country. Public and private converge in the characterization of Lismahago, who, Martz argues, is the principal vehicle for Smollett's praise of Scotland.[4] While it is true that Lismahago's defence of his homeland is important, Bramble commends the northern kingdom almost as much as the Scot does. Their dialogue, nevertheless, is sometimes critical of Scotland. For example, when the captain defends the Scottish dialect and Scottish law and asserts that oatmeal and poverty are Scottish blessings, Bramble disagrees: "I should be glad to see the day when your peasants can afford to give all their oats to their cattle . . . and indulge themselves with good wheaten loaves" (pp. 275–80) [284]. The conversations between Lismahago and Bramble are central to the treatment of Scotland in the text, and the key to understanding the link between the personal and the public is to be found in their last major discussion.

The climactic exchange between these two occasional antagonists, which takes place after the travellers have returned to England, centres upon the issue of the unification of the two nations, achieved by acts of both parliaments in 1707. Lismahago condemns the Union in the strongest possible terms. He denies Bramble's assertion that the recent increase in Scottish material well-being is ascribable to the Union and argues instead that it derives from "the natural process of improvement." According to the captain, the Scots gained one advantage from the Union—"the privilege of trading to the English plantations"—but realized few benefits, and meanwhile lost "the independency of their state, the greatest prop of national spirit; . . . their parliament and their courts of justice." Lismahago asserts that the English reaped the benefits of the Union: political security, territorial expansion, increase of population. But Bramble argues again that material benefits to Scotland justify the Union—"many of them [the Scots] in England, as well as in her colonies, amassed large fortunes, with which they returned to their own country." Lismahago denies that on balance Scotland realized any gain, since so much money leaves the northern kingdom to pay the "grievous impositions" of and to buy "superfluities" from the English. But, while Bramble grants that Lismahago is right to decry "the contempt for Scotland, which prevails too much

4. Martz, pp. 168–70.

on this side of the Tweed," he insists upon "the happy effects of the Union" (pp. 275–80) [280–85].

This exchange between the Welshman and the Scot has its roots in Smollett's own historiographical labours. Lismahago's denunciation of the Union echoes the report in Smollett's *History of England* of the arguments of Scottish noblemen, who, with the loss of their parliament, "found themselves degraded in point of dignity and influence"; of Scottish merchants, who worried about being "saddled with heavy duties and restrictions"; and of "the people in general," who believed "that the independency of their nation had fallen sacrifice to treachery and corruption."[5] Bramble's assertion that "the people lived better, had more trade, and a greater quantity of money circulating since the union, than before" (p. 276) [282] is akin to the arguments in the Scottish parliament of the "noblemen attached to the union," who "magnified the advantages that would accrue to the kingdom from the privileges of trading to the English plantations, and being protected in their commerce by a powerful navy."[6] More important, Bramble's expression of "satisfaction at the happy effects of the union" (p. 275) [280] is identical with the *British* point of view enunciated by the narrator of the *History of England*, who ends his discussion of these events with the sanguine conclusion that the Union "quietly took effect and fully answered all the purposes for which it was intended."[7]

Lismahago is having none of it, but if the reader looks back upon both the censure of England and the praise of Scotland and ahead to the harmonious ending based ostensibly on three marital unions, the discussion of political union will be seen as a focal point in the narrative, one that effects the convergence of many elements in the text that might otherwise seem disparate and unrelated. To begin with, Bramble's defence of the Union suggests the possibility of harmony between the apparently despised southern kingdom and the beloved northern realm. Indeed Bramble's pro-Union stance undermines the argument that an essentially negative view of England is elaborated in the text. From the perspective of the debate over the Union, one can begin to make sense of the hints at a balanced assessment that we find in the midst of the supposed censure of the southern kingdom.[8]

Throughout the journey Bramble acknowledges one feature of English life that is admirable and deserves to be emulated— England's material progress. John Sena argues that Bramble's praise

5. Smollett, *The History of England from the Revolution in 1688 to the Death of George II*, 2 vols (Philadelphia: Edward Parker, 1822), 1:381.
6. *History of England*, 1:384.
7. *History of England*, 1:385.
8. Spector, 137–38.

for Blackfriars Bridge is an exception to the Welshman's generally negative view of English architecture, and Bramble himself thinks the bridge an anomaly: "I wonder how they stumbled upon a work of such magnificence and utility" (p. 87) [94].[9] But elsewhere Bramble, however grudgingly, expresses admiration for other indications of English material well-being. "It must be allowed," he acknowledges, "that London and Westminster are much better paved and lighted than they were formerly. The new streets are spacious, regular, and airy; and the houses are generally convenient" (p. 87) [94]. In the north of England, furthermore, Bramble finds between Durham and Newcastle "the highest scene of cultivation that ever I beheld," and he admits that the latter town has been "rendered populous and rich by industry and commerce" (p. 202) [210]. Once in Scotland, furthermore, Bramble looks back at England and discovers features of English life to praise. About wheat farming, he tells Dr Lewis: "that agriculture in this country is not yet brought to that perfection which it has attained in England" (pp. 215–16) [223]. In Dunbar, although the town is "well situated for trade," he notices that there is "little appearance of business in the place," and, while it is faint praise of England, Bramble admits that "the public inns of Edinburgh, are still worse than those of London" (pp. 216, 219) [223, 226]. Bramble also grants that "an Englishman . . . refers every thing he sees to a comparison with the same articles in his own country; and this comparison is unfavourable to Scotland in all its exteriors" (p. 231) [238]. The clothing, dwellings, and agricultural theories of peasants, as well as the treatment of servants, all point to the fact that Scotland is woefully behind England in material terms (pp. 244–45, 274) [251–52, 262]. In fact, Brambles's favourable comment on Edinburgh's expansion shows that he uses English towns (possibly even Bath!) as a model to be emulated by the Scots. Bramble also avers that Scotland's "gardens and parks are not comparable to those of England" (p. 234) [241].

Remarks by the other correspondents keep the question of England in suspense even as the country comes in for severe criticism. The other letter-writers remind us both that England may not be as bad as Bramble sometimes suggests and that Scotland may not be as wonderful as Lismahago asserts. Although he has much good to say about the northern kingdom, when Jery compares the farmers of Northumberland and Scotland, he finds the former "lusty fellows, fresh complexioned, cleanly, and well-cloathed" but the latter "lank, lean, hard-featured, sallow, soiled, and shabby" (p. 214) [221]. Tabitha holds up Scotland as a model in a way which emphasizes the country's backwardness and poverty: "I don't see why the sarvants of Wales

9. Sena, p. 100.

should'n't drink fair water, and eat hot cakes and barley cale, as they do in Scotland, without troubling the botcher above once a quarter" (p. 274) [279–80]. The cumulative effect of the letters dealing with Scotland and its relationship to England—and this becomes clearer if the reader has Bramble's endorsement of the union of the two kingdoms in mind—is to suggest that unqualified praise for Scotland and denigration of England are not justified; a more balanced view is necessary.[1] In political terms, this perspective is the British point of view embraced by Bramble in his clash with Lismahago.

This British perspective, however, is not rooted solely in Bramble's recognition of English superiority "in all exteriors"; it also derives from the Welshman's conviction that Scotland is a repository of ancient and essential values. Scotland's moral superiority becomes apparent in the course of a comparison of English and Scottish versions of hospitality. Not surprisingly, the treatment of guests is one of the central concerns of this travel narrative. With respect to English hospitality, Bramble, at the home of squire Burdock, finds proof that the English are "as a people totally destitute of this virtue." The host is inattentive; the hostess is hateful; the house is "like a great inn." "I would rather dine upon filberts with a hermit, than feed upon venison with a hog," declares Bramble (pp. 164–65) [174]. But of Scotland, Bramble tells Dr Lewis, "I have met with more kindness, hospitality, and rational entertainment, in a few weeks, than I ever received in any other country during the whole course of my life" (p. 231) [238].

Another instance of the corrupted relations between guest and host in the southern kingdom—one that also illuminates the ways in which *Humphry Clinker* functions as a fictional record of many aspects of mid-eighteenth-century English life—is the Duke of Newcastle's levee. Fallen from grace and in a state of virtual stupefaction, the Duke entertains his guests because he wants them "to support the shadow of that power, which he no longer retains in substance." The guests, for their part, are contemptuous of their host. The leering captain C— says of him: "This wise-acre is still a-bed; and, I think, the best thing he can do, is to sleep on till Christmas; for, when he gets up, he does nothing but expose his own folly." In addition, the nearly total absence of clergymen, noted by Jery ("there was no more than one gown and cassock"), is a sign of the rank ingratitude of the churchmen who enjoyed Newcastle's bountiful patronage for many years (pp. 110–11) [118–19].[2] England,

1. Jack, p. 226.
2. See Paul-Gabriel Boucé, "The Duke of Newcastle's Levee in Smollett's *Humphry Clinker*," *Yearbook of English Studies* 5 (1975), 136–41. That *Humphry Clinker* functions as a work of (fictional) contemporary history has been noted by a number of critics, including Jerry C. Beasley ("Smollett's Novels: *Ferdinand Count Fathom* for the Defense," *Papers on Language and Literature* 20 [1984], 182), who has pointed out that the narrative "fairly hums with historical and topical allusions."

then, is deficient in hospitality and gratitude—a clear sign of its depravity. Scotland is merely lagging behind in material development: Bramble calls the northern kingdom "a paradise" (p. 252) [257].

The comments upon the two countries by the letter-writers focus our attention, then, upon the quite distinct strengths and weaknesses of the two kingdoms. Bramble argues that Scotland has benefited materially from the union; Lismahago worries about the ill effects of English luxury on the Scottish nation. Their inconclusive exchange—each stubbornly asserts his own view—leaves the reader to decide. Living in a post-Union world, however, and generally disposed to side with Bramble rather than with the "comic grotesque" Lismahago, the reader is likely to view the Union as efficacious and beneficial to both sides, even if not unproblematically so.[3] England may threaten Scotland's comparative moral health even as it holds out the promise of necessary progress. Yet the narrative suggests that influence need not always be baneful; Scotland's moral superiority presents itself as a potential remedy for England's ills. The unity that Folkenflik finds in this narrative is, he argues, the result of "a *discordia concors* in which distinct individuals, like the nations England, Scotland, and Wales, come together in a union which gives health to all."[4] The projected concord arises from Smollett's representation and endorsement within the narrative of a change of great historical significance—the gradual creation of the United Kingdom.

The rejuvenating and healing effects of union are most clearly suggested in Smollett's novel in personal terms, but the personal embodies the social and political. Tabitha Bramble, a Welshwoman and therefore someone from south of the Tweed, marries the Scotsman Lismahago. Both Tabitha and her husband are thus happily settled in life, and Matthew Bramble is closer to finding the peace and comfort that he seeks. This and the other marriages, then, should not be dismissed as mere "plot contrivances," but, rather, should be seen as images of what Smollett represents as the best hope for Britain.[5] The link between the marriages and the historical destiny of the United Kingdom is unmistakable; in the letter in which Bramble and Lismahago air their views on the Union, Bramble announces the coming marriage of Tabitha and the Scottish veteran. And the other marriages—not just the union of the two grotesques—also reinforce the arguments that Smollett elaborates in the text about the historical importance of the Union, thereby

3. Davis, p. xxi; Robert Hopkins, "The Function of the Grotesque in *Humphry Clinker,*" *Huntington Library Quarterly* 32 (1968–69), 168–70.
4. Folkenflik, p. 204.
5. Davis, p. xxii.

suggesting the real possibility of the future health of both family and polity. In choosing Clinker, Jenkins rejects (English) luxury represented by Jery's foppish manservant in favour of (Scottish) sincerity and fellow-feeling, while Liddy's marriage to Dennison is, given the character of the Dennisons, an embracing of the country and of the old ways.

The Dennison estate is the clearest and the most important representation of the harmonious ideal that Bramble celebrates in the novel. He tells Dr Lewis that Mr Dennison "has really attained to that pitch of rural felicity, at which I have been aspiring these twenty years." Dennison's success, however, is not simply the attainment of peace and simplicity; it is also the achievement of plenty and comfort through industry and the application of scientific principles. Dennison works hard, conducts "experiments in agriculture," reforests and encloses his land. Bramble proposes enclosure as the solution to the problems of Scottish agriculture (p. 245) [251]. The Dennison estate is consequently a model of "industry and commerce" in a rural setting (pp. 320–28) [324–31]. It is also, of course, a garden. The Dennisons are city people and residents of England who combine the scientific spirit, industry, and activity of the city, of England, of the new age, with the values of the country, of Scotland, of the past. The garden is an image of the ideal espoused by Bramble in *Humphry Clinker*. But the gardens of Scotland are deficient when compared with those of England, and this deficiency is consonant with the backward state of development of the northern kingdom. The Dennison estate, after all, is in England and is therefore an affirmation that the ideal can be achieved in that country. For this reason, the letter-writers can and indeed must return to England. "Their future is in England," as Davis points out.[6] So too is that of Lismahago. And so too is that of Scotland.

Of course, Lismahago himself does not see it that way and in some ways he has the better of his exchange with Bramble on the Union. Bramble's word, however, is the last one, and it is, for him, a somewhat uncharacteristically English word. Lismahago ends by lamenting the ill effects of unbridled personal freedom and commerce on a society, and Bramble answers that "by proper regulations, commerce may produce every national benefit, without the allay of such concomitant evils" (p. 280) [285]. England's commerce can be beneficial if it is suitably regulated—restrained, that is, by a proper sense of value. In *Humphry Clinker* moral values are represented as Scotland's greatest treasure; England is redeemable if the values of Scotland, the country, and the past are embraced along with the benefits of modernity. Baynard, the Welshman's English

6. Davis, p. xxii.

friend, who is being destroyed by his surrender to a life of luxury, is rescued by Dennison and Bramble, who urge him to adopt Dennison's ways and apply them to his own estate. Dennison's methods constitute a felicitous mix of English and Scottish strengths. So the union of Liddy and "Young Mr. Dennison" means that Bramble's niece, who was at first dangerously taken by Bath and London, is now joined to the scion of the family which represents social order and personal well-being in the narrative. Liddy is, therefore, safe, and her return to Bath need not make Bramble anxious about her future. Old and new, city and country, Scotland and England are harmonized in the series of unions that Smollett uses to end *Humphry Clinker*, valorizing both union—harmonious, moral human society—and the Union in the process.

Underlying, then, the satirical depiction of England and the loving portrait of Scotland, underlying the familial disputes and love interests, underlying the movement through space (city and country) and time (old and new), underlying all the seemingly disparate elements in *Humphry Clinker* is an historical vision. England is to be admired for its material progress; Scotland, at an earlier stage of development, might well emulate the southern kingdom on that score. But England as it grows and changes is being corrupted and can only be saved by a return to the values that are preserved in Scotland. The Union in all its ramifications, *Humphry Clinker* suggests, is a potential solution to the woes besetting England and the challenges confronting Scotland. This historical argument might well be regarded as an illusion, as Byron Gassman has suggested in a rather different context, but if so, it is an illusion that is rooted in a vision of the joint destiny of the kingdoms on both sides of the Tweed, one that is elaborated and endorsed within the narrative.[7]

If the claim is accepted that *Humphry Clinker* is more satisfying structurally than Smollett's other fiction because of the historical argument that unfolds in the narrative, should this text therefore be called Smollett's most "novelistic" fiction and his one successfully achieved novel? Several critics have, at least implicitly, already made this point. Alan McKillop suggests that *Humphry Clinker* is Smollett's best essay in the novel form because it is "successfully centered about a humorous character." John Warner, too, argues that in earlier works Smollett was unable "to entrust the serious work of the novel to the story of the individual," whereas in *Humphry Clinker* the focus was not upon "the exterior world for its own sake but upon that scene as it relates to the interior world of

---

7. Gassman, "*Humphry Clinker* and the Two Kingdoms of George III," *Criticism* 16 (1974), 108.

character."[8] These essentially Forsterian arguments—that Smollett's greatest accomplishment as a novelist derives from his having centred *Humphry Clinker* on successfully realized characters—lend credence to the proposition that Smollett's use of history makes *Humphry Clinker* his most fully accomplished novel, since the characterization of Matthew Bramble and the enactment of the historical argument in the narrative depend each upon the other.

We first encounter Bramble at odds with his physical, social, and political environment, including the company of his fellow travellers. His complaint to his doctor that "The pills are good for nothing" opens the novel. Bramble is sick and England is sick; the illness of both will become more apparent as the journey unfolds. In his first letter Bramble observes, "I shall set out tomorrow morning for the Hot Well at Bristol, where I am afraid I shall stay longer than I could wish"; he travels in search of a cure, but the places that he initially visits cause his condition to worsen. Not just Bramble's health is in disrepair, however; Bramble also tells Dr Lewis that "A ridiculous incident that happened yesterday to my niece Liddy, has disordered me in such a manner that I expect to be laid up with another fit of the gout" (pp. 5–6) [11]. The Welshman's relations with his family also contribute to his discomfiture and ill health. These relations too must be improved in the course of the narrative. Bramble is alienated from his environment, his family, and even from himself. Only when his mind and spirit—troubled by the state of his own health and that of his family and his polity—are given relief will his peevishness subside.

The valetudinarian makes real progress in the course of the journey. At the end of the narrative, Bramble's entire family is "happily settled"; Bramble himself has "laid in a considerable stock of health." And not only is Baynard's estate restored to harmony, but Bramble himself is headed back to the "salutary" Brambleton-hall (pp. 350–51) [353–54]. His achievement of a modicum of well-being is linked to the state of his family and both are suggestive of the possibility of social health. When Bramble praises the benefits of society in his penultimate letter to Dr Lewis, he celebrates the new-found harmony within his own family and Baynard's first steps towards the realization of the social ideal represented by the Dennison estate. Bramble provides a centre for this narrative not only because of his relations with the other characters and the richness of his observations and commentary, but also because his health and the well-being of those around him are achieved, like the envisioned health of his polity, by means of a unifying circuit of the

---

8. McKillop, p. 172; John M. Warner, "Smollett's Development as a Novelist," *Novel* 5 (1971–72), 154, 158.

southern and the northern kingdoms. In short, Bramble's fate echoes Britain's fate, and Britain's fate conditions Bramble's; Smollett's most successfully realized character is the efficacious centre of *Humphrey Clinker* in important part because he is crucial to the elaboration of the historical argument enacted within the narrative.

The historical argument in *Humphry Clinker*, then, is a crucial aspect of Smollett's most successful achievement in fictional characterization. Moreover, recognizing that argument also leads to a greater appreciation of Smollett's emplotment of this novel. Sheldon Sacks has argued tellingly that *Humphry Clinker* is "an action with so many digressions of one kind and another that its total effect was somewhat vitiated."[9] Sacks did not indicate what elements in the narrative he regarded as digressions, but Lewis Knapp has commented on "the digressive accounts of the Baynards and the Dennisons" in the latter part of the novel (p. xiv). Having recognized the historical argument of the text, however, one can see that these accounts, as well as the descriptions of Bath, London, Edinburgh, and Loch Leven and the characterizations of Clinker, Lismahago, and the Burdocks, can no longer be regarded as digressive. Elements that heretofore seemed interesting or entertaining, but hardly crucial, in a narrative that seemed to many readers to lack a unifying plan, play an important part in the exacerbation and resolution of the "represented instability" in the relationships of Bramble and the other characters, a relationship that has a public as well as a private, an historical as well as a personal, dimension. In short, recognizing Smollett's elaboration of a historical vision in *Humphry Clinker* makes it clear that the narrative is a better integrated "action" than Sacks allowed.[1]

9. Sheldon Sacks, *Fiction and the Shape of Belief* (1964; reprinted Chicago: University of Chicago Press, 1980), p. 271. For Sacks's definition of an "action," see p. 26.

1. No doubt Sacks was correct about *Humphry Clinker* in the sense that, as he observes, "many readers have felt greater pleasure from the work's parts than from the accomplishment of its artistic ends" (p. 271). This is in part because Sacks's readers were disposed to think of *Humphry Clinker* as seriously deficient in comparison with *Tom Jones*, whereas Smollett's work needs to be seen as something fundamentally different from Fielding's masterpiece. In order to understand how *Humphry Clinker* is different from *Tom Jones*, we may turn to Sacks's fellow Chicagoan, R. S. Crane. Crane identified three possible kinds of plots in novels: those of action, character, and thought. He pointed out that most plots are plots of action and that as a result many critics think of plot in terms of action alone. Indeed, Sacks's definition of a novel as a "represented action" suggests that he identified, to some extent at least, plots of action with novelistic plots. Of Crane's three types, however, clearly it is the third that applies to *Humphry Clinker*. There is no real change in Bramble's situation or in his moral character; but Bramble does feel and think differently at the conclusion of the narrative. Thus *Humphry Clinker* ought to be seen as a successful novel with a plot of thought because the various elements deployed by Smollett in the narrative bear upon the changing views and feelings of the protagonist. Seeing the novel in this light does not, of course, make it any more or less unified, but it may make us more sensitive to the particular unity of Smollett's narrative. See Crane, "The Concept of Plot and the Plot of *Tom Jones*" in *Critics and Criticism: Ancient and Modern*, ed. Crane (Chicago: University of Chicago Press, 1952), pp. 620–21.

Having shown why I think awareness of the historical argument in *Humphry Clinker* lends credence to the claim that Smollett's last work is his most novelistic achievement, let me now propose another, and for me a more compelling, reason for attributing Smollett's accomplishment in *Humphry Clinker* to its historical aspect by focusing briefly on Smollett's several attempts to define the kind of fiction he was writing. Smollett classified *Roderick Random* for his readers by placing it within the picaresque tradition, by identifying it as a species of satire, and, finally, by promising that the satire would be "introduced . . . in the course of an interesting story, which brings every incident home to life; and . . . represent[s] familiar scenes." Smollett thus focused his reader's attention on the imaginative and the literary character of the text. Later, in *Ferdinand, Count Fathom*, Smollett spoke of a novel as "a large diffused picture, comprehending the characters of life, disposed in different groups, and exhibited in various attitudes, for the purposes of a uniform plan, and general occurrence, to which every individual is subservient." At the same time, however, he also used analogies drawn from painting and drama, as McKillop has shown.[2] Here he moved away from a definition of the novel as a satire and towards the realism that has often been associated with the emergent novel.[3] Thus he continued to emphasize the imaginative traditions within which his creations were to be comprehended, but he also began to link his own work with a tradition that includes attempts to define the novel as a fictional form that functions as history.[4]

This latter tendency became more pronounced in *Humphry Clinker*, in which the narrative was presented to the public as a genuine collection of letters. Jonathan Dustwich offers the letters to Henry Davis, a bookseller, but informs him that "with reference to the manner in which I got possession of these Letters, it is a circumstance that concerns my conscience only" (p. 2) [8]. For the first time, Smollett adopted a device that Barbara Foley calls "pseudofactual imposture," a strategy of presentation that we associate with

2. *The Adventures of Ferdinand Count Fathom*, introduction and notes by Jerry C. Beasley, ed. O.M. Brack (Athens: University of Georgia Press, 1988), pp. 4, 9–10; McKillop, pp. 164–65.
3. As in Ian Watt's classic study, *The Rise of the Novel: Studies in Defoe, Richardson and Fielding* (Berkeley: University of California Press, 1957), chap. 1.
4. See Leo Braudy, *Narrative Form in Fiction and History: Hume, Fielding, and Gibbon* (Princeton: Princeton University Press, 1970), pp. 91–212; Jerry C. Beasley, *Novels of the 1740s* (Athens: University of Georgia Press, 1982), pp. 43–84; Michael McKeon, *The Origins of the English Novel, 1600–1740* (Baltimore: Johns Hopkins University Press, 1987), pp. 25–128; and my "The Reception of *A Journal of the Plague Year* and the Nexus of Fiction and History in the Novel," *ELH* 57 (1990), 529–56. Lennard J. Davis, *Factual Fictions: The Origins of the English Novel* (New York: Columbia University Press, 1983) is also apposite.

the fictions of Behn, Defoe, and Richardson.[5] The way in which
Smollett's frame for *Humphry Clinker* could function as a definition of the new form was discussed by Richardson in a letter to
William Warburton. Somewhat dismayed by Warburton's provision
of a preface for the first edition of *Clarissa*, Richardson wrote:

> I could wish that the *Air* of Genuineness had been kept up, tho'
> I want not the letters to be *thought* genuine; only so far kept
> up, I mean, as that they should not prefatically be owned *not* to
> be genuine: and this for fear of weakening their Influence . . .
> [and] that kind of Historical Faith which Fiction itself is gener-
> ally read with, tho' we know it to be Fiction.[6]

Richardson wanted his narrative to be understood as something
other than "mere fiction" or romance; he wanted his text read with
the "Historical faith" of readers of novels. Smollett's reasons for
adopting "pseudofactual imposture" are less clear than Richardson's, but, in appropriating that technique in *Humphry Clinker*, it is
reasonable to conclude that he was insisting upon the historicity of
his fiction. Smollett did not identify his last fiction with literary
genres other than the novel because, like Richardson, he wanted to
induce a "Historical faith" in his readers.

Not only Richardson, of course, but also Fielding and a host of
other writers identified the "new species of writing" which they helped
to create as a kind of history. In implicitly designating *Humphry Clinker* as a "historical" narrative, then, Smollett linked his last work with
a line of development that stretches backward through Defoe to six-
teenth and seventeenth-century anti-romancers and forward to Scott.
Smollett's use of his "editor" constitutes an identification of his own
work with that tradition. In addition, then, to "the ingredients of the
early Scott—humorous realism, precise topographical and social
details about remote and interesting places with a romantic context"—
which McKillop saw in *Humphry Clinker*, Smollett also looked forward to Scott by invoking a convention that indicates to the reader
that this fiction should be read as a kind of history and also acknowledges the paradoxical nature of the novel's claim to historicity.[7]

Thus, the final reason for regarding *Humphry Clinker* as Smollett's most novelistic fictional narrative is because it alone of all
Smollett's works presses us to conceive of the novel as a fictional
form that does the work of history. In doing so, this novel also

5. Barbara Foley, *Telling the Truth: The Theory and Practice of Documentary Fiction*
(Ithaca: Cornell University Press, 1986), p. 118.
6. *Selected Letters of Samuel Richardson*, ed. John Carroll (Oxford: Clarendon, 1964),
p. 85.
7. McKillop, p. 179; also my "The Internal Machinery Displayed: *The Heart of Midlothian*
and Scott's Apparatus for the Waverley Novels," *CLIO* 17 (1987), 1–20.

suggests that the claimed historicity of the novel should be thought of as a necessary element in any theoretical account of the nature of the form. Like many another early English novel, Smollett's last and best work argues for an undeniably problematic but nevertheless constitutive link between the novel and historical discourse. In *Vanity Fair* Miss Rose tells the stiff Mr Crawley that she is reading Smollett's history, "without, however, adding that it was the history of Mr. Humphry Clinker."[8] The joke, it would seem, was on Miss Rose; she said more than she knew. *Humphry Clinker* is indeed historical, and that is an important reason why we still think of it as one of the handful of crucial English novels written in the eighteenth century.

CHARLOTTE SUSSMAN

Lismahago's Captivity:
Transculturation in *Humphry Clinker*[†]

England's colonial possessions seem very far away in Smollett's *Humphry Clinker*. The novel concerns a domestic journey not only in that its path takes it across the domestic spaces of England and Scotland, but also in that it focuses on a domestic group—a household organized around familial relations. This essay will argue, however, that even within such spaces the problems posed by colonial expansion can be perceived, and that, furthermore, it is precisely those problems that provoke the anxiety over the dissolution of English domestic self-sufficiency that is *Humphry Clinker*'s most persistent concern. The primacy of this concern may not be immediately apparent, embedded as it is in a more legible anxiety over England's changing class structure. But, by concentrating on the novel's representation of colonial relations I not only want to make visible the growing connectedness of English and colonial society in the period, but also to reveal the work the novel performs to neutralize any textual evidence of this increasing interdependence, and to erect instead a compensatory fantasy of English self-sufficiency. This fantasy of self-sufficiency, of an impenetrable national identity, seems to me one of the most durable legacies of the eighteenth century, and to hold a central place in the organization of Smollett's novel.

I want to begin with the story of a journey that reverses the usual trajectory of colonial expansion—with Captain Lismahago's voyage

8. William Makepeace Thackeray, *Vanity Fair*, introd. Joseph Warren Beach (New York: Random House, 1950), pp. 87–88.
† From *ELH* 61.3 (Fall 1994): 597–618. © 1994 The Johns Hopkins University Press. Reprinted with permission of The Johns Hopkins University Press.

back from the Native American tribe that adopts him, to the heart of English domestic space as Tabitha Bramble's husband. Captain Lismahago's return is only the novel's most graphic example of the intrusion of the colonial world into English domestic life. Like Lismahago, numerous new commodities made their way back from the New World during the first half of the eighteenth century. To cite one of Smollett's own lists, "Sugar, rum, tea, chocolate, and coffee" all became part of everyday English life during that first phase of imperial expansion.[1] As James Bunn notes, "Tea and porcelain now seem so iconistically English that one must recall . . . [that] what seems to be the very soul of Englishness might recently have been imported and assimilated by a syncretic culture."[2] The influx of these substances, then, was one of many material tokens that intimated that England's colonial expansion not only had created syncretic cultures in the colonial arena, but might also challenge England's idea of itself as a coherent, homogeneous society.[3]

In Smollett's *Humphry Clinker*, published in 1771, one can judge the gravity of such a challenge through the narrative's vision of the dangerous consequences of inter-cultural contact. The novel's anxiety about the economic changes wrought by merchant capitalism centers on the transculturation of England threatened by the foreign luxury goods that mercantile trade brought back into the country. For the text, these luxury goods are most exemplarily food stuffs, whose penetration of individual digestive tracts replicates the penetration of English culture by its supposedly subjugated colonies. Indeed, "By far the largest group [in percentages of total imports during the period] is that which the officials describe as 'grocery' and which consisted of tea, coffee, sugar, rice, pepper and a variety of other tropical, semi-tropical or oriental produce."[4] The growing necessity of such imports undermined England's claim to

---

1. Tobias Smollett, *The Expedition of Humphry Clinker* (Oxford: Oxford Univ. Press, 1988), 279 [284]. All subsequent quotations from this text will be give in parentheses following the citation. [Page numbers in square brackets refer to this Norton Critical Edition.]
2. James Bunn, "The Aesthetics of British Mercantilism," *New Literary History* 11 (1980): 305.
3. The anthropologist, Fernando Ortiz, has labeled this process "transculturation." Transculturation, he argues, "does not consist merely in acquiring another culture, which is what the English word *acculturation* really implies, but the process also necessarily implies the loss or uprooting of a previous culture, which could be defined as a deculturation. In addition it carries the idea of the consequent creation of new cultural phenomena, which could be called neoculturation." The concept of transculturation can account for the way elements of a supposedly subjugated and disappearing culture might enter into the culture of its conquerors. In the process of transculturation, cultures work on one another to produce new social meanings. This essay will argue that in eighteenth-century England commercial exchange became a primary site of transculturation as trade goods were understood and desired through images of foreign cultures. See Fernando Ortiz, *Cuban Counterpoint: Tobacco and Sugar* (New York: Alfred A. Knopf, 1947), 102.
4. Elizabeth B. Schumpeter, *English Overseas Trade Statistics 1697–1808* (Oxford: Oxford Univ. Press, 1960), 11.

national self-sufficiency, especially during the period in which *Humphry Clinker* was written: "Between 1765 and 1774 . . . home-grown supplies [of food] were insufficient to meet the needs of a growing population."[5] I will argue that Smollett's novel views these economic developments as threatening—it figures the process of intercultural exchange as a kind of poisoning, newly possible at the domestic table.

Alongside this fantasy of incorporation, in which cultural difference is fantasmatically transformed into a foreign object looking to take up a destructive residence inside English bodies, we can read a compensatory defense of English national identity. The problem of how to assimilate, or acculturate, other cultures, economically or socially, is redacted into a problem of oral consumption: to avoid becoming the other, one must simply avoid eating the other. I will argue that *Humphry Clinker* enacts a strategy of literalizing, and thus attempting to neutralize, the cultural anxiety surrounding transculturation. Into its insistently corporeal and oral figurations of changing patterns of economic consumption I want to read a nascent fantasy of disconnection—a means by which England could disentangle itself from the cross-cultural connections of mercantilism. Yet behind that fantasy, I believe the novel envisions the collapsing distinctions between foreign sites of capital accumulation and domestic spaces of consumption.

I: *Lismahago's Transculturation*

During the second half of the eighteenth century, England's closest commercial ties were with her American colonies, and it is the peculiar representation of colonial commerce, set against the progress of imperial expansion in Smollett's novel, that I want to discuss. Like almost all eighteenth-century English novels, *Humphry Clinker* refers to the colonies frequently, as a convenient off-stage site for capital accumulation, or as a respectable outlet for entrepreneurial energy.[6] The novel contains only one extended anecdote about colonial life, however: Captain Lismahago's account of his captivity among the Miamis in North America. Critics have often pointed to the topicality of this story, and have used it as evidence of Smollett's extensive knowledge of historical sources. Louis Martz, for instance, claims that Lismahago's adventures are based on episodes from the "History of Canada" which appeared in the *British Magazine* from 1760–63, while T. R. Preston argues for the equal

---

5. Schumpeter, 13.
6. For capital accumulation see the fortunes described on pages 264 [270] and 286 [292]; for entreprenurial energy see the story of Martin the Highwayman's "active and enterprizing disposition" on page 187 [194].

importance of Cadwallader Colden's *History of the Five Nations* (1727) in the formulation of these events.[7] One could undoubtedly find many more relevant historical accounts, given the British pre-occupation with the conquest of North America during the 1760s. I would propose, however, that the multiplicity of possible sources for Lismahago's adventures points as much to the repetition of certain images in eighteenth-century accounts of Native Americans as it does to Smollett's own extensive historical knowledge. I would claim, as well, that these images enact different versions of a problematic scenario for the English during this period: the meeting of two distinctly different cultures in an imperialist setting.

The term "transculturation" seems particularly appropriate for the British experience in North America: the possibility of the "creation of new cultural phenomena" was always present in North America, not least because the indigenous residents of that area were not immediately eradicated, as were those of the Caribbean islands.[8] Instead, although the native tribes were numerically small, James Axtell, for one, has claimed that the battle for hegemony south of the Canadian Shield was primarily waged in terms of cultural conversion: he argues that "the contest for North America was fought largely in times of declared peace, with weapons other than flintlocks and tomahawks."[9] To their advantage in this struggle, the northeastern tribes were disconcertingly capable of absorbing Europeans into their communities.[1] Thus, the colonial encounter in the North American woods was more complicated than simple imperial aggression—as can be seen from Lismahago's adventures.

Indeed, Smollett's rendering of his story takes the form of a parody of the narrative convention that encompassed these complicated relations, the captivity narrative. Captivity narratives, accounts of Europeans forcibly exposed to Native American cultures, themselves encapsulate the ambiguities of transculturation by pointing out a secondary meaning in the word itself: the ability of individuals to move across, or through, cultures. Although the burden of these early American documents was usually to illustrate the protagonist's suffering in a "savage" society, such narratives must somehow accommodate the fact that the protagonist has survived these hardships, having adapted sufficiently to Native American customs to return alive. The tension in these narratives between the fact of

7. Louis Martz, *The Later Career of Tobias Smollett* (London: Archon Books, 1967), 176–80; T. R. Preston, "Smollett Among the Indians," *Philological Quarterly* 61 (1982): 231–41.
8. Ortiz, 102.
9. James Axtell, *The Invasion Within: The Contest of Cultures in Colonial North America* (New York: Oxford Univ. Press, 1985), 4.
1. Axtell, 302–29.

survival, and the cultural imperative to establish the "savagery" of Native American tribes becomes apparent when Rachel Plummer, abducted by the Comanche in 1836, writes: "I have withheld stating many things that are facts, because I well know that you will doubt whether any person could survive what I have undergone."[2] Because the reader must continue to doubt that life as Europeans construe it is possible inside a Native American tribe, Plummer elides material descriptions of the facts of her captivity. The coding of cultural adaptation as inhuman suffering is incompatible with the fact of her survival; the narrative ellipsis can be read as an ideological aporia.

Lismahago's narrative rehearses this central ambivalence in English representations of Native American captivities—the contradiction between documenting the adaptability of cultural identities and reasserting the superiority of European social values. In order to explicate the strategies the text uses to reconcile these positions, I wish to identify two moments as central to many accounts of the tribes of northeastern America: the Algonquin torture ritual of making prisoners "run the gauntlet" (also called "bastinado") and their subsequent practice of either adopting such prisoners into the tribe or cannibalizing them. These rituals, although violent, were seen by eighteenth-century observers as the means by which Native American tribes appropriated and transformed foreign cultures. Europeans saw these rituals as evidence of a tribe's ability to retain its social coherence in the face of a colonizing invasion—a quality they found admirable as well as threatening.

The resonance of the scene of cross-cultural adoption for a culture, like eighteenth-century England, concerned with colonial acquisition becomes apparent in Cadwallader Colden's analysis of the phenomenon. Colden, one-time governor of New York and a contemporary historian of colonial relations during the eighteenth century, links the practice of adopting prisoners of war with imperial expansion. In his *History of the Five Nations*, published in 1727, he remarks:

> They strictly follow one Maxim, formerly used by the *Romans* to increase their Strength, that is, they encourage the People of other Nations to incorporate with them; and when they have subdued any People, after they have satiated their Revenge by such cruel Examples, they adopt the rest of their Captives; who, if they behave well, become equally esteemed with their

---

2. *The Narrative of the Capture and Subsequent Sufferings of Mrs. Rachel Plummer: During a Captivity of Twenty-one Months among the Comanche Indians; With a Sketch of Their Manners, Customs, Laws, &c., &.* (1839; rpt. Waco: Texian Press, 1968), 14.

own people; so that some of their Captives have afterwards become their greatest *Sachems* and *Captains*.[3]

The ability of the northeastern tribes to "incorporate" and "adopt" foreigners into their own society, without diminishing their own cultural integrity, fascinated European observers. This principle of absorption, especially when linked to ideas of "Roman strength," seems to provide a model for a successful, expansionary encounter with another culture. Such native tribes manage to bring foreigners into their culture without challenging their dominant social system, and while continuing to patrol rigorously the borders of that society. Thus, Smollett's Miamis are able to do what the English cannot: in Lismahago's words,

> The Indians were too tenacious of their own customs to adopt the modes of any nation whatsoever . . . neither the simplicity of their manners, nor the commerce of their country, would admit of those articles of luxury which are deemed magnificence in Europe; and that they are too virtuous and sensible to encourage the introduction of any fashion which might help to render them corrupt and effeminate. (194) [202–03]

If, according to Smollett's narrative, colonial expansion had occasioned the luxury that corrupted English society, then, in Lishmahago's view, the "tenacity" of the Miamis' belief in their own culture has enabled them to maintain their virtue: in this version, the colonial encounter violates Europe, rather than the New World.

Eighteenth-century commentators' admiration for the strength and durability of native cultures has its double in a contrasting vision of this encounter. In this nightmarish version of social absorption, the captives are eaten: cannibalism too somehow allegorizes the meeting of two cultures. These two possibilities—cannibalism or adoption—seem to function as positive and negative versions of the same event in the eyes of European victims. Both options focus on Native American social tenacity: both adoption and cannabilism ultimately work to maintain social coherence. The eighteenth-century equation of cultural and gastrointestinal absorption implies a certain vision of how such inter-cultural confrontations might be negotiated. On one hand, such images of Native Americans glorify an image of Roman, imperial virtue as the model of cultural expansion, while on the other hand, they outline the threat of the literal disappearance of European culture into the belly of America. But in both cases texts like Colden's imply that when two cultures meet, one must be incorporated, whole, inside the other.

3. Cadwallader Colden, *History of the Five Nations* (London, 1757), 5.

Lismahago's experience, however, represents a third option; his story has more to do with cultural syncretism, than with either destruction or absorption. Jery Melford's transcription of Lismahago's version of these events reads like this:

> [Lismahago and Murphy] fell in with a party of Miamis, who carried them away in captivity. The intention of these Indians was to give one of them as an adopted son to a venerable sachem, who had lost his own in the course of the war, and to sacrifice the other to the custom of the country. Murphy, as being the younger and handsomer of the two, was designed to fill the place of the deceased, not only as the son of the sachem, but as the spouse of a beautiful squaw, to whom his predecessor had been betrothed; but in passing through the different wigwhams [sic] and villages of the Miamis, poor Murphy was so mangled by the women and children, who have the privilege of torturing all prisoners in their passage, that, by the time they arrived at the place of the sachem's residence, he was rendered unfit for the purposes of marriage: it was determined, therefore, in the assembly of the warriors, that ensign Murphy should be brought to the stake and that the lady should be given to Lieutenant Lismahago, who had likewise received his share of torments, though they had not produced emasculation.—A joint of one finger had been cut, or rather sawed off with a rusty knife; one of his great toes was crushed into a mash between two stones; some of his teeth were drawn, or cut out with a crooked nail; splintered reeds had been thrust up his nostrils and other tender parts; and the calves of his legs had been blown up with mines of gunpowder dug into the flesh with the sharp point of a tomahawk. (193) [201][4]

The Miamis then make "a hearty meal upon the musculature which they pared from the victim" (193) [201] and marry Lismahago to the sachem's daughter Squinkinacoosta. Although the passage outlines the usual options of incorporation—Murphy is eaten while Lismahago is adopted—its descriptive focus is on the violence of running the gauntlet. The injuries Lismahago sustains to his extremities form the basis of the text's vision of his transculturation—his movement from one culture into another.

The significance of this particular form of violence is underlined by the fact that these descriptions are the aspect of his historical sources that Smollett most painstakingly replicates in *Humphry Clinker*.[5] Smollett's description of the structure of the gauntlet is so

---

4. For similar accounts, collected from French Jesuits among the Huron Indians, see Elizabeth Tooker, *An Ethnology of the Huron Indians, 1615–1649, American Ethnology Bulletin* 190 (1964).
5. Martz, 176.

similar to Cadwallader Colden's as to seem a simple repetition.[6] The more brutal instances of dismemberment may well have come from Smollett's own *British Magazine*, which began to publish the "History of Canada" in 1760.[7] This serial abounds in the same descriptions of the ripping and tearing of bodies as does *Humphry Clinker*. To cite just one example: "[One prisoner] had been tortured according to custom. One hand had been crushed between two stones, and one finger torn off: they had likewise chopped off two fingers of the other hand; the joints of his arms were burnt to the bone, and in one of them was a dreadful gash or incision."[8] The central role these details play in Lismahago's story suggests that the paring and grinding down of European bodies provide Smollett's novel with appropriate images for the experience of transculturation on the North American frontier. The novel thus emphasizes the corporeal nature of this transition; Lismahago's captivity narrative represents this cultural possibility as the dispersal of the European body in pieces: teeth, fingers and other body parts disappear into the native community. In this way, the diffuse operations of cultural change are reduced to discrete, physical losses.

Lismahago's account, however, wrestles with the central ambiguity of captivity narratives. His absorption into the Miamis, despite the physical suffering it occasions, nevertheless illustrates a historically new transience in cultural identifications. Running the gauntlet of the Miamis rather brutally reshapes him, it is true—leaving him missing a few teeth and fingers; but it does not disempower him, nor, the text stresses, emasculate him. In fact, he is "elected sachem, acknowledged first warrior of the Badger tribe, and dignified with the epithet of Occacanastaogarora, which signifies *nimble as a weasel*" (194) [202]. He enters into a miscegenous union with Squinkinacoosta, and produces a son among the Miamis. Yet, significantly, Lismahago begins his journey back to England when he is "exchanged for an orator of the community, who had been taken prisoner by the indians that were in alliance with the English" (194) [202]. The principle of adoptability thus renders individuals both replaceable and portable—Lismahago is as much a commodity as one of his own furs. In this case, cultural exchange is literalized

---

6. Here, Colden describes the scene: "The Warriors think it for their Glory, to lead [the prisoners] through all the villages of the Nations subject to them, which lie near the Road; and these, to show their affection to the *Five Nations*, and their Abhorrence of their Enemies, draw up in two Lines, through which the poor Prisoners, stark naked, must run the Gauntlet; and on this occasion, it is always observed, the Women are much more cruel than the Men. The Prisoners meet the same sad Reception when they reach their Journey's End" (9).

7. Martz is even "tempted to assign either the compilation or the editorship of this history to Smollett himself" (180).

8. *British Magazine*, June 1760, 352.

by the mobility of bodies through the communities that are no longer able to anchor them.

When Lismahago returns to England, he brings this instability in cultural identifications with him. His first encounter with the Bramble party reveals his physical difference: "His hat and periwig falling off, displayed a head-piece of various colours, patched and plaistered in a woeful condition" (188) [195]. He has, he explains, been scalped. Rendered alien in this way, he gains Othello's skills as a lover: Tabitha "*did seriously incline her ear*—indeed, she seemed to be taken with the same charms that Captivated the heart of Desdemona, who loved the Moor *for the dangers he had past*" (194) [202]. In what is, once again, a syncretic collapse of the many cultures inhabiting North America, Lismahago has the eloquence both of the African Othello, and of the Native Americans among whom he has lived: note that he owes his presence in England to being exchanged with a tribal orator. Along with his external changes, Lismahago has acquired a style of speech associated with exoticism and seduction; he has assumed the Miamis' ability to take captives and so "captivates" Tabitha. If the novel uses these images to satirize the rather ungainly couple of Tabitha and Lismahago, it also, through these images, acknowledges the recognizability of such American concepts in late eighteenth-century England. Through this chain of associations, Lismahago's marriage to Tabitha becomes as much an interracial union as his marriage to Squinkinacoosta—he represents the presence of creolized North America on English domestic soil.

Lismahago's wedding gift to Tabitha, a "fur cloak of American sables, valued at fourscore guineas" (347) [349], reinforces the aura of scandal surrounding their union. Not only does this costume complete the doubling of the two wives by dressing them alike, but it also figures Lismahago's position as a trader (as well as a commodity for trade himself) and therefore points to his part in the machinery of colonial expansion. Due to his transformative experiences, Lismahago is a foreigner both among the Miamis and among the English, but his position as a trader bridges the two worlds. Furthermore, his samples of colonial goods are the tokens of transculturation, and form the links of the chain of commerce binding the sites of colonial production to the sites of domestic consumption.

Humphry Clinker's description of Lismahago's sojourn among the Miamis contains three possible models of inter-cultural contact: an image of cultural expansion, centering on the Native American practice of adopting war captives; a vision of cultural obliteration focused on the threat of cannibalism; and, finally, a scenario of cultural syncretism, which finds its economic equivalent in trading, and its corporeal image in the dispersal of bodies along the gauntlet. The remainder of this essay will examine how these possibilities, particularly the last, function in the greater part of *Humphry Clinker*, which takes place in domestic territory.

II: Domestic Tides

If Lismahago's narrative illustrates the growing, inextricable net of connections linking England to her colonial possessions, then the novel's domestic scenes figure those connections in a particularly mediated way. Using the same strategy of corporealizing cultural change as the inserted captivity narrative, *Humphry Clinker* imagines English bodies to be under attack by the forces of mercantile accumulation. These forces are materialized in the catachrestic "tide of luxury." The instability of the world through which the Bramble party travels is consistently denoted by images of fluidity. Social disintegration is a "flood of luxury and extravagance" that can turn a city into a "mere sink of profligacy and extortion" (57) [64]; the "tide of luxury" (87) [43] ends in "one vile ferment of stupidity and corruption" (88) [96].[9]

In Bath, these metaphors for social instability assume a different guise, one that proves perilous for individual bodies: here, the ebb and flow of commerce is mirrored by the waters of the baths, which become a literal medium of corporeal contamination. But this metaphoric transference, from the economic to the corporeal, does more than simply mirror economic changes in literary terms. I would argue that such literalization works to neutralize the threat of the innovative forms of consumption provoked by new economic connections by figuring them as a danger against which the body can actually defend itself. This representation erects the fantasy that if the baths can be purified, and foreign substances expelled from the body, the changes in English class structure wrought by cross-cultural economic connections can be reversed.

Smollett's Bath is most obviously scandalous because of the indiscriminate mixing of social classes that takes place there; yet the novel makes rhetorical links between this scandal and the process of imperial expansion. Such links can already be seen in Matthew Bramble's claim that:

> All these absurdities arise from the general tide of luxury, which hath overspread the nation, and swept away all, even the

---

9. These metaphors are a typical eighteenth-century method of describing an economy governed by mercantilism, and a society newly reshaped by trade: as Lismahago explains, trade "is a continuous circulation, like that of the blood in the human body, and England is the heart to which all the streams which it distributes are refunded and returned" (278) [284]. In this characteristic trope, trade and the human body are brought into relation through images of fluidity—the individual body becomes a figure for the cultural body of England.

very dregs of the people. Every upstart of fortune, harnassed in the trappings of the mode, presents himself at Bath, as in the very focus of observation—Clerks and factors from the East Indies, loaded with the spoil of plundered provinces; planters, negro-drivers, and hucksters, from our American plantations, enriched they know not how; agents, commissaries and contractors, who have fattened on two successive wars, on the blood of the nation; usurers, brokers, and jobbers of every kind; men of low birth, and no breeding, have found themselves suddenly translated into a state of affluence, unknown to former ages. (36–37) [43]

All of these "upstarts of fortune," aside from the usurers, brokers and jobbers, have been "translated" into affluence either in or through colonial and foreign ventures.[1] Bramble's method of description itself underlines the disruption such an influx of mercantile wealth produces at Bath. He lists the types of people to be found in the city in no particular order, as if they themselves were random commodities adrift in the "tide of luxury." Laura Brown has identified the presence of such random lists in eighteenth-century texts like "The Rape of the Lock" as the "rhetoric of acquisition": she claims that in such "catalogues the simple list of goods carries a raw and inherent fascination" for "mercantilist discourse."[2] But in Smollett's list, such acquisition has taken on a threatening edge. The "blood of the nation" is set in a negative economy with the various oceans the traders and soldiers cross to make their profits: the former is depleted to swell the "tides of luxury." To account for such anxiety, James Bunn proposes that the danger surrounding random collections was in fact part of the threat mercantilism posed to English cultural identity:

---

1. The historical specificity of Smollett's anxiety over the influx of capital from colonial trade can be seen by comparing two satirical poems about Bath by Christopher Anstey. While the first of these poems, *The New Bath Guide*, published in 1766, may have influenced *Humphry Clinker* in other ways, it contains no references to colonial capital. The second, however, "An Election Ball," published in 1776, contains many such references, not only concrete instances, like "Miss CURD [danced] with a partner as black as OMIAH," but also extended similes, such as:

> Alas! my dear wife, I can never describe
> Bath's beautiful Nymphs, that adorable Tribe,
> Who like Mexican Queens in the picture you may
> Have seen of the Court of the great Montezuma
> Set in solemn array, and diversify'd plume
> That shed o'er their charms its delectable gloom. (28)

One might speculate that the density of such references in both Smollett and Anstey is related to the end of the Seven-Year's War and its related American conflicts. See Christopher Anstey, *The New Bath Guide* (London, 1766) and "An Election Ball: in poetical letters in the Zomersetshire Dialect, from Mr. Inkle, a Freeman of Bath, to his Wife at Glouscester" (Dublin, 1776).

2. Laura Brown, *Alexander Pope* (Oxford: Basil Blackwell, 1985), 12.

> So prodigious, yet so patternless seemed the import of luxu-
> ries from cultures distanced in space and time, that the effect
> seemed to have a life of its own, as if Pygmalion's beloved grew
> grotesque. According to that kind of metaphorical thinking, a
> growing mass of exotic imports overburdened the foundation
> of native English liberties and made them "precarious."[3]

The very patternlessness of the collection of riches at Bath, and the
syntax of iteration this accumulation provokes, signal irreversible
cultural changes. The source of such changes is located in wealth
imported from abroad. In the half century between "The Rape of
the Lock" and *Humphry Clinker*, the not-so-metaphorical oceans of
trade have ceased to swell the English spirit, and begun to dissolve
its cultural borders.

The new, dangerous implications of colonial capital may be
associated with the results of the Seven-Year's War. This war was
unique among eighteenth-century conflicts in that it did not disrupt colonial trade, but rather expanded it. Yet, this mid-century
imperial expansion finally worked to demonstrate the limits of
Britain's fiscal control of her colonies. The North American tax
policies that led to the American War of Independence were a
result of Britain's need to make the colonies pay for the war that
had been fought to defend and increase them. Paradoxically, then,
the very wealth that streamed into British cities, like Bath, after
the war became a sign of Britain's dependence on her colonial
subjects.[4]

The corrosive effects of these tides of luxury are literalized in
the contaminating waters of Bath. *Humphry Clinker*'s extensive
description of the baths transforms economic developments into
waters that break through the physical defenses of the body just
as mercantile accumulation has broken down the social barriers
between landed gentry like the Brambles and the world of commercial enterprise. Matthew Bramble exclaims that "we know not what
sores may be running into the water while we are bathing, and what
sort of matter we may thus imbibe; the king's evil, the scurvy, the
cancer and the pox" (46) [52].[5] Here, a particularly virulent form of
social mixture becomes a problem of ingestion—the mouth can no

---

3. Bunn, 303.
4. See John Brewer, *The Sinews of Power: War, Money and the English State, 1688–1783*
   (London: Unwin Hyman, 1989), 174–75.
5. Smollett says much the same thing in his medical treatise on the Bath waters: "Some
   [women] may be apprehensive of being tainted with infectious distempers; or disgusted
   with the nauseating appearances of the filth, which, being washed from the bodies of
   the patients, is left sticking to the sides of the place." See Tobias Smollett, "An essay on
   the external use of water, in a letter to Dr. ****" (London, 1767), 34.

longer control what it "imbibes." On an only slightly more hysterical note, Bramble declares:

> It is very far from being clear with me, that the patients in the Pumproom don't swallow the scourings of the bathers. I can't help suspecting, that there is, or may be, some regurgitation from the bath into the cistern of the pump. In that case, what a delicate beveridge is every day quaffed by the drinkers; medicated with the sweat, and dirt, and dandriff, and abominable discharges of various kinds, from twenty different diseased bodies, parboiling in the kettle below. (46) [52]

What is perhaps most horrible about this description of uncontrollable oral intake is the promiscuity of contact within the baths. "Twenty different diseased bodies," rather than simply one, combine in what "the patient" unwittingly drinks. Boiled together, these bodies form an indistinguishable mass; not only are individual bodies indiscriminately mixed without regard for social hierarchy, as in Bramble's description of the crowds at Bath, but bits of originally discrete bodies also combine in threatening ways. By swallowing this "beveridge," the patient incorporates the matter of social reorganization, which will begin to destroy him from within his own body.

Thus, the tides of luxury are conflated with the tides of bodily fluid that seek to breach corporeal barriers. At times in *Humphry Clinker*'s Bath, it is impossible to tell where bodily fluids end and the tide of luxury begins:

> Imagine to yourself a high exalted essence of mingled odours, arising from putrid gums, imposthumated lungs, sour flatulencies, rank arm- pits, sweating feet, running sores and issues, plasters, assafoetida drops, musk, hartshorn, and sal volatile; besides a thousand frowzy streams, which I could not analyse. (66) [72]

Here, using the same rhetorical technique with which he listed the components of threatening crowds, and alluding to the same social disruption, Matthew Bramble describes the smell of a typical ball. The channels that normally contain such bodily fluids seem to have dissolved, leaving "running sores" to stream uncontrolled into a public space. No longer attached to a discrete body, such "issues" are indistinguishable from commercially available liquids. Once again, the incoherent mixture of smells, as much as their disgusting nature, heightens the disturbing quality of this description. This anxiety is syntactically marked: names for contaminating bodily fluids slide into names for medications, without even a semi-colon to signal the transition.

This confusion over the limits of individualized bodies links
social disruption inside England with the cultural confusion of the
colonial arena. The dissection of bodies into their component parts
at Bath narratively replicates the results of the gauntlet Lismahago
runs in North America. In Bath, as in Miami territory, the decom-
position of the English body becomes a sign for the dissolution of
English social structure. The scrofulous flakes of skin Matthew
Bramble fears simply represent an even more radical atomization
of the human body; in fact, Bramble's opening sentences refer to
his own battered state, he is "as much tortured in all [his] limbs
as if [he] were broke upon the wheel" (5) [11]. Yet, in both situations,
such fragmentation is triggered by the promiscuous proximity of
bodies. The threat posed by the crowds at Bath partly arises from
the surprise of such undisciplined activity in a supposedly regulated space: the streets of an English town suddenly resemble
uncharted colonial territory, spaces alternately deserted and strangely
overpopulated.

The connection between such isolated crowds and colonial
expansion is reinforced by Smollett's autobiographical account of
the European experience in the Americas, as described in *Roderick
Random*. Here, in a description of Smollett's own stint as a naval
doctor on the English expedition to Cartagena, English bodies are
crowded into dissolution:

> The sick and wounded were squeezed into certain vessels,
> which thence obtained the name of hospital ships, though
> methinks they scarce deserved such a creditable title, seeing
> none of them could boast of either surgeon nurse or cook; and
> the space between decks so confined, that the miserable patients
> had not room to sit upright in their beds. Their wounds and
> stumps being neglected, contracted filth and putrefaction,
> and millions of maggots were hatched amid the corruption of
> their sores.[6]

Like Lismahago's fingers, these sailors' limbs have been amputated
in their voyage to the New World, their bodies radically reshaped.
In fact, ironically enough, their presence in the Caribbean is due to
a war itself instigated by the crime of dismemberment—the War of

---

6. Tobias Smollett, *The Adventures of Roderick Random* (Oxford: Oxford Univ. Press,
1979), 187. The disturbing resemblance between this description and descriptions of
the middle passage of the slave trade is reinforced by Smollett's later assertion that
"such was the oeconomy in some ships, that, rather than be at the trouble of interring
the dead, their commanders ordered their men to throw the bodies overboard, many
without either ballast or winding-sheet; so that numbers of human carcasses floated in
the harbour, until they were devoured by sharks and carrion crows; which afforded no
agreeable spectacle to those who survived" (189).

Jenkins' Ear.[7] Obviously, the injuries done to these soldiers are much more extreme than the damage done to bodies at Bath. Furthermore, the agents for their injuries are clear in the colonial arena—they are at war with the Spanish—while in England, bathing bodies seem to disintegrate of their own accord. Yet, the underlying similarity between these images of corporeal dissolution may allow us to posit that the bodies in Bath are also subject to the consequences of imperial expansion; they are as liable as Lismahago to the loss of physical and cultural integrity seemingly attendant on intercultural contact. If the scenes in Bath represent such effects without a cause, it may be because they refer metonymically to colonial violence.

The similar tropes the novel employs in these geographically disparate scenes can be read as its strategy for representing the actual economic links between English cities such as Bath and British imperialism in the Americas. Robert Giddings notes that "colonial expansion by means of war, and the wealth from the West Indian slave trade—these are the major sources of the wealth and luxury so frequently noted by commentators of the time."[8] The connections formed by the Atlantic trade routes between Bath and the Americas introduce a third term to the text's representation of the forces changing English culture. Just as the tides of luxury have their internal equivalent in contaminated bodily fluids, they have an external equivalent in the ocean waters that facilitate trade. Thus, the anxiety surrounding liquid images in *Humphry Clinker* becomes totalizing and insistent: any stream, either inside or outside the body, becomes a literalization of the problem of social fluidity.

For this reason, when the Bramble party escapes from a watery grave the event carries far more ideological weight than a simple accident: Jery Melford explains that

---

7. This war began when "Jenkins's brig, *Rebecca*, returning from Jamaica to London, was boarded by the [Spanish] guarda-costa off Havana on April 9, 1731. The brig was plundered, and one of Jenkins's ears was cut off. This outrage caused considerable stir in London, where Jenkins finally arrived on the Thames, minus his ear. The affair died down, only to be revived in 1738, when Jenkins was examined before a committee of the House of Commons. The story lost nothing in the telling; the ear was even produced for the benefit of the committee. Public indignation was aroused and the 'War of Jenkins's Ear' ensued." See Henry Veits, M.D., "Smollett, the 'War of Jenkin's Ear,' and 'An Account of the Expedition to Cartagena of 1743,'" *Bulletin of the Medical Library Association* 28 (1940): 187–89 (quoted in David McNeil, *The Grotesque Depiction of War and the Military in Eighteenth-Century English Fiction* [Cranbury, NJ: Associated Univ. Press, 1990], 231).

8. Robert Giddings, "Matthew Bramble's Bath: Smollett and the West Indian Connection," in *Smollett: Author of the First Distinction*, ed. Alan Bold (London: Vision Press, Ltd., 1982), "Smollett's associations with both are clear—he served in the West Indian campaign [to Cartagena in 1740] and it was at Jamaica that he met and fell in love with the handsome Creole Anne Lascelles, who became his wife in 1747. She was the heiress of an estate and slaves valued then at 3,000 pounds. He was to experience great difficulties in laying hands on that wealth" (54).

in crossing the country to get into the post road, it was necessary to ford a river, and we that were a-horseback passed without any danger or difficulty; but a great deal of rain having
fallen last night and this morning, there was such an accumulation of water, a millhead gave way, just as the coach was
passing it, and the flood rushed down with such impetuosity, as first floated, and then fairly overturned the carriage.
(312–13) [317]

This swollen stream seems another version of the putrid waters—
internal and external—of Bath, which also constantly overflow
their bounds, and thus another embodiment of the ravaging ebb and
flow of trade. The Bramble party's submersion in the stream litera-
lizes their experience in the disorganization of English culture. But
they are rescued from this particular mishap—"Humphry flew like
lightning to the coach, that was by this time filled with water, and
diving into it, brought up the poor 'squire, to all appearances deprived
of life" (313) [317]. Although the revelation of Humphry's paternity
that this incident triggers seems largely irrelevant to the plot of the
novel, the fact that Humphry is Matthew Bramble's illegitimate son
does reassert the importance of familial connections in a world where
all non-economic relationships seem to be disintegrating. Only the
power of filial loyalty, and the stable social hierarchy it implies, can
pump the river water out of Matthew Bramble's lungs, and stem the
tide of luxury.

The references to liquid in *Humphry Clinker* may seem to work on
many discursive levels, through metaphors, images, and descriptions
of events. Yet, when this diffuse group of tropes is read through
the organizing framework of a late eighteenth-century ideology of
colonialism, they can be seen as figuring the causes of the cultural
changes brought about by colonial expansion and the mercantile
wealth such expansion produced. Both the new fluidity of cultural
space, and the new fluidity of social classes are rhetorically literalized
in the fluids, bodily and otherwise, that seem to be carrying out a
concerted attack against the Bramble party. Any moment in which
one of the party can deny these fluids access into his or her own body,
or gain control over his or her own oral intake—such as Humphry's
rescue of Matthew Bramble, or Matthew's refusal to participate in
Bath society—can be read as the text's imagined solution to the problem of class structures rendered unstable by mercantile accumulation
and colonial capital. In this way, I would argue, the novel's insistently
corporeal representations of transculturation perform the textual
work of neutralizing these socio-economic disruptions; the novel's literalizing rhetoric promises that otherness will never be assimilated as
long as it is denied access to the individual body. Yet, the fact that the

novel imagines the need for such a promise can be seen as a reaction to the disappearance of any contained site of cultural exchange; the images of dismemberment we might associate only with Lismahago's narrative appear in descriptions of England as well as in descriptions of America. What might be called the material effects of transculturation are not localized, but occur across English culture—in the colonies and on domestic soil.

III: Cannibalism and Home-grown Food

I have been arguing that *Humphry Clinker* transforms the social effects of economic consumption into a physiological problem of oral consumption. This transposition allows the novel to imagine a solution to those problems—a fantasy of harmless ingestion. If it figures the transculturation of English culture as a kind of poisonous physical incorporation of cultural difference, then it describes, in compensation, an ideal of cultural self-sufficiency centering on "pure" English food. While the narrative recounts with horror the uncontrollable intake of various fluids, not least the diseased bodily fluids ubiquitous at Bath, it also extends that horror to contaminated foods. Perhaps the most succinct example of the danger of eating occurs in Scotland, where the haggis puts Jery Melford "in mind of the history of the Congo, in which [he] had read of negro's heads sold publically in the markets" (222) [230]. The alien nature of Scottish culture is amplified by its figuration as Africa. Here, eating the haggis becomes cannibalism, literally taking the colonized other inside oneself. The destructive presence of that other inside is signified as well by the suggestion that the British have, through their economic practice of trading with "inferior" nations, adopted the eating rituals of "savages."

Throughout the novel, food, as a possible agent of the collapsing difference between England and the colonial arena, is suspect. This suspicion is not confined to food actually produced in the colonies, but rather extends to any food associated with the growing intercourse between different social classes occasioned by colonial capital. One can begin to see the formulation of this problem, and its corresponding "solution" in Matthew Bramble's tirade on the corruption of London town life:

> If I would drink water, I must quaff the maukish contents of an open aqueduct, exposed to all manner of defilement; or swallow that which comes from the river Thames, impregnated with all the filth of London and Westminster. . . . The bread I eat in London, is a deleterious paste, mixed up with chalk, alum and bone ashes. . . . I shall conclude this catalog of London dainties, with that table-beer, guiltless of hops and

malt; much fitter to facilitate the operation of a vomit, than to quench thirst and promote digestion . . . [Londoners] may, for aught I care, wallow in the mire of their own pollution. (120–22) [129–31]

Even these excerpts from what is a three-page rant demonstrate that the same tropes operate here as in Bramble's description of Bath. Contaminated liquids not only create internal discomfort, but also coagulate into an external "mire." Furthermore, it is not clear whether the contents of that mire are simply contaminated food stuffs, or also the "vomit" they provoke. There is no way of knowing, in London, whether the food one consumes is human waste or other organic matter. I would argue that an anxiety about class mobility, expressed as a fear of the incorporation of poisonous objects, emerges in the novel whenever, as in London and Bath, the difference between human and non-human substances dissolves into a continuum of contaminated matter.

Matthew Bramble reveals that it is the foreign nature of such food, its importation, which is so destructive, when he contrasts London to his nutritional ideal. At Brambleton Hall, he claims:

> I drink the virgin lymph, pure and crystalline as it gushes from the rock, or the sparkling beveridge, home-brewed from malt of my own making . . . my bread is sweet and nourishing, made from my own wheat, ground in my own mill, and baked in my own oven; my table is, in a great measure, furnished from my own ground; my five-year-old mutton, fed on the fragrant herbage of the mountains, that may vie with venison in juice and flavor; my delicious veal, fattened with nothing but the mother's milk, that fills the dish with gravy; my poultry from the barn-door, that never knew confinement, but when they were at roost; my rabbits panting from the warren; my game fresh from the moors; my trout and salmon struggling from the stream; oysters from their native banks; and herrings, with other sea-fish, I can eat in four hours after they are taken—My sallads [sic], roots and pot-herbs, my own garden yields in plenty and perfection; the produce of the natural soil and moderate cultivation. The same soil affords all the different fruits England may call her own, so that my dessert is every day fresh-gathered from the tree; my dairy flows with nectarious tides of milk and cream, from whence we derive abundance of excellent butter, curds and cheese; and the refuse fattens my pigs, that are destined for hams and bacon. (118–19) [128]

I quote this description at such length in order to demonstrate that Bramble's description of rural purity is at least as excessive as his description of metropolitan corruption. Here, however, colonial food stuffs are replaced by the "fruits England may call her own" and the tides of luxury by the "nectarious tides of milk." Syntactically, Bramble's reiteration of possession—"my veal . . . my sallads . . . my desert . . . my pigs"—adds coherence to a list which in its iterative construction resembles his description of the confusion at Bath. Furthermore, his documentation of the original location of each item, and of its exact distance from his table, inscribes a precise loop of consumption—from orchard to refuse to bacon in a model of self-sufficiency. This contained domesticity seems a refuge from the contaminated and contaminating food of London and, metonymically, from the social changes that disrupt that urban space.

Yet it is exactly this self-contained nutritional system that is already, from the start of the novel, undermined at Brambleton Hall. The "nectarious tides of milk" do not always end up on Bramble's table because Matthew's sister Tabitha often sells them at the local market. Here, another step in the novel's systematic localization of the sources of social change becomes clear: if women have control of the family food intake, then the guilt of contamination falls on them. The depth of Tabitha's transgression thus becomes clear: instead of a domestic manager, facilitating the passage from field to table, she is a "domestic daemon" (77) [84], breaking the barriers between Brambleton Hall and the world of commerce.

Moreover, Tabitha's unpaid and denigrated domestic labor, occasioned by her dependence on her brother, links her to colonial labor forces and to the contaminating world of trade, even before her marriage to Lismahago; she is a domestic entrepreneur, even as he is a colonial entrepreneur. Significantly, Tabitha recognizes her exchange-value on the marriage market, just as Lismahago acknowledges his own exchangability in the colonial arena: this repeated moment of reification links Tabitha's transgression of her gender and class roles—her attempt to alter her dependent spinsterhood into independent wealth and marriage—with the cultural transgressions of colonial captivity.

The central part played by women in the transfer of external corruption into internal physical systems is illustrated as well by the only distinct figure to emerge from Matthew Bramble's catalogue of London muck. Towards the conclusion of his description he notes,

> It was but yesterday that I saw a dirty barrow-bunter in the street, cleaning her dusty fruit with her own spittle; and who knows but some fine lady of St. James parish might admit into her delicate mouth those very cherries which had been rolled and moistened between the filthy and perhaps ulcerated chops of a St. Giles huckster. (122) [131]

The fruit dangerously mediates social mixture[1]—it carries the spittle of a poor woman into the mouth of a rich one. This oral transmission of bodily fluid by the agency of a cherry once again implies that the mouth is the primary orifice by which social corruption passes into the human body. But this exchange occurs between women, who here occupy both ends of a distasteful trade. In this instance women are made responsible for both the contamination of food, and the appearance of that contaminated food at the domestic meal. Thus Tabitha, who herself both sells food at market, and provides a market for luxurious colonial goods, marks the disappearance of distinctions between the fine lady and the St. Giles huckster. The domestic space, although ideologically privileged, is never secured, never purified, never self-sufficient.

In 1713, after the signing of the Treaty of Utrecht, Pope wrote, in "Windsor Forest," that

> The Times shall come, when free as Seas or Wind
> Unbounded Thames shall flow for all Mankind,
> Whole nations enter with each swelling Tyde,
> And Seas but join the regions they divide;
> Earth's distant ends our Glory shall behold,
> And the new World launch forth to seek the old.[2]

Pope's seas are English seas, indistinguishable from the Thames itself. In his view, trade will be both unifying and glorifying: the new world will "seek the old" on the old world's terms. But, by the end of the eighteenth century, this image of the Atlantic as cooperative with English imperialism has begun to be less persuasive. Two years after the publication of *Humphry Clinker*, in 1773, the abolitionist Thomas Day wrote, in the voice of a "Dying Negro":

> And may these fiends, who now exulting view
> The horrors of my fortune, feel them too!
> Be theirs the torment of a ling'ring fate,
> Slow as thy justice, dreadful as my hate,
> Condemned to grasp the riven plank in vain
> And chac'd by all the monsters of the main,
> And while they spread their sinking arms to thee,
> Then let their fainting souls remember me![3]

---

1. For a similar reading of this episode, see John P. Zomchick, "Social Class, Character and Narrative Strategy in *Humphry Clinker*," *Eighteenth-Century Life* 10 (1986), 182.
2. Alexander Pope, *The Poetry and Prose of Alexander Pope*, ed. Aubrey Williams (Boston: Houghton Mifflin Co., 1969), 76.
3. Thomas Day, "The Dying Negro: a poetical epistle, supposed to be written by a Black (Who lately shot himself on board a vessel in the river Thames;) to his intended Wife" (London, 1773), 19.

Here, the ocean is identified with the violent vengeance of one of the victims of colonialism. In what may be the limit case of the destruction caused by the "tides of luxury" the sea literally rises to destroy the (slave) traders who have profited by it. The Atlantic, which carries luxury items, and thus produces cultural confusion, is also the point at which the balance might tilt in favor of the colonized. If Pope's Atlantic is merely an extension of the Thames, then Day's Thames, into which the Negro throws himself, is an extension of the Atlantic, an intrusion into the heart of England itself.

It is this inherent instability in the balance of power between England and her colonial possessions that provokes *Humphry Clinker*'s deepest fear. The text works through problems of inter-cultural contact according to the paranoid logic of incorporation: it imagines that when two cultures meet one must inevitably overwhelm, swallow, or otherwise incorporate the other. This process is dangerous for both the culture swallowed and the culture swallowing, as the former becomes a destructive object lodged within the latter. Smollett's novel is organized around this distiction between a cultural inside and outside, embodied in the inside and outside of the English body, but I read the emphasis the text places on these boundaries as a response to an ongoing process of transculturation, as a textual strategy to neutralize the changes that two cultures work on one another, no matter what the power differential. We must develop a discourse to describe this subterranean process of social change if we hope to escape the oppositional structure of eighteenth-century discussions of inter-cultural contact—discussions that relentlessly strengthen the distinction between self and other, inside and outside, and conquerer and conquered.

DAVID M. WEED

Sentimental Misogyny and Medicine in *Humphry Clinker*[†]

On one level, *The Expedition of Humphry Clinker* (1771) presents its readers with a cast of scraggly, wryly drawn "originals" roaming Britain, including the tatterdemalion Humphry Clinker himself, the quixotic Obadiah Lismahago, and the curmudgeonly Matthew

† From *SEL Studies in English Literature, 1500–1900* 37.3 (Summer 1997): 615–37. Reprinted with permission from *SEL Studies in English Literature, 1500–1900*.

Bramble. It also, however, provides a rare eighteenth-century portrait of England as a "body politic."[1] The connection between an
individual's physical health and moral well-being, for example, an
issue often discussed in criticism of the novel, also correlates to the
health of the nation's social body, which, in the novel's view, is diseased and in need of a cure.[2] In *Humphry Clinker*, Tobias Smollett's
medical and literary knowledge meets his perception of England's
cultural and social condition, and the combination holds important
ramifications for an analysis of eighteenth-century masculinity. In
writing his only novel of sensibility, Smollett may have been yield-
ing to popular taste,[3] but within the form he also discovered a way
to extend the meaning of sensibility by constructing a distinctly
masculine man of feeling who resists infection from the femininity intertwined with England's commercial society. The novel represents commerce as the underlying source of England's social
ills. I will argue that England's social body incorporates the ill
effects of commercialism into its public institutions and civic and
social life, and that it produces effeminate men who participate in
an epidemic spread of luxury, bodily waste, consumption, and
"cannibalism."

   The gendering of the novel's attack on commercial society is not
unique to eighteenth-century political discourse. Indeed, eighteenth-
century economic man "was seen as on the whole a feminised, even
an effeminate being, still wrestling with his own passions and hys-
terias and with interior and exterior forces let loose by his fantasies and appetites . . . [I]n the eighteenth-century debate over the
new relations of polity to economy, production and exchange are
regularly equated with the ascendancy of the passions and the

---

1. Roy Porter, "The Body Politic; Medicine and Political Cartoons" (paper presented at
   the Wellcome Institute for the History of Medicine, London, 28 September 1994).
   Although Porter agrees with historians who argue that the trope of the "body politic"
   generally loses its importance as a metaphor in the seventeenth and eighteenth centuries, he also notes that it appears frequently in eighteenth-century political cartoons by
   William Hogarth, James Gilray, Thomas Rowlandson, and others.
2. I am attempting to broaden the numerous readings that have investigated the medical
   theme in the novel in terms of Bramble's individual journey to bodily and psychological
   health. Besides George S. Rousseau's article on the medical background to the novel
   ("Matt Bramble and the Sulphur Controversy in the Eighteenth Century," *Journal of the
   History of Ideas* 28 [1967]: 577–99), see B. L. Reid, "Smollett's Healing Journey," *VQR*
   41, 4 (Autumn 1965); 549–70; John F. Sena, "Smollett's Matthew Bramble and the
   Tradition of the Physician-Satirist," *PLL* 11, 4 (Fall 1975): 380–96; and William A.
   West, "Matt Bramble's Journey to Health," *TSLL* 11, 2 (Summer 1969): 1197–208. Ronald Paulson, in *Satire and the Novel in Eighteenth-Century England* (New Haven: Yale
   Univ. Press, 1967), mentions in passing the connection between individual and societal
   health: "Bodies, houses, cities, and the whole nation are organisms that are sick or
   conducive to sickness" (p. 196).
3. Robert Donald Spector, *Tobias George Smollett: Updated Edition* (Boston: Twayne,
   1989), p. 104.

female principle."[4] In contrast to eighteenth-century economic man, the virtuous, landowning citizen, who is shaped in particular by the republican discourse that has come to be known as civic humanism, was often criticized by "the polite man of commercial and cultivated society" as resting on an "archaic and restrictive" precommercial foundation.[5] In his debate with this republican, patriot ideal, the advocate of commerce and culture gave names such as "savagery" to his demonstrations that "what had preceded the rise of commerce and culture was not a world of virtuous citizens, but one of barbarism."[6] Interestingly, Smollett's novel intervenes in this debate by applying the notion of the sensible man of feeling to its landowning men, which places a formidably polite face on them: in effect, *Humphry Clinker* critiques economic man by usurping the terms on which he positions himself as civilized in order to construct a model male landowner who is at once more cultivated and more masculine than his allegedly "modern" counterpart. The novel essentially inverts the terms of the debate between republican "country" ideology and commercial "court" ideology by associating England's commercial society with cannibalistic savagery.[7]

The road in *Humphry Clinker*, then, leads continually farther away from England's corrupt and effeminate commercial culture, in which the stress on modernity occludes a real lack of civility. Divided, self-interested, and self-absorbed, the novel's urban Englishmen, painted especially by Bramble in broad strokes that suggest a general disapproval of all of them (except in a few instances, such as Serle), in particular appear incapable of developing or sustaining the kinds of close male bonds that finally emerge among the men in Wales. Comprised of Bramble, Jery Melford, Charles Dennison, Baynard,

---

4. J. G. A. Pocock, "The Mobility of Property and the Rise of Eighteenth-Century Sociology," in *Virtue, Commerce, and History: Essays on Political Thought and History, Chiefly in the Eighteenth Century* (Cambridge: Cambridge Univ. Press, 1985), pp. 103–23, 114; originally published in slightly different form in Anthony Parel and Thomas C. Flanagan, eds., *Theories of Property: Aristotle to the Present* (Waterloo ON: published for the Calgary Institute for the Humanities by Wilfred Laurier Univ. Press, 1979), pp. 141–66.

5. Pocock employs the term "civic humanism," particularly in *The Machiavellian Moment: Florentine Thought and the Atlantic Republican Tradition* (Princeton: Princeton Univ. Press, 1975). For work by John Barrell and civic humanism in the fine arts, see *The Political Theory of Painting from Reynolds to Hazlitt: "The Body of the Public"* (New Haven: Yale Univ. Press, 1986).

6. Pocock, *Virtue*, p. 115.

7. Pocock writes: "When the polite man of commercial and cultivated society looked back into his past, what he necessarily saw there was the passions not yet socialised, to which he gave such names as 'barbarism' and 'savagery': and his debate against the patriot ideal could be far more satisfactorily carried on if he could demonstrate that what had preceded the rise of commerce and culture was not a world of virtuous citizens, but one of barbarism" (*Virtue*, p. 115).

and Clinker—and the Scotsman Lismahago—the group of men that dominates the end of *Humphry Clinker* implicitly rejects England as a place in which successful male social and political relations can be maintained. The maladies of English culture—its luxury and effeminacy in particular—lead the expedition inexorably toward Britain's geographical margins, where the novel formulates a model of masculinity based on rational male control of a landed economy and polite manly camaraderie rather than commercial passion and effeminate, vain self-interest.

Just as the novel is perhaps the last full-scale indictment of luxury in the "classical" sense[8] then, the model of landed, virtuous, republican masculinity that it eulogizes also seems destined for marginalization, forced both geographically and ideologically outside a rapidly expanding commercial English culture that the novel represents as a "monster." The novel rarely compromises its position that men must renounce their ties to commerce, which means, in effect, renouncing their ties to overwhelmingly commercialized England, in order to remain civilized, unified, healthy, and organized around principles of virtuous masculine reason rather than corrupt effeminate passion. Despite the novel's innovative masculinization of the discourse of sensibility and its depiction of the exodus from England as the construction of a civilized, masculine haven in a falsely modern world, *Humphry Clinker* also isolates its men outside civic life. Although land in the eighteenth century generally signifies leisure and independence for its owner, it also assumes the landed man's political engagement. In *Humphry Clinker*, the management of private land—especially the management of strictly demarcated gender roles in the family—becomes such a crucial task that the novel redefines the virtuous man as a privately active rather than a civic-minded individual.

The novel's strategic use of medicine to describe the ills of England's urban culture connects these problems of public and private political economy especially to the question of what it means bodily to be a man in the eighteenth century. The novel locates the problem of managing social waste particularly in Bramble's body and sexuality; I read Bramble's personal expedition as an unconscious discovery of ways that he may safely produce bodily waste and legitimate his production of the bastard Humphry Clinker,

---

8. John Sekora, *Luxury: The Concept in Western Thought, Eden to Smollett* (Baltimore: Johns Hopkins Univ. Press, 1977). Sekora's examination of the concept of luxury in Western history ends with Smollett's works, particularly *Humphry Clinker*. "For nearly two decades [Smollett] had used the classical concept of luxury to express a revulsion against certain aspects of historical change. This sense of the concept, infused into *Humphry Clinker*, was becoming increasingly ineffectual by the time the novel appeared in 1771. It was increasingly difficult, that is, for a ruling elite to demand effort and expansion while simultaneously urging restraint and retrenchment" (p. 285).

who is figured as a waste product in the system of inheritance. Only after "waste" is brought under the control of rational, virtuous, masculine men may Bramble allow himself to become a "man of feeling," triumphing over his misanthropy and his metaphorically violent masculine satire, which he affects during the expedition in reaction to England's effeminate culture.

To be a man of feeling in *Humphry Clinker* especially means regarding friendships between virtuous men as the highest social ideal. While Smollett's novel and Adam Smith's *The Theory of Moral Sentiments* (1759) are at opposite ends of the ideological spectrum regarding the virtue of the commercial man, they share an affinity for classical republican models of masculinity in their estimations that friendships based on "esteem and approbation" can "exist only among men of virtue," which, for Smith, are "by far, the most respectable" attachments a man can make.[9] In *Humphry Clinker*, these virtuous attachments between men are far more closely connected to the English landed republican ethic, which urges men's renunciation of both consumer and sexual desire in the name of virtue and independence. The vocabulary of civic humanist discourse "could describe acquisitive and especially commercial activity in the same terms as it described sexual indulgence (the attractions of both could be termed 'luxury'; their effects on men could both be described as 'effeminacy')."[1] John Barrell argues that this model of republican asexual "virile virtue" in the early eighteenth century begins to compete with a model of bourgeois "virile virtue," which legitimates men's desire for women (and, by extension, for material possessions) as a masculine rather than an effeminate pursuit. While Smith's moral man slips between a masculinized Stoic virtue and a more feminine commercial "prudence" throughout *The Theory of Moral Sentiments*, Smollett's men of feeling in *Humphry Clinker*, curiously, resist indulgent, overly sentimental relations with women in order to bond with other men, which suggests that civic humanist and bourgeois discourses on masculine virtue cross and overlap in specific eighteenth-century texts. Just as Smith's Stoicism in the last instance assures the masculinity of the commercial man, then, Smollett provides the masculine, virtuous republican with civilized and amiable sensibilities.

Of course, because *Humphry Clinker* adamantly disapproves of luxury, indulgence, and desire, the novel dramatizes the eradication of those "feminine" qualities in its major male characters and

---

9. Adam Smith, *The Theory of Moral Sentiments* (Oxford: Oxford Univ. Press, 1976), pp. 224–5.
1. Barrell, "'The Dangerous Goddess': Masculinity, Prestige, and the Aesthetic in Early Eighteenth-Century Britain," *CultCrit* 12 (Spring 1989): 101–31, 103–4.

their suppression by men in the women of the expedition, creating an atmosphere in which the men are able to form virtuous, amiable bonds. In constructing a vision of a world ordered rationally by men, which depends in particular upon limiting both men's and women's "feminine" desires, the novel castigates English culture for its associations, through commerce and luxury, with femininity, and dramatizes the ways that the major male characters restrain the women from their supposedly natural attraction to England's femi-nized culture. At all levels, whether in culture or through the male and female agents of that culture, the "female principle" in commer-cial society becomes the underlying cause of corruption in English social life and public institutions; the novel's relegation of women to minor, comic, subordinate roles reflects its urge to discover a corner of the British island in which manly men may manage women's desires and keep England's corrupt public world at bay.

The young, impressionable Lydia Melford provides the novel's primary example of the way men may teach women to reject an attraction to "vanity, expense, and disorder," which *Humphry Clin-ker* associates with "female nature,"[2] and to reconcile themselves willingly to their subordinate position as women. In the novel's terms, Lydia has the intelligence to understand the requirement that she subordinate herself to men: even though she is "as soft as butter, and as easily melted" because she has "a languishing eye, and reads romances," according to Bramble, she is also not a fool.[3] Lydia in particular has the sense to allow men to protect her from her sexual and consumer desires.

Lydia's brother, Jery, functions as the principal agent of her con-tainment. Bramble's initial reaction to his niece and nephew col-lapses them into the same category: "I an't in a condition to take care of myself; much less to superintend the conduct of giddy-headed boys and girls" (p. 13) [18]. Significantly, his reading of Jery proves to be inaccurate: less "giddy-headed" than Bramble must have been in his libertine youth, Jery, the group's dispassionate observer,[4] seems unmoved by sexual desire and is thus untroubled by any poten-tially dangerous sentimental entanglements with women. Though

---

2. John P. Zomchick, "Social Class, Character, and Narrative Strategy in *Humphry Clin-ker*," *ECL* 10, 3 (October 1986): 172–85, 185 n. 15.

3. Tobias Smollett, *The Expedition of Humphry Clinker*, ed. O. M. Brack Jr. (Athens: Univ. of Georgia Press, 1990), p. 13 [18]. Subsequent references will be to this edition and appear parenthetically in the text. [Page numbers in square brackets refer to this Nor-ton Critical Edition.]

4. Paul-Gabriel Boucé makes the case for Jery's role as the observer of the group: "Jery does not *want* to get involved in the problems of the group. The only time he makes an exception to this rule of conduct is when he yields to a blind impulse of social and per-sonal hatred for Wilson . . . Jery's vocation—and mission—is to hold himself aloof from events and human problems in order the better to *observe* them" (*The Novels of Tobias Smollett*, trans. Antonia White [New York: Longman, 1976], p. 205).

Smollett generally provides a "gynophobic . . . critique of the social and economic changes he perceives,"[5] Jery's relationship with Lydia depicts the novel's most effective lesson in the way that men may avoid misogyny. That avoidance, however, depends upon women's willingness to relinquish the power that accrues from their natural desires. In other words, the novel suggests that men are free to love and respect women as long as they agree to remain socially subservient and under men's protection.

Throughout the novel, Jery fulfills his brotherly duties to his sister by exerting control over her "languishing eye": he confronts Wilson and protects Lydia from the "boldness" of Captain O'Donaghan's "look and manner." He is so keenly observant and anxious about patrolling Lydia's sexual desires, in fact, that he seems able to enter his sister's thoughts: Lydia writes that, to prevent her from having to dance with Captain O'Donaghan, Jery excuses himself "by saying I had got the headach; and, indeed, it was really so, though I can't imagine how he knew it" (p. 41) [48]. Jery also knows why Lydia faints at the sight of Mr. Gordon, who resembles the character Lydia had seen George Dennison, disguised as Wilson, play on stage: "the cause of my disorder remained a secret to every body but my brother, who was likewise struck with the resemblance, and scolded after we came home" (p. 250) [264].

Over the course of the novel, Lydia comes to understand the reasons that men restrain women's desires. Lydia particularly learns to see Tabitha, the novel's comically grotesque "domestic daemon" (p. 74) [000], as frivolously irresponsible in her sexual desires. Indeed, the novel counterpoints the two women in relation to their brothers: while Jery effectively regulates Lydia's desires, Bramble is continually frustrated in his attempts to control Tabitha. Before managing to negotiate one of the novel's "patriarchally approved marriages" between Tabitha and Lismahago,[6] Bramble resorts to tactics such as undeceiving Ulic Mackillgut about the state of Tabitha's fortune, in which "he had been misled by a mistake of at least six thousand pounds" in order to undermine the blossoming affair (p. 61) [70]. Tabitha's relentless commodification of herself on the marriage market particularly helps Lydia to position herself finally as a female misogynist: "My dear Willis, I am truly ashamed of my own sex—We complain of advantages which the men take of our youth, inexperience, sensibility, and all that; but I have seen enough to believe, that our sex in general make it their business to ensnare the other; and for this purpose, employ arts which are by no means

5. James P. Carson, "Commodification and the Figure of the Castrato in Smollett's *Humphry Clinker*," *ECent*, 1 (Spring 1992): 24–46, 25.
6. Carson, p. 30.

to be justified—In point of constancy, they certainly have nothing to reproach the male part of the creation" (p. 251) [265].

Rather than being a publicly active citizen engaged in civic concerns, then, the virtuous man who wishes to maintain masculine order must privately prevent women from exercising their indiscriminate desires for sex and luxury. The novel's comparison between the Baynards and Dennisons, which contains "essentially the thesis of the novel in miniature,"[7] particularly exploits the difference between the virtuous, assertive Mr. Dennison and the weak, passive Mr. Baynard to support the argument that only masculine male control of land and the household economy produces rational order and profit. The Baynards' marriage suggests that the husband who does not control his wife's desires invests her with the power to turn his real property into wasteland. Mr. Baynard's sentimentality toward his wife produces an inversion of gendered economic roles. In the name of "taste and connoisseurship," Mrs. Baynard's "improvements" to the estate have turned profitable land into an item that requires costly upkeep. Bramble's initial, impressionistic view of the Baynard estate provides a striking sense of the economic disaster that Mrs. Baynard has wrought:

> when we arrived at the house, I could not recognize any one of those objects, which had been so deeply impressed upon my remembrance . . . The house itself, which was formerly a convent of Cistercian monks, had a venerable appearance; and along the front that looked into the garden, was a stone gallery, which afforded me many an agreeable walk, when I was disposed to be contemplative—Now the old front is covered with a screen of modern architecture; so that all without is Grecian, and all within Gothic—As for the garden, which was well stocked with the best fruit which England could produce, there is not now the least vestige remaining of trees, walls, or hedges— Nothing appears but a naked circus of loose sand, with a dry bason and a leaden triton in the middle. (p. 275) [291–92]

Bramble's aesthetic sensibility, of course, is also a gendered political sensitivity to the kinds of ruin that a woman such as Mrs. Baynard produces when given the opportunity: her "naked circus" is immodest, costly, tasteless, and dead. Equally important, Mrs. Baynard's disruption of the landed masculine order robs Bramble of the use of private, aestheticized spaces such as the "stone gallery, which afforded me many an agreeable walk, when I was disposed to be contemplative." In civic humanist theory, the private is "appropriate to

---

7. Thomas R. Preston, *Not in Timon's Manner: Feeling, Misanthropy, and Satire in Eighteenth-Century England* (University: Univ. of Alabama Press, 1975), p. 117.

the contemplative, not the active life," and art is a primary medium for man's contemplation.[8] The novel suggests, however, that landed men cannot afford to follow "what the citizen *should* do in his private capacity,"[9] because men must be privately active, especially in managing their wives, to prevent losing the objects of their contemplation.

On the other hand, Mr. Dennison is the foremost example of a man who renounces commerce and public life in order to focus his attention on his private land, which becomes the last stronghold of masculine control in *Humphry Clinker*. In this economy, wives become rubber-stamp legislators of their husbands' executive decisions: Charles Dennison, "with the approbation of his wife . . . determined to quit business, and retire into the country" (p. 308) [325]. Mr. Dennison controls all aspects of this economy: by entering into "a minute detail and investigation" (p. 309) [326], he saves money on household expenses. The ideal family government, using the Dennisons as the model, is not "patriarchal" in the seventeenth-century sense of the term (so that "the family is established by the enclosure of private property, and that family is under the absolute control of the father"),[1] but the man must certainly circumscribe his wife's economic role. The "uncommon" Mrs. Dennison provides the novel's only example of a woman fit to participate in family government (though we may read Lydia, who marries the Dennisons' son, as a potential future candidate). Rather than the excessive love and tears that mark Baynard's relationship with his wife, the Dennisons' marriage is based on friendship and is marked by its formality and absence of overt sexual desire: Mrs. Dennison is "admirably qualified" to be her husband's "companion, confidant, counsellor, and coadjutrix" (p. 307) [324].

Marriage to the (more common) wife who exercises her desires produces a life that is "expensive and fantastic" (p. 281) [297]. The eighteenth-century man who pursues overly sentimental relations with women risks revealing a weakness that allows them potentially devastating power. But what is a man to do when, filled with sensibility and feeling (as is Baynard, who is surrounded by cold servants and a wife who sits "in silence like a statue, with an aspect of insensibility" [p. 283] [300], he loves the very being that threatens his economic happiness? For the man necessarily tied to such a woman by blood, as is Bramble to Tabitha, the answer is for him to find her a proper husband: the alliance of the brother and the husband then

8. Barrell, "'Dangerous Goddess,'" p. 116.
9. Barrell, "'Dangerous Goddess,'" p. 125.
1. Peter Stallybrass, *The Politics and Poetics of Transgression* (Ithaca: Cornell Univ. Press, 1986), p. 131.

insures that her desires are regulated.[2] But marriage to the female economic tyrant is a seemingly intractable problem. Baynard's excessive tenderness, the "greatest defect of his nature" and "the weak side of his soul" (pp. 277, 278) [293, 294], allows his wife to enlarge her role from titular legislator to tyrannical executive. Within the domestic unit, Baynard abdicates his rule, and the threat to the Englishman's property rights becomes a private drama in which the wife confiscates the husband's land and property, which she controls *de facto* if not *de juris*. Women's economic power inverts family government and places it under the absolute control of the mother: Mrs. Baynard wields an "absurd tyranny" over her husband, whose acquiescence is "unmanly" (p. 281) [298].

Bramble's own propensity toward sentimentality, then, in some measure explains his statements that he will not marry: an attachment to a wife like Mrs. Baynard could unman him and entail his estate, heart, and health in a similar sickening corruption. Indeed, the novel characterizes Bramble and Baynard in the same terms: Bramble has a propensity toward a "sensibility of [the] heart, which is tender, even to a degree of weakness." On the expedition, Bramble conceals his sensibility by using satire and "spleen" to defend against the individuals he meets in England's effeminate culture. In Jery's view, Bramble's satire becomes a particularly brutal, masculine, phallic weapon of defense: when provoked, Bramble will "let fly the shafts of his satire, keen and penetrating as the arrows of Teucer" (p. 29) [35]. Mrs. Baynard's death provides Bramble with the opportunity to vent his spleen upon the figure of the economically incompetent woman: "I arrived about four in the afternoon, and meeting the physician at the door, was informed that his patient had just expired.—I was instantly seized with a violent emotion, but it was not grief" (p. 325) [342]. Her death also allows her husband to recover from his sentimentality toward her: "His heart . . . was still subject to vibrations of tenderness, which returned at certain intervals, extorting sighs, and tears, and exclamations of grief and impatience: but these fits grew every day less violent and less frequent, 'till at length his reason obtained a complete victory over the infirmities of his nature" (p. 327) [345]. Tenderness toward and love of women are the "infirmities" of the sentimental man's "nature" which threaten his mental health and over which he must obtain a "complete victory" if he is to maintain his "reason."

Though generally unrealized in the novel, women's potential to exert power in a feminine culture also threatens men's bodies through

---

2. My argument here about male homosocial bonds, which casts the female character as an intermediary figure between two male characters, is strongly indebted to Eve Kosofsky Sedgwick's *Between Men: English Literature and Male Homosocial Desire* (New York: Columbia Univ. Press, 1985).

scatological language. For Win Jenkins and Tabitha, for example, that power is diverted unconsciously into the malapropisms in their letters. Critics have frequently noted that Win's and Tabitha's language is particularly scatological. Win produces writing filled with unintentional puns, "sexual innuendoes, and . . . scatological suggestiveness . . . Writing 'paleass' for 'palace,' describing the family as being in a 'constipation'; dismissing her unfaithful French lover as not worth a 'farting'; and making a 'turd' of 'third' and 'ass of editida' of 'asafetida,' Win does indeed allow 'her innocent pen [to] pursue its anal fixation.' In the same way, Tabby refers constantly to the hired hands as 'hinds,' declares that she will ignore Dr. Lewis's attempts to conciliate her 'though he beshits me on his bended knees,' and gets a great deal of unintended sexual meaning into her description of Humphry."[3] Importantly, though Win and Tabby produce scatological language, their referents are uniformly men. In this reading of the linguistic effects of the women's letters, the problem of bodies in *Humphry Clinker* becomes principally a problem of men's bodies. For Humphry, the problem appears in his name: as a lump of coal, "Clinker" may refer to his employment as a farrier, but the word also refers scatologically to excrement in the eighteenth century.[4] Bramble's bodily problem relates to his health: as he travels through England, where the excesses of excrement and dead bodies merge with the water to be consumed by others, Bramble is constipated. Bramble's constipation, as we will see, is a physical reaction to England's urban diarrhea, and it particularly counterpoints the urban Englishman, who is unwittingly infected by female nature and cannot produce a "healthy" control over his wasteful, indulgent feminine desires.

The novel constructs the bodily excesses and waste of England's commercial society as the savagery underlying its mask of culture, and the collapse of "the extremes of refinement and of savagery" in the novel is most pronounced in the power of women and the propensity toward bodily excesses, marked at its extreme by cannibalism, in both savage and refined cultures.[5] Among the Miami Indians, for example, the strict gender *and* age distinctions that signify a healthy social body are inoperative. Men, at the apex of the cultural hierarchy in a healthy society, suddenly become victims: "[P]oor Murphy was so mangled by the women and children, who have the privilege of torturing all prisoners in their passage, that, by the time they arrived at the place of the sachem's residence, he was rendered

---

3. Spector, p. 112.
4. Sheridan Baker, "*Humphry Clinker* as Comic Romance," *Papers of the Michigan Academy of Science, Arts, and Letters* 66 (1961): 645–54, 653.
5. Carson, p. 31.

altogether unfit for the purposes of marriage" (p. 188) [201]. Worse than Murphy's castration, a sure signifier of his disempowerment, however, the Miamis cannibalize him: the "warriors and matrons" make "a hearty meal upon the muscular flesh which they pared from the victim," and Lismahago's bride distinguishes herself by vying with "the stoutest warrior in eating the flesh of the sacrifice" (p. 188) [201]. Smollett envisions the Miami society as one in which men and women are equally cannibalistic, and any culture, savage or refined, that feminizes itself by basing itself on consumption—an ethos that women in the novel naturally and particularly desire—is bound to consume human beings. The refined savages of urban England do not pare and eat the muscular flesh from the victim, but they consume, diluted in the water, the sloughed-off flesh and excrement of their society's members, as well as the microscopic remains of dead bodies.

Bramble recognizes that microscopic body parts float in Bath's waters, and his attempt to find pure water becomes a nightmarish vision in which he cannot seem to escape cannibalizing the living and the dead:

> I can't help suspecting, that there is, or may be, some regurgitation from the bath into the cistern of the pump. In that case, what a delicate beveridge is every day quaffed by the drinkers; medicated with the sweat, and dirt, and dandriff; and the abominable discharges of various kinds, from twenty different diseased bodies, parboiling in the kettle below. In order to avoid this filthy composition, I had recourse to the spring that supplies the private baths on the Abbey-green; but I at once perceived something extraordinary in the taste and smell; and, upon inquiry, I find that the Roman baths in this quarter, were found covered by an old burying ground, belonging to the Abbey; thro' which, in all probability, the water drains in its passage: so that as we drink the decoction of living bodies at the Pump-room, we swallow the strainings of rotten bones and carcasses at the private bath. (p. 45) [52]

The "medicinal" water is diseased, and refinement is covert, cannibalistic savagery; the unruly bodies of the living and dead regurgitate and discharge themselves into the water supply as sacrifices to a luxurious culture.

Bramble figures Thames' water, an "agreeable potation, extolled by the Londoners, as the finest water in the universe," literally as the female bearer of contagion insofar as it is "impregnated with all the filth of London and Westminster." The metaphorically female body of water contains animal corpses, human bodies, and humans' industrial waste: "Human excrement is the least offensive part of the concrete, which is composed of all the drugs, minerals, and poisons, used in mechanics and manufacture, enriched with the putrefying carcases [sic] of beasts and men; and mixed with the scourings of all the washtubs, kennels, and common sewers, within the bills of mortality" (p. 119) [129]. In the same letter, Bramble contrasts the pregnant and diseased urban female water with the sexually pure female water at Brambleton-hall. Although "she" is pure, rural water provides Bramble with a curiously sexual pleasure: "I drink the virgin lymph, pure and crystalline as it gushes from the rock" (p. 118) [128]. He idealizes the country as a haven from the effects of women's physical and sexual corruption, to which both men and women fall victim through a symbiosis between the human body and the drinking water. If Dr. L———n is any indication, female nature is even more dangerous to men than to women. In a novel where the humor centers on grotesque characters and the laughter elicited by impolitely exposing the scatological realities of eighteenth-century life, Dr. L———n is perhaps the most thoroughly corrupted of all Smollett's figures. He proposes implicitly to cannibalize Bramble: "Sir, (said he) you seem to be of a dropsical habit, and probably will soon have a confirmed *ascites:* if I should be present when you are tapped, I will give you a convincing proof of what I assert, by drinking without hesitation the water that comes out of your abdomen." Worse than the woman who collapses refinement into savagery, the man who does so takes cannibalistic excesses to their most disgusting degree, causing even the "ladies" to make "wry faces at this declaration" (p. 19) [25].

Bramble generally succeeds at avoiding London's and Bath's waters, but urban Englishmen consume luxury goods and produce waste, which are consumed again by the urban cannibal in a cycle of disease and corruption. Gail Kern Paster writes that seventeenth-century economic discourse focuses particularly upon the place of women's bodies, which may be understood "as a 'streamlining' of the patriarchal family for the economic efficiency required by emerging capitalist modes of production. Representations of the female body as a leaking vessel display that body as beyond the control of the female subject, and thus as threatening the acquisitive goals of the family and its maintenance of status and power. The crucial problematic was whether women as a group could be counted on to manage their behaviors in response to historically emergent demands of bodily self-rule."[6] In Smollett's novel, on the other hand, the fears about the "body's moisture, secretions, and productions as shameful

6. Gail Kern Paster, *The Body Embarrassed: Drama and the Disciplines of Shame in Early Modern England* (Ithaca: Cornell Univ. Press, 1993), p. 15.

tokens of uncontrol" are located in urban England's effeminate men.[7] The "acquisitive goals of the family and its maintenance of status and power" are less important to *Humphry Clinker* than *men's* acquisitive goals (particularly of real property) and power, and the figures who prove least able to meet the demands are urban Englishmen. They have been "intoxicated" by finding themselves "suddenly translated into a state of affluence." Besides their dissoluteness and their effeminacy, inscribed particularly in the repeated mention of their vanity, urban Englishmen reproduce their corrupt society by impregnating the diseased urban waters with the "discharge" of their wealth "through every channel of the most absurd extravagance" (p. 36) [43].

Bramble's illness, on the other hand, is caused by a physical reaction against England's social distemper. Refusing to excrete normally, Bramble's body retains its integrity by obstructing his normal, porous intercourse with England's "body." To diagnose Bramble's illness correctly, we must understand that Smollett wrote *Humphry Clinker* at a time of transition involving medicine's older model of bodily "humors": the novel relies on this model to suggest that Bramble's body has sealed itself off from England's troubled culture. Humoral theory envisions the body as "characterized by corporeal fluidity, openness, and porous boundaries."[8] The health of the body depends on a balance in the transfer of liquids between its interior and the world outside it: "Every subject grew up with a common understanding of his or her body as a semipermeable, irrigated container in which humors moved sluggishly. People imagined that health consisted of a state of internal solubility to be perilously maintained."[9] Bramble places gout within a series of diseases that Bath's waters will not affect, using humoral theory to prove his argument: "If these waters, from a small degree of astringency, are of some service in the *diabetes, diarrhœa*, and *night sweats*, when the secretions are too much encreased, must not they do harm in the same proportion, where the humours are obstructed, as in the *asthma, scurvy, gout*, and *dropsy*?" (p. 25) [29–31]. Bramble's gout, therefore, prevents him from being purged and thus cannibalized, but it also places him in a double bind. Though his reaction to the society that threatens his body and, in the novel's connection between physical and psychological illness, his mind, saves him from being cannibalized, his protector also endangers his health.

The passage in which Clinker rescues his father after the coach overturns in the river marks an important resolution to the humoral

7. Paster, p. 52.
8. Paster, p. 8.
9. Ibid.

irregularities of Bramble's body. The crisis forces Bramble, through Clinker's agency, to emit water and bodily fluid. Jery writes that, after Clinker pulls Bramble from the river, "[H]e was laid upon the grass, and turned from side to side, [and] a great quantity of water ran out at his mouth, then he opened his eyes, and fetched a deep sigh—Clinker perceiving these signs of life, immediately tied up his arm with a garter, and, pulling out a horse-fleam, let him blood in the farrier stile.—At first a few drops only issued from the orifice; but the limb being chafed, in a little time the blood began to flow in a continued stream, and he uttered some incoherent words, which were the most welcome sounds that ever saluted my ear" (p. 301) [317–18]. Bramble's body at first will not release its blood, but finally, through the agency of his son and surrounded by a group of male relatives, friends, and servants, he can emit the fluid that he has needed to excrete throughout the expedition. He has found a social structure in which he can safely release fluids within a larger culture in danger of being flooded. In a sense, Clinker's purgation of his father's body also repays Bramble for his earlier rescue of Clinker from the bodily excesses that make the lower classes, a seething background tableau in the novel, a potentially disruptive social force within commercial society. By employing Clinker, Bramble saves him from illness and famine, but he also rescues him from "shewing his bare posteriors" (p. 78) [87], to which poverty and, thus, his identification with the "mob" has led him.[1] Bramble is "conscious of no sins that ought to entail . . . family-plagues upon me" (p. 13) [18], but Clinker, as the unconscious sin that follows Bramble for decades, is in atonement clothed and given the opportunity to exhibit bodily self-rule.

In *Humphry Clinker*, then, men must rescue each other from the excesses of England's corrupt and effeminate culture in order to keep each other healthy, balanced, under control, and masculine. This rescue mission also requires that they prevent women from drowning men. In the same scene in which Clinker purges Bramble, Jery writes that when Lismahago tries to rescue Tabitha from the overturned coach, the couple falls "head and ears in each other's arms. [Lismahago] endeavoured more than once to get up, and even to disentangle himself from the embrace, but [Tabitha] hung about his neck like a mill-stone (no bad emblem of matrimony), and if my man had not proved a staunch auxiliary, those two lovers would in all probability have gone hand in hand to the shades

---

1. Of course, Smollett also disassociates Clinker from the mob by placing the blame for Clinker's condition on the landlord of the inn at Marlborough, for whom Clinker had worked until he became ill. Bramble tells the landlord, "So that the fellow being sick and destitute . . . you turned him out to die in the streets" (p. 80) [88].

below" (p. 301) [317]. Jery recognizes the metaphorical power of the incident's gender politics, and his depiction is "no bad emblem" of the novel's practice of matrimonial regulation through male bonds: men must be staunch auxiliaries to husbands to ensure that their wives do not drown them. In the novel's Utopian vision of male relations, however, the servant class generally performs no more than a supernumerary function: like Jery's servant, they act as "auxiliaries," or they lend silent, nameless support, thereby tacitly legitimating both cooperation between men and hierarchy of male power.

Even women's names and legal involvement in property relations threaten to corrupt men and prevent the smooth functioning of masculine order, which we see through Bramble's narration of his own history. As a young man, Bramble involved himself in the world that he now finds contemptible. In the novel, he wonders whether a peevish nostalgia induces him to see the "morals of mankind" as diseased, as having "contracted an extraordinary degree of depravity within these thirty years," or what is "more probable, the impetuous pursuits and avocations of youth have formerly hindered me from observing those rotten parts of human nature, which now appear so offensively to my observation" (p. 104). Because the novel does not provide us with a thorough portrait of Bramble as a youthful libertine, we do not know precisely the extent to which he was part of the corrupt social body against which he now declaims. We do know, however, that Bramble committed "the sins of youth . . . under his maternal name Lloyd [sic], which he later abandoned for his paternal name, Bramble—symbolizing his moral reformation."[2] Maternal lineage, therefore, becomes associated with moral depravity: economic control by women, even after death through their bequeathed property and names, endangers men and, moreover, constitutes a false state of affairs: "I took my mother's name, which was Loyd, as heir to her lands in Glamorganshire; but, when I came of age, I sold that property, in order to clear my paternal estate, and resumed my real name; so that I am now Matthew Bramble of Brambleton-hall in Monmouthshire, at your service" (p. 305) [322]. To be a "moral" man, therefore, Bramble must purge the maternal and the female, severing their connection with real property. Like the goods of luxury, the maternal estate becomes a waste product, which is only useful insofar as it is disposable. Maternal inheritance is only useful in upholding and servicing the paternal estate for the man who wishes to meet the moral criteria of masculinity in *Humphry Clinker*. In addition, Bramble's previous nominalization

2. Preston, p. 109.

as Matthew Loyd prevents Clinker from recognizing Bramble as his father: the revelation of Bramble's past "fictional" name removes the screen of the maternal from between Bramble and Clinker and unites them as father and son.

Clinker never attains the full standing of a gentleman: not only is he a bastard, but also he takes Bramble's maternal name of Loyd, which signifies his deviance from the "real" Bramble paternal line. Nonetheless, the name change significantly improves his status in that it disinfects him by ending his association with the noisome Clinker name. Clinker's recuperation also signifies Bramble's atonement for the "sins" that have entailed him in "family-plagues" and the transformation of another of Bramble's bodily fluids (p. 13) [18], sperm, into a legitimate social product, a male heir to his property. Bramble's recognition and validation of Clinker's existence provides him finally with masculine control of the system of inheritance and of the sexual economy that produces Clinker—and offspring like him[3]—in the first place. Crucially, Clinker's identity is revealed and verified in the company of Lismahago, Dennison, and Jery, while Tabitha and Lydia have temporarily left the room. The scene takes the form of a judicial proceeding, an exclusively male ceremonial atmosphere in which Bramble acknowledges and recuperates his youthful production of (a) Clinker: "Then, laying his hand on Clinker's head, he added, 'Stand forth, Matthew Loyd—You see, gentlemen, how the sins of my youth rise up in judgment against me'" (p. 305) [322]. The troubling effects of male waste production that pursue and plague a man are nullified within the arena of this informal male legal proceeding. Here Bramble removes the stench of the name Clinker by commanding Humphry to "stand forth" as Matthew Loyd and welcoming him into the community of men. As the model male private citizen and father of "a very hopeful young gentleman" (p. 304) [320], Dennison cannot fully approve of Bramble and Clinker: he only "facetiously" congratulates them. Jery, however, shakes his newfound cousin's hand "heartily," and Lismahago "compliment[s]" Clinker "with the tears in his eyes," although his tears may be "occasioned by the fall of the coal-scuttle upon his foot" (p. 305) [322].

This ceremony, which unites father and son and bonds Clinker to Bramble's nephew and male friends, contrasts in important ways to

---

3. Early in the novel, Bramble and Jery discuss the financial problems that arise for men in connection with their alleged production of illegitimate children. Jery must pay a monetary penalty for allegedly producing a child with a woman he says he does not know: "far from having any amorous intercourse with the object in question, I never had the least acquaintance with her person" (p. 28) [34]. Bramble tells Jery "with great good-humour, that betwixt the age of twenty and forty, he had been obliged to provide for nine bastards, sworn to him by women whom he never saw" (p. 29) [35].

Bramble's portrait of Englishmen's divisiveness. Englishmen do not make worthy companions because their self-interest fosters duplicity and argument rather than honesty and cohesion.

> A companionable man will, undoubtedly, put up with many inconveniences for the sake of enjoying agreeable society . . . [But all] the people I see, are too much engrossed by schemes of interest or ambition, to have any room left for sentiment or friendship . . . Conversation is reduced to party-disputes, and illiberal altercation—Social commerce, to formal visits and card-playing—If you pick up a diverting original by accident, it may be dangerous to amuse yourself with his oddities—He is generally a tartar at bottom; a sharper, a spy, or a lunatic. Every person you deal with endeavours to over-reach you in the way of business; you are preyed upon by idle mendicants, who beg in the phrase of borrowing, and live upon the spoils of the stranger—Your tradesmen are without conscience, your friends without affection, and your dependants without fidelity.
>
> (p. 121) [131–32]

Men's individual "schemes and pursuits" lead to broken connections, and political differences lead to "altercation" (p. 121) [132]. Most of all, Englishmen have no capacity for affection, sentiment, and friendship because they construct a society based on dispute and division, squabbling in order to attain individual affluence and position. Indeed, the expedition's continual movement away from England and the kinds of male relations Bramble encounters among "[a]ll the people" he sees suggests that commercial society has become powerful and corrupt enough to make coexistence impossible: the virtuous man who attempts to live among and befriend the modern urban Englishman is subject to disappointment, loneliness, and financial loss.

Such is the case, for example, with the goodhearted and honorable Mr. Serle. Bramble and Jery meet him as he sits alone in a coffeehouse, uninvited to the tea in the next room hosted by his friend Paunceford. Serle, who once "rescued Paunceford from the lowest distress, when he was bankrupt, both in means and reputation" by providing him with the assistance that allowed him to embrace "the opportunity, which has raised him to this pinnacle of wealth" (p. 66) [75–76], has been repaid with gratitude but not money: "Paunceford carefully and artfully avoided particular discussions with his old patron, who had too much spirit to drop the most distant hint of balancing the account of obligation" (p. 67) [76]. The virtuous Serle has "hurt" his "originally small fortune" a number of times "by a romantic spirit of generosity, which he has often displayed, even at the expence of his discretion, in favour of worthless individuals" (p. 66) [75]. One of the few virtuous urban Englishmen in Smollett's novel, Mr. Serle is recompensed for his generosity and good nature with rejection and isolation. Mr. Serle, representative of a kind of friendship that Paunceford now considers "generally too plain and home-spun" (p. 65) [74], becomes an object of abuse and dishonesty. The ungrateful Paunceford is the novel's most precisely sketched effeminate, social-climbing Englishmen: he "lives in a palace, feeds upon dainties, is arrayed in sumptuous apparel, appears in all the pomp of equipage, and passes his time among the nobles of the land" (p. 67) [76].

The novel generally concludes that the only way for "plain and home-spun" men to avoid the personal and financial losses imposed upon them by the now-dominant urban Englishmen is to make a private haven at the geographical margins in the country. Lismahago, however, articulates a more public solution to England's problems that closely follows the eighteenth century's standard, oppositional "Tory" position. Particularly in his use of water metaphors, Lismahago's rhetorical devices for describing England's corruption match those we have seen elsewhere in the novel. In his discourses on parliament, commerce, and the press, he continually refers to "channeling" public institutions in order to render them manageable. For Lismahago, male law has the potential to restrain the effects of the flood that commerce has produced within England's social body, if only it would exercise its power. For instance, he owns that although he will always consider "liberty of the press" a "national evil . . . under due restrictions, it would be a valuable privilege; but affirmed, that at present there was no law in England sufficient to restrain it within proper bounds" (p. 199) [212]. Importantly, Lismahago's generally more conciliatory position toward commerce and English public institutions erases the association between women and water that particularly characterizes Bramble's tirades against luxury in Bath and London: "He affirmed, the nature of commerce was such, that it could not be fixed or perpetuated, but, having flowed to a certain height, would immediately begin to ebb, and so continue till the channels should be left almost dry; but there was no instance of the tide's rising a second time to any considerable influx in the same nation. Mean while the sudden affluence occasioned by trade, forced open all the sluices of luxury and overflowed the land with every species of profligacy and corruption; a total pravity of manners would ensue, and this must be attended with bankruptcy and ruin" (p. 198) [212]. Lismahago's political theory remains only theoretical, however, and though Bramble generally agrees with Lismahago, they do not return to England to channel public institutions. The novel as a whole suggests that the eighteenth-century "Country" political position, which envisions trade as a corrupting influence but a "necessary evil," has allowed commerce and its influence in public institutions to spread and nearly overwhelm the landed man, who needs to return to and maintain his land as a local bulwark against the nation's opened sluices of luxury and effeminacy.

Part of the novel's answer to the problem of unrestrained corruption, especially in relation to keeping women in their place, lies instead in Edinburgh's apartment houses. Scots women become the novel's model domestic guardians: they remain (or have been placed) in the home, where they labor to provide a refuge from the public. In Edinburgh's apartment houses, the common stairs are "generally left in a very filthy condition . . . Nothing can form a stronger contrast, than the difference betwixt the outside and inside of the door; for the good-women of this metropolis are remarkably nice in the ornaments and propriety of their apartments, as if they were resolved to transfer the imputation from the individual to the public" (p. 210) [225]. Scotland's public spaces may be dirty, but its private environments exclude the filth that contaminates all departments of urban English life.[4] In its representation of Edinburgh, Smollett's novel provides a vision of women's ideal social place, which involves severing their ties to the public and, in turn, marking them as the repositories of cleanliness in private spaces. Rather than being allowed to follow their "natural" luxurious desires in public, as Tabitha and Lydia threaten to do in Bath and London, Scotland's proprietary private women remain within their apartments keeping commerce, filth, and, presumably, their own desires "outside the door." Bramble learns, then, partly from the Scottish model, that the private functions as the arena in which men most effectively circumscribe women's power.

Despite Lismahago's theories, then, the novel's men finally abandon England's commercial centers as spaces in which all things feminine—including women—may be rendered subservient to rational, virtuous male control. Instead, by the novel's end, Bramble orchestrates a cohesive male "little society" in which men associate amiably while they either divide (p. 324) [342], privatize, and observe women, or exclude them altogether. Sentiment between men becomes the basis of this little society; in fact, Bramble states that it is his highest ideal: "I know nothing of equal value with the genuine friendship of a sensible man" (p. 37) [44]. The novel's Utopian vision ensures a controlled interchange of male feeling. Bramble

4. Zomchick provides an excellent detailed analysis of the differences between England and Scotland: "In Bath, Bramble worries about drinking others' bodily discharges . . . In Edinburgh, on the other hand, the public filth does not enter the private space nor threaten the health and welfare of the polite observer." He does not, however, consider the gender implications (pp. 179–80).

plans to acquire "the collector's place" in the neighborhood of Brambleton-hall for Lismahago and Tabitha so that the friendship between the two men may grow: "[Lismahago] seems to mend, upon further acquaintance. That harsh reserve, which formed a disagreeable husk about his character, begins to peel off in the course of our communication . . . I make no doubt but that he will prove a valuable acquisition to our little society, in the article of conversation, by the fire-side in winter" (p. 324) [342]. Thus, proper marriage provides *men* with access to each other's sensibilities. Dr. Lewis, that "sensible man," will continue as Bramble's friend and medical adviser, and Bramble acquaints Baynard with Dennison, "whose goodness of heart would not fail to engage his esteem and affection" (p. 328) [346]. Baynard in particular is now safe from the "ridiculous pride and vanity of silly women." He is no longer a "sacrifice" to his tyrannical wife (p. 283) [299].

Within the framework of affective male friendship, men happily exclude women from finances, discourse, and the bedroom. Together, Baynard and Bramble erase the memory of Mrs. Baynard and, in turn, create an atmosphere of sentimentality that is both safe and productive because it takes men rather than women as its object. Bramble helps his friend to forget "my dear Harriet" by endeavoring "to beguile his attention by starting little hints and insinuating other objects of discourse imperceptibly." Adding to the sexual undertones of Bramble's beguiling and insinuating discourse, Bramble usurps Mrs. Baynard's physical place in the bedroom: "That he might not, however, relapse into weaknesses for want of company, I passed the night in his chamber, in a little tent bed brought thither on purpose" (p. 326) [343]. Bramble and Baynard discover male sensibility through the healing of the psychic trauma caused by a wife.

Baynard, Bramble, and "a reputable attorney" will rebuild Baynard's estate along the lines of utility, "and the pleasure-ground will be restored to its original use of corn-field and pasture" (p. 328) [345]. Economic control by men bonded together in virtuous friendship insures production and "use" rather than consumption and frivolity. Under male guidance, Baynard will "find himself perfectly at ease in mind and body, for the one had dangerously affected the other." In addition, now that Baynard's mind and body are undergoing a cure, the kind of society that he helps produce will be free from disease. Such a rescue from the "misery and contempt" caused by Mrs. Baynard is Bramble's "exquisite pleasure" (p. 335) [354]. Men's sentimental bonds, therefore, protect their bodies, which, in the collapse of physical, mental, and social health, make them also psychologically and culturally safe. "Feeling for other men" involves men's mutual assurances that bodily— and thus societal–production remains under male auspices. By making the production of bodily fluids and waste, from blood to excrement to bastards, safe for men, *Humphry Clinker* asserts a masculine, homosocial, rational society that restores male prerogative, but it can only do so by marginalizing and privatizing its own economy in order to avoid the dreadful connection between commerce and public institutions that, in the novel's terms, has terminally corrupted English society. Finally, *Humphry Clinker* joins other mid–eighteenth-century texts by connecting the question of men's economic desires to their bodies and sexuality. Through their private bonds, the novel's men create a place in which production and waste—bodily, sexual, and economic—are balanced and harmonized, a masculine Utopian vision of a world of possession and production made safe and healthy for men.

EVAN GOTTLIEB

"Fools of Prejudice": Sympathy and National Identity in the Scottish Enlightenment and *Humphry Clinker*[†]

During the middle decades of the eighteenth century, London became an increasingly attractive destination for Scottish-born Britons looking to make their fortunes south of the Tweed. As Scotland continued to lag behind England's more sophisticated economy, the exodus of educated Scots grew apace.[1] Their greater presence in the southern metropolis, however, did not necessarily mean that the post-Union ideal of a united British citizenry had been achieved. As late as 1770, Samuel Johnson could announce that "he considered the Scotch, nationally, as a crafty, designing people, eagerly attentive to their own interest, and too apt to overlook the claims and pretensions of other people." Describing the Scots as "confin[ing] their benevolence, in a manner, exclusively to those of their own country," Johnson's remarks demonstrate the persistence of the xenophobic idea that the Scots were a separate people from the English, possessing distinct (and distinctly suspect) national characteristics and loyalties.[2]

[†] From *Eighteenth-Century Fiction* 18.1 (Fall 2005): 81–106. Reprinted by permission of *Eighteenth-Century Fiction*. www.humanities.mcmaster.ca/~ecf.

1. T. M. Devine provides a detailed analysis of the economic effects of the Union in *The Scottish Nation: A History, 1700–2000* (New York: Viking, 1999), 49–63; on the southern emigration of Scots, see Linda Colley, *Britons: Forging the Nation, 1707–1837* (London: Vintage, 1996), 129–32.

2. James Boswell, *Life of Johnson*, ed. R. W. Chapman (New York: Oxford University Press, 1980), 439.

Supporters of the Union, especially Scots, had long struggled with the problem of how to convince people on both sides of the Tweed to think of themselves as British together. Centuries of feuding and ill will had given way to the incorporative Anglo-Scottish Union of 1707, but neither government policy nor the threat of a common enemy could force the English and the Scottish to resolve their differences and learn to think of themselves as a single nation.[3] According to conventional Whig narratives of "English" history, the tensions and animosities between these two former states dissipated naturally as the superior economic, political, and military might of England simply overwhelmed its northern partner; more recently, advocates of the "internal colonialism" model of post-Union Anglo-Scottish relations advanced a counter-narrative in which England's aggressive absorption of the so-called "Celtic fringe" foreshadowed its later imperial expansion.[4] In the past few years, however, eighteenth-century scholars—influenced in part by new postcolonial theories that contest the assumptions of the old centre-periphery model of national relations—have discovered a renewed interest in how the Scots, far from being merely passive victims of Anglicization, in reality played a formative role in shaping the cultural contours of the new British nation.[5] Building on such revisionist work, in this article I will suggest that David Hume's and Adam Smith's influential formulations of sympathy had significant implications for fostering a sense of shared national identity between the English and the Scots. Appreciating the political ramifications of Enlightened sympathy, in turn, helps shed new light on the nation-building work of the most famous novel of another eighteenths-century Scot, Tobias Smollett's *The Expedition of Humphry Clinker* (1771). Smollett's final novel can be seen as a virtual experiment, in which the sympathetic theories of Hume and Smith are summoned, staged, and tested to determine the most effective way to promulgate more harmonious relations between the citizens of the two former states. Yet even as *Humphry Clinker*

3. Colley's thesis is that anti-French and anti-Catholic sentiments alone were enough to bring Britons together; for an effective rebuttal of this position, see Murray G. H. Pittock, *Inventing and Resisting Britain: Cultural Identities in Britain and Ireland, 1685– 1789* (New York: St Martin's Press, 1997).
4. Michael Hechter, *Internal Colonialism: The Celtic Fringe in British National Development*, rev. ed. (New Brunswick: Transaction Publishers, 1999).
5. See Robert Crawford, *Devolving English Literature*, 2d ed. (Edinburgh: University of Edinburgh Press, 2000); Leith Davis, *Acts of Union: Scotland and the Literary Negotiation of the British Nation, 1707–1830* (Stanford: Stanford University Press, 1998); Susan Manning, *Fragments of Union: Making Connections in Scottish and American Writing* (Houndmills: Palgrave, 2002); Janet Sorensen, *The Grammar of Empire in Eighteenth-Century British Writing* (Cambridge: Cambridge University Press, 2000); and Katie Trumpener, *Bardic Nationalism: The Romantic Novel and the British Empire* (Princeton: Princeton University Press, 1997).

settles on Smithian sympathy as its favoured mode of intra-national relations, Smollett's fiction reveals the difficulties and dangers inherent in the attempt to bring the people of Britain together in feeling as well as in name.

Humean Sympathy and the Dangers of Emotional "Communication"

Sympathy has recently received increased attention from eighteenth-century scholars, but such criticism, with a few notable exceptions, has generally focused on sympathy's role in the sentimental novelistic tradition.[6] Sentimentalism, however, is only one product of the philosophical discourse of sympathy as theorized by the Scottish Enlightenment. Since the Scottish Enlighteners were "traditional intellectuals" in the Gramscian sense of being employed by the hegemonic institutions (church, law, and university) left to Scotland after the Union, their position was both exhilarating and disorienting.[7] Generally supportive of Scottish initiatives at English-style "improvement," but wary of achieving progress at the cost of eradicating the Scottish culture that supported their intellectual endeavours, the Enlightenment literati had personal as well as political motivations to seek ways to heal the fractures still splintering the British state. While their English counterparts could largely afford to ignore the ramifications of the northern expansion of the United Kingdom (the two Jacobite rebellions and the Wilkite Scottophobia of the 1760s notwithstanding), educated Scots had much to gain from the increased access to both the real and cultural capital promised by a shared national identity in which all parties could participate equally.[8]

In this milieu, it is fitting that sympathy explicitly forms the basis of Hume's conception of the workings of both the individual and society, as first put forward in book 2, part 1, section 11 of his

---

6. Studies that (despite other virtues) move too quickly from sympathy to sentimentality include G. J. Barker-Benfield, *The Culture of Sensibility: Sex and Society in Eighteenth-Century Britain* (Chicago: University of Chicago Press, 1992); Ann Jessie Van Sant, *Eighteenth-Century Sensibility and the Novel: The Senses in Social Context* (New York: Cambridge University Press, 1993); and Janet Todd, *Sensibility: An Introduction* (London: Methuen, 1986). Exceptions to this trend include David Marshall, *The Figure of Theater: Shaftesbury, Defoe, Adam Smith and George Eliot* (New York: Columbia University Press, 1986); Marshall, *The Surprising Effects of Sympathy: Marivaux, Diderot, Rousseau, and Mary Shelley* (Chicago: University of Chicago Press, 1988); and John Mullan, *Sentiment and Sociability: The Language of Feeling in the Eighteenth Century* (Oxford: Clarendon Press, 1998).

7. See Richard Sher, *Church and University in the Scottish Enlightenment* (Edinburgh: Edinburgh University Press, 1985).

8. Hence, while many Scots took to calling themselves "North Britons," few, if any, English seem to have regularly referred to themselves as "South Britons" (Crawford, 45–46). Christopher Harvie makes a similar point in "Anglo-Saxons into Celts: The Scottish Intellectuals 1760–1930," in *Celticism*, ed. Terence Brown (Amsterdam: Rodopi, 1996), 23.

Treatise: "No quality of human nature is more remarkable, both in itself and in its consequences, than that propensity we have to sympathize with others, and to receive by communication their inclinations and sentiments, however different from, or even contrary to our own."[9] For Hume, sympathy is a mechanism of emotional connection whereby people assume each other's psychological states by an occult process of the transmission of feelings. Significantly, the mode of such communication is unclear: although Hume initially seems to suggest that sympathy travels primarily by way of oral transmission (his first example cites how children are easily swayed by others' opinions), he subsequently asserts that sympathy can also work "in an instant" through the vehicles of countenance and other non-verbal "external signs" (316–17). These productive ambiguities, which give sympathy the privilege of being the medium, rather than the message, of social contact, may help explain why Hume declines to give sympathy a hard-and-fast definition; instead, he invites the reader to "take a general survey of the universe, and observe the force of sympathy thro' the whole animal creation, and the easy communication of sentiments from one thinking being to another" (363). Later, Hume draws an analogy between this process and sound waves: "As in strings equally wound up, the motion of one communicates itself to the rest; so all the affections readily pass from one person to another, and beget corresponding movements in every human creature" (576). This idea of the natural, involuntary transfer of emotions between individuals provides a simple solution to the problem of accounting for human sociability, as well as a plausible rationale for the moral impetus of civil society: because we can feel others' feelings, by extrapolation we have sympathy with "the interests of society" at large (580).

From communal identity, it is theoretically only a short step to even more capacious forms of belonging. Accordingly, Hume quickly reveals sympathy's implications for the formation of national identity, using the latter as the premier example of his theory's explanatory power:

> To this principle [sympathy] we ought to ascribe the great uniformity we may observe in the humours and turn of thinking of those of the same nation; and 'tis much more probable, that this resemblance arises from sympathy, than from any influence of the soil and climate, which, tho' they continue invariably the same, are not able to preserve the character of a nation the same for a century together. (316–17)

9. David Hume, *A Treatise of Human Nature*, ed. L. A. Selby-Bigge and P. H. Nidditch, 2d ed. (1739–40; Oxford: Oxford University Press, 1978), 316. References are to this edition.

Contrary to many contemporary explanations of national identity, which understood shared characteristics in terms of physical causes such as geography and climate, Hume proposes that national character is established primarily by human causes.[1] Understood as a discourse of extended and shared identity, Humean sympathy thus becomes an integral part of the solution to what Etienne Balibar calls "the fundamental problem" of modern nations: "to produce the effect of unity by virtue of which the people will appear, in everyone's eyes, 'as a people', that is, as the basis and origin of political power."[2]

Hume's most direct expression of sympathy's usefulness as a force for promulgating national identity can be found, not in the *Treatise* itself, but in his later, self-consciously popular essays. "Of National Characters," published in 1753, contains a lengthy discussion of sympathy's role in the formation of national identities. After explaining that "The propensity to company and society is strong in all individuals," causing "like passions and inclinations to run, as it were, by contagion," Hume unveils the full nation-forming potential of sympathy: "Where a number of men are united into one political body, the occasions of their intercourse must be so frequent, for defence, commerce, and government, that, together with the same speech or language, they must acquire a resemblance in their manners, and have a common or national character, as well as a personal one, peculiar to each individual."[3] Once the peoples of two nations have spent enough time living under the same government, sharing the same institutional infrastructures, belief systems, and language, Hume suggests that it is only a matter of time until such contact renders the differences between the two nations null.[4] The implication for Britain is clear: a unified national identity will eventually coalesce as local attachments and habits give way to wider-reaching national sympathies.

Even as Hume was theorizing sympathetic Britishness, Smollett was devoting himself to its popularization; as James P. Carson has indicated, "Smollett is a central writer for the study of early British

---

1. See Roxann Wheeler, *The Complexion of Race: Categories of Difference in Eighteenth-Century British Culture* (Philadelphia: University of Pennsylvania Press, 2000), 184–86.

2. Etienne Balibar, "The Nation Form: History and Ideology," trans. Chris Turner, in *Race, Nation, Class: Ambiguous Identities*, ed. Étienne Balibar and Immanuel Wallerstein (New York: Verso, 1991), 93–94.

3. Hume, "Of National Characters," in *Essays: Moral, Political and Literary*, ed. Eugene Miller, rev. ed. (part 1: 1742; part 2: 1752; combined: 1777; Indianapolis: Liberty Fund, 1985), 202.

4. Of course, such assimilation was often achieved, or at least attempted, by violently coercive means; for example, the activities of the SSPCK (Society in Scotland for the Propagation of Christian Knowledge) were primarily aimed at the conversion of Catholic, Gaelic-speaking Highlanders to Protestantism and standard English. See Sorensen, 28–43.

patriotism."[5] Editor of the powerful *Critical Review* from 1756 to 1763, as well as a popular novelist and prolific non-fiction writer, Smollett exerted considerable influence on London's burgeoning print culture industry. Critics have long agreed that *Humphry Clinker* expressly sets out to repair the damage caused by mid-century Anglo-Scottish tensions; indeed, the work was famously derided by Horace Walpole as a "party novel," too explicitly intent on praising Scotland to be of any lasting literary value.[6] Yet every reader of *Humphry Clinker* quickly realizes that the perspectives presented by the novel's various fictional letter writers initially clash. On the one hand, Bramble and his young niece Lydia Melford, for example, offer radically different depictions of Bath and London: while the former is disgusted, the latter is awed by these English centres of luxury and social congregation. When the travelling party moves into Scotland, on the other hand, their "case studies" of their various destinations begin to complement rather than contradict one another. Much of the effectiveness of Smollett's novelistic investigation into the possibility of establishing a sense of British identity (especially after the Seven Years War, which left Britons "wondering if they had overstretched themselves")[7] stems from the ways in which it encourages the reader to piece together its variously authored letters into a continuous narrative, thus providing a generic model for how English and Scottish readers could learn to reconcile their various perspectives into a united British world view. Moreover, Smollett's choice of his letters writers' Welsh ethnic identity further enhances the impression of consensus enabled by epistolarity. Combining an intimate knowledge of the English with "occasional stirrings of a sentiment of celtic solidarity" with the Scots, Smollett treats his Welsh characters as a neutral subnationality within the larger British nation.[8] Neither English nor Scottish, Bramble and his extended family represent a generalizable British identity.

If the formal organization and national characterization of Smollett's novel seem to support the harmonizing ideals of the Scottish Enlightenment, so does his use of sympathetic discourse in *Humphry Clinker*. A member of "the solid middle order in society,"[9] Bramble begins the novel already well-versed in conducting sympathetic social relations, as demonstrated by his benevolent treatment of a

5. James P. Carson, "Britons, 'Hottentots,' Plantation Slavery, and Tobias Smollett," *Philological Quarterly* 75 (Fall 1996): 472.
6. See Wolfgang Franke, "Smollett's *Humphry Clinker* as a 'Party Novel,'" *Studies in Scottish Literature* 9 (1971–72): 97–106.
7. Colley, 109.
8. Franke, 191.
9. R. S. Krishnan, "'The Vortex of the Tumult': Order and Disorder in *Humphry Clinker*," *Studies in Scottish Literature* 23 (1988): 241.

widow and her consumptive daughter at Bath. By contrast, his nephew Jery Melford's sympathetic instincts need to be reawakened, apparently having been deadened by riotous living and cynical habits at Oxford. Reporting Bramble's unaffected sympathy, the younger man initially describes his uncle as being in "a state of frailty, as would ill become his years and character," and claims to be somewhat puzzled by the "croaking tone of voice" with which Bramble offers the widow twenty pounds of unsolicited charity.[1] Even so, Jery soon recognizes that gentlemen should not be ashamed of participating in, even encouraging, sympathetic social relations: "I feel a strong inclination to follow my uncle's example, in relieving this poor widow; but betwixt friends, I am afraid of being detected in a weakness, that might entail the ridicule of the company" (23) [29]. By the novel's end, Jery has fully imbibed the lessons of his uncle's sympathetic behaviour, regularly joining the older man in sympathetic approbation with various virtuous characters (see 265, 330) [271, 336].

Throughout the novel, Jery benefits from the effects of the spontaneous communication of feelings best described by Humean sympathy. Although he does not initially get along with his famously testy uncle, their relationship improves within a few weeks: "The truth is, [Bramble's] disposition and mine, which, like oil and vinegar, repelled one another at first, have now begun to mix by dint of being beat up together" (17) [22]. Jery's culinary metaphor aptly illustrates the process of involuntary emotional conversion that Humean sympathy ideally involves.[2] Such sympathy asserts itself on a more nationally significant scale when the Bramble family travels to Scotland. At first, Jery is forcibly struck by the Scots' cultural strangeness, exclaiming that "their looks, their language, and their customs, are so different from ours, that I can hardly believe myself in Great-Britain" (214) [222]. Yet through the instinctive workings of sympathy, facilitated by regular contact with actual Scots and immersion in the rituals of daily life, he soon finds such difference replaced by identification. After only a few weeks in Scotland, Jery can proudly proclaim that "If I stay much longer at Edinburgh, I shall be changed into a downright Caledonian," explaining in perfectly Humean terms

1. Tobias Smollett, *The Expedition of Humphry Clinker*, ed. Louis M. Knapp and Paul-Gabriel Boucé (1771; New York: Oxford University Press, 1984), 20–21. References are to this edition. [Page numbers in square brackets refer to this Norton Critical Edition.]
2. While the evidence for Smollett's familiarity with Hume's theories of sympathy is less certain than the evidence of his knowledge of Smith's ideas (see below), it is likely that he was well acquainted with Hume's *Treatise* as well as the better-known *Essays* and *History of England* (1754–62). Not only is Hume named, along with Smith, in *Humphry Clinker* as one of the Edinburgh luminaries "as agreeable in conversation as they are instructive and entertaining in their writings" (233) [240], but his "moral system" is cited explicitly in the *Critical Review* notice of Smith's *Theory* (see below). In any case, sympathy was a prominent part of the discourse of mid-eighteenth-century British literary culture, in which Smollett was fully immersed.

that "I am insensibly sucked into the channel of their manners and customs." Even the usual southern complaint about the harsh Scots dialect has been dropped: "That difference, however, which struck me very much at my first arrival, I now hardly perceive, and my ear is perfectly reconciled to the Scots accent, which I find even agreeable in the mouth of a pretty woman" (221) [229]. Although the last clause shows that Jery has not abandoned his womanizing ways, the passage as a whole demonstrates his ability to adapt sympathetically to his new environment.[3]

Given that, as I will argue, Humean sympathy does become problematic for the other members of the Bramble party, we need to ask why it functions so well for Jery. As a young man, Jery is not only fashionably educated and heir to a prosperous Welsh estate, but also exempt from the excessive sensibility that has effectively driven his uncle from the public sphere. I invoke the "public sphere" here specifically in the spirit of Habermas's original formulation to emphasize that Jery is ideally situated to make maximum use of his class and gender authority in eighteenth-century British society. According to Habermas, *"The fully developed bourgeois public sphere was based on the fictitious identity of the two roles assumed by the privatized individuals who came together to form a public: the role of property owners and the role of human beings pure and simple."*[4] The phrase "fictitious identity," it must be noted, implies that the public sphere was always an illusory formation; since the conflation of "property owners" and "human beings pure and simple" was never fully realized, Habermas is arguably suggesting that the public sphere never existed as anything more than an eighteenth-century masculine ideal.[5] Nevertheless, or perhaps as a result, the concept helps explain how male bourgeois subjects constructed and maintained their sense of selfhood. It also helps explain why Jery is much better equipped to benefit from the effects of Humean sympathy than his travelling companions. As Catherine Gallagher has indicated, a major paradox of Humean sympathy is that it simultaneously requires, and breaks down, the basic differences between self and other. Observing that Hume reverses the usual direction of empirical thought (in which we receive our ideas from our sense impressions) to claim that the sympathetic process turns the idea of someone else's emotion into our own sense impression, Gallagher

---

3. The limit of Jery's assimilation is gustatory: "I am not yet Scotchman enough to relish their singed sheep's head and haggice" (222) [230].
4. Jürgen Habermas, *The Structural Transformation of the Public Sphere: An Inquiry into a Category of Bourgeois Society,* trans. Thomas Burger with Frederick Lawrence (1962; Cambridge: MIT Press, 1989), 56.
5. As Christian Thorne succinctly states, "Habermas is interested in the public sphere as a promise that is never fulfilled," Thorne, "Thumbing Our Nose at the Public Sphere: Satire, the Market, and the Invention of Literature," *PMLA* 116 (May 2001): 542.

explains that "another's internal state becomes 'intimately present' only by losing its distinct quality of belonging to somebody else. . . . That is, when the process occurs, the very relationships of ownership on which it depends seem at once stretched out of recognizable shape and reasserted."[6] In other words, Humean sympathy paradoxically destabilizes the concept of ownership—of feelings and, by extension, of property—by blurring the very boundary between self and other that makes sympathy possible in the first place. As if to correct this tendency, however, Hume carefully reasserts traditional hierarchies by ensuring that the balance of sympathy, so to speak, frequently favours the wealthy and privileged. As the *Treatise* suggests, given that "the minds of men are mirrors to one another . . . because they reflect each other's emotions," such reflections typically work to the advantage of those who shine most brightly: "Thus the pleasure, which a rich man receives from his possessions, being thrown upon the beholder, causes a pleasure and esteem; which sentiments again, being perceiv'd and sympathiz'd with, encrease the pleasure of the possessor" (365), ad infinitum. Since Jery flawlessly combines his public identity as a masculine property owner with his private identity as an educated human being, the potential ontological and proprietary instabilities created by Humean sympathy are literally not his problems: his status as the ideal bourgeois subject means that he can take on others' emotional states without losing his own sense of self. Even when he admits that George Dennison, Lydia's fiancé, is "one of the most accomplished young fellows in England," for example, he maintains that "the comparison [between his own character and Dennison's] excites no envy—I have endeavoured to recommend myself to his friendship, and hope I have already found a place in his affections" (332) [335]. Humean sympathy thus reinforces Jery's sense of community with others, without threatening his firm conviction regarding his privileged place in civil society.

For the other *Humphry Clinker* characters, however, such sympathetic absorption is more disturbing. Unlike his nephew, Bramble begins the novel in retreat from active public life. Wary and disdainful of the market forces that are beginning to reconfigure British culture, he has already more or less withdrawn from the public sphere when the novel opens, instead taking up a more self-consciously private social role: the "man of feeling." I purposefully use this term to describe Bramble's character, since Henry Mackenzie's novel of the same name appeared concurrently with *Humphry Clinker* in 1771. Although Smollett (writing in self-imposed exile in

6. Catherine Gallagher, *Nobody's Story: The Vanishing Acts of Women Writers in the Marketplace, 1670–1820* (Berkeley: University of California Press, 1994), 170.

Italy) likely had no knowledge of Mackenzie's production, his novel clearly avails itself of a similar interest in the effects of emotional sensitivity. Smollett's and Mackenzie's central protagonists share several important qualities, including an acute sensitivity to the distresses of the lower social ranks and a desire to alleviate such suffering, especially through charity.

At the same time, Bramble also represents a trenchant criticism of the sensibility embodied by Mackenzie's protagonist.[7] As Jery describes him, Bramble "is as tender as a man without a skin; who cannot bear the slightest touch without flinching. What tickles another would give him torment" (49) [56]. Jery's ticklish metaphor is doubly meaningful: not only can Bramble hardly bear close physical contact with other people, but he is also incapable of being amused (like Jery), much less awed (like Lydia), by his encounters with modern English society at Bristol, Bath, and London. Ironically, Bramble's increased capacity for sympathy ultimately renders him unfit for society. Recalling Hume's memorable description of the mechanical workings of sympathy—"As in strings equally wound up, the motion of one communicates itself to the rest" (575–76)—it would seem that Bramble is wound *too* tightly for this process to benefit him.

The burden of excessive emotional sensitivity under which Bramble suffers even leads him to resent the demands of his family. An early letter finds him complaining about all of his relations before exclaiming "why the devil should not I shake off these torments at once? I an't married to Tabby, thank Heaven! nor did I beget the other two: let them choose another guardian: for my part, I an't in a condition to take care of myself; much less to superintend the conduct of giddy-headed boys and girls" (12) [18]. Although Bramble has no intention of enacting such threats, his irritation with his patriarchal responsibilities demonstrates that something has already gone awry with the Humean-style sympathy that the novel initially seems to endorse. After all, in his *Treatise*, Hume is adamant that familial sympathy naturally takes precedence over all others: "Whoever is united to us by any connection is always sure of a share of our love, proportion'd to the connexion, without enquiring into his other qualities. Thus the relation of blood produces the strongest tie the mind is capable of in the love of parents to their children, and a lesser degree of the same affection, as the relation lessens" (352). Bramble's hyper-sensitivity to

7. For an acute reading of Mackenzie's novel that finds it to be equally sceptical of sensibility, see Maureen Harkin, "Mackenzie's *Man of Feeling*: Embalming Sensibility," *ELH* 61 (1994): 317–40; on the broader implications of sentimental masculinity in Smollett's novel, see David M. Weed, "Sentimental Misogyny and Medicine in *Humphry Clinker*," *SEL* 37 (1997): 615–36.

emotional stimuli, which finds symptomatic expression in his health problems as well as in his declarations of ill will towards his extended family, suggests the potential for dysfunction in the Humean model of sympathy as a mechanism of involuntary emotional connection.

Furthermore, Hume's insistence that people are constantly open to others' emotions imbues his theory with the potentially troubling tendency to break down barriers between self and other. In this, it bears a marked resemblance to the processes of mixing, both physical and social, that Bramble famously dreads. His fear of bodily contagion in the waters at Bath is certainly the objective corollary of his disgust at the contamination of social rank that he sees taking place in English cities; as Charlotte Sussman explains, "*Humphry Clinker's* extensive description of the baths transforms economic developments into waters that break through the physical defenses of the body just as mercantile accumulation has broken down the social barriers between landed gentry like the Brambles and the world of commercial enterprise."[8] Additionally, Bramble's fears of contamination arguably reflect his aggravation with the involuntary Humean sympathy that mercilessly afflicts him throughout the early stages of the novel. In contradistinction to Mackenzie's Harley, who is destroyed by the very society with which he cannot help sympathizing, Bramble has developed a coping mechanism for reducing his excessive sensitivity to others' emotional states: "He affects misanthropy, in order to conceal the sensibility of a heart, which is tender, even to a degree of weakness. This delicacy of feeling, or soreness of the mind, makes him timorous and fearful" (28) [35]. Bramble's occasional misanthropic performances—underscored by his prickly name—must be understood as protective attempts to enforce the physical and social distance between himself and the rest of humankind that he needs in order to maintain his fragile sense of self.[9] This distance, however, creates a conflict between Bramble's private acts of sympathetically motivated charity and his public displays of disaffection with society—a contradiction that is particularly disturbing for a landed gentleman otherwise well positioned to be an active member of the bourgeois public sphere. Until this conflict is resolved, Bramble is condemned to experience the

8. Charlotte Sussman, "Lismahago's Captivity: Transculturation in *Humphry Clinker*," *ELH* 61 (1994): 607. See also Daniel Cottom's analysis of the Bath episodes as enacting a perverse but effective purification ritual for both the Brambles and the reader, "an object lesson in how to create distinction out of disgusting excess." Cottom, *Cannibals and Philosophers: Bodies of Enlightenment* (Baltimore: Johns Hopkins University Press, 2001), 115.

9. Eileen Douglas argues that Bramble attempts to exert an analogous control over his body throughout *Humphry Clinker* in *Uneasy Sensations: Smollett and the Body* (Chicago: University of Chicago Press, 1995), 162–84.

poor mental and physical health that is symptomatic of his self-divided character.[1]

For Bramble, then, Humean sympathy ironically obstructs the social functioning of the very type of masculine subject upon whose participation the public sphere depends. In addition, whereas we have already seen that Humean sympathy tends to strengthen and reproduce already existing social hierarchies, in *Humphry Clinker* Humean-style sympathetic activities are just as often presented as subversive to the established order.[2] When Bramble finds that the female members of his household have become followers of Clinker's emotionally evocative Methodist preaching, for example, he angrily explains to Lydia that "I don't think my servant is a proper ghostly director, for a devotee of your sex and character" (137) [146]. With its sympathetic powers (Tabitha Bramble's maid Winifred Jenkins, in a notable turn of phrase, calls it "the infectual calling" [155] [164]), Clinker's Methodism threatens to undermine hierarchical social relations; thus, an outburst of patriarchal authority must curb this threat. The deleterious effects of Humean-style sympathy are also seen in the behaviour of Jenkins. As Jery observes, echoing the language of Humean sympathy, "Nature seems to have intended Jenkins for something very different from the character of her mistress; yet custom and habit have effected a wonderful resemblance betwixt them in many particulars . . . [Jenkins] seems to have adopted Mrs Tabby's manner with her cast cloaths" (208) [215]. Like Clinker's preaching, Jenkins's unconscious emulation of her social superiors promulgates an unsettling sympathetic breakdown of traditional class distinctions. Accordingly, she receives a violent lesson in the dangers of identifying with her betters: after dressing up and attending an opera with Jery's Frenchified manservant, she is insulted and attacked by hostile onlookers who mistake her for a prostitute.

While Humean sympathy serves Jery's purposes as a blossoming member of the public sphere, for Bramble and the other members of his travelling party, it clearly causes more problems than it solves. Bramble's excessive sensibility, combined with the disruptions caused by Clinker's and Jenkins's susceptibilities to involuntary sympathy, demonstrates Smollett's mistrust of Humean-style sympathy as an

1. See also Geoffrey Sill's account of the eighteenth-century medical theory informing Smollett's delineation of Bramble's symptoms in *The Cure of the Passions and the Origins of the English Novel* (Cambridge: Cambridge University Press, 2001), 13–18. Sill's assessment that Bramble's "partial derangement contains its own cure in the form of a counter-infection of 'good humour'" (17), however, declines to explain how Bramble converts his painful hyper-sensibility into beneficial sympathy.

2. See the *Treatise* sections "Of external advantages and disadvantages" and "Of property and riches" (303–16) for examples of what Adela Pinch calls "the obedience of Humean sympathy to traditional forms of authority." Pinch, *Strange Fits of Passion: Epistemologies of Emotion, Hume to Austen* (Stanford: Stanford University Press, 1996), 25.

effective force for social, much less national, cohesion. However, *Humphry Clinker* does not abandon sympathy altogether as a mechanism for facilitating collective identification. To see how Smollett retains this ideal while rejecting its specifically Humean manifestations, I will now turn to those moments in *Humphry Clinker* in which sympathy emerges in its more intentional, Smithian form.

Smithian Sympathy and the Dialogue of National Union

Like Hume, Adam Smith was also convinced of the importance of sympathy for social and national cohesion. His frequent laudatory references to Hume's work throughout *The Theory of Moral Sentiments* (1756) make his intellectual debts overt; nevertheless, he significantly develops and alters Hume's ideas concerning the nature of the relationship between society and the individual.[3] The opening sentence of Smith's *Theory* immediately registers the centrality of sympathy to his idea of human nature: "How selfish soever man may be supposed, there are evidently some principles in his nature, which interest him in the fortune of others, and render their happiness necessary to him, though he derives nothing from it except the pleasure of seeing it" (9). Unlike Hume, however, Smith consistently and explicitly stresses that feelings do not travel directly from person to person:

> As we have no immediate experience of what other men feel, we can form no idea of the manner in which they are affected, but by conceiving what we ourselves should feel in the like situation. Though our brother is upon the rack, as long as we ourselves are at our ease, our senses will never inform us of what he suffers. They never did, and never can, carry us beyond our own person, and it is by the imagination only that we can form any conception of what are his sensations. (9)

For Smith, the imagination liberates us from the constraints of our monistic existences, allowing us to experience a sense of the feelings of others. Yet we do not actually feel their emotions; rather, we experience a copy of their feelings that our imagination produces for us. No longer physical, sympathy is now primarily a mental experience.

In a further development from Hume, Smith clarifies the utility of sympathy by claiming that people actively seek the sympathy of others. Individuals must willingly enter a psychological give-and-take of

---

3. A straightforward account of the relations between Hutcheson, Hume, and Smith is found in D. D. Raphael, introduction to *The Theory of Moral Sentiments*, by Adam Smith, ed. D. D. Raphael and A. L. Macfie (1756; 6th ed. 1790; Indianapolis: Liberty Fund, 1984), 12–14. References are to this edition of Adam Smith, *The Theory of Moral Sentiments*. See also Glenn R. Morrow, "The Significance of the Doctrine of Sympathy in Hume and Adam Smith," *Philosophical Review* 32 (1923): 60–78.

complementary attempts to imagine what the other is thinking and feeling: "In all such cases, that there may be some correspondence of sentiments between the spectator and the person principally concerned, the spectator must, first of all, endeavour, as much as he can, to put himself in the situation of the other, and to bring home to himself every little circumstance of distress which can possibly occur to the sufferer" (21). The injunction to "bring home" the circumstances of another's situation, to domesticate metaphorically the feelings (and by extension the perspective) of the other, is the keystone of Smith's sympathetic process. Nonetheless, Smith also recognizes that, since "the emotions of the spectator will still be very apt to fall short of the violence of what is felt by the sufferer," total identification is available only theoretically. The particular genius of Smithian sympathy is that it both acknowledges and accounts for sympathy's partial inoperability:

> The [agent] is sensible of this [lack of correspondence between his feelings and those of the spectator], and at the same time passionately desires a more complete sympathy. He longs for that relief which nothing can afford him but the entire concord of the affections of the spectators with his own. . . . But he can only hope to obtain this by lowering his passion to that pitch, in which the spectators are capable of going along with him. He must flatten, if I may be allowed to say so, the sharpness of its natural tone, in order to reduce it to harmony and concord with the emotions of those who are about him. (22)

The agent recognizes that the spectator cannot fully sympathize with him, so in his desire to receive the spectator's sympathy and approbation, he modifies the tenor of his feelings appropriately. Smith's musical metaphors not only provide rhetorical unity, but also emphasize how eighteenth-century society ideally functions like an orchestra: the various sections may be performing different parts, but the end result is a harmonious whole.[4]

Just as Hume broadens his vision of sympathy to include national as well as personal relations, so Smith expands achieved sympathetic social harmony to encompass the newly enlarged nation-state of Great Britain. As Luke Gibbons observes, "On the face of it, the notion of sympathy would appear to be the ideal means of understanding other societies, and conducting cross-cultural

---

4. Smith's most famous formulation of this idea, of course, is the "invisible hand" that ensures the general benefit of society in the unintentional activities of primarily self-interested individuals; see *Theory*, 184–85; Smith, *The Wealth of Nations*, vol. 1, ed, R. H. Campbell and A. S. Skinner (Indianapolis: Liberty Fund, 1981), 456, The charge that Smith's sympathetic and economic theories are somehow at odds with one another—repeated in a recent and otherwise perceptive article by Julie Murray, "Governing Economic Man: Joanna Baillie's Theater of Utility," *ELH* 70 (2003): 1044—is clearly undone by this link.

dialogue."[5] Accordingly, Smithian sympathy is clearly useful for encouraging the English and the Scots to identify with one another. Although the first edition of the *Theory* makes few explicit references to Britain, when Smith notes "how uneasy are we made when we go into a house in which jarring contention sets one half of those who dwell in it against the other" (39), his allusion to the 1745 rebellion would not have been lost on his contemporaries. Perhaps in response to the growing conflict with Revolutionary France, Smith's belief in sympathy's ability to facilitate national unity is made even more clear in the final 1790 edition of the *Theory*. In a new section, Smith forcefully asserts that national allegiance takes precedence over all others: "The state or sovereignty in which we have been born and educated, and under the protection of which we continue to live is . . . by nature, most strongly recommended to us" (227). Moreover, in an obvious gesture to the Union, Smith asserts that the greatest thing a public servant can do for his country is to ally it as closely as possible with its nearest neighbours: "The most extensive public benevolence which can commonly be exerted with any considerable effect, is that of the statesmen, who project and form alliances among neighbouring or not very distant nations, for the preservation either of, what is called, the balance of power, or of the general peace and tranquility of the states" (230). The message for both the Scots and the English is clear: now is the time to put aside past differences and truly become one nation. Interestingly, Smith's desire to naturalize national sentiment is so strong here that he temporarily abandons his usual intersubjective approach to sympathy, in favour of an appeal to more abstract sensibilities: "We do not love our country merely as a part of the great society of mankind: we love it for its own sake, and independent of any such consideration" (229). But he soon reintroduces a more explicitly sympathetic understanding of how national identity is formed and maintained: "The love of our country seems, in ordinary cases, to involve in it two different principles; first, a certain respect and reverence for that constitution or form of government which is actually established; and secondly, an earnest desire to render the condition of our fellow-citizens as safe, respectable, and happy as we can" (231). Even as the phrase "respect and reverence" for the political status quo evokes Smith's patriotic wish to ensure that civil war within Britain does not recur, "desire" for the well-being of others looks back to the sympathy that makes people want to live in harmony with each other; ideally, each principle reinforces the other. In this way, Smithian sympathy

---

5. Luke Gibbons, "The Sympathetic Bond: Ossian, Celticism, and Colonialism," in *Celticism*, 279.

simultaneously naturalizes and encourages the moral basis of both social and national unions.[6]

We have already seen that Smith's version of sympathy differs from Hume's in several ways, including how it demands more concerted efforts from the persons involved. Such sympathy is aptly described, in John Dwyer's phrase, as "achieved sympathy," the result of a concerted attempt at harmonious social relations, rather than merely the mechanical product of the supposedly contagious nature of human feelings.[7] Significantly, this is precisely the way sympathy is depicted by the anonymous author—likely Smollett himself—of the *Critical Review*'s lengthy and laudatory review of the first edition of Smith's *The Theory of Moral Sentiments*. The reviewer not only agrees with Smith that sympathy is "a principle in human nature which surely, without the greatest obstinacy, cannot be disputed," but also confirms that "such an evident concurrence of daily observation with our author's theory, must be regarded as a strong proof of its solidity."[8] As such, it is fitting that, after indicating some of the dangers and inadequacies of Humean sympathy, *Humphry Clinker* looks to Smithian sympathy for a more workable model of social and national relations. Much of this modelling, in turn, is accomplished through the relations between the "South British" Brambles and the character embodying Scottish difference in the novel, Obadiah Lismahago.

The Bramble travelling party first spots Lismahago outside an inn at Durham, on the way to Scotland. Here is Jery's initial description:

> we were joined by another character, which promised something extraordinary—A tall, meagre figure, answering with his horse, the description of Don Quixote. . . . Perceiving ladies at the window above, he endeavoured to dismount with the most graceful air he could assume; but the ostler neglecting to hold the stirrup when he wheeled off his right foot, and stood with the whole weight on the other, the girth unfortunately gave

6. Evidence that the unifying imperatives of Smith's *Theory* were understood by colonial administrators (often Scottish) of the British Empire can be deduced from its frequent appearance on required curricula in government and missionary institutions in India throughout the nineteenth century. See Gauri Viswanathan, *Masks of Conquest: Literary Study and British Rule in India* (New York: Columbia University Press, 1989), 128–29.

7. John Dwyer, "Enlightened Spectators and Classical Moralists: Sympathetic Relations in Eighteenth-Century Scotland," in *Sociability and Society in Eighteenth Century Scotland*, ed. John Dwyer and Richard B. Sher (Edinburgh: Mercat Press, 1993), 102.

8. *Critical Review* 7 (May 1759): 385, 388. The review of Smith's *Theory* is attributed to Smollett by Susan Bourgeois in *Nervous Juyces and the Feeling Heart: The Growth of Sensibility in the Novels of Tobias Smollett* (New York: Peter Lang, 1986), 10. Interestingly, the review makes no mention of the "impartial spectator," an aspect of Smith's theory that has elicited a disproportionate amount of commentary from contemporary critics; for that reason, it does not enter into my analysis here.

> way, the saddle turned, down came the cavalier to the ground,
> and his hat and periwig falling off, displayed a head-piece of
> various colours, patched and plaistered in a woeful condition,
> (188) [195]

Jery's depiction is purposefully amusing, evoking an archetypal
comic character and involving Lismahago in a stock situation of
physical humiliation. He is thus dismissed at the outset as merely
"another character" among the cast that the Brambles have already
encountered. While Jery is quick to write off Lismahago as "a high-
flavoured dish" (191) [279], however, Bramble is intrigued by the veteran's unusual biography and wide range of polemical opinions,
especially concerning the detrimental effects of the Union. Critics
have often pointed to the debates between Lismahago and Bramble
as a central feature of Smollett's desire to facilitate dialogue between
Scotland and the rest of Britain, air grievances on both sides, and
even suggest possible solutions to current problems.[9] Rather than
focus on the content of these debates, I want to draw attention to
how Smollett stages them. By exploring the ways in which Bramble
and Lismahago regulate their behaviour towards one another, we
can learn much about Smollett's understanding of the benefits of
Smithian-style sympathy for the formation of a shared national
identity.

Upon learning of Lismahago's wartime sufferings in North America, Bramble feels that the Scottish soldier has been grievously
wronged by the neglect he experienced upon his return to Britain.
The latter, conversely, refuses to think of himself as a victim. After
several unsuccessful attempts to convince Lismahago of his misfortune, the discussion becomes heated:

> "So you have spent the best part of your life, (cried Mr Bram-
> ble) your youth, your blood, and your constitution, amidst the
> dangers, the difficulties, the horrors and hardships of war, for
> the consideration of three or four shillings a-day—a consider-
> ation—" "Sir, (replied the Scot, with great warmth) you are the
> man that does me injustice, if you say or think that I have been
> actuated by any such paltry consideration. . . . If I have not
> been lucky in the lottery of life, so neither do I think myself
> unfortunate—I owe to no man a farthing; I can always com-
> mand a clean shirt, a mutton-chop, and a truss of straw; and
> when I die, I shall leave effects sufficient to defray the expence
> of my burial." (189–90) [198]

---

9. Robert Mayer, "History, *Humphry Clinker,* and the Novel," *Eighteenth-Century Fiction*
   3 (1992): 243–45, 249–50. The most complete account of *Humphry Clinker* as a plea
   for tolerance is Eric Rothstein's "Scotophilia and *Humphry Clinker*: The Politics of
   Beggary, Bugs and Buttocks," *University of Toronto Quarterly* 52 (1982): 63–78.

Habituated to assuming that anyone in poor circumstances must be desperate for assistance from his or her social superiors, Bramble is highly surprised to encounter a subject who, despite being marginalized by the bourgeois public sphere for his poverty, eccentricity, and nationality, nevertheless refuses to become the latest recipient of Bramble's habitual sympathy. While Jery wryly suggests that Lismahago protests a little too much—"his moderation was all affected; for, whatsoever his tongue might declare, his whole appearance denoted dissatisfaction" (190) [198]—by asserting his status as an active agent rather than merely as the passive object of another's sympathies, Lismahago effectively alters the terms upon which sympathy can be utilized as a mode of social unification. The difference that Lismahago makes to Bramble's understanding of how to engage in sympathetic relations becomes even clearer when Jery reports that the two men have become frequent verbal sparring partners:

> [Lismahago] and Mr Bramble discoursed, and even disputed, on different subjects in war, policy, the belles lettres, law, and metaphysics; and sometimes they were warmed into such altercation as seemed to threaten an abrupt dissolution of their society; but Mr Bramble set a guard over his own irascibility, the more vigilantly as the officer was his guest; *and when, in spite of all his efforts, he began to wax warm, the other prudently cooled in the same proportion.* (191; emphasis added) [199]

Here we see sympathy being practised in a new manner. Replacing the monologue that announced Bramble's earlier presentation of charity to the passive, speech-deprived widow in Bath, the novel introduces a fresh model of social relations. In fact, Bramble and Lismahago's new-found dialogue implicitly follows Smith's instructions in the *Theory* for maximizing sympathetic relations: "With regard to those objects, which affect in a particular manner either ourselves or the person whose sentiments we judge of, it is at once more difficult to preserve this harmony and correspondence, and at the same time, vastly more important" (20). Furthermore, to avoid the "abrupt dissolution of their society," Bramble and Lismahago clearly engage in voluntary, Smithian-style regulation of their emotions, each "lowering his passion to that pitch, in which [the other is] capable of going along with him" (22).

This harmonious formula is repeated later in the book when, faced with a potentially embarrassing situation, the two men again engage in Smithian dialogue and self-control to keep the peace. Enraged by the callous treatment that Lismahago receives at the dinner table of Lord Oxmington, Bramble asks Lismahago to present the peer with an invitation to a duel. When the challenge is contemptuously dismissed, Lismahago, "half mad with his disgrace," berates Bramble for causing him embarrassment. The Welshman becomes angry in his turn, and they nearly come to blows before Tabitha intervenes: "'Is this your regard for me, (said she to the lieutenant) to seek the life of my brother?' Lismahago, *who seemed to grow cool as my uncle grew hot,* assured her he had a very great respect for Mr Bramble, but he had still more for his own honour, which had suffered pollution; but if that could be once purified, he should have no further cause of dissatisfaction" (283; emphasis added) [288]. Again calibrating their passions to meet each other's sympathetic needs, Bramble and Lismahago are subsequently able to work together to exact their revenge on the obnoxious Oxmington.

To maintain their unlikely friendship, then, the two men become adept at harmonizing their emotional states. As well, they implicitly begin to follow Smith's directions for facilitating sympathy's effectiveness. For Hume, we recall, feelings travel spontaneously between people, meaning that the spectator actually feels the emotions of others, without needing to be sensitive to potential differences in their subject positions. Smithian sympathy, by contrast, demands the spectator's imaginative recreation of the full emotional situation of the other. The extent of Bramble's new investment in this more complete style of sympathy is seen when his travelling party, approaching Scotland from the south, discovers that the windowpanes of all the inns in the north of England are covered with anti-Scottish verses. While Lismahago maintains a calm demeanour, Bramble becomes incensed on the Scottish veteran's behalf:

> My uncle's jaws began to quiver with indignation.—He said, the scribblers of such infamous stuff deserved to be scourged at the cart's tail for disgracing their country with such monuments of malice and stupidity.—"These vermin (said he) do not consider, that they are affording their fellow-subjects, whom they abuse, continual matter of self-gratulation, as well as the means of executing the most manly vengeance . . . . For my part, I admire the philosophic forbearance of the Scots, as much as I despise the insolence of those wretched libellers." (198) [206]

Imagining and appreciating the feelings of North Britons, who show stoic forbearance in the face of such insults, Bramble models for Smollett's readers how "to put himself in the situation of the other," as Smith wrote, "and to bring home to himself every little circumstance of distress which can possibly occur to the sufferer" (21). Significantly, Lismahago's response to the situation is couched in similar terms: "The captain, with an affectation of candour, observed, that men of illiberal minds were produced in every soil; that in supposing those were the sentiments of the English in general, he should pay too great a compliment to his own country, which was not of consequence enough to attract the envy of such a flourishing and powerful people" (198) [206]. While Jery again finds Lismahago's modesty forced, the latter nonetheless responds to the tenor of Bramble's speech by reciprocally entering into and articulating the sentiments of the party that he believes Bramble represents: those South Britons who do not share the "illiberal," xenophobic feelings of their less enlightened brethren. This act of imaginative mutual identification exemplifies Smith's guidelines for establishing a sympathetic relationship, in which "we place ourselves in the situation of another man, and view it, as it were, with his eyes and from his station" (109–10).

The result of Bramble and Lismahago's sympathetic mutual identification is just as Smith would have it: they become fast friends. Critics have often noted that Bramble's physical and mental ailments improve as the travelling party moves towards and through Scotland; I would add that his rehabilitation also accompanies his growing bond with Lismahago. As Bramble becomes more comfortable practising Smithian-style sympathetic relations, he becomes more at ease with the social world around him. No longer at the mercy of involuntary Humean sympathy, Bramble learns to engage in real, substantive dialogue with others. In the process, the differences that once separated him from Lismahago, and by extension divided South Britons from North Britons in general, are reduced to manageable ones. Of course, Lismahago never loses his distinctively Scottish outlook, especially his resistance to the Union itself; at the same time, the imagery of death consistently attached to him—Lismahago is described as "a resurrection of dry bones," has been scalped by the Miamis, and is later mistaken for a ghost—suggests that he embodies an antiquated Scottish perspective that is demonstrably obsolete (188–89, 272–73) [197, 272].[1] More significant than the questionable truth-value of Lismahago's opinions is the moral that Bramble ultimately draws from them: "I cannot help acquiescing in his remarks so far as to think, that the contempt for Scotland, which prevails too much on this side of the Tweed, is founded on prejudice and error" (279) [284]. Bramble's tolerant response to Lismahago's anti-Unionism confirms that the solution to the continuing problem of establishing Britishness is not to dissolve the Union, as Lismahago nearly suggests, but rather to strengthen it through the concerted expansion of mutually sympathetic relations.

1. On the obsolescence of Lismahago's political views, see Paul-Gabriel Boucé, *The Novels of Tobias Smollett*, trans. Antonia White in collaboration with the author (New York; Longman, 1976), 221.

Sympathetic Union: For Better and for Worse

In one of *Humphry Clinker*'s early letters, Jery confidently asserts that "You know we are the fools of prejudice" (50) [56]. By the end of the novel, however, he too affirms that such prejudices can be overcome through learning to identify with others' perspectives. For Jery, personal experience has made this transformation possible: "Without all doubt, the greatest advantage acquired in travelling and perusing mankind in the original, is that of dispelling those shameful clouds that darken the faculties of the mind, preventing it from judging with candour and precision" (332) [335]. Jery is specifically remarking on the improved light in which he views Lydia's mysterious suitor, Wilson, when the latter is finally revealed to be George Dennison, the son of a respectable English country gentleman. Smollett knew that the majority of his readers, English and Scottish alike, were unlikely to have many opportunities to meet their national counterparts in the flesh. This becomes the work of the novel itself: its hybridization of epistolary novel and travel narrative makes *Humphry Clinker* the ideal medium for allowing readers to "peruse" their fellow Britons at as close to first-hand as possible. Despite its use of sympathetic rhetoric, of course, Smollett's novel remains a work of fiction, not a philosophical treatise. What it lacks in philosophical rigour, however, it makes up for in its ability to show sympathy at work, not in abstract "thought experiments," but in the lives of its fictional characters, which provide readers with countless opportunities for identification as well as criticism. In these ways, Smollett's final novel both disseminates the Scottish Enlightenment sympathetic philosophy, especially in its Smithian mode, and points the way forward to a capacious, dialogic, modern conception of Britishness as a national identity to which all citizens of Britain have equal access.

Such access, however, has always been more available theoretically than practically. Like its Humean counterpart, Smithian sympathy has its disadvantages, and these too are distinctly registered in Smollett's novel. James Chandler has observed that Smith's conception of sympathy involves a "reconstitution of the [idea of the] case . . . [that] takes it out of the domain of Christian casuistry, but not into the domain of history"; Smithian sympathy may be case sensitive, so to speak, but it is not calibrated to account for the full effects of historical contextualization.[2] Not surprisingly, given the public sphere for which he was writing, Smith's idea of sympathy

---

2. James Chandler, *England in 1819: The Politics of Literary Culture and the Case of Romantic Historicism* (Chicago: University of Chicago Press, 1998), 290.

turns out to be inherently homosocial in nature: practised almost exclusively between men, it leads primarily to tighter communal bonds between them. Jery's positive revaluation of Dennison, for example, is dependent on the revelation of the latter's true identity as a member of the masculine, bourgeois public sphere; when Dennison was disguised as an itinerant actor or a Jewish peddler, Jery saw him only as an object of scorn. Unlike Dennison, however, Smollett's female characters do not have the option of casting off their subaltern status; as a result, their marginal positions in the public sphere mean that their letters, characterized by abundant malapropisms and feminine naïveté, are never given the same narrative authority or attention as those of their male counterparts. Even the novel's epistolary format, which encourages readers to evaluate the different letter writers' perspectives as "case studies" (to adapt Chandler's terminology) forming a consensus-based whole, does not adequately compensate for its gender bias: more than 80 per cent of the novel is written in the voices of its two central male characters.[3]

Despite (or perhaps because of) these patriarchal underpinnings, *Humphry Clinker* ends in archetypal comic fashion with multiple marriages between Lismahago and Tabitha, Clinker and Jenkins, and Lydia and Dennison.[4] The unions that these marriages create, not coincidentally, reproduce on a personal level the political configuration of Britain itself.[5] Nevertheless, this seemingly happy fact further damages the novel's case for sympathy as an effective facilitator of national unity. Just as the Derridean supplement always reveals "deficiency and infirmity" in the thing it supplements,[6] so the supplementation of sympathetic by contractual familial bonds reveals the former's dependence on the latter. The marriages that so neatly conclude the novel thus parallel the revelation that Humphry Clinker is actually Bramble's bastard son. As John P. Zomchick observes, "with the surprising discovery of relation where no relation was to be expected, the narrative suggests that the Bramble/Clinker or the master/servant relation is a natural one."[7] Similarly, once the novel's sympathetic relations are absorbed into familial ones, the potential for national rifts to be healed by

3. Douglas, 116n9.
4. See esp. Gillian Skinner, *Sensibility and Economics in the Novel, 1740–1800: The Price of a Tear* (New York: St Martin's Press, 1909), 84–90.
5. Jerry C. Beasley, "Tobias Smollett: The Seat in England," *Studies in Scottish literature* 29 (1997): 27.
6. Jacques Derrida, *Of Grammatology*, trans. Gayatri Chakravorty Spivak (Baltimore: Johns Hopkins University Press, 1976), 144.
7. John P. Zomchick, "Social Class, Character, and Narrative Strategy in *Humphry Clinker*," *Eighteenth-Century Life* 10, no. 3 (1986): 183.

the encouragement of mutual sympathy, Humean or Smithian, is inevitably compromised.[8]

Reviving the familial model of social unity, moreover, means revisiting two "primitive" social formations that *Humphry Clinker* initially rejects as un-British: the North American Indians, whose tribal values force Lismahago to marry the chieftain's daughter, and the Highlanders, whose clan system facilitates a form of belonging that is both attractive and worrying to Bramble. Lismahago's North American adventure, as Sussman convincingly argues, clearly indicates an anxiety about cross-cultural contamination; Bramble's attitude towards the Highlands is less clear.[9] His ambivalent response to clan society stems from what he perceives as its defining quality: its close-knit, sympathetic organization—"The clan consider the chief as their father, they bear his name, they believe themselves descended from his family, and they obey him as their lord, with all the ardour of filial love and veneration; while he, on his part, exerts a paternal authority, commanding, chastising, rewarding, protecting, and maintaining them as his own children" (255) [261]. While Bramble admires the Highlanders' fealty, he also recognizes that it runs counter to Britain's need to establish among its citizens larger loyalties to the nation-state as a whole. As a result, clan sympathy must be destroyed in order for national sympathy to be spread equally to all of Britain. Bramble's suggestions for this destruction, which focus on demolishing the Highlanders' feudal lifestyle by introducing modern economic practices, lead to his infamous observation that "Our people have a strange itch to colonize America, when the uncultivated parts of our own island might be settled to greater advantage" (256) [262]. Moreover, the Bramble party never proceeds farther north than Inverary; by leaving so much of the Highlands out of his characters' itinerary, Smollett effectively reduces its geographical significance, delegating its assimilation to the tender mercies of Bramble's proposed economic and legal reforms.

While the novel itself does not end in the Highlands, the Highland episodes represent the geographical as well as political limit of the Bramble party's sympathetic trajectory. The ideological price of Smollett's commitment to a united Britain is now clear; *Humphry Clinker* can conclude with an optimistic vision of Britons joined together by sympathetic bonds, only by proposing that the recalcitrant Highlands,

---

8. A similar transformation occurs in Frances Burney's *Evelina* (1778), where the eponymous English heroine learns to sympathize with a poverty-stricken Scottish poet, only to discover that the young man is her brother. As Evelina explains to the astonished Macartney, "You see, therefore, the claim we mutually have to each other's regard; we are not merely bound by the ties of friendship, but by those of blood." Frances Burney, *Evelina*, ed. Kristina Straub (New York: Bedford Books, 1997), 395.
9. See Sussman, 599–605.

the original site of such "clannish" attachments, must be relegated to the status of an internal colony. The Highlands, in other words, represents an internal "other" against which the rest of the nation can define itself.[1] In this way, even as it seeks to convert otherness to sameness, *Humphry Clinker* ultimately demonstrates that the process of nation formation is not only permanently ongoing (since "others," external or internal, can always be found), but also necessarily constituted by a fundamental exclusionary violence with which fiction, even in its most self-consciously sympathetic manifestations, is never wholly uncontaminated. Even Lismahago finds that full assimilation has an ever-receding horizon. In a short series of letters that introduces the novel proper, Jonathan Dustwich, a Welsh clergyman, offers to a London bookseller a bundle of letters that turns out to be the contents of *Humphry Clinker* itself. Despite having presumably read the letters and therefore witnessed the transformative sympathetic relations between Bramble and Lismahago, Dustwich nevertheless refers to Lismahago as a "vagrant foreigner" who "may be justly suspected of disaffection to our happy constitution, in church and state" (1) [8]. Furthermore, Dustwich intimates that he recently had a violent encounter with the North Briton at a dinner party. Despite his acceptance by the Bramble family, then, Lismahago's absorption into "British" society continues to be problematic, With characteristic humour, this seems to be Smollett's way of saying that, Jery's more hopeful pronouncements notwithstanding, we may inevitably remain the fools of prejudice.

TARA GHOSHAL WALLACE

"About savages and the awfulness of America": Colonial Corruptions in *Humphry Clinker*[†]

Tobias Smollett's last novel, *The Expedition of Humphry Clinker*, articulates a deeply felt and acerbic indictment of British society. From the cesspools of Bath to the superficiality of London to the poverty of Scotland, Matthew Bramble and his family discover, in

---

1. Franco Moretti observes that "Internal borders define modern states as composite structures, then, made of many temporal layers: as *historical* states—that need historical novels." Moretti, *Atlas of the European Novel, 1800–1900* (Verso: London, 1998), 40. It is thus a nice coincidence of literary history that 1771, the year of Smollett's death and the publication of *Humphry Clinker*, is also the year of Walter Scott's birth.

† From *Eighteenth-Century Fiction* 18.2 (Winter 2005–06): 229–50. Reprinted by permission of *Eighteenth-Century Fiction*. www.humanities.mcmaster.ca/~ecf.

their travels, a nation suffering from the corrosive effects of institutional and systemic corruption. Even the country squirearchy,
as represented by the Burdocks, the Baynards, and Lord Oxmington, spectacularly fails to provide the kind of hospitality and
serenity so prized by traditionalists like Bramble. Given the par-
lous state of the kingdom, the sensible and sensitive Briton can
only disengage and retreat . . . but not too far. While condemning
widespread anarchy and degeneracy in Britain, *Humphry Clinker*
emphatically rejects a solution embraced by many disappointed or
marginalized citizens: it abjures escape to the place where Moll
Flanders and Jemy can "live as new People in a new World," where
Clarissa might hide her scandalous elopement until "all is blown
over," and where Henry Esmond finds serenity "far from Europe
and its troubles, on the beautiful banks of the Potomac."[1] For
Smollett, writing in 1771 during an alarming exodus from Scotland to the colonies, America represents a double danger: it
siphons off manpower that could otherwise help build a strong
post-Union Scotland, and it distributes wealth in the home country in a destructively egalitarian way. In *Humphry Clinker*, Smollett
joins the argument against emigration by showing how colonial
adventuring has damaged the social and political health of the
mother nation and by depicting life in America as dangerously
savage.

Lismahago, during his debate with Bramble about the 1707
Union, asserts that England gained more than Scotland because
Scotland provided a most valuable resource, an army of imperial
workers:

1. Daniel Defoe, *Moll Flanders*, ed. David Blewett (1722; London: Penguin, 1989), 383;
Samuel Richardson, *Clarissa*, ed. Angus Ross (1747–48; Harmondsworth: Penguin,
1985), 1256; William Makepeace Thackeray, *The History of Henry Esmond*, ed. John
Sutherland and Michael Greenfield (1852; Harmondsworth: Penguin, 1970), 513. Critics have pointed out the extent to which Smollett participates in the eighteenth-century
topos of revulsion and retreat: Byron Gassman points out that Smollett, "alarmed at the
threat to established modes and institutions . . . foresees social chaos and political
anarchy if England continues its reckless course," and John Sekora adds, "When
national values have been twisted, personal choices alone remain, and these cannot
represent the ideal but merely the inevitable. Hence *Humphry Clinker* ends, for Bramble and Lismahago, with retreat and self-exile in Monmouthshire." Gassman, "Religious Attitudes in the World of *Humphry Clinker*," *Brigham Young University Studies* 6
(1965): 65; Sekora, *Luxury: The Concept in Western Thought, Eden to Smollett* (Baltimore: Johns Hopkins University Press, 1977), 238. Maurice Lévy argues that Bramble
(and Smollett) opt out of history: "Ce qu'il [Bramble] découvre, c'est le changement
qu'impose aux hommes, aux moeurs et aux choses le cours inexorable de l'histoire. Mais
Bramble, comme son géniteur, déteste le changement et l'histoire." Lévy, "*Humphry
Clinker*," *Roman et Société en Angleterre au XVIII Siècle* (Paris: Presses Universitaires
de France, 1978), 129. Paul Theroux's protagonist Allie Fox, whose words are quoted in
the current article's title, removes his family further and further away from the corrupt
civilization of twentieth-century America, only to descend into madness. Theroux, *The
Mosquito Coast* (London: Penguin, 1982), 11.

they got an accession of above a million of useful subjects, constituting a never-failing nursery of seamen, soldiers, labourers and mechanics; a most valuable acquisition to a trading country, exposed to foreign wars, and obliged to maintain a number of settlements in all the four quarters of the globe. In the course of seven years, during the last war, Scotland furnished the English army and navy with seventy thousand men, over and above those who migrated to their colonies, or mingled with them at home in the civil departments of life.[2]

For once, Lismahago does not exaggerate. While early attempts at establishing Scottish settlements in America failed, the "turning point in Scottish emigration was the Seven Years' War," according to Ned C. Landsman, "which attracted large numbers of Scottish soldiers after mid-century. . . . Perhaps 40,000 Scots ventured to America during the next dozen years."[3] This enormous outflow created a problem of depopulation that contemporary witnesses deplored. Samuel Johnson and James Boswell, travelling in Scotland in 1773, repeatedly encounter signs of escalating emigration, including a dance called "America. Each of the couples . . . successively whirls round in a circle, till all are in motion; and the dance seems intended to shew how emigration catches, till a whole neighbourhood is set afloat." Johnson laments that "all that go may be considered as subjects lost to the British crown; for a nation scattered in the boundless regions of America resembles rays diverging from a focus."[4] Like Johnson, who finds that "oppression might produce a

---

2. Tobias Smollett, *The Expedition of Humphry Clinker*, ed. Angus Ross (1771; London: Penguin, 1967), 317 [283]. References are to this edition. [Page numbers in square brackets are to this Norton Critical Edition.]
3. Ned C. Landsman, "Immigration and Settlement," in *Scotland and the Americas, 1600–1800*, intro. Michael Fry (Providence: John Carter Brown Library, 1995), 16. Linda Colley also estimates that 40,000 Scots, as well as 55,000 Protestant Irish and 30,000 English and Welsh, went to America between 1760 and 1776. Colley, *Captives: Britain, Empire, and the World, 1600–1850* (New York: Anchor Books, 2002), 200. Alan Taylor calculates that "Scots emigration soared to 145,000 between 1707 and 1775," outnumbering by far English emigrants to the colonies. Taylor, *American Colonies* (New York: Viking Penguin, 2001), 294, 316. For a detailed analysis of numbers, distribution, and motivations of emigrants, see David Dobson, *Scottish Emigration to Colonial America, 1607–1785* (Athens: University of Georgia Press, 1994). Dobson says that "By the early 1770s the British government was becoming so concerned by the level of emigration from the Highlands that it at times discouraged or hindered it" (155). Peter N. Miller points out that eighteenth-century writers such as James Abercromby and Thomas Pownall went so far as to question the legality of emigration. Miller, *Defining the Common Good: Empire, Religion and Philosophy in Eighteenth-Century Britain* (Cambridge: Cambridge University Press, 1994), 197, 205.
4. *Johnson's Journey to the Western Islands of Scotland and Boswell's Journal of a Tour to the Hebrides with Samuel Johnson, LL.D*, ed. R.W. Chapman (London: Oxford University Press, 1970), 346, 119. Taylor refers to the alarm of "imperial officials" during the 1770s: "elite observers . . . saw no profit to the mother country in the loss of British labourers and tenants into the woods of America" (441).

wish for new habitations," Smollett ascribes this massive exodus at least in part to English punitive policies in the wake of the Jacobite uprisings of 1715 and 1745, policies which de-cultured Highlanders by disarming them and depriving them "of their ancient garb . . . the government could not have taken a more effectual method to break their national spirit" (277) [246].[5] Unlike Johnson, who fears that "nobody born in any other parts of the world will choose this country for his residence,"[6] Smollett believes that proper economic incentives can indeed repopulate the Highlands: "Our people have a strange itch to colonize America, when the uncultivated parts of our own island might be settled to great advantage" (294) [262]. Bramble eagerly praises the superior quality of Scottish produce and the beauty of Scottish women (260–61) [225] and compares Scottish systems of justice, education, and social welfare favourably with those in England. This list of advantages, Smollett seems to argue, should convince Scots not to abandon their home for uncertain futures and dangerous confrontations in the colonies.

To a large extent, then, *Humphry Clinker* participates in a polemical dialogue about the American colonies as refuge and opportunity. As Michael Zuckerman points out, promotional literature extolling America competed with negative images of the colonies: "chiaroscuro constructions, damning European darkness and blazoning American brilliance, were responses to equal but opposite condemnations of the new continent."[7] *Humphry Clinker* joins the voices attempting to stanch the flow of useful manpower from Scotland to America, and, like other texts that Bruce McLeod labels "anti-empire," "negotiates the impact of having an empire, especially when consumer culture kicks in and social divisions appear to wobble precariously."[8]

5. Samuel Johnson, *Johnson's Journey to the Western Islands of Scotland*, 85. See Dobson, 154: "The Highlanders, clearly wishing to maintain their traditional culture and society, preferred to emigrate to the New World rather than be assimilated into the culture and society of Lowland Scotland." Elaine Jordan cites a correspondent in *The Military Register* who characterizes Scottish emigrants as "*all old soldiers* . . . obliged to contemplate transporting themselves into a new and precarious existence in the woods and wilds of North America." Jordan, "The Management of Scott's Novels," in *Europe and Its Others: Proceedings of the Essex Conference on the Sociology of Literature, July 1984*, 2 vols., ed. Francis Barker, Peter Hulme, Margaret Iversen, and Diana Loxley (Colchester: University of Essex, 1985), 2:149.
6. Johnson, *Johnson's Journey to the Western Islands of Scotland*, 87.
7. Michael Zuckerman, "Identity in British America: Unease in Eden," in *Colonial Identity in the Atlantic World, 1500–1800*, ed. Nicholas Canny and Anthony Pagden (Princeton: Princeton University Press, 1987), 123.
8. Bruce McLeod, *The Geography of Empire in English Literature, 1580–1745* (Cambridge: Cambridge University Press, 1999), 30. This assessment is echoed by Robert Giddings, who argues that *Humphry Clinker* is "a portrait of a society at a particular stage of development, as the nation slowly changed from supporting itself . . . into a country which fed its population and provided for its luxuries by overseas trade." Giddings, "Matthew Bramble's Bath: Smollett and the West Indian Connection," in *Smollett: Author of the First Distinction*, ed. Alan Bold (London: Vision Press, 1982), 49.

Matthew Bramble, in one of his many diatribes against the new social (dis)order, connects the collapse of traditional hierarchies with the agents of Empire:

> All these absurdities arise from the general tide of luxury, which hath overspread the nation, and swept away all, even the very dregs of the people. Every upstart of fortune, harnessed in the trappings of the mode, presents himself at Bath. . . . Clerks and factors from the East Indies, loaded with the spoil of plundered provinces; planters, negro-drivers, and hucksters, from our American plantations, enriched they know not how; agents, commissaries, and contractors, who have fattened in two successive wars, on the blood of the nation; usurers, brokers, and jobbers of every kind. (65) [43]

Of course, Bramble targets the whole phenomenon of commercialism with its attendant "plethora of political, social, religious, and moral corruptions,"[9] but significantly, most of the "dregs" he lists are those who engage in the imperial project. One of the few upstarts individualized in Bramble's narrative is "a negro-driver, from Jamaica, [who] pay[s] overnight, to be the master of one of the rooms, sixty-five guineas for tea and coffee to the company, and leave[s] Bath next morning, in such obscurity, that not one of his guests had the slightest idea of his person" (87) [64]. Another is the ungrateful Paunceford, who makes a fortune abroad and turns his back on his early benefactor Serle (97–100) [74–77]. And of course Bramble's first antagonist at Bath is "a Creole gentleman," whose Negro servants are beaten by Bramble as punishment for their insolence as well as their "dreadful blasts" on the French horn, and who, despite being a colonel, "prudently declined any farther prosecution of the dispute" (60–61) [37–38]. Each of these imperial profiteers represents an aspect of what ails England: extravagance, ingratitude, incivility, and cowardice.

Even those who have honourably served their nation in imperial wars are scarred by the engagement. In a coffee house in Bath, Bramble encounters old friends who bear the marks of their

---

9. Susan L. Jacobsen, "'The Tinsel of the Times': Smollett's Argument against Conspicuous Consumption in *Humphry Clinker,*" *Eighteenth-Century Fiction* 9, no, 1 (1996): 72. David M. Weed associates commercialism with debilitating feminization: "England's social body incorporates the ill effects of commercialism into its public institutions and civic and social life, and . . . it produces effeminate men who participate in an epidemic spread of luxury, bodily waste, consumption, and 'cannibalism,'" Weed, "Sentimentalism, Misogyny and Medicine in *Humphry Clinker,*" *SEL* 37, no. 3 (1997): 615. John Dwyer suggests that Scots were particularly disturbed by the new economic order: "Luxury, Scottish writers believed, was spreading . . . alongside the commercialization of Great Britain, as wealth began to find itself in the hands of 'nabobs' and 'contractors' who, it was argued, had neither the training nor the temper of mind to use it properly." Dwyer, *Virtuous Discourse: Sensibility and Community in Late Eighteenth-Century Scotland* (Edinburgh: John Donald Publishers, 1987), 97.

patriotic service: rear-admiral Balderick, "metamorphosed into an old man, with a wooden leg and a weatherbeaten face, which appeared the more ancient from his grey locks," and "what remained of colonel Cockril, who had lost the use of his limbs in making an American campaign" (84–85) [61]. The most egregious example of the human cost of empire is, of course, Lismahago, upon whose body are inscribed the mutilations inflicted by imperial ambition and who epitomizes the forgotten veteran. Bramble says, "our pity was warmed with indignation, when we learned, that in the course of two sanguinary wars, he had been wounded, maimed, mutilated, taken, and enslaved, without ever having attained a higher rank than that of lieutenant" (224) [197].[1] Moreover, the home government, while exploiting the fruits of empire and those who fight to win them, remains deplorably ignorant of the New World that funds British prosperity. The Duke of N——, after being educated in Canadian geography by Captain C——, exclaims, "Egad! I'll go directly, and tell the king that Cape Breton is an island" (145) [119]. Not only does the Duke mangle the names of the tribes that the League of the Iroquois comprises, he facetiously mocks rituals that are crucially important to making alliances with native Americans: "Let 'em have plenty of blankets, and stinkubus, and wampum; and your excellency won't fail to scour the kettle, and boil the chain, and bury the tree, and plant the hatchet—Ha, ha, ha!" (144–45) [121]. Like the East India Company director, who asked Clive whether "Sir Roger Dowlat" (Siraj-ud-daula) was a baronet,[2] the Duke of N—— epitomizes the ignorance of the governing class at home.

1. Jonathan Swift, in book 3 of *Gulliver's Travels*, also refers to ungrateful governments: those who have provided the best service to princes and states "all appeared with dejected Looks and in the meanest Habit; most of them telling me they died in Poverty and Disgrace, and the rest on a Scaffold or a Gibbet." Swift, *The Writings of Jonathan Swift*, ed. Robert A. Greenberg and William Bowman Piper (New York: W. W. Norton, 1973), 172. The prematurely aged Balderick may prefigure Admiral Baldwin in Jane Austen's *Persuasion*, whom Sir Walter Elliot describes as "the most deplorable looking personage you can imagine, his face the colour of mahogany, rough and rugged to the last degree, all lines and wrinkles, nine grey hairs of a side, and nothing but a dab of powder at top." Austen, *Persuasion*, in vol. 5 of *The Novels of Jane Austen*, ed. R. W. Chapman (London: Oxford University Press, 1933), 20.
2. P. J. Marshall, *Problems of Empire: Britain and India, 1757–1813* (London: George Allen and Unwin, 1968), 26. Colley points out that Britons at home evinced very little interest in colonial conditions, including captivity by indigenous Americans, until mid-century: "once troops from Britain and their families began crossing the Atlantic in substantial numbers, after the outbreak of the Seven Years War in 1756, the metropolitan market for tales of captivity by native Americans, as for other information about North America, would sky-rocket. With large numbers of their own kind now flooding over to America . . . this vast territory and all its complex dangers came to seem to Britons at home infinitely more real and absorbing" (161). For a fascinating study of the literary effects of the new interest in captivity narratives, see Nancy Armstrong and Leonard Tennenhouse, "The American Origins of the English Novel," *American Literary History* 4, no. 3 (1992): 386–410. Captivity narratives, they argue, developed precisely those attributes most commonly associated with the rise of the English novel: epistolarity, individualism, middle-class domesticity, and the feminized consciousness.

The home country, as represented in *Humphry Clinker*, suffers from a range of ills brought on by imperial wealth, which produces social chaos and political corruption. Colonial wars have maimed British soldiers, who are then abandoned by an ungrateful government; and the commercialism attending imperial ambition has so disrupted traditional rural life that it has led to an amassing of the lower classes in urban areas, where they *"all tread upon the kibes of one another:* actuated by the demons of profligacy and licentiousness, they are seen every where rambling, riding, rolling, rushing, justling, mixing, bouncing, cracking in one vile ferment of stupidity and corruption" (119) [96]. So-called economic progress has dispossessed rural populations of homes and employment and set them adrift, and this influx to metropolitan areas has led not only to a blurring of class markers but also to rampant consumerism, greed, crime, and disease.

Yet, when Lismahago, finding that his half-pay cannot support him in either England or Scotland, contemplates returning to the colonies to "pass the rest of his days among his old friends the Miamis, and amuse himself in finishing the education of the son he had by his beloved Squinkinacoosta," Bramble thinks "it very hard, that a gentleman who had served his country with honour, should be driven by necessity to spend his old age, among the refuse of mankind, in such a remote part of the world" (305–6) [272–73]. According to this text, whatever the corruptions and dangers of life in the mother country, they are tolerable compared to the violent and barbaric world confronting the European settling in North America. To deflect the impulse to emigrate, *Humphry Clinker* sets out a multiplicity of arguments that articulate the danger and futility of the American mission while promoting national pride.

Paul-Gabriel Boucé argues that "The ritual mutilations described by Lismahago are on the shady borderline between sadism and buffoonery"; Robert Hopkins finds that Lismahago "serves as a catharsis" because "his Thurberlike mythic reduction of Indian captivity converts English anxieties about Indian massacres to a ludicrous, demonic myth"; Joanne Lewis sees Lismahago as "belonging, at least in part, to the world of *commedia dell'arte*" and his captivity as a "scenario for *commedia*, the domestic violence reminiscent of Punch and Judy . . . [and] Smollett's narrative transmute[s] history to farce."[3]

---

3. Paul-Gabriel Boucé, *The Novels of Tobias Smollett* (London: Longman, 1976), 240; Robert Hopkins, "The Function of Grotesque in *Humphry Clinker*," *Huntington Library Quarterly* 32 (1969): 173–74; Joanne Lewis, "Death and the Comic Marriage: Lismahago in Harlequin Skeleton," *Studies in Eighteenth-Century Culture* 18 (1988): 406,

These characterizations of Lismahago's captivity fail to take into account Smollett's deep knowledge of contemporary discourse about native Americans and the congruence of Lismahago's story with reports about captured Europeans. They also fail to recognize that, while accurately transmitting some known indigenous practices, Smollett tilts the narrative towards the grotesque for propaganda purposes: the account of Lismahago in captivity addresses English anxieties about colonial rivalries and transculturation, and concludes that the attempt to win the hearts and minds of native Americans is inherently doomed.

Writers on American colonial history point out that in an ironical reversal of British fantasies about the conversion and assimilation of indigenous populations, native Americans were distressingly successful at converting colonizers to their way of life. James Axtell writes that "Most of the Indians who were educated by the English—some contemporaries thought *all* of them—returned to Indian society at the first opportunity. . . . On the other hand, large numbers of Englishmen had chosen to become Indians."[4] J. Norman Heard prefaces his summary accounts of eighteenth- and nineteenth-century captivities by quoting a 1753 letter from Benjamin Franklin, in which Franklin recounts the recidivism of rescued captives: "tho' rescued by their Friends, and treated with all imaginable tenderness to prevail with them to stay among the English, yet in a short time, they become disgusted with our manner of life, and the care and pains that are necessary to support it, and take the first opportunity of escaping again into the Woods, from whence there is no reclaiming them."[5] Among those who chose the indigenous way of life were captives as disparate as Mary Jamison, captured by Shawnees in 1758, who married a Delaware and lived happily until her death at age seventy-five; David Boyd, captured by

---

411. In a similar vein, Kenneth Simpson, commenting on Smollett's coarse humour, says, "an account of atrocities perpetrated upon the lieutenant and his companion by the American Indians, is a sequence which is certainly offered as ironic comment on the vogue of the travel adventure." Simpson, *The Protean Scot: The Crisis of Identity in Eighteenth-Century Scottish Literature* (Aberdeen: Aberdeen University Press, 1988), 16. John Richetti takes a more complex view: "Comprised of literary and documentary materials that encompass the contradictory areas of Cervantic caricature, the horrors of North American captivity narrative, and the inequities of advancement in the eighteenth-century British army, Lismahago points to his own complicated status as a character simultaneously comic and deeply serious, both grotesque and engagingly pathetic in his pride and considerable intelligence." Richetti, *The English Novel in History, 1700–1780* (London: Routledge, 1999), 186.

4. James Axtell, *The European and the Indian: Essays in the Ethnohistory of Colonial North America* (New York: Oxford University Press, 1981), 170.

5. J. Norman Heard, *White into Red: A Study of the Assimilation of White Persons Captured by Indians* (Metuchen: Scarecrow Press, 1973), 10. McLeod echoes Franklin; "New England leaders worried over the European captives who refused to return to 'civilized' society, since Indian life appeared attractive to some in contrast to the discipline and drudgery of life for the majority of English colonists" (152).

Delawares in 1756, who, brought back to white society by his adoptive father, "had to be closely guarded for weeks before he relinquished his plan" to return to the tribe; and eight-year-old John McCullough, captured in 1756, who had to be forced to visit his white family.[6] As an exasperated Cadwallader Golden remarks in 1717, "The English had as much Difficulty to persuade the People, that had been taken Prisoners by the French Indians, to leave the Indian manner of living, though no People enjoy more Liberty, and live in greater Plenty, than the common Inhabitants of new-York do."[7]

Even narratives about gruesome torture refer to kind treatment from captors, which leads, in turn, to a degree of adaptation: Robert Eastburn is fed chocolate because "I was unwell, and could not eat their coarse food"; John Leeth is well looked after by his Delaware father; John Gyles's frostbite is treated with fir-balsam; and Thomas Morris is presented with, of all things, a volume of Shakespeare.[8] Pierre Esprit Radisson, when his adoptive family dresses him in native garb, admits that "I could not but fall in love wth myselfe, if not yt I had better instructions to shun the sin of pride."[9] Some of Smollett's literary contemporaries write laudatory accounts of life among native Americans. Arthur Young's heroine Emmera lives secluded from all but Indians, who "adore" her and rescue her from a villainous European, while Henry Mackenzie's young hero Annesley regrets leaving "the perfect freedom subsisting in this rude and simple state of society . . . where greatness cannot use oppression, nor wealth excite envy."[1] Lismahago himself, of course, leaves his "advantages and honours" in the Badger tribe only "in consequence of being exchanged for the orator of the community, who had been taken prisoner by the

---

6. Heard, 25–30, 65, 130.
7. Cadwallader Colden, *The History of the Five Indian Nations of Canada, Which are Dependent on the Province of New York, and Are a Barrier between the English and the French in that Part of the World* (New York: Allerton Books, 1904), 263. Colley writes that so many British soldiers had been assimilated into tribal culture that a rescued or ransomed soldier could face court-martial "unless he could somehow prove that he really had been forced to cross the culture line against his will" (196).
8. Robert Eastburn, *A Faithful Narrative*, in *The Garland Library of Narratives of North American Indian Captives*, 111 vols., ed. Wilcomb E. Washburn (New York: Garland Publishing, 1978), 8:10; Ewell Jeffries, *A Short Biography of John Leeth, with an Account of His Life among the Indians*, ed. Reuben Gold Thwaites (1831; New York: Benjamin Blom, 1972), 27; John Gyles, *The Memoirs of Odd Adventures, Strange Deliverances, &c. in the Captivity of John Gyles, Esq.; Commander of the Garrison on St. George's River* (Boston: S. Kneeland and T. Green, 1736), 17; Thomas Morris, *Journal of Captain Thomas Morris* (1791; Ann Arbor: University Microfilms, 1966), 12.
9. Pierre Esprit Radisson, *Voyages of Peter Esprit Radisson, Being an Account of His Travels and Experiences among the North American Indians, from 1652–1684*, ed. Gideon D. Scull (1885; New York: Burt Franklin, 1967), 34.
1. Arthur Young, *The Adventures of Emmera, or The Fair American. Exemplifying the Peculiar Advantages of Society and Retirement*, 2 vols. (1773; New York: Garland Publishing, 1974), 1:221, 2:80; Henry Mackenzie, *The Man of the World*, 2 vols. (New York: Garland Publishing, 1974), 2:182–83.

Indians that were in alliance with the English" (229) [202]. Both
historical and literary accounts, then, attest to a disturbing inversion: instead of "civilizing" the native population, British immi-
grants in America manifest a tendency to admire and assimilate
into tribal culture.[2]

Moreover, and perhaps more gallingly, while native Americans
rejected English attempts to convert them, they responded more
favourably to French blandishments, Morris, writing in 1764,
admires the French for winning native Americans' affections by
intermarrying and "prohibiting the sale of spiritous liquors to Indians"; he contrasts this to the "scandalous practices" of some
English traders, who alienate the indigenous people by "imposing
on the drunken Indian in trade, abusing his drunken wife, daughter, or other female relation."[3] Robert Rogers's play *Ponteach; or
the Savages of America* (1766) explicitly lauds French colonial
customs—

> The French are all subdued,
> But who are in their Stead become our Lords?
> A proud, imperious, churlish, haughty Band,
> The French familiarized themselves with us,
> Studied our Tongues, and Manners, wore our Dress,
> Married our Daughters and our Sons their Maids,
> Dealt honestly, and well supplied our Wants,
> Used no one ill, and treated with Respect . . .

—while excoriating the English as "false, deceitful, knavish, insolent."[4] Gordon M. Sayre points out that Catholic missionaries
embraced martyrdom in a way that was impressive to Indians and
alien to Protestants: "For French Catholics, suffering for one's faith
led naturally to death. . . . The privations of the new environment
were part of the holy suffering of his [the Jesuit's] mission. If his

---

2. In a subtle analysis of Lismahago's story, Charlotte Sussman argues that, in *Humphry
Clinker*, "The problem of how to assimilate, or acculturate, other cultures . . . is
redacted into a problem of oral consumption"; not only is the English body poisoned by
imported food, but native Americans' ritualistic cannibalism is seen as "evidence of a
tribe's ability to retain its social coherence in the face of a colonizing invasion. . . . The
colonial encounter violates Europe, rather than the New World." Sussman, "Lismahago's Captivity: Transculturation in *Humphry Clinker,*" *ELH* 61, no. 3 (1994): 598, 600–1.
For another reading of European anxieties and captivity narratives, see Helen Carr,
"Woman/Indian: 'The American' and His Others," in *Europe and Its Others*: "the Indians are the ones in . . . potential sexual possession, and the narrative can enact and
resolve the colonists' deep fears of being dominated and mastered by the Indian, of
having their identity and power as European men destroyed" (2:52).
3. Morris, 26–27.
4. Robert Rogers, *Ponteach; or the Savages of America*, in *Representative Plays by American
Dramatists*, ed. Montrose J. Moses (New York: E.P. Dutton, 1918), 143.

reception turned from hospitable to hostile, the objective of captivity was not resistance and redemption, but martyrdom."[5] Thus the French were succeeding where the English were failing. Even the hostile voice of the *British Magazine* concedes the efficacy of French missionaries:

> The missionaries scattered among the Indian tribes were generally strong, hale, and active, patient of hunger, cold, and fatigue: all of them were, moreover, enthusiasts who courted danger, and gladly exposed themselves to all manner of afflictions. They attended the Indians in all their martial excursions, appeared always in the hottest part of the battle, baptizing the infidels, and comforting the converts in their last moments: they themselves were generally wounded, often killed, sometimes taken and tortured to death by the most hideous torments. The example of men acting in this manner, from a spirit of benevolence, could not fail to make deep impressions upon sensible minds; and accordingly they soon acquired the veneration of the Indians.[6]

So intertwined were French and indigenous American cultures in some places that, according to Heard, one Eunice Williams, taken by the Iroquois from Massachusetts to Canada in 1704, was doubly transculturated: "The daughter of a steadfast Protestant minister had become converted to Catholicism and learned to love her Indian masters."[7]

Confronted by the alarming and embarrassing spectacle of the wrong sorts of transculturation, British writers embarked on a discourse of rationalization and recuperation. One useful strategy was to paint the French as both cunning and savage, thereby explaining their success with native Americans. In 1762, Peter Williamson complains of the tactics of a French priest, who assures Amerindians that the English killed the son of God, and "that if the *English*, were, all destroyed, the son of the Good-man, who is God, would

5. Gordon M. Sayre, *Les Sauvages Américains: Representations of Native Americans in French and English Colonial Literature* (Chapel Hill: University of North Carolina Press, 1997), 22, 260.
6. "The History of Canada," *British Magazine*, June 1760, 351. The failure of English missionaries would be particularly painful for those who, like John Eliot of Massachusetts, saw "in the conversion experiences of the Indians themselves a model for the spiritual renewal of a colony struggling to cope with both the internal strife of ecclesiastical conflict and the anxiety over England's uncertain future in the wake of the Restoration. . . . Missionary work not only seemed to exempt itself from the bitter debates within English Protestantism. It also offered the English a way of imagining themselves as a Protestant nation united against Roman Catholicism." Thomas Scanlan, *Colonial Writing and the New World, 1583–1671: Allegories of Desire* (Cambridge: Cambridge University Press, 1999), 155, 159.
7. Heard, 20.

come again, and banish all evil spirits from their lands."[8] Thus also, early in "The History of Canada" in the *British Magazine*, appears an account of Le Caron and his fellow Jesuits who, instead of "explaining and enforcing the divine and amiable doctrines of the Gospel," have "inflamed the animosities subsisting between the different nations of the Indians": "They have taught them the arts of fraud, and the refinements of cruelty . . . misrepresented the neighbouring subjects of Britain, as monsters of impiety and brutality . . . they have supported and extended their own influence among those ignorant creatures by craft and hypocrisy, false miracles, and all variety of Jesuitical imposture."[9] This comprehensive indictment of French perfidy not only explains French inroads among native Americans, but also can actually make a merit of British failures, since presumably British missionaries never resorted to such sordid practices.[1] "The History of Canada" contains much more in this vein, emphasizing the ignorance of the Amerindians and the cunning ambition of the Jesuits, as well as their fanatical desire for "the crown of martyrdom."[2] Even when the narrative praises the fortitude and perseverance of French missionaries, as in the account of Father Jogues's bravery under torture, it follows with a reiteration of Catholic zeal for martyrdom, which, of course, undermines the priest's heroism. Colden provides an example of the barbarity of the secular arm of French power when he recounts the Comte de Frontenac's decision to burn a native American prisoner according to

---

8. Peter Williamson, *French and Indian Cruelty: Exemplified in the Life and Various Vicissitudes of Fortune of Peter Williamson*, intro. Michael Fry (1762; Bristol: Thoemmes Press, 1996), 45. The French, writes Williamson, "were sent to dispossess us in that part of the world, [are] indefatigable in their duty, and continually contriving, and using all manner of ways and means to win the *Indians* to their interest" (8). Eastburn complains of the French governor of Quebec: "even in Times of *Peace*, he gives the *Indians* great Encouragement to *Murder* and *Captivate* the poor Inhabitants on our Frontiers" (8:38). William Fleming's Delaware captors tell his wife "that the French were better off than the English, for they had a great many Old Men among them that could forgive all their Sins, and these Men had often assured the Indians it was no Sin to destroy Hereticks, and all the English were such." William and Elizabeth Fleming, *A Narrative of the Sufferings and Surprizing Deliverance of William and Elizabeth Fleming*, in *The Garland Library*, 8:16. Gyles, on the other hand, encounters a good Franciscan priest who has told Amerindians "that excepting their errors in Religion, the English were a better people than themselves," and that God will punish those who hurt the English (19).
9. "The History of Canada," *British Magazine*, April 1760, 198.
1. In his "Address to the British Colonists in North America" (1777), Edmund Burke spells out this notion of British restraint: "born in a civilized country, formed to gentle manners, trained in a merciful religion. . . . We rather wished to have joined you in bringing gradually that unhappy part of mankind into civility, order, piety, and virtuous discipline, than to have confirmed their evil habits, and increased their natural ferocity, by fleshing them in the slaughter of you, whom our wiser and better ancestors had sent into the wilderness, with the express view of introducing, along with our holy religion, its humane and charitable manners." *The Portable Edmund Burke*, ed. Isaac Kramnick (Harmondsworth: Penguin, 1999), 278.
2. "The History of Canada," *British Magazine*, May 1760, 132.

indigenous custom; Colden includes a description of the gruesome torture and execution "to shew on one Hand, what Courage and Resolution, Virtue, the Love of Glory and the Love of one's Country can instill into Mens Minds, even where Knowledge of true Religion is wanting; and on the other Hand, how far a false Policy, under a corrupt Religion, can debase even great Minds" (169–70). The French, in these accounts, are even more barbaric than the Amerindians, since they torture and kill in the full knowledge that they are committing atrocities. In the end, however, the problem lies with the native Americans themselves, whose inherent incapacity foils any attempt to "civilize" them: "the American natives are extremely dull; their faculties circumscribed, their sentiments incapable of refinement; and they seem to be very ill provided with the power of imagination."[3] In a gesture towards European unity, the *British Magazine* concludes that "The truth is, neither France nor England could derive much honour from any connexion with such cruel and irreclaimable savages, whom no precepts could enlighten, and no example humanize."[4]

Humphry Clinker participates in and even exceeds the kind of logical gymnastics that claim that Amerindians cannot be converted at all, except by Europeans who bring their own brand of savagery to the task. At the same time that the text represents appalling Amerindian barbarity, it shows native culture responding with dignity and even intellectual sophistication to French missionary incursions. In a masterly restructuring of familiar materials, Smollett manages to both depict Catholic zeal and trivialize it. In Lismahago's narrative, the Jesuits ignore the Miamis' peaceful attempt to dismiss them, "persist[ing] in saying mass, in preaching, baptizing, and squabbling with the conjurers . . . till they had thrown the whole community into confusion" (232) [204]. The exasperated native Americans then try,

3. "The History of Canada," *British Magazine*, June 1760, 352.
4. "The History of Canada," *British Magazine*, March 1761, 153. Francis Jennings works out the murderous implications of such an attitude: "their mode of existence and cast of mind were such as to make them incapable of civilization and therefore of full humanity . . . the savage creatures of the wilderness, being unable to adapt to any environment other than the wild, stubbornly and viciously resisted God or fate, and thereby incurred their suicidal extermination." Jennings, *The Invasion of America: Indians, Colonialism, and the Cant of Conquest* (Chapel Hill: University of North Carolina Press, 1975), 15. T. H. Breen points to another result of Amerindian resistance to European culture. Unlike imported slaves, they were not part of the labour system in the colonies and therefore of no practical use to the settlers; once the fur trade collapsed, "the Indians, now dependent upon European commerce, had little to offer in exchange for guns and cloth, kettles and knives. Under these conditions, Indians were easily exploited, abused, and cheated out of whatever they still possessed." Breen, "Creative Adaptation, People and Cultures," in *Colonial British America: Essays in the New History of the Early Modern Era*, ed. Jack P. Greene and J. R. Pole (Baltimore: Johns Hopkins University Press, 1984), 214.

condemn, and burn them at the stake, "where they died singing *Salve regina*, in a rapture of joy, for the crown of martyrdom which they had thus obtained" (232) [204]. By representing the disruptive effects of their interventions in a hitherto stable and contented native society, the narrative recasts missionary enthusiasm as petty interference and thus makes English failure at conversion seem culturally respectful.[5]

In any case, the indigenous people in *Humphry Clinker* are too cynical to be converted. Like the dignified Chief Lontac in Robert Bage's *Hermsprong* (1796) and unlike the docile and easily swayed tribe in *The Female American* (1767), Smollett's native Americans confidently assert the superiority of their own forms of belief.[6] Their primitive tenets—"They . . . worship two contending principles; one the fountain of all Good, the other the source of all evil . . . sensible men pay adoration to a Supreme Being, who creates and sustains the universe" (231) [203–04]—can more than hold their own against canting Catholicism. The natives scoff at the Jesuits' accounts of "miracles," of "mysteries and revelations, which they could neither explain nor authenticate"; they are horrified by a God who would not only inflict mortality on his only son but also allow him "to be insulted, flagellated, and even executed as a malefactor"; and as for the creed of transubstantiation, they consider it impious to pretend "to create God himself, to swallow, digest, revive, and multiply him *ad infinitum*, by the help of a little flour and water" (231) [204].[7] Interestingly, Smollett here projects onto the French an English

5. Axtell points out that stoicism "served the Jesuits well in Indian country. Personal courage, especially in the face of death, was appreciated in Europe, but from the American natives it drew special respect. . . . The Iroquois were even more impressed when Father Jogues, his hands mutilated by torture during his previous captivity, returned to the Mohawks in 1646 to pursue the cause of peace and Christ." Axtell, *The Invasion Within: The Contest of Cultures in Colonial North America* (New York: Oxford University Press, 1985), 86. Sayre takes a less admiring approach when describing the 1649 execution of Jean de Brebeuf, who "complied with the custom of singing the *chanson de mort* by substituting a sermon. . . . By substituting his proselytizing sermon for the *chanson de mort*, Brebeuf subverted the customs of torture, for his heroic forbearance did not enhance the power of those who conquered him when he patronizingly claimed to suffer for their lost souls" (299–300).

6. Robert Bage, *Hermprong; or Man as He Is Not*, ed. Pamela Perkins (Peterborough: Broadview Press, 2002) 250–51; *The Female American; or, the Adventures of Unca Eliza Winkfield*, ed. Michelle Burnham (Peterborough: Broadview Press, 2001). *The Female American* narrator glosses over the fact that she manipulates the native tribe's belief system in order to promulgate Christianity: after exploiting their worship of the sun god to achieve credibility, she tells them that such worship is sacrilegious; at the end of the text, she and her clergyman husband, in an unacknowledged parody of imperial practice, determine "to collect all the gold treasure there, to blow up the subterraneous passage, and the statue, that the Indians might never be tempted to their former idolatry" (154).

7. Speaking of Columbus's description of Hispaniola as "a marvel greater than paradise," Stephen Greenblatt argues that "the marvellous takes the place of the miraculous, absorbing some of its force but avoiding the theological and evidentiary problems inherent in directly asserting a miracle." Greenblatt, *Marvellous Possessions: The Wonder of the New World* (Chicago: University of Chicago Press, 1991), 79.

experience of Amerindian cynicism regarding Christianity. John Oldmixon, writing in 1741, recounts questions addressed to the Reverend John Elliot in 1646: *"How there could be an Image of God, since it was forbidden in the Second Commandment?* This probably arose from Mr *Elliot's* saying Man was created after God's own Image. There is Simplicity in this, but more Reflection than would be found in many of our Peasants under a like Lecture." In fact, these native Americans reject Christianity, *"for the* English, *that are* Christians, *will cheat the* Indians *of their Land . . . your Knowledge of Books does but make you the more cunning to cheat others, and so does more Harm than Good."* Finally, they name two or three preachers in New York, *"who instead of preaching their pious Religion, taught them to drink."*[8] In a series of deft moves, Smollett rewrites such English/Protestant failures as French/Catholic ones; the French missionary project is represented as a social evil undertaken by ridiculously fanatical men, whose risible beliefs are appropriately interrogated and rejected by a suspicious native culture.

While he mocks the notion of French Catholic tenets taking root in native culture, Smollett also portrays the evil practices of that culture. The tortures inflicted upon Lismahago and Murphy resemble the descriptions in other captivity narratives: Gyles writes that "Sometimes an old shrivell'd Squaw will take up a Shovel of hot Embers and throw them into a Captive's Bosom"; Jean Lowry watches the agonies of a fellow captive: "first they Scalp'd him alive. . . . They heated their Daggers in the fire and pushed them into the fleshy parts of his Body"; Peter Williamson recounts that as prisoners are being burnt alive, "one of the villains with his scalping knife, ript open their bellies, took out their entrails, and burnt them before their eyes, whilst the others were cutting, piercing, and tearing the flesh from their breasts, hands, arms and legs, with red hot irons, till they were dead."[9] The *British Magazine* relates the suffering of Father Jogues: "Having tore off his nails with their teeth, they crushed all his fingers, and thrust a sword through his right hand."[1] Lismahago, too, is dismembered and wounded, but he is subjected to even worse torments: "some of his teeth were drawn, or dug out with a crooked nail; splintered reeds had been thrust up his nostrils and other tender parts; and the calves of his legs had been blown up with mines of gunpowder dug in the flesh" (228) [201]. Given the wide availability of narratives describing actual episodes of

8. John Oldmixon, *The British Empire in America: Containing the History of the Discovery, Settlement, Progress and State of the British Colonies on the Continent and Islands of America*, 2 vols. (1741; New York: Augustus M. Kelly, 1969), 1:91, 98–99, 277.
9. Gyles, 7; Jean Lowry, *A Journal of the Captivity of Jean Lowry and Her Children* (1760), in *The Garland Library*, 8:6; Williamson, 19.
1. "The History of Canada," *British Magazine*, September 1760, 538.

excruciating torture, one has to look carefully at the particular
details added in Smollett's fiction. These additions, I suggest, signify something more than a novelist's desire for effect, or for what
Colley calls "the pornography of real or invented Indian violence";[2]
they are part of Smollett's warning about the consequences of
imperial adventuring. The splintered reeds *invade* Lismahago's
body; not only his nostrils but also "other tender parts" suffer
penetration. If these "parts" refer to his penis and anus, the
infliction of pain becomes sexualized, so that monstrous perver-
sion is added to the already grotesque tortures devised by Amerindians. Similarly, while Smollett's description of running the
gauntlet evokes the experience of Father Jogue and his companion
René Goupil, who "were set upon by the women and children, who
mangled them in such a manner, that there was not a spot on their
bodies free of scar or wound,"[3] here again Smollett adds a sexual
dimension rarely included in historical accounts: Murphy has been
castrated by these women while "passing through the different whigwhams [*sic*] or villages of the Miamis" (228) [201].[4] Radisson's story
does include castration—"They cut off yor stones and the women
play wth them as wth balles" (54)—but the victims are emphatically
not, as Murphy is, destined to become "the spouse of a beautiful
squaw" (228) [201]. In *Humphry Clinker*, the women's bloodlust
supersedes the sachem's (chief) need for a son and heir, and their
pleasure in inflicting sexual abuse overrides their desire for an able

2. Colley, 177.
3. "The History of Canada," *British Magazine*, September 1760, 538.
4. Heard tells us that David Boyd "had to run the gauntlet, which amusement, for the
   Indians, consisted in running a prescribed limit between two lines made up of vindictive squaws and young savage rogues armed with sticks, stones, or whatever suited their
   purpose best" (60). There are, however, benign versions of the gauntlet recounted in
   some captivity narratives. For example, James Smith, captured in 1755, reports: "They
   [women] all laid violent hold of me, and I for some time opposed them with all my
   might, which occasioned loud laughter by the multitude that were on the bank of the
   river. At length one of the squaws made out to speak a little English . . . and said, 'no
   hurt you.' On this I gave myself up to their ladyships, who were as good as their word;
   for though they plunged me under water and washed and rubbed me severely, yet I
   could not say they hurt me much" (cited in Axtell, *The European and the Indian*, 186).
   Splinters figure in Heard's description of the gruesome scalping and execution of an
   Englishwoman in 1756: "they laid burning splinters of wood, here and there, upon her
   body" (67). In her case, the splinters inflict terrible pain but do not penetrate her body.
   Describing the progressive luridness of captivity narratives, Richard VanDerBeers
   writes: "The infusion of melodrama and sensibility into the narratives, appropriately
   ornamented and stylistically embellished, capitalized on what became an increasingly
   profitable market for properly 'literary' narratives of Indian captivity in the later eighteenth and early nineteenth centuries. . . . The earlier propagandist impulse deliberately
   played up Indian horrors and outrages, but more to solicit strong anti-Indian sentiments
   than to evoke pity and terror for the captive himself. It was but a short almost inevitable
   step from narrative excesses for the purpose of propaganda to excesses in the interest of
   sensation and titillation, from promoting hatred to eliciting horror, from inspiring
   patriotism to encouraging sales, from chauvinism to commercialism." VanDerBeers,
   Held Captive by Indians: Selected Narratives, 1642–1836 (Knoxville: University of Tennes-
   see Press, 1994), xxxviii.

recruit for the tribe. The "crooked nail" and the "gunpowder dug in the flesh," like the reeds, are also forms of penetration, but they represent more than the native American desire to invade the European body. These instruments of penetration are artefacts of the industrial world brought to America by Europeans, tools provided to the natives by the colonizing culture, now turned against the imperial power in a fitting though appalling way. In a monstrous re-enactment of European incursions into American territories, Amerindians use the invaders' weapons to penetrate and destroy them.

Lismahago, of course, survives his ordeal. His friend Murphy is not so lucky, perhaps because his Irish body is less sturdy than Lismahago's Scottish one. Murphy, "mangled by the women and children [and] rendered altogether unfit for the purposes of marriage" (228) [201], undergoes further tortures until he is mercifully killed, heroically singing his death song. In his treatment of this particular ritual, Smollett once again both replicates and manipulates factual accounts, such as Colden's description of the native American tortured and executed by de Frontenac—the young man dies at the stake, singing about his own courage and his memories of inflicting similar punishment on many Frenchmen (171). The death song, in other words, asserts possession of power, agency, and masculinity, even under horrific circumstances.[5] Smollett, in one economical move, manages to trivialize this crucial aspect of native American culture at the same time that he demonstrates British pluck. Murphy, in the agonies of death, sings not of past military exploits or of Christian salvation but the *Drimmendoo*, Gaelic for "black cow with a white back" (403n67) [201]. This last gesture of defiance and mockery, in its parodic bravura, diminishes both the French Jesuits and the Amerindian warrior.

Murphy's tormentors are also, of course, cannibals: like the trader in Williamson's narrative and Captain Robertson in *The Siege of Detroit*, Murphy becomes "a hearty meal" for his captors (228) [201].[6] Cannibalism, while certainly heard of in tribal cultures, must have been unusual enough that the writer of *The Siege of Detroit* feels compelled to explain, "This shocking piece of barbarity is practiced only by some of the Indian nations to the northward. The Six Nations, who use their prisoners, while alive, much worse than they do, yet never eat human flesh, which *they* do, not for want of food,

5. See Mackenzie, *Man of the World*, in which the dying Amerindian captives sing "the glory of their former victories, and the pleasure they had received from the death of their foes; concluding always with the hopes of revenge from the surviving warriors of their nation" (2:177).
6. [Jehu Hay], *The Siege of Detroit in 1763; The Journal of Pontiac's Conspiracy and John Rutherfurd's Narrative of a Captivity*, ed. Milo Milton Quaife (Chicago: Lakeside Press, 1958), 229.

but as a religious ceremony, or rather from a superstitious idea that it makes them prosperous in war."[7] In *Humphry Clinker*, cannibalism is represented as simply another aspect of the Amerindians' exuberant, drunken pleasure in torturing their victims. Smollett's native Americans, then, are not only as cruel as those described in non-fictional narratives; they are also sadists, sexual perverts, and heartless cannibals.[8]

This is no place for a good British man, and yet Lismahago contentedly makes his home there, marrying Squinkinacoosta, producing a child by her, and succeeding his adoptive father as sachem. Such an outcome is so emphatically undesirable that Smollett needs to make tribal life, even for survivors of horrific tortures, seem no healthy alternative to an admittedly diseased home country. Having constructed a narrative that might be misconstrued as advocating reconciliation to a savage culture and a cannibalistic wife, Smollett provides a corrective accessible to the densest reader: he shows that Lismahago has joined a society also tainted by its own version of feminized commodification. Just as the London citizen's "wife and daughters appear in the richest stuffs, bespangled with diamonds" (119) [95], Amerindian society contains women who consume *goods* as well as flesh.

When Tabitha interrogates Lismahago about Squinkinacoosta's wedding clothes, "whether she wore high-breasted stays or bodice, a robe of silk or velvet, and laces of Mechlin or minionette," whether she "used *rouge*, and had her hair dressed in the Parisian fashion," he replies that neither "the simplicity of their manners nor the commerce of their country would admit of those articles of luxury which are deemed magnificence in Europe" (229–30) [202]. Tabitha's

---

7. [Hay], 229.
8. Interestingly, Smollett omits one of the most gruesome details included in some captivity narratives. Both Gyles (12) and Radisson (53) refer to the practice of forcing captives to eat parts of their own bodies. The omission underscores Sussman's argument about "the threat of the literal disappearance of European culture into the belly of America" (602), since self-cannibalization would not fit the pattern on transculturation. Tzvetan Todorov points out how characterizing natives as savages provides a rationale for enslaving them: "We can say that this line of argument unites four descriptive propositions as to the Amerindians' nature to a postulate that is also a moral imperative. These propositions: the Amerindians have a slave's nature; they practice cannibalism; they make human sacrifices; they are ignorant of the Christian religion. The postulate imperative: one has the right or even the duty to impose good on others." Todorov, *The Conquest of America: The Question of the Other*, trans. Richard Howard (Norman: University of Oklahoma Press, 1999), 154. Greenblatt, referring to Columbus's letter proposing trading slaves for beasts, echoes Todorov's analysis: "Those Indians identified as cannibals will be hunted down, seized, torn from their lands and their culture, loaded onto ships still stinking of the animals for whom they are being exchanged, and sent into slavery. But the economic transaction as Columbus conceives it will be undertaken for the welfare of the souls of the enslaved: the Indians are exchanged for beasts in order to convert them into humans" (72).

persistent queries elicit the information "that his princess had neither shoes, stockings, shift, nor any kind of linen" (230) [203]. Squinkinacoosta, then, seems to represent a positive alternative to the kind of European fashion that requires Lydia to sit "above six hours under the hands of a hair-dresser, who stuffed [her] head with as much black wool as would have made a quilted petticoat" (125) [101] and brings Tabitha to an Edinburgh ball dressed "in a full suit of damask, so thick and heavy, that the sight of it alone, at this season of the year, was sufficient to draw drops of sweat from any man of ordinary imagination" (261) [232]. Juxtaposed to these excesses of female finery, the relative nakedness of Squinkinacoosta might be seen as a virtue, especially in a text that, according to David Weed, posits a robust masculinity, which "resists infection from the femininity intertwined with England's commercial society."[9] A woman who can devise and execute tortures with the best of her tribe, who "vied with the stoutest warrior in eating the flesh of the sacrifice," and who can hold her liquor better than anyone (229) [201–02] must at least be free of the feminine vanity and desire for ornament so distressing to eighteenth-century males. Indeed, Squinkinacoosta's lack of linen fits the picture of simplicity drawn by Jean de Léry in 1578: "Léry asserts that the shamelessness with which the Indians display their bodies is more easily defended than the 'sumptuous display' in dress exhibited by many Europeans."[1] Squinkinacoosta, however, is just as wedded to wedding finery as any English miss—only the nature of ornamentation differs. In place of stays, lace, and rouge, she adorns herself with "bobbins of human bone—one eye-lid was painted green, and the other yellow; the cheeks were blue, the lips white, the teeth red . . . a couple of gaudy parrot's feathers were stuck through the division of the nostrils—there was a blue stone set in the chins." Lismahago's bride bedecks herself with earrings, bracelets, and necklaces, and "about her neck was hung the fresh scalp of a Mohawk warrior, whom her deceased lover had lately slain in battle—and finally, she was anointed from head to foot with bear's grease, which sent forth a most disagreeable odour" (230) [203]. Rather than representing native simplicity as a counter to European female vanity, Squinkinacoosta demonstrates that native American women too crave cosmetics, jewels, and scents, some of which are even more repellent than those adorning Swift's Celia and Corinna. When M. A. Goldberg argues that "Smollett is posing the same kind of cultural relativism that the Scottish critics and historians employed in examining

---

9. Weed, 615.
1. Thomas Scanlan, *Colonial Writing and the New World, 1583–1671: Allegories of Desire* (Cambridge: Cambridge University Press, 1999), 47.

and evaluating 'the noble savage,'" thereby making an "analogy between the American Indians and the Scots," he misreads, I believe, this part of Lismahago's narrative. The grotesque adornments of Squinkinacoosta underline the text's conviction that, bad as commercialism might be in Britain, life among the savages of America provides no escape from it.[2]

In any case, the barbarians have already stormed the gate, not only in the persons of those "planters, negro-drivers and hucksters, from our American plantations" (65) [43], but also in the shape of products and practices that penetrate and pervert British life as they have Lismahago's body. Medicines from America turn out to be overpriced and useless, like the Genzeng that Bramble orders, "though I doubt much, whether that which comes from America is equally efficacious with what is brought from the East Indies" (66–67). [44] Some newfangled medical practices, in fact, borrow the murderous habits of Amerindians, and must be energetically resisted by John Bull. When Squire Burdock is injured, the good apothecary Grieve employs traditional British methods such as letting blood and applying poultices. The squire's snobbish wife and worthless son, however, insist on calling in a surgeon who "could not tell whether there was a fracture, until he should take off the scalp" (200) [174]. Unlike Lismahago at the hands of Amerindians, Burdock escapes a scalping, returning to consciousness just before the operation. Significantly, as he overpowers the surgeon's assistants, he asserts his national character, exclaiming, "in a bellowing tone, 'I ha'n't lived so long in Yorkshire to be trepanned by such vermin as you'" (200) [175]. Burdock, the vigorous English squire, reclaims control over his body, foiling the possibly homicidal intentions of his son ("signor Macaroni") and wife. The barbaric native American practice of scalping may have invaded British shores, but "an

2. M. A. Goldberg, *Smollett and the Scottish School: Studies in Eighteenth-Century Thought* (Albuquerque: University of New Mexico Press, 1959), 165–67. Williamson finds that Amerindians "are very proud, and take great delight in wearing trinkets" (21), and Mary Rowlandson writes of the woman named Wettimore: "A severe and proud Dame she was, bestowing every day in dressing herself neat as much time as any of the Gentry of the land: powdering her hair, and painting her face, going with Neck-laces, with Jewels in her ears, and Bracelets upon her hands." Rowlandson, *The Sovereignty and Goodness of God: Together with the Faithfulness of His Promises Displayed. Being a Narrative of the Captivity and Restoration of Mrs Mary Rowlandson, and Related Documents*, ed. Neal Salisbury (Boston: Bedford/St Martin's Press, 1997), 97.

3. Lismahago bears the monstrous scars of his encounter with hostile Amerindians in Ticonderoga, who "rifled him, broke his scull with the blow of a tomahawk, and left him for dead . . . so that scull was left naked in several places, but these he covered with patches" (224) [197]. Axtell points out that "Contrary to popular belief, scalping was not necessarily a fatal operation; the historical record is full of survivors" (*The European and the Indian*, 34–35). Perhaps the most comic version is Williamson's story of the Irishman who was too drunk to realize he had been scalped (72). Rutherfurd carefully explains that "The scalp is not, as is commonly believed, the whole skin of the head, but is only the uppermost part of the crown" ([Hay], 241).

old fox in the West Riding" (200) [175] can and does protect him-self from it.[3]

At the end of the novel, on the occasion of his marriage to Tabitha, Lismahago distributes gifts to his new family. Matthew Bramble gets "a fine deer's skin, and a Spanish fowling-piece"; Jery is given "a case of pistols curiously mounted with silver"; and Win-ifred Jenkins is presented with "an Indian purse, made of silk grass, containing twenty crown pieces." Tabitha becomes the proud pos-sessor of "a fur cloak of American sables, valued at fourscore guin-eas" as well as a wedding ring, "a curious antique, set with rose diamonds [which] had been in the family two hundred years" (390) [350]. Except for the ring, the gifts all represent colonial spoils: the guns are the detritus of a previous imperial presence in North America—the technology of power of that imperial presence has dwindled to the status of souvenirs—and Winifred's purse is an artefact of transculturations, the Amerindian receptacle that houses (or perhaps swallows?) British coins. Tabitha's cloak is mul-tivalent, since "An Indian wearing clothes made from marten (a species of weasel related to the sable) was clad in a commodity reserved for royalty in Europe. . . . Yet pelts were not fully clothes to the explorers' eyes, as they simply covered one's skin with anoth-er's and seemed more like raw materials than finished garments."[4] Where the guns might serve as a salutary *memento mori*, and the purse as a symbol of the financial cost of maintaining colonies, the bridal gift both disrupts the social hierarchies so dear to the text's heart *and* connects the Welshwoman Tabitha to the savage Squinki-nacoosta. The produce and refuse of America penetrate even the hallowed grounds of Brambleton Hall, and Tabitha, like the nation itself, adorns herself with the elegant relic of a rich Celtic past as well as with the shedding of the colonial present. In *Humphry Clin-ker*, Smollett suggests that the American colonies have damaged the home country much more than they have benefited it: they have enriched the wrong kinds of Britons, thereby destabilizing social relations and endangering the national health, and, as Lismahago's captivity narrative demonstrates, they have mutilated the British body (and body politic—for emigration and transculturation can only jeopardize the wholeness of the state). In the end, America's contribution to Britain consists of trinkets and carcases . . . and ultimately, the degradation of the nation itself.

4. Sayre, 154. Like the sable skins they wore, Amerindians' hunting habits presented another social problem for England. Axtell points out that "the Indians' greatest offence was the usurpation of aristocratic privilege, the disorderly jumping of class lines. For in England the only people who hunted were members of the upper classes, who did not kill to eat, or poachers who did and risked their ears—or necks—in the attempt" (*The European and the Indian*, 53).

MISTY G. ANDERSON

From A Usable Past: Reconciliation in *Humphry Clinker* and *The Spiritual Quixote*[†]

On Friday, October 10, 1766, Horace Walpole wrote to his friend Chute the following description of the Countess of Huntingdon's new Methodist Chapel at Bath:

> The chapel is very neat, with true Gothic windows (yet I am not converted); but I was glad to see that luxury is creeping in upon them before persecution: they have very neat mahogany stands for branches [candelabra], and brackets of the same in taste. At the upper end is a broad haut-pas of four steps, advancing in the middle; at each end of the broadest part are two of *my* eagles with red cushions for the parson and clerk.
>
> (*Correspondence* 35: 118)

After heaping scorn on the movement so often in his correspondence, Walpole's suggestion that the Methodists are becoming more like midcentury "cultured" Britons, subject to luxury and capable of taste, almost sounds like peacemaking. His observations about the Bath chapel are echoed in *The Historical and Local New Bath Guide*, which announced the chapel displayed "taste and elegance in the interior part."[1] Like his own Strawberry Hill, the Bath chapel is an architectural testament to changing constructions of the past for use within the cultural present. The Calvinist Methodists who built the Bath chapel wanted to recuperate the medieval Gothic style of the cathedral and to redeploy it as, among other things, a sign of historical authenticity from within a self-conscious experience of being modern. Its gothic windows, candelabra, and cushions indicate the chapel's affinity for Anglo-Catholic space over what Paulson calls the "barnlike structures" of Protestant architecture, "monochrome with only clean white walls and sober woodwork," the style that spreads through London after the Great Fire.[2] Walpole finds much to admire in Lady Huntingdon's chapel on Harlequin Row, much he identifies as versions of his own furnishings ("*my* eagles"), so much, in fact, that he jokes parenthetically about not being converted.

[†] From *Imagining Methodism in Eighteenth-Century Britain: Enthusiasm, Belief, and the Borders of the Self*, 200–220, 230–31 (Baltimore, MD: The Johns Hopkins University Press, 2012). © 2012 The Johns Hopkins University Press. Reprinted with permission of The Johns Hopkins University Press. Notes have been edited for this volume.

1. *The Historical and Local New Bath Guide* (n.p., 1801), 51–52.
2. Ronald Paulson, *Hogarth's Harlot: Sacred Parody in Enlightenment England* (Baltimore: The Johns Hopkins VP, 2003), 13.

In *A Useable Past*, William Bouwsma observes that "Religious symbolism and practice seem to . . . concentrate and integrate singularly well what a society is finally 'about.'"[3] Walpole's reading of the Bath chapel suggests that Methodism is participating productively in modern British society through symbols and architectural choices that negotiate their relationship with British religious history as one of continuity. Methodism's greatest appeal was still among the working classes, but it had also managed to speak to figures as diverse as the Countess of Huntingdon, Samuel Johnson, Benjamin Franklin, Sir John Phillips, David Garrick, and Lord Bolingbroke, without necessarily converting them. Methodism, even by Walpole's reluctant admission, had become a part of what modern Britain was about. George Whitefield died in 1771, curtailing the most vicious strains of anti-Methodist writing and leaving the future of Methodism in the domain of John Wesley's managerial genius. The free-floating *idea* of Methodism, that taunt for what was emotionally excessive and psychologically troubling in British religious practice, was beginning to settle into denominationalism. John Wesley, whose 1758 *Reasons Against a Separation from the Church of England* had made a spiritual and practical plea for continuing to regard Methodism as a movement within the Church of England, was reinvited to preach in some Anglican pulpits in the 1770s and was surprised at the number of offers that came his way. After preaching at All Hallows Church in London, he remarked in his journal "How is this? Do I 'yet please men'? Is the offence of the cross ceased? It seems, after being scandalous near fifty years, I am at length growing into an honourable man!" (*Abingdon Works* 23:41). The establishment of institutional structures also formalized a move from a revival movement within the Anglican church to denominational identity. The Countess of Huntingdon registered her sixty-seven chapels as dissenting places of worship under the Toleration Act, and they became part of her "Connexion" in 1781. This decision, along with the 1784 Deed of Declaration, with which Wesley established a governing infrastructure for the movement after his death, formalized Methodism as a denomination, which in some ways managed the threat it posed to national religious identity by finally separating it out from the Church of England.[2] The softer comic representations of the 1770s reflect on Methodism's appeal across classes and communities within Britain, and in so doing begin to redeem Methodism as a mediating force in British society.

The Expedition of Humphry Clinker (1771) and The Spiritual Quixote, or The Summer's Ramble of Geoffry Wildgoose (1773) signal

3. William J. Bouwsma, *A Useable Past: Essays in European Cultural History* (Berkeley: University of California Press, 1990), 2.

a shift in tone from earlier, more satiric representations of Methodism by their laughable but usable "heart religion." Even though the novels restore traditional class hierarchy, they reflect appreciatively on Methodism's potential to forge connections between people. Similarly, Henry Brooke's Shandian *The Fool of Quality* (1765–1770), with its evangelical vignettes of the life of the Clements, and Mr. Fenton's Christian Rousseauian pedagogical plan for his nephew, sought to reconcile a Methodist-style evangelicalism to public morality, charity, and civic sociability. Christopher Anstey continues to make some sport out of Methodists as part of the amusements of Bath, along with "bathing, tumblers, auctions, apes, or players, New fiddlers, Methodists, or dancing bears," but he also suggests they have become one divertissement among many that might tempt "the nymph abroad"; their threat level is now on par with that of apes and auctions.[4] *Clinker* and *Wildgoose* take up the question of Methodism's cultural place in modern Britain in much greater detail through the specific adventures of the title characters. In these novels, Methodism provides an affective supplement to a more materialist account of mind that isolated individual consciousness, as well as a response to the economic materialism of early capitalism. Self-interest or "self-love," in spite of Pope's optimism about its implicit social function, seemed only to be widening the gap between the poor and the rich. These differences were on display in the urban centers of London and Bath, which Matt Bramble calls centers of dissipation and infection, terms he otherwise uses for bodily ailments, Similarly, the transformation of rural life in the modern British capitalist economy, represented in *The Vicar of Wakefield* and *The Village*, was eroding conventional networks of care and economic interdependence without replacing them in kind. Methodist social activism, particularly in the construction of orphanages, poor houses, and charity schools, was a response to the failing system of parish care in an age of urbanization and greater geographic mobility. The Kingswood School for the poor, Whitefield's orphanage in Georgia, The Stranger's Friend Society (which aided the poor who were not attached to a parish), and hundreds of other charitable projects provided relief in London, the countryside, and the colonies to those who would otherwise have been without parish resources.[5] The prison, feeding, and educational commitments of the original Oxford Methodists of the 1730s had, by 1770, developed a national profile and institutional

---

4. See Anstey's *The New Bath Guide: Or, Memoirs of the B-r-d family*, 5th ed. (London: 1767).
5. Richard Heitzenrater, *Wesley and the People Called Methodists* (Nashville: Abingdon Press, 1995), 122–28, 209.

structures for the movement's attempts to intervene in culture of early British capitalism. Methodism in the 1770s was beginning to look more like a social remedy than a social disease.

Smollett and Graves reflect on this shifting perception, which renegotiates Methodism's relationship to British history. The Hudibrastic architecture of the novels provides a comic return to the historical *agon* of the political Puritan revolution but sublimates it into the domestic question of how to bring the British population into a shared sense of community as economic expansion, urbanization, and mobility eroded traditional parish ties. The novels trace an itinerant's path around Great Britain, walking through the topographical and the ideological domains of the nation and synthesizing them through conversation, friendship, and romantic love, all of which can be fostered by Methodism. Instead of a political or psychological threat to the modern British self, here we glimpse a Methodism that mends frayed communities without demanding their conversion. That Methodism, in thirty years of rapid growth, had not become a political movement like old Dissent made it possible for Smollett and Graves to represent Methodism as an affective supplement to British identity, one capable of mediating the nation's relationship to its own religious and political history. In these novels, Methodists unwittingly draw together far-flung communities and help to mend breaches between characters. Like Clinker's literally rent breeches, they show the seams of conflicts over the meaning of religion in the later eighteenth century, but they also provide a sociable patch that unites communities around the somatic, affective values that Methodism shared with the discourse of sensibility. Smollett and Graves may consider Methodism an inferior expression of taste, literacy, or feeling, but they see it as a usable supplement to modern British identity that fosters relationships in a rapidly changing nation.

Smollett and Graves manage the quixotism of Humphry Clinker and Geoffry Wildgoose through the aesthetic confidence of the comic novels themselves. Clinker and Wildgoose still tend to be moved too easily and to read literally. But their aesthetic failures serve as sources of comic pleasure; these novels can accommodate Methodist characters without engaging in the paranoid hostility of Fielding or Foote. The episodic structure of these novels provides the implicit assurance that history goes on, and that even sensational models of the self are more stable than radically malleable. Even though they hold Clinker and Wildgoose at a comic distance, they acknowledge their palliative if not constructive function in modern British society, which can make use of their excesses of enthusiasm. Matt Bramble affirms that his journey with Clinker, about which he has offered so many complaints, has helped to "unclog the wheels of life" [342],[6] and the narrator of *The Spiritual Quixote* confidently affirms at the close of Wildgoose's Methodist escapades that "Providence frequently makes use of our passions, our errors, and even our youthful follies, to promote our welfare, and conduct us to happiness" (473). Regardless of their particular beliefs, Clinker and Wildgoose are men of feeling who create community. The Bramble family's embrace of Clinker eventually cements their own relations in the discovery that Clinker not only makes relationships but *is* a relation. Wildgoose returns to his native village wiser, chastened, yet still able to bring the lessons of Methodist fervor to bear on community life, replicating their charity and piety in subdued, polite tones. In these novels, it seems possible that Methodists themselves might become pious without enthusiasm.

Coming Around: Smollett and Methodism

It is a critical commonplace held by Sekora, Thorson, Lyles, and others that Smollett extended his career-long assault on Methodism from *Launcelot Greaves* in his most famous novel, *Humphry Clinker*, but Smollett's relationship to Methodism is a more complex affair than this narrative suggests. Early in his career, and in keeping with the more hostile zeitgeist of the 1760s, he positioned Methodism as part of an irrational past from which Great Britain was emerging:

> Imposture and fanaticism still hung upon the skirts of religion. Weak minds were seduced by the delusions of a superstition stiled Methodism, raised upon the affection of superior sanctity, and maintained by pretensions of divine illumination. Many thousands in the lower ranks of life were infected with this species of enthusiasm, by the unwearied endeavours of a few obscure preachers; such as Wh——, and the two W——s, who propagated their doctrines to the most remote corners of the British dominions, and found means to lay the whole kingdom under contribution.[7]

Smollett situates Methodism in his history as a remnant of a past in an era of the "progress of reason" under the clerical leadership of Tillotson, Sherlock, Hoadley, Conybeare, and Warburton (121). In his version of the secularization thesis, Smollett pits the modernity of the 1760s against the cultural primitivity of Methodism which, along with Hutchinsonians (a loose affiliation of Trinitarian Christians skeptical about modern science) and Moravians,

---

6. Page references in square brackets refer to this Norton Critical Edition.
7. Tobias Smollett, *A Complete History of England*, vol. 4 (London: 1757–58), 121–22.

"infects" the lower classes and thrives in "remote" parts of the country. Smollett lays anti-Newtonianism at the feet of Hutchinson's followers and accuses the Moravians of sensualism, impurity, and "gross incentives to the work of propagation" (123), leaving Methodism as the more general case of religious delusion, an annoying holdover rather than a live threat. Wesley, after reading some of Smollett's history, wrote in his journal in July of 1770 that "Poor Dr. Smollett! . . . knows nothing about" Methodism, and later chastised him for his impious "manner of speaking against witchcraft" which must be "extremely offensive to every sensible man who cannot give up his Bible" (*Abingdon Works* 22: 238).[8] Smollett sees his era as modern in the main, defined against Methodism insofar as he regards it as a form of superstition that seduces "weak minds" and the "lower ranks," thus perpetuating a cognitive-primitive past within the present. Wesley's point that Smollett "knows nothing" about Methodism gestures to another vision of Methodism as progressively oriented around social justice and its own version of the enlightenment project of improvement in its educational and literacy efforts.

Smollett continued to pick at Methodists in his early novels and periodical publications along the lines of conventional anti-Methodist satire, labeling them hypocrites and maniacs. He began the *Critical Review* around the same time that Whitefield's London Tabernacle opened and he referred to Whitefield as "the grimy apostle of Tottenham-Court" (*The Critical Review*, no. 11, January 1761). In his 1760–61 *Launcelot Greaves*, the quixotic Greaves finds himself in a madhouse and is able to identify it as such when he hears a Methodist inmate denouncing good works:

> He that thinks to be saved by works is in a state of utter reprobation—I myself was a prophane weaver, and trusted to the rottenness of works— . . . but now I have got a glimpse of the new light—I feel the operations of grace—I am of the new birth—I abhor good works—I detest all working but the working of the spirit.[9]

The lunatic, whose dashes and pauses mimic the "ejaculatory" style of a Methodist preacher, is also a weaver, and like Humphry Clinker the farrier or the cobbler Jeremiah Tugwell of *The Spiritual Quixote*, a barely literate working-class figure. The association of Methodism

---

8. Smollett's editorial contribution to the thirty-five-volume *Works of Voltaire* (1761–81) made him familiar with Voltaire's declarations against Christian intolerance and fanaticism, in which the vision of an enlightened, tolerant public space is undercut by religious violence and orthodoxy.
9. Tobias Smollett, *The Life and Adventures of Launcelot Greaves*, ed. Barbara Laning Fitzpatrick (Athens: U of Georgia P, 2002), 176.

with the laboring class here is another dig at Methodists who leave their employment to go hear or follow Methodist preachers and thus "detest all working." This weaver is an impressionable self so open to transformation through the somatic experience of the Methodist conversion that he fails to meet the standard of individualism on which modern liberal society depends. His failure, which is here rendered as insanity, helps shore up the hegemony of a middle class whose feelings should not interfere with work.

The more generalized clerical satire in his Lucretian *The Adventures of an Atom* and *Roderick Random* bounces between deism and atheism. In *The Adventures of an Atom*, a political roman à clef satire of the British government set in Japan, which appeared immediately prior to *Clinker*, Smollett's inanimate narrator, the conscious atom who circulates "without a fixed principle of action," observes the amoral violence and motion of an entirely material world that precludes ethical speculation or remedy. Religion of all description falls under the satiric lash, including politics as religion in the worship of the "White Horse," or house of Hanover. Yet Smollett is also cynical about human nature and the possibility of a secular ethical society; like his Lucretian mode in *Count Ferdinand* and *Launcelot Greaves*, *Adventures of an Atom* holds the notion of character development hostage to material, protonaturalistic determinism. The overall effect pushes us away, to watch the chaos of history from a safe distance as spectators. Smollett himself took a similar position of detached fatalism in a 1761 letter to David Garrick: "We are all the playthings of fortune, and that it depends upon something as insignificant and precarious as the tossing up of a halfpenny whether a man rises to affluence and honors, or continues to his dying day struggling with the difficulties and disgraces of life."[1]

But Smollett's vision of history was not without lingering hopes of some meaningful form of community based on sympathy. Smollett saw his own moment as an age of degeneracy, marked by "luxury and riot" which alienates people from one another and makes then less capable of sympathy (Smollett, *Complete History* 4: 225). In an extreme example of the historical stakes of sympathetic feeling, Smollett wrote in graphic detail about the death of the French regicide Robert Damiens, who remained conscious during his torture with boiling oil, melted lead, and dismemberment. Smollett calls the execution "shameful to humanity" and a violation of sympathetic principles that ought to trump national self-interest with their greater moral purchase. He extends his sympathy with bodies in pain across the human/animal boundary, describing animal vivisection and asking "what benefit has mankind reaped from all

1. *The Letters of Tobias Smollett*, ed. Lewis M. Knapp (Oxford: Clarendon Press, 1970), 98.

this cruelty and torture inflicted on our fellow creatures?" (*Critical Review* I (1756): 414). These are moments where Smollett "brings home to our own breast," as Adam Smith put it in *Theory of Moral Sentiments*, making the case for feeling for the other in terms that have implications for the community. Without the possibility of some reforming historical change, Smollett's sympathetic impulse is undercut by the lack of redemptive vision.

Wesley also encouraged the sympathies of his readers and was similarly willing to judge what he saw as the abuses of the social and economic order. Wesley challenged his readers in *Thoughts Upon Slavery* to translate their affective responses into conscious consumer action in the cause of abolition:

> *The blood of thy brother* (for, whether thou wilt believe it or no, such is he in the sign of Him that made him) *crieth against thee from the earth*, from the ship, and from the waters. . . . Thy hands, thy bed, thy furniture, thy house, thy lands are at present stained with blood."[2]

Wesley asks the sympathetic reader to feel, hear, and see that the other is present, already among "us" through the corrupted economy we share, a system of exchanges similar to the trope of the Bath waters, which symbolizes the corruptions of luxury in its very particles. Wesley grounded his position in the abolition debate of the 1770s in his Arminian belief in universal salvation, which makes all people "brothers" and thus enlarges the domain of human relatedness. Smollett's reflections on torture and animal cruelty, like Wesley's abolitionism as well as his vegetarianism, enlarge codes of sympathy to include a cultural responsibility to feel for the other.[3] What Smollett believes he can do as a writer through the stimulation of sympathetic feeling is limited by the chaos of history in his earlier work, fictional and historical, but in *Clinker*, Smollett shows chaos lurching toward community.

Reading *Humphry Clinker* as the successor in the train of Smollett's representations of Methodists and in the context of his critique of luxury and alienation foregrounds its salvific if messy vision of community, echoed in the novel's epistolarity and the cavalcade of voices that describe the novels events. The novel mocks the luxury and excesses of Bath but maintains an optimism about modern British community at the structural level, which unites the fragmented epistolary perspectives into a more sympathetic community. The stories of Matt, Jery, Lydia, Tabby, and Win are narratively intertwined, and their perspectives softened and mediated by their interactions.

2. John Wesley, *Thoughts upon Slavery* (London: R. Hawes, 1774), 27.
3. Notably, Smollett, the beneficiary of income from a Caribbean plantation in his wife's dowry, avoided a public stance on slavery.

They become, however imperfectly, a family of love. The vigorously comic, Rabelasian landscape of the novel, full of bodies, fluids, and scatological jokes, provides the conditions for communal sympathy. The embodied world of *Clinker*, much like *Tristram Shandy*, engages with discourses of sympathy from both British and Scottish philosophical schools as Gottlieb, Ghoshal Wallace, and Wetmore have variously argued.[4] The capacity to "bring home" another's feelings and circumstances, to identify somatically (although imperfectly) with the other is the source of affective community for Hume, and an idea appropriated by both Smollett and Wesley (Gottlieb, p. 483 in this volume). Though Wesley objected to the Hutchesonian version of the Scottish Enlightenment school of sympathy in his sermon "On Conscience," on the grounds that his formulation of "public senses" excluded God, the analogy between Methodist "heart religion" and discourses of sympathy had become plain by the 1770s.

Matt Bramble experiences a secularized warming of the heart at the sight of another's suffering or need when he gives twenty pounds sterling to the ensign's widow at Hot Wells. Matt, whom Jery describes as like "a man without a skin," has a body that is infamously available to the reader through Matt's hypochondriac obsession with his body's own flows and fluids, which perversely destabilize its boundaries and move him beyond the limits of self. He warns Clinker about letting his religious enthusiasm mislead him "till you are plunged into religious frenzy," but that threat parallels the extremes of sensibility to which Matt is also prone. The result of his confrontation with Clinker is another of Matt's mild fits of enthusiasm: when Clinker declares his loyalty, Matt smiles and promises to take care of him. These affective ties, which turn out to be more intimate than either character could have realized, are only revealed through communication that risks the boundary of the self for the sake of the other. Though Matt Bramble must overcome his prejudice about Methodism as an affront to his traditional views on both religion and class order, he acknowledges the effects of Methodism as socially useful. Matt's secular, sociable sympathy and Clinker's "primitive Christianity" work well together as components of a dialogic cure for the chaos, luxury, and alienation of modern life.

The Social Mix of Bath

Smollett looked to Christopher Anstey's *The New Bath Guide*, a rougher satire of religion as it intersected with the tourist culture

---

4. See the critical essays by Gottlieb and Ghoshal Wallace in this volume, as well as Alex Wetmore, "Sympathy Machines: Men of Feeling and the Automaton," *Eighteenth-Century Studies* 43.1 (2009): 37–54.

of Bath, for the templates of his "family of originals" in *Humphry Clinker*. Martin Day goes so far as to call *Humphry Clinker* "a prose rendering" of Anstey's guide; it includes a traveling family and even a character named Tabby who needs to be dosed at Bath.[5] *The New Bath Guide: Or, Memoirs of the B-r-d Family* (after 1776, changed to *the B-n-r-d Family*) was reprinted regularly from its 1762 debut until the early nineteenth century. This verse satire was itself inspired by *The New Bath Guide, or Useful Pocket-Companion*, an actual guidebook to the city and its inhabitants, with tables for calculating postage, wages, and the phases of the moon. As Peter Borsay has argued, Bath becomes some of the most significant symbolic territory in the eighteenth-century cultural imagination.[6] Both Anstey and Smollett read Bath as a study in a nation newly awash in luxury goods, including the resources for leisure and tourism, which bring with them a spiritual crisis of meaning. The cures that their characters seek are more than material. In the case of Bath, tourism returned new money to an ancient, even primitive site, the Roman Baths, themselves an effort to "modernize" Celtic, primitive western Britain in the first century AD. The secular, commercial pleasures of Bath were built, quite literally, on a site layered with ancient religions, which seem to animate the "primitive" spirituality that emerges as a cultural force in eighteenth-century Bath.

The New Bath Guide uses ribald comic verse to tell the story of the B-n-r-d family (identified as the "Blunderhead" family in Horace Walpole's personal copy) who come to Bath in search of cures for various vague ailments as well as for entertainment. Beyond the general curiosity about domestic tourism in Anstey's poem, religion is one of the main human foibles on display in its portrait of Bath's tourist culture. Beginning with the fifth edition in 1767, Anstey's *The New Bath Guide* included an illustration of Folly in a cap and bells leading several visitors through a colonnade with strings attached to their noses. One of the party, Miss Prudence, carries a hymnbook, and a ministerial figure, identified alternately as a Moravian minister known as "Rabbi Nicodemus" or a generic Methodist minister, follows the crowd with a hand raised in exclamation. Subsequent editions replaced this image with an engraving entitled "Distemper, Pleasure, Methodism, and Fashion dancing round the bust of Bladud, founder of Bath." The inclusion of Methodism by name reflects the prominence of the movement in the Bath–Bristol corridor and its associations with the resort town. In

---

5. Martin Day, "Anstey and Anapestic Satire in the Late Eighteenth Century," *ELH* 15.2 (1948): 122.
6. See Peter Borsay, *The Image of Georgian Bath, 1700–2000: Towns, Heritage, and History* (Oxford: Oxford University Press, 2000).

this image, Methodism is represented by one of the dancing tourists celebrating England's pagan past. He is visually equivalent to the other humorous "dancers": distemper, pleasure, and fashion. The illustration, with its Hogarthian textures and heraldry, including a cornucopia, an asses head, and a cupid, looks on the social revelry and mixing of Bath with critical detachment, turning it into a neoclassical parody of primitive worship. According to Geoffry of Monmouth, Bladud, the Athenian-educated father of King Lear, founded Bath after being exiled from court for leprosy around 860 BC. He found a cure for his leprosy in the Bath waters. In the illustration, his bust returns in Augustan style to situate Bath in a classical past, which modern Britons consume as entertainment. Both the "Nicodemus" and the "Bladud" images use Methodism to mock the modern crazes of Bath and, at the same time, to display the modern consumer's cultural mastery of Britain's past as a commodity. In this world, Methodism's primitive Christianity, an echo of the mystical pagan history of the city, is just one consumer choice among many in the buffet of Bath's cures.

Smollett draws much from Anstey: the character of Tabby (in Anstey's version, she is the maid); the use of different voices to narrate the trip; references to individuals as Hogarth sketches (in *Humphry Clinker*, Matt suggests that Hogarth should draw Tabby and Lydia, [152]; complaints about adulterated wine and food; and the tension between medical and religious cures. Anstey's satire of Moravians and Methodists has a sharp if conventional sexual edge to it. Prudence seeks a religious "cure" for her discomfort, which Anstey parodies as sexual desire for Nicodemus, who is also known suggestively as Roger:

> Now it happens in this very House is a Lodger,
> Whose Name's Nicodemus, but some call him Roger;
> And Roger's so good as my Sister to bump
> On a Pillion, as soon as she comes from the Pump!
> He's a pious good man, and an excellent Scholar,
> And I think it is certain no Harm can befall her;
> For Roger is constantly saying his Pray'rs,
> And singing of spiritual Hymns on the Stairs. (15)

The motives of Roger's piety are on trial as he volunteers "to go out a riding with Prudence behind" and to teach her "Night and Day." He eventually inspires Prudence to have an erotic spiritual encounter:

> For I dream'd an Apparition
>   Came, like Roger, from Above
> Saying, by Divine Commission
>   I must fill you full of Love.

> Just with ROGER's Head of Hair on,
>   ROGER's Mouth, and pious Smile;
> Sweet, methinks, as Beard of AARON
>   Dropping down with holy Oil.
> I began to fall a kicking,
>   Panted, struggl'd strove in vain;
> When the Spirit whipt so quick in,
>   I was cur'd of all my Pain.
> First I thought it was the Night-Mare
>   Lay so heavy on my Breast;
> But I found new Joy and Light there,
>   When with Heav'nly Love possest.
> Come again than, Apparition,
>   Finish what thou hast begun;
> ROGER, stay, Thou Soul's Physician,
>   I with thee my Race will run.
> Faith her Chariot has appointed
>   Now we're stretching for the Goal;
> All the Wheels with Grace anointed,
>   Up to Heav'n to drive my Soul. (128–29)

Prudence is an imprudently bad reader who cannot separate spiritual from material feeling, dream from reality. The comic tetrameter signals to the reader that the joke is on Prudence, who misrecognizes somatic, sexual experience as a spiritual encounter. In the 1762 edition, the poem is followed by this short note: "The Editor, for many Reasons, begs to be excused giving the Public the Sequel of this young Lady's Letter; but if the Reader will please to look into the Bishop of *Exeter's* Book, entitled, *The Enthusiasm of Methodists and Papists Compared*, he will find many Instances (particularly of young People) who have been elected in the Manner above" (107). Bishop Lavington derisively claimed that the Moravian and Methodist emphasis on Jesus as a man reduces Christ to "a hearty Carpenter in Heaven." His disgust that the "final Reward" of the believer is "to sleep in the Arms of Jesus Christ, as a *Man*, in his *human* Nature" is laced with psychosexual panic about Methodism's "love divine" and its fluid rhetories of passion and somatic experience.[7] The problem is at once sexual and theological. On the one hand, Lavington's concern about sleeping in the arms of Christ destabilized gender identity for the heterosexual male believer by eroticizing the body of Christ. Methodist satire, including *The*

---

7. George Lavington, *The Moravians Compared and Detected* (London: Printed for J. and P. Knapton, 1755), 30.

Methodists, Reed's *The Register Office*, and Foote's *The Minor* managed the issue by focusing their attention primarily on female enthusiasts; Clinker's abject, subordinate pose imports some of the gender trouble of the ravished Methodist believer to Smollett's novel. But Lavington also scoffs at the Methodist use of the incarnate Jesus, implying that the "*human* Nature" of Christ is somehow in itself ridiculous. Anstey's citation of Lavington's rant against the Methodists aligns *The New Bath Guide* with a Juvenalian school of anti-Methodist writing as well as with a Latitudinarian theological anxiety about Christian embodiment, which Methodism stoked.

By comparison, the moments of eroticized spiritual language in *Humphry Clinker* are mild. Smollett picks up the joke on "Roger" when Tabitha complains to Dr. Lewis that Roger at Bramble Hall is taking advantage of her dairy: "Roger gets this, and Roger gets that; but I'd have you know, I won't be rogered at this rate by any ragmatical fellow in the kingdom" [84]. However shallow her interest in Methodism may be, this Tabby is only being "rogered" in a fiscal sense. The broad joke here targets Tabby's greed, which is in need of reformation, and not her blossoming interest in Methodism. Other characters are more aware of managing the difference between spiritual and sexual feeling and thus avoiding the comic (or pornographic) collapse of the two terms. Lydia differentiates between "that nameless charm which captivates and controuls the inchanted spirit," romantic/erotic love, and "the inward motions, those operations of grace" that others claim to experience at the Tabernacle [144]. Jery sees that Tabby is trying to convert Mr. Barton to Methodism to establish "a connexion of souls that might be easily improved into a matrimonial union," but this is a transference of spiritual to sexual feeling that both Jery and Tabby comprehend, unlike Prudence, who fails to sort the categories at all.

The character who redeems Methodism in the novel is the unimpeachably pure Clinker. Smollett first establishes Clinker's Methodism by having him preach to the other footmen at St. James, where Matt, with Barton as guide, has taken Jery to observe "all the great men in the kingdom" [104]. Instead of civic order, Jery and Matt see a chaotic parade of political disorder and accidental privilege. As they turn from this scene of politics, they literally walk into the congregation that Humphry has assembled, an embodied alternative to this disappointing political version of the public sphere. Clinker, like Sterne's Trim, with "his hat in one hand and a paper in the other, in the act of holding forth to the people," desists immediately when he sees Matt and runs to get the carriage. Clinker submits his religious identity to a premodern class hierarchy, which, paradoxically, allows him to continue a critique of social inequality in Methodist terms. When pressed about his preaching, Clinker tells Matt he hopes to cure working people of swearing by making them understand his disinterestedness. "Make them first sensible that you have nothing in view but their good, then they will listen with patience" [108]. When Matt objects that oratory from an undereducated laborer like himself will "leave little or nothing . . . to distinguish their conversation from their betters," Clinker replies that "at the day of judgment, there will be no distinction of persons" (95) [00]. Within the temporality of the novel, Humphry's evangelical prophesy comes true; the "distinction of persons" that grounds his own servitude turns into a comic version of the evangelical trope of family when he is revealed as Matt's son. Clinker's potential for radicalism, implicit in his squarely Wesleyan Methodist message, is undercut by traditional obedience, loyalty, and piety, values that provide cover for Clinker's implicitly political statement.

Clinker's appeal to women, his ability to ingratiate himself with Tabby, the revelation of his body in the infamous breeches-splitting scene, and his charismatic preaching, which Matt suggests he can use "to impose on silly women . . . who will contribute lavishly for your support," embody him and render him an object of desire, a feminized commodity of sorts. But unlike Mary/George Hamilton, Mrs. Cole, or Mr. Barvile, Clinker's sexuality doesn't threaten to become roguish. Because he submits so fully to a traditional, even feudal notion of social hierarchy, his enthusiasm can be entertaining and useful by infusing old families with new life. He is also cleared from suspicion about his ulterior motives because he is not a writer in the novel. Eponymous but voiceless, he is artlessly present as a function of his actions and the impressions he makes on others. Those impressions become the fabric of affection that unites the Bramble clan, making the unaccountable interiority of heart religion both sociable and accountable in its effects.

Matt confronts Clinker's theology as a breach of the principles of reason, which he casts in terms of Clinker's relationship to his master. As Jery reports, Matt reproaches Clinker with being deceived by "the new light of grace," which he calls,

> a deceitful vapour, glimmering through a crack in your upper story—In a word, Mr. Clinker, I will have no light in my family but what pays the king's taxes, unless it be the light of reason, which you don't pretend to follow." "Ah, sir! (cried Humphry) the light of reason, is no more in comparison to the light I mean, than a farthing candle to the sun at noon."
>
> "Very true (said uncle) the one will serve to shew you your way, and the other to dazzle and confound a weak brain— Heark-ye, Clinker, you are either a hypocritical knave, or a wrong-headed enthusiast: and in either case, unfit for my service." [147]

Clinker's naïve, loyal response to Matt's tirade is to conclude that
he must be mad and to submit to Matt's traditional authority by
allowing him to define, quite literally, the terms of their interac-
tion. Tabby then chides Clinker for not being willing to stand up for
Methodism, allowing Smollett to stage Clinker's submission to
Matt's authority. Clinker replies that even though "she [Tabby] and
lady Griskin sing psalms and hymns like two cherubims" that he is
"bound to love and obey your honor," invoking a serf-like relation to
Matt [148]. Clinker's abject loyalty stabilizes the Bramble family's
relationships into an affective version of traditional patriarchy and,
through that order, paradoxically authorizes Clinker as a preacher.
Though Matt takes exception to the idea of a servant preaching, he
soon makes a kinder evaluation that his Methodism is "simplicity
warmed with . . . gratitude" based on the effects of Clinker's beliefs
[163]. His assurance is underwritten by Clinker's deference to his
authority. Lydia goes even further and sees "no harm in hearing a
pious discourse, even if it came from a footman." Jery follows suit in
volume 3; he dismisses Lismahago's "sarcastic remark" about Clinker's Methodism as hypocritical.

Clinker, as part of the cure Matt seeks, is woven into the medical
tropology of the novel, what Paul-Gabriel Boucé has called its
"therapeutic function."[8] The novel opens with Matt Bramble's pro-
testation to Dr. Lewis that "The pills are good for nothing—I might
as well swallow snow-balls to cool my reins." His reference to the
self-dosing culture of eighteenth-century popular medicine is
exemplified in the phrase "Every Man His Own Doctor," which is
included in the titles of at least eight different herbals, medical
guides, and recipe books circulating in the eighteenth century, as
well as Wesley's tremendously popular *Primitive Physic*. Matt's
ambiguous complaint, what Aileen Douglas calls "the apprehensions of disorder," involve a mélange of physical, psychological, and
metaphysical symptoms.[9] Clinker is an unstable figure in this democratic medical landscape, a quack who may actually have a useful
cure. Matt first mistakes him for a mountebank (Win later says
"monkey-bank") and laughs that "he'll make Merry Andrews of us
all—" [108]. The slip between mountebank and Methodist preacher
is both conventional in Methodist satire and a reminder of the more
material connections between Methodists and medicine, which
echoes in Clinker's basic veterinary training as a farrier's assistant.
Clinker proves that he can be an agent of a more material salvation
after his second (and urgently necessary) rescue of Matt from

8. Paul-Gabriel Boucé, *The Novels of Tobias Smollett* (London: Longman, 1976), 209.
9. See Aileen Douglas, *Uneasy Sensations: Smollett and the Body* (Chicago: University of
   Chicago Press, 1995).

drowning when a millhead gives way and a river that the Bramble coach was fording swells to a flood [317]. Clinker carries him from the water "as if he had been an infant of six months," helps expel the water from his lungs, then bleeds him "farrier stile," laughing, weeping, and dancing with joy once Matt regains consciousness. The scene unites the material and symbolic economies of the novel and puts Matt and Clinker at their center. It is a baptism that brings Matt into and then through the liquid nightmare of the other that drives his fears with the help of Clinker, who is the remedy and the other that he seeks.

With Methodism mellowing into a more familiar sociability, Smollett was free to recuperate enthusiasm generally as an unsophisticated but functional engine of civic good in both Methodists and Scots, who become the torchbearers of an enthusiasm that channels a native "primitivity" into modern social uses. Jery enjoys Lismahago's "enthusiasm of altercation" in defense of oatmeal, virtuous poverty, and Scotland. Enthusiasm differentiates the "cool" Lowlanders from the "fiery" Highlanders, whose passion "serves only to inflame the zeal of their devotion to strangers, which is truly enthusiastic" [259]. Scotland in general becomes a sign of enthusiasm redeemed over time, as the nation "so long reproached with fanaticism and canting, [which] abounds at present with ministers celebrated for their learning, and respectable for their moderation" [239]. Matt's reflections on Edinburgh churches, which had "admitted such ornaments as would have incited sedition, even in England, a little more than a century ago," are optimistic about national unity, which depends on the triumph of ecumenism and toleration over orthodoxy [239–40]. The political and religious differences that could still, in 1771, be a cause for paranoia, particularly in the form of Jacobitism, are here reduced to native habits of affect that can fuel national unity within difference. As Evan Gottlieb has argued, Smollett's investments in Scotland's future vis-à-vis the Act of Union lead him to Humean and Smithian theories of sympathy to unite the British population in feeling. Though Gottlieb argues that Smollett is closer to Smith's more cognitively distinct form of sympathy that leaves the "I" autonomous than he is to the near mysticism of Hume's "occult process of the transmission of feelings," a touch of this enthusiasm is good, it seems, for a society. Similarly, his sense that the Presbyterian kirk has been reconciled to good sense prefaces his encomiums to the geniuses of Edinburgh: "the two Humes, Roberton, Smith, Wallace, Blair, Ferguson, Wilkie, &c." Matt Bramble is convinced that whatever "fanaticism" might be found in Scotland's past, it was not an inevitable trajectory but a misstep corrected by education, moderation, and good taste. He observes that he would not be surprised ("in a few years") to hear psalms accompanied by organ at the cathedral of Durham [240]. His pleasant experience of the churches of the kirk, like Walpole's surprise in the Bath chapel, mends the rift in religious practice between Presbyterians and modern British Anglicans. In this vision, denomination and Dissent are not fixed directions in history or epistemic shifts but parts of an ongoing intranational conversation that remains open.

Smollett maintains an aesthetic high ground over Methodists in his comic mastery of language and, more particularly, literacy, to which Win Jenkins and Tabby Bramble have only incomplete access. They communicate through comically inspired malapropisms that hearken back to a class-coded Methodist "material" form of writing from Mrs. Cole and Shamela, into which the body erupts. Win chides Molly to mind "your vriting and your spilling," complains with Rabelaisian flair of "lying in damp shits at sir Tummas Ballfart's," and urges Molly to "pray without seizing for grease." Methodism is guilty by association in Win's poor English, which capitalizes on what were by then old saws about semiliterate Methodists and their misuse of language in phrases like "the grease of God" and "imp-fiddles" who mock the "pyebill" (322, 282) [355, 165].

By contrast, Matt's and Jery's letters are peppered with allusions to Horace, Virgil, and Cicero, quotations from Dryden and Shake-speare, and references to continental painting. Jery's and Matt's verbal mastery allows them to play with language and read jokes, providing the self-consciously literary and masculine standard of literacy in the novel in contrast to Win and Tabby's feminized evan-gelical homonyms and literalisms. Jery's letters take a particular pleasure in playing with cultural references from popular and clas-sical vocabularies (Cropdale looks like "captain Pistol in the play," and Bute is the northern star "Shorn of his beams") as well as his running religious and collegiate joke about his "Jesuitical" educa-tion. As a student in Jesus College, Cambridge, Jery is a "Jesuit," a joke that both speaks to his comfortable distance from anti-Catholic anxieties and the ongoing reality of anti-Catholic sentiment that gives the joke its bite. Even more than Matt, who is ashamed of his first name because it "savors of those canting hypocrites, who in Cromwell's time, christened all their children by names taken from scripture" [199], Jery feels free to play with the reli-gious past of England in a series of puns and word games. Notably, Humphry stands outside this linguistic game because he does not write and can thus have no "I." Clinker and Methodism are not a threat to this project, even though they may convert Tabby and Win Jenkins, because Jery's critically self-reflexive "I" tutors the fit reader out of Methodist literalism and into a more playful literacy.

As editors and writers, Smollett and Wesley both were at the center of a public project of taste-making and history, in which they differed in content but not basic approach. Smollett carried out this work in his energetic, often fearless reviewing and writing in *The Critical Review*, *The Briton*, and *The British Magazine*, as well as his *The Present State of All Nations*, multiple *Histories of England*, collections, and translations. For Wesley, collecting and editing was similarly a way of life. Dozens of hymnals, hundreds of sermons, his *Collection of Moral and Sacred Poems*, *The Arminian Magazine*, treatises, tracts, abridgements, his published and private *Journals*, and the monumental *Christian Library* in its fifty volumes are, among other projects, evidence of his drive to catalogue and shape the beliefs and perspectives of the people called Methodists. The unlikely similarities between Wesley and Smollett burst forth in the one moment we see Smollett as a character in the novel. On Sunday, he opens his house to "all unfortunate brothers of the quill" for a lavish dinner on the one day the debtors were free from fear of arrest [133]. In this scene, Smollett provides a secular version of the "prison ministry" for which Methodists were famous. His Sunday hospitality includes a "Babel" of accents and voices from shady characters to whom he has supplied money, credit, and his good name, though some of his guests continue to abuse him in print. When Jery presses Dick Ivy for an explanation of Smollett's sacrificial giving, he concludes there is no reasonable motive, that Smollett must be "a most incorrigible fool," and that he did not have the resolution "to resist the importunity of even the most worthless" [141]. Smollett's imagined self and his imagined writer's community of hard-luck cases is a vision of remedying the cruelties of the public sphere through his irrational hospitality. Matt expresses the hope that literature and education in general could provide a secular pedagogy of feeling that will transform society, but he is "shocked to find a man have sublime ideas in his head, and nothing but illiberal sentiments in his heart" [114]. In practice, it is Humphry and his "simplicity, warmed with a kind of enthusiasm," like the example of Smollett's "foolish" charity, that provides the missing social glue (the role of religion as Durkheim posits it) even though these acts are not in themselves rational. Matt, Wesley, and Smollett (as fictional character and real citizen) each seek some remedy for the heartlessness of the modern economy through compassion connected to material action that print culture can preach but that individuals must choose to practice—feeding, clothing, and paying one another's debts.

History in *Humphry Clinker* literally comes home in the person of Clinker himself, the "love begotten babe" [88] of Bramble's passionate youth. He refers to the "sins of his past," but fathering Clinker turns out to have been his *felix culpa*. Matt's personal history of feeling walks back into his present, answering his unspoken desire for progeny to embody the future for him and redeeming his youthful sexual enthusiasm as the means to community. For Matt Bramble, class in a traditional patriarchal order is already complicated as he has forgone the paternal "Lloyd" for the maternal "Bramble" in order to inherit, a move that also keeps Humphry's mother from finding Matt. But this wrinkle keeps Matt open to the possibility of a broader notion of community in the midst of his conservatism. The revelation of his own fatherhood is a comic echo of the pattern of accidental family in this previously unacquainted "family of originals." Structurally, it upsets the distinctions between self and other, which Matt's passion for propriety tries to control. But it also cements Matt's position as *pater familias*, renewing his family and the promise of community in the mixed logic of the emerging definitions of class.

Clinker's sociable enthusiasm patches fractures in a plot created by multiple refusals of connection: the characters with one another; Matt with his own past; and the future of a public sphere that seems lost amid paroxysms of consumerism, epitomized in the story of the Baynards. Clinker returns Matt's affection to enthusiastic extremes that mirror Matt's own generous outbursts and create a gift economy of ethical obligation, eventually leading to the comic but narratively satisfying discovery of family. Like Wesley's call for universal brotherhood in the context of universal redemption, Matt's experience of sympathy has called up and then annihilated the distinction between self and other, leaving him with a son, a glimpse of paradise (which turns out to be Scotland), and authentic community among the initially alienated Bramble party. Clinker's enthusiasm helps to offset Matt's, providing a useful contrast in degree but not kind that props up and improves Matt's moderate, polite, and secular heart religion. Clinker backs away from his more Whitefieldian street preaching as the novel progresses, but he continues to attend Methodist meetings in Scotland and to evangelize the family, mostly by example. In a parallel movement, Matt observes that Tabby is still a Methodist but that her religious enthusiasm has been tempered by romantic love, the emotion that "is resolved to assert his dominion over all the females of our family." While Matt (and Smollett) cannot brook the extremes of Humean sympathy, just as they cannot embrace Methodism entirely, both find themselves drawn to it as a missing ingredient. Smollett appropriates Methodism's populist gospel in order to relieve the pains of social class and to patch the gaps in his narrative of British history.

*   *   *

From her nineteenth-century vantage point, George Eliot observed that Methodism provided a useful, nonthreatening connection between past and present. Eliot waxes lyrical about the way that Methodism's heart religion opened up an inner life as well as a sense of historical continuity for working people. In *Adam Bede*, she describes Methodism as "a faith which was a rudimentary culture, which linked their thoughts with the past, lifted their imagination above the sordid details of their own narrow lives, and suffused their souls with the sense of a pitying, loving, infinite Presence, sweet as summer to the houseless needy" (39). Far from Fielding's concerns about Methodism unleashing queer passions, Eliot reflects a cultural reconciliation with a movement that the novels of Smollett and Graves have glimpsed, a version of Methodism that takes its place imaginatively under a banner of British sensibility in the national "family of originals." As Goring notes, *The Spiritual Quixote* brings together Cervantic and Fieldingesque cultural critique with more sentimental literary textures, a claim that also applies to *Humphry Clinker*.[1] The result is a portrait of Methodism's community-making energy compatible with traditional familial relations and comfortably mastered by the polite aesthetic practices of literary reading that the novel models. The specific theological content of Humphry Clinker's beliefs gives way to their affective results, which unite the Bramble-Lloyd clan. For Graves, the quixotic Wildgoose, instead of converting the nation, is himself converted to nationalism. These comic novels reconcile satiric vigor with the language of the warmed heart in a reading practice that trains the reader to critique enthusiastic excess while appreciating the capacity it has for drawing people together and reconciling differences.

For both Smollett and Graves, Methodism is a movement neutralised of politically revolutionary potential while still capable of doing significant cultural and social work. In 1785, fourteen years after Henry Mackenzie published *The Man of Feeling*, he admitted that "in the enthusiasm of sentiment there is much the same danger as in the enthusiasm of religion, of substituting certain impulses and feelings of what may be called a visionary kind, in the place of real practical duties."[7] Both Smollett and Graves avoid the old bromide of Methodist antinomianism and instead connect the domains of enthusiasm and social action, which makes it easier for them to grant the religious movement its legitimate social effects and uses. Methodism is still making something happen in *The Spiritual Quixote* and *Humphry Clinker*, but that something turns out to be community. Mastered in both novels by a literary critical set of strategies that checks its excess, these Methodists energize

---

1. Paul Goring, *The Rhetoric of Sensibility in Eighteenth-Century Culture* (Cambridge: Cambridge University Press, 2005).

rather than challenge the emerging *sensus communis* of a modern Britain.

ANNIKA MANN

From Waste Management: Tobias Smollett and Remediation[†]

Anxiety about writing inhabits Tobias Smollett's *Essay on the External Use of Water* (1752), anxiety focused on the number of medical texts already produced on the waters of Bath. Smollett, a non-practicing doctor, who by 1752 was already a prolific novelist, journalist, and reviewer, explains that Bath has "been investigated by so many different pens, and [has] produced such a variety of opinions among physicians and chemists, that there is very little encouragement for any man to commence author on the same branch of natural knowledge, because he must run a very great risque of feeling his sentiments neglected among the number of those vague *Hypotheses* which are looked upon as the children of idle imagination."[1] "Such diversity of opinions," Smollett writes, "cannot fail to perplex and embarrass" (3) the prospective essayist. At the outset of his *Essay* (the only medical text he published), Smollett expresses nervousness over the confusion and perhaps even misrecognition caused by the surfeit of medical texts in circulation, an excess that can cause even good ideas to appear as "children of idle imagination." Smollett's medical advice, which presents strategies for avoiding contagious physiological waste, is framed by his awareness of textual proliferation. By opening in this way, Smollett raises the possibility—the "risque"—that an overabundance of textual matter might work analogously to the operations of other wasteful matter by contaminating the world of ideas.

This article takes up the possibility of textual contamination raised by Smollett in his *Essay*, arguing that his anxiety over this form of contamination represents a growing uncertainty in later eighteenth-century society at large about the act of reading, an act under pressure not only from the sheer proliferation of print production during this period, but also from new understandings of the human body caused by scientific advances in the study of

---

[†] From *Eighteenth-Century Fiction* 25.2 (Winter 2012–13): 359–71, 378–82. Reprinted by permission of *Eighteenth-Century Fiction*. www.humanities.mcmaster.ca/~ecf.

1. Tobias Smollett, *Essay on the External Use of Water* (London, 1752), 1–2.

"mediums."[2] Medical professionals, scientists, and laypersons during the eighteenth century increasingly emphasized that the human body was profoundly porous and involuntarily affected by its surrounding environment. By examining the later career of the notoriously filth-obsessed Smollett, a writer active in almost every print format of the period, as well as founder in 1756 of the *Critical Review*, we can see the ways in which this change affected him and other writers. As descriptions of the human body underscored the diffuseness, invisibility, and involuntary nature of its processes, it became increasingly difficult to use that body as a figure for enforcing proper textual relations. Effectively, the behaviour of the human body could no longer be the primary grounds for regulating textual consumption. For those writers attempting to bring order to print production, understanding reading via comparison to other bodily processes ceases to be desirable as a method for inculcating "healthy" textual consumption. In response to this development, at the end of his literary career, Smollett experiments with remedies that replace earlier assertions about the comparability of textual and physical matter. In his final texts (published in 1769 and 1771), Smollett turns to new strategies to distinguish reading from other physiological processes; specifically, he turns to remediation in order to depict how print can absorb or refuse other mediums.[3] In so doing, Smollett makes visible the contested, perhaps irreconcilable status of the act of reading at the outset of the Romantic period: reading is either that which immediately affects the body or that which holds the physiological world at bay.

Earlier in his writing career, in his 1752 *Essay*, Smollett appears to offer conflicting evidence about the comparability of reading and more physical forms of ingestion and contamination. His opening remarks about textual proliferation raise the possibility that his readers will view the physical processes described in the succeeding middle sections of the *Essay* as offering an analogous means to confront textual excess. In this intermediary section, Smollett provides lengthy descriptions of physiological contagion and advocates bathing in pure rather than mineral water to purge the body of unwanted waste matter, which he identifies as the primary cause of

2. I follow Kevis Goodman in my use of "mediums" as the plural of medium, which was common usage during the period. Goodman, *Georgic Modernity and British Romanticism: Poetry and the Mediation of History* (Cambridge: Cambridge University Press, 2004). A portion of this article was previously presented at the annual workshop of the Center for Eighteenth-Century Studies at Indiana University (2009).

3. I define remediation (following digital remediation theorists Jay Bolter and Richard Grusin) as the inclusion of one medium, or media form, inside another. I also emphasize that the term "remediation" connotes a specifically physiological remedy: to remediate is also to cure or heal the body of a disease. Jay Bolter and Richard Grusin, *Remediation: Understanding New Media* (Cambridge: MIT Press, 2000).

disease. Smollett argues that the "coldness, pressure, and moisture" of pure water "communicates a spring to the decayed or diseased solids, by which the vessels are enabled to propel their
contents, and renew the circulation, which had been impeded" (5).
Bathing is both curative and preventative, and it works "by washing
away those unctuous and *acrid* impurities . . . which [are] apt to
obstruct the pores, corrode the nerves and disorder the perspiration" (16), leading to disease and eventually death. Smollett explains
that this "unctuous" or "diseased" matter is actually physiological
waste, matter expelled by both animal bodies and the earth itself,
which the surrounding air absorbs and then communicates to the
body. He argues that "air is always impregnated with the finer
parts, and native spirit of those vegetables that grow upon the surface of the earth," and these "finer parts" are "adapted for entering
the smallest order of vessels" (27), the pores. For Smollett, the
pores render the body excessively open to its environment: "What
millions of *inhaling Vessels* gape upon the surface of the skin," he
marvels, "upwards of one hundred thousand of them may be covered with one grain of sand" (26). These gaping apertures allow
dangerously "impregnated" air access to the body and to its delicate
organs, infecting the body's circulation.

By framing these descriptions of omnipresent, "impregnated" air
with remarks about an overabundance of textual material, Smollett
links bad texts and infected air, encouraging his readers to see how
both are sources of dangerous contagion because they continually
absorb and communicate, or mediate, waste matter, carrying
sloughed-off skin or outmoded ideas to unsuspecting persons and
forming a repeating cycle of absorption, communication, and infection. Reading Smollett's *Essay* as an example of such likeness would
fit with early eighteenth-century aesthetic theories of taste, which
are also underpinned by the analogy between the physiological,
or corporeal, and the aesthetic. In his "Of the Standard of Taste,"
David Hume argues that universal agreement is possible because
all persons possess the same bodily organs, and "there is a great
resemblance between mental and bodily taste."[4] Relying on this
resemblance, Smollett's description of the powers of a cold bath in
the middle portion of his *Essay* might be read as a description of the
purgation that his own text will accomplish in the realm of ideas:
washing the body in a cold bath could be like the shock of reading
a good text, "renewing circulation" to the communication of ideas
by exposing and expelling spurious medical opinions. After reading
his *Essay*, readers would be able to see and identify diseased textual

4. David Hume, "Of the Standard of Taste," *Four Dissertations* (London, 1757), 217.

material, such as "false reasoning," "idle sophistry" and "false quotations" (33), in the same way that "an *unctuous* matter is observ-
able in the *baths* . . . after they have been used by persons apparently
in health" (17).

But this is not the case. After giving his medical advice on bathing and the reformation of Bath, Smollett returns to his initial concerns about writing, where he somewhat surprisingly explains that
he has written his *Essay* only in support of ideas that already
appeared in print: Archibald Cleland previously published these
recommendations in "a memorial to the mayor, and corporation . . .
desiring they would petition the parliament, to enable them to
make several alterations in Baths, which are necessary for the good
of the public" (31). At the end of his *Essay* readers find that Smollett
merely parrots Cleland's ideas, and that these ideas have already
been debated: "the cruel treatment [Cleland] underwent upon that
occasion [presenting his ideas to the corporation], compelled him
to appeal to the public, and the whole contest betwixt him and his
adversaries appeared in print" (33). Smollett's *Essay* reignites a
pamphlet war from the 1740s, when Cleland first presented his recommendations. With this revelation, the purifying clarity that
Smollett's text works to produce (that is, making ideational waste
visible) is muddied, as readers are now unable to tell which ideas in
the text are Smollett's and which are recycled from Cleland. Smollett's *Essay* appears to participate in, and perhaps encourage, the
very cycle of textual absorption and communication that his medical advice works to forestall in the physiological realm. The analogy
between the physiological and the textual initially implied by the
framing of the *Essay* is called into question, when readers are asked
to see Smollett's own act of textual mediation—his absorption and
communication of the matter of Cleland's text—as a cure for,
rather than an infection of, the circulation of ideas. Textual mediation appears poised in Smollett's *Essay* between being identified as
the problem—as contaminating as physiological mediation—and
identified as the solution to, or the cure for, infected ideological
communication.

Smollett's inconsistent use of the resemblance between the physical and the textual, or more broadly between the physiological and
the aesthetic, can be read as a first tentative response to changing
understandings of the human body during this same period. We
can identify these shifts in his descriptions of that body in the *Essay*
itself. As I will explain in more detail, medical and technological
advances in the study of mediums during the first half of the eighteenth century make managing bodily health increasingly time-
consuming and difficult, because those advances question the
body's ability to perceive and thereby control how it participates in

its physical environment. The act of distinguishing between texts by comparing their physiological effects shares in that difficulty because bodies are understood to slip continually and imperceptibly into disorder. In response to this shift, in his final texts—*The History and Adventures of an Atom* (1769) and *The Expedition of Humphry Clinker* (published posthumously in 1771)—Smollett supplements analogy with remediation and investigates the unique capacity of print for absorbing and communicating other mediums.

Exploring Smollett's final textual experiments with remediation challenges an increasingly dominant, intertwined literary and historical narrative about the rise of the novel and of commercialization during the eighteenth century. Recent historical work has established that the eighteenth century underwent a "Consumer Revolution," when an influx of consumer goods, especially from other nations, spurred the creation and consumption of recognizably British products. Historians of consumer culture argue that the creation of these products, combined with changing lending practices and an increase in speculative capitalism, created a specifically British identity that certain individuals could participate in by purchasing these products.[5] Literary historians have built productively on this historical work by focusing on one such consumer product, the novel, which novel critics have argued develops into a recognizable genre that readers purchase for the pleasure of identifying with specifically British characters.[6] Studies of the novel have emphasized reading as voluntary identification, an intimate participation on the part of willing persons. According to these critical narratives, the novel appears as one of many specialty products that individuals choose to consume for the pleasure of a sense of belonging.

Closer attention to eighteenth-century writers who were anxious about the ever-increasing production of printed matter during their lifetimes—particularly satirists, including Alexander Pope, Jonathan Swift, and Smollett—tells a different story about print culture during this period. These writers, who perceive the dangerously leveling (and thereby corrupting) possibilities of textual overproduction and

---

5. See John Brewer and Neil McKendrick, *The Birth of a Consumer Society: The Commercialization of Eighteenth-Century England* (Bloomington: Indiana University Press, 1982); and Maxine Berg, *Luxury and Pleasure in Eighteenth-Century Britain* (Oxford: Oxford University Press, 2005).

6. See Lynn Festa, *Sentimental Figures of Empire in Eighteenth-Century Britain and France* (Baltimore: Johns Hopkins University Press, 2006); Deidre Lynch, *The Economy of Character: Novels, Market Culture, and the Business of Inner Meaning* (Chicago: University of Chicago Press, 1998); Liz Bellamy, *Commerce, Morality, and the Eighteenth-Century Novel* (Cambridge: Cambridge University Press, 1998); and Judith Frank, *Common Ground: Eighteenth-Century Satiric Fiction and the Poor* (Palo Alto: Stanford University Press, 1997).

consumption, regularly employ analogies between textual and physical matters in their efforts to ensure intellectual health through
good reading habits.[7] Likewise, Smollett, as editor of the *Critical
Review* (1756–63), instructed his readers which texts to read and
which to avoid based on a logic that noxious books and noxious food
have similar bodily consequences.[8] However, for Smollett, writing a
generation after Pope and Swift, controlling textual consumption by
analogy to bodily consumption was becoming an increasingly difficult manoeuvre because of his growing awareness that the body is
characterized by its continual, involuntary absorption of omnipresent mediums, rather than by its voluntary purchases. This difficulty spurs an exploration of new textual strategies to account for
and elicit new relations with readers. The character of these new
relations helps to explain why Smollett continues to exist uneasily
alongside current studies of the novel in the eighteenth century;
even *Humphry Clinker*, while the most frequently discussed work
by Smollett in literary studies, has remained on the outskirts of literary criticism about the development of the novel: critics describe
Humphry Clinker as "part of an older literary tradition,"[9] its characterizations "elegiac."[1] In his attempts to find a means to slow textual
absorption, to make readers conscious of print as a unique medium,
Smollett illuminates a different literary history than that typically
emphasized by studies of the novel.

7. Extended analogies that figure the similitude of noxious bodily and textual consumption are common in the early eighteenth-century satires of the Scriblerus Club, especially in the work of Alexander Pope, Jonathan Swift, and John Arbuthnot. For a
virulent example of such analogizing, see the scatological "heroic games" played by
booksellers, poets, and critics in book 2 of Pope's *The Dunciad* (1728).
8. In the preface to the first volume of the *Critical Review; Or, Annals of Literature* (1756),
Smollett writes that the editors' "aim has been to exhibit a succinct plan of every performance; to point out the most striking beauties and glaring defects; to illustrate their
remarks with proper quotations," so that readers know which performances (or texts) to
avoid. Smollett then makes an analogy between bodies and texts to describe the work of
the *Critical Review* (and the response of its audience) by claiming that the editors
"value themselves upon having reviewed every material performance, immediately
after its first appearance, without reserving productions for a dearth of articles, and
then raising them, like stale carcasses from oblivion, after they have been blown upon
by every minor critic, and the curiosity of the public is gorged even to satiety." Smollett,
preface to *Critical Review* 1 (January 1756): i–ii. In his preface to the 1761 volume,
Smollett baldly states that "*True criticism* aims at nothing else but diminishing the
number of useless volumes." Smollett, preface to *Critical Review* 11 (January 1761): 2.
For a list of the reviews and prefaces attributed to Smollett and evidence of their attribution, see James Basker, "Appendix A," in *Tobias Smollett: Critic and Journalist* (Newark: University of Delaware Press, 1988), 220–78.
9. K. G. Simpson, "Tobias Smollett: The Scot as English Novelist," in *Smollett: Author of
the First Distinction*, ed. Alan Bold (Totowa: Vision Press, 1982), 102.
1. Lynch, 110. According to Ian Watt, "Smollett has many merits as a social reporter and
as a humorist, but the manifest flaws in the central situations and the general structure
of all his novels except *Humphry Clinker* (1771) prevent him from playing a very important role in the main tradition of the novel." Watt, *The Rise of the Novel: Studies in
Defoe, Richardson, and Fielding* (London: Pimlico, 1957), 290.

Unnatural Circulation and the Problem of Visibility

In his descriptions of the dangerously infectious quality of air, Smollett's *Essay* is consonant with its contemporary medical theory, which held that the health of the body was ensured only by a continual management of what were termed, following Hippocrates, the "non-naturals": food and drink, evacuations and obstructions, sleeping and waking, exercise, air, and the passions. As this list illustrates, the human body stays healthy by regulating its functions, its continual inter- and intra-bodily exchanges, both voluntary (exercise) and involuntary (breathing). The concept of managing the body via the non-naturals arose only at the end of the seventeenth century, when medical professionals (led by Thomas Sydenham and others) argued for a return to Hippocratic ideals and methods, a "Neo-Hippocratic method" that absorbed fifteenth- and sixteenth-century humoral theory. While both lay and professional writers continued to use humoral terminology, doctors now attempted to improve the body's internal functions by regulating the interactions between the body and the surrounding world, instead of seeking solely to balance the body's humors.[2]

By attempting to treat the body with interventions at the level of function, the medical community in Britain participated in an intense, renewed interest in mediums, particularly (as we have seen in Smollett) those with which the human body involuntarily comes into contact, such as air, which might contain invisible, infectious waste matter. George Cheyne, perhaps Britain's most famous eighteenth-century advocate of bodily management, writes in his *Essay on Health and Long Life* (1724) that "all *animal* Bodies, from an *active* and self-moving *Principle* within them, as well as from the *Rubs* of Bodies without them, are constantly throwing off some of their superfluous and decayed Parts."[3] Inter- and intra-bodily circulation causes bodily detritus—"superfluous and decayed parts"—to be thrown off into the air, where they are absorbed, becoming in the process a dangerous effluvia or miasma. Cheyne explains that "our Bodies *suck* and *draw* into them, the good or bad qualities of the *circumambient Air*, through the Mouths of all the *perspiratory Ducts* of the Skin. And if we were to view an *animal* Body with a proper Glass, it would appear with an *Atmosphere* quite round it, like the *Steam* of a boiling Pot" (81–82). For Cheyne, the body becomes diseased because air mediates the waste matter of other organisms back into

2. For more on this transformation, see Roy Porter and Dorothy Porter, *In Sickness and Health: The British Experience, 1650–1850* (New York: B. Blackwell, 1989).
3. George Cheyne, *Essay on Health and Long Life* (London, 1724), 77.

the body. By absorbing the "good or bad qualities" that the air has mediated, the human body becomes infected.

Cheyne's desire for a "proper Glass" to view the body illustrates how medical writing and the investigation of mediums during the eighteenth century draws upon late seventeenth-century scientific advancements, particularly in the field of optics. Recent work on mediation, including that by Kevis Goodman, William Warner, and Clifford Siskin, has pointed out that technological advances in optics during the seventeenth century encouraged, in Britain, an intense interest in mediums, when instruments such as the microscope revealed tiny, unknown particulates within larger organic materials. As this critical work has shown, however, these technological advances also changed the term "medium" itself, which expanded to include both passive material through which an element passes (such as water or air) and those instruments (such as the microscope) that perform functions in experiments, allowing one to see those organic mediums in the first place.[4] The term "medium" became increasingly understood to signify conduits both passive and determinative; a medium becomes an in-between space, a middle layer, an intermediary through which material passes, but also an instrument, a solvent, or a means of communication (like language) that can change the constitution or reception of what is moving through it.[5] And so, while the term medium designates a means to aid vision or communication, that same medium has the power to deform what it is attempting to illuminate. Within the very concept of mediation, there is implied transparent communication as well as malfunction, visibility, and impeded vision.

Late seventeenth- and early eighteenth-century advances in mediums only increased the visibility problems they were invented to resolve: not only could a medium alter what it was meant to communicate, but also, as Goodman notes, a sense of spatial dislocation arises because new technological mediums, or sensory extensions, "bring home information not verifiable by the ordinary powers of vision, hearing, or touch . . . simulat[ing] sense-experience from positions or vantages where the body cannot literally be situated, dislocating both body and place."[6] This dislocation was particularly acute in the discovery of the nervous system. The use of the

---

4. For more on the expanding definition of the term "medium," see Goodman; and William Warner and Clifford Siskin, "This is Enlightenment: An Invitation in the Form of an Argument," in *This is Enlightenment* (Chicago: University of Chicago Press, 2010), 1–36. For more on the linked terms "medium," "milieu," and "atmosphere," see Leo Spitzer, "Milieu and Ambiance: An Essay in Historical Semantics," *Philosophy and Phenomenological Research* 3, no. 2 (1942): 169–218. www.jstor.org/stable/2103127.
5. Goodman, 19–20.
6. Goodman, 12.

microscope and other technological mediums in anatomical experiments by Thomas Willis, Richard Blackmore, and Robert Whytt produced a new conception of anatomy by the mid-eighteenth century, one in which motion and sensation were diffused: the body was apprehended as a conglomerate of tensile fibres, or nerves, responsible for transmitting sensation to the brain and dispersed along the surface of the body. Cheyne, in *The English Malady* (1733), invites readers to "consider the Number of *Veins, Arteries, Lymphaticks, Nerves, Fibres, Tendons, Ligaments, Membranes, Cartilages, Bones, Muscles* and *Glands* discovered in every Animal, and this infinite Number still increased and made further conspicuous by *Injections* and *Microscopes*."[7] The microscope simultaneously dislocates the interior of the body and that which envelops it; the interior of the body has become "infinite," surrounded not by what it can actually perceive, but by an invisible *"Atmosphere."*

Insomuch as doctors and laypersons writing during this period participate in this anxiety over mediums, they primarily focus on the human body's involuntary consumption of waste matter. Two nonnaturals, air and the passions, become the focus of intense medical attention because they threaten to mediate what should be absolutely voided and avoided: diseased matter or undesirable feelings—what Smollett would describe as waste, or "filth." For Smollett, however, who was a literary critic concerned with ideational as well as physiological corruption, the discourse of the non-naturals during the 1750s appears to provide him with a way to make bad ideas visible in his *Essay* by placing them alongside physiological waste, thus encouraging the analogizing of one as the other. As Barbara Stafford argues, analogy is a process that ultimately relies upon and produces visibility: an analogy is a comparison that allows one to see resemblances or correspondences between an abstraction and a material form. Whether visualizing proportion (part to whole) or mimetic participation (recognizing likeness), for Stafford "all of analogy's simile-generating figures are thus incarnational. They materialize, display, and disseminate an enigma that escapes words."[8] Analogy as a strategy uses and depends upon visuality, and, in his use of its incarnational power, Smollett follows in the wake of such satirists as Pope and Swift, who repeatedly used analogy to figure (as bodily) the corrosive effects of unrestrained print production. Because of the way in which Smollett frames his medical text, it is possible to read his *Essay* as positing an implicit analogy between

7. Cheyne, *George Cheyne: The English Malady* (1733), ed. Roy Porter (London: Routledge, 1991), 92–93. References are to this edition.
8. Barbara Stafford, *Visual Analogy: Consciousness as the Art of Connecting* (Cambridge: MIT Press, 1999), 24.

ideational and physiological waste—or "vague *Hypotheses*" as "unctuous matter"—that works to make textual filth visible during the time of reading. Such an analogy would encourage readers to see and recognize literary waste through descriptions of bodily waste and cause them to be disgusted by bad ideas in the same way that they are "disgusted with the nauseating appearance of the filth, which, being washed from the bodies of the patients, is left sticking to the sides of the place" (34).

This defensive strategy against print proliferation—the effort by Smollett to "incarnate" or make visible ideational filth by comparing the medium of print to that of air or water—is already strained in several ways. First, if print is like air, an omnipresent medium carrying noxious waste that the body involuntarily absorbs, then regulating that absorption is difficult if not impossible. Second, making textual waste visible requires ever more text, as is apparent from the revelation of Smollett's own mediation of Cleland's first essay—if the body must repeatedly bathe to isolate and wash away physiological impurities, then it must also repeatedly read texts that will identify and purge ideational waste. This produces the very textual proliferation that Smollett might curtail by recourse to analogy in the first place. The medical community's response to the new disappearance of the human body as a coherent figure was twofold: to narrate incessantly the body's internal processes and to encourage the management of those internal bodily functions by engaging in reading as habitual exercise. Medical practitioners advocated reading as a way to vicariously experience feelings, and to purge those feelings. In *Pamela; or, Virtue Rewarded* (1740), Samuel Richardson, a patient and correspondent of Cheyne, shows Mr B morally and physically realigned by Pamela's "Reflections": "you have touch'd me sensibly with your mournful Relation," he tells her, "and your sweet Reflections upon it."[9] Richardson has Mr B articulate a notion of reading as physio-moral exercise, as a physical realignment of the body via identification. Bodily disorder no longer reveals the negative effects of engaging with print, but instead provides the very rationale for its repeated consumption:

---

9. Samuel Richardson, *Pamela; or, Virtue Rewarded*, ed. Thomas Keymer and Alice Wakely (Oxford: Oxford University Press, 2001), 241. Literary critics emphasize how this medical discourse, particularly the discovery of the nervous system, encouraged the reading and writing of the novel and literature of sensibility more generally. See G.S. Rousseau, "Nerves, Spirits, and Fibres: Towards Defining the Origins of Sensibility," *Studies in the Eighteenth Century III*, ed. R. F. Brissenden (Toronto: University of Toronto Press, 1976), 137–157; John Mullan, *Sentiment and Sociability: The Language of Feeling in the Eighteenth Century* (Oxford: Clarendon Press, 1988); Ann Jessie Van Sant, *Eighteenth-Century Sensibility and the Novel: The Senses in Social Context* (Cambridge: Cambridge University Press, 1993); and Geoffrey Sill, *The Cure of the Passions and the Origins of the English Novel* (Cambridge: Cambridge University Press, 2001).

readers are encouraged to regularly purchase novels in order to experience bodily feelings, to ingest and to purge alongside the novel's central characters.

Even by 1752 the likeness between physical and textual mediums already seems for Smollett to be increasingly troubling rather than helpful, and ill-suited as a means to control the rapid production and consumption of texts, Smollett's *Essay* may show symptoms that the analogy between the physiological and the textual proves unwieldy, but, in texts written less than twenty years later, that comparison has been completely restructured. Composed after his disastrous experience defending the Bute ministry in his periodical *The Briton* (1762–63), when Smollett was repeatedly lampooned in the periodical press by John Wilkes and others, both *The History and Adventures of an Atom* and *The Expedition of Humphry Clinker* represent a departure from the picaresque form typical of Smollett's earlier novels. These texts instead exhibit a different kind of formal experimentation, what we would recognize in our modern digital moment as remediation. In these texts, rather than analogize the printed and the physiological, Smollett illustrates their collapse. In so doing, Smollett creates texts that are alternately hyper-readable (*Humphry Clinker*) and impossible to consume (*Atom*).

* * *

Renew, Reuse, Recycle

If *The History and Adventures of an Atom*, the most "vindictive" and "grotesque"[1] of Smollett's texts, represents the outer limit of communication by being actually incommunicable, *The Expedition of Humphry Clinker* is usually described as the "softest,"[2] gentlest, and most readable of Smollett's texts. *Humphry Clinker* is explicitly about physiological remedies: the novel chronicles the travels of Welshman Matthew Bramble and his family as Bramble traverses England and Scotland in a quest to achieve bodily health. "Prithee send me another prescription," Bramble writes to his doctor at the novel's outset; "I am as lame and as much tortured in all my limbs as if I was broke upon the wheel: indeed, I am equally distressed in mind and body."[3] Most recently, critics have argued that the novel achieves personal and

---

1. Robert Day, "*Ut Pictura Poesis*: Smollet, Satire, and the Graphic Arts, *Studies in Eighteenth-Century Culture* 10 (1981): 309.

2. Ronald Paulson, *Satire and the Novel in Eighteenth-Century England* (New Haven, CT: Yale UP, 1997), 208.

3. Smollett, *The Expedition of Humphry Clinker*, ed. Thomas Preston (Athens: University of Georgia Press, 1990), 7 [11]. References are to this edition. Page references in square brackets are to this Norton Critical Edition.

social health, curing Bramble and his wider social group, by means of figures that rely implicitly upon the analogy between the ideational and the physical. According to Charlotte Sussman and others, Smollett figures the corrupting effects of Britain's consumerist ethos as physical bodies—waters and women—bodies that, once recognized, can either be expelled (waters) or recuperated (women) by the novel's plot.[4] While Bramble incessantly narrates the contagious material flowing through the waters of London and Bath, he also combats the consumptive desires of his sister Tabitha, whose "avarice seems to grow every day more and more rapacious" and who "keeps the whole family in disquiet and uproar" (59) [68]. Tabitha, described as a "domestic plague" (60) [68], finds her own double at the end of the novel in Mrs Baynor, the recently deceased wife of Bramble's old friend, whose estate is on the verge of utter financial ruin because he could not curb his wife's excessive spending. Here the figures of water and women themselves seem to become analogous, as the draining of Baynor's estate cures the devastation wrought by his wife: Bramble writes that after rendering the estate productive, he has no doubt that Baynor "will find himself perfectly at ease both in mind and body" (335) [354]. For his own part, Bramble is also recuperated by his success: he informs his physician that "I have laid in a considerable stock of health, [and so] it is to be hoped that you will not have much trouble with me in the way of physic" (336) [354]. By figuring consumerism as a disease spread by infected waters and rapacious women, the novel can enact a purification of both, when noxious waters are voided and women either die or, in the case of Tabitha, are married off to men who will re-channel their consumptive desires into the desire for having children.

These analogies between a commercial ideology and physical bodies operate through description and plot and imply that Smollett would extend the strategy to texts and bodies. Yet his more pervasive formal devices actually separate the physical from the textual, rendering them distinct for the reader. *Humphry Clinker* is a novel in epistles, consisting of about eighty letters from Bramble, Bramble's niece and nephew Lydia and Jery Melford, his sister Tabitha, and Tabitha's maid, Win Jenkins. But *Humphry Clinker* is what Wolfgang Iser describes as a "one-sided correspondence":[5] it presents letters from each member of the Bramble party, but not

4. Charlotte Sussman, "Lismahago's Captivity: Transculturation in *Humphry Clinker*" *ELH* 61, no. 3 (1994): 597–618. www.jstor.org/stable/2873336. See also Douglas; John Sekora, *Luxury: The Concept in Western Thought, Eden to Smollett* (Baltimore: Johns Hopkins University Press, 1977); and David M. Weed, "Sentimental Misogyny and Medicine in *Humphry Clinker*," *SEL: Studies in English Literature, 1500–1900* 37, no. 3 (1997): 615–36. www.jstor.org/stable/451052.
5. Wolfgang Iser, *The Implied Reader: Patterns of Communication in Prose Fiction from Bunyan to Beckett* (Baltimore: Johns Hopkins University Press, 1977), 60.

the responses to them. One result of this formal device is that language of physiological mediation is contained, rather than diffused,
in the novel as a whole; while *Atom* makes the reader wince with its
ceaseless rush of extended bodily imagery, the language of waste in
Humphry Clinker is much more easily dispensed with because it is
contained only in discrete sections, in the letters written by Bramble. In Bath, for example, Bramble complains about "infected" air
and water: he speculates that "in all probability . . . as we drink
the decoction of living bodies at the Pump-room, we swallow the
strainings of rotten bones and carcasses at the private bath" (45)
[52]. Bramble also sees this gross mediation of waste in London,
where he describes how "faded cabbage-leaves and sour draff [are]
carried through the streets in open pails, exposed to foul rinsings,
discharged from doors and windows, spittle, snot, and tobacco-
quids from foot-passengers" (121) [131]. Bramble's concerns about
waste cause him to claim that "snares are laid for our very lives in
every thing we eat or drink: the very air we breathe, is loaded with
contagion" (46) [53]. These anxieties about contagion do not infil-
trate the novel as a whole, for, while the other characters also meditate on the events presented in Bramble's letters (for example, each
member of the Bramble party writes a letter that describes his or
her experience walking through London), they do not incorporate or
disseminate his concerns about waste and infection. Physiological
mediation fails to proliferate as textual matter as it did in *Atom*,
but is instead contained by textual means, by the structure imposed
on the novel by the letters themselves.

Although the novel stages analogous moments of the physiological expulsion of waters and the social recuperation of women, these
moments are themselves contained by the larger formal structure
of the novel, which works against such wholeness and reconciliation.
The medium of the letter keeps writers separate from one another,
thereby keeping the (absent) physiological distinct from the (present)
textual. While scenes of social integration occur within particular
letters, such as that between Bramble and his son Humphry Clinker,
reunions between letter writers and their correspondents do not, at
least within the text of the novel. *Humphry Clinker* can be considered what Bolter and Grusin describe as a hypermediated text, one
that "multipl[ies] the signs of mediation,"[6] for it continually reminds
readers of its primary remediated medium: the printed letter.
While the epistolary novel is by 1771 already a familiar form of
remediation—incorporating, mimicking, and replacing the earlier
medium of the manuscript—*Humphry Clinker* makes the reader

---

6. Jay Bolter and Richard Grusin, *Remediation: Understanding New Media* (Cambridge,
MA: MIT Press, 2000), 34.

hyperaware of the letter's status as remediation by having each letter shift, without response, to another letter written by a different member of the Bramble party. This strategy disrupts attempts to read the letters as forming a seamless narrative progress; further, it makes visible the remediation of the "original" correspondence, which has been reorganized and transferred to print.

The novel highlights the "signs of its mediation" by proceeding in one-sided epistolary form, while Smollett at the same time stages scenes where the reader has to move between different levels of representation, Midway through the novel, Bramble witnesses a reconciliation involving one of Smollett's other fictional characters: Bramble explains that "Grieve was no other than Ferdinand count Fathom, whose adventures were printed many years ago," but he has become "a sincere convert to virtue," and so "the adventurer Fathom was, under the name of Grieve, universally respected among the commonalty of this district, as a prodigy of learning and virtue" (166) [179]. The readers of *Humphry Clinker* are asked to acknowledge that Bramble is writing about another fictional character ("whose adventures were printed many years ago"), one who is perhaps a more evidently fictional character. And this process is reversed when Bramble's nephew Jery describes a long evening spent with the author of the very text the reader is reading: Tobias Smollett, "Mr. S——."

The strongest prophylactic against infection for the reader of *Humphry Clinker* is not analogy—figuring contagion as waters and female bodies—but remediation, which relocates processes of absorption to literary mediums, thereby containing and transforming the physiological into the textual. Physiological contagion in the novel is diminished by the restriction of the language of physiological waste to particular letters (Bramble's); simultaneously, social contact in the novel is accompanied by an overt acknowledgement of textual or literary mediation (the letter itself, and the patently fictional), which transforms physical contact into purely textual communication. For by reading successive, unanswered letters and experiencing scenes between alternately hyperfictionalized characters and "real" people, the reader of *Humphry Clinker* is forced to acknowledge multiple levels of representation, implying a multiplication of mediums. These formal manoeuvres make literary mediation visible to the reader, while also encouraging readers to substitute textual for physical communication and contact. Whereas *Atom* forced readers to acknowledge the horror of reading as an immediate bodily act, *Humphry Clinker* models reading as an interrupted, self-conscious activity: one where the text is kept always between the bodies of readers, and where print is presented as a container, a buffer. The act of reading is separated from other bodily engagements, and print is made to do the work of distancing one body from another, as well as the social from the textual. Hyper-mediated contact, or a kind of interrupted reading, seems finally to be the kind of social contact advocated by the novel, where readers trade in textual or literary mediums (letters, representations of fictional and real characters, and novels) instead of physical ones.

Humphry Clinker works as an experiment in containment, exposing how literary mediation and physiological mediation do not need to correspond—indeed are different enough that one can be used to counteract the other. Yet both of Smollett's texts appear to be dead ends, because both seem to make reading ultimately undesirable: one creates a bodily feeling so strong that it forestalls reading entirely, and the other encourages readers to visualize reading as an activity that distances and is distant from the physical or the social. These texts work against an interconnected, but ordered, analogical world, one where reading and other physiological acts could be productively considered alongside one another. The texts themselves appear irreconcilable. This irreconcilability is revelatory, however, for it will continue to structure notions of print culture and the act of reading during the Romantic period, although perhaps it lies with the poets rather than the novelists to continue its exploration. Through poems that posit absent listeners and silent interlocutors, and in communication that fails or petrifies, Wordsworth and Coleridge take up this concern with medium and mediation. In their "experiment"[7] with poetic form and language, we again glimpse strategies designed to counter or embrace print's mediating power, its ability to subjugate the reading body, or to keep the hostile world at bay.

---

7. William Wordsworth, "Preface to *Lyrical Ballads* (1802)," *William Wordsworth and Samuel Taylor Coleridge: Lyrical Ballads and Related Writings*, ed. William Richey and Daniel Robinson (Boston: Houghton Mifflin, 2002), 390.

Tobias Smollett: A Chronology

1721	Baptized on March 19, Cardross, Dumbartonshire, Scotland
1727/28	Begins formal education at Dumbarton Grammar School, then University of Glasgow (dates uncertain)
1736	Begins apprenticeship to William Stirling and John Gordon, Glasgow surgeons
1739	Leaves university without matriculating, relocates to London
1740	Commissioned surgeon's second mate in the navy; begins service on the HMS *Chichester*; sails to Jamaica and participates in the Cartagena expedition
1741	Returns to London. Possibly already betrothed to Anne Lassells, heiress daughter of a planter in Jamaica; they marry ca. 1743
1744	Begins practicing as a surgeon in London
1746	Publishes *The Tears of Scotland* and *Advice*, a verse satire
1747	*Reproof*, a sequel to *Advice*
1748	*The Adventures of Roderick Random*; translation of Lesage's *Gil Blas*
1749	*The Regicide*, an unproduced tragedy; tours Flanders, Holland, and parts of France
1750	Receives M.D. from Marischal College, Aberdeen; visits Paris
1751	*The Adventures of Peregrine Pickle*
1752	*Habbakkuk Hilding*, an anonymous pamphlet attacking Henry Fielding (usually attributed to Smollett); *An Essay on the External Uses of Water*
1753	*The Adventures of Fedinand Count Fathom*; visits Scotland for the first time in fifteen years
1755	Translation of Cervantes' *Don Quixote* (begun ca. 1748)
1756	Co-founds, edits, and contributes to the *Critical Review* (until 1763); *A Compendium of Authentic and Entertaining Voyages*
1757	*The Reprisal*, a two-act farce, performed at the Theatre Royal in Drury Lane

1757–58	*A Complete History of England*
1760	*The Adventures of Sir Launcelot Greaves* begins serial publication in *The British Magazine*; serves four months in King's Bench Prison for libel of admiral published in 1758 in *Critical Review*
1762–63	Edits weekly periodical *The Briton* in support of Lord Bute's administration; health begins to deteriorate
1763	Only child, Elizabeth, dies at age fifteen; leaves for France and Italy
1765	Returns to England
1766	*Travels through France and Italy*; makes final trip to Scotland
1768	*The Present State of All Nations* (begun 1760)
1768	Moves to Leghorn, Italy
1769	*The History and Adventures of an Atom*, an anonymous political satire attributed to Smollett
1771	*The Expedition of Humphry Clinker*; Smollett dies and is buried in the English cemetery near Leghorn

Selected Bibliography

• indicates works included or excerpted in this Norton Critical Edition

Tobias Smollett: Works

The most complete scholarly edition of Smollett's writings is the University of Georgia Press edition of *The Works of Tobias Smollett* (general editor, Alexander Pettit; textual editor O. M. Brack Jr.). It currently comprises all of Smollett's novels (except for *The Adventures of Peregrine Pickle*, which is forthcoming); his translations of Cervantes, Lesage, and Fénelon; his poems, plays, and *The Briton*.

Biographical and Critical Studies

Alker, Sharon. "The Geography of Negotiation: Wales, Anglo-Scottish Sympathy, and Tobias Smollett." *Lumen: Proceedings of the Canadian Society for Eighteenth-Century Studies* 21 (2002): 87–103.
• Anderson, Misty G. *Imagining Methodism in Eighteenth-Century Britain: Enthusiasm, Beliefs, and the Borders of the Soul.* Baltimore and London: Johns Hopkins UP, 2012.
Basker, James G. *Tobias Smollett, Critic and Journalist.* Newark: U of Delaware P, 1988.
Beasley, Jerry C. *Tobias Smollett: Novelist.* Athens: U of Georgia P, 1998.
———. "Tobias Smollett: The Scot in England." *Studies in Scottish Literature* 29 (1997): 14–28.
Blackwell, Mark. "Disjecta Membra: Smollett and the Novel in Pieces." *The Eighteenth Century: Theory and Interpretation* 52.3–4 (Fall–Winter 2011): 423–44.
Bold, Alan, ed. *Smollett: Author of the First Distinction.* London and Totowa, NJ: Barnes & Noble, 1982.
Boucé, Paul-Gabriel. *The Novels of Tobias Smollett*, trans. Antonia White and the author. New York: Longman, 1976.
Carson, James P. "Britons, 'Hottentots,' Plantation Slavery, and Tobias Smollett." *Philological Quarterly* 75 (Fall 1996): 471–99.
———. "Commodification and the Figure of the Castrato in Smollett's *Humphry Clinker.*" *The Eighteenth-Century: Theory and Interpretation* 33.1 (Spring 1992): 24–46.
Crawford, Robert. *Devolving English Literature.* 2nd ed. Edinburgh: U of Edinburgh P, 2000.
Davis, Leith. *Acts of Union: Scotland and the Literary Negotiation of the British Nation, 1707–1830.* Stanford: Stanford UP, 1998.
Dickie, Simon. *Cruelty and Laughter: Forgotten Comic Literature and the Unsentimental Eighteenth Century.* Chicago and London: U of Chicago P, 2011.

Douglas, Aileen. *Uneasy Sensations: Smollett and the Body*. Chicago: U of Chicago P, 1995.

Evans, James E. "'An honest scar received in the service of my country': Lismahago's Colonial Perspective in *Humphry Clinker*." *Philological Quarterly* 79 (2000): 483–99.

Felsenstein, Frank. "With Smollett in Harrogate." *Philological Quarterly* 88.4 (Fall 2009): 438–46.

Folkenflick, Robert. "Self and Society: Comic Union in *Humphry Clinker*." *Philological Quarterly* 53 (1974): 195–204.

Gassman, Byron. "*The Briton* and *Humphry Clinker*." *SEL: Studies in English Literature, 1500–1900* 3.3 (Summer 1963): 397–414.

———. "*Humphry Clinker* and the Two Kingdoms of George III." *Criticism* 16 (1974): 95–108.

Gibson, William. *Art and Money in the Writings of Tobias Smollett*. Lewisburg, PA: Bucknell UP, 2007.

• Gottlieb, Evan. "'Fools of Prejudice': Sympathy and National Identity in the Scottish Enlightenment and *Humphry Clinker*." *Eighteenth-Century Fiction* 18.1 (Fall 2005): 81–106.

Irvine, Robert P. *Enlightenment and Romance: Gender and Agency in Smollett and Scott*. Oxford: Peter Lang, 2000.

Iser, Wolfgang. "The Generic Control of the Aesthetic Response: An Examination of Smollett's *Humphry Clinker*." *Southern Humanities Review* 3 (1969): 243–57.

Jacobsen, Susan. "'The Tinsel of the Times': Smollett's Argument against Conspicuous Consumption in *Humphry Clinker*." *Eighteenth-Century Fiction* 9.1 (1996): 71–88.

Jones, Richard J. *Tobias Smollett in the Enlightenment: Travels Through France, Italy, and Scotland*. Lewisburg, PA: Bucknell UP, 2011.

Keener, Frederick. "Transitions in *Humphry Clinker*." *Studies in Eighteenth-Century Culture* 16 (1986): 149–63.

Kelly, Lionel, ed. *Tobias Smollett: The Critical Heritage*. London: Routledge, 1987.

Krishnan, R. S. "'The Vortex of the Tumult': Order and Disorder in *Humphry Clinker*." *Studies in Scottish Literature* 23 (1988): 239–55.

Leissner, Debra. "Smollett Colonizes Scotland: Displacement and Absorption in *Humphry Clinker*." *Eighteenth-Century Novel* 2 (2002): 161–78.

Lutz, Alfred. "Representing Scotland in *Roderick Random* and *Humphry Clinker*: Smollett's Development as a Novelist." *Studies in the Novel* 33 (2001): 1–17.

Lynch, Deidre Shauna. *The Economy of Character: Novels, Market Culture, and the Business of Inner Meaning*. Chicago and London: U of Chicago P, 1998.

• Mann, Annika. "Waste Management: Tobias Smollett and Remediation." *Eighteenth-Century Fiction* 25.2 (2012–13): 359–82.

Markidou, Vassiliki. "Gender and Space in Tobias Smollett's *Humphry Clinker*." *Critical Survey* 22.1 (2010): 58–73.

Martz, Louis. *The Later Career of Tobias Smollett*. New Haven: Yale UP, 1942.

• Mayer, Robert. "History, *Humphry Clinker*, and the Novel." *Eighteenth-Century Fiction* 3 (1992): 239–55.

McInelly, Brett C. "Domestic and Colonial Space in *Humphry Clinker*." *1650–1850: Ideas, Aesthetics, and Inquiries in the Early Modern Era* 10 (2002): 126–42.

Miles, Peter. "The Bookhood of *Humphry Clinker*: The Editor, the Publisher, and the Law." *Eighteenth-Century Life* 18.1 (1994): 48–63.

———. "Smollett, Rowlandson, and a Problem of Identity: Decoding Names, Bodies, and Gender in *Humphry Clinker*." *Eighteenth-Century Life* 20 (1996): 1–20.

Murphy, Michael. "Marriage as Metaphor for the Anglo-Scottish Parliamentary Union of 1707: The Case of *Humphry Clinker*." *Etudes Ecossaises* 3 (1996): 61–65.

Prior, Tim. "Lydia Melford and the Role of the Classical Body in Smollett's *Humphry Clinker*." *Studies in the Novel* 30 (1998): 489–505.

Richetti, John. *The English Novel in History, 1700–1780*. New York: Routledge, 1999.

——. "Representing an Under-Class: Servants and Proletarians in Fielding and Smollett." In Felicity Nussbaum and Laura Brown, eds., *The New Eighteenth Century: Theory, Politics, English Literature*. New York and London: Methuen, 1987.

Rosenblum, Michael. "Smollett's *Humphry Clinker*." In John Richetti, ed., *The Cambridge Companion to the Eighteenth-Century Novel*. Cambridge: Cambridge UP, 1996.

• Rothstein, Eric. "Scotophilia and *Humphry Clinker*: The Politics of Beggary, Bugs and Buttocks." *University of Toronto Quarterly* 52.2 (Fall 1982): 63–78.

Rousseau, George S. *Tobias Smollett: Essays of Two Decades*. London: T&T Clark, 1982.

Rousseau, George S., and P.-G. Boucé, eds. *Tobias Smollett: Bicentennial Essays Presented to Lewis M. Knapp*. Oxford: Oxford UP, 1971.

Schwarzchild, Edward. "'I will Take the Whole upon My Own Shoulders': Collections and Corporeality in *Humphry Clinker*." *Criticism* 36.4 (Fall 1994): 541–68.

Sekora, John. *Luxury: The Concept in Western Thought, Eden to Smollett*. Baltimore: Johns Hopkins UP, 1974.

Sena, John F. "Ancient Design and Modern Folly: Architecture in *The Expedition of Humphry Clinker*." *Harvard Library Bulletin* 27 (1979): 86–113.

——. "Smollett's Matthew Bramble and the Tradition of the Physician-Satirist." *Papers on Language and Literature* 11 (1975): 380–96.

Sharp, Andrew. "Scots, Savages, and Barbarians: *Humphry Clinker* and the Scots' Philosophy." *Eighteenth-Century Life* 18.3 (1994): 65–79.

Siebert, Donald T., Jr. "The Role of the Senses in *Humphry Clinker*." *Studies in the Novel* 6 (1974): 17–26.

Skinner, John. *Constructions of Smollett: A Study of Genre and Gender*. Newark: U of Delaware P, 1996.

Smith, Nicholas. "'The Muses O'lio': Satire, Food, and Tobias Smollett's *The Expedition of Humphry Clinker*." *Eighteenth-Century Fiction* 16.3 (2004): 401–18.

Sorensen, Janet. *The Grammar of Empire in Eighteenth-Century British Literature*. Cambridge: Cambridge UP, 2000.

Spector, Robert. *Smollett's Women: A Study in Eighteenth-Century Masculine Sensibility*. Westport, CT: Greenwood, 1994.

• Sussman, Charlotte. "Lismahago's Captivity: Transculturation in *Humphry Clinker*." *ELH* 61 (1994): 597–618.

Van Renen, Denys. "Biogeography, Climate, and National Identity in Smollett's *Humphry Clinker*." *Philological Quarterly* 90.4 (2011): 395–424.

Wagoner, Mary. "On the Satire in *Humphry Clinker*." *Papers on Language and Literature* 2 (1966): 109–16.

• Wallace, Tara Ghoshal. "'About savages and the awfulness of America': Colonial Corruptions in *Humphry Clinker*." *Eighteenth-Century Fiction* 18 (Winter 2005–06): 229–50.

• Weed, David. "Sentimental Misogyny and Medicine in *Humphry Clinker*." *SEL: Studies in English Literature* 37 (1997–98): 215–34.

• Zomchick, John. "Social Class, Character, and Narrative Strategy in *Humphry Clinker*." *Eighteenth-Century Life* 10.3 (1986): 172–85.